厉德寅 / 著　厉无咎　袁卫　王振 / 编

厉德寅
经济学文集
Tehyin Y. Li's
Essays on Economics

上海社会科学院出版社
SHANGHAI ACADEMY OF SOCIAL SCIENCES PRESS

图书在版编目(CIP)数据

厉德寅经济学文集 / 厉德寅著;厉无咎,袁卫,王振编. — 上海：上海社会科学院出版社，2022
ISBN 978-7-5520-3913-9

Ⅰ.①厉… Ⅱ.①厉… ②厉… ③袁… ④王… Ⅲ.①经济学—文集 Ⅳ.①F0-53

中国版本图书馆 CIP 数据核字(2022)第 130717 号

厉德寅经济学文集

著　　者：厉德寅
编　　者：厉无咎　袁　卫　王　振
出 品 人：佘　凌
责任编辑：陈如江　包纯睿
封面设计：KeliStudio　柯珂
出版发行：上海社会科学院出版社
　　　　　上海顺昌路 622 号　邮编 200025
　　　　　电话总机 021-63315947　销售热线 021-53063735
　　　　　http://www.sassp.cn　E-mail:sassp@sassp.cn
照　　排：南京理工出版信息技术有限公司
印　　刷：上海颛辉印刷厂有限公司
开　　本：710 毫米×1010 毫米　1/16
印　　张：43
插　　页：1
字　　数：748 千
版　　次：2022 年 9 月第 1 版　2022 年 9 月第 1 次印刷

ISBN 978-7-5520-3913-9/F·704　　　　　定价:168.00 元

版权所有　翻印必究

题咏历德寅巨擘　卢昭明

画水歌山灵气冲　槐堂村里育鸾龙
历序嫡子超侪众　崖廊先鞭向主峰
治学标新开化境　献谋抗戎建战功
谁知运变沧戈壁　坐劲圳杨花怨红

书于壬寅七月十六

序

中国人民大学原常务副校长、教授　袁　卫

厉德寅先生是中国经济学史、中国统计学史都绕不过的一位学者。

一位学者在经济学和统计学两个领域都产生重要影响是不容易的。厉先生凭着在经济学和统计学两个领域的扎实训练和深厚涵养游走在两个学科，在民国时期和新中国成立后，为国家培养专业人才和咨询资政贡献了才智与力量。

厉先生1920年在浙江东阳中学毕业，考入南京高等师范学校物理系，与著名物理学家赵忠尧同班。厉先生各科学习成绩优秀，深受地学系主任竺可桢、物理系主任胡刚复、教授叶企孙等器重。1925年大学毕业后留在数学系任教，编著了《解析几何》，显示出极强的数学天赋。

1929年厉先生考取公费留学，赴美国威斯康星大学经济学系攻读博士学位。1934年以《相关理论的发展及其在经济统计学中的应用》获得经济学博士学位。这篇422页的论文综述了直至20世纪30年代概率统计的重要进展，特别研究了经济统计数据的特征及其应用，是一篇利用现代数理统计方法进行数量经济研究的经典文献。获得博士学位后，先生谢绝了留在美国任教的邀请，返回祖国。在途经英国时，他特别去英国伦敦大学学院（UCL）拜访R.A. Fisher，请教并探讨统计正态分布理论及应用的一些问题。

关于厉先生在经济学领域的研究，本书收录了先生陆续发表的23篇文章，还有关于先生经济思想研究的两篇专稿，特别是本书以《厉德寅经济学文集》命名，读者不难领略先生在经济理论研究与咨询建议方面的贡献。至于先生在统计学领域所下的功夫和付出的心血，特别是被错误地打成右派的前后，我愿意将所知的点滴写出来。

新中国诞生后，厉先生先在复旦大学，1952年高校院系调整后转到上海财经学院，讲授统计学、高等统计学、高等统计方法论、数理统计学、经济统计学、工业产品的统计管制等课程。1956年1月，党中央召开了全国知识分子会议，提出了"百花齐放、百家争鸣"的方针，统计学界也呈现出一片繁荣的景象。厉先生十分兴奋,着手翻译《数理统计导论》,但紧接着1957年就开始了反右运动。在上海财经学院党委召开的座谈会上,厉先生提出了"我们要总结本国经验,学习苏联经验,吸收其他国家的好的东西,来作出今后建设方针","我们不仅要学习苏联的统计,也要加强数理统计在经济研究中的应用","统计调查不要只守着陈旧的全面调查和大样本方法,而把现代数理统计所发展的新的小样本方法放弃不用,应该并用"等建议,结果被扣上"反对学习苏联""复辟资产阶级统计学"等大帽子,1958年3月被错定为右派分子,开除公职。随后又以"历史反革命"罪判处5年徒刑,发配青海德令哈农场。虽然先生在1963年9月刑满释放,但身心俱损,很快"文化大革命"爆发,厉先生再次面临逆境,1976年不幸去世。1979年3月他终于获得平反昭雪。

在我搜集到的民国时期33位获得博士学位的统计学留学生中,有13位获得的是经济学博士学位。在这些博士生的论文中,多数应用的统计方法比较简单,只有厉先生的这篇论文,与其说是一篇经济学博士论文,不如说是一篇数理统计方法研究的统计学博士论文。

先生的长子厉无咎教授级高工嘱我为"文集"写序,我是有些犹豫的。先生的生平和对统计学科的贡献有许多还是说不清楚的。比如先生在复旦大学和上海财经学院开了这么多门统计课程,所用教材及教学内容是什么?再比如1956年先生开始翻译《数理统计导论》,原书是哪一本?翻译的进展如何?等等。如果我们能够查阅到先生的档案,以及其中的个人简历与自传,许多疑问或许能够有所解答,那样的话,我们对先生的介绍就能够更细致、生动、全面。

在先生120周年诞辰纪念日前,先写到这里,但我们对先生生平的研究、对先生治学爱国精神的传承才刚刚开始。

2022年5月23日

目 录

中国数理统计学、计量经济学开拓者——厉德寅博士
.... 厉无咎 厉无忌 胡宋萍 1

THE DEVELOPMENT OF THE CORRELATION THEORY AND
 ITS APPLICATION TO ECONOMIC STATISTICS 1
算学在统计学上之任务.. 353
二项展开式与正态曲线.. 362
相关方法与变量之分析及其在智慧分析上之应用............ 385
新货币政策之史的背景及其将来................................ 394
改进中国国际贸易拟议.. 408
中央银行改组为中央储备银行时应有之认识.................. 414
维持外汇法价与黑市汇价... 418
隔离外汇黑市之建议... 438
再论维持外汇与黑市汇价... 451
树立平价行政机构议... 455
论对日经济制裁.. 462
我国当前外汇问题的出路... 471
国际贸易之理论.. 482
抗战以来之物价现象... 499
战时物价问题... 510

统制贸易之理论与办法 …………………………………………… 516
三年来之农业金融及今后改进之途径 …………………………… 534
我国农业金融制度之展望 ………………………………………… 563
法币与抗战 ………………………………………………………… 581
如何运用中美平准基金 …………………………………………… 593
以物资为中心之我国经济政策 …………………………………… 604
国际货币基金与中国 ……………………………………………… 620

附录 厉德寅经济思想研究 …………………………………… 627
全面抗战时期厉德寅的外汇政策研究 …………… 徐　昂 629
厉德寅农村金融思想及历史价值 ………… 苗书迪　贺水金 646
后记 …………………………………………………………… 厉无咎 660

中国数理统计学、计量经济学开拓者
——厉德寅博士

厉无咎　厉无忌　胡宋萍*

浙江东阳的自然资源并不富饶，境内以丘陵为主，会稽山、大盘山、仙霞岭延伸入境，形成三山夹两谷、两谷涵双江的地理。人众地瘠，出路何在？东阳人选择了以勤学苦读为立身上进之道。迨至清末，东阳累计出过305名进士。民国肇始，东阳领风气之先，兴办现代教育。20世纪二三十年代，从东阳出来了第一代博士杜佐周（1886—1974）、金士宣（1900—1992）、厉德寅（1902—1976），以及第一代硕士严济慈、葛正权等。此后，一代激励一代、一代提挈一代，东阳崇文重教的风气日益光大，耕读传家久、诗书济世长的理念播植人心。

中国计量经济学开拓者厉德寅博士

中国计量经济学和数理统计学的开创者厉德寅，是东阳第一代博士，也是东阳中学培养出来的第一位博士。也许是家学渊源有潜移默化的作用，他的家庭虽几经磨难，但在改革开放政策的阳光滋润下又茁壮起来，有两个子女是计量经济学和数理统计学家，其第三子厉无畏是计量

计量经济学博士生导师、第十一届全国政协副主席厉无畏

---

* 厉无咎，厉德寅长子，教授级高级工程师，1961年毕业于清华大学电机工程系，1992年起享受国务院特殊津贴；厉无忌，厉德寅小女儿，1988年获得美国马萨诸塞州立大学运筹学博士，先后被聘任为贝尔实验室、AT&T、朗讯等公司研究部门研究员；胡宋萍，上海财经大学统计与管理学院行政秘书、助理研究员。

经济学博士生导师、上海社会科学院部门经济研究所所长、第十一届全国政协副主席。他的小女儿厉无忌是美国马萨诸塞州立大学运筹学博士,也精通数理统计学。

1. 早年备尝艰辛,奋力畅游学海,成绩超拔

厉德寅于 1902 年 10 月 10 日在浙江东阳槐堂村诞生,其父厉芷轩(号寿祥)为清末贡生,以务农为生。厉德寅有兄弟姐妹共四人,其为长兄,生而颖慧,自幼便到城里读书,成绩优异。小学毕业后即在设于祠堂的学馆教学幼童一年。后考入东阳中学,其学业名列前茅。平时生活艰苦,常年以梅干菜下饭。课余则相帮父母编织草鞋出售,以补贴家用。

1920 年厉德寅从东阳中学毕业,考入学费、膳宿费全免的南京高等师范学校,和毕业于诸暨县立中学的赵忠尧同在数理化部学习,两人自此建立

英国皇家研究所所长、物理学家 William Bragg 所著《声之世界》,由厉德寅翻译,叶企孙校对,发表于《科学》1927 年第 12 卷第 3 期

了终身友谊。1922年8月至1923年7月曾辍学一年,赴洛阳省立第四师范学校担任数理化教师,挣钱帮助弟妹读书。1923年8月复学,继续在南京高等师范学校和东南大学物理系学习(1921年后南京高等师范学校相继衍变为东南大学和中央大学)。他成绩优秀,深受学校各科老师赞赏。1924年冬天,叶企孙教授从哈佛大学获得博士学位归来,在东南大学讲授近代物理,厉德寅深得叶企孙教授和物理系主任胡刚复教授的赏识。1925经叶、胡两位名师推荐,加入中国科学社。1927年2月,厉德寅翻译了英国皇家研究所所长、物理学家William Bragg所著的《声之世界》,由叶企孙校对,发表于《科学》1927年第3期,并编著《解析几何》一书,由东南大学出版。

2. 不负重托,为重建中国科学社美国分社作贡献

1925年,厉德寅从东南大学(中央大学)毕业后留校任高等数学教师。1929年他考取公费留学美国,于1930年3月赴美国威斯康星大学学习经济学和数理统计学。临行前,领受中国科学社社长竺可桢和总干事杨孝述交托,帮助在美国恢复和发展中国科学社美国分社,遂积极奔走,颇多贡献。

1930年厉德寅等威斯康星大学的研究生和他们的接待老师在等车去沃浦市的合影(前排左二为厉德寅)

美国加州州立理工大学普莫娜分校历史系教授、美国科学史学会理事会理事(2012—2014)王作跃曾在其《中国科学社美国分社历史研究》一文中说道:

中国科学社总部对美国分社的重视,不仅体现在总干事杨孝述与梅贻琦的密切联系上,也从当时社长竺可桢(时任中央研究院气象所所长)和杨孝述与留美学生厉德寅通信上得到反映。厉德寅1925年东南大学物理系毕业,留校任教并加入了科学社,1929年赴美国威斯康星大学攻读经济学博士,行前受到竺可桢"面嘱",要他帮助重建美国分社。1930年8月28日厉德寅写信给竺可桢和杨孝述,报告他在当地试图组织科学社社友的情况。竺可桢回信告知他梅贻琦在组织"东部科学社分会"及8月份在东部开会的消息,希望他与梅贻琦联系。杨孝述则在10月3日给厉德寅的回信中详告梅贻琦重组"美国分社"、8月间在纽约开年会的消息。他并提到康奈尔大学有顾毓琼、刘锴另发展的二十多个新社员,如果厉德寅能在芝加哥地区也组织起来,"则在美分社可有三个中心点,于社务发展大有裨益"。在接到竺、杨回信之前,厉德寅于9月7日又发函竺可桢,具体内容不详,但似乎提到在美建立多个分社以及与其他留美学术团体联合之事。竺可桢在10月10日给厉德寅的回信中,对这些问题作了回复,但态度与杨孝述不完全一样,他更强调科学社的统一性和独立性:"美国幅员辽阔,不妨有数个中心点,则办事上较为灵便,但一切行政上组织则须统一。至于与各学会联合问题,则因历史上关系,势有所难。惟年会则不妨同时同地举行。从前中国工程学会与科学社联合举行年会,凡数年之久也。"接到竺可桢和杨孝述的指示之后,厉德寅写信给梅贻琦,寄去他在当地发展的社员名单,请梅贻琦联系批准这些新发展的学人入会。(见《自然辩证法通讯》2016年第3期)

3. 勇攀高峰,开创中国计量经济学研究

1932年,厉德寅被威斯康星大学授予经济学硕士学位。同时他的指导老师H. Jerome教授介绍他加入了美国统计学社。

1934年他完成博士论文《相关理论的发展及其在经济统计学中的应用》,获得经济学博士学位。这篇422页的论文综述了直至20世纪30年代初数理统计的重要进展,特别研究了经济统计数据的特征及其应用,是一篇经济统计学的经典文献。Paul B. Trescott教授在其专著(*Jingji Xue: The History of the Introduction of Western Economic Ideas into China, 1850 - 1950*, Chinese University Press, 2007)中说,这一时期被国外学者认为"在学位论

文中研究'最尖端'经济理论问题的是厉德寅。其博士论文《相关理论的发展及其在经济统计学中的应用》运用的数理分析最多,是中国经济学由定性分析走向定量分析的里程碑式的成果"。

2003年厉无咎手持其父博士论文在威斯康星大学图书馆借书处

中国人民大学原常务副校长、中国人民大学应用统计科学研究中心一级教授袁卫等,以袁同礼先生于20世纪60年代初编著的《中国留美、留欧同学博士论文目录》为依据,加以分类和归纳,并参考其他文献资料,整理出统计学留学生基本信息,按获取学位时间顺序编成一个表格(见下,原载《治学报国:民国时期的统计留学生》,《统计研究》2021年第7期)。从表格中可见,厉德寅的这篇博士论文是中国第一篇系统地阐明当代最新数理统计理论和方法及其在经济统计学中的应用的论文,是中国经济统计学的开篇之作。

获得博士学位的统计留学生33位(部分为应用统计博士生)

姓名	学校	研究领域	获学位时间	论文题目
陆志韦	美国芝加哥大学	心理学	1920	遗忘的条件
廖世承	美国布朗大学	教育学	1921	非智力需求的数量分析
朱君毅	美国哥伦比亚大学	教育心理学	1922	中国留美学生:成功的要素
陈达	美国哥伦比亚大学	社会学	1923	中国移民研究

续表

姓名	学　校	研究领域	获学位时间	论文题目
唐启宇	美国康奈尔大学	经济学	1924	中国农业的经济学研究
李　昂	美国哥伦比亚大学	心理学	1925	记忆力与智力的实验研究
陈钟声	美国哥伦比亚大学	经济学	1925	中国人口普查：历史性与批判性研究
艾　伟	美国乔治·华盛顿大学	教育心理学	1925	学习中文时影响因素分析
沈有乾	美国斯坦福大学	心理学	1926	眼睛移动的研究
寿景伟	美国哥伦比亚大学	经济学	1926	中国的人口与金融：财政政策发展与目标的研究
吴泽霖	美国俄亥俄州立大学	社会学	1927	美国人对黑人、犹太人和东方人的态度
胡　毅	美国芝加哥大学	教育学	1928	中国成年人的阅读习惯与实验研究
赵人儁	美国哈佛大学	经济学	1928	马萨诸塞州实际工资和成本的变动(1890—1921)：一个统计分析
吴定良	英国伦敦大学学院	生物统计	1928	手和眼的右旋与左旋
袁贻瑾	美国约翰斯·霍普金斯大学	生物统计	1931	遗传对人类寿命的影响——基于1365年至1914年一个中国家族的数据
赵承信	美国密歇根大学	社会学	1933	从分裂到整合的中国生态学研究
赵才标	美国康奈尔大学	经济学	1933	中国十二省粮食产量的统计分析
裘开明	美国哈佛大学	经济学	1933	中国农业资料来源的研究：数据搜集方法和经济条件的获得
黄　钟	德国莱比锡大学	经济学	1933	现代中国人口统计的方式和结果
梁庆椿	美国哈佛大学	经济学	1934	中国人口和食品供应关系的研究

续表

姓名	学 校	研究领域	获学位时间	论文题目
厉德寅	美国威斯康星大学	经济学	1934	相关理论的发展及其在经济统计学中的应用
刘南溟	法国巴黎大学	人口统计学	1935	中国人口研究
齐泮林	美国芝加哥大学	教育学	1936	个性评估的可靠性与有效性
郑名儒	瑞士弗里堡大学	经济学	1936	大战前后中国对外贸易的统计比较
杨蔚	美国康奈尔大学	经济学	1937	1930年7月至1935年6月纽约六十家农场与商店牛奶互助供应的商业分析
陈仁炳	美国密歇根大学	经济学	1937	现代工业社会的人口平衡：美国商业研究机构的结构与功能
罗志如	美国哈佛大学	经济学	1937	电力价格和市场的统计研究
唐培经	英国伦敦大学学院	数理统计	1937	在方差分析与误差风险研究中假设检验问题研究
许宝騄	英国伦敦大学学院	数理统计	1938	双样本问题t检验理论的研究
李景均	美国康奈尔大学	生物统计	1940	棉花产量试验研究——竞争效应、面积和形状以及对照田的使用
徐钟济	美国哥伦比亚大学	数理统计	1941	双变量正态总体的抽样
魏宗舒	美国爱荷华大学	数理统计	1941	具有共同元素的和的回归系统是线性的必要与充分条件
李景仁	美国爱荷华州立大学	数理统计	1943	混杂析因实验的设计与统计分析

获得博士学位后，厉德寅利用平时结余的奖学金去欧洲各国考察经济，以丰富自己的实际知识。这期间拜访了一些著名数理统计学家，其中访问了时任英国伦敦大学学院教授、数理统计学奠基人之一的R.A. Fisher，他们深入讨论了随机变量的概率分布问题。之后返回祖国，受聘担任中央大学和中央政治学校教授，讲授经济统计学等课程。那时期他发表了《算学在

统计学上之任务》(《国立中央大学社会科学丛刊》1935年第2卷第1期)，《二项展开式与正态曲线》(《计政学报》1935年第1卷第4期)，《相关方法与变量之分析及其在智慧分析上之应用》(《科学》1936年第20卷第6期)，"A Theory of Correlation"(《国立中央大学科学研究录》1936年第2卷第2期)等论文。其中三篇中文写就的论文，许多数理统计学的名词术语在中国也是首次应用。当时中国社会的语言文字也处在从文言文过渡到白话文的时期，所以与现在通行的有比较大的差异。综上所述，厉德寅是中国最早学习和掌握当时世界上新兴的数理统计学和计量经济学理论的专家之一，也是中国研究和教学推广该学说的先行者。

4. 恩师竺可桢牵线，与蒋作宾长女喜结连理

1920年，厉德寅考进南京高等师范学校时，竺可桢刚好从武昌高等师范学校调来任气象学和地理学教授，后来兼任东南大学地学系主任，并在1923年后当选为中国科学社讲演委员会主任、中国气象学会理事和副会长等职。由于厉德寅勤奋好学、成绩优秀、诚实守信，深得竺可桢器重。1927年至1928年，竺可桢又重返中央大学(东南大学改为中央大学)任地学系主任，与厉德寅进一步发展了友谊。

1936年秋，竺可桢把自己刚从法国里昂大学毕业回国的内侄女蒋硕德(1915—1988)介绍给厉德寅。蒋硕德生于上海，是辛亥革命元老、民国勋臣蒋作宾的长女。蒋作宾夫人是出身湖南名门的张淑嘉，她的大姐是中国民主革命家、妇女运动先驱、中华民国教育家和诗人张默君，她的小妹是中国第一个乘飞机上天的张侠魂，张侠魂的丈夫便是竺可桢。

蒋硕德端庄秀丽、温婉大方、仪态超卓、知书达理、待人和善。1932年，她与妹妹蒋硕真在上海大同中学毕业后，一同去法国里昂大学留学。1936年获教育学学士后回国。经她姨父竺可桢介绍与厉德寅认识后，二人一见钟情，很快就在次年的一月十五日结婚。厉德寅与蒋硕德共育有三男一女，依次为厉无咎、厉无吝、厉无畏和厉无忌(女)。

青年蒋硕德

蒋硕德1936年从法国留学归来

1946年厉德寅蒋硕德夫妇和他们的三个儿子无咎、无吝和无畏在昆明住宅前

蒋硕德及其儿孙们

5. 苟利国家生死以，岂因祸福避趋之

　　1937年7月7日，日本发动全面侵华战争，8月13日淞沪会战爆发，国军血战三月，终因敌强我弱而失守。11月20日国民政府宣布撤出南京，退至武汉，迁都重庆。同时，还宣布改组长江沿线各省主政官员，以最得力的干将充实前线，直接领导各省抗战。这样，蒋作宾便由内政部长改任安徽省政府主席，兼任省保安队司令，以图挽救时局。在那烽火漫天的时日，他带着重病在身的夫人和次子蒋硕英，冒着敌人的炮火，未带一兵一卒于11月

22日仓促上任,组建省保安部队抵抗日寇。未几,广德和宣城相继失守。当时有如下报道:"1937年11月27日上午8时左右,日寇数批飞机,轮番轰炸宣城,持续到下午4时才告结束,被炸死的男女老少,尸横在地,目不忍睹,大部分商店民房成为废墟。投弹最多的是鳌峰一带及东门火车站和南门学校区。而时任国民党宣城县党部书记雷克展,于11月26日弃职,带着全家逃回湖南,此时全城一片混乱,人心惶惶。"

南京也于1937年12月13日沦陷。安徽第十行政专区(当时又名休宁专区,管辖休宁、屯溪、歙县、绩溪、祁县和黟县,后加入旌德),与已被日寇占领的广德和宣城毗邻。面临日寇大兵压境,潮水般涌入的大批难民与溃散的军人急需安置和疏散,又要组织民工配合守军修筑公路和保障运输,还要组织和训练民兵(保安队)维持治安和进行游击战抵抗日寇的侵略,蒋作宾一时无人可用,急忙电召时任中央大学和中央政治学校教授的厉德寅前来救急。厉德寅接电后本着"苟利国家生死以,岂因祸福避趋之"的信念,不计个人安危,安顿好有孕在身的夫人,投笔从戎,直奔抗日前线。就这样代理了三个月的安徽第十行政专区专员,为抗日战争作出贡献。后来他还应中央政治训练团邀请就这段经历作了"如何做好地区专员"的演讲。1938年4月李宗仁所指挥的第五战区在安徽省部署到位,安徽军政都由李宗仁负责,厉德寅遂辞去第十行政专区专员,回到中央政治学校教授经济统计学。

6. 殚精竭虑,研究战时经济良策

1937年8月,为应对抗日战争金融管理之需要,国民政府设立了四联总处(即中国、中央、交通、中国农民四银行联合办事总处的简称)。四联总处成立之初,它的主要任务是联合国家银行,协调各行业务,配合政府贯彻《非常时期安定金融办法》,对外汇实行初步管制,稳定金融市场以及融通资金,支持工矿企业内迁和扶持生产。至1939年,国民政府为了应对日趋严峻的战争形势,对其进行了改组,由国家财政部、经济部、粮食部、交通部和各个国家银行之负责人共同组织理事会,由蒋介石亲自兼任理事会主席,孔祥熙、宋子文出任理事会常务理事,健全机构,扩展业务。至此,四联总处成为一事权高度集中的、具有权威性的战时金融总枢机构,即所谓"经济作战之大本营",不仅参与各项经济金融大计之决策与筹划,还负责督导国家相关行政机构和银行贯彻执行。厉德寅于1939年11月被调任四联总处统计科科长,主管金融调查、统计、研究工作。

四联总处重要职员名册

厉德寅在四联总处负责统计工作时,设计和编制了许多统计项目,以便尽可能真实、全面和快速地反映社会经济情况。例如他设计的"十五项物价每周指数",采用十五种商品作为代表样本,以1937年上半年为基期,采用加权综合式计算,权数是根据1936—1937年有关生产、进出口和消费的部分资料估计出来,每周发表。这个指数因为所包括的种类少、计算方便,所以较其他物价指数发表得早,及时而准确,一直被沿用到1949年。

民国时期特别是抗日战争时期,面临内忧外患的复杂境况与社会转型的历史背景,中国最需要解决的经济问题主要是整顿货币制度、发展金融,使其适应和促进工商业的发展,吸收外资发展外贸,构建健康完善的财政制度、税收制度及关税自主制度及发展农村经济等。厉德寅胸怀忧国忧民之心,寻求救国图存之道,对上述这些重大的经济政策和制度均有深入研究,精辟分析,就此发表了许多论文,如《新货币政策之史的背景及其将来》《改进中国国际贸易拟议》《中央银行改组为中央储备银行时应有之认识》《论对日经济制裁》《隔离外汇黑市之建议》,以及《维持外汇法价与黑市汇价》《战时物价问题》《统制贸易之理论与办法》,等等。

中国西部地区的经济,历来落后于沿海和中部地区。民国以后,由于军阀割据、兵祸连连,农村经济之凋敝、农业金融之枯竭、高利贷之肆虐,尤其于全国。面对西部地区农村如此严峻的局面,为了增加农业生产以供战时军民衣食和出口创汇之需,为了保证战时兵役、力役的输送,为了稳定广阔的农村社会,国民政府就必须采取有力措施,迅速改变西部农村状况,从战前发展合作、推行农贷的思路和实践出发,把农贷作为复兴农村经济的重要政策和措施。其时,由于战争的影响,各地农贷一时处于停顿状态。战前一些办理农贷业务的商业金融机构,由于战时商业利润的驱使,避害趋利,纷纷收缩和停办农贷业务,国民政府成了在战时国统区发动农贷的主要力量。

厉德寅目睹此情此景,先后发表了《三年来之农业金融及今后改进之途径》《树立兼营式农业金融体系之建议》《我国农业金融制度之展望》等论文。在《三年来之农业金融及今后改进之途径》一文中,厉德寅科学地统计分析了1937—1940年国家行局、各省银行、各省农民银行、各省合作金库、各省政府部门与合作机关等各类农贷机关的放款数据,完整地勾画出了抗战初期农贷机关组织的结构表征,为后续农村金融机构的组织体系调整奠定了基础,也为后世研究战时农业金融提供了丰富的史料。厉德寅在他的这些论文中提出建立国家农业银行及各省分行,各县设立合作金库及下属合作社的一整套农业金融体系,发行农业债券等筹集资金,统筹办理对农户的短期、中期和长期贷款,大力推行农贷以支持农村经济发展,这些建议被其任职的四联总处采纳推进,取得良好成效。

这时期厉德寅还曾任《财政学报》编辑委员会委员和重庆《商务日报》主编,为促进当时经济刊物的成长和普及经济学作了贡献。

7. 监控汇率,辅佐中英美平准基金委员会运行

1941年4月1日,由国民政府、中央银行与英国财政部代表三方签订中英平准基金协定,接着中美签订平准基金协定,随即三方开始着手成立一个统一的中英美平准基金委员会。1941年4月25日,宋子文分别与美国财政部部长摩根索、英国财政次长费立浦在华盛顿换文,宣告中国政府将设立由中、英、美三方代表参加的平准基金委员会,由中方三人(陈光甫、席德懋、贝祖诒)、美英方各一人(美方为福克斯,英方为霍伯奇)组成。平准基金委员会设有研究室,对外汇和金融市场进行统计计算和分析,以及进行相关政策的研究。经由孔祥熙推荐,才学丰富的厉德寅在1941年6月被任命为平准基金委员会研究室主任。1941年8月13日,中英美平准基金委

员会召开了第一次会议,标志着平准基金委员会正式成立。

中英美平准基金协定于1943年6月30日到期,当时孔祥熙和中央银行认为,通过多年的工作实践,他们完全有能力把握中国未来的汇率走势,加以美国同意给中国五亿美元借款,可满足中国对外汇的需求,从而不再保留平准基金委员会。厉德寅则在1943年5月18日向平准基金委员会主席陈光甫提交辞呈后,离开了平准基金委员会,调任经济部参事和交通银行总行设计处副处长,主管该行的设计和统计工作。

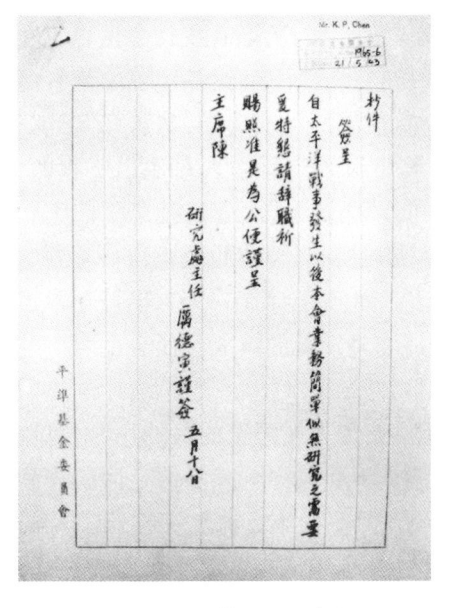

厉德寅向平准基金委员会主席
陈光甫提交的辞呈

厉德寅向平准基金委员会主席
陈光甫提交的辞呈(英文)

1945年10月,厉德寅调任中央银行昆明分行总经理,并在1946年8月开始兼任云南大学国际贸易学教授,直到1948年10月离开昆明为止。他在云南大学还建立以其父名字命名的厉寿祥奖学金,以帮助贫困学生求学。1948年10月,厉德寅调任中央银行上海经济研究处高级专员。

8. 为统计学教育鼓与呼卷入旋涡,冤案终获昭雪

1950年8月起,厉德寅任复旦大学教授,教授统计学、高等统计学方法论和品质管理学。1951年到1952年,全国各大专院校开展"知识分子思想

改造运动",厉德寅因为曾在国民政府机构中任职的经历,成了复旦大学"知识分子思想改造运动"的重点人物。在小会、大会上反复检讨交代,批判自己的学术是资产阶级的、反动的、唯心主义的,最后在群众大会上始得"过关"。随后全国高校进行院系调整,厉德寅被调到上海财经学院,还被降级为四级教授。虽然受此打击,但是他还是抱着为新中国服务、为国家建设多作贡献的愿望,花了一年多业余时间学会了俄文,从而能够阅读俄文的统计学参考书籍,以便编辑统计学新教材。到1956年为止,数理统计学和工业产品品质检查等课程已被停止开课多年。厉德寅一向认为数理统计是统计学的数学基础,为各种应用统计学提供理论支持,数理统计方法在工农业生产、医疗卫生、工程技术、自然科学以及社会经济金融各领域中都有广泛的应用。他认为自己在数理统计学上有很深的学术造诣,是这些需要高深数学知识的课程的专家,是可以为培养高级统计科学人才作出贡献的。1956年1月,中共中央召开了知识分子问题会议,这次会议鼓舞了广大知识分子,激发了他们的政治热情和工作积极性,统计学界也呈现出一片繁荣的景象。厉德寅开始翻译《数理统计导论》,但紧接着在1957年就开始了"反右"运动。1957年5月,厉德寅在上海财经学院的鸣放座谈会上对该院统计学专业的教学计划提出批评意见,他建议要"对学习苏联统计学作出总结",要"总结本国经验,学习苏联经验,吸收其他国家的好的东西,来作出今后建设方针"。他还批评说:"统计调查不要只守着陈旧的全面调查和大样本方法,而把现代数理统计所发展的新的小样本方法放弃不用。"他的这些言论受到了严厉批判,不仅大会、小会批判,还被《学术月刊》上发表的《驳斥厉德寅对学习苏联的诬蔑》和《我们对资产阶统计学的态度和右派对我们的攻击》两篇专论进行批判(见《学术月刊》1958年第2期)。这两篇文章认为厉德寅企图从恢复数理统计来复辟资产阶级统计学,企图推翻工人阶级自己的统计学;还认为"厉德寅说的'学习苏联'不过是一个幌子,他实际是要大家向有传统经验的旧统计学家学习,也就是向厉德寅这样的资产阶级学者学习,再一个就是向资本主义国家学习。学习的结果,当然是在中国建立资产阶级统计学,建立为资产阶级服务的统计工作。那时候像厉德寅辈,就可掌握领导大权,为恢复资本主义开锣喝道"。厉德寅就此被划为右派分子,给予撤销教授职务、开除公职、劳动教养处分。旋即又被上海市虹口区人民法院定为历史反革命分子,判刑5年,送青海省德令哈农场劳动改造。1963年9月2日刑满释放,1964年5月回沪,1976年10月2日不幸病逝。1979年3月厉德寅获得平反昭雪。

厉德寅和蒋硕德 1974 年夏在上海虹口公园

厉德寅是中国最早研究经济统计、经济计量方法的学者之一，在国内大学开设经济统计和数理统计在经济中应用等课程，培养统计应用人才，发表论文40余篇，还著有《解析几何》《高等代数补充教材》《国民经济研究所丛书之五：外汇和贸易问题》等书。他的学术成就得到了国内外学术界的好评。

中南财经政法大学副校长邹进文教授在《近代留学生留学期间的经济学研究——以博士论文为中心的考察》(见《中国社会科学》2010年第5期)一文中说："厉德寅的博士论文《相关理论的发展及其在经济统计学中的应用》运用的数理分析最多，是中国经济学由定性分析走向定量分析的里程碑式的成果。"

复旦大学经济学院的孙大权教授发表的论文《民国时期的中国经济学与经济思想》(载《贵州财经学院学报》2011年第6期)中曾说道："1938—1940年，应否维持法币汇价成为讨论主题。以马寅初、刘大钧为代表的维持法币汇率派，同以叶元龙、厉德寅、陈长蔚为代表的法币贬值派进行了激烈的论辩。1940年后，讨论的中心为如何反通货膨胀，包括：(1)收缩与扩充信贷的论争。谷春帆等认为应紧缩生产信贷，减少货币流通，控制物价上涨；章乃器等却认为应扩充信贷以发展生产，增加物资供应，控制物价上涨。(2)利率高低的论争。刘大钧、吴大业等认为应提高利息，通货膨胀情况下实际利率为负，生产变为没有效益的'负号生产'；厉德寅、朱祖晦等认为应降低利息，鼓励生产。"虽然该文没有深入分析各种观点，但可以看出他列出的这些经济学领军人物讨论的都是攸关国计民生和坚持对日抗战的重大经济问题。

湖南工商大学副校长、博士生导师易棉阳教授在其论文《民国经济学家在构建中国经济学话语体系上的努力——以留学生为中心的考察》(载《中国计量经济史研究动态》2016年第3期)中说:"厉德寅和刘大中对计量经济学的发展也作出了卓越贡献。20世纪初,世界计量经济学方兴未艾,中国留学生敢于攻坚克难,涉足计量经济学研究,其中的佼佼者是厉德寅。他1935年毕业于威斯康星大学,博士论文题为《相关理论的发展及其在经济统计学中的应用》,这篇论文对相关理论的发展历史和内涵做了系统的梳理,剖析了回归分析方法的要领,研究了抽样分布和方差分析方法,就时间序列之间的相关性做了深入的探讨,其数理分析的难度即使是今天也是一般经济学家难以掌握的。时至今日,美国学者仍认为厉德寅的学位论文研究的是'最尖端'的经济理论问题。"

厉德寅不仅对中国计量经济学和数理统计学学科的开创、教学、推广应用和发展作出了卓越贡献,还为民国时期经济适应长期抗日战争和历史转型提出了许多充满真知灼见的政策建议和实施方法。

(本文曾发表于《世纪》2022年第3期,收入此书时作者进行了扩充和修订)

THE DEVELOPMENT OF THE CORRELATION THEORY AND ITS APPLICATION TO ECONOMIC STATISTICS

CHAPTER I INTRODUCTORY

1.1 Scope and Organization

The correlation analysis as a powerful tool in scientific investigation has been widely used in the biological and social sciences. The method has been developed since its discovery from a variety of hypotheses. The major difficulty encountered is not one of deriving the formulas but rather one of establishing a high degree of probability that the hypotheses underlying the derivations are realized in relation to practical problems of statistics. The objective in this thesis is to trace chronologically the development of correlation theory and to elucidate analytically the methods so far developed, so that an accurate concept of correlation, a full knowledge of the assumptions underlying the deduction of the formulas, and an understanding of the limitations to the applications of the method in statistical practice may be secured.

The honor of the discovery① of the theory is attributed to Francis Galton by Karl Pearson, but the mathematical foundations were laid by early mathematicians — Laplace, Plana, Gauss, and Bravais are among the most noted ones.② Indeed, to some of them may rightfully belong the honor of the discovery of the correlation analysis. However, it is of relatively little

---

① "It was not until 1889, ... that Galton published his Natural Inheritance, and with it the first solid foundation of the correlation calculus." And "In his(Galton's) notebook on the sweet-pea experiments occur the first correlation table, the first regression curve, ...". K. Pearson, Frances Galton 1822 – 1922, A Centenary Appreciation.

② See Chapter II.

consequence, exactly who was the discoverer. We are primarily interested in what contributions the different writers have made to the correlation analysis. With this purpose in view, we shall trace the development of the theory under the four headings:

(1) Correlation surface method,
(2) Regression method,
(3) Analysis of variance method,
(4) Vector of matrix method.

In addition to the foregoing, we may mention the graphic method but, in reality, this is one variant of the regression method and therefore will be included in the discussion of that method. These methods differ from each other in the manner of approach, and certain of the methods have distinct advantages of presentation and interpretation, but may, on the other hand, be limited in use for other reasons. In the following paragraphs, we shall attempt to give a general picture of the four methods so as to show how the several methods are related to each other. For the sake of simplicity, we shall in this chapter confine the exposition to the case of two variates (variables), except that the matrix method is more conveniently discussed here for the general case. For the sake of clearness, we shall first explain some fundamental concepts.

1.2 Some Fundamental Concepts

A variable quantity is called a variate. If we make an infinite number of all possible observations on some variable of quantity (if we observe, for example, the atomic weight of hydrogen, or the prices of different samples of a commodity, or the statures of a specified group of men), the aggregate of the results is a population of observations. The observations in a population differ in value, that is to say, the individuals in a population display variation. The manner of the variation is characterized by a scheme, called a frequency distribution, which specifies how frequently the variate takes each of its possible values.

Correlation analysis is the study of the simultaneous variation or <u>covariation</u> of two or more variates.

1.3 The Correlation Surface Method

The manner of covariation of any number of variates is completely known so soon as the simultaneous frequency distribution, called the correlation surface or the compound probability function, of the variates is specified. The correlation surface method seeks to determine such a correlation surface through a sample of available observations on the variates in question.

For the description of the frequency distribution of a variate normally distributed we fit a normal curve of the form:

$$\varphi(x) = \frac{1}{\sigma_1 \sqrt{2x}} e^{\frac{-x^2}{2\sigma_1^2}}. \qquad (1 \cdot 1)$$

In terms of the theory of probability, this means that the probability that an x taken at random will lie in the interval $(x, x+h)$ is

$$P = \frac{1}{\sigma_1 \sqrt{2x}} \int_x^{x+h} e^{\frac{-x^2}{2\sigma_1^2}} dx.$$

By the extension of this method to the case of two variables normally distributed (i.e., any array of y's corresponding to a given x is a normal distribution and vice versa), we may fit a normal surface of the form:

$$\varphi(x, y) = \frac{1}{2x\sigma_1\sigma_2\sqrt{1-r^2}} e^{\frac{-1}{2(1-r^2)}\left(\frac{x^2}{\sigma_1^2} + \frac{y^2}{\sigma_2^2} - \frac{2xy}{\sigma_1\sigma_2}\right)}. \qquad (1 \cdot 2)$$

But if x and y were independent, the frequency surface would be of the form:

$$\varphi(x)\,\varphi(y) = \frac{1}{2x\sigma_1\sigma_2} e^{-\frac{1}{2}\left(\frac{x^2}{\sigma_1^2} + \frac{y^2}{\sigma_2^2}\right)}. \qquad (1 \cdot 3)$$

Since the probability that two independent events will occur simultaneously is equal to the product of their respective probabilities and the probabillty for x to occur is $P_1 = \dfrac{1}{\sigma_1 \sqrt{2x}} e^{\frac{-x^2}{2\sigma_1^2}}$ and that for y to occur is $P_2 = \dfrac{1}{\sigma_2 \sqrt{2x}} e^{\frac{-y^2}{2\sigma_2^2}}$.

Hence the parameter r which makes $(1 \cdot 2)$ different from $(1 \cdot 3)$ is called the coefficient of correlation between x and y. For independent variates the coefficient of correlation is zero.

The above discussion of the characterization of frequency surfaces is limited to normally distributed variates. As to the case of non-normally distributed variates, the Gram-Charlier theory of generalized frequency curves may be extended. Such a generalized correlation surface for two variates may be written in the form:[1]

$$f(x, y) = \varphi(x, y) + \sum\sum_{k+l \geq 3} \Delta_{11} \frac{\partial^{k+l}\varphi(x, y)}{\partial_x^k \partial_y^l}. \quad (1\cdot 4)$$

Where $\varphi(x, y)$ is the normal correlation surface given in equation $(1\cdot 2)$, and the characteristic coefficients A's may be expressed in terms of moments of the distribution.

As in the case of one variate, the correlation surface means that the probability for x, y to occur in the region $(x, x+h)$, $(y, y+k)$ is given by

$$P = \frac{1}{\sigma_1\sqrt{2\pi}} \int_x^{x+h} \int_y^{y+k} f(x, y) \,dx dy.$$

However, we may view it in another way. Let us write the correlation surface $(1\cdot 2)$ as a product

$$\varphi(x, y) = \left[\frac{1}{\sigma_1\sqrt{2x}} e^{\frac{-x^2}{2\sigma_1^2}}\right] \left[\frac{1}{\sigma_2\sqrt{1-r^2}\sqrt{2x}} e^{\frac{-1}{2\sigma_2^2(1-r^2)}\left(y - r\frac{\sigma_2}{\sigma_1}\right)^2}\right]. \quad (1\cdot 5)$$

This shows clearly two things: (1) the values of y corresponding to a given x are normally distributed with the mean at $y = r\dfrac{\sigma_2}{\sigma_1}x$. By definition, the locus of the array-means of y is the regression curve of y on x, and therefore the regression equation is obtained simply by putting the derivative of the exponent of the second factor in $(1\cdot 5)$ equal to zero, or, by performing the integration:

$$\int_{-\infty}^{+\infty} y\varphi(x, y)\,dy + \int_{-\infty}^{+\infty} \varphi(x, y)\,dy.$$

(2) The precision of predicting that a value for y will lie in the interval dy at a given x by means of the regression curve is given by

---

[1] This function may be derived from different assumptions, namely, elementary error hypotheses, hypergeometric series, and Van der Stoke's premises. Cf. Chapter II.

$$P_0 = \frac{1}{2x\sigma_1\sigma_2\sqrt{1-r^2}}e^{\frac{-x_0^2}{2\sigma_1^2}}dy,$$

i.e., P_0 is the probability that an observation y taken at random under conditions where x takes the value x_0, will lie between

$$r\frac{\sigma_2 x_0}{\sigma_1} \pm \frac{1}{2}dy.$$

Nevertheless, in common practice, we use the probable error or the probability integral

$$P = \int_{-p}^{p} \frac{1}{2x\sigma_1\sigma_2\sqrt{1-r^2}} e^{\frac{-1}{2\sigma_2^2(1-r^2)}\left(y-r\frac{\sigma_2}{\sigma_1}x\right)^2} dy = \frac{1}{2}$$

meaning that a half of the N observations made at random will lie within the range $y = r\frac{\sigma_2}{\sigma_1}x - p$ and $y = r\frac{\sigma_2}{\sigma_1}x + p$. Here p is a number defined by the equation

$$\int_{-p}^{+p} f(x, y) dy = \frac{1}{2}.$$

If the correlation surface is normal, then

$$\int_{-p}^{+p} f(x, y) dy = 2\int_{0}^{+p} f(x, y) dy,$$

and p the probable error, which may be shown equal to 0.674 5 times the standard deviation of (1 · 5) at a given value of x, may be used instead of the probability integral.

1.4 The Regression Curve Method

As mentioned above, the regression curve, which is defined as the loci of the means of arrays of y, may be obtained by putting the exponent of second factor in (1 · 5) equal to zero. However, the direct way to find it is to fit a line to the array-means of y. The best estimate of the line obtainable from the sample is the one which yielded with the maximum probability by the sample and the regression line so determined is then interpreted as the regression line in the theoretical population which would yield this line with the greatest frequency.

Suppose we observe n quantities x, y, ... Each of these quantities is assumed to be independent and to follow the normal law. The combined probability of the system is

$$P_n = K_0 e^{-\frac{1}{2}\left\{\left(\frac{x-\bar{x}}{\sigma_1}\right)^2 + \left(\frac{y-\bar{y}}{\sigma_2}\right)^2 + \cdots\right\}}. \tag{1·6}$$

This probability will be maximum when

$$X_n^2 = \sum \left(\frac{x-\bar{x}}{\sigma_1}\right)^2 \tag{1·7}$$

is minimum—the principle of the least squares as developed by Gauss. It follows that the best estimate of the true regression may be obtained by the method of least squares, provided the distributions of the variates are normal as implied in the derivation of the method of the least squares. The regression line thus estimated is exactly the same as would be obtained by equating to zero the derivative of the exponent of the second factor in (1·5). Therefore, from the result of either method, we can easily obtain the solution for the other.

It is thus seen that the regression method is fundamentally the same as the correlation surface method. In a sense, the former may be regarded as revolving from the latter and makes the process of computation simpler by fitting a least squares line to the means of arrays instead of fitting a correlation surface to the cross classified frequencies.

1.5 The Analysis of Variance Method

The squared standard deviation is called the variance, this is used as a measure of variation in preference to the standard deviation because of its associative property. The method of the analysis of variance is to divide the variance in question into parts representing the variations, due, by assumption, to certain specified causes so that we may ascertain, for one cause at a time, if the variance changes as the cause is varied.

If d be the deviation of an observed value of y from its corresponding computed value y_c (the variation of y_c represents the variation in y due to the cause x) on the regression line, as defined in the last section, i.e., $y = \dfrac{r\sigma_2 x}{\sigma_1}$, then for each individual we may write $y = y_c + d$. And it can be shown that

$$\sigma_y^2 = \sigma_{y_c}^2 + \sigma_{y \cdot x}^2,$$

where σ_y^2 is the mean square of the deviations of the observations from the grand mean and will be called the total variance of y, and denoted by σ_t^2; and $\sigma_{y \cdot x}^2$ is the mean square of the deviations of the observed y from the computed y_c or array-means and will be called the intra-array variance (hereafter denoted by σ_s^2), because it owes its source to the variation within arrays; and $\sigma_{y_c}^2$ is the mean square of the deviations of the computed y_c (or the array-means) from the grand mean and will be called the inter-arrays variance (hereafter denoted by σ_r^2), because it owes its source to the variations between arrays. It is the inter-arrays variation which gives rise to the coefficient of correlation; for

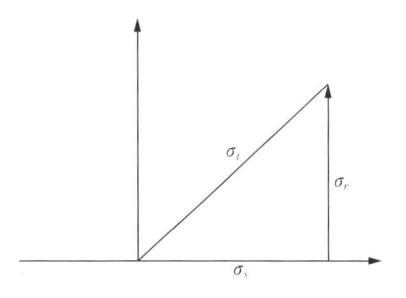

$$\sigma_s^2 = \sigma_t^2 - \sigma_r^2 = \sigma_t^2 \left(1 - \frac{\sigma_r^2}{\sigma_t^2}\right) \qquad (1 \cdot 8)$$

or,
$$= \sigma_t^2 (1 - r^2),$$

$$r^2 = \frac{\sigma_r^2}{\sigma_t^2}. \qquad (1 \cdot 9)$$

If we represent these three variances by a right triangle, as shown in the diagram then the correlation coefficient corresponds to the sine function. However, the important thing is the relative magnitudes of these three variances, and therefore either of the six ratios corresponding to the six trigonometric functions may serve this purpose, because knowing one we can determine the other five. In mathematics, we use the tangent oftener than the sine function because of certain of its advantages. It is perhaps for the same reason[1] that R. A. Fisher

---

[1] The analysis of variance is a generalized method of studying variation, and a function of this ratio $\dfrac{\sigma_r^2}{\sigma_s^2}$ assumes a nearly constant form of distribution and tends to normality rapidly.

uses the ratio $\dfrac{\sigma_r}{\sigma_s}$ instead of $\dfrac{\sigma_r}{\sigma_t}$ in the correlation analysis.

Fisher's method starts by fitting a regression line and therefore involves the assumptions underlying the theory of regression curve method. But his method uses as a measure of correlation the function $z = \dfrac{1}{2}\log\dfrac{\sigma_r^2}{\sigma_s^2}$, which has certain properties making small samples reveal more trustworthy results and telling more accurately the significance of the relationship in question.

1.6 Vector or Matrix Method[①]

The method of studying the correlation among a set of variates by means of the vector and matrix notation is called the vector or matrix method of correlation analysis. This method enables us to make use of the properties of quadratic forms and linear transformations, which have been developed in algebra, in obtaining information concerning correlation.

Now if the intra-array variance σ_s^2, in the last section is zero, then all observed y's are on the regression line and the correlation is perfect. In other words, the triangles formed by the sets of any two vectors or points (x_1, y_1), (x_2, y_2) and the origin (the origin is taken at the grand means $\bar{x}, \bar{y}$) will reduce to segments of a straight line and their areas

$$\Lambda = \frac{1}{2}\begin{vmatrix} x_i & x_j \\ y_i & y_j \end{vmatrix} \qquad (1\cdot 10)$$

---

① For the other reasons see Chapter IV. The method was developed by R. Frisch in 1928, "Correlation and Scatter in Statistical Variables", Nordisk stat. Tid., Bd. B, pp.86 – 102. A vector is a directed quantity. A set of n quantities $x_1, x_2, \cdots, x_n$, represented geometrically in an n-dimensional space determines a point, and the directed segment of the straight line from the origin to this point is a vector, denoted by $x=(x_1, x_2, \cdots, x_n)$. A system of mn quantities arranged in a rectangular array of m rows and n columns is called a matrix:

$$\begin{bmatrix} x_{11} & x_{12} & \cdots & x_{1n} \\ x_{21} & x_{22} & & x_{2n} \\ \vdots & & \ddots & \vdots \\ x_{m1} & x_{m2} & \cdots & x_{mn} \end{bmatrix}$$

If $m=n$, the matrix is called a square matrix of order n. See M. Bocher, Higher Algebra, The Macmillan Company, New York.

are all identically zero. If the N observations are not lying in a straight line, the area $(1 \cdot 10)$ will not vanish for some of the sets. The magnitude of this area $(1 \cdot 10)$ for any set of two points will serve as a measure of how far the triangle constructed on this set is from being a straight line. And the average of all these areas, taken over all possible sets of two points (the number of sets is seen to be equal to the number of combinations of N elements taken 2 at a time or N_2^c) will therefore present itself as a measure of scatter or dispersion of the observation points about a straight line. In order not to have positive and negative areas cancelled out, we may make use of the squares of the determinants in $(1 \cdot 10)$ and define the collective standard deviation σ by

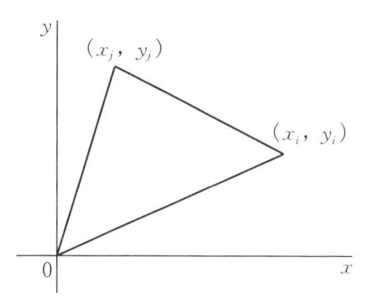

$$\sigma^2 = \frac{1}{2!N^2} \sum_{ij} \begin{vmatrix} x_i & x_j \\ y_i & y_j \end{vmatrix}^2. \qquad (1 \cdot 11)$$

Now let us take the case of two variates in $N=3$ observations and examine the meaning of $(1 \cdot 11)$. The possible determinants in $(1 \cdot 11)$ formed by making i, j run independently through N values are seen to be:

(I)

(1) $i = 1, j = 2.$

$$B = \begin{vmatrix} x_1 & x_2 \\ y_1 & y_2 \end{vmatrix}$$

(2) $i = 2, j = 1.$

$$B' = \begin{vmatrix} x_2 & x_1 \\ y_2 & y_1 \end{vmatrix}$$

(II)

(1) $i = 1, j = 3.$

$$C = \begin{vmatrix} x_1 & x_3 \\ y_1 & y_3 \end{vmatrix}$$

(2) $i = 3, j = 1.$

$$C' = \begin{vmatrix} x_3 & x_1 \\ y_3 & y_1 \end{vmatrix}$$

(III)

(1) $i = 2, j = 3.$

$$D = \begin{vmatrix} x_2 & x_3 \\ y_2 & y_3 \end{vmatrix}$$

(2) $i = 3, j = 2.$

$$D' = \begin{vmatrix} x_3 & x_2 \\ y_3 & y_2 \end{vmatrix}$$

And those determinants corresponding to $i=j=1, 2, 3$ which vanish identically.

Hence there are $N^P n = 3^P 2 = 6$ determinants forming into $N^C n$ groups with $n!$ determinants in each (Here N = number of observations = 3, and n = number of variates = 2). Moreover, the determinants in each group are equal in absolute value.

Now taking a determinant from each group and expanding their squares

$$B^2 = (x_1 y_2 - x_2 y_1)^2 = x_1^2 y_2^2 + x_2^2 y_1^2 - 2 x_1 x_2 y_1 y_2,$$
$$C^2 = (x_1 y_3 - x_3 y_1)^2 = x_1^2 y_3^2 + x_3^2 y_1^2 - 2 x_1 x_3 y_1 y_3,$$
$$D^2 = (x_2 y_3 - x_3 y_2)^2 = x_2^2 y_3^2 + x_3^2 y_2^2 - 2 x_2 x_3 y_2 y_3,$$

and summing up

$$B^2 + C^2 + D^2 = [x_1^2(y_2^2 + y_3^2) + x_2^2(y_1^2 + y_3^2) + x_3^2(y_1^2 + y_2^2)]$$
$$= [x_1 y_1(x_2 y_2 + x_3 y_3) + x_2 y_2(x_3 y_3 + x_1 y_1) + x_3 y_3(x_2 y_2 + x_1 y_1)]$$
$$= \left(\sum_{i=1}^{i=N} x_i^2\right)\left(\sum_{i=1}^{i=N} y_i^2\right) - \left(\sum_{i=1}^{i=N} x_i y_i\right)\left(\sum_{i=1}^{i=N} x_i y_i\right)$$
$$= (m_{11} m_{22}) - (m_{12} m_{21}) = \begin{vmatrix} m_{11} & m_{21} \\ m_{21} & m_{22} \end{vmatrix} \cdots \quad (1 \cdot 12)$$

And then multiplying $(1 \cdot 12)$ by the number of determinants in each group (i.e., $n! = 2!$), we obtain

$$\sigma^2 = \frac{1}{N^2} \begin{vmatrix} m_{11} & m_{12} \\ m_{21} & m_{22} \end{vmatrix} \quad (1 \cdot 13)$$

where $m_{ij} = \sum_{i=1}^{N} x_i y_j$ are the product moments about the means and $m_{ij} = m_{ji}$. The symmetric matrix

$$(M) = (m_{ij}) = \begin{pmatrix} m_{11} & m_{12} \\ m_{21} & m_{22} \end{pmatrix} \quad (1 \cdot 14)$$

will be called the moment matrix of the set-(x, y). if the diagonal matrix of M

$$(D) = \begin{pmatrix} m_{11} & 0 \\ 0 & m_{22} \end{pmatrix} \quad (1 \cdot 15)$$

is non-singular, then the matrix

$$(R) = (D)^{-\frac{1}{2}}(M)(D)^{-\frac{1}{2}} = \begin{pmatrix} \dfrac{m_{11}}{\sqrt{m_{11}m_{22}}} & \dfrac{m_{12}}{\sqrt{m_{11}m_{22}}} \\ \dfrac{m_{21}}{\sqrt{m_{22}m_{11}}} & \dfrac{m_{22}}{\sqrt{m_{22}m_{22}}} \end{pmatrix} = \begin{pmatrix} r_{11} & r_{12} \\ r_{21} & r_{22} \end{pmatrix} \quad (1 \cdot 16)$$

having as its elements the simple correlation coefficients, will be called the correlation matrix of the set of (x, y). The determinant value of (R) is equal to

$$R = \frac{M}{m_{11}m_{22}} = 1 - r^2. \quad (1 \cdot 17)$$

Applying the same consideration to the case of n variates in N observations, we obtain, parallel to equation $(1 \cdot 11)$, the collective standard deviation

$$\sigma^2 = \frac{1}{n!N^n} \sum_{t_1, t_2, \cdots, t_n} \begin{vmatrix} x_1(t_1) & \cdots & x_1(t_n) \\ x_2(t_1) & \cdots & x_2(t_n) \\ \cdots & \cdots & \cdots \\ \cdots & \cdots & \cdots \\ x_n(t_1) & \cdots & x_n(t_1) \end{vmatrix}^2 \quad (1 \cdot 18)$$

where the n summation subscripts $t_1, t_2, \cdots, t_n$ independently of each other run through all the N values of t and the square root is taken positive to obtain σ. This expression can be shown equal save a constant multiple $\dfrac{1}{N^2}$, to

$$(M) = (m_{ij}) = \begin{pmatrix} m_{11} & \cdots & m_{1n} \\ \cdots & \cdots & \cdots \\ \cdots & \cdots & \cdots \\ m_{n1} & \cdots & m_{nn} \end{pmatrix} \quad (1 \cdot 19)$$

whence, we obtain

$$(R) = (D)^{-\frac{1}{2}}(M)(D)^{-\frac{1}{2}}, \quad (1 \cdot 20)$$

and $$R = M/m_{11}m_{22}\cdots m_{nn},$$

where $x_i(t_j)$ denotes the j-th observation of x_i-variate, $m_{ij} = \sum_t x_i(t) x_j(t)$, and D is the diagonal matrix of (M). The positive square root of R

$$s = + \sqrt{R} \qquad (1 \cdot 21)$$

is called the collective scatter coefficient, and the quantity $r = + \sqrt{(1-R)}$ is called the collective correlation coefficient. In the case where there are only two variates, the collective correlation coefficient reduces to the simple correlation coefficient. Moreover, the collective standard deviation σ and the collective scatter coefficient s are connected by the following relation

$$s = \frac{\sigma}{\sigma_1 \sigma_2 \cdots \sigma_n}, \qquad (1 \cdot 22)$$

that is, the former depends on the units with which the variates are measured while the latter does not and therefore is needed when different scatters are compared. The collective correlation coefficient, like the collective scatter coefficient, is an abstract measure.

This is the manner that Professor R. Frisch approaches the theory of correlation. Thus, Frisch's method may be regarded as starting with the variance analysis, i.e., correlation owes its existence to the inter-arrays variations and therefore a perfectly correlated set of variates must be linearly dependent and assuming the relationship between the variates to be linear, and then setting the moment or correlation matrix as a means for investigating into the most essential features of the statistical material. In this way, the question of correlation merely reduces to the evaluation of the determinant value of the moment or correlation matrix. It does not require the fitting of a regression curve and therefore gets rid of the assumptions involved in the theory of regression curves. The only important underlying assumption is the linearity of the relationship among the variates. It is therefore applicable to time series of economic statistics in cases where the relationship in question can be judged on the ground of a priori reasons or à posteriori experiences to be at least approximately linear. For this reason, Frisch may be said to have taken a step toward the solution of correlation problem in economic statistics. The distributions of the "collective correlation coefficients" have been obtained by S. S. Wilks[1] and accordingly the significance of the computed coefficients can be tested.

---

[1] Wilks, "Certain Generalizations in the Analysis of Variance", Biom., Vol.24, p.471, 1932.

1.7 Summary of the Essential Features of the Four Methods

From the above discussion we may see in what respects the four methods are related and how they differ.

The correlation surface method seeks to determine the frequency distribution whereby may be found (1) the probability for the occurrence of any possible set of values of the variates; (2) the regression line of each variate (considered as the essential variate) on the others (considered as the associate variates); and (3) the precision of a prediction (or estimate) made for the essential variate on the basis of its regression line.

The regression method characterizes the correlation sought (1) by means of a regression line representing the type of relationship, fitted according, usually, to the criterion of least squares, and (2) by the standard error as a measure of the degree of scatter around the regression line and hence of the intensity of relationship[①].

The method of the analysis of variance divides the total variance in the essential variate into parts representing the variances ascribable to the respective associate variates considered as the causes of variation, in order to test whether the variation in each of the associate variates is significantly accompanied by variation in the essential variate.

The matrix method studies the linear type of relationship by means of the matrix which specifies the characteristics of the linear dependence of the variates, and the determinant value of which measures the degree of scatter about the regression line and therefore intensity of correlation.

In cases of normal correlation, the solution obtained by any one of the four methods may easily be derived from that given by any other and therefore we may say that the four methods afford the same results. In other cases, the information about correlation yielded by the several methods is far from being identical.

We shall now trace the development of the first three methods in detail so that their advantages and disadvantages from the point of view of theoretical

---

① If s measures the degree of scatter, then $r = \sqrt{1-s^2}$ denotes the degree of correlation. Thus, in reality, they measure the same thing; the smaller the scatter, the greater the correlation coefficient.

validity and practical applicability may be seen.

CHAPTER II CORRELATION SURFACE METHOD

This chapter is devoted to the development of the correlation surface method. This method, in the writer's opinion, is theoretically the most satisfactory for treating correlation problems and should be recommended for more extensive use, in spite of the fact that it often requires extensive arithmetical calculations in application, which means time, labor, and money to the practical statisticians. For this reason, a brief theory of the correlation surface method will preface the main text, which traces chronologically and analytically the development of the method. Thus, this chapter consists of two constituent parts: An exposition of the theory (Sec.2.1 – 2.12) and a history of the development of the correlation surface method (Sec.2.13 – 2.29).

In the theory part, what we mean by a correlation surface is explained. In order to minimize repetition in the theory and the history, the theory part is necessarily brief and mathematical deductions are to be omitted.

In the historical part, we attempt to present the various contributions of the several contributors, with regard to the manner of deduction, the formulae for use, and the nature of illustrations, if any, given by the author, together with any comment which the present writer may be able to offer. If a certain contribution has been made by several authors, we give a combined description so as to avoid unnecessary repetition. For purpose of clearness, we sometimes deviate from the chronological order and from the original notations used.

2.1 Object of Correlation Analysis

Suppose the corresponding values of two variates, representing two statistical characters, arranged in order according to the magnitude of the first variable x_1 and then separated into classes by selecting class intervals dx_1. The set of values of the second variable x_2, corresponding to values of x_1 in an interval of length dx_1 with the limits $x_{1h} - \frac{1}{2}dx_1$ and $x_{1h} + \frac{1}{2}dx_1$, is called the x_{1h}-array of x_2 and the value x_{1h} is called the type of the array. The frequency distribution of x_2 in the x_{1h}-array is called the array-frequency-distribution of x_2 of the type x_{1h}, and the <u>expected</u> value of x_2 in the x_{1h}- array is called the array-mean of x_2 of the type x_{1h}, denoted by $\bar{x}_{2h}$. The total of the values of the two variates form a whole population. But we can seldom have a whole population at our disposal. The actual data we happen to have is regarded as constituting a random sample of a population of the type under consideration. A whole population usually exists only in theory and is supposed to be infinitely large. The law of distribution of such a theoretical population is specified by relatively few parameters, which are sufficient to describe it exhaustively in respect to all qualities which we may consider. The statistical methods seek to estimate these parameters through the sample. The values so estimated from a particular sample which we happen to have at our disposal should be distinguished from their true values which we should like to know, but can only estimate. Using these estimated values of the parameters, we may arrive at an estimate of the law of distribution for the whole population from which the sample is considered to have drawn.

The correlation analysis as a statistical method seeks to determine those parameters which are required for an adequate description of the correlation between the variates composing the population in question.

2.2   Statistical Data as a Sample

In this thesis, any statistical data will always be regarded as the available observations as a sample from a theoretical infinite population. Let us take some statistical data and arrange them according to the scheme as mentioned above. The frequency distribution in a column is the illustration of an array. Similarly, the set of values of the first variable x_1, corresponding to the values of x_2 in the interval $x_{2k} - \frac{1}{2}dx_2$ and $x_{2k} + \frac{1}{2}dx_2$, is called the x_{2k}-array of x_1's which is illustrated by the frequency distribution of a row in the example given below, and the mean of x_1 in this array is called the array mean of the type x_{2k}, denoted by $\bar{x}_{1k}$. A table of double entry so formed, exhibiting the frequencies of pairs of values lying within given cells is called the correlation table. The number of observations in each cell is called the cell frequency and the ratio of the cell frequency to the total number of observations in the sample is called the relative frequency. Now if we enter a dot in the corresponding cell for each pair of observations, then the density of dots represents the total frequencies in a cell and the resulting swarm of observation points is called the scattered diagram.

2.3 Parity of Frequency Curve and Frequency Surface

Now let us erect at the center of every compartment of the correlation table a vertical pillar of length proportionate to the frequency in that compartment and join up the tops of the verticals, the irregular figure so obtained for the representation of the frequency distribution of two <u>variables is termed a stereogram</u>[①] corresponding to the histogram for a single variable. This stereogram will appear to resemble more and more a continuous surface (just as a histogram will look like a continuous curve), as the size of the sample is increased and at the same time the number of classes and the scale of measurement are changed according to the circumstances of the problem. To reach a true curve, however, not only would the sample have to include an infinite number of individuals, but also each cell must contain an infinite number of observations, and the number of classes (arrays) into which the population is supposed to have divided must be infinite while the frequency in each cell bears a finite ratio to the total frequency. Consequently, it should be clear that the concept of a frequency surface (a frequency curve in the case of a single variate) includes that of a hypothetical infinite population, distributed according to a mathematical law, represented by the surface (the curve in the case of one variate). Further, three infinities have been introduced, namely, the number of arrays, the frequency in a cell, and the total frequency in the population are all made infinite. In this circumstance, the finite ratio which a cell frequency bears to the total frequency is defined as the probability for the simultaneous occurrence of a pair of observations in that cell. Thus, there is an intimate connection between the concept of relative frequency and that of probability. In order to make this relation clear, we give the following definition:

If the observation on a certain object is repeated in a finite number of times

---

① For illustrations, See G.U. Yule, An Introduction to the Theory of Statistics, 9th ed., London.

under the same set of circumstances and the observations so obtained are divided into two classes according as they do, or do not have a certain specified character (in statistical data this character is specified by a fixed set of values assigned to the variates, one for each variate), the ratio in which the number of observations having the specified character bears to the total number of observations made, is defined as the relative frequency of the occurrence of that character in one observation. If this relative frequency approaches a limit when the observation is repeated indefinitely, this limit is defined as the probability of the occurrence of that character in one observation.

The law, according to which the theoretical infinite population is distributed, is specified by assigning to each set or domain of the variates the corresponding element of probability. Thus, in the case of the normal distribution, the probability of an observation falling in the domain $dx_1 dx_2$, is $\varphi dx_1 dx_2$, where

$$\varphi = \frac{1}{2x\sigma_1\sigma_2\sqrt{1-\rho^2}} e^{-\frac{1}{2(1-\rho^2)}\left\{\frac{(x_1-\bar{x}_1)^2}{\sigma_1^2} - \frac{2\rho(x_1-\bar{x}_1)(x_2-\bar{x}_2)}{\sigma_1\sigma_2} + \frac{(x_2-\bar{x}_2)^2}{\sigma_2^2}\right\}}$$

in which expression x_1 and x_2 are the values of the variates, while $\bar{x}_1$ and $\bar{x}_2$, their means, σ_1 and σ_2, their standard deviations, and ρ, the correlation coefficient or the standardized product moment, are the parameters by which the theoretical population is specified. The function φ representing the frequency surface is called the frequency function or probability function. If a sample of n observations be taken from such a population, the data comprise n independent facts. The process of correlation analysis is designed to extract from these data the relevant, ideally the whole, information with respect to the values of $\bar{x}_1$, $\bar{x}_2$, σ_1, σ_2, ρ, and to reject all other information as irrelevant, i.e., to obtain from the sample as best as we can an estimate of the frequency surface representing the law of distribution of the sampled population and the reliance on such an estimate.

The frequency distribution of one variate may be represented by a curve in 2 dimensions and the frequency distribution of two variates may be represented by a surface in 3 dimensions. This reasoning may be extended to the cases of 3, 4, ⋯, n variates. A frequency surface of n variates may be represented by a surface of $n + 1$ dimensions. The frequency surface of n variates which are not independent is called the correlation surface of the n variates.

2.4 Problems of Correlation Analysis

Now it should be clear that the problems in correlation analysis are essentially of the three types:

(i) Problems of Specification. These arise in the choice of the mathematical form of the theoretical population.

(ii) Problems of estimation. These arise in estimating from a sample the values of the parameters of the theoretical population.

(iii) Problems of Reliability. These give rise to discussions of the distribution of the statistical derivates, such as the moments used in estimating the values of the parameters, and the estimated parameters (the latter may also be called the statistical derivates).

2.5 Choice of Theoretical Surfaces

The problems of the first type are entirely a matter for the practical statistician. In some case where the form of the theoretical population is known, there is no problem of this type. In other cases, we may know by experience what forms are likely to be suitable and the adequacy may be tested a posteriori. This gives rise to the need of an objective criterion of goodness of fit like the x^2-test developed by Pearson. For, if we can apply a rigorous and objective test of the adequacy with which the proposed population represents the whole of the available facts, then the arbitrary element in the choice of the mathematical form is cleared of its dangers. Hence the possibility of developing complete and self-contained tests of goodness of fit deserves very careful consideration, since therein lies our justification for the free use which is made of empirical frequency formulae. Of course, we must confine ourselves to those forms which we know how to handle, or for which any table which may be necessary have been constructed. For this reason, the correlation function of Type A (See Sec. 2.24 of this Chapter) is often preferred for treating the moderate skew correlation.

2.6 Frequency Surface Fitting

After the mathematical form is chosen, we know what parameters are required to specify the population from which the sample is drawn. Now the problem before us is to estimate the parameters in the chosen mathematical form from a sample in hand, the process is called frequency surface (curve in case of one variate) fitting. There are three methods which may be used for getting suitable values for the required parameters:

(1) The Least Squares Method.

Let f be the rightly chosen function of known form, involving the parameters θ_1, θ_2, $\cdots$, θ_r and the variates x_1, x_2, and y be the observed frequency in the domain $dx_1\, dx_2$. The criterion of fitting the observations is to make

$$\int_{-\infty}^{\infty} (f - y)^2 dx_1 dx_2$$

a minimum for variations of any θ; or if the observations are made at finite and equal intervals of the respective variates, we should substitute

$$\sum (f - y)^2$$

for the integral.

This method will obviously give a good result wherever a good result is possible. However, the equations to which the minimum condition gives rise are often practically insolvable, a difficulty which renders the method less useful than the simplicity of its principle would suggest.

(2) The Method of Moments.

The method of moments, introduced by K. Pearson, is possibly of more value, though its arbitrary nature is more apparent. The criterion is to equate the moments of the theoretical population respectively to their corresponding moments of a sample from that population:

$$\int_{-\infty}^{\infty} x_1^p x_2^q f\, dx_1 dx_2 = \int_{-\infty}^{\infty} x_1^p x_2^q y\, dx_1 dx_2$$

or,

$$\sum x_1^p x_2^q f = \sum x_1^p x_2^q y$$

$$p, q = 0, 1, 2, \cdots$$

If we solve the r moment equations of lowest order, we may obtain values for the r parameters required. The surface so fitted will look about as good as that obtained by least squares method and the process is in general easier, but for some distributions methods (1) and (3) give better fits.

(3) The Method of Maximum Likelihood.

Since the chance with which any pair of values fall into the specified domain is

$$f(x_1, x_2, \theta_1, \theta_2, \cdots, \theta_r) dx_1 dx_2,$$

the chance that a sample of n observations, n_1 will fall in the domain $dx_{11} dx_{21}$, and n_2 in the domain $dx_{12} dx_{22}$, etc., will be

$$P = \frac{n!}{\prod(n_h!)} \prod \{f(x_{1h}, x_{2h}, \theta_1, \theta_2, \cdots, \theta_r) dx_{1h} dx_{2h}\}^{n_h}.$$

The method of maximum likelihood, developed by R. A. Fisher, [1] consists simply in choosing that set of values for the parameter which makes this quantity a maximum, and since in this expression the parameters are only involved in the function f, we have to make

$$L = \sum (\log f) = \text{maximum} \qquad (2 \cdot 1)$$

for variations of $\theta_1, \theta_2, \cdots, \theta_r$, L being connected to P by the relation $\log P = \log C + L$.

To illustrate the method, let us take a problem of the intraclass correlation. The process of the intraclass correlation analysis is designed to determine the fraternal correlations, and others of a like nature, in which the mean and the standard deviation are presumed to be the same for both variables. If the theoretical infinite population, from which a sample of n pairs $x_1, x'_1, x_2, x'_2, \cdots, x_n, x'_n$ have been drawn, is normal with m, σ, ρ as the mean, standard deviation, and the correlation coefficient, then the chance that any pair of values will fall into specified infinitesimal ranges is

---

[1] "The Mathematical Foundation of Theoretical Statistics", Phil. Trans. Ray. Soe., A. Vol.222, pp.309 – 368, 1922; and also "On an absolute criterion for fitting Frequency Curves" Messenger of Math., New Series, Vol.41, p.155, 1912.

$$fdxdx' = \frac{1}{2x\sigma^2\sqrt{1-\rho^2}} e^{-\frac{1}{2\sigma^2(1-\rho^2)}\{(x-m)^2 - 2\rho(x-m)(x'-m) + (x'-m)^2\}} dx'dx,$$

and the chance that all the observations of the sample have the given values, is

$$P = \frac{1}{(2x\sigma^2\sqrt{1-\rho^2})^n} e^{-\frac{1}{2\sigma^2(1-\rho^2)}\sum\{(x-m)^2 - 2\rho(x-m)(x'-m) + (x'-m)^2\}} dx_1 dx'_1 \cdots dx_n dx'_n.$$

By the criterion of the maximum likelihood as given in equation (2·1), we differentiate L partially with respect to m, σ, and r:

$$\frac{\delta L}{\delta m} = \frac{\delta}{\delta m}\sum(\log f) = \frac{1}{\sigma^2(1-\rho^2)}\sum\{(x-m) - \rho(x+x') + 2m\rho + (x'-m)\}$$

$$= \frac{1}{\sigma^2(1-\rho^2)}\{\sum(x+x') - \rho\sum(x+x') - 2m(1-\rho)\cdot n\}$$

$$\frac{\delta L}{\delta \sigma} = -\frac{2n}{\sigma} + \frac{1}{\sigma^3(1-\rho^2)}\sum\{(x-m)^2 - 2\rho(x-m)(x'-m)(x'-m)^2\}$$

$$\frac{\delta L}{\delta \rho} + \frac{n\rho}{1-\rho^2} + \frac{1}{\sigma^2(1-\rho^2)}\sum(x-m)(x'-m)$$

$$- \frac{\rho}{\sigma^2(1-\rho^2)^2}\sum\{(x-m)^2 + 2\rho(x-m)(x'-m) + (x'-m)^2\}.$$

Introducing the notation,

$$2n\bar{x} = \sum(x+x'),$$

$$2n\mu_2 = \sum\{(x-\bar{x})^2 + (x'-\bar{x})^2\},$$

$$n\mu_2 r = \sum(x-\bar{x})(x'-\bar{x}),$$

the first equation now becomes

$$\frac{1}{\sigma^2(1-\rho^2)} \cdot 2n\{\bar{x}(1-\rho) - m(1-\rho)\} = 0,$$

or, $\qquad m = \bar{x}$, if $1-\rho \neq 0$, $\sigma \neq \infty$

and the last two equations then become,

$$\frac{2n}{\sigma^3(1-\rho^2)}\{\sigma^2(1-\rho^2) + \mu_2(1-r\rho)\} = 0$$

$$\frac{n}{\sigma^2(1-\rho^2)^2}\{-\rho\sigma^2(1-\rho^2)+2\mu_2\rho(1-\rho r)-\mu_2 r(1-\rho^2)\}=0$$

from which we may get the solution:

$$\rho = r = \frac{1}{n\mu_2}\sum(x-\bar{x})(x'-\bar{x}),$$

$$\sigma = \sqrt{\mu_2},$$

if neither $\rho=1$, nor $\sigma=\infty$, other solutions do not satisfy the condition that P is maximum, and therefore are not wanted.

By using geometrical representation in hyperspace, Fisher[1] has found,

$$P = P_0 e^{-\frac{2n}{2\sigma^2(1-\rho^2)}|(\bar{x}-m)^2(1-\rho)+\mu_2(1-r\rho)|} d\bar{x} \times \mu_2^{\frac{2n-3}{2}} d\mu_2 (1-r)^{\frac{n-2}{2}}(1+r)^{\frac{n-3}{2}} dr.$$
$$(2 \cdot 2)$$

This expression specifies the relative frequencies with which any assigned values of $\bar{x}$, μ_2, and r will occur in the process of random sampling. From $(2 \cdot 2)$ it follows that all the samples which have the same values for m, σ, and ρ, must have the same P, the probability of occurrence of a certain specified sample. Let Φ be the total frequency of all samples for which the required parameters have the same set of values as determined by the method of maximum likelihood and denoted by m, σ, ρ, then Φ is proportional to P, that is,

$$\Phi = C_1 P = C e^L.$$

According to Fisher[2], the interpretation is that the likelihood of any set of values of m, σ, ρ is proportional to

$$L \propto e^{-\frac{2n}{2\sigma^2(1-\rho^2)}|(x-m)^2(1-\rho)+\mu_2(1-r\rho)|} \mu_2^{\frac{2n-3}{2}}(1-r)^{\frac{n-2}{2}}(1+r)^{\frac{n-3}{2}}, \quad (2 \cdot 2L)$$

and is therefore a maximum when

$$m = \hat{m} = \bar{x},\ \sigma = \hat{\sigma} = \sqrt{\mu_2},\ \rho = \hat{\rho} = r,$$

---

[1] "The probable Error of a coefficient of correlation deduced from a small sample", Metron. Vol.1, No.4, pp.3–33, 1921.

[2] "Mathematical foundations of the theoretical Statistics", p.236, and "An Absolute Criterion for fitting freq. curves", Op.cit, p.159.

which is the best set of values obtainable from the sample. The word
"likelihood" is not loosely used as a synonym of probability, but simply used to
express the relative frequencies with which such values of the parameters in the
theoretical infinite population would in fact yield the observed sample. The
values $\hat{m}$, $\hat{\sigma}$, $\hat{\rho}$, so determined are called the optimum values of the
parameters respectively. Other sets of values of m, σ, ρ, for which the
likelihood is not much less, cannot, however, be deemed unlikely values for the
true values of m, σ, ρ. We do not, and cannot, know, from the information
supplied by a sample, anything about the probability that m, σ, ρ should lie
between any assigned values. We cannot therefore, multiply this quantity L by
the variations of the parameters to integrate through a region and then compare
the integral over this region with the integral over all possible values of the
parameters. L is a relative probability only, suitable to compare point with point,
but incapable of giving any estimate of absolute probability.

This may be seen, since the same frequency curve or surface might equally
be specified by any s independent functions of the θ's, say φ_1, φ_2, $\cdots$, φ_s, and
the relative values of L would be unchanged by such a transformation, but the
probability that the true values lie within a region must be the same whether it is
expressed in terms of θ's or φ's, so that we should have for all values

$$\frac{\delta(\varphi_1, \varphi_2, \cdots, \varphi_s)}{\delta(\theta_1, \theta_2, \cdots, \theta)} = 1$$

a condition which is manifestly not satisfied by the general transformation.

Hence the solution of the problems of calculating from a sample the
theoretical parameters θ's by the method of maximum likelihood consists simply
of choosing such values of these parameters as have the maximum likelihood.
The optimum value of a parameter so obtained, say $\hat{\rho}$ in the example given
above, is merely that value of ρ for which the observed r occurs with greatest
frequency.

Moreover, Fisher has enumerated three criteria of estimation of parameters,
namely.

(1) The criterion of consistency.

That when applied to the whole population the estimated value should be equal to the parameter.

(2) The criterion of efficiency.

That in large samples, when the distributions of the estimated values for the parameters tend to normality, that estimate should be chosen which has the least probable error.

(3) The criterion of sufficiency.

That the estimate chosen should summarize the whole of the relevant information supplies by the sample.

The estimate by the method of maximum likelihood has been shown by Fisher to be capable of conforming these criteria.

There is another advantage for this method. If θ be the optimum value of a parameter required and be normally distributed, then the standard deviation of θ may be very simply found by the formula[1]

$$\frac{\delta^2 L}{\delta \theta^2} = \frac{-1}{\sigma_\theta^2}.$$

While each of the three methods heretofore mentioned is applicable to the fitting of populations involving any number of variates of continuous or discontinuous distributions, the method of maximum likelihood judged by theoretical considerations seems to be the best one. Yet it has drawbacks, because the equations for solving the parameters are about as impracticable as those required for the least-square method. But it also should be mentioned that Fisher[2] has again shown that, starting from an inefficient estimate, it is possible to obtain by a single process of approximation an efficient estimate of the parameter required, thus making the method of maximum likelihood capable of application in many instances without prohibitive calculations. This approximate method of obtaining efficient estimate from an inefficient estimate has been used by Koshol[3] to improve the estimates obtained by the method of moments in fitting to a coarsely grouped frequency distribution belonging to Pearson's Type I.

---

[1] Fisher, "Math. Found of Theoretical Stat", Op. Cit., pp.328–329.

[2] "Theory of Statistical Estimation", Proc. Camb. Phil. Soe., Vol.22, pp.700–725, 1925.

[3] R. S. Koshal, "Application of the Method of Maximum Likelihood to the Improvement of Curves, Fitted by moment method", Jour., Roy. Stat, Soc., Vol. 46, pp.303–313, 1933.

The method of moments, though of great practical utility, has also its serious limitations. The probable error increases very fast as the order of moments used becomes higher. Any moment higher than the fourth order has, in general, a probable error too great for the moment to be of any practical service. And, in order that the probable error of the fourth moments should not be infinitely great, the first eight moments must be finite. This restriction requires that the class of distribution in which this condition is not fulfilled while the fourth moment is necessary in the fitting should be set aside as "heterotypic". Under these circumstances we must resort to some other method for a satisfactory solution. Moreover, for that class of distribution to which this method can be applied, it has not been shown, except in the case of the normal distribution where the three methods give the same solution, that the best values will be obtained by the method of moments. The method will, in these cases, certainly be serviceable in yielding a fairly good approximation, but to discover whether this approximation is a good or a bad one, and to improve it, if necessary, deserves careful consideration. In this circumstance, we are reminded again of the need to have an objectively efficient and sufficient criterion of goodness of fit and can see the valuable service rendered by Fisher's process of obtaining an efficient estimate from an inefficient estimate.

2.7 Random Sampling Distribution of Statistical Derivates

In the example of intraclass correlation given above, the values found, regarded as estimates of the mean, the standard deviation, and the correlation coefficient of a normal population of which the data is considered as a sample, are effected by errors of random sampling; that is, a second sample will probably not give us the same values. The values for different samples of the same size would be distributed according to some form which, when the number of samples is infinitely large, may be represented by a mathematical law just as is an observational variate. The mean follows the normal law of errors while the intraclass correlation within s fraternal variates (in the given example there are two fraternal variates and therefore it is the case when $s = 2$) is distributed according to[1]

$$C\{1 + (s-2)\rho - (s-1)\rho r\}^{-\frac{sn-1}{2}}(1-r)^{\frac{(s-1)n-2}{2}}\left(\frac{1}{s-1}+r\right)^{\frac{n-3}{2}}dr$$

$$(2\cdot 3)$$

where C is a constant which may be determined by the condition that the integral over the whole range of r should be 1. This may be transformed into a form nearly normal by using the following transformation:

$$2(s-1)r = (s-2) + s\tanh(2-\varphi)$$
$$2(s-1)\rho = (s-2) + s\tanh(\zeta-\varphi)$$
$$\tanh\varphi = \frac{s-2}{s}.$$

$$(2\cdot 4)$$

The resulting distribution becomes

$$\frac{\frac{2n-3}{2}!}{2^{\frac{sn-3}{2}}\cdot\frac{(s-1)n-2}{2}!\frac{n-3}{2}!}e^{-\frac{n(s-2)+1}{2}(2-\zeta-\varphi)}\operatorname{sech}^{\frac{sn-1}{2}}(2-\zeta-\varphi)d(2-\zeta),$$

$$(2\cdot 5)$$

the constant multiplier C is now given such a value that the area of the curve is unity.

When the random sampling distribution is normal, the precision of any one estimate may be satisfactory expressed by its standard error. The standard error may be calculated from the parameters of the population, and in treating large samples we may use the estimates of the parameters as the basis of the calculation. The formulae for the standard errors of random sampling of estimates of the mean and the intra-class correlation of a large normal sample are

$$\sigma_{\bar{x}} = \frac{\sigma}{\sqrt{n}}, \quad \sigma_r = (1-r)\left(\frac{1}{s-1}+r\right)\sqrt{\frac{2(s-1)}{sn}}. \quad [2]$$

---

[1] Fisher, R. A., "The probable error of a coefficient of correlation deduced from a small sample", Metron., Vol.1, pt.4, 1921.

[2] For $s=2$, the standard error is given to be $\dfrac{1}{\sqrt{n-\dfrac{3}{2}}}$. See Fisher, R. A., Metron, Vol.1, No.4, p.3.

Their numerical values are then appended to the estimated parameters to which they refer:

$$\bar{x} - \sigma_{\bar{x}} \text{ and } \bar{x} + \sigma_{\bar{x}},$$

then as interpreted by writers, that the sample shows a significant deviation from any population whose mean lies outside the limits $\bar{x} \pm \sigma_{\bar{x}}$, and it is therefore likely that the mean of the population from which it was drawn lay between these limits.

This interpretation is entirely for practical convenience. From the table of a normal probability integral, it is seen that the chance for a deviation exceeding the standard deviation is about one out of three ($P=0.317\,31$), exceeding twice the standard deviation is about one out of 22 ($P=0.045\,50$), and exceeding the standard deviation sixfold is about one out of a thousand million trials ($P=10^{-8}$, when the deviation $x=6.109\,41$). We cannot set absolute limits beyond which no deviation would occur in cases where one or both of the limits of the distribution, like the normal curve, are infinite. Any point taken as a limit in judging whether a deviation is to be considered significant or not, is entirely arbitrary, but its arbitrary nature may become conventionally established and fully understood of its arbitrary nature. We will take, after Fisher[①], the value for which $P=0.05$ as the significant limit or level of variation. This value when expressed in units of standard deviation is 1.96. Referring again to the interpretation of an estimated mean, we will say that our statistical data from which the mean has been estimated, <u>will not likely</u> come from a population whose mean lies outside the limits $\bar{x} \pm 1.96 \dfrac{\sigma_{\bar{x}}}{\sqrt{n}}$, in other words, the mean of the sampled population will likely lie between these limits. We will also say that a second sample from the same population will not likely give a mean lying outside these limits. So the words "likely" as well as "significant" are used to denote the chance of 19 against 1.

In cases where the estimated parameter such as r is not normally distributed, a positive deviation and a negative deviation are not equally

---

① Fisher, R. A., "Statistical Method for Research Workers", 3d ed., p. 45, 1930.

probable and therefore we must distinguish between a positive significant limit and a negative significant limit of variation. These limits will be denoted by z_1 and z_2 when measured from the mean of the random distribution, $P(r)$, in units of the standard deviation, and may be found from the equations:

$$0.025 = \int_{\bar{r}+z_2}^{+1} P(r)\,dr$$

$$0.025 = \int_{-1}^{\bar{r}+z_1} P(r)\,dr.$$

This formula is equally applicable to both the normal and skew sampling distributions, provided they are known. After having obtained the significant limits of variation, we will interpret the result in the same way as given in the previous paragraph, that is, we will make the deductive inference, from the experience of a sample, with respect to the sampled population and also the probable nature of future samples drawn from the same population. If a second sample belies this expectation, we will infer that it is drawn from a different population. A critical test of this kind is possible only where we know the exact distribution of the estimated parameter and will be called the test of significance, through which we may discover whether a second sample is or is not significantly different from the first or a sample is or is not significantly different from the theoretical population of which the actual data is presumably a sample. Pearsonian test of goodness of fit is one of this kind, because we know its exact distribution. Suppose certain observed distribution fitted by a normal curve and the probability P corresponding to n, the number of degrees of freedom, and

$$x^2 = \sum_{i=0}^{n} \frac{(m'_i - m_i)^2}{m_i},$$

is found to be less than 0.05, we will, according to our convention, infer that our actual data are likely to have been drawn from a non-normal population, if that statistical data are the only available guide.

It must be observed, however, that, using this convention, we should be led to base our conclusion on an erroneous judgement of significance once in 20 trails. Indeed, it is simply an expression of the relative chance measuring our order of preference among different possible populations of which the actual data may be a sample.

Moreover, the problems of estimation and of distribution are intimately related. A knowledge of frequency distribution of different suggested parameters which have similar functions, may guide us in the choice of which parameter it is most profitable to use. For example①, both mean and median may be used for locating a frequency curve, but one is preferred to the other in some cases whereas in some other cases the preference may be reversed. Furthermore, a comparison of random sampling distributions of statistical derivates may show us that, in large samples, one particular method of calculation gives a result less subject to random errors than those given by other methods of calculation, or that the whole of the relevant information contained in one is contained in the other.

However, problems of distribution are of great mathematical difficulty and not all the exact distributions of all the statistical derivates in practical use have not all been found. The known forms of those statistical derivates used in correlation may be found in Chapter IV. If the exact distribution has not been known, a formula for the probable error of any statistical derivate is a practical necessity if that statistical derivate is to be of any service. In the majority of cases such formulae have been determined, chiefly by the labors of Pearson② and his school, by a first approximation which describes the distribution with adequate accuracy if the sample is sufficiently large.

2.8 Normal Correlation

Let $P_m \mathrm{d}x_1 \mathrm{d}x_2 \cdots \mathrm{d}x_m$ be the differential of the probability of the simultaneous occurrence of the system of variates with the n variables lying between x_1 and $x_1+\mathrm{d}x_1$, $x_2+\mathrm{d}x_2$, $\cdots$, $x_m+\mathrm{d}x_m$, respectively, then the general

---

① Fisher has shown that the only curve of the Pearsonian system for which the mean is the best parameter for locating the curve is the normal curve. If the curve is not of this type, the mean is not necessarily of any value whatever. "Math. Foundation", Phil. Trans. Roy. Soc. Vol.222, p.304, 1922.

② "On the Probable errors of Frequency Constants and Correlation", Phil. Trans. Ray. Soc., Vol.191, p.229; and Biom. Vol.2, p.273; Sheppard, W. W. "On the Application of the Theory of Errors", Phil. Trans., Vol.192, p.101; Yule, G. A., Prec. Roy. Soc. A., Vol.89, p. 182; Isserlis, L., Phil. Mag., Vol.34, 1917.

problem of correlation is to determine P from an observed statistical distribution of the variates. Let the distribution be normal,

$$P_m = J_m e^{-\frac{1}{2}\Sigma a_{ij} x_i x_j}$$

$$J_m = \frac{A_m}{\sqrt{(2x)^m}},$$

$$A_m = |a_{ij}|, \qquad (2\cdot 6)$$

the determinant with a_{ij} as its ij-th element. The coefficients a_{ij} can be expressed in terms of the moments of 2nd order. Let the moments of the second order be

$$m_{ij} = \int\int\cdots\int x_i x_j p \, dx_1 dx_2 \cdots dx_m,$$

$$m_{ii} = \sigma_i^2,$$

and
$$M = |m_{ij}|,$$

the m-th order determinant with m_{ij} as its ij-th element, then we have

$$A = \frac{1}{M}, \quad a_{ij} = \frac{M_{ij}}{M} \qquad (2\cdot 7)$$

where M_{ij} is the cofactor of m_{ij} in M.

It is sometimes more convenient to express the parameters in terms of the standardized moments of second order. Thus, if

$$r_{ij} = \frac{m_{ij}}{\sqrt{m_{ii} m_{jj}}}, \quad R = |r_{ij}|,$$

we then have

$$R = \frac{M}{m_{11} m_{22} \cdots m_{mm}},$$

$$A = \frac{1}{R m_{11} m_{22} \cdots m_{mm}},$$

$$a_{ij} = \frac{1}{\sigma_i \sigma_j} \frac{R_{ij}}{R_m}, \quad J = \frac{1}{(\sqrt{2x})^m \sigma_1 \sigma_2 \cdots \sigma_m \sqrt{R}}. \qquad (2\cdot 8)$$

Now let
$$y_i = \frac{x_i}{\sigma_i},$$

and let

$$\Delta = \begin{bmatrix} 1 & r_{12} & r_{13} & \cdots & r_{1m} & y_1 \\ r_{21} & 1 & r_{23} & & r_{2m} & y_2 \\ \vdots & & & \ddots & & \vdots \\ r_{m1} & r_{m2} & r_{m3} & \cdots & 1 & y_m \\ y_1 & y_2 & y_3 & & y_m & 0 \end{bmatrix}, \quad (2\cdot 9)$$

and $\Delta_{ik\cdots s|ji\cdots t}$ the determinant, multiplied by $(-1)^{i+k+\cdots+s+j+i+\cdots+t}$, which is obtained from Δ by cancelling the i-th, k-th, $\cdots$, s-th rows and the j-th, i-th, $\cdots$, t-th columns, then,

$$R = \Delta_{(m+1)\,|\,(m+1)}, \quad R_{ij} = \Delta_{i(m+1)\,|\,j(m+1)},$$

and P_m may be written in the very simple form:[①]

$$P_m = \frac{1}{(2x)^{\frac{m}{2}}\sigma_1\sigma_2\cdots\sigma_m\sqrt{R}}e^{\frac{\Delta}{R}}.$$

For $m=1$,

$$\frac{\Delta_1}{R_1} = \begin{vmatrix} 1 & y_1 \\ y_1 & 0 \end{vmatrix} = -y_1^2 = -\frac{x_1^2}{\sigma_1^2}, \quad R_1 = 1,$$

and, for $m=2$,

$$\frac{\Delta_2}{R_2} = \begin{vmatrix} 1 & r_{12} & y_1 \\ r_{21} & 1 & y_2 \\ y_1 & y_2 & 0 \end{vmatrix} : \begin{vmatrix} 1 & r_{12} \\ r_{12} & 1 \end{vmatrix} = -\frac{y_1^2 - 2r_{12}y_1y_2 + y_2^2}{1-r^2}$$

$$= \frac{1}{1-r^2}\left\{\frac{x_1^2}{\sigma_1^2} - 2r\frac{x_1x_2}{\sigma_1\sigma_2} + \frac{x_2^2}{\sigma_2^2}\right\}.$$

By a well known theorem of determinant,

$$\Delta \cdot \Delta_{(m+1)\,m\,|\,(m+1)\,m} = \Delta_{(m+1)(m+1)}\Delta_{m\,|\,m} - \Delta_{(m+1)\,|\,m}\Delta_{m\,|\,(m+1)}, \text{ we obtain}$$

---

① This form is taken from notes on Professor M. H. Ingraham's Lectures on the Mathematical Statistics for the year 1930–1931.

$$\frac{\Delta}{R} = \frac{\Delta}{\Delta_{(m+1)\mid(m+1)}} = \frac{\Delta_{m\mid m}}{\Delta_{(m+1)m\mid(m+1)m}} - \frac{\Delta_{(m+1)\mid m}\Delta_{m\mid(m+1)}}{D_{(m+1)\mid(m+1)}D_{(m+1)m\mid(m+1)m}} = \frac{\Delta_{m-1}}{R_{m-1}} -$$

$$\frac{\Delta_{(m+1)\mid m}}{R_m R_{m-1}} = \frac{R_{m\mid m}}{R}\left\{y_m + \sum \frac{R_{mj}}{R_{mm}}y_j\right\}^2 - \frac{1}{R_{mm}}\sum (R_{m_i\mid m_j}y_i y_j)$$

where $R_{m-1} = R_{m\mid m} = \mid r_{ij}\mid$ of $(m-1)$-th order, and Δ_{m-1} is the determinant formed by bordering R_{m-1} with y's as Δ, in equation (2·9), is formed from R. Now, putting

$$P_{m-1} = J_{m-1}e^{-\frac{1}{2R_{mm}}\sum R_{m_i\mid m_j}y_i y_j} = J_{m-1}e^{\frac{\Delta_{m-1}}{2R_{m-1}}},$$

$$P_{m;\,(m-1)\cdots 21} = J_{m;\,(m-1)\cdots 21}e^{-\frac{R_{mm}}{2R}\left\{y_m + \sum \frac{R_{mj}}{R_{mm}}y_i\right\}^2}, \qquad (2\cdot 10)$$

$$J_{m;\,(m-1)\cdots 21} = \frac{\sqrt{R_{m-1}}}{\sigma_m\sqrt{R_m(2x)}},$$

$$P = P_{m-1} \cdot P_{m;\,(m-1)\cdots 21}$$

applying the same process to P_{m-1} and so on, we may write

$$P_m = P_{m-1} \cdot P_{m;\,(m-1)\cdots 21} = P_{m;\,(m-1)(m-2)\cdots 21} \cdot P_{(m-1);\,(m-2)\cdots 21}P_{2\cdot 1}P_1.$$

For given values of $x_1, x_2, \cdots, x_{m-1}$, we have the partial distribution of x_m which is evidently given by the equation (2·10).

It is seen to be a normal curve with its variance

$$\sigma^2_{m;\,(m-1)\cdots 21} = \frac{R_m}{R_{m-1}}\sigma^2_m$$

and its mean

$$\frac{\bar{x}_{mr}}{\sigma_m} = \sum_{j=1}^{m-1}\frac{R_{mj}}{R_{mm}}\frac{x_j}{\sigma_j}. \qquad (2\cdot 11)$$

This expression may also be written in the determinant form

$$\frac{1}{R_{mm}}\Delta_{(m+1)\mid m} = 0$$

provided y_m is replaced by $\bar{y}_{mr} = \dfrac{\bar{x}_{mr}}{\sigma_m}$ in Δ.

Thus, the partial or array mean x_{mr} varies with the types while the array variance $\sigma^2(m \cdot 12 \cdots \overline{m-1})$ remains the same for all the arrays. If we define the relation between the array mean (or the expected value) and its type as the expected relationship, commonly called the regression, existing between the essential variate x_m and its associated variates, then the regression, as given in (2 · 11), of normal correlation is linear. The coefficient $R_{mj} = -\dfrac{R_{mj}}{R_{mm}}$ is called the partial regression coefficient of the variate x_m or x_j. Moreover, it should be clear that the regression (or partial mean) may be obtained by integrating x_m over its partial frequency curves.

If f_m be the regression function of the m-th variate on the first $(m-1)$ variates, then

$$P_{m \cdot 123 \cdots (m-1)} = \frac{1}{\sigma_{m \cdot 123 \cdots (m-1)} \sqrt{2\pi}} e^{-\frac{1}{2}\frac{(x_m - f_m)^2}{\sigma^2_{m \cdot 123 \cdots (m-1)}}}$$

$$P_m = P_1 \cdot P_{2 \cdot 1} \cdot P_{3 \cdot 12} \cdots P_{m \cdot 123 \cdots (m-1)}$$

$$= \frac{1}{\sigma_1 \sigma_{2 \cdot 1} \sigma_{3 \cdot 123} \cdots r_{m \cdot 123 \cdots (m-1)} \sqrt{(2x)}^m} e^{-\frac{1}{2}\left\{\frac{x_1^2}{\sigma_1^2} + \frac{(x_2 - f_2)^2}{\sigma_{2 \cdot 1}^2} + \cdots + \frac{(x_m - f_m)^2}{\sigma^2_{\cdot 123 \cdots (m-1)}}\right\}}$$

and, by comparison with (2 · 8),

$$\sigma_1 \sigma_{2 \cdot 1} \sigma_{3 \cdot 12} \cdots \sigma_{m \cdot 123 \cdots (m-1)} = \sigma_1 \sigma_2 \sigma_3 \cdots \sigma_m \sqrt{R}. \qquad (2 \cdot 12)$$

It follows, thus, that in the case of normal correlation, all the partial regressions as well as the total regression must be linear. Indeed, Camp[1] has shown that all the regressions of one variate on another or on several other variates of m correlated variates must be mutually consistent. In other words, as soon as regression f_i is determinate, the others can no longer be arbitrarily assumed.

The correlation surface may be used for predicting x_m at an assigned type of values $x_1, x_2, \cdots, x_{m-1}$. The best value which we shall predict with the

---

[1] Camp, "Mutually Consistent Multiple regression surfaces", biom., Vol. 17, pp. 443 – 458, 1925.

knowledge of a correlation surface estimated from a sample of n observations by the method of moments① is the value x_{mr} which gives the maximum expectation in the probability sense. Evidently the probability for the occurrence of an x_m after the previous occurrence of $(x_1, x_2, \cdots, x_{m-1})$ is $P_{m \cdot m(m-1) \cdots 21}$, equation $(2 \cdot 10)$, and this probability is maximum when

$$x_m = -\sigma_m \sum_{j=1}^{m-1} \frac{R_{mj}}{R_{mm}} \frac{x_j}{\sigma_j}.$$

Hence the best prediction is the value of x_m which satisfies the regression equation $(2 \cdot 11)$. This constitutes the basis for using the regression equation to predict a value for x_m when the values of the other variates are known.

The precision of the prediction so obtained may be stated that an observation made under the conditions that $x_1, x_2, x_3, \cdots, x_{m-1}$ would have assumed the assigned values will not likely deviate from x_{mr}, equation $(2 \cdot 11)$, by an amount greater than l where l is given by

(a) in case of negative deviation,

$$(1 - 0.025) = \int_{(x_{mr} - l_1)}^{x_{mr}} P_m dx_m, \qquad (2 \cdot 13a)$$

(b) in case of positive deviation,

$$(1 - 0.025) = \int_{x_{mr}}^{(x_{mr} + l_2)} P_m dx_m. \qquad (2 \cdot 13b)$$

But the more common practice is the use of the standard error defined by

$$\sigma^2_{m \cdot (m-1) \cdots 321} = \sum_t \left(x_{mt} + \sigma_m \sum_j \frac{R_{mj}}{R_{mm}} \frac{x_{jt}}{\sigma_j} \right)^2$$

in expressing the precision of a prediction.

The significance of a prediction x_m based on the knowledge of a correlation surface estimated from a sample of n observations may be better appreciated if we compare the precision of such a prediction with that of a prediction based on its mean $x_m = \frac{1}{n} \sum_t x_{mt}$. Since x_m follows the normal law of distribution, the

---

① For Normal Surfaces, the result obtained by the method of moments is the same as the method of maximum likelihood.

probability of obtaining an x_m in a specified range dx is given by

$$\varphi_1 = \frac{1}{\varphi_m \sqrt{2x}} e^{-\frac{1}{2}\frac{(x_m - \bar{x}_m)^2}{\sigma_m^2}} dx \qquad (2 \cdot 14)$$

and this probability for $x_m = \bar{x}_m$ is $\sigma_{\bar{x}_m} = \frac{1}{\sigma_m \sqrt{2x}}$. Now the probability for x_m equal to the regression value given in $(2 \cdot 11)$ is, by equation $(2 \cdot 10)$,

$$J_{m \cdot (m-1) \cdots 21} = \frac{1}{\sigma_m \sqrt{2x}} \left(\frac{R_{m-1}}{R_m}\right)^{\frac{1}{2}} = \frac{1}{\sqrt{2x} \, \sigma_{m(m-1) \cdots 21}}.$$

Hence the relative magnitude of these two probabilities,

$$\sqrt{\frac{R_{m-1}}{R_m}} = \frac{\sigma_m}{\sigma_{m \cdot (m-1) \cdots 21}},$$

is a measure of improvement of the prediction based on the correlation surface over that based on the mean. Clearly this quantity becomes unity when the variates are independent and becomes infinitive large when the set of variates approaches linear dependence or approaches a perfect correlation as represented by the regression equation. For this reason, this quantity may be used as a measure of the strength of correlation and called an index of correlation denoted by ξ. Its variation ranges from 1 when there is no correlation, to infinity when the correlation is perfect.

    The above interpretation for a normal correlation surface may easily lend itself to extension to the case of non-normal surface. The regression may be obtained by integrating the surface for the essential variates over its partial frequency curve; the precision of a prediction based upon the regression is obtained by following exactly the same way as shown in equation $(2 \cdot 13a)$ and $(2 \cdot 13b)$ with P to be replaced by the surface concerned; and the probability function corresponding to that in equation $(2 \cdot 14)$ may be found by integrating the surface in question for all the associate variates and the index of correlation may accordingly be obtained.

2.9 A Method of Computing Correlation Determinant

The computation of ξ or R is exceedingly laborious and unconvenient, when the usual developments of determinants is taken into use. There is, however, another method for such computations which is much easier and used by Charlier[1] who found it in the treatise of Norbert Hertz, <u>Wahrscheinlichkeits and Ausgleichungsrechung</u>, p.341. The principle is a very simple one.

$$\text{Let } D = |\, a_{ij} \,|$$

be any determinant of the order n. Subtract from the i-th row the elements of the first row multiplied by $\dfrac{a_{i1}}{a_{11}}$ and put

$$b_{ij} = a_{ij} - \frac{a_{i1}}{a_{11}} a_{ij} \, (i, j = 1, 2, \cdots, n),$$

then $D = a_{11} |\, b_{ij} \,|$, where now $|b_{ij}|$ is a determinant of the order $(n-1)$.

Proceeding in like manner we put

$$c_{ij} = b_{ij} - \frac{b_{i2}}{b_{22}} b_{2j},$$

and get

$$D = a_{11} b_{22} |\, c_{ij} \,|,$$

where $|c_{ij}|$ is of order $(n-2)$. Then we get

$$D = a_{11} b_{22} c_{33} |\, d_{ij} \,|,$$

a.s. f. till at least a determinant of the first order is reached.

The factors a_{11}, b_{22}, c_{33}, etc. may evidently be expressed as quotients of determinants. We have, indeed,

$$b_{22} = \begin{vmatrix} a_{11} & a_{12} \\ a_{21} & a_{22} \end{vmatrix} \div a_{11}$$

$$c_{33} = \begin{vmatrix} a_{11} & a_{12} & a_{13} \\ a_{21} & a_{22} & a_{23} \\ a_{31} & a_{23} & a_{33} \end{vmatrix} \div \begin{vmatrix} a_{11} & a_{12} \\ a_{21} & a_{22} \end{vmatrix}, \qquad (2 \cdot 15)$$

---

[1] "On Multiple Correlation", So. Ak. Tid, p.18, 1915.

etc. which relations may be used for obtaining the values of certain sub-determinants necessary for the solution. As a numerical illustration, Charlier gives the cor. between mean temperature of July, June, May, April, March in Lund. If S_4 be the determinant to be computed, then

$$S_4(12345) = \begin{vmatrix} 1 & 0.586\,0 & 0.409\,0 & 0.209\,0 \\ 0.586\,0 & 1 & 0.429\,0 & 0.303\,0 \\ 0.409\,0 & 0.429\,0 & 1 & 0.421\,0 \\ 0.209\,0 & 0.303\,0 & 0.421\,0 & 1 \end{vmatrix}$$

	0.586 0	0.343 4	0.239 7	0.122 5
	0.409 0	0.239 7	0.167 3	0.085 5
	0.209 0	0.122 5	0.085 5	0.043 7
1.523 0		0.056 6	0.189 3	0.180 5
0.288 3		0.189 3	0.832 7	0.335 5
0.274 0		0.180 5	0.335 5	0.956 3
		0.189 3	0.054 6	0.052 0
		0.180 5	0.052 0	0.049 6
1.285 2			0.778 1	0.283 5
0.364 4			0.283 5	0.906 7
			0.283 5	0.103 3
				0.803 4

the first 4 lines give the determinant to be computed. The next three lines give the elements of the 1st line of the determinants multiplied by the factors 0.586 0, 0.409 0, 0.209 0 respectively. Subtracting from the corresponding elements of the determinant, we get the next three lines. The first number (0.656 6) gives the value b_{22} in (2 · 15). Taking the inverse value of this element (+1.523 0) from Barlow's tables and multiplying it by the elements of the first column, we obtain the factors 0.288 3 and 0.274 9 by which now the first (8th) row is to be multiplied. Thus, we get a determinant of 2nd order, which is in like manner reduced to a determinant of let order (0.803 4). We now get

$$s_{11} = 1 \times 0.656\,6 \times 0.778\,1 \times 0.803\,4 = 0.410\,5.$$

The same table gives simultaneously the values of the following determinants of lower order:

$$s_{11}(12) = 1$$
$$s_{11}(123) = 0.656\ 6$$
$$s_{11}(1234) = 0.656\ 6 \quad 0.778\ 1 = 0.510\ 9.$$

2.10 Distribution of a Correlation Index

The distribution of ζ in a sample from a normal population of m variates may be derived from that $R = |r_{ij}|$. Dr. S. S. Wilks has shown that the distribution of R in a sample of n observations from an m-variate normal population is given by

$$P(R) \frac{\Gamma^{(n-1)}\left(\frac{n-1}{2}\right) R^{\frac{n-m}{2}-1}(1-R)^{\frac{n(n-1)}{4}-1}}{\prod_{i2}^{m}\left[\Gamma\left(\frac{n-i}{2}\right)\Gamma\left(\frac{i-1}{2}\right)\right]} \int_0^1\int_0^1\cdots\int_0^1 v_1^{\frac{1}{2}-1} v_2^{1-1} \cdots v_{m-2}^{\frac{m-2}{2}-1} \cdot$$

$$(1-v_1)^{\frac{m(m-1)}{4}-\frac{3}{2}}(1-v_2)^{\frac{m(m-1)}{4}-\frac{5}{2}} \cdots (1-v_{m-2})^{\frac{m-3}{2}} \{1-v_1(1-R)\}^{-\frac{1}{2}} \cdot$$

$$[1 - \{v_1 + v_2(1-v_1)\}(1-R)^{-1}\cdots] \cdot$$

$$[1 - \{v_1 + v_2(1-v_1) + \cdots + v_{m-2}(1-v_1) \cdots (1-v_{m-3})\}(1-R)^{-\frac{m-2}{2}}] \cdot$$

$$dv_1 dv_2 \cdots dv_{m-2} \qquad (2\cdot 16)$$

from which we may deduce the distribution of ζ, by the simple change of variable

$$\sqrt{\frac{R_{mm}}{R}} = \zeta \text{ or } \frac{R_{m-1}}{R} = \zeta^2.$$

2.11 Analogy of a Correlation Surface to a Physical Law

To summarize the above discussions, we may say that a correlation surface estimated from a sample of n observation enables us, in general, to answer approximately the following questions:

(a) What is the expected relation existing between the variates?

(b) What degree of precision does a prediction based on the

regression equation have?

(c) What is the intensity of the relationship, if any, existing between the variates?

A correlation surface may also be interpreted as a scientific generalization or law. There are 3 classes of laws:

(A) If an event A is known to have occurred, then a second event B must occur. For instance, the law of gravitation.

(B) If an event A is known to have occurred when the events C, D, etc. are present, then the second event B must occur. For instance, Boyle's law, with regard to the volume end pressure of gas, states that if the pressure is increased while the temperature is kept constant, then the volume decreases proportionately.

(C) If an event A is known to have occurred when the events C, D, etc. are present, then the second event B has a definite probability of occurrence. For instance, the economic law of demand for a certain good.

A correlation surface represents a law of the third kind. Of course, a law of the first kind may be considered as a special case of the second kind while the second kind may be considered as a special case of the third kind, i.e., the second kind is the case of the third kind when the probability is of certainty.

2.12 Characteristic Properties of a Correlation Surface

If the correlation function of m variates is geometrically represented in a rectangular system of coordinates in space of $m + 1$ dimensions so that the variates x_1, x_2, x_3, $\cdots$, x_m are reckoned along the m axes and the frequency w of any system of values of x_1, x_2, x_3, $\cdots$, x_m is reckoned along the w-axis [or $(m+1)$th axis] perpendicular to the $(x_1, x_2, x_3, \cdots, x_m)$-hyperplane, the correlation surface of m variates is obtained. If the contours are cut out of the correlation surface by planes parallel to the $x_m w$-plane, we obtain the so-called partial frequency curves, representing the array distributions of $x_{mh}(t)$ of the

$(x_{1h}, x_{2h}, \cdots, x_{(m-1)h})$-type. Their equations are obtained by substituting the assigned type values for the first $(m-1)$ variates

$$w = P(x_m \cdot x_1 x_2 \cdots x_{(m-1)}) = P(x_{1h}, x_{2h}, \cdots, x_{(m-1)h}, x_{mt}).$$

When the correlation surface is of the form (2·6), we have the formula (2·10) for the partial frequency curves of x_m. Now a correlation surface may be considered as the continuance or locus of these partial frequency curves, so its form must depend on their characteristics. A partial frequency curve just as a frequency curve of a single variate depends its position on the mean and its form on the variance, the skewness, and the kurtosis. The locus of the partial mean is, as we have seen above, called the regression curve (surface in cases where $m > 2$), and the loci of variance, skewness, and kurtosis are respectively defined as the scedastic, clitic, and kurtic curves.① Therefore these curves must be at least among the determinate characteristics of a correlation surface. For normal correlation function, the regression is linear, scedasticity is homogeneous, i.e., all the partial variances are equal to each other, and the clisy and kurtosis vanish. Furthermore, if the contours cut out of the correlation surface by planes parallel to the $(x_1, x_2, x_3, \cdots, x_m)$-hyperplane are projected on that plane we obtain the so-called curves of equal frequency. Their equations are obtained by putting

$$w = P(x_1, x_2, x_3, \cdots, x_m) \text{ const.}$$

When the correlation is normal, we have for the curves of equal frequency the formula:

$$C' = J_m e^{-\frac{1}{2R}\sum \frac{R_{ij}}{\sigma_i \sigma_j} x_i x_j} \qquad (2 \cdot 17)$$

or

---

① Pearson originally defined the scedastic curve as the curve in which the ratio of the standard deviation of the array to the standard deviation of the character in the population at large is plotted to position, and clitic curve as the curve in which the skewness of the array is plotted to position. The kurtic curve was first discussed by Wicksell who called it the synergic curve. Pretorius prefers the term "kurtic curve" to the term "synergic curve" for the locus of kurtosis. Pearson, K. "On the Theory of Skew Cor. and non-linear Regression", Drapers' Co. Res. Mem. II; Wicksell, S. D., "The Cor. Function of Type A", K. Sv. Vet. Handl., Vol.58, p. 10; Pretorius, "Skew Bivariate Freq. Surface", Biom. 22, p.111.

$$c = \sum \frac{R_{ij}}{\sigma_i \sigma_j} x_i x_j, \quad i, j = 1, 2, 3, \cdots, m. \qquad (2 \cdot 18)$$

This is a system of similar and similarly placed ellipsoids in the m dimensional space. Clearly the curves of equal frequency must be also a determinate characteristic of a correlation surface. Indeed, the equal frequency curves may be regarded as an analogous case of partial frequency curves, because the latter are the contours cut out of the correlation surface by planes parallel to the (w, x_1, x_2, x_3, $\cdots$, x_{m-1})-planes while the former are the contours cut out of the correlation surface by planes parallel to the (x_1, x_2, x_3, $\cdots$, x_m)-hyperplane and therefore they are cross-secetions from the same correlation surface in different directions.

Theoretically it may seem possible to determine any correlation surface, normal as well as skew, through the determination of these determinate characteristics, namely, the regression, scedastic, clitic, kurtic, and equal frequency curves. But the theory is not yet satisfactorily developed, as we shall see as we proceed. Nevertheless, it may be mentioned that the Scandinavians have developed quite fully the theory of characterization of skew correlation surfaces by series, parallel to the theory of characterization of the skew frequency curves by the series of type A and type B. The weakness of such a method lies mainly in the fact that the representation of a correlation surface by a series is an approximation process and the accuracy of such an approximation depends upon the rapidity of convergency. If the series converges slowly, a satisfactory representation would require a great number of terms of which the computation demands too much labor to be practicable.① The problem has also been approached from other points of view and some progress has been made. But the interpretation of a correlation surface which has set forth in sections 8 and 11, will still hold regardless of the line which further development of the theory may take.

Now let us trace the history of the correlation surface method.

---

① For further comment, see J. P. Van der Stok, "On the Analysis of Frequency Curves according to a General Method", Kon. Ak. Van. Wet. Amst. Proc., Sec. of Sciences, p.10, 1908.

2.13 Laplace's Contributions

Laplace's memoir[①] on some definite integrals and their applications to probabilities, so far as the present writer is aware, gives the first mathematical derivation of the bivariate normal correlation surface. It was a result of his investigation on the theory of errors.

Laplace's investigation is on a prior process. He assumes that an error (deviation), as actually occurring in an observation, is not of simple origin, but is produced by the algebraical combination of a great many independent contributory causes of error, each of which, according to the chance which affects it independently, may produce an error, of either sign and of different magnitude. These errors are supposed to be integral multiples of a common measure ε so that they admit of being treated by the usual theory of chances, then supposing the common measure ε to be indefinitely small, and the range of their multiples to be indefinitely great, the conditions ultimately approach to the state of graduated errors. Suppose then that, for one source of error, the errors in units ε may be

$$-n, -n+1, -n+2, \cdots, -1, 0, +1, 2, \cdots, n-2, n-1, n$$ with probabilities respectively $\varphi\left(\dfrac{x}{n}\right)$, $x = \pm 1, \pm 2, \cdots, \pm n$, i.e., $\varphi\left(\dfrac{n}{n}\right)$, $\varphi\left(\dfrac{-n+1}{n}\right)$, $\varphi\left(\dfrac{-n+2}{n}\right)$, $\cdots$, $\varphi\left(\dfrac{-1}{n}\right)$, $\varphi\left(\dfrac{0}{n}\right)$, $\varphi\left(\dfrac{1}{n}\right)$, $\cdots$, $\varphi\left(\dfrac{n-2}{n}\right)$, $\varphi\left(\dfrac{n-1}{n}\right)$, $\varphi\left(\dfrac{n}{n}\right)$.

Suppose that for another source of error, the errors may also be,

$$-n, -n+1, -n+2, \cdots, -1, 0, +1, 2, \cdots, n-2, n-1, n$$

with respective probabilities:

$\varphi\left(\dfrac{n}{n}\right)$, $\varphi\left(\dfrac{-n+1}{n}\right)$, $\varphi\left(\dfrac{-n+2}{n}\right)$, $\cdots$, $\varphi\left(\dfrac{-1}{n}\right)$, $\varphi\left(\dfrac{0}{n}\right)$, $\varphi\left(\dfrac{1}{n}\right)$, $\cdots$,

---

[①] The complete title of the memoir is "Mémoir sur les Intégrales Définies et leur application aux Probabilities, et specialement à la recherche du milieu qu'il fant choisir entre les résultats des observations", published in the Memoires de l'Institute Imperial de France for 1810. It occupies pages 279 – 347 of the volume. The derivation is also reproduced in his book *Theorie Analytique des Probabilite's*, Chapter 4. The word "error" corresponds in meaning to this word "deviation" in statistics.

$$\varphi\left(\frac{n-2}{n}\right), \varphi\left(\frac{n-1}{n}\right), \varphi\left(\frac{n}{n}\right).$$

And so on for s sources of error, and suppose that we wish to ascertain what is the probability that, upon combining algebraically one error taken from the first series, with an error taken from the second series, and with one error taken from the third series, and so on, we can produce an error ℓ. The first step is to ascertain how many are the different combinations which will each produce ℓ.

Now, if we watch the process of combination, we shall see that the numbers are added by exactly the same law as the addition of indices in the successive multiplications of the polynomial

$$\varphi\left(\frac{n}{n}\right)e^{-n\theta i} + \varphi\left(\frac{n-1}{n}\right)e^{-(n-1)\theta i} + \varphi\left(\frac{n-2}{n}\right)e^{-(n-2)\theta i} + \cdots + \varphi\left(\frac{n-2}{n}\right)e^{(n-2)\theta i}$$
$$+ \varphi\left(\frac{n-1}{n}\right)e^{(n-1)\theta i} + \varphi\left(\frac{n}{n}\right)e^{n\theta i}$$

by itself, supposing the operation repeated $s - 1$ times. And therefore the number of combinations required will be the coefficient of $e^{i\ell\theta}$ (which is also the same as the coefficient of $e^{-i\ell\theta}$ because the polynomial is symmetrical with respect to θ in the sense that the polynomial remains unchanged if $-\theta$ is substituted for θ), in the expansion of

$$\left\{\varphi\left(\frac{n}{n}\right)\left(e^{-in\theta} + e^{in\theta}\right) + \varphi\left(\frac{n-1}{n}\right)\left(e^{-(n-1)\theta i} + e^{(n-1)\theta i}\right) + \cdots\right.$$
$$\left. + \varphi\left(\frac{0}{n}\right)\left(e^{-i\theta} + e^{i\theta}\right) + \varphi\left(\frac{0}{n}\right)\right\}^s$$
$$= \sum_{x=1}^{n}\left\{\varphi\left(\frac{x}{n}\right)\left(e^{ix\theta} + e^{-ix\theta}\right) + \varphi\left(\frac{0}{n}\right)\right\}^s. \quad (2 \cdot 19)$$

This coefficient will be exhibited as a number uncombined with any power of $e^{i\theta}$, if we multiply the expansion either by $e^{i\ell\theta}$, or by $e^{-i\ell\theta}$, or by $\left(\frac{e^{i\ell\theta} + e^{-i\ell\theta}}{2}\right)$. The number of combinations required is therefore the same as the term independent of θ in the expansion of

$$\frac{1}{2}(e^{i\ell\theta} + e^{-i\ell\theta}) \left\{ \varphi\left(\frac{0}{n}\right) + 2\varphi\left(\frac{1}{n}\right)\cos\theta + 2\varphi\left(\frac{2}{n}\right)\cos 2\theta + \cdots + \varphi\left(\frac{n}{n}\right)\cos n\theta \right\}^s$$

$$= \cos\ell\theta 2 \left\{ \sum_{x=1}^{n} \varphi\left(\frac{x}{n}\right)\cos\theta + 2\varphi\left(\frac{0}{n}\right) \right\}^s. \qquad (2\cdot 20)$$

And, remarking that if we integrate this quantity with respect to θ, from $\theta = 0$ to $\theta = x$, the terms depending on θ will entirely disappear, and the term independent of θ will be multiplied by x, it follows that the number of combinations required is the definite integral:

$$P_\ell = \frac{1}{x}\int_0^x d\theta \cos\ell\theta \left\{ \varphi\left(\frac{0}{n}\right) + 2\varphi\left(\frac{1}{n}\right)\cos\theta + 2\varphi\left(\frac{2}{n}\right)\cos 2\theta + \cdots \right.$$

$$\left. + 2\varphi\left(\frac{n}{n}\right)\cos n\theta \right\}^s = \frac{1}{x}\int_0^x \cos\ell\theta \left\{ \varphi\left(\frac{0}{n}\right) + 2\sum_{x=1}^{n}\varphi\left(\frac{x}{n}\right)\cos x\theta \right\}^s d\theta = P_\ell.$$

$$(2\cdot 21)$$

Now, let $x' = \dfrac{x}{n}$, $dx' = \dfrac{1}{n}$ and expand $\cos x\theta$ in the power series of $x\theta$:

$$2\varphi\left(\frac{x}{n}\right)\cos x\theta = 2\varphi\left(\frac{x}{n}\right) - \frac{x^2}{n^2}\varphi\left(\frac{x}{n}\right)n^2\theta^2 + \text{etc.}$$

Then,

$$\varphi\left(\frac{0}{n}\right) + 2\sum_{x=1}^{n}\varphi\left(\frac{x}{n}\right)\cos x\theta = 2n\int_0^1 \varphi(x')\,dx' - n^3\theta^2\int_0^1 x'^2\varphi(x')\,dx' + \text{etc.}$$

$$(2\cdot 22)$$

Moreover, let

$$k = 2\int_0^1 \varphi(x')\,dx', \quad k'' = \int_0^1 x'^2\varphi(x')\,dx', \quad \text{etc.} \qquad (2\cdot 23)$$

The preceding series $(2\cdot 22)$ becomes

$$nk\left(1 - \frac{k''}{k}n^2\theta^2 - \text{etc.}\right)$$

and the integral $(2\cdot 21)$ becomes

$$P_\ell = \frac{n^s k^s}{x}\int_0^x d\theta \cos\ell\theta \left(1 - \frac{k''}{k}n^2\theta^2 - \text{etc.}\right)^s. \qquad (2\cdot 24)$$

Suppose

$$\left(1 - \frac{k''}{k}n^2\theta^2 - \text{etc.}\right)^s = e^{-t^2}, \qquad (2\cdot 25)$$

when s is large, we may write

$$s\frac{k''}{k}n^2\theta^2 = t^2$$

whence

$$\theta = \frac{t}{n}\sqrt{\frac{k}{k''s}}.$$

Now if we observe that $nk = 2\int_0^n dx\varphi\left(\frac{x}{n}\right)$ expresses the total probability that an error will lie between the limits $\pm n$, this quantity nk must be equal to unity, and

$$P_\ell = \frac{1}{nx}\sqrt{\frac{k}{k''s}}\int dt\, e^{-t^2}\cos\left(\frac{\ell t}{n}\sqrt{\frac{k}{k''s}}\right) \qquad (2\cdot 26)$$

the integral being taken from $t = 0$ to $t = nx\sqrt{\frac{k''s}{k}}$ or to $t = \infty$ because n is supposed infinitely large. But

$$\int_0^\infty dt\, e^{-t^2}\cos\left(\frac{\ell t}{n}\sqrt{\frac{k}{k''s}}\right) = \frac{x}{2}e^{-\frac{\ell^2}{4n}\frac{k}{k''s}} \qquad (2\cdot 27)\,①$$

so $(2\cdot 26)$ becomes $\qquad P_\ell = \frac{1}{2n\sqrt{x}}\sqrt{\frac{k}{k''s}}\,e^{-\frac{\ell^2}{4n^2}\frac{k}{k''s}}.$

This expression gives the probability that an error, produced by the combination of numerous errors will be ℓ, is based upon the supposition that the changes of magnitude of ℓ proceed by a unit at a time. If now we pass from errors of integers to graduated errors, we may consider that we have thus obtained all the probabilities that an error will lie between ℓ and $\ell + 1$. In order to obtain all the probabilities that an error will lie between ℓ and $\ell + a\ell$, we derive the following expression from the above,

$$\frac{1}{2n\sqrt{x}}\sqrt{\frac{k}{k''s}}\,e^{-\frac{k}{4n^2k''s}\ell^2}\,a\ell. \qquad (2\cdot 27a)$$

Hence an error, compounded of elementary errors from a large number of

---

① Laplace, Op. Cit., No.25 of BK. I.

independent sources, follows the normal law of distribution with the variance (the square of the standard deviation) equal to $\dfrac{2n^2k''s}{k}$.

Moreover, if we observe that the variance of an error from one of the s sources is

$$\frac{2\sum_{x=1}^{n} x^2 \varphi\left(\dfrac{x}{n}\right)}{2\sum_{n=1}^{r} \varphi\left(\dfrac{x}{n}\right)} = \frac{2n^2 \sum \dfrac{x^2}{n^2}\varphi\left(\dfrac{x}{n}\right)\dfrac{1}{n}}{2n \sum \varphi\left(\dfrac{x}{n}\right)\dfrac{1}{n}} = \frac{2n^2 \int_0^1 x'^2 \varphi(x')\,\mathrm{d}x'}{2\int \varphi(x')\,\mathrm{d}x'} = \frac{2n^2 k''}{k},$$

and that the variances of these component errors are equal to each other, we see that the variance of the resultant error compounded of a number of elementary errors is simply equal to the sum of the variances of these elementary errors.

Let
$$\frac{2k''n^2 s}{k} = \sigma^2$$

and
$$\frac{\ell}{\sigma} = y,$$

then we have the following formula for the probability that an error will fall between y and $y + \mathrm{d}y$:

$$w = \varphi(y) = \frac{1}{\sqrt{2x}} e^{-\frac{1}{2}y^2} \mathrm{d}y. \tag{2 · 28}$$

Now if we plot (y, w) in a rectangular system of coordinates, a bell-shaped curve is obtained. This curve is called the normal curve and the function $\varphi(y)$ called the normal probability function. In the derivation, there are three fundamental suppositions involved.

(1) There are an indefinitely great number of sources of error.
(2) The positive and negative errors have equal probabilities of occurrence, i. e., the error from each source follows symmetrical law of distribution.
(3) The total probability of errors in one source is equal to unity and the errors from different sources are independent of each other.

It may be a convenient opportunity to point out that, although the independent component errors x in the derivation are non-observed theoretical notions, the conclusions reached above are applicable to the case where the component errors are observations provided they satisfy the underlying assumptions as mentioned above.

Now suppose s observations on a quantity z be taken and denoted by z_1, z_2, $\cdots$, z_s. Let $x_j = z_1 - z$ be the error (deviation) or the j-th observation, then a linear function of these deviations (errors) may be written

$$\ell = m_1 x_1 + m_2 x_2 + \cdots + m_s x_s = \sum_{j=1}^{s} m_j x_j, \qquad (2 \cdot 29)$$

where m's are positive or negative integers, it is now required to determine the probability for the occurrence of a resultant deviation equal to given magnitude: $\sum m_j x_j = \ell$, or, to find the probability for the occurrence of the mean deviation $\bar{x}$ defined by

$$\bar{x} \sum_{j=1}^{s} m_j = \sum_{j=1}^{s} m_j x_j = \ell.$$

In doing so, Laplace considers the product①

$$\int_{-a}^{a} \varphi\left(\frac{x}{a}\right) e^{m_1 x \theta i} \cdot \int_{-a}^{a} \varphi\left(\frac{x}{a}\right) e^{m_2 x \theta i} \cdots \int_{-a}^{a} \varphi\left(\frac{x}{a}\right) e^{m_s x \theta i}$$

where $\pm a$ are the common limits of x's and $\varphi\left(\dfrac{x}{a}\right)$ is the probability for the occurrence of a deviation x. This expression is thus seen to be equivalent to that in equation $(2 \cdot 19)$ of the preceding section. It is therefore clear that the coefficient of any term $e^{\ell \theta i}$ in the development of this product will be the

---

① The integral sign as used by Laplace is understood to be the summation; i.e.,

$$\int \varphi\left(\frac{x}{a}\right) e^{mx\theta i} = \sum \varphi\left(\frac{x}{a}\right) e^{mx\theta i},$$

if the deviation x takes integral values only. Moreover, if $\varphi\left(\dfrac{x}{a}\right)$ is a constant, $\sum \varphi\left(\dfrac{x}{a}\right) e^{m_j x \theta i}$ may be simply written as $\sum e^{m_j x \theta i}$, leaving out the constant. This is the case which Plana considered in his paper "Mémoire sur divers problémes de probabilité", Memoires de l'Académie Impériale des Science, Litterature at Beaux-Arts de Turin, pous les Années 1811–1812, Vol.20, Turin, pp.355—408, 1813. It added nothing new to the result of Laplace. In fact, it is much narrower in assumption. So H.M. Walker's discussions in history of Statistics are misleading.

probability that the sum of the errors of the observations multiplied respectively by m_1, m_2, etc. will be equal to ℓ. In multiplying therefore, the preceding product by $e^{-\ell\theta i}$, the term independent of $e^{\theta i}$ and its powers in the new product will be this probability. As we did before, we assume the probability of a positive error x is the same as that of a negative error $-x$ and unite every term of the form $e^{mx\theta i}$ with $e^{-mx\theta i}$, then the probability that the sum $\sum_{x=1}^{i=s} m_j x_i$ will be equal to ℓ is

$$P_\ell = \frac{1}{2x} \int_{-x}^{x} d\theta\, e^{-\ell\theta i} 2 \left[\int \varphi\left(\frac{x}{a}\right) \cos m_1 x\theta \cdot 2\int \varphi\left(\frac{x}{a}\right) \cos m_2 x\theta \cdots \right.$$
$$\left. 2\int \varphi\left(\frac{x}{a}\right) \cos m_s x\theta \right]. \qquad (2 \cdot 30)$$

Now let
$$\frac{x}{a} = x',$$

$$k = 2\int_0^1 \varphi(x')\,dx' = 2\sum_0^a \varphi\left(\frac{x}{a}\right) \cdot \frac{1}{a}$$

$$k'' = \int_0^1 \varphi(x')\, x'^2 dx' = \sum \varphi\left(\frac{x}{a}\right) \frac{x^2}{a^2} \frac{1}{a}$$

and expand the cosine function in series

$$\int \varphi\left(\frac{x}{a}\right) \cos mx\theta = \int \varphi\left(\frac{x}{a}\right) - \frac{1}{2} m^2 a^2 \theta^2 \int \frac{x^2}{a^2} \varphi\left(\frac{x}{a}\right) + \text{etc.}$$
$$= ak\left(1 - \frac{k''}{k} m^2 a^2 \theta^2 + \frac{k^{(IV)}}{12k} m^4 a^4 \theta^4 - \text{etc.}\right).$$

The logarithm of the second member of this equation is

$$-\frac{k''}{k} m^2 a^2 \theta^2 + \frac{kk^{(IV)} - 6k''^2}{12k^2} m^4 a^4 \theta^4 - \text{etc.} + \log ak.$$

But $ak = 2\sum_{x=0}^{a} \varphi\left(\frac{x}{a}\right)$ is the total probability of all errors between the limits and therefore is equal to unit. So the expression becomes

$$\log\left\{\int \varphi\left(\frac{x}{a}\right) \cos mx\theta\right\} = -\frac{k''}{k} m^2 a^2 \theta^2 + \frac{kk^{(IV)} 6k''^2}{12k^2} m^4 a^4 \theta^4 - \text{etc.}$$

Hence,

$$2\int\varphi\left(\frac{x}{a}\right)\cos m_1 x\theta \cdot 2\int\varphi\left(\frac{x}{a}\right)\cos m_2 x\theta \text{ etc.}$$

$$= e^{\sum_{j=1}^{j=s}\left\{-\frac{k''}{k}m^2 a^2\theta^2 + \frac{kk^{(\text{IV})} - 6k''^2}{12k^2}m^4 a^4\theta^4 + \text{etc.}\right\}}$$

$$= e^{-\frac{k''}{k}a^2\theta^2 \sum m_j^2} \cdot e^{\frac{kk^{\text{IV}} - 6k''^2}{12k^2}a^4\theta^4 \sum m_j^4} + \text{etc.}$$

$$= e^{-\frac{k''}{k}a^2\theta^2 \sum m_j^2 \{1 + \frac{kk^{\text{IV}} - 6k''^2}{12k^2}a^4\theta^4 \sum m_j^4 + \text{etc.}\}}$$

and, from equation (2 · 30),

$$P_\ell = \frac{1}{2x}\int_{-x}^{+x} a\theta\left\{1 + \frac{kk^{\text{IV}} - 6k''^2}{12k^2}a^4\theta^4 \sum m_j^4 + \text{etc.}\right\} e^{-\ell\theta i - \frac{k''}{k}a^2\theta^2 \sum m_j^2}. \quad (2\cdot 31)$$

Neglecting the terms in $a^4\theta^4 \sum m_j^4$ and higher orders, ① we have

$$\Omega(\theta) = \frac{1}{2x}\int_{-x}^{+x} a\theta e^{-\frac{k''}{k}a^2\theta^2 \sum m_j^2 - \ell\theta i}$$

Putting ②
$$\frac{2k''a^2}{k}\sum m_j^2 = \sigma^2$$

---

① If the terms $a^4\theta^4 \sum m_j^4$ and higher orders are not negligible, the equation (2 · 31) may be expressed in the form

$$P_\mu = \Omega(\theta) + A_3 \frac{a\Omega}{a\theta^3} + A_4 \frac{a\Omega}{a\Omega^3} + \text{etc.}$$

which is the well-known Type A function of Charlier. Cf. Charlier, C. V. L., "Die Strange Form des Bernoullis'-chen Theorems", Meddeland fran Lunds Astro. Observatorium, No.43, which is also reprinted in Arkiv for Math. Astronomie och Fysik, Bd. 5, Nov.15, 1909. The same series may also be obtained by developing the generating function of a simple hypergeometric series just as Charlier developed the generating function of a binomial series into his type A function. Cf. S. D.

S. D. Wicksell, "Analytic Theory of Sampling", Ark. Math. Astr. och. Fysik, Bd.17, Nov.19, 1917.

② The variance of $m_j x$ is

$$\sigma_{mx}^2 = \left\{\sum_{x=-a}^{a}(m_j x)^2 \varphi\left(\frac{x}{a}\right)\right\} : \left\{\sum_{x=-a}^{a}\varphi\left(\frac{x}{a}\right)\right\}$$

$$= \left\{2m_j^2 \sum_{x=a}^{a} a^2\left(\frac{x}{a}\right)^2 \varphi\left(\frac{x}{a}\right)\right\} : \left\{2a \sum \varphi\left(\frac{x}{a}\right)\frac{1}{a}\right\}.$$

Let $\frac{x}{a} = x'$, $\frac{1}{a} = dx'$, then

$$\sigma_{m_j x}^2 = \frac{2m_j^2 a^3 \int_0^1 x'^2 \varphi(x') \, dx'}{2a \int_0^1 \varphi(x') dx'} = m_j^2 \cdot \frac{2a^2 k''}{k} = m_j^2 \sigma_x^2,$$

but $u = \sum_{j=1}^{s} m_j x$, so $\sigma_u^2 = \sum_{j=1}^{s} m_j^2 \cdot 2a^2 \frac{k''}{k} = \sigma_x^2 \sum_{j=1}^{s} m_j^2.$

and changing① the limits of integration from $\pm x$ to $\pm\infty$, we obtain, if σ^2 is not small,

$$\varphi(\ell) = \frac{1}{2x}\int_{-\infty}^{\infty} d\theta\, e^{-\frac{\sigma^2}{2}\theta - \ell\theta i}$$

$$= \frac{1}{2x}\int_{-\infty}^{\infty} d\theta\, e^{-\frac{\sigma^2}{2}\left(\theta - \frac{\ell i}{\sigma}\right)^2} = \frac{1}{\sigma\sqrt{2x}} e^{-\frac{\ell^2}{2\sigma^2}}.$$

If u is a graduated variate, the probability for ℓ to lie between u and $u+du$ is

$$\varphi d\ell = \frac{1}{\sigma\sqrt{2x}} e^{-\frac{\ell^2}{2\sigma^2}} d\ell. \qquad (2\cdot 32)$$

For the linear regression equation

$$Y = a + bx,$$

the regression coefficient

$$b = \frac{\sum xy}{\sum x^2} = \sum\left(\frac{x}{\sum x^2}\right) y$$

may be considered as a weighted aggregate of y with weight $\dfrac{x}{\sum x^2}$ which corresponds to m in $(2\cdot 29)$. It is then easy to see that the linear regression coefficient b follows the normal distribution with standard deviation

$$\sigma_b^2 = \sigma_y^2 \sum\left(\frac{x}{\sum x^2}\right)^2 = \sigma_y^2 \frac{\sum x^2}{\left(\sum x^2\right)^2} = \frac{\sigma_y^2}{\sum x^2}.$$

For this reason, it may be said that Laplace in 1810 has developed the mathematics for the law of the distribution of the simple linear regression coefficient.

Moreover, the weighted mean $\bar{x}$ may be considered as a weighted aggregate with $\dfrac{m_j}{\sum m_j}$ as the weight of x_j. Thus, the weighted mean is seen to be normally

---

① For a study of the effect of such a change of limits of integration upon the result, see Wicksell, "Analytic Theory of Sampling", Op.Cit.

distributed with standard deviation

$$\sigma_{\bar{x}} = \frac{\sum m_j^2}{(\sum m_j)^2}\sigma_x^2,$$

σ_x being the standard deviation of an individual observed error. It is clear that when $m_j = 1$, the weighted mean becomes simple mean which follows the normal law of errors with standard deviation $\sigma_{\bar{x}} = \dfrac{\sigma_x}{\sqrt{s}}$.

Next Laplace investigates the probability of the simultaneous occurrence of a pair of resultant errors ℓ and ℓ', each being a linear function of a large number of component errors

$$\begin{cases} \ell = m_1 x_1 + m_2 x_2 + \cdots + m_s x_s \\ \ell' = n_1 y_1 + n_2 y_2 + \cdots + n_s y_s \end{cases}$$

where x_j and y_j are the respective errors① of j-th observations on the two variates X and Y. The process of investigation is merely an extension of what he used in the investigation of the probability that a resultant error will occur. So the required probability is equal to the constant term of the following product

$$e^{-i\ell\theta - i\ell'\theta'}\left\{\int_{-a}^{a}\varphi\left(\frac{x}{a}\right)e^{-(m_1\theta + m'_1\theta')ix} \cdot \int_{-a}^{a}\varphi\left(\frac{x}{a}\right)e^{-(m_2\theta + n\theta')ix}\cdots\int_{-a}^{a}\varphi\left(\frac{x}{a}\right)e^{-(m_s\theta + n_s\theta')ix}\right\}$$

$$(2 \cdot 33)$$

or

$$\frac{1}{(2x)^2}\int_{-x}^{x}\int_{-x}^{x}d\theta d\theta' e^{-i\ell\theta - i\ell'\theta'}\left\{2\int\varphi\left(\frac{x}{a}\right)\cos(m_1\theta + n_1\theta')x + \cdots\right.$$
$$\left. + 2\int\varphi\left(\frac{x}{a}\right)\cos(m_s\theta + n_s\theta')x\right\}.$$

Following the procedures of the preceding section, we reduce this function approximately to the form:

$$\frac{1}{4x^2}\int_{-x}^{x}\int_{-x}^{x}d\theta d\theta' e^{-i\ell\theta - i\ell'\theta - \frac{k''}{k}a^2(\theta^2\sum m_j^2 + 2\theta\theta'\sum m_j n_j + \theta'^2\sum n_j^2)}.$$

---

① These errors x_j and y_j may also be considered the non-observed theoretical elementary errors as in the preceding section if the problem in consideration requires doing.

Changing the variables

$$t = a\theta + \frac{a\theta \cdot \sum m_j n_j}{\sum m_j^2} + \frac{ik\ell}{2k''a \sum m_j^2},$$

$$t' = a\theta' - \frac{k}{2k''a} \cdot \frac{i(\ell \sum m_j n_j - \ell' \sum m_j^2)}{\sum m_j^2 \sum n_j^2 - (\sum m_j n_j)^2},$$

we obtain

$$e^{-\frac{k(\ell^2 \sum n_j^2 - 2\ell\ell' \sum m_j n_j + \ell'^2 \sum m_j^2)}{4ak''[\sum m_j^2 \sum n_j^2 - (\sum m_j n_j)^2]}} \iint \frac{dt dt'}{4x^2 a^2} e^{\frac{k'' \sum m_j^2}{k} t^2 - \frac{k'' m_j^2[\sum n_j^2 (\sum m_j n_j)^2]}{k \sum m_j^2} t'^2}$$

$$= \frac{k}{4sk''a^2 [\sum m_j^2 \sum n_j^2 - (\sum m_j n_j)^2]^{\frac{1}{2}}} e^{-\frac{k}{4a^2 k''} \frac{\ell^2 \sum n_j^2 - 2\ell\ell' \sum m_j n_j + \ell'^2 \sum m_j^2}{[\sum m_j^2 \sum n_j^2 - (\sum m_j n_j)^2]}}.$$

(2 · 34)

As in the preceding section, let

$$\sigma_\ell^2 = \frac{2a^2 k''}{k} \sum m_j^2,$$

$$\sigma_{\ell'}^2 = \frac{2a^2 k''}{k} \sum n_j^2,$$

$$r_{\ell\ell'} = \frac{\sum m_j n_j}{\sqrt{\sum m_j^2 n_j^2}},$$ (2 · 35)

we obtain finally the probability of the simultaneous occurrence of ℓ and ℓ':

$$\frac{1}{2x\sigma_\ell \sigma_{\ell'} \sqrt{(1-r^2)}} e^{-\frac{1}{2(1-r^2)}\left(\frac{\ell^2}{\sigma_\ell^2} - 2r\frac{\ell\ell'}{\sigma_\ell \sigma_{\ell'}} + \frac{\ell'^2}{\sigma_{\ell'}^2}\right)}.$$ (2 · 36)

In order to obtain all the probabilities that a pair of errors will lie respectively between ℓ and $\ell + a\ell$ and between ℓ' and $\ell' + a\ell'$, we derive the following expression by multiplying by $a\ell\, a\ell'$

$$\frac{1}{2x\sigma_\ell \sigma_{\ell'} \sqrt{(1-r^2)}} e^{-\frac{1}{2(1-r^2)}\left(\frac{\ell^2}{\sigma_\ell^2} - 2r\frac{\ell\ell'}{\sigma_\ell \sigma_{\ell'}} + \frac{\ell'^2}{\sigma_{\ell'}^2}\right)} a\ell a\ell'.$$ (2 · 36a)

It may be of general interest to point out that in the correlation analysis there are three problems:

(ⅰ) The investigation of the general form of a correlation function based on some reasonable assumptions.①

(ⅱ) The determination of the parameters in such a correlation function in terms of the observed distribution.

(ⅲ) The determination of the precision of these estimated parameters.

Laplace solved the first problem in case of two variates by giving the equation (2・34), i.e.,

$$\varphi(x_1, x_2) = J_2 e^{-\frac{1}{2}X(x_1, x_2)}$$
$$X(x_1, x_2) = a_{11}x_1^2 + 2a_{12}x_1x_2 + a_{22}x_2^2, \qquad (2 \cdot 34a)$$

a homogeneous function of the two variates of 2nd degree, as the general form of a frequency function of correlated variates, if the elementary errors are large in number, independent of each other, and follow the symmetrical law of distribution. But he made no attempt at the solution of the second problem.

In the 1880s, Galton, interested in the human inheritance problem, found the bivariate normal surface to be the appropriate formula for representing the correlation between the organs in parents and in their off-springs, determined then the parameters in this expression in terms of the observed data, and interpreted it in light of biological knowledge with regard to the measurements obtained from other organism in which experimental breeding could be practiced, as the law of heredity in man respecting its form and its intensity. Making use of general formulas with proper interpretation is a different art from their establishment by mathematical proof. This formula, through Galton's use for establishing the law of inheritance for man at a time when nothing was known about the mechanism of inheritance, immediately caught the attention of the scientists and spread its use rapidly in every observational quantitative sciences. In this sense Galton was the first one to supply the solution of the second problem of the correlation analysis in case of bivariate normal correlation. After we have determined the parameters of a correlation function in terms of the

---

① The problem may be stated in its inverse form, i.e., the investigation of the most general conditions under which a given form of distribution is fulfilled. Edgeworth's memoir on "The Law of Error and The Cor. Average" is of this nature. Also See Part I of this chapter.

moments of the distribution, we may write, by using the familiar notation, the equation (2 · 36) in place of (2 · 34). Equation (2 · 36) is comprehensible to every student of statistics. This seems to emphasize the importance of the standardized notation, yet the point is that the transformation from equation (2 · 34) is equation (2 · 36) is a solution of the second problem in the investigation of correlation analysis.

In the case of three variates, Edgeworth was the first to solve problem (ii) of the correlation analysis and then Pearson solved the same for the case of m variates in his memoir "Regression Heredity, and Panmixia", which we shall consider as we proceed.

Problem (iii) has been solved by Fisher, Pearson, and "Student", as we shall see in Chapter 4.

It may be observed that Laplace's investigation in reality assumed linear regression between the two variates ℓ and ℓ'; because he assumed two quantities u and u' being so related to ℓ and ℓ' that

$$\ell \sum m_i x_i = (\sum p_i m_i) u + (\sum q_i m_i) u'$$
$$\ell' \sum n_i y_i = (\sum p_i n_i) u + (\sum q_i u_i) u'.$$

In fact, Laplace's object is to determine u and u' through the determination of ℓ and ℓ'. The probability function for u and u' is given by

$$\iint \frac{k}{4k''x} \frac{I}{E} \frac{dudu'}{a^2} e^{\frac{k(Fu^2 + 2Guu' + Hu'^2)}{4k''a^2 E}} \tag{2 · 34b}$$

where

$$F = Sn_i^2 (Sm_i p_i)^2 - 2Sm_i n_i Sm_i p_i Sn_i p_i + Sm_i^2 (Sn_i p_i)^2$$
$$G = Sn_i^2 Sm_i p_i Sm_i q_i + Sm_i Sn_i p_i Sn_i q_i - Sm_i n_i [Sn_i p_i Sm_i q_i$$
$$\qquad + Sm_i p_i \cdot Sn_i q_i]$$
$$H = Sn_i^2 (Sm_i q_i)^2 - 2Sm_i n_i Sm_i q_i \cdot Sn_i q_i + Sm_i^2 (Sn_i q_i)^2$$
$$I = Sm_i p_i Sn_i q_i - Sn_i p_i Sm_i q_i.$$

Laplace did not use a single symbol and therefore gave no definition to what we now call the coefficient of correlations, but the object of his investigation was to determine the probability of the simultaneous occurrence of ℓ and ℓ' and accordingly he must have had in view whether the two variates ℓ and ℓ' are dependent or correlated since the function (2·36) is in reality a measure of dependence when compared to

$$\frac{1}{2x\sigma_\ell\sigma_{\ell'}}e^{-\frac{1}{2}\left(\frac{\ell^2}{\sigma_\ell^2}+\frac{\ell'^2}{\sigma_{\ell'}^2}\right)} \qquad (2\cdot 37)$$

which is the probability of the simultaneous occurrence of ℓ and ℓ' when they are independent. Moreover, it can not be denied that Laplace knew that the difference between (2·36) and (2·37) is a measure of dependence or correlation between the two variates ℓ and ℓ' in question. But this difference is evidently due to the existence of the coefficient of the product term in the exponent which is, in Laplace's own natation, $\sum mn$, or more complete

$$\frac{1}{\frac{2a^2k''}{k}}\frac{\sum m_j n_j}{E}$$

where $$E = \sum m_j^2 \sum n_j^2 - \left(\sum m_j n_j\right)^2.$$

Therefore, he must have recognized that the coefficient of the product term in the exponent is a measure of dependence of the two variates ℓ and ℓ'. But it was given an altogether new importance by Galton's use as a means for demonstrating the existence of inheritance and measuring its intensity.

One may ask① whether the variables ℓ and ℓ' in Laplace's treatment can be considered variables in the modern conception of correlation. The answer is of course positive. We often deal with index numbers in economics. An index number of prices② is usually a weighted mean, of individual prices, and an

---

① Pearson has pointed out in his "Historical note on Correlation" that the variables in the treatises of Gauss and Bravais are not themselves susceptible of direct measurements and therefore their treatments are almost the inverse of our modern conception of correlation. Blom., Vol.13:35. Helen M. Walker says: "In correlation the variables upon which we make direct observations are those whose relationship we wish to study and we assume (in normal correlation at least) that each of them is a function of a number (perhaps a very large number), of independent variables not themselves susceptible of direct measurement." "The Relations of Plana and Bravais", Isis., Vol.10, p.477.

② W. C. Mitchell, U. S. B. L. S. Bulletin 284.

index number of production① is commonly a weighted mean of relatives of physical quantities of individual commodities. Evidently, Laplace's ℓ and ℓ' correspond to the weighted means, m_i, n_i to the weights x_i, y_i, to the observed quantities or the relatives of the observed quantities. Moreover, we often deal with variables which are not directly observable. The index numbers of wholesale prices and of physical productions are certainly not themselves susceptible of direct measurement; they are merely mathematical abstractions from the observed quantities.

Laplace's analysis is especially significant in view of the fact that his method has been extended by the Scandinavian scholars, especially Gram (1897), Thiele (1889), Charlier, and Wicksell, to the derivation of the generalized frequency function for the representation of frequency distributions of a variable of two or more variables with linear regression. But this method has often been criticized as not being exact [See the approximation process (2·31), (2·32)]. This criticism becomes less weighty when it is noted that some formulas so obtained are identical with those obtained through exact procedure.

In practical statistics, we are concerned, not so much with the fact that the mathematical approximation process in the derivation of a formula in use is capable of being shown to be accurate to a degree sufficiently high for practical purpose, as with the question whether or not the hypotheses underlying the derivation are with a high degree of probability realized in actual statistical problems. Laplace's assumption that an error consists of a large number of independent and equally likely elementary errors is a plausible and useful one, although it does not necessarily hold theoretically. Furthermore, Wicksell② has made an attempt to deduce the form of a correlation function of variates when their component errors are correlated. The logarithmic correlation is a fruitful result.

2.14 Gauss

The next important work is Gauss' fundamental memoir on least squares.③

---

① E. E. Day, Rev. Eco. Stat. Sept. 1920, Jan., 1921, Jul., 1922.
② Wicksell. S. D., "On the Genetic Theory of Correlation", Ark. for Math, etc., Bd. 12, No.20.
③ Gauss, Theonia Combinations Observationum Errorihus Minimis obnoxiae of 1823 and the Supplementum of 1826.

In this memoir Gauss, starting with the normal curve as the law of distribution of errors, reached the method of least squares. The result of his analysis may be regarded, on the other hand, as giving the normal correlation function of n variates. The method[①] of deduction may be summarized as follows:

"We observe or measure directly a certain number of quantities a, b, c, d, $\cdots$ Each of these quantities is supposed by Gauss to be independent and to follow the normal law. The combined probability of the system is accordingly

$$P \propto e^{-\frac{1}{2}\left(\frac{a-\bar{a}}{\sigma_a}\right)^2 + \left(\frac{b-\bar{b}}{\sigma_b}\right)^2 + \left(\frac{c-\bar{c}}{\sigma_c}\right)^2 + \cdots} \quad (2 \cdot 38)$$

or the product of the independent probabilities, where σ_a, σ_b, σ_c, $\cdots$ are the variability in errors of a, b, c, $\cdots$ and $\bar{a}$, $\bar{b}$, $\bar{c}$, $\cdots$ the means. This probability will be a maximum when

$$u^2_{a,\,b,\,c,\,\cdots} = s\left(\frac{a-\bar{a}}{\sigma_a}\right)^2 \quad (2 \cdot 39)$$

is a minimum. This is really the principle of weighted least squares. Its validity depends upon the normal law of distribution of error. Without this law holding it may be a utile method, but we have no means of proving it the 'best'."

The investigator in Gauss' case is, however, not interested in the quantities observed, but in certain <u>indirectly</u> ascertained quantities x_1, x_2, x_3, $\cdots$, x_n, which are functions of them.

Thus,

$$x_1 = f_1(a, b, c, \cdots)$$
$$x_2 = f_2(a, b, c, \cdots)$$
$$x_3 = f_3(a, b, c, \cdots)$$
$$\cdots\cdots\cdots\cdots\cdots \quad (2 \cdot 40)$$

where f_1, f_2, $\cdots$ are <u>known functions</u>. Now Gauss cannot as a rule express from these general equations a, b, c, $\cdots$ in terms of x_1, x_2, x_3, $\cdots$, x_n.

He assumes that all of them differ slightly from their mean or "true" values and accordingly expands by Taylor's theorem

---

① Pearson, K., "History of Cor.", loc. cit.

$$x_1 - \bar{x}_1 = \alpha_1(a - \bar{a}) + \beta_1(b - \bar{b}) + \gamma_1(c - \bar{c}) + \cdots$$
$$x_2 - \bar{x}_2 = \alpha_2(a - \bar{a}) + \beta_2(b - \bar{b}) + \gamma_2(c - \bar{c}) + \cdots$$
$$\cdots\cdots\cdots\cdots \quad (2\cdot 41)$$

where the α, β, γ, $\cdots$ are $\dfrac{df}{da}$, $\dfrac{df}{db}$, $\cdots$ and can be ascertained a priori. Clearly Gauss supposes that <u>a linear relationship is adequate</u>, in other words he replaces <u>statistical differentials by mathematical differentials</u>, a step he does not really justify.

From these linear equations we can find the $a - \bar{a}$, $b - \bar{b}$, $c - \bar{c}$, $\cdots$ in terms of the indirectly observed variables $x_1 - \bar{x}_1$, $x_2 - \bar{x}_2$, $x_3 - \bar{x}_3$, $\cdots$ by solution in determinantal form, say

$$a - \bar{a} = A_1(x_1 - \bar{x}_1) + B_1(x - \bar{x}_2) + C_1(x_3 - \bar{x}_3) + \cdots$$
$$b - \bar{b} = A_2(x_1 - \bar{x}_1) + B_2(x_2 - \bar{x}_2) + C_2(x_3 - \bar{x}_3) + \cdots$$
$$\cdots\cdots\cdots\cdots$$

substituting in u^2 we find

$$u^2_{x_1, x_2, x_3 \cdots} = s\left(\frac{A_1^2}{\sigma_a^2}\right)(x_1 - \bar{x}_1)^2 + s\left(\frac{B_1^2}{\sigma_a^2}\right)(x_2 - \bar{x}_2)^2$$
$$+ 2s\left(\frac{A_1 B_1}{\sigma_a^2}\right)(x_1 - \bar{x}_1)(x - \bar{x}_2) + \cdots \quad (2\cdot 42)$$

Hence the probability of x_1, x_2, $\cdots$ occurring is

$$P \propto {}^{-\frac{1}{2}u^2 x_1, x_2, x_3, \cdots}$$

This is a normal surface which contains the product terms. As we now interpret it we sat that the x's are correlated variates. And in this sense Gauss in 1823 reached the normal surface of n correlated variates. But he does not seek to express all his relations in terms of the S. D.' σ_{x_1}, σ_{x_2}, $\cdots$ and the correlations r_{12}, r_{23}, $\cdots$ or these variates. These x-variates are not for Gauss, nor for those who immediately followed him, the directly observed quantities. What he is seeking is the expression for σ_x, or the probable error of an indirectly observed variate in terms of

$$S\left(\frac{A_1}{\sigma_a^2}\right), \ S\left(\frac{B_1^2}{\sigma_a^2}\right), \ S\left(\frac{A_1 B_1}{\sigma_a^2}\right), \ \cdots$$

In this case A, B, C, are ratios of minors and determinants of the $\alpha, \beta, \gamma, \cdots$ which are Gauss' known quantities. His object therefore, is to express σ_x not from direct observations but in terms of through the sums of determinantal terms.

Commenting on Gauss' work with regard to correlation analysis, Pearson says in his historical note on correlation:

"That the Gaussian treatment leads (1) to non-correlated surface for the directly observed variates, (2) to a correlation surface for the indirectly observed variates. This occurrence of product terms arises from the geometrical relations between the two classes of variates, and not from an organic relation between indirectly observed variates appearing on our direct measurement of them."

"It will be seen that Gauss' treatment is almost the inverse of our modern conceptions of correlation. For him the observed variables are independent, for us the observed variables are associated or correlated. For him the non-observed variables are correlated owing to their known geometrical relations with observed variables; for us the non-observable variables may be supposed uncorrelated causes, and to be connected by unknown functional relations with correlated variables. In short, there is no trace in Gauss' work of observed physical variables being—apart from equations of conditions—associated organically which is the fundamental conception of correlation."

2.15 Plana

Plana is erroneously designated by Helen M. Walker[①] as the discoverer of the equation for the probability of the simultaneous occurrence of two variates. If we examine Plana's[②] paper "Memoire sur divers problémé de probabilité", we will see that Plana simply reproduces a special case of Laplace's investigation (cf. footnote in p.41 of this book), and adds nothing whatever new.

[①] "Evidently Plana did not cherish highly his discovery of a formula which becomes extremely interesting in the light of modern correlation theory", p.472, and similar statements in p.465, "The relation of Plana and Bravais", Isis, Vol.10, 1928.

[②] Loc. cit.

Plana supposes that an error ε from a contributory cause of error is the same as may be obtained by throwing a $2n$ faced dice whose faces carry the numbers:

$$-n, -(n-1), \cdots, -2, -1, 1, 2, \cdots, (n-1), n.$$

If $\varepsilon_1, \varepsilon_2, \varepsilon_p$ be the exposed face-values in a throw of p uniform similar $2n$ faced dice, and $q_1, q_2, \cdots, q_p$ one system of purely numerical factors, and $q'_1, q'_2, \cdots, q'_p$ a second like system, then Plana introduces two dependent variates Q and Q' as linear functions of these ε's so that

$$Q = q_1\varepsilon_1 + q_2\varepsilon_2 + \cdots + q_p\varepsilon_p, \qquad (2 \cdot 43)$$
$$Q' = q_1'\varepsilon_1 + q_2'\varepsilon_2 + \cdots + q'_p\varepsilon_p,$$

and attempts to find the probability that the foregoing two equations shall be satisfied simultaneously. Thus, Plana assumes, in precisely the same manner as Laplace did in deducing the normal curve and the bivariate normal surface, p similar but independent contributory causes each of which may give $2n$ equally likely half positive and half negative deviations so that the probability for the occurrence of each ε is $\frac{1}{2n}$, $\left[\text{i.e.}, \varphi\left(\frac{x}{n}\right)\right.$ in Laplace's problem is replaced by the constant probability $\left.\frac{1}{2n}\right]$ and that the means of the ε's are zero and the variances are all equal to $\frac{1}{6}(n+1)(2n+1)$.

On these hypotheses he now deduces, in the manner in which Laplace deduced the normal curve and surface, the bivariate normal surface

$$Z = \frac{N}{4xa\sqrt{E}} e^{-\frac{1}{4aE}(CQ^2 - 2BQQ' + AQ'^2)} \qquad (2 \cdot 44)$$

where

$$A = \frac{\sigma_Q^2}{\sigma_\varepsilon^2}, \quad C = \frac{\sigma_{Q'}^2}{\sigma_\varepsilon^2},$$

$$B = \frac{\sigma_{Q'}\sigma_Q\sigma_{QQ'}}{\sigma_\varepsilon^2}, \quad E = AC - B^2,$$

$$a = \frac{\sigma_\varepsilon^2}{2} = \frac{1}{12}(n+1)(2n+1).$$

Further, Walker is in error when she supposes Plana's Q's corresponding to Laplace's u's, because Q's here used correspond to Laplace's ℓ's. Consequently, the two equations given in her book, *The History of Statistical Methods*, p.94, are not comparable.①

2.16 Bravais

The next important work is Bravais' memoir entitled "Sur les Probabilités des erreurs de situation dún point".② In this memoir, Bravais derived the normal correlation surfaces for 2 and 3 variates and discussed the properties of the surfaces whereby he found the line or plane of maximum probability now known as the regression line or plane. His method of approach is geometrical as the title of his memoir indicates.

Let x_1, x_2, x_3 be the errors of the three quantities x_1, x_2, x_3, and each is a linear function of independent errors $u_1, u_2, \cdots, u_\ell$:

$$x_1 = a_{11}u_1 + a_{12}u_2 + \cdots + a_{1\ell} = \sum_{i=1}^{\ell} a_{1i}u_i$$

$$x_2 = \sum_{i=1}^{\ell} a_{2i}u_i$$

$$x_3 = \sum_{i=1}^{\ell} a_{3i}u_i.$$

Bravais said that Laplace had shown that a variation of x_1 between $x_1 + \mathrm{d}x_1$ will be of the form:

$$\frac{\mathrm{d}}{\mathrm{d}x_1} w(x_1) = \frac{1}{\sigma_1 \sqrt{2x}} e^{-\frac{x_1^2}{2\sigma_1^2}}$$

where σ_1^2 is given by

---

① Pearson, commenting on Walker's work, says: "Miss Walker has, I venture to think, at the same time under-estimated and over-estimated Plana's contributions to the subject. The under-estimation arises from her misreading of what Plana is doing; a misreading to some extent justified by his vogue language and awkward choice of symbols. Her over-estimation arises from slips in her own algebra, when she comes to interpret in modern symbols Plana's results." Biom., Vol.20, p.295.

② Memoires des Divers Savants a l'Academie Royale des science de l'Institute de France, 2nd series, Vol.9, pp.255−332, 1846.

$$\sigma_1^2 = a_{11}^2 \sigma_{u_1}^2 + a_{12}^2 \sigma_{u_2}^2 + \cdots + a_{1\ell}^2 \sigma_{u_\ell}^2. \qquad (2 \cdot 45)$$

But he did not say that Laplace had obtained the same probability function for two variables he developed the expression for the surface of two dimensions:

$$\frac{dw(x_1, x_2)}{dx_1 dx_2} = \frac{1}{x \left\{ \sum_{i \neq j}^{\ell} (a_{1i}a_{2j} - a_{2i}a_{1j})^2 \sigma_{u_i}^2 \sigma_{u_j}^2 \right\}^{\frac{1}{2}}} \cdot x$$

$$e^{-\frac{1}{2} \frac{x_1^2 \sum_i a_{2i}^2 \sigma_{u_i}^2 - 2x_1 x_2 \sum_i a_{1i}a_{2i}\sigma_{u_i}^2 + x_2^2 \sum_i a_{1i}^2 \sigma_{u_i}^2}{\sum_{i \neq j}(a_{1i}a_{2j}-a_{2i}a_{1j})^2 \sigma_{u_i}^2 \sigma_{u_j}^2}}$$

$$i, j = 1, 2, 3, \cdots, \ell \qquad (2 \cdot 46)$$

$\sum$ = summation over all ℓ values of i and j.

Although he did not mention Gauss' work, his method of procedure was the same as Gauss' which has been outlined above.

Now, if you take

$$\sigma_1^2 = \frac{1}{N}\sum_t^N x_{1t}^2 = \frac{1}{N}\sum_t \left(\sum_i a_{1i}u_{it}\right)^2 = \frac{1}{N}\left(\sum_t \sum_i a_{1i}^2 u_{it}^2\right)$$

$$= \sum_i a_{1i}^2 \frac{1}{N}\left(\sum_t u_{it}^2\right) = \sum_i a_{1i}^2 \sigma_{u_i}^2$$

$$\sigma_2^2 = \frac{1}{N}\sum_t x_{2t}^2 = \sum_i a_{2i}^2 \sigma_{u_i}^2$$

$$r_{12}\sigma_1\sigma_2 = \frac{1}{N}\sum_t(x_{1t}x_{2t}) = \frac{1}{N}\sum_t\left(\sum_i a_{1i}u_{it}\right)\left(\sum_i a_{2i}u_{it}\right)$$

$$= \frac{1}{N}\sum_t \sum_i a_{1i}a_{2i}u_{it}^2 = \sum_i a_{1i}a_{2i}\sigma_{u_i}^2$$

whence

$$\sigma_1^2\sigma_2^2(1 - r_{12}^2) = \left(\sum_i a_{1i}^2 \sigma_{u_i}^2\right)\left(\sum_i a_{2i}^2 \sigma_{u_i}^2\right) - \left(\sum_i a_{1i}a_{2i}\sigma_{u_i}^2\right)^2$$

$$= \sum_{i \neq j} a_{1i}^2 a_{2j}^2 \sigma_{u_i}^2 \sigma_{u_j}^2 - 2 \sum_{i \neq j} a_{1i}a_{2i}a_{1j}a_{2j} \sigma_{u_i}^2 \sigma_{u_j}^2$$

$$= \sum_{i \neq j}(a_{1i}a_{2j} - a_{2i}a_{1j})^2 \sigma_{u_i}^2 \sigma_{u_j}^2$$

$$i, j = 1, 2, 3, \cdots, \ell.$$

Hence, Bravais' expression in our familiar notation becomes

$$\frac{dw(x_1, x_2)}{dx_1 dx_2} = \frac{1}{2x\sigma_1\sigma_2(1-r_{12})} e^{-\frac{1}{2(1-r^2)}\left\{\frac{x_1^2}{\sigma_1^2} - 2r_{12}\frac{x_1 x_2}{\sigma_1 \sigma_2} + \frac{x_2^2}{\sigma_2^2}\right\}}. \qquad (2 \cdot 47)$$

Now he proceeds to discuss the properties of the surface. Thus, he found the loci of equal probabilities, that is, curves drawn on the surface at a constant height. These curves are a family of concentric ellipses, obtained by equating the exponent to a constant: $\sigma_2^2 x_1^2 - 2r\sigma_1\sigma_2 x_1 x_2 + \sigma_1^2 x_2^2 = k^2$.

This family of ellipses has its center at the origin and its principal axes making an angle θ with the coordinate axes, θ being given by

$$\tan 2\theta = \frac{2\sigma_1\sigma_2 r_{12}}{\sigma_1^2 - \sigma_2^2}. \qquad (2\cdot 48)$$

By rotating the coordinate system through an angle θ so defined, the correlation surface is thrown into an uncorrelated surface:

$$\varphi(x_1)\varphi(x_2) = \frac{1}{2x\sigma_1\sigma_2} e^{-\frac{1}{2}\left(\frac{x_1^2}{\sigma_1} + \frac{x_2^2}{\sigma_2}\right)}.$$

Besides, he determines the probability of point lying in areas bound by similar ellipses and in angular sectors.

Now Bravais proceeds to find the value of y at which the probability is maximum for a given x. To do so, he maximizes the expression $(2 \cdot 47)$ and obtains

$$x_2 = \frac{\sigma_1}{\sigma_2} x_1$$

which, now called the regression of x_2 on x_1, shows the type of relationship between x_1 and x_2.

Bravais also gives a similar analysis for three variates and obtains the trivariate normal surface:

$$w(x_1, x_2, x_3) = \frac{G}{\sqrt{x^3}} e^{-(ax_1^2 + bx_2^2 + cx_3^2 + 2ex_1 x_2 + 2fx_1 x_3 + 2gx_2 x_3)}. \qquad (2\cdot 49)$$

The loci of equal probability in this case is a family of concentric ellipsoids

$$ax_1^2 + bx_2^2 + cx_3^2 + 2ex_1 x_2 + 2fx_1 x_3 + 2gx_2 x_3 = k^2$$

and the locus of x_3 with maximum probability for given values x_1 and x_2 is

$$x_3 = \frac{1}{e}(fx_1 + gx_2) \qquad (2\cdot 50)$$

which we now call the multiple linear regression equation of x_3 on x_1 and x_2.

With regard to Bravais' regression equation, Pearson[1] remarks that "This is not a result of observing x_1 and x_2 and determining their association, but of the fact that x_1 and x_2 are functions of certain independent and directly observed quantities. When he (Bravais) thinks of u_i's at all, it is not in terms of observations on x_1 and x_2 but of the differential coefficients a_{ij} [corresponding to α's, β's $\cdots$ in Gauss' procedure, see equation (2·41)] of the geometrical relations between positions in space and the angles by which the position is found". Pearson also says in comment on both Gauss and Bravais: "In the case of both these distinguished men the quantities they were observing were absolutely independent, they neither of them had the least idea of correlation between observed quantities. The product terms in their expressions—never analyzed in the sense of correlation—arise solely not from organic relationship, but from the geometrical relationships which exist between their observed quantities and the indirectly observed quantities they deduce from them $\cdots$ They contributed nothing or real importance to the problem of[2] correlation..." But we must not forget that in correlation analysis we are not always to deal with the directly observed values, as has already been remarked in connection with Laplace's work. Moreover, Bravais' regression equations are the results of his investigation into the properties of the correlation surfaces, he must have comprehended the significance of these equations, at least as a property of the correlation surface. Indeed, these regression equations represent the manner of interdependence between the variates. We cannot see how Pearson can be sure that Bravais' regression equations are not the results of determining the association of the indirectly observed x quantities. On the contrary, Bravais was the first to have a notion of the causes[3] of correlation; namely, the coexistence

---

[1][2] Pearson, "Historical Note or Correlation", Loc. Cit., p.31.

[3] At the outset of determining the correlation surface and the regression equation, Bravais says: "La coexistence des memes variables u_1, u_2, $\cdots$ dans les equations simultanees en x_1 et x_2, amene une correlation telle que les modules

$$h\left(=\frac{1}{2\sigma_1^2}\right), h_2\left(=\frac{1}{2\sigma_2^2}\right)$$

cessent de representer la possibilite des voleurs simultanees de (x, x) saus le vrai point de vue de la question." Loc. Cit., p.263.

of some elementary errors in the variables brings a correlation among the variables. This explanation of the source or origin of correlation is clearly based on the Laplacian theory of elementary errors, namely, an error (deviation) is the resultant of a large number of elementary errors. So far as I am aware, no writer on correlation has pointed it out and corrected Pearson's erroneous statement.

It may be a convenient opportunity to point out the meaning of a regression equation with regard to law or relationship. An equation is a mathematical expression of relationship. To determine the relationship between variates in statistics is to determine such an equation. So soon as the equation is rightly determined, the type of relationship among the variates is known. If all the values which the variates may take, satisfy the equation so determined, we say that there is a perfect relationship existing between the variates in question; or we say that there is an imperfect relationship between the variates, the degree of perfectibility or intensity of such a relationship being given by the form of the correlation surface. A perfect relationship, in logic, is one of the following forms:

> (i) If an event A happens, then a certain second event B must happen;
> (ii) If an event A happens when certain definite conditions C and D exist, then a certain second event B must happen.

And an imperfect relation may be translated into the following form:

> (iii) If the event A happens and certain conditions exist, then a certain second event B has a definite probability (in correlation analysis, this probability is given by the correlation surface) of happening.

When the probability approaches certainty, the intensity of relationship approaches perfection. Regression equations in statistics are generally in the domain of the third class.

It may be observed that Bravais' functional variables x_i's correspond to Laplace's ℓ's and the former's independent variables correspond to the latter's observed errors. But there is a difference in that Laplace does not assume the observed variables independent while Bravais does. In practical statistics, we can hardly have such a case, even in Bravais' own case, the measurements of different stellar magnitudes are probably not uncorrelated. Therefore, the application of Bravais' results are necessarily limited.① However, his contribution cannot be denied. He was the first to use the term correlation and to discuss the properties of correlation surfaces. Indeed, if Galton had been aware of Bravais' work, he would have had no difficulty in formulating his results in 1886.

2.17 Schols

Schols' Theory of Errors② dealt generally with the principal axes of inertia, and showed that for the normal surface they were axes of independent probability. Generalizing this it would signify that if $Z = F(x, y)$ be the expression for the frequency surface, then by a rotation of axes it could be put into the form:

$$Z = f_1(x') \cdot f_2(y').$$

Sections parallel to the principal axes are thus not only similar but also similarly situated. But Schols did not justify this generalization.

2.18 Galton

In Memories of My Life, Galton writes: "In 1886 I contributed two papers of which one is 'Family Likeness in Stature' to the Roy. Soc. on family likeness, having by that time got my method for measuring heredity into satisfactory shape. I had given much time and thought to tables of correlations, to display the frequency of cases in which the various deviations say in stature, of an adult person, measured along the top, were associated with the various deviations of stature in his mid-parent, measured along the side. But I could not see my way to express the results of the complete table in a single formula. At length, one

---

① Bravais did mention the limitation in application of the results in the resume, p.331.

② Schols, C. H. M., "Theorie des erreurs daus le plan et dans l'espace", Ann de l'ecole Polytechn de Delft, 1886, pp.123 − 175. Published in Dutch in the Verhandelingen van de Koninklijke Akademie van Wetenschappen, Deel 15, Amsterdam, 1875.

morning, while waiting at a roadside station near Ramstage for a train, and pointing over a small diagram in my notebook, it struck me that the lines of equal frequency ran in concentric ellipses…"

The concentric ellipses of equal frequency are properties of a correlation surface as had been found by Bravais. But Galton did not know this and had to submit his problem, under the form of a problem of mechanics, to G. Hamilton Dickson for the solution. Dickson worked it out on the basis of the law of error, and the solution being the well-known bivariate normal surface, was published in the appendix of Galton's "Family Likeness in Stature".[1] Thus, Galton says: "It had appeared from observation, and it was fully confirmed by this theory, that such a thing existed as an 'Index of correlation'."[2]

It is thus seen that Galton's contribution to the correlation analysis was a result of his investigation in the problems of inheritance. On the other hand, Laplace's work on correlation was an extension of his investigation in the theory of probability on a product of his research on error theory and Gauss and Bravais continued Laplace's investigation in the theory of error because their work in astronomy employs this theory as the criterion for formulating results and thus become early contributors to correlation theory. By the very nature of this work, Galton's attention was focused on the direct observations while the astronomers were concerned with the indirect observations. Moreover, Galton started a new method of approach, namely, the regression method. Thus, he used the regression $x_2 = b_{21} x_1$ and did not trouble to determine the correlation surface for expressing the correlation. We shall give the detail of the regression method in the next chapter.

2.19 Edgeworth

Edgeworth, in his paper "Correlated Average"[3], reverts to the correlation

---

[1] Galton, Francis, "Family Likeness in Stature with an appendix by J.D. Hamilton Dickson", Proc. Roy. Soc. Vol. 40, pp. 42 – 73, 1886. This solution was also reproduced in Galton's *Natural Inheritance*, London, 1889.

[2] Galton, F., Memories of My Life. pp.303 – 304, Methuen and Co., 3rd Ed., London, 1909.

[3] Edgeworth, F. Y., "Correlated Average", Phil. Mag., Vol.34, Pages 199 – 201, 429 – 438, 518 – 526, 1892.

surface method although Galton and his immediate follower Weldon had developed and used the regression method. His paper is not easy to read; he did not give the requisite attention to the wording or printing to make it clear to the readers.

Pearson says "It was doubtful, analysis not errors of printing which led to his obscure conclusion"①. Nevertheless this statement is unfair to the author. Although Edgeworth did not explain the meaning of his symbols, $\Delta p_{13} = + \Delta^3_{(p_{24}p_{31}p_{42})}$ etc., nor show the derivations of these relations, nor give the final form for the n-correlation surface as we would expect, his analysis from the beginning until the appearance of these obscure relations (which appear in the last paragraph of his theoretical analysis, see p.201) is correct and the way for generalization is already clear. Moreover, the final form which we would anticipate from his analysis in the text was given in a subsequent paper "Compound Law of Error".② Now we shall show his method of procedure.

Giving justification③ later, Edgeworth assumes

$$x = Je^{-R} dx_1 \, dx_2 \, dx_3 \cdots \qquad (2 \cdot 51)$$

to be the probability that any particular values of x_1, x_2, $\cdots$ should occur. Where $R = p_1(x_1 - \bar{x}_1)^2 + p_2(x_2 - \bar{x}_2) + \cdots 2q_{12}(x_1 - \bar{x}_1)(x_2 - \bar{x}_2) + 2q_{13}(x_1 - \bar{x}_1)(x_3 - \bar{x}_3) + \cdots$, $p_1, p_2, \ldots, q_{12}, q_{13}, \ldots$ are constants to be obtained from observations; J is a constant deduced from the condition that the integral between extreme limits should be unity. Then he states that Galton, taking means as the origin and the respective quartile (it should be the modulus $= 2\sigma$ as Pearson pointed out in his historical note on correlation) as the unit of measurement, had reduced in the case of two variables

$$R_2 = \frac{x_1^2}{1 - \rho^2} - \frac{2\rho x_1 x_2}{1 - \rho^2} + \frac{x_2^2}{1 - \rho^2} \qquad (2 \cdot 52)$$

---

① History, Ibid.

② Edgeworth, Phil. Mag. Vol.51, 5th series, p.211, 1896. Pearson gave e similar formula in his Memoir "Reg., Heredity, Panmixia" in the same year. These, I think, are independent contributions.

③ The justification, mainly in the Manner of Laplace's Line of thinking, was given in a subsequent memoir "The Law of Error and the Correlated Average". Phil. Mag., 5th series, Vol.34, pp.429–438, pp.518–526, 1892. After giving the proof, he stated clearly that this was to fulfill his promise as he says: "Assuming the appropriateness of this form, I have in a former article shown how to calculate the coefficient from the measurements of correlated organs. I now justify that assumption." (p.523) But Pearson seems not to have seen this article as he said in his history that "he (Edgeworth) does not justify this assumption but hopes to do so in a subsequent paper". Biom., Vol.13, p.42.

to an expression with a single parameter ρ. He calls ρ the "coefficient of correlation" instead of Galton's term "Ende of correlation". Edgeworth says: "the parameter (ρ) is found by observing the value of x_1, say δ_1, which most frequently corresponds to assigned value of x_2, say x_2' (or vice versa). From the equation

$$\frac{\partial R}{\partial x_1} = 0 \qquad (2 \cdot 53)$$

we have $\qquad \delta_1 = \rho x_2' \qquad \rho = \dfrac{\delta}{x_2'}.$ " ①

Thus, Edgeworth determines the regression equation in the same way as Bravais did.

Now Edgeworth shows how the exponent R or the constants $p_1, p_2, \cdots, q_{12}, q_{13}, \cdots$ in R may be found in the case of three variables. It may be remarked here that he did not give the value of the constant J in the correlation surface $(2 \cdot 51)$ throughout his analysis, except he indicated in the beginning of this paper how it may be deduced.

Let the coefficients $\rho_{12}, \rho_{13}, \rho_{14}$ of correlation for each pair $(x_1 x_2)$, $(x_1 x_3)$ and $(x_2 x_3)$ be determined. Then, by equation $(2 \cdot 52)$, the probability for simultaneous occurrence of any particular values (x_1, x_2) is

$$W_{12} = J_2 e^{-S} dx_1 x_2 \qquad (2 \cdot 54)$$

where $\qquad S = \dfrac{x_1^2}{1-\rho_{12}^2} - \dfrac{2 x_1 x_2 \rho_{12}}{1-\rho_{12}^2} + \dfrac{x_2^2}{1-\rho_{12}^2}.$

Now the expression above must be derived from the sought expression

$$J e^{-R} dx_1 dx_2 dx_3$$

where $R = p_1 x_1^2 + p_2 x_2^2 + p_3 x_3^2 + 2 q_{12} x_1 x_2 + 2 q_{13} x_1 x_3 + 2 q_{23} x_2 x_3$, by integration with respect to x_3 between extreme limits $+\infty$ and $-\infty$. But we may write R in the form:

---

① To find this regression equation from the correlation surface is one of his objects in this memoir. He says: "It (the expression x) enables us to answer the questions: what is the most probable value of one deviation x_r corresponding to assigned values $x_1', x_2', \cdots$ of the other variables? And what is the dispersion of the values of x_r about its mean (the other variables being assigned)? "

$$R = p_3\left(x_3 + \frac{q_{13}}{p_3}x_1 + \frac{q_{23}}{p_3}x_2\right)^2 + \frac{p_1p_3q_{13}^2}{p_3}x_1^2 + 2\frac{q_{12}p_3 - q_{13}q_{23}}{p_3}x_1x_2$$
$$+ \frac{q_{13}p_3 - p_{23}^2}{p_3}x_3^2.$$

Hence

$$W_{12} = \int_{-\infty}^{+\infty} Je^{-R}dx_3 = J_2 e - \left(\frac{p_1p_3q_{13}^2}{p_3}x_1^2 + 2\frac{q_{12}p_3 - q_{13}q_{23}}{p_3}x_1x_2 + \frac{p_2p_3 - q_{23}^2}{p_3}x_3^2\right),$$
(2·55)

where $\quad J_2 = J\int_{-\infty}^{+\infty} e^{-p_3\left(x_3 + \frac{q_{13}}{p_3}x_1 + \frac{q_{23}}{p_3}x_2\right)^2} dx_3 = \text{Const.} \times J.$

Hence, comparing (2·54) and (2·55), we have

$$\begin{cases} \dfrac{p_1p_3 - q_{13}^2}{p_3} = \dfrac{1}{1 - \rho_{12}^2} \\ \dfrac{q_{13}q_{23} - q_{12}p_{33}}{p_3} = \dfrac{\rho_{12}}{1 - \rho_{12}^2} \\ \dfrac{p_2p_3 - q_{23}^2}{p_3} = \dfrac{1}{1 - \rho_{12}^2}. \end{cases} \quad (2·56)$$

Employing the exponent in (2·55) to determine the most probable x_1 corresponding to any assigned x_2, we have[1]

$$\rho_{12} = \frac{q_{13}q_{23} - q_{12}p_3}{p_1p_3 - q_{23}^2} = \frac{Q_{12}}{P_1}, \quad (2·57)$$

where P_1 and Q_{12} are the cofactors of p_1 and q_{12} in the determinant Δ:

$$\Delta = \begin{vmatrix} p_1 & q_{12} & q_{13} \\ q_{12} & p_2 & q_{23} \\ q_{13} & q_{23} & p_3 \end{vmatrix}, \quad (2·58)$$

---

[1] This equation may be directly obtained from (2·56): From the second equation of (2·56), $\rho_{12} \times \dfrac{p}{1-\rho_{12}^2} = q_{13}q_{23} - q_{12}p_3$, and from the first and third equation of (2·56), $p_1p_3 - q_{13}^2 = \dfrac{p_3}{1-\rho_{12}^2}$
$= p_2p_3 - q_{23}^2, \therefore \rho_{12}(p_1p_3 - q_{13}^2) = q_{13}q_{23} - q_{12}p_3.$

which is the discriminant of the exponent R. How if we integrate W_{12} in (2·55) with respect to x_2 between the extreme limits, we shall find for the probability of any x_1 the expression①:

$$L\,e^{-\frac{\Delta}{P_1}x_1^2}dx_1. \qquad (2\cdot 59)$$

But, by convention, the modulus of the probability curve under which the values of x_1 range, is unity. Therefore, $P_1 = \Delta$.

By parity of reasoning,

$$P_1 = P_2 = P_3 = \Delta$$

$$\rho_{13} = \frac{Q_{13}}{P_1} = \frac{Q_{13}}{P_3}$$

$$\rho_{24} = \frac{Q_{23}}{P_2} = \frac{Q_{23}}{P_3}, \qquad (2\cdot 60a)$$

therefore

$$Q_{12} = \Delta\rho_{12},\ Q_{13} = \Delta\rho_{13},\ Q_{23} = \Delta\rho_{23}.$$

Thus, we may write the adjoint Δ' (Edgeworth called it reciprocal) of the determinate Δ in the form:

$$\Delta' = \begin{vmatrix} P_1 & Q_{21} & Q_{13} \\ Q_{21} & P_2 & Q_{23} \\ Q_{31} & Q_{23} & P_3 \end{vmatrix} = \begin{vmatrix} \Delta & \Delta\rho_{12} & \Delta\rho_{13} \\ \Delta\rho_{12} & \Delta & \Delta\rho_{23} \\ \Delta\rho_{13} & \Delta\rho_{23} & \Delta \end{vmatrix}$$

$$= \Delta^3 \begin{vmatrix} 1 & \rho_{12} & \rho_{13} \\ \rho_{12} & 1 & \rho_{23} \\ \rho_{13} & \rho_{23} & 1 \end{vmatrix}. \qquad (2\cdot 60b)$$

---

① The exponent of (2·55) may be written:

$$S = -\frac{p_2 p_3 - q_{23}^2}{p_3}\left(x_2 + \frac{q_{12}p_3 - q_{13}q_{13}}{p_2 p_3 - q_{23}^2}x_1\right)^2 + \left[\frac{p_1 p_3 - q_{13}^2}{p_3} - \frac{q_{12}p_3 - q_{13}q_{23}}{p_3(p_2 p_3 - q_{23}^2)}\right]^2 x_1^2.$$

The coefficient of $x_1^2 = \dfrac{P_1 P_2 - Q_{12}^2}{P_3 P_1} = \dfrac{1}{P_3 P_1}\begin{vmatrix} P_1 & Q_{12} \\ Q_{12} & P_2 \end{vmatrix} = \dfrac{\Delta P_3}{P_3 P_1} = \dfrac{\Delta}{P_1}$, where P_i and Q_{ij} are cofactors of p_i and q_{ij} in Δ. Edgeworth's expression $L\,e^{-\frac{\Delta}{P_2}x_1^2}dx_1$ (p.195) should be of the form given in (2·59). But for this equation in the original paper P_2 was used in the place of P_1.

By a well-known theorem of determinant, ①

$$\Delta' = \Delta^2 \text{ (In general, } \Delta' = \Delta^{n-1} \text{ for the } n\text{-th order determinant)}.$$

$$\Delta^{-1} = \frac{1}{\Delta} = \begin{vmatrix} 1 & \rho_{12} & \rho_{13} \\ \rho_{12} & 1 & \rho_{23} \\ \rho_{13} & \rho_{23} & 1 \end{vmatrix} = (1-\rho_{12}^2)(1-\rho_{12}^2) - (\rho_{12}\rho_{13} - \rho_{23})^2.$$

$$(2\cdot 61)$$

How if $(\Delta)_{ij}$ be the cofactor of the ij-th element in Δ', then we have, by a theorem of determinant,

$$\Delta'_{ii} = \Delta p_i, \quad \Delta'_{ij} = \Delta q_{ij} \qquad (2\cdot 62)$$

(in general, $\Delta'_{ij} = q_{ij}\Delta^{n-2}$ for the n-th order determinant).

But, by direct calculation from $(2\cdot 60)$,

$$\Delta'_{11} = \Delta^2 \begin{vmatrix} 1 & \rho_{23} \\ \rho_{23} & 1 \end{vmatrix} = \Delta^2 (\Delta^{-1})_{11}, \quad \Delta'_{12} = \Delta^2 (\Delta^{-1})_{12}, \text{ etc.} \quad (2\cdot 63)$$

Hence, from $(2\cdot 62)$ and $(2\cdot 63)$,

$$p_1 = \frac{\Delta^2 (\Delta^{-1})_{ii}}{\Delta} = \frac{(\Delta^{-1})}{\Delta^{-1}}, \quad q_{ij} = \frac{(\Delta^{-1})_{ij}}{\Delta^{-1}}, \qquad (2\cdot 64)②$$

where Δ^{-1} being deduced from the adjoint, Δ', of the discriminant determinant Δ of the exponent R, is as is commonly called, correlation determinant given in $(2\cdot 61)$.

Hence Edgeworth's analysis is to determine the coefficients $p_i's$, $q_i's$, of the exponent R, being a quadratic form, in terms of the correlation coefficients. He first expresses $p's$, $q's$ in terms of Δ and the minors of its adjoint Δ' and then shows that both Δ and Δ' can be expressed in terms of the correlation determinant Δ^{-1}. The course of analysis is exact and the way for generalization is clear, although unfortunately the last part of his paper is mysteriously obscure. Thus, in the case of 4 variables, to obtain "the adjoint determinant Δ' of the discriminant Δ

---

① See Bôcher, Mexime, Higher Algebra, p.33.
② These formulas are written in different forms from those given by Edgeworth, see p.195.

$$\Delta' = \begin{vmatrix} \Delta & \Delta\rho_{12} & \Delta\rho_{13} & \Delta\rho_{14} \\ \Delta\rho_{12} & \Delta & \Delta\rho_{23} & \Delta\rho_{24} \\ \Delta\rho_{12} & \Delta\rho_{23} & \Delta & \Delta\rho_{34} \\ \Delta\rho_{14} & \Delta\rho_{24} & \Delta\rho_{34} & \Delta \end{vmatrix}$$

we have merely to border with a new row and column the determinant used for the case if three variables" (see p.201). The general solutions for p's and q's were not given by Edgeworth, but we might expect that by his foregoing analysis,

$$p_i = \frac{(\Delta')_{ii}}{\Delta} \quad \text{and} \quad q_{ij} = \frac{(\Delta')_{ij}}{\Delta}.$$

Indeed, he did give in other connections① the exact solutions for the law of error relating to any number of variables $x_1, x_2, \cdots, x_n$,

$$Z = \frac{1}{(2x)^{\frac{\pi}{2}}\sqrt{\Delta}} e^{\frac{-(K_1 x_1^2 + L_{12} x_1 x_2 + 2L_{13} x_1 x_3 + K_2 x_2^2 + \cdots)}{2\Delta}} \qquad (2\cdot 65)$$

where Δ is the determinant.

$$\begin{vmatrix} K_1 & l_{12} & \cdots \\ l_{21} & k_2 & \cdots \\ \vdots & \vdots & \\ & & \cdots \end{vmatrix},$$

$\zeta_i = f_i(x_1, x_2, \cdots x_n)$ the law of distribution

$$K_1 = \sum_{i=1}^{n} \iint \cdots \int \zeta_i x_1^2 dx_1 dx_2 \cdots dx_n = \sigma_1^2$$

$$K_2 = \sum_{i=1}^{n} \iint \cdots \int \zeta_i x_2^2 dx_1 dx_2 \cdots dx_n = \sigma_2^2$$

$$\vdots$$

$$l_{12} = \sum_{i=1}^{n} \iint \cdots \int \zeta_i x_1 x_2 dx_1 dx_2 \cdots dx_n = l_{21} = r\sigma_1 \sigma_2$$

K_i and L_{ij} are cofactors of k_i and l_{ij} in Δ.

After giving this result, Edgeworth remarks: "If the units of the variables be taken so that $k_1, k_2, \cdots$ each $= \frac{1}{2}$, then $l_{12}, l_{13}, \cdots$ will be replaced by $\frac{1}{2}\rho_{12}$,

---

① "Compound law of error", Phil. Mag., p.211, 1896.

$\frac{1}{2}\rho_{13}$, ⋯ the coefficients of correlation which have been discussed in a former paper (namely the paper on "correlated average" we have just discussed)."

Edgeworth's proof of the function (2 · 65) following the method he used to derive the asymmetrical law of error, ① consists in solving a system of partial differential equations which must be satisfied by such a function. He assumed that x_1, x_2 ⋯ each follows the normal law of distribution. But he did not explicitly assume the existence of a linear relation between these variables.

Thus, Edgeworth has generalized the correlation surface of (linearly) correlated variables following the normal law of distribution in such a way that the coefficients in the exponent of the frequency function can be systematically expressed in terms of cofactors or minors of the correlation determinant, convenient for computation in practical statistics. He has also shown how the simple coefficient of correlation may be determined from a given correlation surface. For instance, if we are required to determine the simple correlation coefficient r_{12} between x_1 and x_2, we first integrate $x = Je^{-R} dx_1 dx_2 \cdots dx_n$ with respect to all the $n - 2$ variables. x_3, x_4, ⋯x_n between the extreme limits and then differentiate the resultant exponent with respect to x_1 (or x_2). The coefficient of x_2 so obtained is the required coefficient of correlation provided the variables are measured with their standard deviations as the unit. This may also be viewed as a proof that any set of variables x_1, x_2, ⋯x_n if their law of distribution can be represented by an exponential with a quadratic form as its exponents are linearly related to each other, i.e., the regression is linear.

2.20 Pearson

Pearson, the eminent statistician whose works cover and contribute to every field, had also, in 1896, given an independent proof② for the n-variate normal surface on the hypotheses of elementary errors and expressed the parameters in the surface in terms of the moments of the distribution. On account of his proneness to emphasize the regression method, his contributions to that approach

---

① "The Asymmetrical Probability Curve", Phil. Mag., Vol.41, p.90, 1896.
② Pearson, K., "The Mathematical Contributions to the Theory of Evolution", III. Regression, Heredity, and Panmixia, Phil. Trans. Roy. Soc., Vol.187, pp.253−318, 1896.

will be discussed in Chapter III.

In 1923, Pearson[1] took

$$z = z_0 \left(1 + b_1 \frac{x^2}{\frac{1}{2}} + 2b_2 \frac{xy}{\sigma_1 \sigma_2} + b_3 \frac{y^2}{\sigma_2^2} \right)^{-n}$$

for describing the non-skew correlation between x and y. The constants are given by

$$z_0 = \frac{N}{x} \frac{(n-1)\sqrt{b_1 b_3 - b_2}}{\sigma_1 \sigma_2}, \quad N = \text{No. of observations},$$

$$b_1 = b_2 = \frac{1}{1-r^2} \frac{1}{2(n-2)}$$

$$b_2 = -\frac{r}{1-r^2} \frac{1}{2(n-2)}.$$

The correlation surface may thus be written in the following form:

$$Z = \frac{N}{2x\sigma_1\sigma_2\sqrt{1-r^2}} \frac{n-1}{n-2} \left[1 + \frac{1}{2(n-2)(1-r^2)} \left(\frac{x_1^2}{\sigma_1^2} - \frac{2rxy}{\sigma_1\sigma_2} + \frac{y^2}{\sigma_2^2} \right) \right]^{-n}.$$

$$(2 \cdot 66)$$

It is seen that both x-arrays of y's and y-arrays of x's are the Pearsonian Type III curves and that, when n is infinite, this becomes the ordinary normal surface for two variates.

When n is finite, n may be expressed in terms of marginal totals β_2 and β_2' for x and y variates respectively. The results as given by Pearson are:

$$\beta_2 = \beta_2' m \quad n = \frac{\alpha(\beta_2 - 2)}{\beta_2 - 3}.$$

Pearson has also found the marginal distributions for x and y:

$$\varphi_1(x) = \frac{\sqrt{2N}}{x\sigma_1} \frac{2\beta_2 - 3}{\sqrt{\beta_2(\beta_2 - 3)}} I_{2n-2} \left(1 + \frac{(\beta_2 - 3)x^2}{2\beta_2 \sigma_1^2} \right)^{-\frac{5\beta_2 - 9}{\beta_2 - 3}},$$

the y-marginal $\varphi_2(y)$ is obtained from $\varphi_1(x)$ by merely changing $\dfrac{x}{\sigma_1}$ into $\dfrac{y}{\sigma_2}$.

---

[1] Pearson, K., "On Non-skew Frequency Surfaces", Biom., Vol.15, p.231, 1923.

The first two characteristic curves are given as follows:

(i) the regression curves

$$\bar{x}_y = -\frac{b_2}{b_1}\frac{\sigma_1}{\sigma_2}y, \quad \bar{y}_x = -\frac{b_2}{b_3}\frac{\sigma_2}{\sigma_1}x, \quad (2\cdot 67a)$$

(ii) the scedastic curves are parabolas:

$$\frac{\sigma_{ay}^2}{\frac{2(n-2)}{2n-3}\sigma_2^2(1-r^2)} - \frac{x^2}{2(n-2)\sigma_1^2} = 1 \quad (2\cdot 67b)$$

σ_{ay}^2 being the array variance.

Just as the distribution of a single variable may not be Gaussian, the distribution of two or more variables cannot be assumed normal for all cases. In a normal surface, the contours of equal probability, as we have seen in the discussions given by Bravais for cases of two and three variables and in Galton's empirical contours of equal frequency drawn from a correlation table for long series of sweet peas, are families of mathematical curves or surfaces with symmetrical axes—in case of two dimensions they consist in a family of concentric ellipses with two symmetrical axes and in case of three dimensions they belong to a family of concentric ellipsoids with three symmetrical axes. But in a skew surface, the contours of equal probability do not possess, in general, more than one axis of symmetry. For instance, in the bivariate correlation surface, these contours of equal probability may be a family of ovals not ellipses, which do not possess more than one axis of symmetry. Many of the statistical problems present the second type of distribution. Therefore, it is necessary to have an appropriate system of surfaces which will give skew frequency.

2.21 Perozzo

Perozzo's Analysis[1] of the number of marriages contracted in Italy during the years 1878 – 1879 was, according to S.G. Pretorius[2], the first attempt to

---

[1] S. G. Pretorius, Skew Bivariate Frequency Surfaces, Biom. 22, p.131, 1931.
[2] Perozzo, Lurgi, "Nuove Applicazioni del calcolo delle Probabilità", Acta, Reale Accademia dei Lincei, pp.1–33, 1881–1882.

analyze graphically a skew bivariate distribution and to give a general formula for its representation. From the contours of equal probability exhibited in the correlation table, he points out that they are not concentric and are tending to symmetry with respect to one axis only. Accordingly, the normal surface no longer applies. As an approximation to the binomial, Perozzo gives the asymmetrical curves:

$$Z = z_0 e^{\pm a_1 x - a_2 x^2 \pm a_3 x^3 \cdots}$$

And
$$Z = a\left(x - \sqrt{\frac{n}{2a_2}}\right) e^{-a_2\left(x - \sqrt{\frac{n}{2a_2}}\right)^2}.$$

Similarly for the asymmetrical surface

$$Z = Z_0 Z_0' e^{-a_2 x^2 \pm a_3 x^3 - \cdots - a_2' y^2 \pm a_3' y^3 - \cdots}$$

and

$$Z = a \cdot a' \left(x - \sqrt{\frac{n}{2a_2}}\right)^n \left(y - \sqrt{\frac{n'}{2a_2'}}\right)^{n'} e^{-a_2\left(x - \sqrt{\frac{n}{2a_2}}\right)^2 - a_2'\left(y - \sqrt{\frac{n'}{2a_2'}}\right)^2}.$$

Perozzo gives no underlying theoretical basis for these formulae, nor does he fit them to his observations.

2.22 Pearson

Contributions to skew correlation surface analyses. Pearson has made several attempts to solve the problem of skew correlation since the publication of his memoir on *Skew Variation*[1] in 1895, where he called attention to the need of an analytical description of skew bivariate distributions by the remark that "if material obeys a law of skew distribution, the theory of correlation[2] as developed by Galton and Dickson requires very considerable modification". Pearson's first attempt started with the idea of independent probability. By analyzing skew correlation data, he was led to conclude that "if the skew frequency surface was $Z = f(x, y)$, it in most cases could not be thrown into the form $Z = f_1(x') \cdot f_2(y')$ by a rotation of axes"[3]—i.e., a generalized surface could not be obtained by taking the product of two of the Pearsonian skew

---

[1] Phil. Trans. Roy. Soc. 186^A, 1895. The quotation is from p.411.
[2] See the following Chapter on Regression Method and also Section 2.18.
[3] Pearson, "Notes on Skew Freq. Surface", Biom. 15, pp.222–230, 1923.

frequency curves and rotating the axes—as we might expect by analogy to the case of normal correlation surface. As a second attempt, he endeavored to extend the idea underlying his system of frequency curves, i.e., to determine a system of surfaces from the two general differential equations to a certain double hypergeometrical series by an analogy to the development of his system of frequency curves from a differential equation to a single hypergeometric series. These differential equations, as given by Rhodes, were of the form:

$$\frac{1}{Z}\frac{dZ}{dx} = \frac{\text{cubic in } x, y}{\text{Quartic in } x, y}$$

$$\frac{1}{Z}\frac{dZ}{dy} = \frac{\text{another cubic in } x, y}{\text{the same quartic in } x, y}. \qquad (2\cdot 68)$$

But the integration of these differential equations has hitherto proved impossible. However, special forms were considered by Pearson, Filon (1901), Isserlis (1913) and Rhodes (1923). These surfaces are of little value, as Pearson has pointed out that in each case there exists a relation between the β's of the two marginal distributions while also the correlation can be expressed as a function of them, that these and similar restrictions upon the characteristics of the distribution cannot lead to satisfactory bivariate frequency surfaces, and that freedom can be given to the variation of the characteristics only by having enough independent constants in the equation of the surfaces. It is perhaps this last belief which has led Pearson to the development of "The Fifteen Constant Bivariate Frequency Surface".[1]

The results obtained by Filon and Isserlis have not been published, but Pearson has given a summary of their analyses in his "Notes on Skew Frequency Surfaces". One of the Filon-Isserlis Surfaces is

$$Z = Z_0 \left(\frac{x}{b_1}\right)^{p_1} \left(\frac{y}{b_2}\right)^{p_2} \left(1 - \frac{x}{b_1} - \frac{y}{b_2}\right)^q, \qquad (2\cdot 69)$$

here

$$\frac{\beta_{20} + 3}{\beta_{10} + 4} = \frac{\beta_{02} + 3}{\beta_{01} + 4}$$

$$r = \pm \frac{\sqrt{(p_1 + 1)(p_2 + 1)}}{(p_1 + q + 2)(p_2 + q + 2)}.$$

---

[1] Biom., Vol. 17, pp.268−313, 1925.

The marginal total and partial distributions are Pearson Type I curves. Regressions are linear and scedasticity is parabolic.

The surface obtained by Rhodes is

$$Z = Z_0 e^{-lx-my} \left(1 - \frac{x}{a} + \frac{y}{b}\right)^p \left(1 + \frac{x}{a'} - \frac{y}{b}\right)^{p'}. \quad (2 \cdot 70)$$

For the determination of the constants in terms of the moments, he gives the following equations:

$$\beta_{10} = \frac{4(\varphi^3 + \lambda)^2}{s(\varphi^2 \cdot \lambda)^3} \quad \beta_{01} = \frac{4(\theta^3 + \lambda)^2}{s(\theta^2 + \lambda)^3}$$

$$r = \frac{\theta_\varphi + \lambda}{(\theta^2 + \lambda)(\varphi^2 + \lambda)} \quad Z_0 = \frac{N \cdot X \cdot p^s (p')^s}{e^{R-2} r'(s) r'(s')}$$

$$\frac{q_{21} - r\sqrt{\beta_{10}}}{\sqrt{1-r^2}} = \frac{2\sqrt{\lambda}}{\sqrt{s}} \frac{\varphi(1-\varphi)}{(\varphi^2 + \lambda)^{\frac{3}{2}}}$$

$$\frac{q_{12} - r\sqrt{\beta_{01}}}{\sqrt{1-r^2}} = \frac{2\sqrt{\lambda}}{\sqrt{s}} \frac{\theta(1-\theta)}{(\theta^2 + \lambda)^{\frac{3}{2}}}, \quad (2 \cdot 71)$$

where

$$\theta = \frac{ap'}{a'p}, \quad \varphi = \frac{bp'}{b'p} = \frac{s'}{s}$$

$$x = \frac{1}{a'b} - \frac{1}{ab'}, \quad R = p + p' + 2, \quad s' = p' + 1, \quad s = p + 1.$$

In the illustration one equation is derived from the two equations $(2 \cdot 71)$ so as not to give greater weight to one part of the table, but Rhodes does not explain how he combines them.

The following relations hold amongst the moments of the surface:

$$\frac{q_{21} - r\sqrt{\beta_{10}}}{\sqrt{1-r^2}} 3 = \sqrt{2\beta_{20} - 3\beta_{10} - 6}$$

$$\frac{q_{12} - r\sqrt{\beta_{01}}}{\sqrt{1-r^2}} \sqrt{3} = \sqrt{2\beta_{02} - 3\beta_{10} - 6}. \quad (2 \cdot 72)$$

These identical relations may serve as the criteria when the surface may be used for the representation of an observed distribution. In other words, a necessary condition justifying the use of Rhode's surface for the representation of an observed frequency distribution is that certain parameters, say, β_{20} and β_{02}, have within the limits of sampling error the same values whether they are computed from the conditions $(2 \cdot 72)$ when the other parameters are given the observed values (which will hereinafter be called the condition values) or obtained directly from the observed distribution. To judge the significance of the difference between the observed and the condition values, Pretorius[1] makes use of the formula:

$$\varepsilon = \frac{\text{observed-condition value}}{\text{s.d. of condition value}}. \qquad (2 \cdot 73)$$

This formula may be applied to all cases where there are identical relations existing between the moments of the distribution.

The mode is given by

$$1 - \frac{x}{a} + \frac{y}{b} = \frac{pp'\left(\dfrac{1}{ab'} - \dfrac{1}{a'b}\right)}{-\left(\dfrac{mp'}{a'} + \dfrac{lp'}{b'}\right)}$$

$$1 + \frac{x}{a'} - \frac{y}{b'} = \frac{pp'\left(\dfrac{1}{ab'} - \dfrac{1}{a'b}\right)}{-\left(\dfrac{lp}{b} + \dfrac{mp}{a}\right)}.$$

The distance of the mean from the mode is

$$u'_{10} = \frac{1}{x}\left(\frac{1}{pb'} + \frac{1}{p'b}\right)$$

$$u'_{01} = \frac{1}{x}\left(\frac{1}{pa'} + \frac{1}{p'a}\right).$$

The marginal and regression curves are expressed in infinite series:

y-marginal curve:

$$Z_y = ce^{-pa'u}\left[u^{-R-1} - \frac{aa'ls'}{R}u^R + \frac{(aa'l)^2 s'(s'+1)}{2! \, R(R+1)}u^{R+1} - \cdots\right].$$

Regression curve of x on y:

---

[1] Pretorius, S.G., "Skew Bivariate Frequency Surfaces", Biom. 22, p.205, 1930.

$$u'_1(x) = a'\left(\frac{y}{b'} - 1\right) + \frac{as'}{R} \cdot \frac{S_{R+1, s'+1}}{S_{R, s'}},$$

where
$$u = \frac{1}{a} + \frac{1}{a'} + xy$$

$$S_{R, s'} = u^{R-1} - \frac{aa'ls'}{R}u^R + \cdots$$

$$S_{R+1, s'+1} = u^R - aa'l\frac{s'+1}{R+1}u^{R+1} + \cdots$$

An example is given based on the distribution of barometric heights at Landale and Southampton. The cell mid-ordinates and frequencies are computed, and the goodness of fit test is applied to the whole surface as well as to the marginal totals.

Both the Filon-Isserlis and the Rhodes surfaces suffer from the defect that the small number of parameters they contain requires certain relations between at least the fourth and lower order momental constants to be satisfied, and these relations limit the freedom in the variation of the array and marginal distributions and consequently the breadth of application. Furthermore, it is unlikely that these relations would exist in practical statistics. Pretorius has tested those pertaining to the Rhodes surface with six sets of statistical data, only one distribution seems to satisfy them approximately. Apart from these limitations resulting from some identical relations between moments, Rhodes surface has another serious disadvantage in that the array moments and marginal curves are not finite expressions and thus not of any direct practical use.

To bring out the range of applicability had Pearson's differential equations admitted a general solution, we may quote Wicksell's[1] comment on Pearson's attempt at the extension of his general theory of univariate skew variation to the bi-variate or multi-variate skew variation.

"As is well known, when Pearson invented his general theory of skew variation his main idea was that the variation should be given by the binomial and the hypergeometrical series. His Types I to V are continuous functions for these series. An attempt at extending this idea to variation surfaces was no doubt

---

[1] "The correlation function of Type A", Kungl. So. Vet., Akademiens Handlingar, Bd.58, No.3, p.4.

the next step taken. If the object was to find continuous functions giving the multinomial(the extension of binomial) and the solid hypergeometrical series (the extension of hypergeometrical series), it may easily be understood, that the attempt met with great difficulties, though, at least in case of the multinomial, the difficulties are surmountable... Really, the case would have been the same had there been continuous correlation functions available, if they had been built up on the schemes giving rise to multinomial or hypergeometrical series. Pearson's was a work on non-linear regression, but as I have endeavored to prove in another place correlation surfaces to which the multinomial or hypergeometrical series may be applied must necessarily have linear regression."

"Hence it may be seen that though binomial and hypergeometrical series give fairly general frequency curves their extension to frequency surfaces can cover only very special cases."

In short, any solution whatever derived from Pearson's differential equations (2 · 68) based on the hypergeometrical series must subject its application to the limitations arising from the characteristics of the hypergeometric series. Let us consider the hypergeometrical series for a moment.

2.23 Hypergeometrical Series—Isserlis, Wicksell

The solid hypergeometrical series have been considered by Isserlis, Wicksell, Pearson, and Pretorius.[①] Isserlis applied the series to bivariate correlation surfaces by expressing its parameters in terms of the moments. Wicksell demonstrated that the regression of a solid hypergeometrical series is strictly linear, that its corresponding probability problem may be considered as an extension of Bernoulli's problem to multivariate distributions, and that the series may be analytically represented by functions of Type A and of Type B. Pearson attempted to represent the series by continuous frequency surfaces. Pretorius found some additional relations between the moments which may serve

---

① Isserlis, "The Application of Solid Hypergeometrical Series to Freq. Distributions in Space", Phil. Mag., Vol.28, pp.379−403, 1914. Wicksell, "Some Theorems in Theory of Probability", Sv. Ak. Tid., pp.12−213, 1916. "The Application of Solid Hypergeometrical Series to Frequency Distributions in Space", Phil. Mag., Vol.31, pp.389−393, 1917.

as a guide to the use of the series.

The problem in probability corresponding to the solid hypergeometrical series may be stated as follows:

Problem I

Suppose a limited population of size N to contain m marked individuals; a sample of size n is found to contain s of these marked individuals. Suppose a second sample of size n' to be extracted, the first sample not being replaced, what is the probability for the simultaneous occurrence of s marked individuals in the first sample and s' in the second?

The chances of drawing $0, 1, 2, 3, \cdots, s, \cdots$ marked individuals in the first sample are given by the successive terms of the series:

$$x\left[1 + n\frac{m}{N-m-n+1} + \frac{n(n-1)}{1\cdot 2}\frac{m(m-1)}{(N-m-n+1)(N-m-n+2)} + \cdots \right.$$
$$\left. + \frac{n!}{s!(n-s)!}\frac{m(m-1)\cdots(m-s+1)}{(N-m-n+1)(N-m-n+2)} + \cdots\right]$$

where $x = \dfrac{N-m}{N}\dfrac{N-m-1}{N-1}\dfrac{N-m-2}{N-2}\cdots\dfrac{N-m-n+1}{N-n+1}$

$$= \sum_s \frac{n!}{s!(n-s)!}\frac{(N-m)!}{(N-m-n)!}\frac{(N-n)!}{N!}\frac{m!}{(m-s)!(N-m-n+s)!}$$

$$= \sum_s H(s). \qquad (2\cdot 74)$$

Let the probabilities be $p = \dfrac{m}{N}$, $q = \dfrac{n-m}{N}$. Then it can be shown that $H(s)$ becomes

$$H(s) = \frac{n!}{(n-s)!s!}p^s q^{n-s} \text{ when } N\to\infty.$$

Let the hypergeometrical series $F(\alpha, \beta, \gamma, x)$ be

$$F(\alpha, \beta, \gamma, x) = 1 + \frac{\alpha\cdot\beta}{1\cdot\gamma}x + \frac{\alpha(\alpha+1)\beta(\beta+1)}{1\cdot 2\cdot \gamma(\gamma+1)}x^2 + \cdots$$
$$+ \frac{\alpha(\alpha+1)\cdots(\alpha+s-1)\beta(\beta+1)\cdots(\beta+s-1)}{1\cdot 2\cdot 3\cdots s\cdot \gamma(\gamma+1)\cdots(\gamma+s-1)}x^s$$
$$= 1 + h_1 x + h_2 x^2 + \cdots + h_s x^s.$$

Now put $-n = \alpha$, $-m = \beta$, $N - m - n + 1 = \gamma$, then

$$\sum_{S} H(S) = \sum_{S} \frac{(N-m)!(N-n)!}{N!(N-m-n)!} \frac{\alpha(\alpha+1)\cdots(\alpha+s-1)\beta(\beta+1)\cdots(\beta+s-1)}{1\cdot 2\cdot 3\cdots s\cdot \gamma(\gamma+1)\cdots(\gamma+s-1)}$$

$$= \frac{(N-m)!(N-n)!}{N!(N-m-n)!} \sum_{S} h_s = \frac{(N-m)!(N-n)!}{N!(N-m-n)!} F(\alpha, \beta, \gamma, 1)$$

when $F(\alpha, \beta, \gamma, 1)$ is the value of $F(\alpha, \beta, \gamma, x)$ when $x = 1$.

After the draw of the first sample of n with s marked individuals, the population now consists of $(N-n)$ individuals of which $(m-s)$ are marked, we have the probabilities:

$$p_s = \frac{m-s}{N-n}, \quad q_s = \frac{N-m-n+s}{N-n}. \tag{2·75}$$

The chances of drawing $0, 1, 2, 3, \cdots, s'\cdots$ marked individuals in the second sample are given by

$$H_S(S' \cdot S) = \frac{N-n-(m-s)}{N-n} \frac{N-n-1-(m-s)}{N-n-1} \frac{N-n-2-(m-s)}{N-n-2} \cdots$$

$$\frac{N-n-n'+1-(m-s)}{N-n-n'+1}$$

$$\cdot \left\{1 + n' \frac{m-s}{N-n-n'+1-(m-s)}\right.$$

$$+ \frac{n(n-1)}{1\cdot 2} \frac{(m-s)(m-s-1)}{[(N-n-n'+1)-(m-s)][N-n-n'+2-(m-s)]}$$

$$+ \cdots$$

$$\left. + \frac{n!}{(n-s)!s!} \frac{(m-s)(m-s-1)\cdots(m-s-s'+1)}{[N-n-n'+1-(m-s)][N-n-n'+2-(m-s)]\cdots[N-n-n'+s'-(m-s)]}\right\},$$

$$\tag{2·76}$$

which is the array of distribution of the second sample corresponding to a definite number s of marked individuals in the first sample.

Hence the chance for the simultaneous occurrence of s marked individuals in the first sample and s' in the second is

$$H = (s, s') = H(s) \cdot H_s(s') = \frac{n!n!}{s!s'!(n-s)!(n'-s')!} \cdot$$

$$\frac{(N-n-n')!}{N!} \frac{m!}{(m-s-s')!} \frac{(N-m)!}{(N-n-n'-m+s+s')!}. \tag{2·77}$$

The usual formulae for the moments of a hypergeometrical series (2·74) are

$$\mu_1 = \frac{nm}{N}$$

$$\mu_2 = \sigma_1^2 = npq\left(1 - \frac{n-1}{N-1}\right)$$

$$\mu_3 = \sigma_1^3 \sqrt{\beta_1} = npq(p-q)\left(1 - \frac{n-1}{N}\right)\left(1 - \frac{2(n-1)}{N-2}\right)$$

$$\mu_4 = npq\left(1 - \frac{n-1}{N-1}\right)\left\{1 - \frac{6(n-1)}{N-2}\left(1 - \frac{n-2}{N-3}\right)\right.$$

$$\left. + 3pq(n-2)\left[1 - \frac{n-1}{N-2}\left(\frac{n-10}{n-2} + \frac{9}{N-3}\right)\right]\right\}.$$

If we substitute $(N-n)$ for N, $(m-s)$ for m, s' for s, n' for n, and p_s for p in (2·75); we may easily obtain the moments of (2·76), i.e., the array moments of (2·77).

$$p'_{01} = n' \frac{(m-s)}{N-n}$$

$$p'_{02} = n' \frac{N-n-n'}{N-n-1}\left[\frac{1}{4} - \left(\frac{m-s}{N-n} - \frac{1}{2}\right)^2\right]$$

$$p'_{03} = n' \frac{N-n-n'}{N-n-1} \frac{N-n-2n'}{N-n-2} \frac{m-s}{N-n}\left(1 - \frac{m-s}{N-n}\right)\left[1 - \frac{2(m-s)}{N-n}\right]$$

$$= \frac{N-n-2n'}{N-n-a}\left[1 - \frac{2(m-s)}{N-n}\right] p_{02}$$

$$p'_{04} = n' \frac{N-n-n'}{N-n-1} \frac{m-s}{N-n}\left(1 - \frac{m-s}{N-n}\right)\left[1 - \frac{6(n'-1)(N-n-n'-1)}{(N-n-2)(N-n-3)}\right.$$

$$+ 3(n'-2) \frac{m-s}{N-n}\left(1 - \frac{m-s}{N-n}\right)\left(1 - \frac{n'-1}{N-n-2} \cdot \frac{n'-10}{n'-2}\right.$$

$$\left.\left. + \frac{9}{N-n-3}\right)\right]$$

$$= p_{02}\left\{1 - \frac{6(n'-1)(N-n-n'-1)}{(N-n-2)(N-n-3)}\right.$$

$$\left. + 3(n'-2) \frac{N-n-1}{n'(N-n-n')} p_{02}\left[1 - \frac{n'-1}{n-n-2}\left(\frac{n'-10}{n'-2} + \frac{9}{N-n-3}\right)\right]\right\}$$

Hence,

$$\beta_{01} = \frac{p'^2_{03}}{p'^3_{02}} = \left(\frac{N-n-2n'}{N-n-2}\right)^2 \frac{N-n-1}{n'(N-n-n')}\left[\frac{(N-n)^2}{(m-s)(N-n-m+s)} - 4\right]$$

$$\beta_{02} = \frac{p'_{04}}{p'^2_{02}} = \frac{N-n-1}{n'(N-n-2)(N-n-3)(N-n-n')} \cdot$$

$$\left\{3\left[n'(N-n-n')(N-n+6) - 2(N-n)^2\right]\right.$$

$$\left. + \frac{(N-n)^2\left[(N-n)(N-n-6n'+1)\right] + 6n'^2}{(m-s)N-n-(m-s)}\right\}.$$

From these moments we may obtain the regression, scedastic, clitic and kurtic curves. Moreover, between β_{01} and β_{02} there exists the following relation:

$$\beta_{01} + \frac{(N-n-3)(N-n-2n')^2}{(N-n-2)\left[(N-n)(6n'-N+n-1)+6n'^2\right]}\beta_{02}$$

$$= \frac{(N-n-1)(N-n-2n')^2\left[3n'^2-(N-n)(3n'-2)\right]}{n'(N-n-2)(N-n-n')\left[(N-n)(N-n-6n'+1)+6n'^2\right]}.$$

Denoting by x and y the deviations from the means $s-np$ and $s'-n'p_s$, then we have as the regression line of s' on s:

$$y = bx = \frac{p_{11}}{p_{20}}x = r\frac{\sigma_2}{\sigma_1}x,$$

where p_{ij} denotes the moments about the means of $H(s, s')$. As a consequence of the linearity of the regression, Wicksell finds the following relations existing between the moments

$$p_{21}p_{20} = p_{\alpha+1}, 0p_{11}$$

$$\alpha_{1\beta}p_{02} = p_0, s + 1p_{11}. \qquad (2 \cdot 78)$$

Now if we put $-n = \alpha$, $-n' = \alpha'$, $-m = \beta$, $N-m-n-n'+1 = \gamma$ and

$$h_{s, s'} = \frac{\alpha(\alpha+1)\cdots(\alpha+s-1)\alpha'(\alpha'+1)\cdots(\alpha'+s'-1)\beta(\beta+1)\cdots(\beta+s+s'-1)}{s!s'!\gamma(\gamma+1)\cdots(\gamma+s+s'-1)},$$

we see that the equation $(2 \cdot 77)$ becomes

$$H(s, s') = \frac{(N-m)!(N-n-n')!}{(N-m-n-n')! N!}h_{s, s'}.$$

Employing the double hypergeometrical series

$$F(\alpha, \alpha', \beta, \gamma, x, y) = \sum_s \sum_{s'} h_{s, s'} x^s y^{s'},$$

we find that $H(s, s')$ is the coefficient of $x^s y^{s'}$ in

$$\frac{(N-m)!(N-n-n')!}{(N-m-n-n')!(N!)} F(\alpha, \alpha', \beta, \gamma, x, y)$$

or

$$\sum_s \sum_{s'} H(s, s') = \frac{(N-m)!(N-n-n')!}{(N-m-n-n')!(N!)} \sum_s \sum_{s'} F(\alpha, \alpha', \beta, \gamma, 1, 1). \quad (2\cdot 79)$$

Isserlis expresses the parameters n, n', m and N in terms of the moments for purposes of application. To transfer the moments about some convenient origin to the mean, we have the following equations:

$$p_{02} = p'_{02} - p'^2_{01}$$
$$p_{03} = p'_{03} - 3p'_{02}p'_{01} + 2p'^3_{01}$$
$$p_{04} = p'_{04} - 4p'_{03}p'_{01} + 6p'_{02}p'^2_{01} - 3p'^4_{01}$$
$$p_{05} = p'_{05} - 5p'_{04}p'_{01} + 10p'_{03}p'^2_{01} - 10p'_{02}p'^3_{01} + 4p'^4_{01}$$
$$p_{11} = p'_{11} - p'_{01}p'_{10}$$
$$p_{21} = p'_{21} - p'_{20}p'_{01} - 2p'_{11}p'_{10} + 2p'^2_{10}p'_{01},$$

and similar forms may be obtained by interchanging the suffixes. To determine the necessary parameters for fitting we calculate:

$$\sigma = \sqrt{p_{20}}, \quad \sigma' = \sqrt{p_{02}}, \quad r = \frac{p_{11}}{\sigma\sigma'}$$

$$\lambda = \frac{\sigma p_{12}}{\sigma' p_{21}} \text{ (of same sign as } r\text{)}$$

$$a = \frac{(1 + r\lambda)}{r(r + \lambda)}, \quad b = \frac{1}{r^2 a}$$

$$d = \frac{p_{21}p_{12}}{p^3_{11}(a-1)(b-1)}.$$

N is determined by either group of equations A, B, C:

(A)
$$\beta_{10} = \frac{p_{30}^2}{p_{20}^3}, \quad \beta_{01} = \frac{p_{03}^2}{p_{02}^3}$$

$$\beta_{20} = \frac{p_{40}}{p_{20}^2}, \quad \beta_{02} = \frac{p_{04}}{p_{02}^2}$$

$$Q = \frac{(1+a)^2 b}{(1+b)^2 a}$$

$$\frac{N}{6} = \frac{Q(\beta_{01} - \beta_{02} + 1) - (\beta_{10} - \beta_{20} + 1)}{Q(3\beta_{01} - 2\beta_{02} + 1) - (3\beta_{10} - 2\beta_{20} + 6)}$$

(B)
$$\beta_{30} = \frac{p_{50}}{p_{20} p_{30}}$$

$$\beta_{03} = \frac{p_{05}}{p_{02} p_{03}}$$

$$N^2 = \frac{(4\beta_{30} - 10\beta_{20} + 6\beta_{10} + 2)(4\beta_{03} - 10\beta_{02} + 6\beta_{01} + 2)}{(\beta_{30} - 4\beta_{20} + 3\beta_{10} + 2)(\beta_{03} - 4\beta_{02} + 3\beta_{01} + 2)}$$

(C)
$$\frac{1}{K} = p_{11}(a+1)(p+1)$$

$$N^2(d - K) + 4N(1 - d) + 4(d - 1) = 0.$$

The parameters $m = \frac{p}{N}$, n, n' are given by

$$\frac{1}{p(1-p)} = \frac{4 + d(N-2)^2}{(N-1)}$$

$$n = \frac{N}{(a+1)}, \quad n' = \frac{N}{(b+1)}.$$

The starting point of the series is at

$$p'_{10} = c(1 + np)$$
$$p'_{01} = c'(1 + n'p)$$

from the means, where c and c' are given by

$$c = \frac{\sigma \sqrt{N-1}}{\sqrt{n(N-n)p(1-p)}}$$

$$c' = \frac{\sigma'\sqrt{N-1}}{\sqrt{n'(N-n')p(1-p)}}.$$

Equations (C) will in general give the best value of n when $cc' = 1$, since the errors of the lower moments are less, but may fail to give a real value of n. (A) and (B) on the other hand always give a real n. As the right-hand side of (B) must always be positive, it is only used for symmetrical distributions. Isserlis evaluates them for three numerical examples but to only one of the examples is the equivalent series fitted, namely the distribution in 25 000 deals of trumps in the first two hands in whist with ordinary shuffling.

The probability function $H(s, s')$ in (2.79) may be looked upon from another point of view. Wicksell states the problem in probability as follows:

Problem II

A bag contains N balls of which Nx_1 are white, Nx_2 are red, and Nx_3 are black; s balls are drawn without replacement. To find the probability that m_1 balls are white and m_2 balls are red, the rest ($s - m_1 - m_2$ balls) being black.

The solution is

$$H(m_1, m_2) = \frac{s!(x_1N)!(x_2N)!(x_3N)!(n-s)!}{N!(m_1!m_2!)(s-m_1-m_2)!(x_1N-m_1)!(x_2N-m_2)!(x_3N-s+m_1+m_2)!}.$$

Putting

$$-s = a, \quad -x_1N = b_1, \quad -x_2N = b_2, \quad x_3N - s + 1 = c$$

$$hm_1m_2 = \frac{a(a+1)\cdots(a+m_1+m_2-1)b_1(b_1+1)\cdots(b_1+m_1-1)b_2(b_2+1)\cdots(b_2+m_2-1)}{1\cdot 2\cdot 3\cdots m_1 \cdot 1\cdot 2\cdot 3\cdots m_2 c(c+1)\cdots(c+m_1+m_2-1)},$$

we see that

$$H(m_1, m_2) = \frac{(N-s)!(x_3N)!}{N!(x_3N-s)!}hm_1m_2$$

or

$$\sum_{m_1}\sum_{m_2}H(m_1, m_2) = \frac{(N-s)!(x_3N)!}{N!(x_3N-s)!}F(a, b_1, b_2, c, 1, 1)$$

(2·79a)

where $F(a, b_1, b_2, c, 1, 1)$ is the double hypergeometrical series $\sum_{m_1} \sum_{m_2} x^{m_1} y^{m_2} h m_1 m_2$ for $x = 1$, $y = 1$. If we exchange

$$s \text{ against } m$$
$$3^N \text{ against } N - n - n'$$
$$N - s \text{ against } N - m$$
$$x_3 N - s \text{ against } N - n - n' - m,$$

the equations $(2 \cdot 79)$ and $(2 \cdot 79a)$ are identical. Thus, we may conclude that the problem I and II are equivalent.

While probability in Problem I itself is an extension of a probability problem containing a single variate, it may be extended to a problem in probability containing 3 or more variates.

<u>Problem III</u>

A bag contains N balls of which $x_1 N$ are white, $x_2 N$ are red, $x_3 N$ are blue, and $x_4 N$ are black; s drawings without replacement are made to find the probability that m_1 balls are white, m_2 red, and m_3 blue, the rest $(s - m_1 - m_2 - m_3)$ being black.

The solution is

$$H(m_1, m_2, m_3) = \frac{s'(n-s)!(Nx_1)!(Nx_2)!(Nx_3)!(Nx_4)!}{m_1! m_2! m_3!(s - m_1 - m_2 - m_3)!(Nx_1 - m_1)!(Nx_2 - m_2)!(Nx_3 - m_3)!(Nx_4 - s + m_1 + m_2 + m_3)! N!}$$
$$(2 \cdot 80)$$

As before, putting

$$-s = \alpha, \ -x_1 n = \beta_1, \ -x_2 n = \beta_2, \ -x_3 n = \beta_3, \ x_4^{n-s+1} = \gamma$$

$$h m_1 m_2 m_3$$
$$= \frac{\alpha(\alpha+1) \cdots (\alpha + m_1 + m_2 + m_3 - 1) \beta_1(\beta_1 + 1) \cdots (\beta + m - 1) \beta(\beta + 1) \cdots (\beta + m)}{m_1! m_2! m_3!}$$

$$\cdot \frac{\beta_3(\beta_3 + 1) \cdots (\beta_3 + m_3 - 1)}{\gamma(\gamma + 1) \cdots (\gamma + m_1 + m_2 + m_3 - 1)}$$

$$F(\alpha, \beta_1, \beta_2, \beta_3, \gamma, x_1, x_2, x_3) = \sum_{m_1} \sum_{m_2} \sum_{m_3} x_1^{m_1} x_2^{m_2} x_3^{m_3} h m_1 m_2 m_3,$$

we have $\sum_{m_1} \sum_{m_2} \sum_{m_3} H(m_1 m_2 m_3) = F(\alpha, \beta_1, \beta_2, \beta_3, \gamma, 1, 1, 1)$.

And the way is clear for the extension or the probability problem and its solution to the m variates.

Wicksell has given analytic functions for the representation of the series $H(m_1)$, $H(m_1, m_2)$, and $H(m_1, m_2, m_3)$. These functions give the essentials of the original series and are also continuous functions of the variates m_1, m_2, m_3 when they are varied continuously. We shall reproduce the case of two variates as illustration.

As shown by Isserlis[1], $F(\alpha, \beta_1, \beta_2, \gamma_1, x, y)$ satisfies the system of differential equations

$$x(1-x)\frac{\partial^2 F}{\partial x^2} + y(1-x)\frac{\partial^2 F}{\partial x \partial y} + [\gamma - (\alpha + \beta_1 + 1)x]\frac{\partial F}{\partial x} - \beta_1 y \frac{\partial F}{\partial y} - \beta_1 \alpha F = 0$$

$$y(1-y)\frac{\partial^2 F}{\partial y^2} + x(1-y)\frac{\partial^2 F}{\partial x \partial y} + [\gamma - (\alpha + \beta_2 + 1)y]\frac{\partial F}{\partial x} - \beta_2 x \frac{\partial F}{\partial y} - \beta_2 \alpha F = 0,$$

substituting $x = e^{W_1 i}$, $y = e^{W_2 i}$, and putting

$$\frac{(n-s)!x_3 n!}{n!(x_3 n - s)!} F(\alpha, \beta_1, \beta_2, \gamma, e^{W_1 i}, e^{W_2 i}) = x(w_1, w_2),$$

we find

$$(1 - e^{W_1 i})\frac{\partial^2 x}{\partial w_1^2} + (1 - e^{W_1 i})\frac{\partial x}{\partial w_1 \partial w_2} + i[\gamma - 1 + (\alpha + \beta_1)e^{w_1 i}]\frac{\partial x}{\partial w_1}$$

$$- i\beta_1 e^{w_1 i}\frac{\partial x}{\partial w_2} + \beta_1 \alpha e^{w_1 i} x = 0$$

$$(1 - e^{W_2 i})\frac{\partial^2 x}{\partial w_2^2} + (1 - e^{W_2 i})\frac{\partial x}{\partial w_1 \partial w_2} + i[\gamma - 1 + (\alpha_2 + \beta_2)e^{w_2 i}]\frac{\partial x}{\partial w_2}$$

$$- i\beta_2 e^{w_2 i}\frac{\partial x}{\partial w_1} + \beta_2 \alpha e^{w_2 i} x = 0. \qquad (2 \cdot 81)$$

Inserting the old parameters s, n, x_1, x_2, x_3 instead of α, β_1, β_2 and γ, we have

$$(1 - e^{W_1 i})\left(\frac{\partial^2 x}{\partial w_1^2} + \frac{\partial^2 x}{\partial w_1 \partial w_2}\right) + i[n - (s + x_1 n)(1 - e^{W_1 i})]\frac{\partial x}{\partial w_1}$$

---

[1] Loc. Cit., p.383.

$$+ ix_1 n e^{W_1 i} \frac{\partial x}{\partial w_2} - ix_2 n \frac{\partial x}{\partial w_1} + snx_1 e^{W_1 i} x = 0$$

$$(1 - e^{W_2 i}) \left(\frac{\partial^2 x}{\partial w_2^2} + \frac{\partial^2 x}{\partial w_1 \partial w_2} \right) + i[n - (s + x_2 n)(1 - e^{W_2 i})] \frac{\partial x}{\partial w_2}$$

$$+ ix_2 n e^{W_2 i} \frac{\partial x}{\partial w_1} - ix_1 n \frac{\partial x}{\partial w_2} + snx_2 e^{W_2 i} x = 0. \qquad (2 \cdot 82)$$

Equations $(2 \cdot 81)$ will now be used in order to get $\log x(w_1, w_2)$ expanded[①] in powers of w_1 and w_2. To this end we put

$$\Pi(w_1, w_2) = e^{\sum \frac{b_{k'l}}{k'l'}(w_1 i)^k (w_2 i)^l}$$

where, as $\Pi(0, 0) = 1$, $b_{0,0} = 0$. We have now

$$\frac{\partial \Pi}{\partial w_1} = i\Pi \cdot \sum \sum \frac{b_{k+1, l}}{k'l'} (w_1 i)^k (w_2 i)^l$$

$$\frac{\partial \Pi}{\partial w_2} = i\Pi \cdot \sum \sum \frac{b_{k, l+1}}{k'l'} (w_1 i)^k (w_2 i)^l$$

$$\frac{\partial \Pi}{\partial w_1^2} = -\Pi \cdot \left[\sum \sum \frac{b_{k+1, l}}{k'l'} (w_1 i)^k (w_2 i)^l \right]^2 - \Pi \cdot \left[\sum \sum \frac{b_{k+2, l}}{k'l'} (w_1 i)^k (w_2 i)^l \right]$$

$$\frac{\partial \Pi}{\partial w_1 \partial w_2} = -\Pi \sum \sum \frac{b_{k+1, l}}{k'l'} (wi)^k (wi)^l \cdot \sum \sum \frac{b_{k, l+1}}{k'l'} (w_1 i)^k (w_2 i)^l -$$

$$\Pi \sum \sum \frac{b_{k+1, l+1}}{k'l'} (w_1 i)^k (w_2 i)^l$$

$$\frac{\partial \Pi}{\partial w_2^2} = -\Pi \left[\sum \sum \frac{b_{k, l+1}}{k'l'} (w_1 i)^k (w_2 i)^l \right]^2 - \Pi \sum \sum \frac{b_{k, l+2}}{k'l'} (w_1 i)^k (w_2 i)^l.$$

Inserting this in $(2 \cdot 81)$ and arranging in powers of w_1 and w_2, we find, putting the coefficients equal to zero,

$$b_{10} + x_1 b_{01} - x_2 b_{10} - sx_1 = 0$$

$$b_{01} + x_2 b_{10} - x_1 b_{01} - sx_2 = 0$$

$$b_{10}^2 + b_{10} b_{01} + b_{20} + b_{11} - nb_{20} - (s + x_1 n) b_{10} - x_1 n b_{11}$$

$$- x_1 n b_{01} + x_2 n b_{20} + snx_1 = 0$$

[①] This is the first case of reduction resulting in the formula called type A. If we expand $\log px(W_1, W_2)$ in powers of $\left(x_1 + \frac{s}{n} \right)$ and $\left(x_2 + \frac{s}{n} \right)$, the reduction will result in formula of type B.

$$b_{01}^2 + b_{10}b_{01} + b_{02} + b_{11} - nb_{02} - (s + x_2 n)b_{01} - x_2 n b_{11}$$
$$- x_2 n b_{10} + x_1 n b_{02} + sn x_2 = 0$$
$$b_{11} + x_1 b_{02} + x_2 b_{11} = 0$$
$$b_{11} + x_2 b_{20} + x_1 b_{11} = 0.$$

Solving these equations, we find

$$b_{10} = sx_1$$
$$b_{01} = sx_2 \qquad (2\cdot 83)$$

$$b_{20} = sx_1(1 - x_1)\frac{n - s}{n - 1}$$

$$b_{11} = -sx_1 x_2 \frac{n - s}{n - 1}$$

$$b_{02} = sx_2(1 - x_2)\frac{n - s}{n - 1} \qquad (2\cdot 83\text{a})$$

For the coefficients of the third order, we get the sufficient equations easily, and the solution will be found to be

$$b_{30} = b_{20}(1 - 2x_1)\frac{n - 2s}{n - 2}$$

$$b_{21} = b_{11}(1 - 2x_1)\frac{n - 2s}{n - 2}$$

$$b_{12} = b_{11}(1 - 2x_2)\frac{n - 2s}{n - 2}$$

$$b_{03} = b_{02}(1 - 2x_2)\frac{n - 2s}{n - 2}. \qquad (2\cdot 83\text{b})$$

Further we write

$$e^{\sum_{k+l\geqslant 3}\sum \frac{b_{k,l}}{k!\,l!}(w_1 i)^k (w_2 i)^l} = 1 + \sum_{k+l\geqslant 3}\sum (-1)^{k+l} A_{kl}(w_1 i)^k (w_2 i)^l.$$

Expanding the left-hand member, we find

$$A_{30} = -\frac{b_{30}}{3!} = -\frac{1}{6}b_{20}(1 - 2x_1)\frac{n - 2s}{n - 2}$$

$$A_{21} = -\frac{b_{21}}{2!} = -\frac{1}{2}b_{11}(1 - 2x_1)\frac{n - 2s}{n - 2}$$

$$A_{12} = -\frac{b_{12}}{2!} = -\frac{1}{2}b_{11}(1-2x_2)\frac{n-2s}{n-2}$$

$$A_{03} = -\frac{b_{03}}{3!} = -\frac{1}{6}b_{02}(1-2x_2)\frac{n-2s}{n-2}. \qquad (2\cdot 84)$$

Hence we have

$$\Pi(w_1, w_2) = e^{b_{10}(w_1 i) + b_{01}(w_2 i) - \frac{1}{2}(b_{20}w_1^2 + 2b_{11}w_1 w_2 + b_{02}w_2^2)} \cdot$$
$$\left[1 + \sum_{k+l \geqslant 3} \sum (-1)^{k+l} A_{kl}(w_1 i)^k (w_2 i)^l \right]. \qquad (2\cdot 85)$$

To obtain an analytical development for $H(m_1 m_2)$, we put

$$H_0(x_1, x_2) = \frac{1}{(2x)^2} \int_{-x}^{+x} dw_1 \int_{-x}^{+x} dw_2 \Pi(w_1, w_2) e^{-(x_1 w_1 + x_2 w_2) i}. \qquad (2\cdot 86)$$

As

$$\Pi(w_1, w_2) = \sum_{m_1=0}^{s} \sum_{m_2=0}^{s} H(m_1, m_2) e^{(m_1 w_1 + m_2 w_2) i},$$

it is seen that $H_0(m_1, m_2) = H(m_1, m_2)$.
Writing

$$\Omega_0(x_1, x_2) = \frac{1}{(2x)^2} \int_{-x}^{+x} dw_1 \int_{-x}^{+x} dw_2 \cdot e^{-(x_1 - b_{10})(w_1 i) - (x_2 - b_{01})(w_2 i) - \frac{1}{2}(b_{20}w_1^2 + 2b_{11}w_1 w_2 + b_{02}w_2^2)},$$
$$(2\cdot 87)$$

we evidently get

$$H_0(x_1, x_2) = \Omega_0(x_1, x_2) + \sum_{k+l} \sum_{3} A_{kl} \frac{\partial^{k+l} \Omega_0(x_1, x_2)}{\partial x_1^k \partial x_2^l}. \qquad (2\cdot 88)$$

Here we may extend the limits of integration to $\pm \infty$, when b_{20} and b_{02} are not exceedingly small quantities, so as to obtain a good approximation of the function $\Omega_0(x_1, x_2)$. We have then, putting

$$\varphi(x_1, x_2) = \frac{1}{(2x)^2} \int_{-\infty}^{\infty} dw_1 \int_{-\infty}^{\infty} dw_2 e^{(-x_1 - b_{10})w_1 i - (x_2 - b_{01})w_2 i - \frac{1}{2}(b_{20}w_1^2 + 2b_{11}w_1 w_2 + b_{02}w_2^2)}$$
$$(2\cdot 89)$$

$$H_0(x_1, x_2) = \varphi(x_1, x_2) + \sum_{k+l} \sum_{3} A_{kl} \frac{\partial^{k+l} \varphi(x_1, x_2)}{\partial x_1^k \partial x_2^l}, \qquad (2\cdot 90)$$

as well known the function $\varphi(x_1, x_2)$ is given by

$$\varphi(x_1, x_2) = \frac{1}{2x\sigma_1\sigma_2\sqrt{1-r_{12}}} e^{-\frac{1}{2(1-r^2)}\left[\frac{(x_1-b_{10})^2}{\sigma_1^2} - 2r\frac{(x_1-b_{10})(x_2-b_{01})}{\sigma_1\sigma_2} + \frac{(x_2-b_{01})^2}{\sigma_2^2}\right]},$$

where $\quad \sigma_1 = \sqrt{b_{20}}; \; \sigma_2 = \sqrt{b_{02}}; \; r = \dfrac{b_{11}}{\sqrt{b_{20}b_{02}}}.$ $\qquad(2 \cdot 91)$

The series $(2 \cdot 90)$ is the series of type A in two dimensions. Its parameters are here

$$b_{10} = sx_1 \qquad b_{01} = sx_2$$

$$\sigma_1^2 = sx_1(1-x_1)\frac{n-s}{n-1}$$

$$\sigma_2^2 = sx_2(1-x_2)\frac{n-s}{n-1}$$

$$r = -\sqrt{\frac{x_1 x_2}{(1-x_1)(1-x_2)}}$$

$$A_{30} = -\frac{1}{6}\sigma_1^2(1-2x_1)\frac{n-2s}{n-2}$$

$$A_{21} = -\frac{1}{2}\sigma_1\sigma_2 r(1-2x_1)\frac{n-2s}{n-2}$$

$$A_{12} = -\frac{1}{2}\sigma_1\sigma_2 r(1-2x_2)\frac{n-2s}{n-2}$$

$$A_{03} = -\frac{1}{6}\sigma_2(1-2x_2)\frac{n-2s}{n-2},$$

where r is the coefficient of correlation. It is negative independent of the size s of the sample, and also independent of the size n of the population. Hence, we have the same coefficient of correlation whether the drawings are performed with replacement or not.

A condition for rapid convergency is that the coefficients b_{20} and b_{02} are not small. If any one of these parameters is small while s is great, recourse must be had to developments of $\log \text{II}(w_1, w_2)$ in powers of $\left(x_1 + \dfrac{s}{n}\right)$ and $\left(x_2 + \dfrac{s}{n}\right)$ which result in series of type B. But Wicksell has given this development only for the case of a single variate.

Wicksell also proves the formula of type A for three variates by the same method of procedure. Therefore, it is fair to say that the way is already clear for the development of a similar formula of type A for the case of m variates.

So far as the correlation function of type A is an analytic expression for a corresponding hypergeometrical series, its applications must be restricted by the basic characteristics of that series, namely, linear regression, parabolic scedasticity, clisy of cubic parabolic type, kurtosis of quartic parabolic type. In other words, their applications can cover only limited cases. However, the theory of the correlation function of type A is not restricted to the above scheme. It has been developed on the basis of elementary errors by Charlier and called by him the genetic theory of frequency. Furthermore, the developments of Charlier have, indeed, the properties that make them more or less independent of their hypothetical foundation. His functions have in a very high degree the properties of rather elastic developments of arbitrary functions, being in that respect in a way analogous to Fourier series.①

Moreover, it may be added that we may obtain the same probability function $H(m_1, m_2)$ from a probability problem in still another form.

Problem IV

A bag contains n balls. The balls in the bag are distinguishable by two different kinds of attributes, i.e., each ball is either black or white and is moreover marked with either an even or an odd number. In the bag nx_1 balls are white and "even", nx_2 balls are white and odd, nx_3 balls are black and even, and nx_4 balls are black and odd. If s drawings are made without replacement, what is the probability $H'(h, k)$ that h balls have white color and k balls have an even number written on them?

Evidently the probability that the combination white-even occurs m_1 times, white-odd m_2 times, black-even m_3 times, and black-odd m_4 times, is, as these combinations are mutually exclusive, given by the function $H(m_1, m_2, m_3)$ in (2·80). The solution hence is

$$H'(h, k) = \sum_{m_1} \sum_{m_2} \sum_{m_3} H(m_1, m_2, m_3)$$

---

① Charlier, Convergence of the development in series of type A, Med. Lund. Observatelum, No.71.

where the sum is to be taken for all values of m_1, m_2, m_3, which are subject to the conditions

$$m_1 + m_2 = h,$$
$$m_1 + m_3 = k;$$

or,
$$H'(h, k) = \sum_{m_1} H''(h, k, m_1).$$

Putting $x_1 + x_2 = p$, $x_1 + x_3 = p_1$, $1 - p = q$, $1 - p_1 = q_1$, and following the procedure done for $H(m_1, m_2)$, Wicksell finds

$$H'(x, y) = \varphi(x, y) + \sum_{k+l \geq 3} \sum A'_{k, l} \frac{\partial^{k+l} \varphi(x, y)}{\partial x^k \partial y^l}$$

where

$$\varphi(x, y) = \frac{1}{2x\sigma'_1 \sigma'_2 \sqrt{1-r^2}} e^{-\frac{1}{2(1-r^2)} \left[\frac{(x-b'_{10})^2}{\sigma'^2_1} - 2r \frac{(x-b'_{10})(y-b'_{01})}{\sigma'_1 \sigma'_2} + \frac{(y-b'_{01})^2}{\sigma'^2_2} \right]},$$

and the parameters are

$$b'_{10} = sp, \quad b'_{01} = sp_1,$$

$$\sigma'^2_1 = spq \frac{n-s}{n-1}, \quad \sigma'^2_2 = sp_1 q_1 \frac{n-s}{n-1}$$

$$r' = \frac{x_1 - pp_1}{\sqrt{pqp_1 q_1}},$$

$$A'_{30} = -\frac{1}{6} \sigma'^2_1 (1 - 2p) \frac{n - 2s}{n - 2} = \frac{1}{6} \sigma'^2_1 (p - q) \frac{n - 2s}{n - 2}$$

$$A'_{21} = \frac{1}{2} \sigma'_1 \sigma'_2 r'(p - q) \frac{n - 2s}{n - 2},$$

$$A'_{12} = \frac{1}{2} \sigma'_1 \sigma'_2 r'(p_1 - q_1) \frac{n - 2s}{n - 2},$$

$$A'_{03} = \frac{1}{6} \sigma'^2 (p_1 - q_1) \frac{n - 2s}{n - 2}.$$

This is the same as $H_0(x_1, x_2)$ above.

The Problem IV is clearly a problem of correlation between two attributes, and thus a theory of correlation or association of attributes may be developed along this line. However, our point is to bring out the connections between probability Problems I, II, IV.

If the drawings in Problem IV are made with replacement, the solution will clearly be:

$$B(m_1, m_2, m_3) = \frac{s!}{m_1!m_2!m_3!m_4!} x_1^{m_1} x_2^{m_2} x_3^{m_3} x_4^{m_4}.$$

This is the coefficient of

$$x_1^{m_1} x_2^{m_2} x_3^{m_3} x_4^{m_4}$$

In the development of

$$(x_1 x_1 + x_2 x_2 + x_3 x_3 + x_4 x_4)^s.$$

But the probability that we find

h individuals in white color

k individuals in even number

is the sum of all such terms for which

$$m_1 + m_2 = h, \ m_1 + m_3 = k.$$

Thus, it is the coefficient $x^h y^k$ in the development of

$$(x_1 xy + x_2 x + x_3 y + x_4)^s.$$

Hence the probability $B(h, k)$ may now be obtained by summing for all value of m_1:

$$B(h, k) = \sum_{m_1} B(m_1, m_2, m_3) = \sum_{m_1} B'(h, k, m_1)$$

$$= \sum_{m_1} \frac{s!}{m_1!(h - m_1)!(k - m_1)!(s + m_1 - h - k)!}$$

$$\cdot x_1^{m_1} x_2^{h-m_1} x_3^{k-m_1} x_4^{(s+m-h-k)}.$$

Wicksell has developed this probability function $B(h, k)$ into Charlier Type A and Type B functions according to whether $s(x_1 + x_2)(1 - x_1 - x_2)$ and $s(x_1 + x_3)(1 - x_1 - x_3)$ are great or small.

It is well known that, in case of a single variate, the frequency distribution will be binomial if the drawings are made with replacement and hypergeometrical if the drawings are made without replacement. As known above, this has been extended by Wicksell to two and more variates, i.e., the distribution will be multi-nomial if the drawings are made with replacement and solid hypergeometrical if the drawings are made without replacement. Moreover, all these distributions, binomial or multi-nomial and single hypergeometrical or multi-hypergeometrical, may be developed into functions of Type A and Type B and thus provide a wider basis for the Type A and Type B functions in the theory of correlation, which have originally been built upon the hypothesis if elementary errors as we shall see as we proceed.

2.24 Narumi and Pretorius

Being not satisfied with the results obtained by Filon, Isserlis, and Rhodes, Pearson put the problem in the hands of Professor Narumi for solutions. Narumi[①] approached the problem on the assumption that the array distributions are similar. On the basis of this assumption, Narumi naturally starts his investigation from a consideration of the regression and scedastic curves, having no regard for the clisy and kurtosis. The regression curve need not be restricted to the curve of means; it can be any series of points defined in the same manner for each array. Let $x = f_1(y)$, $y = f_2(x)$ be the two regression curves. Now if the frequency curve of any array be transferred to the regression curve as the origin, then the equation to the y-arrays will be of the form:

$$\psi_2[y - f_2(x)].$$

Now if the arrays are heteroscedastic, they can be transformed into a homoscedastic system through the modification of the units in which we measure variation in each array. Thus, if the variate be measured in terms of its standard deviation, the arrays will now be homoscedastic. We need not however, think in terms of standard deviations; we may simply alter the scale of measurement of the variation in each array, the scale in the y-arrays varying with x and in the x-arrays varying with y. Let these scales of measurement, which reduce arrays to complete scedasticity, be $\dfrac{1}{F_2(x)}$ and $\dfrac{1}{F_1(y)}$. Then the equation to the y-arrays expressed in this scale will now be

---

① "On General Forms of Bivariate Frequency Distribution", Biom., Vol.15, pp.77 − 88, 209 − 222.

$$\psi_2\{[y - f_2(x)]F_2(x)\}.$$

If the distribution of x when considered independent of y is $\Phi_2(x)$, then, by the theorem of compound probability, the most general functional equation to the frequency surface will be

$$Z = \Phi_2(x)\psi_2\{[y - f_2(x)]F_2(x)\}$$
$$= \Phi_1(y)\psi_1\{[x - f_1(y)]F_1(y)\}.$$

Narumi works from this functional equation with given forms of $f_1(y)$, $f_2(x)$, $F_1(y)$, $F_2(x)$ back to the frequency surface and concludes (i) that the possible mathematical surfaces are very narrowly limited; (ii) that we cannot combine arbitrary regression curves with quite arbitrary array variation; and (iii) that if we know the nature of the regression and of the array variation we can predict what type of frequency surface is alone possible, without any appeal to the general law of probability. In this way observation of regression and of the scedasticity of arrays lead us directly to the suitable frequency surface. Thus,

(a) homoscedasticity and linear regression correspond to normal surface.

(b) homoscedasticity and rectangular parabolic regression both ways correspond to

$$Z = Z'_0 x^{n_1} y^{n_2} e^{-\gamma\left(\frac{1}{1m_1} - \frac{y}{2}\right)\left(\frac{1}{2m_2} - \frac{x}{1}\right)},$$

the arrays are Pearson Type III curves.

(c) Linear regression both ways:

$$f_1(y) = m_1 y + c_1, \quad f_2(x) = m_2 x + c_2,$$

and parabolic scedasticity

$$\beta(1 \cdot 2) = \left[\frac{1}{F_1(y)}\right]^2 = \lambda_1^2 (y + a)^2, \quad \beta(2 \cdot 1) = \left[\frac{1}{F_2(x)}\right]^2 = \lambda_2^2 (x + a_2)^2,$$

leads to Filon-Isserlis surface:

$$Z = Z_0 (x + g_1)^{P_1} (y + g_2)^{P_2} \{[(g_1 - a_2)(y + a_1) + g_2 - a_1](x + a_2)\}^q.$$

The arrays both ways are Pearson Type I curves.

(d) Regression curves of equilateral hyperbolas:

$$x + \frac{f_1 y + c_1}{y + g_1} = 0, \quad y + \frac{g_2 x + c_2}{x + f_2} = 0,$$

and scedasticity of the form

$$\frac{1}{F_1(y)} = \frac{1}{y+g_1}, \quad \frac{1}{F_2(x)} = \frac{1}{x+f_2}$$

leads to a surface of the form:

$$Z = Z_0(x+f_1)^{\gamma_1}(y+g_2)^{\gamma_2} e^{\gamma(x+f_2)(y+g_1)}$$

with arrays of Pearson Type III curves.

(e) linear regression and parabolic scedasticity of the form:

$$\beta(1 \cdot 2) = y^2 + c_1, \quad \beta(2 \cdot 1) = x^2 + c_2,$$

leads to Pearson's non-skew frequency surface[1]:

$$Z = Z_0 \left\{ 1 + \frac{\dfrac{x^2}{\sigma_1^2} - \dfrac{2\gamma xy}{\sigma_1 \sigma_2} + \dfrac{y^2}{\sigma_1^2}}{2\lambda(1-\gamma^2)} \right\}^{-2}.$$

Clearly the validity of Narumi's theory depends upon the validity of his assumption that the array distributions have the same shape or form so that if they are brought to a common origin as determined by the regression line and modified in scale of measurement, they will be a system of similar and similarly placed curves defined by their origin as the center of similitude. If this hypothesis was valid, then correlation would be completely characterized by a regression surface, scedastic surface, and the marginal curves without any appeal to the frequency surface of the variates. Any justification for this assumption must rest on the analysis of observed date. Since the assumption of similarity of array curves is almost equivalent to the assumption of homoclisy and homokurtosis of arrays, an examination of the clisy and kurtosis of the arrays will provide us with a practical test as to the generality of Narumi's hypothesis. In this way Pretorius[2] has examined four sets of statistical date, namely, the correlation between ages of bride and groom, between ages of father and mother, between barometric heights of the first and third day, between the breadth and length of beans. For the first two distributions, the variation in the clisy and

---

[1] "On Non-Skew Frequency Surface", Biom., Vol.15, p.231, 1923.
[2] Op. Cit.

kurtosis is remarkably regular; for the barometric data a quite defined trend, other than constant, is noticeable, and it is only for the distribution of length and breadth of beans, where both the number of points on the graphs and the total number of observations are small, that these two measures seem to be scattered at random. "This finding", Pretorius concludes, "of a fairly regular variation in the shape of array distributions disproves, beyond doubt, the generality of Narumi's hypothesis".

We may also test Narumi's theory through an examination of the regression and scedasticity associated with the theoretical surfaces. According to Narumi's theory, the frequency surface for a linear regression and parabolic scedasticity (case c and case e given above) must be either Filon-Isserlis surface or Pearson's non-skew surface. Therefore, to the data for the whist experiment which has linear regression and parabolic scedasticity, we should expect a good fit by either of these two surfaces. But the actual fitting by Pearson[1] does not seem to be good. "From a comparison of the contours, of the array variations, and of the marginal distributions," Pearson concludes, "neither of the two surfaces seems to be really adequate. This inadequacy is not solely because of the replacing a discrete series by a continuous surface, but because of neglecting either value β_1 or β_2 (the non-skew frequency surface does involve β_1 while Filon-Isserlis surface does not involve β_2 in the representation)." This certainly disproves Narumi's theory in another way, and also indirectly the Filon-Isserlis surface and the non-skew frequency surface. A satisfactory theory of correlation surface cannot be obtained without giving due consideration to each of the basic characteristics: regression, scedastic, clitic, kurtic, and the equal frequency contours, if we attempt to work from the functional equation back to the frequency surface.

2.25 Pearson's 15-Constant Bivariate Surface

In order to be free from the restrictions imposed on the array distributions,

---

[1] Op. Cit., "On a Certain Hypergeometrical Series".

it is needful, according to Pearson, to have an adequate number of parameters in the function. His memoir on "The Fifteen Constant Bivariate Frequency Surface"① seems to be a result of his efforts towards this goal. The surface is assumed to be of the form

$$w = g(y_1 y_2) \begin{Bmatrix} 1 - a_0 + a_1 y_1 + a_2 y_2 + b_1 y_1^2 + 2b_2 y_1 y_2 + b_3 y_2^2 \\ + c_1 y_1^3 + c_2 y_1^2 y_2 + c_3 y_1 y_2^2 + c_4 y_2^3 \\ + d_1 y_1^4 + d_2 y_1^3 y_2 + d_3 y_1^2 y_2^2 + d_4 y_1 y_2^3 + d_5 y_2^4 \end{Bmatrix} \quad (2 \cdot 92)$$

where

$$g(y_1, y_2) = \frac{1}{2x\sqrt{1-r^2}} e^{-\frac{1}{2(1-r^2)}(y_1^2 - 2ry_1 y_2 + y_2^2)},$$

$$y_1 = \frac{x_1}{\sigma_1}, \quad y_2 = \frac{x_2}{\sigma_2}.$$

The parameters are expressed in terms of the first five moments. Thus, if

$$p_{hk} = \int\int_{-\infty}^{\infty} w x_1^h x_2^k dx_1 dx_2$$

or

$$q_{hk} = \frac{m_{hk}}{\sigma_1^p \sigma_2^q} = \int\int_{-\infty}^{\infty} w y^h y^k dy_1 dy_2$$

and

$$Q_{40} = \frac{1}{24}(q_{40} - 3), \quad Q_{04} = \frac{1}{24}(q_{04} - 3)$$

$$Q_{31} = \frac{1}{6}(q_{31} - 3r), \quad Q_{13} = \frac{1}{6}(q_{13} - 3r)$$

$$Q_{22} = \frac{1}{12}(q_{22} - 1 - 2r^2), \quad (2 \cdot 93)$$

the fifteen parameters are given by:

$$a_1 = \frac{1}{2(1-r^2)^2} \{3rq_{21} - q_{30} - (1 - 2r^2)q_{12} + rq_{03}\}$$

---

① Pearson, K., "The fifteen Constant Bivariate Frequency Surface", Biom., Vol.17, pp.268 – 313, 1925.

$$a_2 = \frac{1}{2(1-r^2)^2}\{3rq_{12} - q_{03} - (1-2r^2)q_{21} + rq_{30}\}$$

$$c_1 = \frac{1}{6(1-r^2)^3}\{r^2(3q_{12} - rq_{03}) - (3rq_{21} - q_{30})\}$$

$$c_2 = \frac{1}{2(1-r^2)^3}\{(1+2r^2)q_{21} - rq_{30} - r[(2+r^2)q_{12} - rq_{03}]\}$$

$$c_3 = \frac{1}{2(1-r^2)^3}\{(1+2r^2)q_{12} - rq_{03} - r(2+r^2)q_{21} - r^2 q_{30}\}$$

$$c_4 = \frac{1}{6(1-r^2)^3}\{r^2(3q_{21} - rq_{30}) - (3rq_{12} - q_{03})\}$$

$$a_0 = -\frac{3}{(1-r^2)^2}\{Q_{40} + Q_{04} - r(Q_{31} + Q_{13}) + (1+2r^2)Q_{22}\}$$

$$b_1 = -\frac{3}{(1-r^2)^3}\{2Q_{40} + 2r^2 Q_{04} - 2rQ_{31} - r(1+r^2)Q_{13} + (1+5r^2)Q_{22}\}$$

$$2b_2 = -\frac{3}{(1-r^2)^3}\{4r(Q_{40} + Q_{04}) - (3r^2+1)(Q_{31} + Q_{13}) + 4r(2+r^2)Q_{22}\}$$

$$b_3 = -\frac{3}{(1-r^2)^3}\{2r^2 Q_{40} + 2Q_{04} - r(1+r^2)(Q_{31} - 2rQ_{13}) + (1+5r^2)Q_{22}\}$$

$$d_1 = \frac{1}{(1-r^2)^4}\{(Q_{40} - r^4 Q_{04} - rQ_{31} - r^3 Q_{13}) + 3r^2 Q_{22}\}$$

$$d_2 = \frac{-1}{(1-r^2)^4}\{4rQ_{40} + 4r^3 Q_{04} - (1+3r^2)Q_{31} - r^2(3+r^2)Q_{13} + 6r(1+r^2)Q_{22}\}$$

$$d_3 = \frac{1}{(1-r^2)^4}\{2r^2(Q_{40} + Q_{04}) - r(1+r^2)(Q_{31} + Q_{13}) + (1+4r^2+r^4)Q_{22}\}$$

$$d_4 = -\frac{1}{(1-r^2)^4}\{4r^3 Q_{40} + 4rQ_{04} - r^2(3+r^2)Q_{31} - (1+3r^2)Q_{13} + 6r(1+r^2)Q_{22}\}$$

$$d_5 = \frac{1}{(1-r^2)^4}\{r^4 Q_{40} + Q_{04} - r^3 Q_{31} - rQ_{13} + 3r^2 Q_{22}\}. \quad (2\cdot 94)$$

Integrating $(2\cdot 92)$ for y_2 from $-\infty$ to $+\infty$, we obtain the marginal curve of y_1:

$$w_1(y_1) = g(y_1)\left\{1 + \frac{1}{6}Q_{30}(y_1^3 - 3y_1) + \frac{1}{24}Q_{40}(y_1^4 - 6y_1^2 + 3)\right\}.$$

Using the tetrachoric functions of which the k-th order is defined to be

$$k^{(y)} = \frac{1}{\sqrt{k!}}\left(-\frac{d}{dx}\right)^{k-1} g(y) = \frac{1}{\sqrt{k!}} g(y) \cdot H_{k-1}(y) \qquad (2\cdot 95)$$

where $H_{k-1}(y)$ is called the Hermite polynomial of the $(k-1)$-th order:

$$H_{k-1} = y^{k-1} - \frac{(k-1)(k-2)}{2\cdot 1} y^{k-3} + \frac{(k-1)(k-2)(k-3)(k-4)}{2\cdot 2!} y^{k-5} \text{etc.},$$

$$(2\cdot 95a)$$

we may write the marginal curve of y_1 as:

$$w_1 = \tau_1 + \frac{4}{\sqrt{24}} q_{30}\tau_4 + \frac{5}{\sqrt{120}}(q_{40} - 3)\tau_5.$$

Similarly, we have for marginal curve of y_2,

$$w_2 = \tau_1 + \frac{4}{\sqrt{24}} q_{03}\tau_4 + \frac{5}{\sqrt{120}}(q_{04} - 3)\tau_5.$$

The regression of y_1 on y_2 is of the form:

$$\bar{y}(1\cdot 2) = ry_2 + \frac{\frac{1}{2}(q_{12} - rq_{03})(y_2^2 - 1) + \frac{1}{6}(q_{31} - rq_{04})(y_2^3 - 3y_2)}{1 + \frac{1}{6}q_{03}(y^3 - 3y_2) + \frac{1}{24}(q_{04} - 3)(y_2^4 - 6y_2^2 + 3)}$$

$$= ry_2 + \frac{\sqrt{\frac{3}{2}}(q_{12} - rq_{03})\tau_3 + \frac{2}{3}(q_{12} - rq_{04})\tau_4}{w_2}$$

$$= ry_2 + \frac{U_2}{w_2}, \qquad (2\cdot 96a)$$

and the scedastic curve of y_1 on y_2 is

$$U(1\cdot 2) = (1 - r^2) - \frac{\sqrt{2}[r(q_{12} - rq_{03}) - (q_{21} - rq_{12})]\tau_2}{w_2}$$

$$+ \frac{\sqrt{6}\{r(q_{13} - rq_{04}) - \frac{1}{2}[q_{22} - r^2(q_{04} - 1) - 1]\}\tau_3}{w_2}$$

$$-\frac{\sqrt{\frac{3}{2}}(q_{12}-rq_{03})\tau_3 + \sqrt{\frac{2}{3}}(q_{13}-rq_{04})\tau_4}{w_2}$$

$$=(1-r^2)-\frac{V_2}{w_2}\left(\frac{U_2}{w_2}\right)^2. \qquad (2\cdot 96\text{b})\text{①}$$

Pearson gives two illustrations; namely, the distribution of trumps in 25 000 deals of whist and the distribution of contemporaneous barometric heights at Southampton and Landale. In both illustrations, the theoretical frequencies and contours are computed and constructed. It fits remarkably well the cancrine forms of the contours for the whist distribution. But the barometric distribution does not give such a good result: the observations, for one thing, seem bimodal. However, the goodness of fit test shows that the graduation is better than that obtained by Rhodes with his surface.

So far as theoretical validity is concerned, the fifteen-constant surface is far from being satisfactory. No basis for the selection of

$w=$ (normal cor. function)   (polynomial of the variates)

as a general correlation surface, is set forth by Pearson. And also there is no reason given as to why the polynomial should be of 4th order. The only defense for so assuming would lie in a demonstration that the polynomial consists of terms of a convergent, rather rapidly convergent, series so that the terms higher than the 4th order are negligible. To this end, Pearson gives a discussion② from a practical point of view and tends to conclude that the series is likely divergent and as a consequence the fifteen constant surface will not likely give highly satisfactory results, notwithstanding its fifteen momental identities. Furthermore, it is unwarranted to say that the fifteen constant surface will fit better than a surface with fewer constants for the same reason that, we cannot say without qualification that a curve with more constants will fit better to a uni-variate frequency distribution than a surface with fewer constants.

---

① A printer's error in the numerical coef. of the third term occurs as 3 for 6.

② The discussion is on the case of a single variate and the conclusion is generalized the bivariate case.

In fact, Pearson has expressed his surface in another form. Thus, if φ be normal correlation function of two variates and

$$\varphi_{hk} = \frac{\partial^{h+k}\varphi}{\partial y_1^h \partial y_2^k},$$

then, the equation (2 · 92) becomes

$$w = \varphi - \frac{1}{6}[q_{30}\varphi_{30} + 3q_{21}\varphi_{21} + 3q_{12}\varphi_{12} + q_{01}\varphi_{03}]$$
$$+ Q_{40}\varphi_{40} + Q_{31}\varphi_{31} + 3Q_{22}\varphi_{22} + Q_{13}\varphi_{13} + Q_{04}\varphi_{04}$$
$$= \varphi + \sum_{h+k}\sum_{3} A_{hk}\frac{\partial^{h+k}\varphi}{\partial y_1^h \partial y_2^k},$$

which is apparently identical to the correlation function of Type A. For this reason, one may surmise that Pearson borrowed the form of his fifteen constant surface from the Type A correlation function which has already been referred to in connection with the solid hypergeometrical series and will be fully discussed immediately.

2.26 The Correlation Function of Type A

While Pearson's unceasing efforts to solve the skew correlation problem have not given a quite satisfactory result, they have certainly aroused interest in different quarters and have continued to be an influential inspiration in the statistical world for making progress toward a complete and satisfactory solution. Ever since 1896, this urgent task has indeed been undertaken by a number of prominent mathematical statisticians of whom we may mention Edgeworth[1], Van der Stok[2], Charlier[3],

---

[1] Edgeworth, F. Y., "The Compound Law of Error", Phil. Mag., Vol.41, pp.207 – 217, 1896; "The Law of Error", Camb. Phil. Trans., Vol. 20, pp. 116 – 119, 1905; "On the Mathematical Representation of Statistical Data", Jour. Roy. Stat. Soc., Vol.80, pp.266 – 288, 1917; "Edgeworth's Contributions to Math. Stat.", Roy. Stat. Soc., London, 1928.

[2] Van der Stok, "On the Analysis of Frequency Curves according to a general method", Proc. Kon. Ak. V. Wet., Amsterdam, pp.799 – 817, 1907.

[3] Charlier, C. V. C., "Contributions to the Mathematical Theory of Statistics. The Cor. Func. of Type A", Akiv for Math. etc., Bd. 9, No.26, pp.1 – 18, 1914.

Jorgensen①, Wicksell②, Steffensen③, Van Uven④, Rhodes⑤, and Camp⑥. Their contributions together with those discussed above constitute the main developments in Skew Correlation Theory. But it is still far from completion. The validity and the applicability of the contribution of any of them depend upon whether the hypotheses underlying the deduction are likely realized in relation to the problems in statistics and whether the surfaces so deduced are adequate to represent the observed data.

Pretorius⑦ has examined the adequacy of the mathematical surfaces by testing the regression, scedastic, clitic, kurtic, and the marginal curves associated with them. On account of the scantiness of the material, the result cannot be expected to give a final conclusion, rather only a possibility. This kind of work is still much needed in the theory of correlation.

2.26.1 Edgeworth and the Scandinavian on the Type A and B Curves

Before proceeding to the development of the Type A correlation function, it may be advantageous to discuss briefly the case when the Type A function contains one variate.

Starting from the hypothesis of elementary errors, Charlier⑧ deduces two

---

① Jorgensen, N. R., Undersogelen over Frequency fladen og Korrelation Kobenhavn, Arnold Busck, 1916.

② Wicksell, S. D., "The Cor. Function of Type A, and the Regression of its Characteristics", Kungl. So. Vet. Akad. Handl., Bd. 58, No.3, pp.1−48, 1917; "The construction of the curves of equal frequency in case of type A correlation", Sv. Ak. Tid., pp.122−140, 1917; "Some Theorems in the Theory of Probability with Special reference to their importance in the theory of homograde correlation", Sv. Ak. Tid., pp.165−213, 1916; "The General Characteristics of the Frequency Function of Astronomiska Observatorium", Series II, No.12, 1915; "Multiple Cor. and Non-Linear Regression", Arkiv for Math. etc., Bd. 14, No.10, 1919.

③ Steffensen, J. F., "A Correlation Formula", Sk. Akt. Tid., 1922.

④ Van Uven, M. J., "On Treating Skew Correl", Proc. Kon. Ak. v. Wet., Amsterdam, Vol.28, No.8−9, pp.797−811, 1925; No.10, pp.919−935; Vol.29, No.4, pp.580−590, 1926; Vol.32, No.4, pp.408−413, 1929. "Skew Correlation between Three and More Variables", Proo. Kon. Ak. v. Wet., Vol.32, pp.793−807, 1929; No.7, pp.995−1007; No.8, pp.1085−1103.

⑤ Rhodes, E. C., "On a Certain Skew Cor. Surface", Biom., Vol.14, pp.355−377, 1922−1923; "On a Skew Cor. Surface", Biom., Vol.17, pp.314−326, 1925.

⑥ Camp, B. H., "Mutually Consistent Multiple Regression Surface", loc. cit.

⑦ Loc. cit.

⑧ For the work of Charlier on Type A and Type B functions see: Meddeland fran Lunds Astronomiska Observatorium, Series I, Nos. 25, 26, 27, 34, 43, 49, 50, 51, 52, 57, 58, 61, 66, 71, and Series II, Nos. 4, 8, 9, 14, Lund, 1905−1915.

generalized forms of frequency function, called respectively by him Type A and Type B. These two types may be written in the following forms:

Type A

$$w(x) = \varphi(x) + \sum_{k \geq 3} (-1)^k \frac{A_k}{k!} \frac{d^k \varphi(x)}{dx^k} \qquad (2 \cdot 97a)$$

where

$$\varphi(x) = \frac{1}{\sigma \sqrt{2x}} e^{-\frac{x^2}{2\sigma^2}}$$

$$A_k = \sigma \int_{-\infty}^{\infty} w(x) H_k(x) \, dx .$$

$H_k(x)$ is the Hermite polynomial $(2 \cdot 95)$, and $A_3 = p_3$, $A_4 = p_4 - 3p_2^2$, $A_5 = p_5 - 10p_3 p_2$, $A_6 = p_6 - 30p_2^3 - 15p_4 p_2$, and p_j is the j-th moment of $w(x)$.

Type B

$$w(x) = B_0 \psi_\lambda(x) + \sum_{k \geq 1} (-1)^k \frac{B_k}{k!} \Delta^k \psi_\lambda(x) \qquad (2 \cdot 97b)$$

where

$$\psi_\lambda(x) = \frac{e^{-\lambda}}{x} \int_0^x e^{\lambda \cos w} \cdot \cos(\lambda \sin w - xw) \, dw$$

$$= \frac{e^{-\lambda} \lambda^m}{m!},$$

which is the Poisson exponential for non-negative integral values of x, and where Δ^k denotes the k-th finite difference of $\psi_\lambda(x)$ with its first order equal to $\Delta \psi_\lambda(x) = \psi_\lambda(x) - \psi_\lambda(x-1)$. If the series $w(x)$ converges rapidly so that it may be broken off at $k=2$, we have for the values of the coefficients:

$$B_0 = 1, \ B_1 = 0, \ B_2 = \frac{1}{2}(p_2 - \lambda).$$

Charlier has also introduced in place of $\psi_\lambda(x)$ a more general function:

$$I_{\lambda\mu}(x) = \frac{e^{-\lambda}}{x} \int_0^x e^{\lambda \cos w} \cdot \cos(\mu \sin w - xw) \, dw . \qquad (2 \cdot 97c)$$

But Charlier confined his treatment to the function $\psi_\lambda(x)$ and determined the coefficients of B by an approximate method. The more general function $I_{\lambda\mu}(x)$

has been discussed by Jorgensen.① He finds the exact values of the coefficients and considers special cases of a linear transformation of the argument. But Steffensen② has shown that the moments

$$P_k = \int_{-\infty}^{\infty} I(x) x^k dx$$

are lacking.

Thus,

$$I(x) = \frac{e^{-\lambda}}{x} \int_0^x e^{\lambda \cos w} \cos(\mu \sin w - xw) dw$$

$$= e^{-2} \frac{\sin x}{xx} - \mu e^{-2\lambda} \frac{\sin xx}{xx} + \frac{f(x)}{x^3}$$

where the function $f(x)$ is finite for real values of x. Now the k-th moment is lacking, because

$$\int_{-\infty}^{-1} I(x) x^k dx, \int_{+1}^{+\infty} I(x) x^k dx$$

are, according to the above relation, decomposed into three integrals of which the first two are convergent but the third one is divergent.

"Indeed," as Wicksell③ has said, "at the present date there is not even any quite satisfactory theory of applications of B-functions available. The reason for this lies in the fact that… the integrals for the continuous moments of the B-function are indeterminate or generally even divergent…" For this reason, we shall not give a detailed account of the Type B correlation.

The Type A function of a single variate has been deduced by several other writers on the hypothesis of elementary errors of which Laplace was the originator. Among them, we shall particularly mention Edgeworth, for the reason that he was the first to show the order of magnitude of the characteristic coefficients by which we are enabled to know where the A series are to be broken off in order to get a certain degree of approximation. Thus, as mentioned

---

① "Note Sur la fonction de repartition de Type B de M. Charlier", Ark. for Math. etc., Bd.10, No.15, 1914, and also Op. Cit.

② Svenska Ak. Tid., No.4−5, 1916.

③ Wicksell, "On the Genetic Theory of Frequency", Ark. for Math. etc., Bd.12, No.20.

in connection with Laplace, Edgeworth assumes an error to be the resultant of a large number, s of error contributing sources which satisfy the following conditions:

(i) the selections from the different sources are independent of each other,

(ii) the chance of obtaining a particular magnitude from one source is independent of the previous selections,

(iii) $\dfrac{p_k}{\sigma^k}$ is finite for all values of k in the elementary groups.

On these assumptions the frequency functions of the resultant error is found to be

$$w(y) = e^{\sum_{k \geq 3}(-1)^k \frac{c_k \, d^k}{k! \, dy^k}} \varphi(y) \qquad (2 \cdot 98)$$

and the parameters C_k are shown in the following order of magnitude:

$$C_3 \text{ is of the order of magnitude } S^{-\frac{1}{2}}$$
$$C_4 \text{ is of the order of magnitude } S^{-1}$$
$$C_6 \text{ is of the order of magnitude } S^{-1}$$
$$C_5 \text{ is of the order of magnitude } S^{-\frac{3}{2}}$$
$$C_k \text{ is of the order of magnitude } S^{-\frac{k}{2}}.$$

Now S may be assumed to be a great number and C_6 happens to have the form

$$C_6 = \frac{C_3^2}{2} + \text{term of order } \frac{1}{S^2}$$

so that, to an approximation of the order S^{-1}, we have for the A-function of a univariate:

$$w(y) = \left\{ 1 - \frac{C_3}{3!} \frac{d^3}{dy^3} + \frac{C_4}{4!} \frac{d^4}{dy^4} + \frac{1}{2} \left(\frac{C_3}{3!} \right)^2 \frac{d^6}{dy^6} \right\} \varphi(y),$$

or, introducing the tetrachoric functions,

$$w(y) = \tau_1 + \sqrt{\frac{2}{3}} q_3 \tau_4 + \sqrt{\frac{5}{24}} (q_4 - 3) \tau_5 + \sqrt{\frac{35}{36}} q_3^2 \tau_7, \qquad (2 \cdot 98a)$$

which is not quite identical with $(2 \cdot 96)$. The relation between A_k and C_k is evidently $A_k = \sigma^k C_k$. Edgeworth extends his theory to two variates, but he does not investigate the order of magnitude and retains terms only involving moments up to the third order.

The order of magnitude of the characteristic coefficients A or C in the bivariate correlation function is investigated by Wicksell[①]. There are two possible cases: In one case the characteristic coefficients do not depend in their order of magnitude upon the number of error sources s and in the other case they do. For the former case the series may be broken off at A_4 while for the latter case the series should include the term A_6 or rather a part of A_6 as stated in (2·98) in order to obtain an approximation of the order $\dfrac{1}{s}$.

2.26.2 Charlier-Wicksell-Esscher on the Correlation Function of Type A

The correlation A-functions as deduced by Chartier have a genetic foundation which is provided by the hypothesis of elementary errors. According to this method in its most general form as we have seen the discussion in connection with Laplace, each variate (z), eventually reduced by a constant, may be considered as the result of the summation of an indeterminate, but large, number of elementary or contributory variates, the frequency functions of which it is not, however, necessary to know.

Let $t_1, t_2, \cdots, t_s$ be s contributory variates and let $f_1(t_1), f_2(t_2), \cdots, f_s(t_s)$ be their frequency functions. Let further z_1 and z_2 be two variates defined by the relations:

$$z_1 = k_1 t_1 + k_2 t_2 + \cdots + k_s t_s,$$
$$z_2 = l_1 t_1 + l_2 t_2 + \cdots + l_s t_s,$$

then the frequency function $F(z_1, z_2)$ is

$$F(z_1, z_2) = \frac{1}{(2x)^2} \int_{-\infty}^{\infty} \int dw_1 dw_2 X_1 X_2 \cdots X_s e^{-(z_1 w_1 + z_2 w_2)i}$$

where

$$X_j(w_1, w_2) = \int_{-\infty}^{\infty} dt f_j(t) e^{(k_j w_1 + l_j w_2)ti} = e^{\sum \frac{a_h^{(j)} (k_j w_1 + i_j w_2)^h i^h}{h!}} \quad (2 \cdot 99)$$

and $X(w_1, w_2) < 1$ for all real values of w_1 and w_2, but $X(0, 0) = 1$; and a_h are

---

① "The Correlation Function of Type A", loc. cit.

identical to the semi-invariants of Thiele.

Using the notation

$$a_{pq} = \sum_{j=1}^{s} a_{p+q}^{(i)} k_j^p l_j^q,$$

we then have

$$X_1 X_2 \cdots X_s = e^{(a_{10}w_1 i + a_{01}w_2 i) + \frac{1}{2!}[a_{20}(w_1 i)^2 + 2a_{11}(w_1 i)(w_2 i) + a_{02}(w_2 i)^2]}$$

$$\times\ e^{\frac{1}{3!}[a_{30}(w_1 i)^3 + 3a_{21}(w_1 i)^2 (w_2 i) + 3a_{12}(w_1 i)(w_2 i)^2 + a_{03}(w_2 i)^3]}$$

$$\times\ e^{\frac{1}{4!}[a_{40}(w_1 i)^4 + 4a_{31}(w_1 i)^3(w_2 i) + 6a_{22}(w_1 i)^2(w_2 i)^2 + 4a_{13}(w_1 i)(w_2 i)^3 + a_{04}(w_2 i)^4]}$$

etc.

Now if we put

$$e^{\frac{1}{3!}[a_{30}(w_1 i)^3 + 3a_{21}(w_1 i)^2(w_2 i) + 3a_{12}(w_1 i)(w_2 i)^2 + a_{03}(w_2 i)^3] + \cdots}$$

$$= 1 - (A_{30}w_1^3 + A_{21}w_1^2 w_2 + A_{03}w_2^3) + (A_{40}w_1^4 + A_{31}w_1^3 w_2$$
$$+ A_{22}w_1^2 w_2 + A_{22}w_1^2 w_2 + A_{13}w_1 w_2^3 + A_{04}w_2^4) - \cdots \quad (2 \cdot 100)$$

and

$$\varphi(z_1, z_2) = \frac{1}{(2x)^2} \int_{-\infty}^{\infty} \int dw_1 dw_2\, e^{-[(z_1 - a_{10})w_1 + (z_2 - a_{01})w_2]i}$$
$$- \frac{1}{2}[a_{20}w_1^2 + 2a_{11}w_1 w_2 + a_{02}w_2^2], \quad (2 \cdot 101)$$

it is seen that

$$F(z_1, z_2) = \varphi(z_1, z_2) + \sum_{h+k \geq 3} A_{hk} \frac{\partial^{h+k} \varphi}{\partial z_1^h \partial z_2^k}, \quad (2 \cdot 102)$$

which is the general form of bivariate correlation function of Type A. It can also be written in a symbolic form parallel to the univariate A-function:

$$F(z_1, z_2) = e^{-\frac{1}{3!}(a_{30}D_{30} + 3a_{21}D_{21} + 3a_{12}D_{12} + a_{03}D_{03}) + \frac{1}{4!}a_{40}D_{40} + \cdots} \varphi(z_1, z_2) \quad (2 \cdot 103)$$

where

$$D_{pq} = \frac{\partial^{p+q}}{\partial z_1^p \partial z_2^q}.$$

The expression $\varphi(z_1, z_2)$ through the reduction of the double integral as has already been shown in connection with the discussion of Laplace work, becomes

$$\varphi(z_1, z_2) = \frac{1}{2\pi\sqrt{a_{20}a_{02} - a_{11}^2}} e^{-\left[\frac{a_{02}(z_1-a_{10})^2 - 2a_{11}(z_1-a_{10})(z_2-a_{10}) + a_{20}(z_2-a_{01})^2}{2(a_{20}a_{02}-a_{11}^2)}\right]}.$$

$$(2 \cdot 104)$$

It will be convenient to write this generating function in the following way:

$$\varphi(z_1, z_2) = Je^{-\frac{1}{2}X} \qquad (2 \cdot 104a)$$

where

$$X = c_{20}(z_1 - b_1) + 2c_{11}(z_1 - b_1)(z_2 - b_2) + c_{02}(z_2 - b_2)^2.$$

The investigation given above can without essential modifications be directly generalized to an arbitrary number of variates. Thus, let $t_1, t_2, \cdots, t_s$ be variates with frequency functions of Type A; let $z_1, z_2, \cdots, z_m (m<s)$ be linear functions of $t_1, t_2, \cdots, t_s$; then the probability function for the simultaneous occurrence of $z_1, z_2, \cdots, z_m$ is

$$F(z, z, \cdots, z) = \varphi(z, z, \cdots, z) + \sum A_{k_1 k_2 \cdots k_m} \cdots D_{k_1 k_2 \cdots k_m} \varphi, \quad (2 \cdot 105)$$

where the generating function φ has the form

$$\varphi = Je^{-\frac{1}{2}X} \qquad (2 \cdot 106)$$

where

$$X = \sum c_{ij}(z_i - b_i)(z_j - b_j), \ i, j = 1, 2, \cdots, m.$$

The lowest order of the differential coefficient in right member of $(2 \cdot 105)$ is 3.

This is the solution for the problem: what is the general form of the Type A correlation function? The second problem to be solved now consists in the determination of the parameters; namely, the generating coefficients C_{ij} and the characteristic coefficients A_{hk} in terms of the moments.

The determination of the characteristic coefficients may formally be performed for any value of the generating coefficients, but the convergence is dependent on the choice of these parameters. For obtaining the expansion $(2 \cdot 105)$ or $(2 \cdot 102)$, we suppose that the values of the generating coefficients are chosen in such a manner that the terms after the first one vanish. Thus, we have the following conditions for determining the generating coefficients J, b_1, b_2, c_{20}, c_{11}, c_{02} in the case of two variates:

$$A_{10} = A_{01} = 0,$$
$$A_{20} = A_{11} = A_{02} = 0. \qquad (2 \cdot 107)$$

Moreover, we suppose that

$$\iint_{-\infty}^{+\infty} F(z_1, z_2) \, dz_1 dz_2 = 0$$

so that also

$$\iint_{-\infty}^{\infty} \varphi(z_1, z_2) \, dz_1 dz_2 = 1. \qquad (2 \cdot 108)$$

The generating coefficients so determined in terms of the moments are

$$b_1 = \bar{z}_1, \ b_2 = \bar{z}_2$$

$$c_{20} = \frac{1}{\sigma_1^2(1 - r^2)}$$

$$c_{02} = \frac{1}{\sigma_2^2(1 - r^2)}$$

$$c_{11} = -\frac{r}{\sigma_1 \sigma_2 (1 - r^2)} \qquad (2 \cdot 109)$$

and therefore, the generating function takes the form of bivariate normal correlation function:

$$\varphi(z_1, z_2) = \frac{1}{2\pi\sigma_1\sigma_2\sqrt{1-r^2}} e^{-\frac{1}{2(1-r^2)}\left\{\frac{(z_1-\bar{z}_1)^2}{\sigma_1^2} - \frac{2r(z_1-\bar{z}_1)(z_2-\bar{z}_2)}{\sigma_1\sigma_2} + \frac{(z_2-\bar{z}_2)^2}{\sigma_2^2}\right\}}.$$

$$(2 \cdot 110)$$

This conclusion holds for an arbitrary member of variates. Thus, the b's in the formulae $(2 \cdot 106)$ are respectively the means of the variates, the c's have the values of the parameters in a normal correlation function which as already given in $(2 \cdot 6)$ are

$$C_{ij} = \frac{M_{ij}}{M} \qquad (2 \cdot 111)$$

where M_{ij} is the cofactor of the ij-th element in the determinant $M = |m_{ij}|$ where m_{ij} is the second moment of the normal correlation function φ

$$m_{ij} = \iint \cdots \int (z_1 - \bar{z}_1)(z_2 - \bar{z}_2) \varphi \mathrm{d}z_1 \mathrm{d}z_2 \cdots \mathrm{d}z_m \qquad (2 \cdot 112)$$

and therefore, the generating function takes the form:

$$\varphi(z_1, z_2, \cdots z_m) = \frac{1}{(2x)^{\frac{m}{2}}\sqrt{M}} e^{-\frac{1}{2M}\sum M_{ij}(z_i - \bar{z}_i)(z_j - \bar{z}_j)}. \qquad (2 \cdot 113)$$

For purpose of simplicity, we may suppose the variates to be measured from their means and use the variates x_i in place of $z_i - \bar{z}_i$.

In practice and also in theory we may use the second moment p_{ij} of the observed frequency function F instead of the second moment m_{ij}, defined in $(2 \cdot 112)$ of the normal correlation function. This procedure is strictly allowable on account of the following equation:

$$\begin{aligned}p_{ij} &= \iint \cdots \int x_i x_j F \mathrm{d}x_1 x_2 \cdots \mathrm{d}x_m \\ &= \iint \cdots \int x_i x_j \varphi \mathrm{d}x_1 x_2 \cdots \mathrm{d}x_m = m_{ij}.\end{aligned} \qquad (2 \cdot 114)$$

However, it should not be assumed that the general relation between the moments of F and φ is given by

$$p_{abc\cdots l} = m_{abc\cdots l} + \sum A_{k_1 k_2 \cdots k_m}(-1)^{k_1 + k_2 + \cdots + k_m} \frac{a!b!\cdots l!}{(a-k_1)!\cdots(l-k_m)!} \qquad (2 \cdot 115)$$

because

$$\iint \cdots \int x_1^a x_2^b \cdots x_m^l D_{k_1 k_2 \cdots k_m} \varphi \mathrm{d}x_1 \mathrm{d}x_2 \cdots \mathrm{d}x_m$$
$$= (-1)^{k_1 + k_2 + \cdots k_m} \frac{a!b!\cdots l!}{(a-k_1)!(b-k_2)!\cdots(l-k_m)!} m(a-k_1)(b-k_2)\cdots(l-k_m)$$

when simultaneously $a\ k_1$, $b\ k_2$, $\cdots l\ k_m$. Whenever either $a\ k_1$, or $b\ k_2$, $\cdots$, $l\ k_m$ the integral becomes zero. As $m_{ab\cdots c} = 0$ when $a + b + \cdots + l$ is an odd number, we see that the integral also vanishes whenever $(a - k_1) + (b - k_2) + \cdots + (l - k_m)$ is an odd number.

The characteristic coefficients $A's$ have been determined for the bivariate A-function by Charlier and Wicksell, and for the general case of the multivariate A-function by Esscher.[1]

---

[1] Esscher, K. S. F., "Some General formulae in the Theory of Multiple Correlation", Ark for Math., etc., qd.15, No.19, 1920.

Introducing the reciprocal normal functions which are defined by

$$\varphi(x_1, x_2, \cdots, x_m) = \frac{\sqrt{C}}{(2\pi)^{\frac{m}{2}}} e^{-\frac{1}{2}\sum c_{ij} x_i x_j}, \quad C = |c_{ij}|$$

$$\psi(x_1, x_2, \cdots, x_m) = \frac{\sqrt{A}}{(2\pi)^{\frac{m}{2}}} e^{-\frac{1}{2}\sum a_{ij} x_i x_j}, \quad A = |a_{ij}| \quad (2 \cdot 116)$$

whose parameters are so related that

$$c_{ij} = \frac{A_{ij}}{A}, \quad a_{ij} = \frac{c_{ij}}{c} \quad (2 \cdot 117)$$

and making use of the Hermite polynomials H and G defined by

$$D_{k_1 k_2 \cdots k_m} \varphi = H_{k_1 k_2 \cdots k_m}(x_1, x_2, \cdots, x_m) \varphi(x_1, x_2, \cdots, x_m),$$
$$D_{k_1 k_2 \cdots k_m} \psi = G_{k_1 k_2 \cdots k_m}(x_1, x_2, \cdots, x_m) \psi(x_1, x_2, \cdots, x_m). \quad (2 \cdot 118)$$

The characteristic coefficients $A_{k_1 k_2 \cdots k_m}$ is given by

$$k_1! k_2! \cdots k_m A_{k_1 k_2 \cdots k_m} = \int\!\!\int_{-\infty}^{\infty}\!\!\cdots\!\int dx_1 dx_2 \cdots dx_m \cdot H_{k_1 k_2 \cdots k_m}(x_1 x_3 \cdots x_m) F_{(x_1 \cdots x_m)}$$

$$(2 \cdot 119)$$

where

$$x_i = \sum_{j=1}^{m} c_{ij} x_j .$$

As $H_{k_1 k_2 \cdots k_m}(x_1, x_2, \cdots, x_m)$ is found to be

$$H_{k_1 k_2 \cdots k_m}(x_1, x_2, \cdots, x_m)$$
$$= \sum_{r_1=1}^{k_1} \sum_{r_2=1}^{k_2} \cdots \sum_{r_m=1}^{k_m} (-1)^{\frac{[k]+[r]}{2}} \binom{k_1}{r_1}\binom{k_2}{r_2}\cdots\binom{k_m}{r_m} x_1^{r_1} x_2^{r_2} \cdots x_m^{r_m} m_{k_1-r_1 \cdots k_m-r_m}$$

$$(2 \cdot 120)$$

where $[k] = \sum_{i=1}^{m} k_i$, $[r] = \sum_i r_i$ and m denotes the moment of $\varphi(x_1, x_2, \cdots, x_m)$, we have

$$k_1! k_2! \cdots k_m! A_{k_1 k_2 \cdots k_m}$$
$$= \sum_{r_1} \sum_{r_2} \cdots \sum_{r_m} (-1)^{\frac{[k]+[r]}{2}} \binom{k_1}{r_1}\binom{k_2}{r_2}\cdots\binom{k_m}{r_m} m_{k_1-r_1 \cdots k_m-r_m} \cdot P_{r_1 r_2 \cdots r_m} .$$

$$(2 \cdot 121)$$

A formula which gives the characteristics $A_{k_1 k_2 \cdots k_m}$ as a function of the m- and p-

moments. From $(2 \cdot 115)$, all the m-moments may be expressed by means of the p-moments. The first four orders of m-moments in terms of p are:

$$m_{200\cdots 0} = p_{2000\cdots 0}$$
$$m_{1100\cdots 0} = p_{1100\cdots 0}$$
$$m_{400\cdots 0} = 3p^2_{2000\cdots 0}$$
$$m_{3100\cdots 0} = 3p_{200\cdots 0}p_{1100\cdots 0}$$
$$m_{2200\cdots 0} = p_{200\cdots 0}p_{0200\cdots 0} + 2p^2_{1100\cdots 0}$$
$$m_{2110\cdots 0} = p_{200\cdots 0}p_{0110\cdots 0} + 2p_{1100\cdots 0}p_{1010\cdots 0}$$
$$m_{11110\cdots 0} = p_{1100\cdots 0}p_{0011\cdots 0} + p_{1010\cdots 0}p_{0101\cdots 0}$$
$$+ p_{0110\cdots 0}p_{1001\cdots 0}. \qquad (2 \cdot 122)$$

Using these values, we get the form from $(2 \cdot 121)$ the following values of the A-characteristics of the third and fourth order in terms of p's

$$3! \quad A_{3000\cdots 0} = - p_{3000\cdots 0}$$
$$2! \quad A_{2100\cdots 0} = - p_{2100\cdots 0}$$
$$\quad\quad A_{11110\cdots 0} = - p_{1110\cdots 0}$$
$$4! \quad A_{4000\cdots 0} = p_{4000\cdots 0} - 3p^2_{200\cdots 0}$$
$$3! \quad A_{3100\cdots 0} = p_{3100\cdots 0} - 3p_{2000\cdots 0}p_{1100\cdots 0}$$
$$2!2! \quad A_{22000\cdots 0} = p_{2200\cdots 0} - 2p^2_{1100\cdots 0} - p_{2000\cdots 0}p_{02000\cdots 0}$$
$$2! \quad A_{2110\cdots 0} = p_{2100\cdots 0} - 2p_{1100\cdots 0}p_{1010\cdots 0} - p_{2000\cdots 0}p_{0110\cdots 0}$$
$$\quad\quad A_{1111\cdots 0} = p_{11110\cdots 0} - p_{1100\cdots 0}p_{0011\cdots 0} - p_{1010\cdots 0}p_{0101\cdots 0}$$
$$- p_{0110\cdots 0}p_{1001\cdots 0}. \qquad (2 \cdot 123)$$

Any other characteristics of the third and fourth order are obtained by permutation of indices.

When the variates are expressed in their respective dispersions as units, the correlation function is given by

$$F(y_1, y_2, \cdots, y_m) = \varphi(y_1, y_2, \cdots, y_m) + \sum_{[k]_3} \beta_{k_1 k_2 \cdots k_m} D_{k_1 \cdots k_m} \varphi(y_1 \cdots y_m)$$
$$(2 \cdot 124)$$

where the generating parameters in $(2 \cdot 124)$ are given by

$$c_{ij} = \frac{R_{ij}}{R}$$

where $R = |r_{ij}|$ and $r_{ij} = \dfrac{P_{ij}}{\sqrt{P_{ii}P_{jj}}}$, which is the corresponding coefficient between y_i, y_j, and the β-characteristics are given by

$$\beta_{k_1 k_2 \cdots k_m} = \frac{A_{k_1 k_2 \cdots k_m}}{\sigma_1^{k_1} \sigma_2^{k_2} \cdots \sigma_m^{k_m}} \qquad (2\cdot125)$$

where σ_i is the standard deviation of the variate x_i.

The characteristic properties of the surface constitute the criteria when the surface may be applied. So long as the method of fitting frequency curves, we are justified to take the partial moment curves as the practical criteria for applying the surface.

The n-th partial moment curve obtained by plotting out the n-th moment of the arrays of x_m against the other variates is called the n-th regression curve of x_m on the others. In mathematical equations it may be defined by

$$\theta[m^n \cdot 12\cdots(m-1)] = \int_{-\infty}^{\infty} y_m^n F(y_1, y_2, \cdots, y_m)\,dy_m$$

$$: \int_{-\infty}^{\infty} F(y_1, \cdots, y_m)\,dy_m. \qquad (2\cdot126)$$

Using the notation

$$I^{(n)} = \int_{-\infty}^{\infty} y_m^n \varphi(y_1 \cdots y_m)\,dy_m \qquad (2\cdot127)$$

we get for the regression formula:

$$\theta[m^n \cdot 12\cdots(m-1)] = \Big\{ I^{(n)} + \sum_{k_1} \sum_{k_2} \cdots \beta_{k_1 k_2 \cdots k_m}(-1)^{k_1}$$

$$\cdot \frac{n!}{(n-k_1)!} D_{k_2 k_3 \cdots k_m} I^{(n-k_1)} \Big\}$$

$$: \Big\{ I^0 + \sum_{k_1} \sum_{\substack{k_2 \\ k \geq 3}} \cdots \sum_{k_m} \beta_{0 k_2 \cdots k_m} D_{k_2 k_3 \cdots k_m} I^0 \Big\}$$

$$(2\cdot128)$$

where $k = k_1 + k_2 + \cdots + k_m$.

Let

$$I^0 = \int_{-\infty}^{\infty} dy_m \varphi(y_1, y_2, \cdots, y_m) = \varphi_{m-1}(y_1, y_2, \cdots, y_{m-1}), \qquad (2\cdot129)$$

which is the normal function of $(m-1)$ variates. The general expression for $I^{(n)}$ is found to be

$$I^{(n)} = \sum_{t=0}^{n} (-1)^t \binom{n}{t} \frac{m(n-t), 0, \cdots, 0}{\sigma_1^{(n-t)}} \cdot$$

$$\left(\sum_{j=1}^{m-1} r_{mj} \frac{\partial}{\partial y_j} \right) \varphi_{m-1}(y_1, y_2, \cdots, y_{m-1}) \qquad (2 \cdot 130)$$

since

$$\frac{m(n-t), 0, \cdots, 0}{\sigma_1^{(n-t)}} = \begin{cases} 0 & \text{when } n-t \text{ is odd,} \\ \dfrac{(n-t)!}{\left(\dfrac{n-t}{2}\right)! 2^{\frac{n-t}{2}}} & \text{when } (n-t) \text{ is even,} \end{cases}$$

we distinguish between the two cases when n is even and n is odd:

$$I^{(2n)} = \sum_{t=0}^{n} \frac{(2n)!}{(2t)!(n-t)!2^{n-t}} \left(\sum_{j=1}^{m-1} r_{mj} \frac{\partial}{\partial y_j} \right)^{2t} \varphi_{m-1}(y_1, y_2, \cdots, y_{m-1})$$

$$(2 \cdot 130a)$$

$$I^{(2n+1)} = \sum_{t=0}^{n} \frac{(2n+1)!}{(2t+1)!(n-t)!2^{n-t}} \left(\sum_{j=1}^{m-1} r_{mj} \frac{\partial}{\partial y_j} \right)^{2t+1} \varphi_{m-1}(y_1, y_2, \cdots, y_{m-1}) \cdot$$

$$(2 \cdot 130b)$$

For the case of two variates, i. e., $m=2$, we have:

(i) $n=1$, the regression curve of means,

$$\bar{y}_{2 \cdot 1} = \theta(2^1 \cdot 1) = \frac{ry_1 - r\beta_{30} H_4(y_1) - \beta_{21} H_2(y_1) - r\beta_{40} H_5(y) - \beta_{31} H_3(y)}{1 + \beta_{30} H_3(y_1) + \beta_{40} H_4(y_1)} \cdot$$

(ii) $n=2$, the regression curve of variances,

$$\theta(2^2 \cdot 1) = \{1 + r^2 H_2(y_1) + \beta_{30}[H_3(y_1) + r^2 H_5(y_1)] + \beta_{40}[H_4(y_1) + r^2 H_6(y_1)] + 2\beta_{21} r H_3(y_1) + 2\beta_{31} r H_4(y_1) + 2\beta_{12} H_1(y_1) + 2\beta_{22} H_2(y_1)\} \div$$
$$[1 + \beta_{30} H_3(y_1) + \beta_{40} H_4(y_1)] \cdot$$

These two equations expressed in tetrachoric functions have also been given by Pearson in his fifteen constant frequency function.

(iii) $n=3$, the regression curve of the 3rd order,

$$\theta(2^3 \cdot 1) = \{-3rH_1(y_1) - r^3H_3(y_1) - \beta_{30}[3rH_4(y_1) + r^3H_6(y_1)]$$
$$- \beta_{40}[3rH_5(y_1) + r^3H_7(y_1)] - 3\beta_{21}[H_2(y_1) + r^2H_4(y_1)]$$
$$- 3\beta_{31}[H_3(y_1) + r^2H_5(y_1)] - 6r\beta_{12}H_2(y_1) - 6r\beta_{22}H_3(y_1)$$
$$- 6\beta_{03} - 6\beta_{13}H_1(y_1)\} : [1 + \beta_{30}H_3(y_1) + \beta_{40}H_4(y_1)].$$

(iv) for $n = 4$, the regression of the 4th order,

$$\theta(2^4 \cdot 1) = \{3 + 6r^2H_2(y_1) + r^4H_4(y_1) + \beta_{03}24rH_1(y_1)$$
$$+ \beta_{12}12[H_1(y_1) + r^2H_3(y_1)] + \beta_{21}[12rH_3(y_1) + 4r^3H_5(y_1)]$$
$$+ \beta_{30}[3H_3(y_1) + 6r^2H_5(y_1) + r^4H_7(y_1)] + 24\beta_{04}$$
$$+ \beta_{13}24rH_2(y_1) + \beta_{22}12[H_2(y_1) + r^2H_4(y_1)]$$
$$+ \beta_{31}[12rH_4(y_1) + 4r^3H_6(y_1)] + \beta_{40}[3H_3(y_1)$$
$$+ 6r^2H_6(y_1) + r^4H_8(y_1)]\} : [1 + \beta_{30}H_3(y_1) + \beta_{40}H_4(y_1)].$$

And the marginal frequency curve of y_1 in this case is given by

$$w_1 = 0(2^0 \cdot 1) = \varphi(y_1) + \beta_{30}\varphi'''(y_1) + \beta^{(iv)}(y_1).$$

These regression curves of various orders may be directly constructed. The characteristic coefficients as defined by $(2 \cdot 125)$ and $(2 \cdot 123)$ are found from the moments of the observed date, and a table of $H_n(y)$ has been provided by Wicksell[1] to facilitate the computation for the values of y in the interval $-3 \cdot 5$ to $+3 \cdot 5$. The curves will be applicable within the whole range where the correlation A-function is applicable. Nevertheless, it will very seldom be of any practical use to construct the regression curves further than to $3 \cdot 5$ times the dispersion reckoned from the mean, because the number of terms included in the formulae will generally not be enough to give a sufficient degree of approximation when $|y| > 3 \cdot 5$.

When the correlation surface is not very considerably skew, the regression equations of the various orders may be transformed into other forms which are somewhat easier to handle numerically. Wicksell has inverted the denominator and developed the regression function into a power series of $\beta_{30}H_3(y_1) + \beta_{40}H_4(y_1)$ and found that this series will be convergent so long as the denominator does not become zero or exceed 2. The resulting expressions

---

[1] "Correlation Function of Type A", p.24, loc. cit.

arranged according to powers of y show that the first regression is cubic and becomes linear when the correlation coefficients of 3rd and 4th order are zero:

$$r(1^3 2^0) = \beta_{21} - 3r\beta_{30} = 0, \ r(1^0 2^3) = \beta_{12} - 3r\beta_{03} = 0;$$
$$r(1^4 2^0) = \beta_{31} - 4r\beta_{40} = 0, \ r(1^0 2^4) = \beta_{13} - 4r\beta_{04} = 0;$$

that the second regression is parabolic; that the third e regression is linear, and that the fourth regression disappears.

But in common practice the scedastic, clitic, and kurtic curves, instead of the second, third, and fourth regressions, are considered as the basic characteristics.

Let $\nu[m^n \cdot \overline{123\cdots(m-1)}]$ be the n-th array moments of x_m about their array means. Then the scedasticity skewness, and kurtosis of arrays are respectively proportional to

$$\nu[m^2 \cdot \overline{12\cdots(m-1)}] = \theta[m^2 \cdot \overline{123\cdots(m-1)}] - \theta^2[m^1 \cdot \overline{123\cdots m-1}]$$
$$\nu(m^3 \cdot \overline{12\cdots m-1}) = \theta(m^3 \cdot \overline{123\cdots m-1}) - 3\nu(m^2 \cdot \overline{12\cdots m-1})$$
$$- \theta^3(m^1 \cdot \overline{12\cdots m-1})$$
$$\nu(m^4 \cdot \overline{123\cdots m-1}) - 3\nu^2(m^2 \cdot \overline{12\cdots m-1}) = \delta(m \cdot \overline{123\cdots m-1}).$$
$$(2 \cdot 131)$$

In order to obtain the scedastic, clitic, and kurtic curves, it is needful to have expressions for ν's which may be derived from the θ's through the following relations:

$$\nu(m^2 \cdot \overline{123\cdots m-1}) = \theta(m^2 \cdot \overline{12\cdots m-1}) - \theta(m^1 \cdot \overline{12\cdots m-1})$$
$$\nu(m^4 \cdot \overline{12\cdots m-1}) = \theta(m^4 \cdot \overline{12\cdots m-1})$$
$$- 4\nu(m^3 \cdot \overline{12\cdots m-1})\theta(m^1 \cdot \overline{12\cdots m-1})$$
$$- 6\nu(m^2 \cdot \overline{12\cdots m-1})\theta^2(m^1 \cdot \overline{12\cdots m-1}) - \theta^4(m^1 \cdot \overline{12\cdots m-1}),$$

which are the ordinary relations between the moments about the mean and any other arbitrary origin.

Expressed in tetrachoric functions, defined in $(2 \cdot 95)$, of which the values may be found in Pearson's Tables for Statisticians and Biometricians, we have for the case of $m=2$:

(i) The marginal curve when $n=0$,

$$\theta(2^0 \cdot 1) = w_1(y_1) = \tau_1 + \sqrt{\frac{2}{3}} q_{30} \tau_4 . \qquad (2\cdot 131\text{a})$$

(ii) The regression of y_2 on y_1 when $n=1$,

$$\theta(2^1 \cdot 1) = ry_1 + \left\{ \sqrt{\frac{3}{2}} (q_{21} - rq_{30}) \tau_3 + \sqrt{\frac{2}{3}} (q_{21} - rq_{40}) \tau_4 \right\} : w_1(y_1)$$

$$= ry_1 + U_1 / w_1(y_1) . \qquad (2 \cdot 131\text{b})$$

(iii) The array scedasticity when $n=2$,

$$\nu(2^2 \cdot 1) = (1-r^2) - U_1^2 : w_1^2 + \left\{ \sqrt{2} [r(q_{21} - rq_{30}) - (q_{12} - rq_{21})] \tau_2 \right.$$

$$\left. + \sqrt{6} \left[r(q_{31} - rq_{40}) - \frac{1}{2}(q_{22} - 1 - r^2) q_{40} - 1 \right] \tau_3 \right\} : w_1$$

$$= (1-r^2) - U_1^2 : w_1^2 - v_1 : w_1 . \qquad (2 \cdot 131\text{c})$$

(iv) The third array moment about mean when $n=3$,

$$\nu(2^3 \cdot 1) = 3U_1 V_1/w_1^2 + 2U_1^3 + w_1^3 + \{[q_{03} - r^3 q_{30} - 3r(q_{12} - rq_{21})]\tau_1$$

$$+ 6\sqrt{2}[Q_{13} - 6rQ_{22} + 3rQ_{31} + 4r^3 Q_{40}] \cdot \tau_2\}$$

$$: w_1 = 3U_1 V_1/w_1^2 + 2U_1^3/w_1^3 + X_1 / w_1 . \qquad (2 \cdot 131\text{d})$$

(v) The fourth array moment about the array mean,

$$\nu(2^4 \cdot 1) = 3(1-r^2)^2 + (q_{04} - 3)(1 - 4r^2) - 3r^4(q_{40} - 3)$$

$$+ 6r^2(q_{22} - 1 - 2r^2) - 4r(q_{13} - rq_{04}) - 4r^3(q_{31} - rq_{40})\tau_1$$

$$: w_1 - 6(1-r^2) V_1/w_1 + U_1^2/w_1^2 - 4U_1 X_1/w_1^2 - 6U_1^2 V_1/w_1^3$$

$$- 3U_1^3 w_1^3 = 3(1-r^2)^2 + Y_1/w_1 - 6(1-r^2) V_1/w_1 + U_1^2/w_1^2$$

$$- 4U_1 X_1/w_1^2 - 6U_1^2 V_1/w_1^3 - 3U_1^3/w_1^3 \qquad (2 \cdot 131\text{e})$$

where q_{hk} are moments defined in $(2 \cdot 93)$.

When the correlation is moderately skew and the denominator of the regressions are expanded, as already indicated above, in powers series and arranged according to powers of y_1, then they become approximately

$$\nu(2^1 \cdot 1) = \beta_{21} - 3r\beta_{30} + y_1[r - 3(\beta_{31} - 4r\beta_{40})] - y_1^2(\beta_{21} - 3r\beta_{30})$$

$$+ y_1^3(\beta_{31} - 4r\beta_{40})$$

$$\nu(2^2 \cdot 1) = 1 - r^2 - 2\beta_{22} + 6r\beta_{31} - 12r^2\beta_{40} - y_1(2\beta_{12} - 4r\beta_{21} + 6r\beta_{30})$$
$$+ y_1(2\beta_{22} - 6r\beta_{31} + 12r^2\beta_{40})$$
$$\nu(2^3 \cdot 1) = -6\beta_{03} + 6r\beta_{12} - 6r^2\beta_{21} + 6r^3\beta_{30} + y_1(6\beta_{13} - 12r\beta_{22} + 18r^2\beta_{31} - 24r^3\beta_{40})$$
$$\nu(2^4 \cdot 1) = 3 + 24\beta_{04} - 12\beta_{22} - 6r^2 + 3r^4 + 36r\beta_{31} - 24r\beta_{13} + 36r^2\beta_{22}$$
$$- 72r^2\beta_{40} - 60r^3\beta_{31} + 96r^4\beta_{40} - y_1(12\beta_{12} - 24r\beta_{21} - 12r^2\beta_{12}$$
$$+ 36r^2\beta_{30} + 24r^3\beta_{21} - 36r^4\beta_{30}) + y_1^2(12\beta_{22} - 36r\beta_{31} - 12r^2\beta_2$$
$$+ 72r^2\beta_{40} + 36r^3\beta_{31} - 72r^4\beta_{40}). \qquad (2 \cdot 131f)$$

From these moments the clitic and kurtic curves can easily be obtained.

The curves of equal frequency of bivariate Type A correlation have been investigated by Wicksell. The equations of these curves are obtained by putting $F(y_1, y_2) = $ constant.

If the system of coordinates is rotated about the centroid though an angle θ given by

$$\tan 2\theta = \frac{2r_1\sigma_1\sigma_2}{\sigma_1^2 - \sigma_2^2},$$

then the A function may be written in the form

$$F'(\xi', \eta') = \frac{1}{\sqrt{2x}} e^{-\frac{\xi'^2}{2}} \cdot \frac{1}{\sqrt{2x}} e^{-\frac{\eta'^2}{2}} \{1 + \sum \beta_{ij} R_i(\xi') R_j(\eta')\}$$

where ξ', η' are new normal coordinates after rotation and $R_i(\xi')$ is the Hermite polynomial of i-th order.

Neglecting the powers of the sum $\sum_{ij} R_i(\xi') R_j(\eta')$ which is allowed when the correlation is moderately skew, we may put

$$1 + \sum \beta_{ij} R_i(\xi') R_j(\eta') = e^{\sum \beta_{ij} R(\xi') R(\eta')}$$

and the equations of equal frequency curves are

$$F'(\xi', \eta') = C' = \frac{1}{2x} e^{-\frac{1}{2}\xi'^2 + \eta'^2 - 2\sum \beta_{ij} R_i(\xi') R_j(\eta')}$$

or,

$$\rho^2 = \xi'^2 + \eta'^2 - 2\sum \beta_{ij} R_i(\xi') R_j(\eta') \qquad (2 \cdot 132)$$

where

$$\rho^2 = -2 \log 2xC'.$$

If we put

$$\xi'^2 + \eta'^2 = R^2, \qquad (2 \cdot 133)$$

R will be the radius vector of the curve equal frequency, making use of the circle:

$$\rho^2 = \xi_1'^2 + \eta_1'^2, \qquad (2 \cdot 134)$$

we may, when ρ is not small, insert the coordinates of this circle in the terms multiplied with the β_{ij} in $(2 \cdot 132)$.

Thus, we have with fair approximation

$$R^2 - \rho^2 = 2 \sum_{i+j \geq 3} \beta_{ij} R_i(\xi_1') R_j(\eta_1'). \qquad (2 \cdot 135)$$

When the β_{ij}' are small we may put

$$\Delta_\rho = \frac{\sum \beta_{ij} R_i(\xi_1') R_j(\eta_1')}{\rho}. \qquad (2 \cdot 136)$$

Here Δ_ρ are the quantities to be added to the radial vectors of the circle $(2 \cdot 134)$ in order that the radii of the curves of equal frequency be obtained.

The method of constructing the curves of equal frequency will now be: First the circle $(2 \cdot 134)$ is drawn. A number of radii vectors to the circle are drawn at equal angels. The coordinates (ξ_1', η_1') where the radii cut the circle are inserted in the polynomials $R_i(\xi_1')$ and $R_i(\eta_1')$. Now Δ_ρ is found from $(2 \cdot 136)$ and if it be added to the corresponding radius of the circle, we get a point and the points thus constructed are then joined by a smooth line. The abscissa ξ' of this curve is multiplied by σ_1' and the ordinates η' by σ_2'. The pairs of coordinates thus obtained are plotted out and a curve laid though the points. We then get a curve of equal frequency in the $x'y'$-plane. To facilitate the work, Wicksell gives at the end of the paper, a table of the values of $R_i(\xi_1') \cdot R_j(\eta_1')$ for $i+j=3$ and 4 in the points where the circles for which $\rho=1$, $1 \cdot 5$, 2, $2 \cdot 5$ are intersected by a system of 24 radii at $15°$ angles. The angle of any radius with the ξ'-axis is called a.

We thus see that the curves of equal frequency in case of type A correlation are disturbed ellipses with their center in the point $x = m_1$, $y = m_2$ (m_1 and m_2 are the means). These curves will be valid as far out in the xy-plane as the A-function is valid and as far as the square of the sum $\sum \beta'_{ij} R_i(\xi') R_j(\eta')$ can be neglected.

For small values of ρ, that is for large frequencies, the method given above can, however, not be used. The equal frequency curves are given according to Wicksell by the circles

$$\rho^2 + 2E = (\xi' - \delta_\xi)^2 + (\eta' - \delta_{\eta'})^2.$$

Here $E = 3\beta'_{40} + \beta'_{22} + 3\beta'_{04}$ is the total excess of the correlation surface. Multiplying the abscissa of (ξ') by σ'_1 and the ordinate η' by σ'_2 we find the equation

$$\rho^2 + 2E = \frac{(x' - \delta_{x'})^2}{\sigma'^2_1} + \frac{(y' - \delta_{y'})^2}{\sigma'^2_2}.$$

Here $\delta_{x'}$ and $\delta_{y'}$ are coordinates of the mode in the $x'y'$-plane. They are

$$\delta_{x'} = m'_1 + \sigma'_1(3\beta_{30} + \beta_{12}),$$
$$\delta_{y'} = m'_2 + \sigma'_2(3\beta_{03} + \beta_{21}).$$

Hence, we see that in the vicinity of the mode, the curves of equal frequency are ellipses with their center in the mode. According to the previous result the frequency in the rest of the xy-plane, say beyond $\rho = 1$ are disturbed ellipses with their center in the mean. Of course, they may also here be regarded as disturbed ellipses with their center in the mode.

Wicksell illustrates the method with two examples. The first example is the correlation between weight of new-born boy and weight of placenta. There are 1 223 cases in all. The second example is the correlation between the number of trumps on the first two hands in whist recorded by Pearson. But he did not compare the actual with the computed contours so that we are not able to judge as to the goodness of it.

2.26.3 Van der Stoke on A-Function

It is seen now that the correlation A functions as developed by Charlier are entirely based upon the premises of the theory of probability and a generalization in the use of definite integrals. Furthermore, the development seems to be the method indicated for frequency distributions with indefinite limits. Now we shall see how the A function has been developed by Van der Stoke from another point of view without any appeal to the general law of probability.

The method of development used by Van der Stoke is based on the following premises:

(i) The frequency function shall be in series form.

(ii) The series takes place according to polynomial of an ascending degree.

(iii) For the determination of the constants, the calculation of means (moments) of different orders is used, in relation to an origin favorably selected according to the requirements of the various cases.

Van der Stoke classifies the distributions of statistical data into three classes according to

Class i, the frequencies between definite limits.

Class ii, the frequencies between a definite limit on one side and an infinite limit on the other.

Class iii, the frequencies between the infinite limits $\pm\infty$.

And has deduced a frequency function for each class on the basis of the above-mentioned premises.

For the representation of the frequency distribution of class i, he takes the series

$$u = A_0 Q_0 + A_1 Q_1 + A_2 Q_2 + \cdots \qquad (2 \cdot 137)$$

where Q_n represents a polynomial of n-th degree, and is assumed to be of the form:

$$Q_n = x^n + a_1 x^{n-1} + a_2 x^{n-2} + \cdots + a_n.$$

In order to determine the A-coefficients in a finite form, the unique and sufficient condition is that the a-coefficients be determined so that the condition

$$\int Q_n x^m dx = 0 \qquad (2 \cdot 138)$$

is satisfied for all values of m n. Thus, by taking $m = 0, 1, 2, \cdots, (n-1)$, we obtain n equations for solving the n constants $a_0, a_1, \cdots, a_n$. If the origin be conveniently taken at the mean, as then, on integrating between the limits, all odd terms vanish, we find for the general expression of the polynomial:

$$Q_n = x^n - \frac{n(n-1)}{2 \cdot (2n-1)} x^{n-2} + \frac{n(n-1)(n-2)(n-3)}{2 \cdot 4 \cdot (2n-1)(2n-3)} x^{n-4} + \cdots$$

$$(2 \cdot 139)$$

It is evident from $(2 \cdot 139)$ that

$$\int Q_m Q_n dx = 0$$

for all values of m different from n and, further, that

$$A_n = B \int u Q_n dx$$

where

$$B^{-1} = \int Q_n Q_n dx = \int Q_n x^n dx = \frac{2^{2n+1}(n!)^4}{(2n+1)!(2n)!}.$$

If the moments of different order are denoted by

$$P_u = \int u x^n dx,$$

we find

$$A_n = B \left\{ P_n - \frac{n(n-1)}{2 \cdot (2n-1)} P_{n-2} + \frac{n(n-1)(n-2)(n-3)}{2 \cdot 4 \cdot (2n-1)(2n-3)} P_{n-4} - \cdots \right\}.$$

For the representation of the frequency distribution of class ii, he simply multiplies the series $(2 \cdot 137)$ by a suitable factor e^{-x} which satisfies the bounding limits of the distribution: zero for the smallest and infinite for the largest. Thus, the equation of frequency becomes

$$u = e^{-x}(A_0 Q_0 + A_1 Q_1 + \cdots).$$

The conditions to be satisfied by the a-coefficients are then

$$\int e^{-x} Q_n x^m = 0$$

for all values of m n.

And Q_n and A_n are found to be:

$$Q_n = x^n - \frac{n^2}{1!}x^{n-1} + \frac{n^2(n-1)^2}{n!2!}x^{n-2} - \cdots + (-1)^n n!$$

$$A_n = \frac{P_n}{(n!)^2} - \frac{n}{1!\,n!(n-1)!}P_{n-1} + \frac{n(n-1)}{2!}\frac{P_{n-2}}{n!(n-2)!} - \cdots (-1)^n \frac{1}{n!}.$$

For the distribution of class iii, he takes e^{-x^2} for the factor by which the limits are determined and takes the origin at the mean so that the polynomial can be separated into even and odd functions, because then, on integrating between the limits, the odd functions vanish.

The series becomes then

$$u = e^{-x^2}\{A_0 Q_0 + A_2 U_2 + A_3 U_3 + \cdots\}.$$

The conditional equation for the determination of the a-coefficients is

$$\int x^m Q_n e^{-x^2} = 0 \qquad \text{for all } m<n,$$

The polynomial and the A-coefficients are found to be

$$Q_n = x^n - \frac{n(n-1)}{2^2 \cdot 1!}x^{n-2} + \frac{n(n-1)(n-2)(n-3)}{2^4 \cdot 2!}x^{n-4} + \cdots$$

$$A_n = B\int_{-\infty}^{\infty} uU_n dx, \quad B^{-1} = \int_{-\infty}^{\infty} e^{-x^2}Q_n Q_n dx = \frac{n!}{2^n}\sqrt{x}$$

or

$$A_n = \frac{2^n}{x}\left\{\frac{P_n}{n!} - \frac{P_{n-2}}{2^2 \cdot 1!(n-2)!} + \frac{P_{n-4}}{2^4 \cdot 2!(n-4)!} - \cdots\right\}.$$

According to Van der Stoke, the extension of this treatment to two dimensions offers no difficulties as, in calculating the means of different order, the two variables (projected upon two axes arbitrarily chosen) can always be separated and the method remains in all other respects quite the same. Only instead of one mean of each order, we can now dispose of $p+1$ means of order p. Thus, if by R_n be denoted the same function of y as Q_n is of x, the equation of the surface in case of distribution of class iii assumes the form

$$w(x, y) = e^{-x^2-y^2}\{A_0 + A_{10}Q_1 + A_{01}R_1 + A_{20}Q_2 + A_{11}Q_1R_1 + A_{02}R_2 + A_{30}Q_3 + A_{21}Q_2R_1 + \cdots\}$$

The general expression for the polynomial is

$$Q_nR_m$$

and as, evidently

$$\int_{-\infty}^{\infty}\int e^{-x^2-y^2}(Q_nR_m)(Q_{n'}R_{m'})\,dxdy = 0$$

for all values of n' different from n and of m' from m, we find for the A-coefficient:

$$A_{nm} = B\int_{-\infty}^{\infty}\int e^{-x^2-y^2}(Q_nR_m)^2\,dxdy = \frac{n!m!}{2^{n+m}}x .$$

If the origin is conveniently taken at the means, then the terms with coefficients A_{10} to A_{01} vanish from (2 · 140).

If we wish to alter the scale values according to the nature of the date, we have to write everywhere, hx and ky, instead of x and y, whence

$$B^{-1} = \frac{n!m!}{2^{n+m}}\frac{x}{hk} .$$

The scale factors h and k can then be determined by putting

$$A_{20} = A_{02} = 0$$

and the second power moments can be disposed of for the determination of these constants:

$$p_{20} = \frac{1}{2h^2}, \quad p_{02} = \frac{1}{2k^2} .$$

The series now becomes

$$w(hx, ky) = e^{-h^2x^2-k^2y^2}\{A_0 + A_{11}Q_1(hx)R_1(ky) + A_3Q_3(hx), + \cdots\} .$$

(2 · 140)

He further points out that if the system is rotated about the origin so that they coincide with the principal axes of inertia, then, also A_{11} has to be put equal to zero and the frequency surface now becomes

$$w(x', y') = e^{-x'^2-y'^2}\{A_0 + A_{30}Q_3 + A_2Q_2R_1 + A_{12}Q_1R_2 + A_{03}R_3 + \cdots\}$$

$$(2 \cdot 141)$$

where x', y' are measured from the means in units of standard deviation along the principal axes of inertia.

Of course, Van der Stoke's method does not provide a genetic foundation and the convergency of the series has also been neglected. Any justification for applying the series to a statistical data will entirely rest upon the goodness of fit. Theoretically, it simply provides another basis for the A-function in dealing with the correlation problem.

2.26.4 Jorgensen

Jorgensen has also considered the correlation A-function. According to him, the general formula $(2 \cdot 124)$ is not so well adopted to numerical application as the formula $(2 \cdot 140)$ because of the fact that the variables and differential coefficients in the latter form are separable and consequently with tables of the normal curve and of its derivatives at hand, the arithmetical work can be greatly diminished. He gives one example as the illustration. It may also be pointed out that Jorgensen also considers the possibility of making some of the higher coefficients in the expression negligibly small by rotating the coordinate axes to coincide with the principal axes of inertia, e.g., by transforming from the form $(2 \cdot 140)$ into $(2 \cdot 141)$. However, in his particular illustration, nothing is gained by such a transformation. The mid-ordinates of the frequency cells are calculated and compared with the observed frequencies. Even if allowance be made for the paucity of the observations, the fit does not seem to be satisfactory.

2.26.5 The Range of Applicability of the A-Function

From the examples given by Wicksell in his memoir on "The Correlation Function of Type A", we may obtain some knowledge about the range of applicability of the A-functions. There are four examples, of which one is of linear regression and the other three are of non-linear regression. The regression curves are fitted for all four examples, and the scedastic curves for two only. The fit seems to be satisfactory for all of the four cases. The degrees of skewness and kurtosis for the marginal distributions in the instances of non-linear regression are found to be:

(i) $S_{10} = \dfrac{-1}{2} q_{30} = 0.1064$ $K_{10} = \dfrac{1}{8}(q_{40}^{-3}) = 0.0834$

$S_{01} = -0.1704$ $K_{01} = 0.0093$,

(ii) $S_{10} = 0.2199$ $K_{10} = 0.0816$

$S_{01} = 0.4545$ $K_{01} = 0.2316$,

(iii) $S_{10} = 0.0660$ $K_{10} = 0.0357$

$S_{01} = -0.2412$ $K_{01} = -0.0138$.

These values indicate that the examples are representative of slightly and moderately skew correlations. Hence the A-functions may be said to have a range of applicability from slightly to moderately abnormal skew correlation, if we call, after Professor Edgeworth, slightly abnormal those frequency distributions for which $q_3 = 2S$ is less than 0.5, and moderately abnormal those distributions for which q_3 lies between 0.5 and 0.85 roughly.

Moreover, Wicksell fits his regression formula (the approximate formula 2·131f) to three of the examples given by Pearson in his memoir on "Skew Correlation and Non-Linear Regression" so as to afford a comparison. The result shows that his formulae, with moments only up to the fourth order, give virtually as good a description of regression curves as Pearson's involving moments up to the sixth, even though two of the examples are not of A-Type correlation, and that the arithmetics are much less. So far as these examples go, we are led to doubt the efficiency of the regression method, including the correlation ratio.

The correlation function of Type B.

Jorgensen has discussed in his treatise on frequency surfaces and correlation the three types of correlation surfaces:

(i) Type AA, where the array distributions both ways are curves of Type A;

(ii) Type BB, where the array distributions both ways are curves of Type B;

(iii) Type AB, where the array distributions of one variate are curves of Type A while the array distributions of the other variate are curves of Type B.

For similar reasons given for the case of Type AA correlation, Jorgensen takes the generating function of Type BB and of Type AB to be respectively

$$\vartheta(x_1, x_2) = \vartheta(x_1)\vartheta(x_2)$$
$$\varphi(x_1, x_2) = \varphi(x_1)\vartheta(x_2)$$

where $\varphi(x)$ and $\vartheta(x)$ have the same meaning as previously defined. He determined the parameters, the regression and scedastic curves. But he did not discuss the convergency of the series, nor he gave no numerical example.

2.27 The Transformed Correlation Surface

Let $w = F(u)$ be the frequency function of a variate u, F being a known function. Now if u can be determined as a function of the observed variate, say, $u = f(z)$, z being the observed variate, so that

$$F(u)du = F[f(z)]f'(z)dz = G(z)dz, \qquad (2 \cdot 142)$$

i.e., the areas between the corresponding ordinates under the respective frequency curves $F(u)$ and $G(z)$ are equal, then the curve $F(u)$ is called the generating curve and the curve $G(z)$ is called the generated or transformed curve. If $F(u)$ is the normal curve, it is called the method of translation developed by Edgeworth[①], and if the $f(z) = \log z$, it is called the method of logarithmic transformation expounded by Wicksell. Both methods have been extended to the cases of two variates. Moreover, Wicksell has established a connection between the transformed frequency functions and a genetic theory of frequency by means of a generalized hypothesis about elementary errors.

2.27.1 Kapteyn-Wicksellian Generalized Hypothesis about Elementary Errors

Thus, Wicksell assumes that a statistical variate is built up of a number of elementary errors emanating from a corresponding number of sources, and that the elementary errors are only impulses whose effects are proportional to the strength of the impulses but also are dependent on the size at the time of action

---

[①] "Method of Translation", Jour. Roy. Stat. Soc., Dec.1898, Mar., Jun., Sep. 1899, and March 1900.

of the organ (or statistical quantity) on which they are at work. A similar device has also independently been developed by Kapteyn[①].

For the following analysis there is no loss in the generality of the hypothesis if the sources of error impulses at work are thought of as ordered in time. Let the sources be taken in the following order in which they are at work: Q_1, Q_2, Q_3, $\cdots$, Q_s. The corresponding error impulses we denote by t_1, t_2, t_3, $\cdots$, t_s and suppose the probability of t_i falling within the limits $t - \dfrac{1}{2} dt$ to $t + \dfrac{1}{2} dt$ is $f_i(t)\,dt$. Further we suppose that at the time of action of the source Q_i, the variate has reached the value z_{i-1}, and that the effect of Q_i is proportional to a certain $\theta(z_{i-1})$ of this value. Thus, t_i being the error impulse of Q_i, we have the effect on the variate equal to $t_i \theta(z_{i-1})$.

Then the variate z is the sum of all such effects, so that if

$$z_i = z_{i-1} + t_i \theta(z_{i-1}), \qquad (2\cdot 143)$$

we have

$$z = z_0 + t_1 \theta(z_0) + t_2 \theta(z_1) + \cdots + t_s \theta(z_{s-1}). \qquad (2\cdot 144)$$

Supposing further $\theta(z_i)$ to be expressed in the same unit as z (for instance of the form $a\theta_1\left(\dfrac{z_1}{a}\right)$ where a is expressed in the units employed), the impulses t_i will be abstract numbers.

It is now required to find the frequency function of z. Postulating that there exists a hypothetical variate u which comes forth as a simple aggregate of the error impulses themselves

$$u = t_1 + t_2 + \cdots + t_s \qquad (2\cdot 145)$$

and that there exists a function connecting the variate z and u:

$$u = f(z). \qquad (2\cdot 146)$$

Now, this function $f(z)$ must have the property that when the character z on account of the impulse t_i changes from z_{i-1} to z_i, it wil be changed by the

---

① Kapteyn, J. C., "Skew Frequency Curves in Biology and Statistics", Astronomical Laboratory at Groningen, 1903, 1916.

value t_i itself. Hence, we have

$$f(z_i) - f(z_{i-1}) = t_i. \qquad (2\cdot 147)$$

But also we have from $(2\cdot 143)$

$$z_i - z_{i-1} = t_i \theta(z_{i-1}).$$

Thus, we obtain the following equation to determine $f(z)$:

$$\frac{f(z_i) - f(z_{i-1})}{z_i - z_{i-1}} = \frac{1}{\theta(z_{i-1})}$$

or

$$\frac{df(z)}{dz} = \frac{1}{\theta(z)} \qquad (2\cdot 148)$$

or

$$f(z) = \int_{z_0}^{z} \frac{dz}{\theta(z)}. \qquad (2\cdot 149)$$

According to the theory of Charlier, the frequency function of the variate $u = f(z)$, which is the aggregate of the elementary errors, will be of either the type A or of the type B.

Denoting the frequency function of the actual variate z by $G(z)$ and knowing that

$$G(z) = \frac{df(z)}{dz} = F[f(z)],$$

then we have for the frequency function of the actual variate z the two alternative forms according as $F(u)$ is of type A or of type B:

$$G(z) = f'(z) F[f(z)] = \frac{1}{\theta(z)} \left\{ \varphi[f(z)] + A_3 \frac{d^3\varphi}{df(z)^3} + A_4 \frac{d^4\varphi}{df(z)^4} + \cdots \right\}$$

$$(2\cdot 150a)$$

$$G(z) = \frac{df(z)}{dz} = F[f(z)] = \frac{1}{\theta(z)} \{ \vartheta[f(z)] + B_1 \Delta_1 \vartheta[f(z)] + B_2 \Delta_2 \vartheta[f(z)] + \cdots \}$$

$$(2\cdot 150b)$$

where the functions φ, ϑ are given in $(2\cdot 97a)$ and $(2\cdot 97c)$. It is seen thus that they are forms of (2 · 142) and that (2 · 41) is Wicksell's logarithmic transformation when $f(z) = \log z$.

Through z will generally be distributed according to (2 · 150a), there is even a certain plausibility that $u = f(z)$ is approximately normally distributed, so that we may write

$$F[f(z)] = \varphi[f(z)].$$
$$G(z) = f'(z)\varphi[f(z)] = \frac{1}{\theta(z)}\{\varphi[f(z)]\}. \qquad (2 \cdot 151)$$

This is exactly the formula which Edgeworth has developed in his method of translation.

It seems therefore, that when z cannot be treated by A-functions, it has a great chance to be treated by (2 · 151) or (2 · 150a) where the transformation function $f(z)$ in some way or other is by trial determined so as to have normal or approximately normal frequency. In this circumstance lies the connection of the method of translation with the genetic theory of frequency. The generalized theory of elementary errors for the case of two variates may be stated as follows:

$Q_1, Q_2, \cdots, Q_s$ are s sources of disturbance operating on the two variates u and v by the impulses $t_1, t_2, t_3, \cdots, t_s$. The chance for an arbitrary source Q_i giving rise to an impulse of the magnitude $t - \frac{1}{2}dt$ to $t + \frac{1}{2}dt$ is as before $f_i(t)\,dt$.

The effects of an impulse on the two variates are proportional to functions of the variates at the time of action. These functions[①] we denote by $\theta_1(u)$ and $\theta_2(v)$. If the variates at the time of action of the source Q_i are respectively u_{i-1} and v_{i-1}, we should have

$$u_i = k_i\theta_i(u_{i-1})t_i + u_{i-1}$$
$$v_i = l_i\theta_2(v_{i-1})t_i + v_{i-1}$$

---

① In order that we should find a general theory of correlation from the standpoint of the generalized hypothesis of elementary errors, it is necessary to assume that effects of the error impulses on, say, the variate u is dependent, not only on u, but also on v, that is on the sizes of both the variates at the time of action. This will lead to the following case: in each v-array of u, there will be found a function $f(u, v)$ of u, that is normally distributed. The parameters of this function, which has the same form in all arrays, will be functions of v. In the case treated in the text only the means of the resulting (array) normal curves were functions of v.

so that for the final values of the variates, we have

$$u = u_0 + k_1\theta_1(u_0)t_1 + k_2\theta_1(u_1)t_2 + \cdots + k_s\theta_1(u_{s-1})t_s$$
$$v = v_0 + l_1\theta_2(v_0)t_1 + k_2\theta_2(v_1)t_2 + \cdots + l_s\theta_2(v_{s-1})t_s.$$

The coefficients k_i and l_i are constants characteristic for each source.

Postulating now that there exist two functions $z_1 = f_1(u)$ and $z_2 = f_2(v)$ of u and v that come forth as the sum of the impulses multiplied by the constants k_i and l_i we should have

$$z_1 = f_1(u) = k_1t_1 + k_2t_2 + \cdots + k_st_s$$
$$z_2 = f_2(v) = l_1t_1 + l_2t_2 + \cdots + k_st_s.$$

If s is a great number of the existence of $f_1(u)$, and $f_2(v)$ will be safe for the great bulk of the observations where the error impulses are small.

As before we shall then have

$$\frac{df_1(u)}{du} = \frac{1}{\theta_1(u)}, \quad \text{or} \quad f_1(u) = \int_{u_0}^{u} \frac{du}{\theta_1(u)}.$$

$$\frac{df_2(v)}{dv} = \frac{1}{\theta_2(v)}, \quad \text{or} \quad f_2(v) = \int_{v_0}^{v} \frac{dv}{\theta_2(v)}.$$

From the work of Charlier the correlation function of z_1 and z_2 will, in the general case, be of the A-type given in equation $(2 \cdot 102)$ and the parameters may all be determined from the observations.

Hence the correlation function of u and v will be

$$G(u, v) = \frac{df_1(u)}{du} \cdot \frac{df_2(v)}{dv} \cdot F[f_1(u) \cdot f_2(v)]$$

$$= \frac{1}{\theta_1(u)\theta_2(v)} \left\{ \varphi(z_1, z_2) + \sum_{i+j\geq 3} A_{ij} \frac{\delta^{i+j}\varphi(z_1, z_2)}{\delta z_1^i \delta z_2^j} \right\}. \quad (2 \cdot 152)$$

At times also correlation functions for z_1 and z_2 of the type B will occur.

Of course, here, as in the case of the single variable, the functions $\theta_1(u)$ and $\theta_2(v)$ are generally not known. Here as there, however, is plausibility for the function $f_1(u)$ and $f_2(v)$ to be nearly normally distributed. By determining empirical functions of u and v, that are normally distributed, we may obtain plausible approximations to the functions $f_1(u)$ and $f_2(v)$ and then, by

(2·152), approximations to the functions $\theta_1(u)$ and $\theta_2(v)$.

In practice there seem to be two cases likely to occur:

(i) We have no knowledge about the forms of $f_1(u)$ and $f_2(v)$, but seek by trial to find them. If we seek the solution by aid of the method of moments, the number of constants in f_1 and f_2 must be so limited that there are a sufficient number of moment equations for determining both the parameters in f_1 and f_2 and the parameters in the distribution of f_1 and f_2 while no moment higher than the fourth order is used. Thus, if the distribution of f_1 and f_2 is assumed to be normal and the moments up to the fourth order are used, there are 14 moment equations available and consequently we cannot allow more than 13 constants in f_1 and f_2 in addition to the parameter p involved in the normal surface.

Further, a successful determination of the parameters in $f_1(u)$ and $f_2(v)$ so as to make, as far as possible, $F(f_1, f_2)$ a normal distribution depends largely on the functions f_1 and f_2 being reversible functions, that is, on the possibility of expressing u and v as functions of f_1 and f_2.

(ii) We may know or suspect beforehand the forms of f_1 and f_2. In this case, the problem reduces itself to the determination of the parameters both in f_1, f_2 and in the distribution of $F(f_1$ and $f_2)$. It is merely a special case of (i).

Edgeworth's method of translation belongs to case (i). In this circumstance, the method of translation has been provided a genetic foundation for characterization of frequency distributions. Wicksell's method of logarithmic transformation belongs to the case (ii).

2.27.2 Edgeworth's Method of Translation[①]

Edgeworth measures the variates from the median in units of the modulus $(2\sigma^2)$. The generating function is now of the form:

$$\varphi(u) = \frac{1}{\sqrt{x}} e^{-u^2}.$$

Since the forms with which we have to deal do not for the mose part deviate widely from the normal type, there is propriety in assuming for the transformation function, or the operator as Edgeworth calls it, a Taylor

---

① "Method of Translation", Loc. Cit.

expansion:

$$z = a(u + bu^2 + cu^3 + \cdots), \qquad (2 \cdot 153)$$

z being the actual variate. It will not in general be necessary to proceed beyond the third order, and therefore we may regard z as a cubic function of u. Thus each element or small rectangular strip of the generating curve at the point u with the base Δu is translated to the distance $a(u+bu^2+cu^3)$; its base being changed from Δu to $\Delta z = \dfrac{dz}{du}\Delta u = a(u + 2bu + 3cu^2)\Delta u$, and its height altered in the inverse ratio. This transformation is seen to have kept the areas between the corresponding ordinates of the generating and the generated curves unchanged, so that

$$\varphi(u)\,du = G(z)\,dz$$

or,

$$G(z) = \varphi(u)\frac{du}{dz} = \frac{1}{\sqrt{x}}e^{-u^2} \cdot \frac{1}{a(u + bu^2 + cu^3)}. \qquad (2 \cdot 154)$$

The parameters, a, b, c, of the transformation may be determined by the method of moments. Let the n-th moment of $G(z)$ about its median be

$$M_n = \int_{-\infty}^{\infty} Z^n G(z)\,dz = \frac{1}{\sqrt{x}}\int_{-\infty}^{\infty} a^n(u + bu^2 + cu^3)^n \cdot e^{-u^2}du. \qquad (2 \cdot 155)$$

For $n=1, 2, 3$, we obtain the necessary equations for solving the parameters a, b, c:

$$M_1 = \frac{1}{2}ab,$$

$$M_2 = a^2\left(\frac{1}{2} + \frac{3}{4}b^2 + \frac{3}{2}c + \frac{15}{8}c^2\right),$$

$$M_3 = a^3\left(\frac{9}{4}b + \frac{15}{8}b^3 + \frac{45}{4}bc + \frac{315}{16}bc^2\right).$$

Expressed in terms of the moments, u_n, about the mean, they become

$$u_1 = M_1 = \frac{1}{2}ab$$

$$u_2 = M_2 - M_1^2 = a^2 \frac{1}{2}\left(1 + b^2 + 3c + \frac{15}{4}c^2\right)$$

$$u_3 = M_3 - M_1^3 - 3M_1 u_2 = a^3 b\left(\frac{3}{2} + b^2 + 9c + \frac{135}{8}c^2\right).$$

Putting

$$\beta_3^2 = \frac{u_3^2}{u_2^3}, \qquad \beta_4 = \frac{u_4}{u_2^2}, \qquad x = b^2,$$

we obtain the simplified expressions connecting the observed moments with the required constants x and c which are to be determined:

$$8x\left(\frac{3}{2} + x + 9c + \frac{135}{8}c^2\right)^2 - \beta_3^2\left(1 + x + 3c + \frac{15}{4}c^2\right)^3 = 0$$

$$4\left(6x + 3c + 3x^2 + 54xc + 27c^2 + 135xc^2 + \frac{405}{4}c^3\right.$$

$$\left. + \frac{1215}{8}c^4\right) - \beta_4\left(1 + x + 3c + \frac{15}{4}c^2\right)^2 = 0. \qquad (2\cdot 156)$$

The area or frequency under the translated or generated curve $G(z)$ between any two ordinates may be computed, after solving the cubic $(2\cdot 153)$, from tables of the normal probability integral according to the formula $(2\cdot 154)$. An ambiguity arises when the values of b and c are such that for a certain range of z, the cubic has three real roots. The translated curve then loses its typical shape of rising continuously from a practically zero value to a maximum and falling at the same or at a different rate down to zero again. The singularities that may occur are of two types. In Edgeworth's terminology: there is a "break" if $\frac{dz}{du}$, the quadratic expression in the denominator of $(2\cdot 154)$, becomes negative; there is a "stop" if the ordinate of the curve has a relative minimum value, that is to say, if $\frac{dG(z)}{dz}$ has real roots other than the mode. After passing through the minimum value, the curve ascends and ultimately changes abruptly from $+\infty$ to $-\infty$ at that point of z which corresponds to a root of $\frac{dz}{du} = 0$. Edgeworth claims that the method of translation is applicable especially to slightly and moderately abnormal curves, and that the construction is sufficiently accurate if no peculiarity occurs within a distance from the median of the translated curve corresponding to a distance of $|u| = 2$ from the median of the generating curve. The tails cut off outside this range of about 283 times the standard deviation of the normal curve from its mean amounts to only about 5 per mille of the total frequency, and are therefore practically insignificant as compared to the central portion of the curve. They are folded over or swung around, so to speak, in the process of translation, the central portion being extended or contracted according to the nature of the data.

Now $\dfrac{dz}{du}$ will be positive for all values of $|u| \leqslant 2$, provided $b^2 < 9\left(c + \dfrac{1}{12}\right)^2$. Also, the derived function of (2·154)

$$\frac{1}{G(z)} \frac{d}{du} G = \frac{-2[3cu^3 + 2bu^2 + (3c+1)u + b]}{1 + 2bu + 3cu^2}$$

will have no real root within the region $|u| \leqslant 2$ other than the mode, provided $b^2 < \dfrac{100}{9}\left(c + \dfrac{1}{15}\right)^2$. These conditions, together with $b^2 < 3\lambda$, form a lower boundary to the x, c domain within which the method can be applied. By assuming $\beta_4 = 15$ to be a fairly extreme case, Edgeworth obtained from the second of equations (2·156) an upper boundary to the x, c domain which is to be searched for values of x and c, satisfying equations (2·156). Professor Bawley[1] utilized these conditions in constructing a table which shows the values of x and c to three decimal places for given $\dfrac{\beta_3}{8}$ and $\varepsilon = \dfrac{1}{12}(\beta_4 - 3)$ by intervals of 01. Those who are accustomed to think in terms of the Pearsonian $\beta_1\beta_2$-plane, may get a clear picture of what portion in that plane will uphold Edgeworth's hypothesis if they construct a $\beta_1\beta_2$-curve by computing the values of $\beta_1 (= \beta_3^2$ in our notation) and $\beta_2 (= \beta_4 + 3$ in our notation) from equations (2·156) corresponding to the values of x and c which satisfy the lower boundary of the restricted xc-domain. The locus so obtained will constitute the lower boundary of

---

[1] Edgeworth's Contributions to Math. Stat., pp.123 – 128.

a domain in the Pearsonian $\beta_1\beta_2$-plane within which the method of translation may be applied satisfactorily.

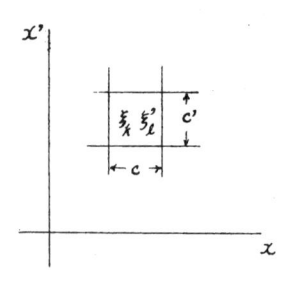

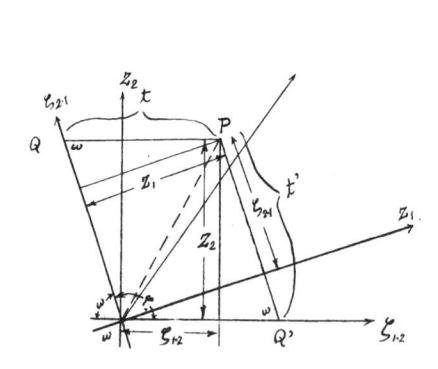

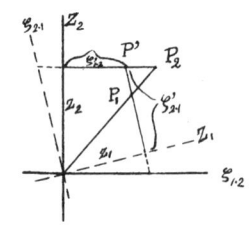

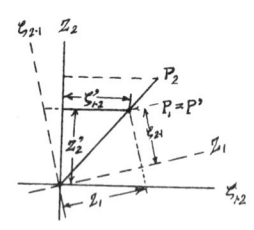

For the analogue of the preceding method in cases where the given statistics relate to two (or more) characters, say z_1 and z_2, it would seem proper to use as the equations of transformation up to the fourth order:

$$Z_1 = a_1(u_1 + b_1 u_1^2 + c_1 u_1 u_2 + d_1 u_1^3 + e_1 u_1^2 u_2 + f_1 u_1^4 + g_1 u_1^3 u_2 + h_1 u_1^2 u_2^2)$$
$$Z_1 = a_2(u_2 + b_2 u_2^2 + c_2 u_1 u_2 + d_2 u_2^3 + e_2 u_1 u_2^2 + f_1 u_2^4 + g_2 u_1 u_2^3 + h_2 u_1^2 u_2^2) .$$

Substituting these expressions in the values of the moments up to the fourth order given by the observation, we obtain 14 equations for solving the 17 parameters.

It is therefore, needful to drop certain terms of the transformation system in order that a definite solution may be obtained for the parameters. The question as to what terms should be retained in the transformation system has not received a theoretically satisfactory solution and therefore has to be answered by subjective judgment based on a sort of sense acquired by experience.

The solution may be simplified in cases where we know that the product moments of the type $z_1^2 z_2$, $z_1 z_2^2$, $z_1^3 z_2$, etc., may be ignored (perhaps we do not know the contrary), for then the distribution will depend only on the power moments. Edgeworth has elucidated such a case including up to the third moments and calls it the method of simple translation as distinguished from the composite translation which retains the product moments.

It is to be noted that the procedure in two variates differs from the translation in one variate in that the generating normal surface

$$\varphi(u_1, u_2) = \frac{1}{x\sqrt{1-p^2}} e^{-\frac{1}{1-p^2}(u_1^2 - 2pu_1 u_2 + u_2^2)}$$

is not now given beforehand. The modulus for each variate is indeed still made unity, but the other constant, p the coefficient of correlation, has to be determined from parameters of the transformation system.

Let the transformation system be of the form:

$$Z_1 = a_1(u_1 + b_1 u_1^2 + c_1 u_1^3),$$
$$Z_2 = a_2(u_2 + b_2 u_2 + c_2 u_2^3). \qquad (2 \cdot 157)$$

The parameters are determined separately from their respective marginal distributions. In other words, if $G(z_1, z_2)$ be the generated surface, the parameters in the first of the equations $(2 \cdot 157)$ shall be so determined that the marginal distribution of z_1, namely,

$$G_1(z_1) = \int_{-\infty}^{\infty} G(z_1, z_2) \, dz_2$$

is generated from the normal curve:

$$\varphi_1(z_1) = \int_{-\infty}^{\infty} \varphi(z_1, z_2) \, dz_2.$$

The process is therefore exactly the same as the translation in one variate, except that we have now to do it twice, one for each variate.

Let u_{11}, u_{20}, u_{02} be the product and power moments of the second order of the actual variates, z_1, z_2, about their means. Edgeworth finds

$$u_{11} = r\sqrt{u_{20}u_{02}} = a_1 a_2 \left\{ \frac{\rho}{2} + \frac{3}{4}(c_1 + c_2)\rho + \frac{1}{2}b_1 b_2 \rho^2 + \frac{1}{8}c_1 c_2 (9\rho + 6\rho^3) \right\}.$$

From this cubic equation, ρ may be solved. If the cubic terms in b and c are neglected, then

$$\rho = r\left\{ 1 + \frac{3}{4}(c_1^2 + c_2^2) + \frac{1}{2}(b_1^2 + b_2^2) - b_1 b_2 r^2 - \frac{3}{2}c_1 c_2 r^3 \right\}. \quad (2 \cdot 158)$$

This is regarded as the correlation coefficient between z_1 and z_2, on the assumption that when a normal surface is translated so as to represent an abnormal frequency distribution, the correlation coefficient of the generating normal surface may be taken as the measure of the connection between the actual variates whose distribution is represented by the generated surface.

The composite translation considered by Edgeworth is of the form:

$$Z_1 = a_1(u_1 + b_1 u_1^2 + d_1 u_2^2),$$
$$Z_2 = a_2(u_2 + b_2 u_2^2 + d_2 u_1^2). \quad (2 \cdot 159a)$$

But Bowley[1] has investigated a composite translation to include the third power terms; namely,

$$Z_1 = a_1(u_1 + b_1 u_1^2 + d_1 u_2^2 + c_1 u_1^3),$$
$$Z_2 = a_2(u_2 + b_2 u_2^2 + d_2 u_1^2 + c_2 u_2^3). \quad (2 \cdot 159b)$$

Substituting these expressions in the values of the moments given by observation, we obtain as many equations as there are variables:

$$M_{hk} = \iint z_1^h z_2^k G(z_1, z_2)\,dz_1 dz_2$$
$$= \iint a_1^h a_2^k (u_1 + b_1 u_1^2 + d_1 u_2^2 + c_1 u_1^3)^h \cdot (u_2 + b_2 u^2 + d_2 u_1^2$$
$$+ c_2 u_2^3)\varphi(u_1, u_2)\,du_1 du_2. \quad (2 \cdot 160)$$

---

[1] Edgeworth's Contributions to Math. Stati., Op. Cit.

In order to obtain the integrals of the product terms such as $u_1 u_2 \varphi$ or generally $u_1^h u_2^k \varphi$, the system is first rotated by putting

$$u_1 = v_1 \cos\theta - v_2 \sin\theta,$$
$$u_2 = v_1 \sin\theta + v_2 \cos\theta,$$

where

$$\cos\theta = \sin\theta = \frac{1}{\sqrt{2}},$$

so that the coordinate axes coincide with the principal axes. Thus

$$\iint_{-\infty}^{\infty} u_1 u_2 \varphi \, du_1 \, du_2 = \iint_{-\infty}^{\infty} dv_1 \, dv_2 \, \frac{v_1^2 - v_2^2}{2} \, \frac{1}{x(1-\rho^2)} e^{-\frac{v_1^2}{1+\rho} - \frac{v_2^2}{1-\rho}},$$

where v_1 and v_2 are independent variates with modulus $\sqrt{1+\rho}$ and $\sqrt{1-\rho}$ respectively. By a well-known formula the transformed integral is equal to $\frac{1}{2}\left\{\frac{1}{2}(1+\rho) - \frac{1}{2}(1-\rho)\right\} = \frac{1}{2}\rho$. Likewise, the integral

$$\iint_{-\infty}^{\infty} u_1^h u_2^k \varphi \, du_1 \, du_2 = \iint_{-\infty}^{\infty} dv_1 \, dv_2 \, \frac{(v_1 - v_2)^h (v_1 + v_2)^k}{(\sqrt{2})^h (\sqrt{2})^k} e^{-\frac{v_1^2}{1+\rho} - \frac{v_2^2}{1-\rho}} \qquad (2 \cdot 161)$$

may be evaluated.

It would be a tremendous task to solve for the parameters, including ρ, from the moment equations considering the high powers of the variables in each of these equations. However, fairly simple expressions can be found for them if the squared or higher power terms in b, c, d may be neglected, i.e., if the correlation is moderately skew.

After we have found the values of the transformation parameters and the correlation coefficient ρ, the values of u_1 and u_2 corresponding to any given values of z_1 and z_2 can be found from $(2 \cdot 160)$ and then the cell frequencies may be found from the generating normal surface with the aid of tables for the normal curves.

From what we have discussed above, it is seen that the composite translation reduces to the simple translation when the d-coefficients vanish. As a consequence, we obtain the following equations:

$$q_{21} = \frac{1}{3}(2q_{30}\rho + q_{03}r^2) = \frac{q_{11}}{3}(2q_{30} - q_{03}q_{11}),$$

$$q_{12} = \frac{1}{3}(2q_{03}\rho + q_{03}r^2) = \frac{q_{11}}{3}(2q_{03} - q_{30}q_{11}), \quad (2 \cdot 162)$$

where q's are moments of the observed distribution with reference to their standard deviations as the units and $r = q_{11}$, and ρ being the translated correlation coefficient may be replaced by r, since r in general differs only by a small quantity from ρ. Edgeworth calls (2 · 162) the simple criterion for the adequacy of the simple translation.

The methods are illustrated on a few cell frequencies of some examples given by Isserlis and Pearson. The general agreement between theory and observations so far as these frequency groups are concerned seems to be quite satisfactory.

Theoretically, the method of translation has been provided a genetic foundation by Wicksell's generalized hypothesis of elementary errors and is supplementing the theory of Type A and Type B functions. Actually, the inadequacy of simple translation and the impracticability of the composite translation constitute an important point—that in the application of the method of the translation, there is a limit beyond which the elaborateness of the machinery is not compensated for by the value of the return.

2.27.3 Wicksell's Method of Logarithmic Transformation

Now we come to Wicksell's method of logarithmic transformation[①]. It is the case where f_1 and f_2 in (2 · 152) are assumed to be the logarithms of the observed variates.

We shall first describe briefly the method in one variate to which we shall refer when we discuss the correlation surface. Let u be the observed variate with $\bar{u}$ and σ as its mean and standard deviation. Let $\xi = f(u) = \log_{10}(u - a)$ which is expected to have normal distribution. Denoting by $\bar{\xi}$ and s the mean and dispersion of ξ and by u'_p the moments of u about the point $u = a$, we may find

---

① "On Genetic Theory of Freq.", Ark. for Math., 1917, and "On Logarithmic Cor.", Sv. Ark. Tid., 1917.

$$u'_p = \int_0^\infty du(u-a)^p G(u) = \int_{-\infty}^\infty e^{pb\xi}\varphi(\xi)d\xi = e^{\bar{\xi}pb} + \frac{a^2}{3}p^2b^2$$

$$(2 \cdot 163)$$

where

$$b = \frac{1}{\log_{10}e} = \frac{1}{0.434\,3} = 2.302\,6.$$

If u'_p are the moments about its mean $\bar{u}$, we have

$$\mu'_1 = \bar{u} - a = e^{\bar{\xi}b + \frac{1}{2}s^2b^2}$$

$$\mu'_2 = \mu_2 + (\bar{u} - a)^2 + e^{2\bar{\xi}b + 2s^2b^2}$$

$$\mu'_3 = \mu_3 + 3\mu_2(\bar{u} - a) + (\bar{u} - a)^3 = e^{3\bar{\xi}b + \frac{9}{2}s^2b^2}.$$

By aid of these three equations, the three parameters a, s, $\bar{\xi}$ may be determined.

Eliminating ξ and s it will be found that $(\bar{u} - a)$ is equal to the real root of the following cubic(which always has one real and two imaginary roots)

$$\mu_3 x^3 - 3\mu_2^2 x^2 - \mu_2^3 = 0 \qquad (2 \cdot 164)$$

and that ξ and s are given by

$$\bar{\xi} = 2\log(\bar{u} - a) - \frac{1}{2}\log\{\mu_2 + (\bar{u} - a)^2\},$$

$$bs^2 = 2\log(\bar{u} - a) - 2\bar{\xi} = \log\{u + (\bar{u} - a)^2\} - 2\log(\bar{u} - a).$$

$$(2 \cdot 165)$$

Introducing $y = \dfrac{x}{\sqrt{\mu_2}}$ and $S(\text{skewness}) = -\dfrac{\mu_3}{2\sqrt{\mu_2^3}}$, we obtain a simpler form from the equation $(2 \cdot 164)$ for solving

$$y^3 + 3y + 2s = 0. \qquad (2 \cdot 166)$$

The frequency function of u will now be:

$$F(u) = \frac{1}{6s\sqrt{2x}} \frac{1}{(u-a)} e^{-\frac{|\log(u-a)-\bar{\xi}|^2}{2s^2}}. \qquad (2 \cdot 167)$$

In order that the method shall be successful, the identity between the moments

$$\mu'_4(\bar{u} - a)^2 = \mu'^2_3$$

or,

$$(u - a)^2(u - 9\mu_2^2) = \mu_3^2 + 2\mu_3[3\mu_2(\bar{u} - a) - (u - a)^3]$$

should be approximately fulfilled.

In the logarithmic correlation, a fairly extensive case will be covered by assuming the two functions $\xi = \log_{10}(u - a_1)$ and $\eta = \log_{10}(v - a_2)$ to have normal correlation, while the general case is that they are of Type A-correlation. We shall describe the former case first.

Denoting by μ'_{pq} the moments about the points $u = a_1$ and $v = a_2$, we may find

$$\mu'_{pq} = \iint_{-\infty}^{\infty} d\xi d\eta e^{pb\xi} e^{qb\eta} \varphi(\xi, \eta) = e^{b\xi + b\eta q + \frac{b^2}{2}(p^2 s_1^2 + 2rpq s_1 s_2 + q^2 s_2^2)}. \quad (2 \cdot 168)$$

From this it follows, as in the case of a single variate, that the two parameters a_1 and a_2 should be determined from the following equations (μ_{pq} denoting moments about the mean of u and v)

$$\mu_{30}(\bar{u} - a_1)^3 - 3\mu_{20}^2(u - a_1) - \mu_{20}^3 = 0$$
$$\mu_{03}(\bar{v} - a_2)^3 - 3\mu_{02}^2(\bar{v} - a_2) - \mu_{02}^3 = 0. \quad (2 \cdot 169)$$

If we have recourse to the original observations, we may hence compute the $\log(u - a_1)$ and $\log(v - a_2)$ for each individual and by ordinary methods find the values of the parameters s_1, s_2, $\bar{\xi}$, $\bar{\eta}$, and ρ. If we have not the original observations but only a correlation table of u and v, the first four parameters are determined as in the case of a single variate, by the aid of the marginal moments (2 · 168) up to the third order, and the correlation coefficient of the logarithms by the aid of the moment μ_{11}^2. Thus, we obtain

$$\bar{\xi} = 2\log(\bar{u} - a_1) - \frac{1}{2}\log\{\mu_{20} + (\bar{u} - a_1)^2\}$$

$$\bar{\eta} = 2\log(\bar{v} - a_2) - \frac{1}{2}\log\{\mu_{02} + (u - a_2)^2\}$$

$$bs_1^2 = 2\log(\bar{u} - a_1) - 2\bar{\xi}$$

$$bs_2^2 = \log(\bar{v} - a_2) - 2\bar{\eta}$$

$$\rho = \frac{-\log(\bar{u} - a_1) - \log(\bar{v} - a_2) + \log[\mu_{11} + (\bar{u} - a_1)(\bar{v} - a_2)]}{\sqrt{\{\log[\mu_{20} + (\bar{u} - a_1)^2]\} - 2\log(\bar{u} - a_1)} \sqrt{\{\log[\mu_{02} + (v - a_2)^2]\} - 2\log(\bar{v} - a_2)}}.$$

$$(2 \cdot 170)$$

Writing the frequency function of ξ and η in the form

$$\varphi(\xi, \eta) = \varphi(\xi)\varphi_\eta(\eta)$$

where

$$\varphi(\xi) = \frac{1}{s_1 \sqrt{2x}} e^{-\frac{1}{2s_1^2}(\xi-\bar{\xi})^2}$$

$$\varphi_{\eta\xi}(\eta) = \frac{1}{s_2\sqrt{2x(1-\rho^2)}} e^{-\frac{1}{2s_2^2(1-\rho^2)}|(\eta-\bar{\eta})-\rho\frac{s_2}{s_1}(\xi-\bar{\xi})|^2},$$

the regression of v on u will then be given by

$$(v_u - a_2) = \int_{-\infty}^{\infty} \frac{1}{\sqrt{2x}\,s_2\sqrt{1-\rho^2}} e^{-\frac{1}{2s_2^2(1-\rho^2)}|(\eta-\bar{\eta})-\rho\frac{s_2}{s_1}(\xi-\bar{\xi})|^2} e^{b\eta} d\eta$$

$$= e^{b\bar{\eta}+\frac{1}{2}bs_2^2+b\rho\frac{s_2}{s_1}|\log(u-a)-\bar{\xi}|-\frac{b^2}{2}\rho^2 s_2^2}$$

$$= (\bar{v} - a_2) e^{b\rho\frac{s_2}{s_1}|\log(u-a_1)-\bar{\xi}|-\frac{b^2}{2}\rho^2 s_2^2}$$

or,

$$\log(v_u - a_3) - \bar{\eta} = \rho\frac{s_2}{s_1}\{\log(u - a_1) - \bar{\xi}\} + \frac{b}{2}s_2^2(1-\rho^2). \quad (2\cdot 171)$$

Mutatis mutandis we have for the regression curve of u on v the equation

$$\{\log(u_v - a_1) - \bar{\xi}\} = \rho\frac{s_1}{s_2}\{\log(v - a_2) - \bar{\eta}\} + \frac{b^2}{2}s_1^2(1-\rho^2).$$

As a condition for $\log(u - a_1)$ and $\log(v - a_2)$ having normal correlation, we should have the following relations between the moments fulfilled

$$\mu'_{21}\mu'^2_{10}\mu'_{01} = \mu'^2_{11}\mu'_{20}$$
$$\mu'_{12}\mu'_{10}\mu'^3_{01} = \mu'^2_{11}\mu'_{02}$$
$$\mu'_{40}\mu'^2_{10} = \mu'^2_{30}$$
$$\mu'_{22}\mu'^3_{10}\mu'^2_{01} = \mu'_{20}\mu'^4_{11}\mu'_{02}$$
$$\mu'_{13}\mu'_{10}\mu'^3_{01} = \mu'^3_{11}\mu'_{03}$$
$$\mu'_{04}\mu'^2_{01} = \mu'^2_{03}. \quad (2\cdot 172)$$

The regression curves, put on the natural scale, are of the form

$$u_v - a_1 = a_1 r_1 \left(\frac{v - a_2}{a_2}\right)^{\beta_1},$$

$$v_u - a_2 = a_2 r_2 \left(\frac{n - a_1}{a_1}\right) \beta_2,$$

where

$$a_1 = \frac{(\bar{u} - a_1)^2}{\sqrt{v_{20} + (\bar{u} - a_1)^2}},$$

$$a_2 = \frac{(\bar{v} - a_2)^2}{\sqrt{\mu_{02} + (\bar{v} - a_2)^2}},$$

$$\beta_1 = \rho \frac{s_2}{s_1}, \quad \beta_2 = \rho \frac{s_2}{s_1},$$

$$r_1 = \left(\frac{\bar{u} - a_1}{a_1}\right)^{1-\rho^2}, \quad r_2 = \frac{(\bar{v} - a_2)^{1-\rho^2}}{(a_2)^{1-\rho^2}}.$$

They do not have inflexions (which the regression curves of skew correlation will, by experience, have) and they will intersect at two points

$$u = a_1, \quad v = a_2,$$

$$u = a_1 + \left(\frac{\bar{v} - a_2}{a_2}\right)^{\beta_1}(\bar{u} - a_2), \quad v = a_2 + \left(\frac{\bar{u} - a_2}{a_1}\right)^{\beta_2}(\bar{v} - a_2).$$

On account of the peculiar form of the regression curve which is not very often observed in practical statistics and on account of the requirement to fulfill the identical relations between the moments not used in the solution, the method can hardly be expected to apply to very many practical cases. Later in the same year, Wicksell published a second paper to improve the method. There the correlation function of $\xi = \log_{10}(u - a_1)$ and $\eta = \log(v - a_2)$ is assumed to be of the type A instead of the normal surface. Thus, by equation $(2 \cdot 152)$,

$$G(u, v) = \frac{1}{(u - a_1)(v - a_2)b^2} \varphi^{[\log(u-a_1), \log(v-a_2)]} + \sum_{b+j=3} A_{ij} \frac{\delta^i + j_\varphi}{\delta^i_\xi \delta^j_\eta}$$

$$-\frac{1}{2(1-\rho^2)}\left\{\frac{(\xi - \bar{\xi})^2}{S_1^2} - \frac{2\rho(\xi - \bar{\xi})(\eta - \bar{\eta})}{s_1 s_2} + \frac{(\eta - \bar{\eta})^2}{s_2^2}\right\}$$

$$(2 \cdot 173)$$

where

$$\varphi(\xi, \eta) = \frac{1}{2s_1 s_2 \sqrt{1 - \rho^2}} e.$$

Let the moments of u and v about the point a_1 and a_2 be

$$m_{pq} = \iint_{-\infty}^{\infty} (u-a_1)^p (v-a_2)^q G(u,v) \, du \, dv = \iint_{-\infty}^{\infty} e^{pb\xi} e^{pb\eta} F(\xi, \eta) \, d\xi \, d\eta.$$

It will easily be found by integration per partes that

$$\iint d\xi d\eta \, e^{pb\xi} e^{pb\eta} \frac{\delta^{i+j} \varphi(\xi, \eta)}{\delta \xi^i \delta \eta^j} d\xi d\eta = (-1)^{i+j} (pb)^i (qb)^j u'_{pq}$$

where u'_{pq} is defined in (2·168).

Hence, we find for the moments m'_{pq} about the point (a_1, a_2) the formula:

$$m'_{pq} = \left[1 + \sum A_{ij} (-1)^{i+j} (p^b)^i (q^b)^j \right] e^{b\bar{\xi}p + b\bar{\eta}q + \frac{b^2}{2}(p^2 s_1^2 + 2rpqss_2 + q^2 s_2^2)}. \qquad (2 \cdot 174)$$

These moments are functions of a_1, a_2 and the known moments m_{pq} about the mean. They are

$$m'_{10} = \bar{u} - a_1, \quad m'_{01} = \bar{v} - a_2,$$
$$m'_{20} = m_{20} + m'^2_{10}, \quad m'_{02} = m_{02} + m'^2_{01},$$
$$m'_{11} = m_{11} + m_{10} m_{01}, \quad m'_{30} = m_{30} + 3 m_{20} m'_{10} + m'^3_{10},$$
$$m'_{21} = m_{21} + 2 m_{11} m'_{10} + m_{20} m'_{01} + m'_{01} + m'^2_{10} m'_{01}; \text{ etc.}$$

Substituting these expressions for m'_{pq} in (2·174), we obtain the moment equations for solving the parameters.

Let the point (a_1, a_2) be so chosen that A_{30} and A_{03} vanish. This condition as in the previous case, gives rise to the following equations for solving a_1 and a_2:

$$m_{30}(\bar{u} - a_1) - 3 m_{20}(\bar{u} - a_1) - m_{20}^3 = 0$$
$$m_{03}(\bar{v}_2 - a_2) - 3 m_{02}(\bar{v} - a_2) - m_{02}^3 = 0.$$

Further, we get, as in equation (2·170),

$$\bar{\xi} = 2\log(\bar{u} - a_1) - \frac{1}{2}\log m_{20} + (\bar{u} - a_1)^2,$$

$$\bar{\eta} = 2\log(\bar{v} - a_2) - \frac{1}{2}\log m_{02} + (\bar{v} - a_2)^2,$$

$$bs_1^2 = \log[m_{20} + (\bar{u} - a_1)^2] - 2\log(\bar{u} - a_1),$$

$$bs_2^2 = \log[m_{02} + (\bar{v} - a_2)^2] - 2\log(\bar{v} - a_2). \qquad (2 \cdot 175)$$

Let us introduce the notations

$$k'_{11} = \frac{m'_{11}}{m'_{10}m'_{01}} = (1 - b^3 A_{21} - b^3 A_{12})e^{\rho s_1 s_2 b^2}, \qquad (2\cdot 176a)$$

$$k'_{21} = \frac{m'_{21}}{m'_{20}m'_{01}} = (1 - 4b^3 A_{21} - 2b^3 A_{12})e^{2\rho s_1 s_2 b^2}, \qquad (2\cdot 176b)$$

$$k'_{12} = \frac{m'_{12}}{m'_{02}m'_{10}} = (1 - 2b^3 A_{21} - 4b^3 A_{12})e^{2\rho s_1 s_2 b^2}, \qquad (2\cdot 176c)$$

where k's are known numbers because the m's are known.

Neglecting $(b^3 A_{12})^2$ and $(b^3 A_{21})^2$ which are small compared to unity, we have approximately

$$k'^2_{11} = (1 - 2b^3 A_{12} - 2b^3 A_{21})e^{2\rho s_1 s_2 b^2}$$

and

$$k'_{21} - k'^2_{11} = \alpha_1 (2k'^2_{11} - k'_{21}) + v(k'^2_{11} - k'_{21}),$$
$$k'_{12} - k'^2_{11} = \alpha_2 (k'^2_{11} - k'_{12}) + v(2k'^2 - k'_{12}),$$

where

$$\alpha_1 = -2b^3 A_{21}, \qquad \alpha_2 = -2b^3 A_{12}.$$

From these equations u and v, and therefore A_{21} and A_{12} may be determined. Now from the equation $(2\cdot 176a)$, or

$$e^{\rho s_1 s_2 b^2}\left(1 + \frac{\alpha_1}{2} + \frac{\alpha_2}{2}\right) = k'_{11},$$

we obtain

$$\rho = \frac{\log k'_{11} - \log(1 - b^3 A_{21} - b^3 A_{12})}{bs_1 s_2}.$$

The successful application and the mathematical validity of the solution depends on the following conditions:

(i) The parameters a_1 and a_2 may be varied until A_{30} and A_{03} disappear without the simultaneous occurrence of terms of an order higher than the third in $(2\cdot 173)$ which cannot be neglected.

(ii) That $(b^3 A_{21})$ and $(b^3 A_{12})^2$ are negligibly small when compared to 1. If this condition be not fulfilled, then A_{21}, A_{12}, and ρ must be solved from

$(2 \cdot 176)$. Thus ρ is given by

$$e^{\rho s_1 s_2 b^2} = \frac{3}{4}k'_{11} + \sqrt{\frac{1}{16}(9k'^2_{11} - 4k'_{21} - 4k'_{12})} \qquad (2 \cdot 177)$$

and subsequently A_{21} and A_{12} are found from two linear equations.

(iii) The following identical relations, to which the moments of the fourth order are subject, must be approximately fulfilled:

$$m'_{40}(m'_{10})^8 = (m_{20})^6,$$

$$m'_{31}(m'_{10})^6(m'_{01})^2 = (m'_{11})^3(m'_{20})^3 \frac{1 - 3b^3(3A_{21} + A_{12})}{[1 - b^3(A_{21} + A_{12})]^3},$$

$$m_{22}(m'_{10})^4(m'_{01})^4 = (m'_{11})^4 m'_{20} m'_{02} \frac{1 - 8b^3(A_{21} + A_{12})}{[1 - b^3(A_{21} + A_{12})]^4},$$

$$m'_{13}(m'_{01})^6(m'_{10})^2 = (m'_{11})^3(m'_{02})^3 \frac{1 - 3b^3(A_{21} + 3A_{12})}{[1 - b^3(A_{21} + A_{12})]^3},$$

$$m'_{04}(m'_{01})^8 = (m'_{02})^6, \qquad (2 \cdot 178)$$

where the moments m'_{pq} about the point (a_1, a_2) are computed from the moments about the mean by the formulae:

$$m'_{40} = m_{40} + 4m_{30}(\bar{u} - a_1) + 6m_{20}(\bar{u} - a_1)^2 + (u - a_1)^4,$$

$$m'_{31} = m_{31} + 3m_{21}(\bar{u} - a_1) + m_{30}(\bar{v} - a_2) + 3m_{11}(\bar{u} - a_1)^2$$
$$+ 3m_{20}(\bar{u} - a_1)(\bar{v} - a_2) + (\bar{u} - a_1)^3(\bar{v} - a_2),$$

$$m'_{22} = m_{22} + 2m_{21}(\bar{v} - a_2) + 2m_{12}(\bar{u} - a_1) + 4m_{11}(\bar{u} - a_1)(\bar{v} - a_2)$$
$$+ m_{20}(\bar{v} - a_2) + m_{02}(\bar{v} - a_1)^2 + (\bar{u} - a_1)^2(v - a_2)^2.$$

Mutatis mutandis we have the expressions for m'_{13} and m'_{04}.

The marginal curves are ordinary logarithmic curves of the form given in $(2 \cdot 167)$.

The regression or partial moment curve of the i-th order of v on u is defined by

$$\theta(2^i \cdot 1) = \int_{-a_2}^{\infty}(v - a_2)^i G(u, v)\,dv : \int_{-a_2}^{\infty} G(u, v)\,dv$$

$$= \int_{-a_2}^{\infty} e^{ib\eta} F(\xi, \eta)\,d\eta : \int_{-a_2}^{\infty} F(\xi, \eta)\,d\eta$$

where

$$F(\xi, \eta) = \varphi(\xi, \eta) + A_{21} \frac{\delta^3 \varphi(\xi, \eta)}{\delta \xi^2 \delta \eta} + A_{12} \frac{\delta^3 \varphi(\xi, \eta)}{\delta \xi^2 \delta \eta^2}.$$

By the same procedure which has been used in finding the various regressions for the Type A correlation surface, Wicksell finds

$$\theta(2^i \cdot 1) = e^{ib\bar{\eta} + ib\rho \frac{s_2}{s_1}[\log(u-a_1) - \bar{\xi}] + \frac{1}{2}i^2 b^2 s_2^2 (1-\rho^2)}$$

$$\cdot \left\{ 1 - ib \frac{A_{21}}{s_1^2} \left[\left(\frac{\log(u - a_1) - \bar{\xi}}{a_1} - ib\rho s_1 \right)^2 - 1 \right] \right.$$

$$\left. - ib^2 \frac{A_{12}}{s_1} \left(\frac{\log(u - a_1) - \bar{\xi}}{s_1} - ib\rho s_2 \right) \right\}. \qquad (2 \cdot 179)$$

Observing

$$e^{ib\bar{\eta} + \frac{1}{2}i^2 b^2 s_2^2} = m'_{0i}$$

and introducing the notations

$$a^{(i)} = ibr \frac{s_2}{s_1}, \quad \beta^{(i)} = ib\rho \frac{s_2}{s_1} \bar{\xi} + \frac{1}{2} i^3 b^2 s_2^2 \rho^2,$$

$$D_0^{(i)} = 1 + ib \frac{A_{21}}{A_{12}}, \quad D_1^{(i)} = - i^2 b^2 \frac{A_{12}}{s_1^2},$$

$$D_2^{(i)} = - ib \frac{A_{21}}{s_1^4}, \quad d^{(i)} = \bar{\xi} + ibs_1 s_2 \rho. \qquad (2 \cdot 180)$$

We may write the regression of any order about the origin a_2:

$$\theta(2^i \cdot 1) = m'_{0i} e^{a^{(i)} \log(u-a_1) - \beta^{(i)}}$$

$$\cdot \{ D_0^{(i)} + D_1^{(i)} [\log(u - a_1) - d^{(i)}]$$

$$+ D_2^{(i)} [\log(u - a_1) - d^{(i)}]^2 \}. \qquad (2 \cdot 181)$$

Putting $i = 1, 2, 3, 4$, we may obtain the first four regressions about the origin a_2. From these regressions we may compute the regressions about the array means and subsequently the scedasticity, the clitic, and the kurtic curves by the same procedure as used in connection with the correlation A-functions (see formula $2 \cdot 140$).

The method is illustrated by the correlation between the ages of the spinsters and bachelors at marriages in Sweden 1901 – 1910. From the good agreement of the theory with the marginal distribution and with the regression of the means and the close fulfillment of the identical relations between the higher moments, it may be said that the logarithmic correlation A function has given a satisfactory fit and that it seems to have remarkable powers of accommodation.

2.28 Transformation by the Graphic Method—Van Uven

Van Uven's treatise on skew correlation follows the same principle as used by Kapteyn in dealing with the skew frequency distributions of a single variable Kapteyn, like Edgeworth, conceived the idea that the normal law may be maintained in the most general case, provided it be granted that the quantity which is normally distributed is not necessarily the directly observed quantity x, but rather a function $f(x)$ of this quantity. Kapteyn① has succeeded in deriving the normal distribution of a function of x from the simple supposition that the elementary increment of x depends on the value already reached. But Kapteyn, Edgeworth, and also, to certain extent, Wicksell in finding the function $f(x)$ which is expected to follow the normal distribution have confined themselves to certain concrete types of functions. Then Van Uven, in the second paper of Kapteyn's "Skew Frequency Curves",② developed a scheme to determine this function graphically without any premised supposition with regard to its analytical structure. Only some simplifying suppositions upon finiteness, continuity, etc., are introduced in order to make the problem determinate. This method has been extended to treat skew correlations of two or more variates.

Since the method of treating skew correlation will depend on the method of analyzing skew frequency curves, it may be profitable first to sketch the latter in its principal outlines.

Let x be the variate whose observed values are grouped in n classes with the same interval c. Let ξ_1, ξ_2, ξ_3, $\cdots$, ξ_n be the class centers and denote the class

---

① "Skew Frequency Curves in Biology and Stat.", Op. Cit. and Cf. Wicksell's generalized hypothesis of elementary errors, Op. Cit.

② Kapteyn and Van Uven, Skew Freq. Curves in Biology and Statistics, Groningen, 1916, Noordhoff.

limits by X_0, X_1, $\cdots$, X_n so that

$$X_k = \xi_k + \frac{c}{2}, \quad X = \xi_k - \frac{c}{2}.$$

The theoretical lower limit X_0 ought not to be equal to $\xi_1 - \frac{c}{2}$, but may be smaller, since the theoretical frequencies may sink beneath the empirical minimum value 1. For the same reason the theoretical upper limit X_n may surpass $\xi_n + \frac{c}{2}$.

Let the frequency in the k-th class be Y_k so that the frequency scheme is:

Class Center	ξ_1	ξ_2	ξ_3	$\cdots$	ξ_k	$\cdots$	ξ_n
Frequency	Y_1	Y_2	Y_3	$\cdots$	Y_k	$\cdots$	Y_n

and the cumulative frequency below X_k will be

$$Y_1 + Y_2 + \cdots + Y_k = \sum_{i=1}^{k} Y_i.$$

Now it is required to determine a function $z = f(x)$, which will be normally distributed around the mean value zero with the modulus of precision equal to unity, on the premise that the corresponding intervals from X_0 to X_k and from $Z_0 = f(X_0)$ to $a_k = f(X_k)$ be equally probable. This is the same premise used by Edgeworth and Kapteyn as already expressed in equation (2 · 142).

As a simplifying supposition, it is also assumed that the variable z is a continuous, univalent, ever-increasing function of x. Then Z_0 is the theorotical lower limit of the variable z normally distributed, thus $Z_0 = -\infty$; likewise, we have $Z_n = +\infty$. So the class limit Z_k corresponding to X_k is determined by

$$P_k = \frac{1}{N} \sum_{i=1}^{k} Y_i - \frac{1}{\sqrt{x}} \int_{-\infty}^{z_k} e^{-z^2 dz} = H(Z_k) \qquad (2 \cdot 182)$$

where N is the total frequency. The values X_0 and X_n, corresponding to $Z_0 = -\infty$ and $Z_n = +\infty$ being indeterminate, we obtain $n-1$ equations $P_k = H(Z_k)$ for $k = 1, 2, 3, \cdots, n - 1$, and therefore $(n - 1)$ pairs (X_1, Z_1), $(X_2, Z_2), \cdots, (X_{n-1}, Z_{n-1})$ of the function $Z = f(x)$ are known.

Representing the pairs (X_k, Z_k) by the rectangular coordinate system, the problem now reduces itself to find a curve which will pass through these $(n - 1)$

points. The problem is therefore quite indeterminate, nevertheless it is possible in a good many cases to draw a simple curve through these points. Then the analytical expression of this curve is a suitable solution of the function $f(x)$ required. In choosing $f(x)$ we also have particularly in mind the obtaining of a simple form for the so-called "reaction function".

By following the same principle, a skew correlation[1] in transformed into a normal correlation between two functions t and t', which in general may depend on both of the observed variates. The problem, is therefore to construct the two functions t and t'. Let both quantities x and x' be observed with each of N individuals forming the frequency scheme as shown in the diagram.

The class centers $\xi_1, \xi_1, \cdots, \xi_n$ of x increase, by the same interval c and the class centers $\xi'_1, \xi'_2, \cdots, \xi'_n$, of x' by the same interval c'. Likewise, the class limits are respectively given by

$$X_k = \xi_{k+\frac{c}{2}} \qquad X_{k-1} = \xi_{k-\frac{c}{2}}$$
$$X'_l = \xi'_{l+\frac{c}{2}} \qquad X'_{l-1} = \xi'_{l-\frac{c}{2}}. \qquad (2 \cdot 183)$$

The frequency Y_{kl} in the cell (ξ_k, ξ') means the number of observations on x and x' which lie between the rectangle, the sides of which are:

$$x = x_{k-1}, \qquad x = x_k;$$
$$x' = x'_{l-1}, \qquad x' = x_l.$$

Thus, the sum of the frequencies in the k-th row of x' is:

$$Y_{k1} + Y_{k2} + \cdots + Y_{kl} + \cdots + Y_{kn'} = \sum_{j=1}^{n'} Y_{kj} = R_k.$$

And the cumulative frequency of the same array is:

$$Y_{k1} + Y_{k2} + \cdots + Y_k = \sum_{j=1}^{l} Y_{kj} = P_{k \cdot l}.$$

The cumulative relative frequency of x in this array is therefore

$$\sigma_{k \cdot l} = \frac{P_{k \cdot l}}{R_k}. \qquad (2 \cdot 184)$$

---

[1] Van Uven, M. G., On Treating Skew Correlation, Proc. Kon. AK. V. Wet., Amsterdam, Vol.28, pp.797−811, 919−935; Vol.29, pp.580−590; Vol.32, p.408.

The cumulative marginal frequency of x is

$$S_k = R_1 + R_2 + \cdots + R_k = \sum_{i=1}^{k} R_i = \sum_{i=1}^{k} \sum_{j=1}^{n'} Y_{ij}$$

whence

$$N = S_n = \sum_{i=1}^{n} R_i.$$

Then, the relative cumulative marginal frequency of x is

$$S_k = \frac{S_k}{S_n} = \frac{S_k}{N}. \qquad (2 \cdot 185)$$

By making proper changes in the index, we may obtain the similar formulas for the variate x'.

If $D(x, x')$ be the theoretical probability function, so that the chance that the point (x, x') lies within the infinitesimal domain $\left(x - \frac{1}{2}dx, x + \frac{1}{2}dx; x' - \frac{1}{2}dx', x' + \frac{1}{2}dx'\right)$ is

$$dW = D(x, x')dxdx',$$

then we have the following equation connecting this probability function and the actual relative frequency:

$$Y_{kl} = N \int_{X_{k-1}}^{X_k} \int_{X'_{l-1}}^{X'_l} D(x, x')dxdx' = N \int_{X_{k-1}}^{X_k} \int_{X'_{l-1}}^{X'_l} dW. \qquad (2 \cdot 186)$$

Now the problem before us is to determine two functions $t = f_1(x, x')$ and $t' = f_2(x, x')$ in such a way that

$$dW = D(x, x')dxdx' = \frac{\sqrt{1-\rho^2}}{x} e^{-(t^2 - 2\rho tt' + t'^2)} \frac{\partial(t, t)}{\partial(x, x')} dxdx$$

$$= \frac{\sqrt{1-\rho^2}}{x} e^{-(t^2 - 2\rho tt' + t'^2)} dtdt' = \varphi(t, t')dtdt' \qquad (2 \cdot 187)$$

where

$$\frac{\partial(t, t')}{\partial(x, x')} = \begin{vmatrix} \dfrac{\partial t}{\partial x} & \dfrac{\partial t'}{\partial x} \\ \dfrac{\partial t}{\partial x'} & \dfrac{\partial t'}{\partial x'} \end{vmatrix}, \rho = \text{coef. of correlation between } t \text{ and } t'.$$

$$(2 \cdot 188)$$

Putting

$$t\sqrt{1-\rho^2} = Z_1, \qquad t' - \rho t = \xi_{2\cdot 1} \qquad (2\cdot 189)$$

or

$$t'\sqrt{1-\rho^2} = Z_2, \qquad t + \rho t' = \xi_{1\cdot 2}$$

so that

$$\frac{\partial(t, t')}{\partial(z, \xi)} = \frac{1}{\sqrt{1-\rho^2}}.$$

Defining a function $H(u)$ by the integral

$$H(u) = \int_{-\infty}^{u} \varphi(v)\,dv = \frac{1}{\sqrt{x}}\int_{-\infty}^{u} e^{-v^2}\,dv, \qquad (2\cdot 190)$$

then

$$dW = \frac{1}{x}e^{-(z^2+\zeta_{2\cdot 1}^2)}\,dz_1 d\zeta_{2\cdot 1} = d\{H(z_1)\}\,d\{H(\zeta_{2\cdot 1})\} \qquad (2\cdot 191)$$

or

$$dW = d\{H(z_2)\}\,d\{H(\zeta_{1\cdot 2})\} = \frac{1}{x}e^{-(z_2^2+\zeta_{1\cdot 2}^2)}\,dz_2 d\zeta_{1\cdot 2}.$$

From the equation

$$dW = D(x, x')\,dxdx' = d\{H(z_1)\}\,d\{H(\zeta_{2\cdot 1})\} = d\{H(z_2)\}\,d\{H(\zeta_{1\cdot 2})\},$$

we may conclude

$$D(x, x') = \frac{\partial\{H(z_1), H(\zeta_{2\cdot 1})\}}{\partial(x, x')} \frac{\partial\{H(z_2), H(\zeta_{1\cdot 2})\}}{\partial(x, x')}. \qquad (2\cdot 192)$$

Admitting $D(x, x')$ to be known, the equation $(2\cdot 192)$ will enable us to determine $H(\zeta_{2\cdot 1})$ if $H(z_1)$ is chosen. Moreover, z and ζ will be known after $H(z_1)$ and $H(\zeta_{2\cdot 1})$ are so obtained. Then the correlation coefficient ρ may be determined from the values of z_1, and $\zeta_{2\cdot 1}$ and z_2, $\zeta_{1\cdot 2}$. Since the formulae for the set z_2, $\zeta_{1\cdot 2}$ may be obtained from those for z_1, $\zeta_{2\cdot 1}$ by symmetry, we may omit the index for the sake of simplicity.

If the original variables x and x' are not linearly correlated, the scheme yet pointing to some dependence, we will first try to establish a normal correlation between a function t only of x, and another function t' only of x'. Should this prove to be impossible, we shall try to obtain at least one function t (or t') depending on only one variable x(or x'). If this attempt also fails, we shall try to introduce one function t(resp. t') which varies but little by the influence of x'

(resp. x), and, at the same time, "to obtain a correlation as large as impossible, since just a high degree of correlation in interpretation will give interesting results".

Substituting $(2 \cdot 191)$ in $(2 \cdot 186)$, we have the equation connecting the theoretical probability to its empirical value:

$$Y_{kl} = N \int_{x_{k-1}}^{x_k} \int_{x'_{l-1}}^{x'_l} D(x, x') \mathrm{d}x \mathrm{d}x' = N \int_{z_{k-1}}^{z_k} \int_{\zeta_{k-1, l-1}}^{\zeta_{k, l}} \cdot \mathrm{d}\{H(z)\} \mathrm{d}\{H(\zeta)\}.$$
$(2 \cdot 193)$

Now if we integrate over the entire range of x' and then integrate for x from x_0 to x_k,

$$\sum_{i=1}^{k} \sum_{j=1}^{n'} Y_{ij} = N \int_{-\infty}^{x_k} \int_{-\infty}^{\infty} D(x, x') \mathrm{d}x \mathrm{d}x' = N D_1(x_k)$$
$$= \int_{-\infty}^{z_k} \mathrm{d}\{H(z)\} \int_{-\infty}^{\infty} \mathrm{d}\{H(\zeta)\}$$
$$= H(z_k), \qquad (2 \cdot 194)$$

we see that $H(z_k)$ and z_k are functions of x only. Hence, to each value x_k we obtain a corresponding value for $H(z_k)$, from which a value for z_k may be found.

Besides the pairs $(x_0, z_0 = -\infty)$, $(x_n, z_n = \infty)$, we thus have $n - 1$ pairs

$$(x_1, z_1), (x_2, z_2), \cdots, (x_{n-1}, z_{n-1}),$$

from which we may construct a function $z = z(x)$ of x in the manner the function z has been constructed for the case of non-normal frequency distribution of a single variate. We may denote $H(z) = H[z(x)] = u(x)$, with

$$\begin{aligned}
&z(x_k) = z_k, & &u(x_k) = u_k = H(z_k) = H_k, \\
&z(x_0) = z_0 = -\infty, & &u_0 = H_0 = 0, \\
&z(x_n) = z_n = +\infty, & &u_n = H_n = 1.
\end{aligned} \qquad (2 \cdot 195)$$

Now from $(2 \cdot 192)$ it follows that $H(\zeta)$ and also ζ are functions of x and x', and we may introduce the notation:

$$\begin{aligned}
&\zeta(x_k, x'_l) = \zeta_{kl}, H(\zeta_{kl}) = H_{kl} = H\zeta(x_k, x'_l) = v(x_k, x') = v_{kl}, \\
&\zeta(x_k, x'_0) = \zeta_{k0} = -\infty, \quad v_{k0} = H_{k0} = 0, \\
&\zeta(x_k, x'_n) = \zeta_{kn'} = +\infty, \quad v_{kn'} = H_{kn'} = 1.
\end{aligned} \qquad (2 \cdot 196)$$

Integrating $(2 \cdot 193)$ over x' in the x_k-array, we obtain the cumulative frequency of that array:

$$P_{kl} = \int_{x_{k-1}}^{x_k} \int_{x'_0}^{x'_l} D(x, x') \,dx\,dx' = \int_{z_{k-1}}^{z_k} d\{H(z)\} \int_{\zeta_{k0}}^{\zeta_{kl}} d\{H(\zeta)\} \quad (2 \cdot 197)$$

or $\quad P_{kl} = \{H(z_k) - H(z_{k-1})\}\{H(\zeta_{kl}) - H(\zeta_{k0})\} = \{H_k - H_{k-1}\}H_{kl}.$

But integrating along this same array over x' from x'_0 to x'_n, we obtain the total frequency of that array:

$$R_k = (H_k - H_{k-1})H_{kn'} = H_k - H_{k-1}.$$

Thus,

$$\frac{P_{kl}}{R_k} = H_{kl} = H(\zeta_{kl}) \quad (2 \cdot 198)$$

which connects the cumulative probability of x' in the x_k-array to its empirical value. By means of this relation, we may determine a value ζ_{kl} corresponding to each pair (x_k, x'_l). From the $(n-1)(n'-1)$ sets of value so obtained, we may construct a function $\zeta(x, x')$ of x and x'.

If x and x' are of normal distribution, then t and t' must be linear functions respectively of x and of x' and thus, z and ζ must satisfy linear equations:

$$z = t\sqrt{1-\rho^2} = h(x-m)\sqrt{1-\rho^2} = ax + c,$$
$$\zeta = t' - \rho t = h'(x'-m') - \rho h(x-m) = a'x + b'x' + c'.$$
$$(2 \cdot 199)$$

These furnish a criterion to judge whether the observed variates are of normal correlation.

If x and x', by the above test, are not normally correlated, we have to seek a set of functions $t(x, x')$ and $t'(x, x')$ which are normally correlated. The method consists in making use of two rectangular coordinate system: $(z_1, \zeta_{2 \cdot 1})$ and $(z'_2, \zeta_{1 \cdot 2})$ having the same origin.

The way in which z_1, z_2, $\zeta_{2 \cdot 1}$, $\zeta_{1 \cdot 2}$ are defined (equation $2 \cdot 190$) indicates that they are permanently increasing functions respectively of $H(z_1)$, $H(z_2)$, $H(\zeta_{2 \cdot 1})$, $H(\zeta_{1 \cdot 2})$. Moreover, from $(2 \cdot 194)$ and $(2 \cdot 198)$ it follows that $H(z)$ and $H(\zeta)$ are permanently increasing functions of x and therefore z and ζ are permanently increasing functions of x and vice versa. Hence ζ, being a permanently increasing function of x and x', is a permanently increasing function of z and consequently we obtain

$$dz_1 d\zeta_{2 \cdot 1} = dz_1 \frac{d\zeta_{2 \cdot 1}}{dz_1} dz_1, \qquad \frac{d\zeta_{2 \cdot 1}}{dz_1} > 0, \qquad (2 \cdot 200a)$$

and, by symmetry,

$$dz_2 d\zeta_{2 \cdot 1} = dz_2 \frac{d\zeta_{1 \cdot 2}}{dz_2} dz, \qquad \frac{d\zeta_{1 \cdot 2}}{dz_2} > 0. \qquad (2 \cdot 200b)$$

These inequalities geometrically mean that the z_1-axis and the $\zeta_{2 \cdot 1}$-axis on the one hand, and z_2-axis and the $\zeta_{1 \cdot 2}$-axis on the other hand, must include an acute angle. We denote it by φ and its supplement by w.

Introducing the polar coordinates r and θ with its polar axis at the bisector of the z_1- and z_2-axis, we obtain

$$\begin{cases} z_1 = r_1 \cos\left(\dfrac{w}{2} + \theta\right) \\ \zeta_{2 \cdot 1} = r_1 \sin\left(\dfrac{w}{2} + \theta\right) \end{cases} \qquad \begin{cases} z_2 = r_2 \cos\left(\dfrac{w}{2} - \theta\right) \\ \zeta_{1 \cdot 2} = r_2 \sin\left(\dfrac{w}{2} - \theta\right) \end{cases} \qquad (2 \cdot 201)$$

whence

$$A \equiv z_1 z_2 - \zeta_{2 \cdot 1} \zeta_{1 \cdot 2} = r_1 r_2 \cos w$$
$$B \equiv z_1 \zeta_{1 \cdot 2} + z_2 \zeta_{2 \cdot 1} = r_1 r_2 \cos w, \qquad (2 \cdot 202)$$

whence

$$\tan w = \frac{z_1 \zeta_{1 \cdot 2} + z_2 \zeta_{2 \cdot 1}}{z_1 z_2 - \zeta_{2 \cdot 1} \zeta_{1 \cdot 2}} = \frac{A}{B}. \qquad (2 \cdot 203)$$

Expressing $\zeta_{2 \cdot 1}$ as a function of z and z'

$$\zeta_{2 \cdot 1} = \frac{z_2 - z_1 \cos w}{\sin w}, \qquad (2 \cdot 204)$$

we have

$$r_1^2 = z_1^2 + \zeta_{2 \cdot 1}^2 = \frac{z^2 - 2z_1 z_2 \cos w + z_2^2}{\sin^2 w}. \qquad (2 \cdot 205)$$

Now putting

$$t = \frac{z_1}{\sin w}, \quad t' = \frac{z_2}{\sin w}, \quad \rho = \cos w = -\cos \varphi \qquad (2 \cdot 206)$$

we obtain
$$t^2 - 2ptt' + t'^2 = r^2.$$

Geometrically interpreted, t and t' are the coordinates of the point P in an oblique coordinate system with $\zeta_{1 \cdot 2}$ and $\zeta_{2 \cdot 1}$ as the axes.

When the functions t and t' determined by (2 · 201) are of normal correlation, the following relations must be fulfilled:

$$r_1^2 = z_1^2 + \zeta_{2 \cdot 1}^2 = z_2^2 + \zeta_{1 \cdot 2}^2 = r_2^2, \qquad (2 \cdot 207)$$

$$\tan w = \frac{z_1 \zeta_{1 \cdot 2} + z_2 \zeta_{2 \cdot 1}}{z_1 z_2 - \zeta_{1 \cdot 2} \zeta_{2 \cdot 1}} = \text{const. or } \cos w = \rho = \text{const.} \qquad (2 \cdot 208)$$

and inversely.

If these conditions are not fulfilled, adjustments must be made. Among the innumerable possible methods, Van Uven recommends the following two:

(i) The first method is:
(A) to leave the functions $z_1(x)$ and $z_2(x')$ unaltered,
(B) to introduce a constant angle $\bar{w}$ which is the weighted mean of the variable w computed from (2 · 203), the weight being the corresponding frequency at the point whose coordinates are used in the computation of w.

Then the points P_1 and P_2 are shifted to a point P' so that $z_1' = z_1$, $z_2' = z_2$ and that $\zeta'_{2 \cdot 1} = \dfrac{z_2 - z_1 \cos w}{\sin w} = -z_1 \cot w + \dfrac{z_2}{\sin w}$. The variables $t(x)$ and $t'(x, x')$ expressed in terms of z_1, z_2 are:

$$\begin{cases} t = \dfrac{z_1}{\sin w}, \\ t' = \dfrac{\sin(w - \bar{w})}{\sin w \sin \bar{w}} z_1 + \dfrac{1}{\sin w} z_2. \end{cases} \qquad (2 \cdot 209\text{i})$$

(ii) The second method is:
(A) to hold z_1 and $\zeta_{2 \cdot 1}$ unchanged,
(B) to introduce the mean angle $\bar{w}$ as in the first method,
(C) to shift P' to P.

Thus, the unadjusted values z_2 and $\zeta_{1.2}$ are only used in conjunction with z_1 and $\zeta_{2.1}$ to determine w. The value z_2 is afterwards adjusted to $z'_2 = \dfrac{r_1}{r_2} z_2$, becoming in this way a mixed function of x and x'.

The functions $t(x)$ and $t'(x, x')$ which will be of normal correlation, with correlation coefficient equal to $\rho = \cos \bar{w}$, are determined by

$$\begin{cases} t = \dfrac{z_1}{\sin w}, \\ t = \dfrac{\sin(w - \bar{w})}{\sin w \sin \bar{w}} z_1 + \dfrac{r_1}{r_2} \dfrac{z_3}{\sin w}. \end{cases} \qquad (2 \cdot 209\text{ii})$$

By this method we may obtain precisely the given frequencies by computing back from $(z_1, \zeta_{2.1})$. But there is a drawback, because the comparatively accurate quantity z_2 is almost wholly neglected in the process (according to Van Uven, z_1 and z'_2 are determined more accurately that $\zeta_{2.1}$ and $\zeta_{1.2}$ because the latter is computed from small frequencies and affected by the uncertainties of interpolation).

Van Uven[①] has established his method for treating skew correlation between an arbitrary number (n) of variates by following the same process of transformation.

Suppose the frequency distribution of the observed n variables x_1, x_2, $x_3, \cdots, x_n$ so that

$$\mathrm{d}W = G(x_1, \cdots, x_n)\mathrm{d}x_1\cdots\mathrm{d}x_n = \dfrac{\sqrt{A}}{\sqrt{x^n}} e^{-f} \mathrm{d}t_1 \mathrm{d}t_2 \cdots \mathrm{d}t_n \qquad (2 \cdot 210)$$

where

$$f = \sum_{i=1}^{n} \sum_{j=1}^{n} a_{ij} t_i t_j$$

with $\quad a_{ii} = 1, \ a_{ij} = a_{ji}, \ a_{ij}^2 = 1, \ A = a_{ij}.$

Now f may be divided into a sum of n squares in the manner we have noted in the case of two variates [see also equation $(2 \cdot 9)$]:

---

① "Skew Correlation between Three and More Variables", Proc. Kong. Ak. v. Wet. Amst., Vol.32, pp.793–807, 995–1007, 1085–1103, 1929.

$$f = \zeta^2_{n \cdot 12\cdots,(n-1)} + \zeta^2_{(n-1) \cdot 12\cdots(n-2)} + \cdots + \zeta^2_{b \cdot 12\cdots(b-1)} + \cdots + \zeta^2_1. \qquad (2 \cdot 211)$$

Parallel to equation $(2 \cdot 191)$, we have here

$$\begin{aligned} \mathrm{d}W &= \frac{1}{\sqrt{x}^n} e^{-\zeta^2_1 + \zeta^2_{2 \cdot 1} + \cdots \zeta^2_{n \cdot 12 \cdots n-1}} \mathrm{d}\zeta_1 \mathrm{d}\zeta_{2 \cdot 1} \cdots \mathrm{d}\zeta_{n \cdot 12 \cdots n-1} \\ &= \mathrm{d}\{H(\zeta_1)\}\mathrm{d}\{H(\zeta_{2 \cdot 1})\}\cdots\mathrm{d}\{H(\zeta_{n \cdot 12 \cdots n-1})\}. \end{aligned} \qquad (2 \cdot 212)$$

Let us assume the variates $x_{b+1}, x_{b+2}, \cdots, x_n$ to be arbitrary and have the partial set of variates $x_1, x_2, \cdots, x_b$. The frequency distribution of this partial set, called the $(n-b)$-th partial correlation surface, will be given by

$$\begin{aligned} \mathrm{d}_{n-b} W &= \int_{x_{b+1,0}}^{x_{b+1,n}} \cdots \int\int_{x_{n,0}}^{x_{n,n_1}} G(x_1 \cdots x_n) \mathrm{d}x_{b+1} \cdots \mathrm{d}x_n \\ &= \mathrm{d}\{H(z_1)\}\mathrm{d}\{H(\zeta_{2 \cdot 1})\}\cdots\mathrm{d}\{H(\zeta_{b \cdot 12 \cdots b-1})\} \\ &\quad \cdot \int\int \cdots \int_0^\infty \mathrm{d}\{H(\zeta_{b+1 \cdot 12 \cdots b})\}\cdots\mathrm{d}\{H(\zeta_{n \cdot 12 \cdots n-1})\} \\ &= \mathrm{d}\{H(z_1)\}\mathrm{d}\{H(\zeta_{2 \cdot 1})\}\cdots\mathrm{d}\{H(\zeta_{b \cdot 12 \cdots b-1})\}. \end{aligned} \qquad (2 \cdot 213)$$

Hence the total (cumulative) probability of x_b, $x_b(k_b)$ in an array of x_b of the $\{x_1(k_1), x_2(k_2), \cdots, x_{b-1}(k_{b-1})\}$-type is, parallel to equation $(2 \cdot 198)$, connected to its empirical value by the following equation

$$H\zeta_{b \cdot 12 \cdots b-1}(k_1, k_2, \cdots, k_{b-1} \cdot k_b)$$

$$= \frac{\sum_{i_b=1}^{k_b} \sum_{i_{b+1}=1}^{n_{b+1}} \cdots \sum_{i_n=1}^{n_n} Y(k_1, k_2, \cdots, k_{b-1}, i_b, i_{b+1}, \cdots, i_n)}{\sum_{i_b=1}^{n_b} \sum_{i_{b+1}=1}^{n_{b+1}} \cdots \sum_{i_n=1}^{n_n} Y(k_1, k_2, \cdots, k_{b-1}, i_b, \cdots, i_n)} \qquad (2 \cdot 214)$$

where b may be assigned successively, values $1, 2, \cdots, n$; and $n_1, n_2, \cdots, n_n$ denote the number of classes of the variates $x_1, x_2, \cdots, x_n$ respectively.

From the equations $(2 \cdot 214)$, we may determine values for $\zeta_{n \cdot 12 \cdots n-1}$, $\zeta_{n-1 \cdots n-2}, \cdots, \zeta_{2 \cdot 1}$ and ζ_1 corresponding to the combinations of $x_1, x_2, \cdots, x_n$ and then construct the functions $\zeta_1(x_1)$, $\zeta_{2 \cdot 1}(x_1, x_2), \cdots, \zeta_{n \cdot 12 \cdots (n-1)}(x_1 \cdots x_n)$ graphically.

As the construction will hold no matter in what order we have taken up the variates, we may permutate the subscripts to obtain the other system of functions:

$$\zeta_i, \zeta_{j\cdot i}, \zeta_{k\cdot ij}, \cdots, \qquad (i, j, k, \cdots = 1, 2, \cdots, n),$$

which may result as we build them in various orders.

Following the same procedure as in the case of two variates we may introduce

$$\overline{\zeta_i \zeta_j} - \overline{\zeta_{ji} \zeta_{ij}} = B'_{ij}$$
$$\overline{\zeta_i \zeta_{j\cdot i} \zeta_j \zeta \zeta_{i\cdot j}} = B_{ij}$$

and obtain

$$M_{ij} = \tan w_{ij} = \frac{B_{ij}}{B'_{ij}} \left(\frac{\cos w_{ij}}{A_{ij}} \; 0 \right) \qquad (2 \cdot 215)$$

$$r_{ij} = \cos w_{ij} = \text{coef. of cor. between } t_i \text{ and } t_j.$$

In order to express t-functions in terms of ζ-functions, Van Uven makes use of the "polar" expressions for r_{ij}, which may be found in Pearson's①"On the Influence of Natural Selection on the Variability and Correlation of Organs" and Charlier's②"On Multiple Correlation". Thus

$$r_{ij} = \frac{A_{ij}}{\sqrt{A_{ii} A_{jj}}} \qquad (2 \cdot 216)$$

where A_{ij} is the algebraic complement to a_{ij} in the determinant a_{ij}. The relation between r_{ij} and a_{ij} is mutual

$$a_{ij} = \frac{R_{ij}}{\sqrt{R_{ii} R_{jj}}} \qquad (2 \cdot 217)$$

where $R = r_{ij}$. So, by equation $(2 \cdot 210)$,

$$f = \sum_{i=1}^{n} \sum_{j=1}^{n} R_{ij} t_i t_j / \sqrt{R_{ii} R_{jj}}. \qquad (2 \cdot 218)$$

Van Uven has shown that

$$\zeta_{b\cdot 12\cdots b-1} = \frac{\sqrt{R}}{\sqrt{R_b R_{b-1}}} \sum_{i=1}^{b} \frac{(R_b)_{ib}}{\sqrt{R_{ii}}} t_i \qquad (2 \cdot 219)$$

where R_b denotes the principal minor of both order in the determinant r_{ij} and

---

① Phil. Trans., Vol.200, London, 1903.
② So. Ak. Tid., p.78, 1915.

$(R_b)_{ij}$ algebraic complement of the element r_{ij} in R_b. As b takes the values 1, 2,⋯, n, we obtain the expressions:

$$\zeta_1 = \frac{\sqrt{R}}{\sqrt{R_{11}}} t_1 \text{ or, in general, } \zeta_i = \frac{\sqrt{R}}{\sqrt{R_{ii}}} t_i; \qquad (2\cdot 219\text{a})$$

$$\zeta_{2\cdot 1} = \frac{R}{\sqrt{1-r^2}} \frac{r_{12}}{\sqrt{R_{11}}} t_1 + \frac{1}{\sqrt{R_{22}}} t_2;$$

⋯⋯

$$\zeta_{n\cdot 12\cdots n-1} = \frac{1}{\sqrt{R_{n-1}}} \sum_{i=1}^{n} \frac{R_{in}}{\sqrt{R_{ii}}} t_i. \qquad (2\cdot 219\text{b})$$

From these equations, t-functions may be solved in terms of ζ-functions which are known functions of x's.

If t's so determined are of normal correlation, some relations must be fulfilled:

(i) As mentioned above, the ζ-functions are independent of the arrangement of the subscripts 1, 2, ⋯, b, we must have

$$q_{ij}^2 = \zeta_i^2 + \zeta_{j\cdot i}^2 = \zeta_j^2 + \zeta_{i\cdot j}^2 = q_{ji}^2. \qquad (2\cdot 220)$$

(Condition I)

(ii) Moreover, from (2·219a) and (2·219b)

$$\zeta_{j\cdot i} = \frac{-r_{ji}\zeta_1 + \zeta_j}{\sqrt{1-r_{ij}^2}}$$

$$\zeta_{i\cdot j} = \frac{-r_{ij}\zeta_j + \zeta_i}{\sqrt{1-r^2}}, \qquad (2\cdot 221)$$

it follows that

$$q_{ij}^2 = \frac{\zeta_i^2 - 2r_{ij}\zeta_i\zeta_j + \zeta_j^2}{1-r_{ij}^2} \qquad (2\cdot 222)$$

and that

$$\zeta_i\zeta_j - \zeta_{j\cdot i}\zeta_{i\cdot j} = \frac{(1-r_{ij}^2)\zeta_i\zeta_j - r_{ij}\zeta_i\zeta_j + r_{ij}\zeta_j^2 + \zeta_i\zeta_j}{1-r_{ij}^2}$$

$$= r_{ij}q_{ij}^2 \qquad (2\cdot 223)$$

$$\zeta_i\zeta_{j\cdot i} + \zeta_j\zeta_{i\cdot j} = \sqrt{1-r_{ij}^2 q_{ij}^2}. \qquad (2\cdot 224)$$

Hence
$$M_{ij} = \frac{\sqrt{1-r_{ij}^2}}{r_{ij}} = \frac{\zeta_i \zeta_{j\cdot i} + \zeta_j \zeta_{i\cdot j}}{\zeta_i \zeta_j - \zeta_{j\cdot i}\zeta_{i\cdot j}} = \text{constant}. \quad (2 \cdot 225)$$

(Condition II)

(iii) Furthermore, from equations $(2 \cdot 219)$ and $(2 \cdot 219a)$, we obtain the third condition to be fulfilled:

$$\zeta_{b\cdot 12\cdots b-1} = \frac{\sum_{i=1}^{b}(R_b)_{ib}\zeta_i}{\sqrt{R_b R_{b-1}}} \quad (2 \cdot 226)$$

(Condition III)

$$q_{12\cdots b}^2 = \zeta_1^2 + \zeta_{2\cdot 1}^2 + \cdots + \zeta_{b\cdot 12\cdots b-1}^2$$
$$= \left\{ \sum_{i=1}^{b}\sum_{j=1}^{b} R_{ij}\zeta_i\zeta_j \right\} : R_b. \quad (2 \cdot 227)$$

If these conditions in $(2 \cdot 220)$, $(2 \cdot 225)$, and $(2 \cdot 226)$ are fulfilled, then the t_i functions are determined by

$$t_i = \sqrt{\frac{R_{ii}}{R}} \zeta_i. \quad (i = 1, 2, \cdots, n)$$

In the particular case that all the functions $\zeta_i(x_i)$ are linear, there exists normal correlation among the variates themselves.

If conditions I and III are satisfied, but condition II is not, then the constant arcs $\bar{w}_{ij}$ being the weighed mean of arc tang $\overline{M}_{ij}$, are introduced for adjustment.

Putting

$$\zeta_i \sqrt{\frac{R}{R_{ii}}} = u_i,$$

we obtain
$$\zeta_1 = u,$$
$$\zeta_{2\cdot 1} = (-\bar{r}_{12}u_1 + u_2) : \sqrt{R_2},$$
$$\zeta_{b\cdot 12\cdots b-1} = \left(\sum_{i=1}^{b}(\bar{R}_b)_{ib}u_i \right) : \sqrt{R_b \bar{R}_{n-1}}$$
......

$$\zeta_{n \cdot 12 \cdots n-1} = \left(\sum_{i=1}^{n} \overline{R}_{in} u_i \right) : \sqrt{\overline{R}\ \overline{R}_{n-1}}.$$

Substituting in (2 · 219) we obtain in equations to solve for t_i in terms of u_i.

If conditions III are not satisfied, then the adjusted values $\zeta'_{b \cdot 12 \cdots b-1}$ should be used in place of the empirically found values $\zeta_{b \cdot 12 \cdots b-1}$.

$$\zeta'_{b \cdot 12 \cdots b-1} = \left(\sum_{i=1}^{b} (R_b)_{ib} \zeta_i \right) : \sqrt{R_b R_{b-1}}.$$

Now the t's determined from the system of equations (2 · 219) will not give back the original frequency distribution, but an adjusted frequency distribution.

If even condition I is not satisfied, so that $q_{i \cdot j} = q_{j \cdot i}$, then the empirical values $\zeta_{i \cdot j}$ and $\zeta_{j \cdot i}$ must be replaced by their adjusted values determined by (2 · 221), i.e.,

$$\zeta'_{i \cdot j} = \frac{\zeta_i - \zeta_j \cos w_{ij}}{\sin w_{ij}} = \frac{-r_{ij} \zeta_i + \zeta_j}{\sqrt{1 - r_{ij}^2}},$$

$$\zeta'_{j \cdot i} = \frac{\zeta_j - \zeta_i \cos w_{ij}}{\sin w_{ij}} = \frac{-r_{ij} \zeta_j + \zeta_i}{\sqrt{1 - r_{ij}^2}},$$

where w_{ij} is computed from (2 · 215). Clearly, these adjusted values $\zeta'_{i \cdot j}$ together with ζ_i will give the same w_{ij} and therefore the same r_{ji} as the empirical values. But the magnitude q_{ij} in (2 · 222) must now be replaced by

$$q'^2_{ij} = \frac{\zeta_i^2 - 2\zeta_i \zeta_j \cos w_{ij} + \zeta_j^2}{\sin^2 w_{ij}}.$$

Van Uven illustrates his method in the case of two variates. The problem is to determine the correlation between the height and the volume of djati trees with 916 observations. The distribution appears to be g-shaped in one direction and thus representative of extremely skew correlation.

This method seems to be superior to the general method of translation which uses high moments and involves an approximation process. High moments and approximations involved in the determination of constants may often result in incontrollable probable errors. Furthermore, Van Uven's method will in general give a better fit to the observed frequency distribution, and no objection-able negative frequency can result.

2.29 Steffensen's Surface[1]

To represent a slight degree of correlation, Steffensen, in 1922, gave the frequency function of the form

$$F(x, y) = kf_1(x, y)f_2(x, y)$$

which can be reduced to

$$F(x, y) = kf'_1(x)f'_2(y).$$

Suppose x and y to be linearly related, then

$$F(x, y) = kf_1(x + cy)f_2(y + \gamma x)$$
$$= kf_1(\xi)f_2(\eta). \qquad (2 \cdot 228)$$

Let c'_p and γ'_p denote the moment coefficient of the functions $f_1(\xi)$ and $f_2(\eta)$ respectively, μ'_{pq} the pq-th moment coefficient of $F(x, y)$; the primes are to be dropped when the origin is at the mean.

Thus,

$$c'_p = \int \xi^p f_1(\xi) d(\xi), \quad \gamma'_p = \int \eta^p f_2(\eta) d\eta, \quad \mu'_{pq} = \iint x^p y^q F(x, y) dxdy.$$

The constants on which f_1 and f_2 depend are to be found in the usual way from the moments c_p and γ_p.

From the transformation, we have

$$\iint f_1(\xi)f_2(\eta) d\xi d\eta = \int f_1(x + cy)f_2(y + \gamma x) \begin{vmatrix} \dfrac{\partial \xi}{\partial x} & \dfrac{\partial \eta}{\partial x} \\ \dfrac{\partial \xi}{\partial y} & \dfrac{\partial \eta}{\partial y} \end{vmatrix} dxdy$$

$$= \frac{1}{k} \iint F(x, y) \mid 1 - c\gamma \mid dxdy$$

or,

$$k = \mid 1 - c\gamma \mid ; \qquad (2 \cdot 229)$$

and also

$$\iint (x + cy)^p (y + \gamma x)^q F(x, y) dxdy = c'_p \gamma'_q. \qquad (2 \cdot 230)$$

From this last equation, it follows

---

[1] "A Correlation Formula", loc. cit.

$$c_1 = \mu_{10} + c\mu_{01} = 0$$
$$\gamma_1 = \gamma\mu_{10} + \mu_{01} = 0$$
$$\begin{cases}\gamma\mu_{20} + (1 + c\gamma)\mu_{11} + c\mu_{02} = 0 \\ \gamma^2\mu_{30} + \gamma(2 + c\gamma)\mu_{21} + c(2 + c\gamma)\mu_{12} + c^2\mu_{03} = 0 \\ \gamma\mu_{30} + (1 + 2c\gamma)\mu_{21} + c(2 + c\gamma)\mu_{12} + c^2\mu_{03} = 0\end{cases} \quad (2\cdot231)$$

whence c and γ may be solved.

Introducing two new parameters

$$r = \frac{\gamma}{1+c\gamma}, \qquad v = \frac{c}{1+c\gamma}$$

whence

$$c = \frac{1-\sqrt{1-4uv}}{2u}, \qquad \gamma = \frac{1-\sqrt{1-4uv}}{2v},$$

and substituting these expressions for c and γ in $(2\cdot231)$, we obtain

$$u\mu_{20} + v\mu_{02} + \mu_{11} = 0 \quad (2\cdot232)$$

$$\begin{cases}u\mu_{21} + v\mu_{30} + \mu_{12} = 0 \\ u\mu_{30} + v\mu_{12} + \mu_{21} = 0.\end{cases} \quad (2\cdot233)$$

Combine equations $(2\cdot233)$ by making

$$(u\mu_{21} + v\mu_{30} + \mu_{12})^2 + (u\mu_{30} + v\mu_{12} + \mu_{21})^2$$

a minimum. This gives

$$\frac{\mu_{02}}{\mu_{20}} = \frac{u(\mu_{03}\mu_{21} + \mu_{30}\mu_{12}) + v(\mu_{03}^2 + \mu_{12}^2) + \mu_{12}(\mu_{03} + \mu_{21})}{u(\mu_{30}^2 + \mu_{21}^2) + v(\mu_{03}\mu_{21} + \mu_{30}\mu_{21}) + \mu_{21}(\mu_{30} + \mu_{12})} \quad (2\cdot234)$$

which together with $(2\cdot232)$ will determine the values of u and v and therefore the values of c and γ.

The moments c_p and γ_p are obtained by expanding the binomial in $(2\cdot230)$. Thus

$$c_p = \mu_{p0} + \frac{p}{1!}c\mu_{p-1,1} + \frac{p(p-1)}{2!}c^2\mu_{p-2,2} + \cdots + c^p\mu_{0p}$$

$$\gamma_p = \gamma^p\mu_{p0} + \frac{p}{1!}\gamma^{p-1}\mu_{p-1,1} + \frac{p(p-1)}{2!}\gamma^{p-2}\mu_{p-2,2} + \cdots + \mu_{0p}.$$

The method is illustrated on the example treated by Jorgensen for the type

A-function as given in (2·140). The resulting surface is:

$$z = z_0 e^{-d_1 x - d_2 y}(1 - a_1 x + b_0 y)^{p_1}(1 - a_2 x + b_2 y)^{p_2}.$$

From the values of Pearsonian β_1, β_2 coefficients, the marginal distributions are of Pearsonian Type III curves. The cell mid-ordinates are computed for comparison with Jorgensen's results. From an inspection of the table exhibiting these frequencies, it is obvious that Steffensen's method gives an improved graduation. Moreover, it does not give rise to the objectionable negative frequencies.

CHAPTER III THE REGRESSION METHOD

3.1 The Meaning of the Regression Method

In this chapter we shall trace the development of the regression method of approach to the description of relationship between variates. This method is perhaps most commonly used in practical statistics, and an exposition may be found in almost any textbook of statistics.[1] The method mainly seeks to determine whether there is a general tendency or trend for a large x (a variable quantity or variate) to be associated with a large or small y (another variate) and the amount of mean variation of individual observations from the general tendency or trend. In other words, for assigned x larger than the mean value of x's, if a corresponding y taken or observed at random is much more likely to be above than below the mean value of y's, it is said that there is a general tendency for x and y to vary simultaneously in the same direction, or simply that there is a positive covariation or correlation between x and y; if a corresponding y taken at random is much more likely to be below rather than above the mean value of y's, it is said that there is an inverse covariation or correlation between x and y; if a corresponding y taken at random is equally likely to be above as below the mean value of y, it is said that there is no correlation between x and y. If the values of x and y are arranged in a twofold frequency distribution (as explained in Chapter II, part i), this tendency may be revealed by the means or modes, or medians, of the arrays, or any series of points defined in the same

---

[1] For instance, we may find a good exposition of this method in Jerome, H., *Statistical Methods*, Rietz, H. L., *Mathematical Statistics*, Yule, G. U., *An Introduction to the Theory of Statistics*.

manner for arrays. The locus of such points representing such a general tendency of covariation of x and y is called the regression line. However, the means seem to be preferred by statisticians for that purpose, and a regression value (that is the value estimated for the essential variate from the regression line) is then called the expected value of the essential (dependent) variate of a specified type. In dealing with a statistical data, we are making an estimate, according to some criterion, of such a regression line in the sampled population. If a mathematical curve is fitted for the representation of the regression as exhibited by the means, the principle of the least squares is commonly used as the criterion.

It is fairly obvious from the frequency distribution (or correlation table) that for values of x in any given interval dx, the corresponding values or y may differ considerably, and thus the values of y corresponding to a specified type-value of x cannot be given by the regression equation representing the regression line, but form a partial frequency distribution (see Chapter II) which specifies how frequently y takes each of the possible values. If such partial frequency curves are all definitely determined, the variation of y about the regression is then completely specified and accordingly the correlation between x and y is wholly known. Indeed, these partial frequency curves, when put together, will form the surface which will be obtained by the correlation surface method. In this circumstance, the regression method is identical to the correlation surface method. However, the regression method as commonly used does not attempt to specify the variation about the regression by determining these partial frequency curves; instead it simply employs the standard error (the root-mean-square-deviation from the regression line) as the measure of variation. In this respect, the regression method ignores the form, skew or otherwise, of the distribution and thus diverges from the correlation surface method. When the standard error, $\sigma_{2\cdot1}$, about the regression of y on x is measured in units or standard deviation, σ_y, of y, the quantity $\sigma_{2\cdot1}/\sigma_y$ may be used as a measure of the intensity of correlation, the greater is $\sigma_{2\cdot1}/\sigma_y$, the less is the intensity; or, introducing the parameter: $r = \sqrt{1 - \sigma_{2\cdot1}^2/\sigma_y^2}$, the greater is r, the greater is the intensity of correlation. The parameter r so defined is called the correlation coefficient.

It should be observed that the standard error is sufficient to characterize the variation, and therefore the correlation coefficient is adequate to describe the intensity of correlation, only when the distribution is normal. The apparent simplicity of the method is thus gained at the expense or theoretical validity.

The above explanation may be easily extended to the case of any number of variates. The locus of means of the $(x_1, x_2, \cdots, x_{n-1})$ -arrays of x_n's is the regression of x_n on $x_1, x_2, x_3, \cdots, x_{n-1}$, and $\sigma_{n\cdot 123 \cdots n-1}$, the root-mean-square-deviation from the regression line, measures the variation of x_n about the regression line, and $r_{n\cdot 12 \cdots n-1} = \sqrt{1 - \dfrac{\sigma_{n\cdot 12 \cdots n-1}^2}{\sigma_n^2}}$ called the multiple correlation coefficient of $(n-2)$-th order, indicates the intensity of correlation of x_n with x_1, $x_2, \cdots, x_{n-1}$.

The regression is called linear when the regression function $f_n(x_1, x_2, \cdots, x_{n-1})$, is a linear function in $x_1, x_2, \cdots, x_{n-1}$, and curvilinear when the regression function f_n is a nonlinear function in $x_1, x_2, \cdots, x_{n-1}$. The regression is called simple when $n = 2$, and multiple when $n \geq 3$. Thus, $x_2 - b_{21}x_1 = 0$ is a simple linear regression, while $x_2 - (bx_1 + cx_1^2 + \cdots) = 0$, is a simple curvilinear regression of x_2 on x_1; and $x_n - (b_{n1}x_1 + b_{n2}x_2 + \cdots + b_{n(n-1)}x_{n-1}) = 0$ is a $(n-2)$-th order multiple linear regression equation while $x_n - (b_1x_1 + c_1x_1^2 + \cdots) + (b_2x_2 + c_2x_2^2 + \cdots) = 0$ is a $(n-2)$-th order multiple curvilinear regression equation of x_n on $x_1, x_2, \cdots, x_{n-1}$. Since the correlation coefficients are computed by using the regression lines as the basis, the coefficients so obtained are termed accordingly, for instance, we shall speak of a $(n-2)$-th order multiple curvilinear correlation coefficient if it is computed by using a $(n-2)$-th order multiple curvilinear regression as the basis of calculation.

3.2 The Scope of this Chapter

The regression method was Galton's ingenious discovery and has since been developed by Pearson, Yule, and others. We shall describe the various important developments in chronological order. As to the determination of regression lines by mathematical or graphical methods, we cannot hope to describe all the techniques so far developed, since, by the nature of the theory of the regression method, any mathematical curve (or surface) or even a freehand curve may be employed for the representation of the regression if it seems to be appropriate by experience or otherwise. No fitting can be said to be wrong or right, but rather in better or worse "taste".

In view of the fact that the statistical data to be dealt with are often a finite or small sample of available observations while the formulas in use are generally developed for large samples or an infinite population, the number of degrees of freedom used up for the determination of constants cannot be neglected and therefore will be considered in the course of discussion. In view of the fact that the so-called coefficient of determination has been unfortunately used by some quite eminent statisticians on erroneous grounds, the meaning of the correlation coefficient will be explained in contrast to that of the coefficient of determination. Finally, an account of spurious correlation is given so as to show that precautions should be exercised in the use or manipulation of statistical data.

3.3 The Discovery of the Regression Method of Galton[①]

3.3.1 Origins of Galton's Correlation Concept

Pearson[②], Galton came to the conception of correlation from two problems. The first problem which led Galton to the idea of correlation was the problem of measuring the resemblance of offspring to a parent, a partial causation in the sense that a character in the father does not determine absolutely the like character in the son, it is only one out of many contributory factors such as the mother's germplasm and innumerable ancestral stirps. The second problem which impressed itself on Galton's mind was the fact he had noted that two characters measured on a human being are not independent. The femur of man has its characters associated with those of the humerus.

The first problem involves causation while the second does not and the variates in the first problem have the same units of measurement while in the

---

[①] Galton's primary interest was in inheritance. To study the problem, he used as data the seeds of cress and then of sweet-peas, he experimented with the raising of pedigreed moths, studied hounds, and finally offered prizes for records of human families. For a description of his life and works, See Galton, Francis, *The Memories of My Life*, and Pearson, K., *The Life, Letters, and Labors of Francis Galton*, London, 1930.

[②] *Life of Galton*, Vol. III. A., p.3. Galton's earliest attempts at the solution of the problem of inheritance were not published and the available source of information is Pearson's *Life of Galton*, wherein we see that as early as 1875 Galton was conducting experiments with sweet-pea seeds to determine the relation with respect to the size between the mother and daughter peas. An interesting pictorial correlation table of seeds is shown in *Life of Galton*, Vol.II, p.392, on "Typical Laws of Heredity" Galton's lecture at the Royal Institution, Feb.1877, shows that he was then already in possession of sweet-pea data. Twelve years later, in the memoir "Correlation and their measurement" 1888, he succeeded in overcoming the difficulty of different variabilities in variates by using the quartile deviation Q as the unit of measurement.

second they do not.

"Galton did not realize immediately that his two problems admitted of the same solution. His first actual attempts at solution of the inheritance problem were based on the weight of the seeds of mother and daughter plants. In the first place he used, about 1875, some seeds like that of cress, and he started by endeavoring to correlate grades and ranks①. This could not be very successful because the regression curve and the isograms are not linear, but extremely complicated curves. Later in 1875 we find him experimenting, with Darwin's assistance, on the weight and diameter of sweet-pea seeds, and here he reached his first 'regression line'. I reproduce from Galton's data in a note-book the first 'regression line' which I suppose ever to have been computed. I have recalculated the constants and redrawn the line it is for sweet-pea diameters in mother and daughter plants. The correlation coefficient is 0.33, almost exactly one-third, ... Here we have the origin of Galton's 'regression straight line'. We see that as the size of mother pea increases, so does the size of daughter pea, but whether in excess or defect of mean the daughter pea does not reach the deviation of the mother's diameter from the mean value; the offspring is less a giant or a dwarf than the mother pea. This is Galton's phenomenon of regression. In this case the variabilities of mother and daughter peas were approximately equal②, and Galton reached the idea that the slope of the regression line would measure the intensity of resemblance between mother and daughter. If there were no slope, the diameter of daughter pea would be the same for all diameters of mother pea. If it sloped at 45°, i.e., a slope of unity, the daughter pea's diameter would be exactly that of the mother pea's, supposing their means were the same; if they were not, the deviations from their respective means would still be equal."③

---

① He first gives ranks to the observed values of breathing capacity; next he plots the ranks of breathing capacity against their corresponding stature; finally, he obtains the isogram by joining the points of equal breathing capacity.

See Pearson, *Life of Galton*, Vol.II, pp.390 – 391. Here we may also make mention of Pearson's remark in respect to the claims for the honor of the discovery of the correlation of ranks: "It is, I think, sufficient evidence that Galton dealt with the correlation of ranks before he reached the correlation of variates, and the claim that it is a contribution of the psychologist some thirty or forty years later to the conception of correlation does not seem to me valid." *Life of Galton*, Vol.II, p.393.

② If σ_m and σ_d are standard deviations of mother and daughter peas respectively, then $b = b\sigma_d/\sigma_m$ = r, since the s. d. of mothers should be equal to that of daughters.

③ Pearson, K., *Life of Galton*, Vol.III, A., p.3.

This was Galton's first conception of measuring correlation by means of the regression coefficient.

Table The First Correlation Table

Diameter of Parent Seed	Diameter of Filial Seeds							Total	Mean Diameter of Filial Seeds		s.d. of the array
	Under 15	15–	16–	17–	18–	19–	20–	Above 21–			
										observe	smoothed
21	22	8	10	18	21	13	6	2	100	17.5	17.26	1.988
20	23	10	12	17	20	13	3	2	100	17.3	17.07	1.938
19	35	16	12	13	11	10	2	1	100	16.0	16.37	1.896
18	34	12	13	17	16	6	2	0	100	16.3	16.40	2.037
17	37	16	13	16	13	4	1	0	100	15.6	16.13	1.654
16	34	15	18	16	13	3	1	0	100	16.0	16.17	1.594
15	46	14	9	11	14	4	2	0	100	15.3	15.98	1.763

From Appendix of Nat. Inh., p.226.

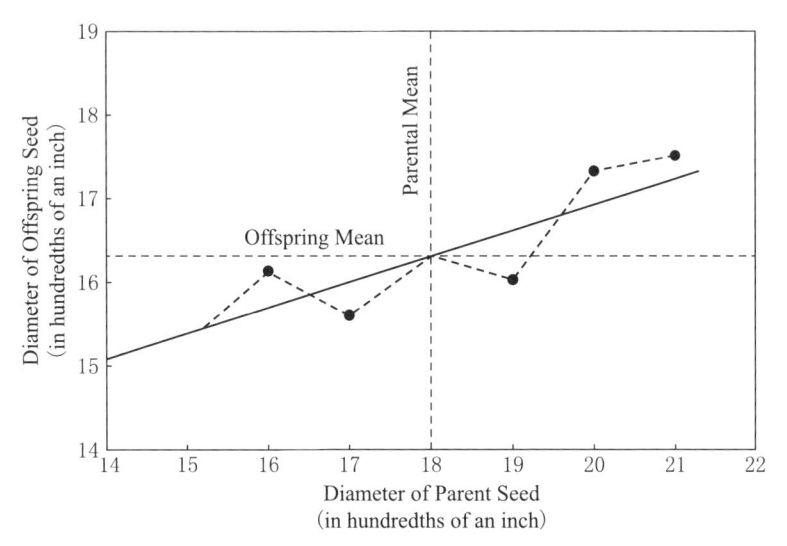

Figure The First Regression line

Inheritance in Size of Sweet-Pea Seeds (Galton-Royal Institution lecture, 1877), From Pearson, *Life of Galton*, Vol.III, A., p.4.

It is thus seen that Galton's first concept of correlation is similarity of

177

variation of the two variates about their medians, that the correlation may be described by a regression line, with the regression coefficient measuring the intensity of correlation, and that he reached the correlation coefficient, as a distinct concept from the concept of regression, at a much later date, namely, in 1886. Moreover, it should also be clear that the regression approach to the correlation analysis in this early stage of development had no connection with the theory of probability or the form or frequency distribution.

3.3.2 Galton's Works on Correlation

Galton might be said to have given a regression line in "notes on the Marlborough school statistics"①, 1874, where he takes the boys for each year of age and finds their means, which give for the central ages $12\frac{1}{2}$, $13\frac{1}{2}$, etc., the law of growth. Nevertheless, we shall assign 1877, when he gave the lecture on "Typical laws of heredity in man" at the Royal Institution, as the date of his formulation of the concept that the coefficient of regression, or reversion, as he called it at that time, is a measure of relationship of two characters. During the immediately following years, he was occupied in collecting material for further investigation of regression and heredity. Thus, beginning with 1885, he returned to the subject and published a number of papers dealing with regression mainly bearing upon the problem of inheritance of stature in man.②

3.3.3 Characteristics of Data used by Galton

Galton was dealing with anthropometric characters whose deviations from type (the median or mean), approximately followed the normal law of

---

① Jour. Anthrop. Inst., Vol.4, pp.130 – 135.

② (a) Address to Anthrop. Section, British Ass. at Aberdeen, Jour. British Association, pp.1206 – 1214, 1885.

(b) "Regression towards Mediocrity in Hereditary Stature", in the Miscellanea of J. Anthrop., Inst. 15, 246 – 263, 1805.

(c) Presidential Address to the Anthrop., Inst.15, pp.489 – 499, 1886.

(d) "Family Likeness in Stature with an Appendix by J. D. Hamilton Dickson", Proc. Roy. Soc. 40, pp.42 – 73, 1886.

(e) "Correlation and Their Measurement", Proc. Roy. Soc. 45, pp.135 – 145.

(f) *Natural Inheritance*, London, 1889. The three memoirs, b, d, e are the more important ones.

distribution (Chart II). So he was justified in assuming the normal curve as describing the deviations of a population or of any conditioned population, e.g., that of an array of offspring from a parent of given character. Secondly, his data approximately constant variability for all arrays of one character for a given value of the second. For instance, the array of standard deviations of the sweet peas as shown in Table II are approximately equal. Thus, Galton says: "I was certainly astonished to find the variability of the produce of the little seeds to be equal to that of the big ones; but so it was, and I thankfully accept the fact; for if it had been otherwise, I cannot imagine from theoretical consideration, how the typical problem could be solved."① As a third feature of his correlation table, he reached the linear regression line. These are in fact the conditions for a normal simple linear correlation surface. Inasmuch as these qualities are present in the heredity problem, he was preserved from any great error.

3.3.4 Evolution of Galton's Concept of Correlation

3.3.4.1 Reversion

In his experiment with the sweet peas,② Galton found from the data that there was a linear regression of daughter peas on maternal seed. He does not yet use the term "regression", but speaks of reversion. "Reversion," Galton says, "is the tendency of the ideal mean filial type to depart from the parental type, reverting towards what may be roughly and perhaps fairly described as the average ancestral type." Instead of supposing the offspring to revert he supposes the parent to revert and then to have offspring of a specified parentage after reversion as the mean type. In other words, if x (measured from the median or simply a deviation from the median) be the character of a parent and r be the reversion coefficient, then rx will be the same parentage after reversion, and the offspring of this parentage will distribute about rx as the type value. Moreover, if the character x in the parentage has a normal distribution and when reproduced, is to have the same normal distribution, then the offspring of this character will

---

① Pearson, *Life of Galton*, Vol.III, p.7; or "Typical Laws of Heredity", Roy. Inst. of Great Britain, Feb. 9, p.10, 1877.
② "Typical Laws of Heredity", Ibid.

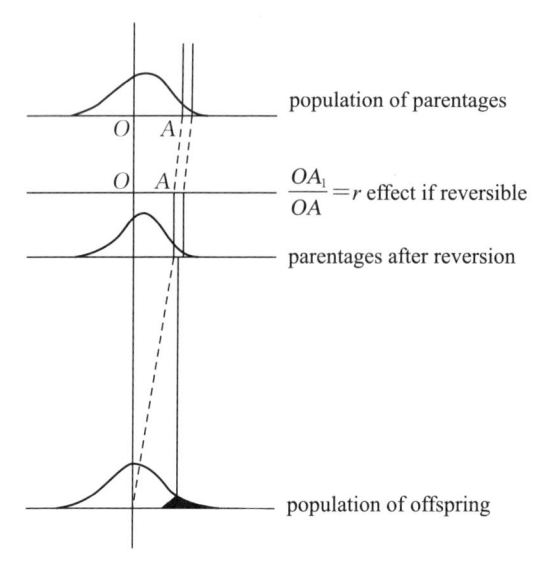

Figure Galtons Quincunx Illustrating the Nature of Regression

also be a normal distribution with rx as the mean and $\sigma_1\sqrt{1-r^2}$ as the standard deviation.① It is also of interest to see the ingenious "Quincunx" by which Galton illustrates the phenomenon of reversion and the continued maintenance by aid of inheritance of a stable population.②

3.3.4.2 Regression

Starting with the memoir "Regression towards mediocrity in Hereditary Stature", Galton speaks of regression instead of reversion. Thus, he says: "It is a universal rule that the unknown kinsman in any degree of any specified man, is probably more mediocre than he. Let the relation be what it may, it is safe to wager that the unknown kinsman of a person whose stature is $68\frac{1}{4} \pm x$ (where $68\frac{1}{4}$ is the median M of the population stature) inches, is of some height

---

① Let x assume the set of value $x_1, x_2, \cdots, x_n$ in the n parentages and the offspring of each x_i be normally distributed with variability σ_a. If $y_1, y_2, \cdots, y_n$, be the population of the offspring of all the n parentages in question, then $y = rx + y_{2\cdot1}$ and $\sigma_2^2 = r^2\sigma_1^2 + \sigma_{2\cdot1}^2$, where $y_{2\cdot1}$ is the residual of y from the regression line and σ_1, σ_2, $\sigma_{2\cdot1}$ are the standard deviations of x, y, and $y_{2\cdot1}$ respectively. By hypothesis the offspring assume the same distribution as the original parents, so $\sigma_1 = \sigma_2$, $\sigma_a^2 = \sigma_{2\cdot1}^2 = \sigma_1^2(1-r^2)$.

② Pearson, K., *Life of Galton*, Vol.III, A., p.9.

$68\frac{1}{4} \pm \bar{x}'$ inches①, where $\bar{x}'$ is less than x. ... $\bar{x}'$ becomes 0 in remote degrees of kinship, ... in intermediate degrees the value of $\bar{x}'/x$ is constant for all statures in the same degree of kinship. This fraction is what I call the ratio of regression, and I designate it by w." ② But in the determination of the regression coefficient w, Galton did not make use of the ratio $\bar{x}'/x$ or of the median of all such ratios. He simply plotted the medians of arrays, fitted graphically these medians with a straight line, and took the slope of this straight line as the regression coefficient. If the filial standard deviation and the parental standard deviation be equal as it should be, then the regression coefficient is the correlation coefficient; but that term was not used by Galton until the publication of the memoir "correlation and their measurement" in 1888 when he recognized the distinction between them.

In the problem of filial regression on the mid-parent, Galton found the regression coefficient w equal to 2/3. The interpretation is that "if $M + (\pm x)$ be the stature of the parent, the stature of the offspring will on the average be $M + (\pm x/3)$". ③ Galton designated this as "the law of regression" in respect to stature.

3.3.4.3 Correlation

In 1888 when the memoir "Correlation and Their Measurement" appeared, Galton fully recognized that the second problem of measuring correlation between variates having different variabilities is equivalent to the first, provided each

---

① Galton's Notation is $68\frac{1}{4} \pm x'$. But by this he really means the array mean of the kinsmen of the specified man of stature $68\frac{1}{4} \pm x$. So we may read: "the unknown kinsman of a person... is, on the average, of height $68\frac{1}{4} \pm \bar{x}'$, ..."

② Roy. Soc. Proc. 40, pp.50–51.

③ *Natural Inheritance*, p.104. It should be observed how Galton has obtained the regression coefficient of offspring on a parent from that of offspring on the mid-parent. A mid-parent is the imaginary mean of the two parents, after the female measurements have been transmuted to their male equivalents by multiplying by the ratio which the male stature bears to the female stature. "As the two parents contribute equally the contribution of either of them can be only one half of that of the two jointly; in other words, only one-half of that of the mid-parent." Nat. Inh., p.6, 98.

character was measured in its own variability as the unit and that the coefficient of correlation is different from the coefficient of regression. This year marks the completion of Galton's method for normal correlation analysis.① In this paper, he starts with the definition of correlation and then gives the practical method of determining the correlation coefficient (he calls it the index of correlation and denotes it by r. Thus, he used r to denote the "reversion" in 1877, and then used w to denote the "regression" until 1888 when he used r for the index of correlation). Thus, he says:

"Two variable organs are said to be correlated when the variation of the one is accompanied on the average by more or less variation of the other, and in the same direction. Thus, the length of the arm is said to be co-related with that of leg, because a person with a long arm has usually a long leg, and conversely. If the correlation be close, then a person with a very long arm would usually have a very long leg; if it be moderately close, then the length of his leg would usually be only long, not very long; and if there were no co-relation at all then the length of his leg would on the average be mediocre." "It is easy to see," he continues in explaining the causes for the correlation, "that co-relation must be the consequence of the variations of the two organs being partly due to common causes. If there were wholly due to common causes, the co-relation would be perfect, as is approximately the case with the symmetrically disposed parts of the body. If they were in no respect due to common causes, the co-relation would be nil. Between these two extremes are an endless number of intermediate cases, and it will be shown how the closeness of co-relation in any particular case admits of being expressed by a simple number."②

Here we notice that he writes "co-relation" for correlation. His then concept of correlation was reciprocal relationship. He says:③

"The relation between the cubit and the stature will be shown to be such

---

① "In 1886 I contributed two papers to the Royal Society on Family Likeness, having by that time got my methods for measuring heredity into satisfactory shape." *Memories of My Life*, p.302. This passage seemed to show that he had completely formulated the correlation method in 1886; but so far as his publications are concerned, the method itself was not in complete shape until the appearance of the memoir on "Correlation and their Measurement".
② "Correlation and their Measurement", p.135.
③ Ibid., p.136.

that for every inch, centimeter, or other unit of absolute length that the cubit deviates① from the mean length of cubits, the stature will on the average deviate from the mean length of statures to the amount of 2·5 units, and in the same direction (e.g., the regression line of stature on cubit is $x_2 = 2·5x_1$ or $b_{21} = 2·5$). Conversely, for each unit of deviation of stature, the average deviation of the cubit will be 0.26 unit (e.g., $x_1 = 0.26x_2$ or, $b_{12} = 0.26$). These relations are not numerically reciprocal (e.g., $b_{21} \neq b_{12}$), but the exactness of the co-relation becomes established when we have transmuted the inches or other measurement of the cubit and of the stature into unit dependent on their respect scales of variability. We thus cause a long cubit and an equally long stature, as compared to the general run of cubits and statures, to be designated by an identical scale value. The particular unit that I shall employ is the value of the probable error [he uses for the probable error the mean quartile deviation $Q = \frac{1}{2}(Q_3 - Q_1)$, where Q_1 and Q_3 are the first and the third quartile deviation] of any single measure in its own group. In that, of the cubit, the probable error is 0.56 inch = 1.42 cm; in the stature it is 1.75 inch = 4.44 cm. Therefore, the measured lengths of the cubit in inches will be transmuted into terms of a new scale, in which each unit = 0.56 inch, and the measured length or the stature will be transmuted into terms of another new scale in which each unit is 1.75 inch. After this has been done, we shall find the deviation of the cubit as compared to the mean of the corresponding deviations of the stature, to be as 1 to 0.8. Conversely, the deviation of the stature as compared to the mean of the corresponding deviations of the cubit will also be as 1 to 0.8. Thus the existence of the co-relation is established, and its measure is found to be 0.8." This measure is called the index of correlation, designated by r.

However, it should be noted that Galton's then concept of "index of correlation" was the same as that of "regression" in his earlier memoirs. "... the index of co-relation, which is what I here (he means the memoir 'Hereditary

---

① Galton fully realized that the correlation exists between the deviations from the mean (median in his usage then) of the variates; the law of regression in stature refers primarily to deviations, that is, to measurements made from mediocrity (medians) to the crown of the head, upwards or downwards as the case may be, and not from the ground to the crown of the head. Nat. Inh., p.104.

Stature') called 'regression', is different in the different cases. In dealing with kinships there is usually no need to reduce the measures to units of Q, because the Q values are alike in all the kinsmen, being of the same value as that of the population at large."①

3.3.5　Generalization of Correlation Table by a Correlation Surface

To examine more closely into the correlation table of parents and offspring, Galton smoothed② the frequencies by writing at each intersection between a horizontal line and a vertical one, the sum of the frequencies in the four adjacent cells. He then noticed that the contour of equal frequencies forms a family of concentric ellipses with center at the common mean of the filial and midparental statures. He also determined from the contours the inclinations of the conjugate axes③ which were recognized to be the regression lines. Galton believed that these relations admitted of mathematics expression, but he failed to find the solution and asked Mr. Dickson to solve for him. The solution being the simple linear correlation surface④ enabled Galton to identify his correlation coefficient with the coefficient of the product term in the exponent of that surface and thus put the regression method in cases where the variates follow the normal distribution upon a sound theoretical basis.

3.3.6　Conclusion

Galton's discovery of the regression method was an empirical process. His creative mind led him to see that there is a partial causal relation between the characters of parents and of their offspring, that the simultaneous variation of such characters as revealed from the statistical data is an evidence of the existence of such relationship and that the average variation of one character

---

① "Correlation and their Measurement", p.143.

② A description appeared in "Hereditary Stature", "Family Likeness", and also in *Natural Inheritance*. Dickson's solution is also found there.

③ See Bravais' method of determination.

④ An account of Galton's attempts to express the correlation table in a single formula which Dickson supplied, he may be also included among those who used the correlation surface approach, and for this reason we did describe her work briefly in Chap. II. However, we should like to point out that there is a slight gap left by Galton in his identification that the regression line derived from the normal bivariate surface as given in Dickson's solution was the same line which he had obtained by his method; the former is the locus of array modes while the latter is the locus of array medians. But only in the normal distribution are these two identical.

relative to the other is a measure of correlation, with the regression coefficient measuring the intensity of the correlation. Next, he came to recognize that this method is equally applicable to cases where the variates are not necessarily causally related and have different variabilities, provided each character be measured in units of its own variability. Finally, he expressed the correlation table by the normal bivariate surface and thereby gave the regression method a sound theoretical basis. In short, Galton did not start with a general definition of correlation and see whether that would lead him; the definition came in "Correlation and their Measurement", 1888, simply to fit the results he had obtained.

Galton's arrangement and analysis of data were systematic and practical. His method of fitting the regression line by observation was a rude one and consequently the correlation coefficient which is the slope of the line so fitted, was only a rough estimate. It is of interest to note, after having identified his correlation coefficient with the coefficient of the product term in exponent of the normal bivariate surface, that he could not see, although we might expect that he would, from the mathematical derivation of the surface that the correlation coefficient should be given by the standardized product moment, namely, $r = \dfrac{m_{11}}{\sqrt{m_{20} m_{02}}}$, where $m_{ij} = \sum \dfrac{x^i y^j}{N}$.

3.4 Weldon, W. F. R. (1860 – 1906)

The immediate follower of Galton was Weldon[1] who published three papers in applying, improving, and extending Galton's method of correlation. The first paper[2] on organs of shrimps was the first application of Galton's method of regression to other zoological types than man. This paper added nothing to the method and meaning of regression or correlation; it did not even give the numerical values of the coefficients computed, but stated that certain biological principles had been established in terms of correlation and variation.

---

[1] For biographical account of Weldon, See Pearson, K., "Biography of Weldon", Biom., Vol.5, pp.1 – 52, 1906.

[2] "The Variation occurring in certain Decaped Crustacea", Proc. Roy. Soc., Vol.47, pp.445 – 453, 1890.

Weldon's second paper[①] on Shrimps followed in 1892, and this gives a brief description of Galton's method of regression and its meaning and also his own method of compulating r. Weldon's method introduces two modifications on Galton's procedure; he uses the mean instead of the median, and determines r from each individual array[②], taking the mean value of these r's as the true r. His own description of the method is an admirable sample of this type of work and will be reproduced as a demonstration of how Weldon proceeds in determining r:

"(1) In the population examined, let all those individuals be chosen in which a certain organ A, differs from its average size by a fixed amount, Y; then, in those individuals, let the deviations of a second organ, B, from its average be measured. The various individuals will exhibit deviations of B equal to x_1, x_2, x_3, $\cdots$ whose mean may be called x_m. The ratio $\dfrac{x_m}{Y}$ will be constant for all values of Y."

"In the same way, suppose those individuals are chosen in which the organ B has a constant deviation, X, then in those individuals y_m, the mean deviation of the organ A, will have the same ratio to X, whatever may be the value of X."

"(2) The ratios $\dfrac{x_m}{Y}$ and $\dfrac{y_m}{X}$ are connected by an interesting relation. Let Q_a represent the probable error of distribution of the organ A about its average, and Q_b that of the organ B; then,

$$\frac{\frac{y_m}{X}}{\frac{x_m}{Y}} = \frac{Q_a^2}{Q_b^2}$$

or

$$\frac{\left(\dfrac{x_m}{Q_b}\right)}{\left(\dfrac{Y}{Q_a}\right)} = \frac{\left(\dfrac{y_m}{Q_a}\right)}{\left(\dfrac{X}{Q_b}\right)} = r, \text{ a constant.''} \qquad (3 \cdot 1)$$

---

① "Certain Correlated Variations in Crangon Vulgaris", Proc. Roy. Soc., Vol.51, pp.2 – 21, 1892.

② The ratio of the mean of an array to the type of that array is r, the deviations of both variates being expressed in units of the quartile deviation.

"So that by taking a fixed deviation of either organ, expressed in terms of its probable error, and by expressing the mean associated deviation of the second organ in terms of its probable error, a ratio may be determined, whose value becomes ±1, when a change in either organ involves an equal change in the other, and 0 when the two organs are quite independent. This constant, therefore, measures the 'degree of correlation' between the two organs."①

From the foregoing paragraph, Weldon seemed to have recognized the domain of negative correlation coefficients.

Weldon's third paper appeared in 1893. Here he dealt with 23 pairs of Naples and Plymouth Shore Crabs and suggested② that "r" be called "Galton's function". This is perhaps the only feature of this paper which is of interest to us.

3.5　Pearson, K.

Pearson's first memoir on correlation was "Mathematical contributions to the Theory of Evolution. III. Regression, Heredity, and Panmixia"③, which summarized, refined, and extended the correlation analysis at that time. He indicated clearly the object of the memoir in the introduction to this article: "The problem of regression and heredity have been dealt with by Mr. Francis Galton in his epoch making work on 'Natural Inheritance', but, although he has shown exact methods of dealing, both experimentally and mathematically, with the problems of inheritance, it does not appear that the mathematicians have hitherto developed his treatment, or that biologists and medical men have yet fully appreciated that he has really shown how many of the problems which perplex them may receive at any rate a partial answer. A considerable portion of the present memoir will be devoted to the expansion and fuller development of

---

　①　"Certain Correlated Variations in Crangon Vulgaris", Proc. Roy. Soc., Vol.51, pp.2－21, 1892.

　②　"The importance of this constant in all attempts to deal with the problems of animal variation was first pointed out by Mr. Galton… and I would suggest that the constant whose changes he has investigated and whose importance he has indicated, may fitly be known as 'Galton's function'." "Correlated Variations in Naples and Plymouth shore crabs", Proc. Roy. Soc., Vol.54, p.325, 1893.

　③　Phil. Trans., Roy. Soc. 187: pp.253－318, 1896.

For Pearson's contributions to correlation surface method of approach, see Sections 20, 22, 23, and 25 of Chapter II.

Mr. Galton's ideas, particularly their application to the problem of bi-parental inheritance."①

Now let us examine this memoir more fully.

3.5.1 Definitions of Correlation and Regression

His definitions for correlation and regression are technical (methodical) and clear-out and may well be cited:

(1) "Correlation. Two organs (meaning measurable characteristic of an organism) in the same individual, or in a connected pair of individuals, are said to be correlated, when a series of the first organ of a definite size being selected, the mean of the sizes of the corresponding second organs is found to be a function of the size of the selected first organ. If the mean is independent of this size, the organs are said to be non-correlated. Correlation is defined mathematically by any constant, or series of constants, which determine the above function."

(2) "Regression. Regression is a term which has been hitherto used to mark the amount of abnormality (deviation which falls on the average to the lot of offspring of parents of a given degree of abnormality). The mathematical measure of this special regression is the ratio of the mean deviation of offspring of selected parents from the mean of all offspring to the deviation of the selected parents from the mean of all parents. This may be further elucidated as follows: Let parents, having an organ or characteristic of given deviation (we call it the type value x_{1h}), from the average or normal, be termed a 'parentage', let the offspring of a parentage be termed a 'fraternity'. Then the coefficient of regression may be defined as the ratio of the mean deviation (we call the mean of the array, $\bar{x}_{2h}$), of the fraternity from the mean offspring to the deviation of the parentage from the mean parent $\left(\text{i.e., reg. coef.} = \dfrac{\bar{x}_{2h}}{x_{1h}}\right)$."②

3.5.2 Derivation of Normal n-variate Correlation

Pearson now proceeds to determine the frequency surface of n linearly related variates. The method and the result were not entirely new, he makes this

---

① Phil. Trans., Roy. Soc.187: pp.254-255, 1896.
② The words in the parentheses are our addition, and the quotation is from p.256, loc. cit.

clear himself as he says: "The investigation of correlation which will now be given does not profess, except at certain stated points, to reach new results. It endeavours, however, to reach necessary fundamental formula with a clear statement of what assumptions are really made, and with special reference to what seems legitimate in the case of heredity."①

Let y_1, y_2, y_3, $\cdots$, y_n be the deviations from their respective means of measurable characteristics. He assumes that the sizes of these characteristics are determined by m independent contributory causes, m being a large number and generally much greater than n. Let x_1, x_2, x_3, $\cdots$, x_m be the deviations from their respective means of these contributory causes, then y_1, y_2, y_3, $\cdots$, y_n will be functions of x_1, x_2, x_3, $\cdots$, x_m. He also assumes that the deviations in intensity of the contributory causes are small as compared with their absolute intensity, and that these variations follow the normal law of distribution. Assuming mean sizes of the characteristics to be reached with the mean intensities of the contributory causes, he obtained by the principle of the superposition of small quantities,②

$$y_1 = a_{11}x_1 + a_{12}x_2 + \cdots + a_{1m}x_m$$
$$y_2 = a_{21}x_1 + a_{22}x_2 + \cdots + a_{2m}x_m \qquad (3\cdot 2)$$
$$\cdots\cdots$$
$$y_n = a_{n1}x_1 + a_{n2}x_2 + \cdots + a_{nm}x_m.$$

Here any of the a's may be zero and $m > n$.

Further, the chance that we have a conjunction of contributory causes lying between $(x_1, x_1 + dx_1)$, $(x_2, x_2 + dx_2)$, $\cdots$, and $(x_m, x_m + dx_m)$ will be given by

---

① Phil. Trans. Roy. Soc. 187: p.261, 1896.

② Cf. Gaussian derivation of n-dimension frequency surface with x's corresponding to a, b, c, and y's to x's. Gauss obtained the system of equation through expansion by Taylor's formula and now Pearson obtained such similar system of equations by assumption as Laplace and Edgeworth did that a characteristic (or deviation) is the weighted aggregate of the contributory causes (or elementary deviations or errors). For a discussion on the derivation of such normal curve or surface, see David Brunt, *The Combination of Observations*, pp. 11 – 24, 1917, Czuber, *Beobachtungsfehler*, pp. 48 – 110, 1891; Pearson, "A Rejoinder", Biom., Vol.4, p.169, and also, Warren Weaver, "The Fundamental Law of Errors", which is expected to be published soon.

$$P = Ce^{-\frac{1}{2}\left(\frac{x_1^2}{s_1^2}+\frac{x_2^2}{s_2^2}+ \cdots +\frac{x_m^2}{s_m^2}\right)} dx_1 dx_2 \cdots dx_m \qquad (3\cdot 3)$$

where the standard deviations of the variation distribution for x_1, x_2, $\cdots$, x_m are respectively s_1, s_2, $\cdots$, s_m, and C is a constant.

Now Pearson assumes that n of the variables x can be solved from equation $(3\cdot 2)$ in terms of y's. Let these be the first n of the x's, then, by substituting these solutions for x_1, x_2, $\cdots$, x_n, in $(3\cdot 2)$, he obtains

$$P' = C'e^{-\frac{1}{2}\varphi^2} dy_1 dy_2 \cdots dy_n dx_{n+1} \cdots dx_m$$

where C' is a constant, a function of C and the a's, and φ^2 consists of the following parts:

(i) A quadratic function of y_1, y_2, $\cdots$, y_n;

(ii) A quadratic function of x_{n+1}, x_{n+2}, $\cdots$, x_m;

(iii) A series of functions of the type:

$$x_{n+1}(b_{1,\,n+1}y_1 + b_{2,\,n+1}y_2 + \cdots + b_{n,\,n+1}y_n),$$
$$x_{n+2}(b_{1,\,n+2}y_1 + b_{2,\,n+2}y_2 + \cdots + b_{n,\,n+2}y_n),$$
$$\cdots\cdots$$
$$x_m(b_{1,\,m}y_1 + b_{2,\,m}y_2 + \cdots + b_{n,\,m}y_n),$$

where some of b's may be zero. And P' will be the chance that we have a complex with organs lying between

$$(y_1, y_1 + dy_1), (y_2, y_2 + dy_2), \cdots, (y_n, y_n + dy_n),$$

together with a series of contributory causes lying between

$$(x_{n+1}, x_{n+1} + dx_{n+1}), \cdots, (x_m, x_n + dx_m).$$

Now if P' be integrated for the values from $-\infty$ to $+\infty$ of all the contributory causes x_{n+1}, x_{n+2}, $\cdots$, x_m, the result will be the chance of a complex with organs falling between $(y_1, y_1 + dy_1)$, $\cdots$, $(y_n, y_n + dy_n)$. But every time we integrate with regard to an x, say x_{n+1}, we alter the constants of each constituent part of φ^2, but do not alter the triple constitution of φ^2, except to cause one x to disappear from its (ii) and (iii) constituents. At the same time, we alter C' without introducing into it any terms in y. Thus, finally, after

m-n integrations, φ^2 is reduced to its constituent, or we conclude that the chance of a complex of organs between $(y_1, y_1 + dy_1)$, $(y_2, y_2 + dy_2)$, $\cdots$, $(y_n, y_n + dy_n)$ occurring is given by

$$P = Ce^{-\frac{1}{2}x^2} dy_1 dy_2 \cdots dy_n \qquad (3 \cdot 4)$$

where x^2 is a quadratic function of the y's. This is the law of frequency for the complex.

Later in 1909, the same law is given a condensed proof by Greiner in the memoir "Uber das Fehlersystem der Collectivmasslehre" *Zeitschr für Mathem. Und Phys. Bd.* 57, 1909, and is called the Edgeworth-Pearson Theorem by Charlier (Cf. "On Mult. Cor." Sv. Ak. Tid., p.19, 1915, in which we find a reproduction of Greiner's proof).

Pearson did not give any interpretation of how the frequency surface $(3 \cdot 4)$ offers a measure of correlation among y's. Moreover, his definition of correlation above does not appear to bear any connection with this frequency surface[①]. Regarding the meaning of the frequency surface $(3 \cdot 4)$, Pearson merely says that P is the probability for the occurrence of a complex of organs between $(y_1, y_1 + dy_1)$, $\cdots$, $(y_n, y_n + dy_n)$; but his concept of correlation is not in terms of probability.

3.5.3 The Formula for Computing r in Case of Normal Distribution

When $n = 2$, the equation $(3 \cdot 4)$ becomes

$$P_2 = Ce^{-g_1 x^2 + 2hxy + g_2 y^2} dxdy \qquad (3 \cdot 4a)$$

which is the familiar form previously obtained[②] by Laplace and Bravais. Let σ_1 and σ_2 be the standard deviations of x and y, treated as independent variations. Let N be the total number of pairs. Integrate P for all values of y from $-\infty$ to $+\infty$, and we must have the normal curve of x-variate, hence

$$\frac{1}{2\sigma_1^2} = g_1 \left(1 - \frac{h^2}{g_1 g_2}\right).$$

Similarly, integrating P for all values of x, we have

---

① For this reason and in view of his interpretation being entirely regression in nature, we classify Pearson's work, not as a correlation surface approach, but as regression approach to correlation.

② See the reduction from $(2 \cdot 27a)$ to $(2 \cdot 28)$, and $(2 \cdot 35)$ to $(2 \cdot 36a)$, and also $(2 \cdot 46)$ to $(2 \cdot 47)$, Chapter II.

$$\frac{1}{2\sigma_2^2} = g_2\left(1 - \frac{h^2}{g_1 g_2}\right).$$

Now integrate P for all values of x and y to obtain the total frequency, and we have

$$N = \frac{\sigma_x}{\sqrt{g_1 g_2 - h^2}}.$$

If we now write r for $-\dfrac{h}{\sqrt{g_1 g_2}}$, we can throw P into the form

$$P_2 = \frac{N}{2x\sigma_1\sigma_2\sqrt{1-r^2}} e^{-\frac{1}{2}\left\{\frac{x_1^2}{\sigma_1^2(1-r^2)} - \frac{2rxy}{\sigma_1\sigma_2(1-r^2)} + \frac{y^2}{\sigma_2^2(1-r^2)}\right\}} dxdy. \qquad (3\cdot 4b)$$

Hence from Laplace's or Bravais' proof ①, $-\dfrac{h}{g_1 g_2} = r$ clearly stands for the expression $\dfrac{\sum xy}{N\sigma_1\sigma_2}$ and cannot be otherwise, so that there is no room for questioning what is the best value for r. Yet Pearson in this memoir shows that the best value of r is given by $\dfrac{\sum xy}{N\sigma_1\sigma_2}$. His so doing is, however, justified on the ground that r "has hitherto been frequently calculated by methods of somewhat arbitrary character, involving only a portion of the observations" ②(p.265).

---

① The form $(3\cdot 4a)$ simply stands for Bravais' expression in p.272:

$$\frac{dw}{dxdy} = \frac{1}{x} \frac{1}{\left\{\sum \frac{AB' - A'B}{h_m h_n}\right\}^{\frac{1}{2}}} e^{-\frac{\left\{x^2 \sum \frac{A'^2}{h_n} - 2xy \sum \frac{AA'}{h_m} + y^2 \sum \frac{A^2}{h_m}\right\}}{\sum\left\{\frac{(AB'-A'B)^2}{h_m h_n}\right\}}}$$

or, for $(2\cdot 36a)$ in Chapter II. Likewise, from Pearson's "r" must be given by $\sum \dfrac{xy}{N\sigma_1\sigma_2}$ since, if it is not, r will no longer be the correlation coefficient.

② Edgeworth in his memoir on "Correlated Average" suggested that it will be adequate to find r by taking some of the ratios of 'subject' and mean 'relatives' instead of the whole series. Galton determines r from regression coefficient which is the slope of the freehand regression line. However, it was sufficient for Pearson to point out that r is merely a notation for $\dfrac{\sum xy}{N\sigma_1\sigma_2}$ and on this account, should be computed from that formula.

Thus, "let the n pairs of organs be x_1, y_1, x_2, y_2, $\cdots$ then the chance of the observed series for a given value of r varies as

$$\frac{1}{(1-r^2)^{\frac{n}{2}}} e^{-\frac{1}{2(1-r^2)}\left\{\frac{x_1^2}{\sigma_1^2} - 2r\frac{x_1 y_1}{\sigma_1 \sigma_2} + \frac{y_1^2}{\sigma_2^2}\right\}} \times e^{-\frac{1}{2(1-r^2)}\left\{\frac{x_2^2}{\sigma_1^2} - 2r\frac{x_2 y_2}{\sigma_1 \sigma_2} + \frac{y_2^2}{\sigma_2^2}\right\}}$$

$$\times e^{-\frac{1}{2(1-r^2)}\left\{\frac{x_3^2}{\sigma_1^2} - 2r\frac{x_3 y_3}{\sigma_1 \sigma_2} + \frac{y_3^2}{\sigma_2^2}\right\}} \times \cdots\cdots$$

or, S denoting summation, since $\sigma_1^2 = \dfrac{S(x_1^2)}{r}$, $\sigma_2^2 = \dfrac{S(y_2^2)}{n}$, the chance varies as

$$\frac{1}{(1-r^2)^{\frac{n}{2}}} e^{-n\left\{\frac{1-\lambda r}{1-r^2}\right\}}$$

where λ is written for $\dfrac{S(xy)}{n\sigma_1 \sigma_2}$."

"Now, assume r to differ by ρ from the value previously selected, and expand by Taylor's Theorem, after expressing the function, in the following manner:

$$u_r = \frac{1}{(1-r^2)^{\frac{n}{2}}} e^{-n\left\{\frac{1-\lambda r}{1-r^2}\right\}} = e^{n\left\{-\frac{1}{2}\log(1-r^2) - \frac{1-\lambda r}{1-r^2}\right\}}.$$

We have

$$\frac{1}{n}\log u_{r+\rho} = \frac{1}{n}\log u_r + \frac{(1+r^2)(\lambda - r)}{(1-r^2)^2}\rho + \frac{1}{2}\frac{\lambda(2r^3 + 6r) - 1 - 6r^2 - r^4}{(1-r^2)^3}\rho^2$$
$$+ \frac{1}{6}\frac{\lambda(6 + 36r^2 + 6r^4) + 4r^5 - 6r^4 - 28r^3 - 18r}{(1-r^2)^4}\rho^3 + \text{etc.}$$

$$(3 \cdot 5)$$

Hence, $\log u_r$ and therefore u_r is a maximum when $r = \lambda$, for the coefficient of ρ^2 is then negative. Thus, it appears that the observed result is the most probable, when r is given the value $\dfrac{S(xy)}{n\sigma_1 \sigma_2}$." We note that the proof involves the assumption of normal distribution for x and y.

3.5.4 An Attempt at Deriving σ_r on a First Approximation

Now Pearson based on the equation $(3 \cdot 5)$ determines the probable error of correlation coefficients. Assuming that r has the value given by $\dfrac{\sum xy}{N\sigma_1\sigma_2}$, then $\lambda = r$ and equation (3·5) becomes

$$u_{r+\rho} = u_r e^{-\frac{n(1+r^2)}{(1+r^2)^2}\frac{\rho^2}{2} - \frac{2nr(r^2+3)}{(1-r^2)^3}\frac{\rho^3}{3} - \text{etc.}}. \qquad (3\cdot 5a)$$

"Now $u_{r+\rho}$ is the chance of the observed series on the assumption that the coefficient of correlation r is $r + \rho$ instead of r. Hence the above is the law of distribution of variation in the coefficient of correlation. If the second term be negligible as compared with the first, we see that ρ follows the normal law of distribution. Thus, we may say that with sufficient accuracy for most cases the standard deviation of a coefficient of correlation is

$$\frac{1-r^2}{\sqrt{n(1+r^2)}}, \qquad (3\cdot 6)$$

or its probable error $= 0.674\,5\,\dfrac{1-r^2}{\sqrt{n(1+r^2)}}$."

"The ratio of the first term neglected to the term retained

$$= \frac{4}{3}\frac{r(r^3+3)}{(r^2+1)(1-r^2)}\rho$$

or to determine the order, giving ρ its probable value on a first approximation, we have

$$\text{ratio} = \frac{4}{3}\frac{r(r^2+3)}{\sqrt{n\,(r^2+1)^{\frac{3}{2}}}}\,0.674\,5."$$

"This may be shown to be a maximum for $r^2 = 1$, and the ratio then takes the value $\dfrac{1.272}{\sqrt{n}}$, or the second term in this most unfavorable case will only be about 4 per cent of the first when $n = 1\,000\,\ldots$"

This was the first attempt to ascertain the distribution of r and its standard deviation in order to test the significance or reliability of the computed correlation coefficient. This formula, as he himself had concluded in a later date, was in error① and ought to be replaced by $\dfrac{1-r^2}{\sqrt{n}}$, and in 1915 R. A. Fisher proved the exact distribution of r and devised a z-test for the significance of an estimated r from a sample.

3.5.5 Correlation Coefficient and Regression Coefficient

In the introduction to his demonstration of the best value for r, Pearson made the remark that "This (equation 3・4b) is the well-known Galton form of the frequency for two correlated variables, and r is the Galton function or coefficient of correlation" (p.264). Pearson seemed to assume that the Galton function or coefficient of correlation and the coefficient of the product term in the exponent of the frequency surface (equation 3・4b) are the same thing without giving any explanation. This can be justified by assuming that Pearson② accepted both Galton's and Edgeworth's theorem and assumed the variates to conform the conditions assumed in their theorems. By Galton's theorem we mean the theorem: if $\dfrac{x_2}{\sigma_2}=\dfrac{rx_1}{\sigma_1}$ is the regression line between x_1 and x_2 and the partial (array) distribution is of normal type with homoscedastic variation, then the law of distribution of the two variates is given by equation (3・4b). By Edgeworth's theorem we mean the theorem: If the law of distribution of the two variates x_1 and x_2 is given by equation (3・4b), then the regression equation of x_2 on x_1 is $x_2 = rx_1$ (the locus of the array mode of x_2) and that of x_1 on x_2 is $x_1 = rx_2$ (the locus of the array mode of x_2). Thus, it follows that by accepting Galton's definition of correlation, the correlation coefficient is the regression coefficient when the variates are measured from their means and in units of their standard deviations, the coefficient of correlation is the coefficient of the product term in exponent of

---

① Pearson and Filon, "On the Probable Errors of Frequency Constant", Roy. Soc. Proc., Oct., 1897. Sheppard, Phil. Trans. A., Vol.192, p.128.

② It is to be observed that Galton's regression, as seen from his explanation, was the locus of the array median, that Edgeworth's regression as seen from his derivation was the locus of the array mode, and that Pearson's regression as defined was the locus of the array mean. So it seems to be needful for Pearson to demonstrate that the regression equation x_2/σ_2 and rx_1/σ_1 may be obtained, according to his definition, by integrating the normal bivariate surface (3・4b) after multiplying by x_2.

equation (3·4b) and vice versa, and furthermore, the correlation surface method and the regression line method are identified to be the same in this particular case, namely when the variates follow the normal law of distribution.

For the same reason, Pearson, referring to the correlation surface of three variates:

$$P = \frac{n\sqrt{R}}{(2x)^{\frac{3}{2}} \sigma_1 \sigma_2 \sigma_3} e^{-\frac{1}{2}R\left\{\frac{x_1^2}{\sigma_1^2}R_{11} + \frac{x_2^2}{\sigma_2^2}R_{22} + \frac{x_3^2}{\sigma_3^2}R_{33} + 2R_{12}\frac{x_1 x_2}{\sigma_1 \sigma_2} + 2R_{13}\frac{x_1 x_3}{\sigma_1 \sigma_3} + 2R_{23}\frac{x_2 x_3}{\sigma_2 \sigma_3}\right\}} dx_1 dx_2 dx_3$$

(3·7)

where

$$R = \begin{vmatrix} 1 & r_{12} & r_{13} \\ r_{12} & r & r_{23} \\ r_{13} & r_{23} & 1 \end{vmatrix},$$

and R_{ij} denotes the cofactor of the ij-th element in R, is also justified in saying that, if h_1 be the deviation of the mean of x_1 organs, selected with regard to values h_2 and h_3 of x_2 and x_3, from the x_1- mean of the whole population, the regression will be

$$h_1 = -\frac{R_{12}\sigma_1}{R_{11}\sigma_2}h_2 - \frac{R_{13}\sigma_1}{R_{11}\sigma_3}h_3 = \frac{r_{12} - r_{13}r_{23}}{1 - r_{23}^2}\frac{\sigma_1}{\sigma_2}h_2 + \frac{r_{13} - r_{12}r_{23}}{1 - r_{23}^2}\frac{\sigma_1}{\sigma_3}h_3 \quad (3 \cdot 8)$$

and that expressions of the forms $\frac{R_{ij}}{R_{11}}$ and $\frac{R_{ij}}{R_{11}}\frac{\sigma_1}{\sigma_j}$ may be respectively called coefficients of double correlation and of double regression.①

3.5.6 Correlation and the Control of Variability

Another important contribution made by Pearson in this memoir is his interpretation of correlation in terms of the restriction of variability. With special reference to the problem of uniparental inheritance where the normal law (equation 3·4b) is followed and h is the deviation of an organ in a parent from

---

① These definitions are developed on the basis of analogy to the case of two variates. Pearson did not explain how they should be interpreted in actual statistics. Later Yule changed the terminology and supplied an explanation. See next section.

the mean, Pearson gives as the frequency of a variation x in the same or any other organ of the offspring

$$z = \frac{N}{2x\sigma_1\sigma_2\sqrt{1-r^2}} e^{-\frac{1}{2}\left\{\frac{x}{\sigma_1^2(1-r^2)} - \frac{2rxh}{\sigma_1\sigma_2(1-r^2)} + \frac{h^2}{\sigma_2^2(1-r^2)}\right\}}.$$

The offspring, therefore, have variation following a normal distribution about the mean

$$x_0 = r\frac{\sigma_1}{\sigma_2}h$$

and with the standard deviation $\sigma_1\sqrt{1-r^2}$.

Hence, by his definition, the coefficient of regression $\frac{x_0}{h} = r\frac{\sigma_1}{\sigma_2}$, and the variability of the offspring of the selected parents is reduced from that of the general population of offspring in the ratio of $\sqrt{(1-r^2)}$ to 1. We thus have a measure of the manner in which selection of parents reduces the variability in offspring, i.e., tends to make the latter closer to a definite type. Further we note that the coefficient of regression and the restriction of variability are the same whatever type of parent be adopted, or the closeness with which selection leads to a given type of offspring is independent of the parent adopted and the type offspring which results from this parent. This seems to indicate a tendency to regard correlation as an analysis of variation or variance (Fisher has developed the theory or correlation as an analysis of variance from another view point which we shall consider in Chapter IV), and that we can reduce the variability of the essential variate through the selection or control of the subordinate variate.

3.5.7 The Distinction between the Correlation Coefficient Afforded by Normal Correlation Surface and that Derived from Regression Method

It seems worthwhile pointing out that Pearson at that time accepted Yule's view as developed in his memoir[①] "On the significance of Bravais' formula for regression, etc." in 1897, although he criticized this view point in his History of

---

① Proc. Roy. Soc. 60: p.477, 1897.

Correlation.① Pearson says in the footnote: "This (the above interpretation) is, of course, true of the regression and variability of the array corresponding to any type whatever, when frequency follows the normal law. Mr. G. U. Yule points out to me that if the coefficient of regression be constant for the arrays of all types, then it follows that whatever be the law of frequency, the coefficient of regression must $= r\sigma_1/\sigma_2$, where $r = \dfrac{S(xy)}{N\sigma_1\sigma_2}$. This much generalizes the formula. At the same time, in the case of skew correlation, the coefficient of regression usually varies with the type, and the fundamental problem is to determine what function it is of the type...."② However, we must not forget that, even though the standard deviation of all arrays be the same and the regression linear, if only the frequency distribution can not be represented by the normal surface (3·4b), then the Galton function or the standardized regression coefficient is not the same thing as the coefficient of the product term in the exponential because this exponential, being not the law of distribution of the two variates in question, has nothing whatever to do with the relationship concerned. Therefore, if Pearson accepted Yule's view, he was on the wrong track to regard the coefficient of the product term in the exponential to be the Galton function or coefficient of the linear regression between two variates expressed in units of their standard deviations, these two views are theoretically not identical. If Pearson took the view of the correlation surface approach and accepted both Galton's and Edgeworth's theorems, then his definition of correlation cannot be considered as satisfactory. If Pearson took the view of regression method and agreed with Yule's suggestion, then his taking the coefficient of the product term

---

① Biom., Vol.13, p.45, 1921.

② Footnote at p.268, Phil. Trans. Roy. Soc., V.187. Pearson has a similar expression on p.287 in connection with correlation among three variables. "The above values for Σ_1 (the array-s.d. $= 3\sigma_1 \dfrac{R}{R_{11}}$) and h (as given in equation 3·8, $h_1 = -\dfrac{R_{12}\sigma_1}{R_{11}\sigma_2}h_2 - \dfrac{R_{13}\sigma_1}{R_{11}\sigma_3}h_3$) are still true, as Mr. G. U. Yule points out to me, whatever be the law of frequency, and provided the standard-deviations of all arrays be the same and h_1 be a linear function of h_2 and h_3."

in the normal correlation surface as the coefficient of correlation was theoretically not broad enough, in this case the coefficient of correlation is simply the regression coefficient of the regression line fitted to the types or averages (mean, or median, or mode, etc.) of the arrays according to certain reasonable criterion when the variates are expressed in units of standard deviations, or, is, according to Yule, the geometrical mean of two regressions, coefficients. It is on account of the existence of such ambiguity that we need to understand the underlying theory in order to know the assumptions and the limitations in the actual uses.

3.5.8 Another Formula for the Correlation Coefficient

It may be recalled that Pearson's proof for the best value of the coefficient of correlation is based on the assumption that the two variates x_1 and x_2 must follow the normal law of distribution. Hence the definition $r = \dfrac{\sum x_1 x_2}{N \sigma_1 \sigma_2}$ as the coefficient of correlation is theoretically correct only when the variates, x_1 and x_2, follow normal law of distribution. And if we take the coefficient of correlation as the regression coefficient of a regression line, fitted by least squares criterion to the variates measured from their means in units of their standard deviation, then the correlation coefficient being still given by the product moment formula as approved by Yule, also depends for its validity[1] on the normal law of distribution for x_1 and x_2. And lastly, if we define the coefficient of the product term in the exponential frequency function as the coefficient of correlation, it clearly assumes the normal law of distribution. Now while the definition[2] $r = \dfrac{\sum xy}{\sqrt{\sum x^2 \sum y^2}}$ as the coefficient of correlation, on the basis of a sort of genetic or analogous development without regard to law of distribution for the variates, may be useful and simple, we may gravely doubt whether it is more accurate

---

[1] See the criticism of Yule's method by Pearson in "History", Biom. 13: p.45, 1921.

[2] Pearson defined the standardized product moment as the correlation coefficient in a tentative manner. "Regression Heredity and Panmixia", Ibid., see also next section and Charlier, "Contributions to the Mathematical Theory of Statistics", 6. Op. cit.

theoretically than the assumption of a normal distribution and whether the coefficient can still preserve a precise meaning. I don't think, however, that this has been observed, either by exponents of the method of Pearson or by his successors.

When Pearson gave another formula for determining r in cases that the normal law is not followed by the two variates in question, he obviously neglected the assumptions involved in defining $r = \dfrac{\sum xy}{N\sigma_1\sigma_2}$ as the coefficient of correlation. On account of the repeated appearances of similar forms in the later works of the author[1] and others,[2] we shall cite the proof and the conclusions in order to make clear what hypotheses have been implied in the derivation.

Let X and Y be two correlated organs and let x and y be corresponding deviations from the mean values m_1 and m_2. Let r be the coefficient of correlation of x and y, σ_1, σ_2 their standard deviations, $v_1 = \dfrac{\sigma_1}{m_1}$, $v_2 = \dfrac{\sigma_2}{m_2}$, their coefficients of variation, and let Z be any function $f(x, y)$ of x and y with a deviation z, corresponding to x and y, and a standard deviation, mean, and coefficient of variation respectively Σ, M, V.

We shall suppose that x and y are so small that the squares of the ratios $\dfrac{x}{m_1}$ and $\dfrac{y}{m_1}$ are negligible as compared with the first powers. Differentiating $z = f(X, Y)$ and remembering the hypothesis as to smallness of the variations, we have:

$$z = f_X x + f_Y y.$$

Squaring:

$$z^2 = f_X^2 x^2 + f_Y^2 y^2 + 2f_X f_Y xy.$$

---

[1] "On the Theory of Errors of Judgment", Phil. Trans. A., Vol. 198, pp. 235–299, and in a Study of Wasps in Biom., Vol. 5, p. 409.

[2] Boas, "Determination of the Coefficient of Correlation", Science, Vol. 29, p. 823, and Thorndike, *Mental and Social Measurement*, p. 158, 1913. Otis, A. S., "The Otis Correlation Chart", Jour. Educational Research, Vol. 8, pp. 440–448, 1923.

Summing for every possible value of x and y, and dividing by n, the total number of correlated pairs:

$$\frac{S(z^2)}{n} = f_X^2 \frac{S(x^2)}{n} + f_Y^2 \frac{S(y^2)}{n} + 2f_X f_Y \frac{S(xy)}{n},$$

or,

$$\Sigma^2 = f_X^2 \sigma_1^2 + f_Y^2 \sigma_2^2 + 2f_X f_Y \sigma_1 \sigma_2 \frac{S(xy)}{n\sigma_1 \sigma_2}.$$

Now, Pearson defined① $r = \dfrac{S(xy)}{n\sigma_1 \sigma_2}$ as the coefficient of correlation and found the following formula for its calculation:

$$r = \frac{\Sigma^2 - f_X^2 \sigma_1^2 - f_Y^2 \sigma_2^2}{2f_X f_Y \sigma_1 \sigma_2}. \qquad (3 \cdot 9)$$

Then Pearson goes on to say: "The question naturally arises as to what is the best value of $f(X, Y)$. This will often be already answered by the data themselves. A common case is that in which the variations in X and Y are given, and the variation in their ratio or the index $\dfrac{X}{Y}$ is calculated. In this particular instance $f_X = \dfrac{M}{m_1}$ and $f_Y = \dfrac{-M}{m_2}$. Hence

$$r = \frac{v_1^2 + v_2^2 - v^2}{2v_1 v_2}.$$

We thus throw back the determination of correlation on ascertaining three

---

① Pearson might think that he has given justification for this definition by saying "Now, if there were no correlation, we should have: $\Sigma^2 = f_X^2 \sigma_1^2 + f_Y^2 \sigma_2^2$; hence any law of frequency whatever which causes $S(xy) = 0$, for example, if it be equally likely that y occurs with an equal negative or positive value of x, will show that x and y are independent variations", p.278. But this statement itself needs justification. I do not see how it can be proved when the law of distribution is not normal. Furthermore, his illustrative statement suggests the question whether "no correlation" and "independence" are identical or two different things in Pearson's theory of correlation. Furthermore, the statement that "if it be equally likely that y occurs with an equal negative or positive value of $x \cdots$" is clearly an assumption of symmetrical distribution, and, accordingly Pearson's conclusion (the last paragraph this section) is unwarranted.

coefficients of variation."

"This formula while less general than the one previously given, in that we have neglected squares of small quantities, is more general in that we have not limited ourselves to any special law of frequency." (p.279, see also our footnote in p.201 of this book) Later in 1909, Pearson comments in the reply to Boas, letter to Science with regard to the formula: "It is quite reliable and often convenient."①

3.5.9 Summary

Pearson's contributions in this memoir consist mainly in giving a proof for the normal n-variate frequency surface so as to provide a theoretical basis for the extension of Galton's Method of Correlation Analysis to the case of any number of variates normally distributed, in giving an interpretation of correlation in terms of restriction of variability, and in attempting to arrive at the derivation of σ_r on a first approximation. The proof that the best value of r is given by $\sum xy/N\sigma_x\sigma_y$, does not have the theoretical value as would at first sight appear. The formula (3·9) is theoretically unsound, since it is derived from an unverified assumption that $\sum xy/N\sigma_x\sigma_y$ is the correlation coefficient. Furthermore, to call the correlation coefficient the Pearsonian coefficient (see footnote in p.234 of this book) is unjustified. So far as I am aware, the justification for defining $\sum xy/N\sigma_x\sigma_y$ as the (linear) correlation coefficient, skew or otherwise, was given by G. U. Yule (see next section), and no other. In the case of non-linear correlation, the use of this formula as the definition of correlation coefficient is merely by analogy.

3.6 Yule's Generalization of the Regression Method

3.6.1 Characteristics of Yule's Theory

As early as 1897, Yule generalized the regression approach to the correlation analysis on the premise that the mean square deviations from the

---

① Pearson, K., Letter on "The Determination of the Coefficient of Correlation", A Reply to Boas, Science, Vol.30, p.23, 1909.

regression curve or line be a minimum. Yule's view is entirely practical, and his theory is unique as compared with the previous development so that it may be called a theory of similarity in the sense that he considers primarily whether the variates rise or fall, directly or inversely, together and pays little attention to the form of distribution.① His justification for so doing lies in the demonstration that the formulas of measuring the correlation obtained through a generalized application of the method of least squares are the same as those are afforded by the normal theory, provided the regression may be reasonably assumed to be linear.②

3.6.2 Definitions of Correlation and Regression Coefficient

Yule's definition of correlation is based on the regression and has no connection with the theory of probability. Thus, Yule defines the regression curve as the curve which may be taken to represent the locus of the array means. But in view of the fact that few statistics would seem worth the labor of calculating any characteristic more complex than the linear regression and that in most cases the deviation from the linear character, at all events near the middle of the table where frequencies are greatest, does not appear to be very serious even though well defined, Yule confines his treatment to the case of linear regression. Now, if $x = a_1 + b_1 y$ is the regression line of x on y (all the variates in Yule's treatment are measured from their means) and $\sigma_{1\cdot 2}$ is the standard error of

---

① In the beginning of his first memoir "On the significance of Bravais' Formula for regression, etc., in the case of Skew Correlation", Proc. Roy. Soc., Vol.60, p.477, 1897, Yule says: "It seems worthwhile noting, ... that in ordinary practice statisticians never concern themselves with the form of the correlation, normal or otherwise, but yet obtain results of interest—though always lacking in numerical exactness and frequently in certainty. Suppose the case to be one in which two variables are varying together in time, curves are drawn exhibiting the history of the two. If these two curves appear, generally speaking, to rise and fall together, the variables are held to be correlated. If on the other hand it is not a case of variation with time, the associated pairs may be tabulated in order according to the magnitude of one variable, and then it may be seen whether the entries of the other variable also occur in order. Both methods are of course very rough, and will only indicate very close correlation, but they contain, it seems to me, the point of prime importance at all events with regard to economic statistics. In all the classical examples of statistical correlation... We are only primarily concerned with the question is a large x usually associated with a large y (or small y); the further question as to the form of this association and the relative frequency of different pairs of the variables is, at any rate on a first investigation, of comparatively secondary importance."

② Ibid.

estimating x from its associated variate y by the regression equation, then the correlation coefficient r is defined by the following equation

$$r = \pm \sqrt{1 - \frac{\sigma_{1\cdot 2}^2}{\sigma_1^2}}, \qquad (3\cdot 10)$$

for the reason that the greater the value of r is, the more nearly are the values of the two variates related by a simple linear law as represented by the linear regression.① The sign is the sign of the regression coefficient, or of the mean product (see equation $3 \cdot 15$), when the slope of the regression line is positive, i.e., if large values or x are associated with large values of y and conversely, negative if small values of x are associated with large values of y and conversely.

Similarly, if $\sigma_{1\cdot 23 \cdots n}$ is the standard error of estimating x_1 from its associated variates $x_2, x_3, \cdots, x_n$ by the regression equation

$$x_1 = b_{12}x_2 + b_{13}x_3 + \cdots + b_{1n}x_n,$$

the multiple correlation coefficient between x_1 and $(x_2, x_3, \cdots, x_n)$ is defined by

$$r_{1\cdot 23 \cdots n} = \pm \sqrt{1 - \frac{\sigma_{1\cdot 23 \cdots n}^2}{\sigma_1^2}}. \qquad (3\cdot 11)$$

Moreover, Yule defines the correlation coefficient in another way. Thus if $x = a_1 + b_{12}y$ and $y = a_2 + b_{21}x$ be the two regression lines, then the correlation

---

① See next section, especially equation ($3 \cdot 17$). It seems worthwhile to quote Yule's concept of a regression line. He says: "…suppose that we take a straight line, RR' (see Figure in p.206 of this book), and fit it to the curve, subjecting the distances of the means from the line to some minimal condition. If the slope of RR' be positive, we may say that large values of x are on the whole associated with small values of y, and vice versa. Further, the slope of RR' to the vertical is a measure of a rough practical kind of the shift of the mean of an x-array, corresponding to a given shift of its type y. The equation to the line RR' consequently gives a concise and definite answer to two most important statistical questions: Can we say that large values of x are on the whole associated with either large values of y or small values of y? And, what is the average shift of the means of an x- array corresponding to a shift of unity in its type? If RR' be vertical, we may call the two variables uncorrelated; so long as it slopes to the vertical, we may call them correlated…" "On the Theory of Correlation", Jour. Roy. Stat. Soc., Vol.60, p.814, 1897. Yule also says that "The regression being, in fact, the fundamental physical quantities, r is a coefficient of correlation because it is a coefficient of regression" when each deviation is measured in terms of its standard deviation. See "On the Significance of Bravais' Formula", Ibid., p.482.

coefficient r is defined as the geometric mean of b_{12} and b_{21}, i.e.,

$$r_{12} = \pm \sqrt{b_{12} \cdot b_{21}} \text{ (the sign is same as } b_{12} \text{ or } b_{21}\text{)}. \quad (3 \cdot 12)$$

By analogy, if

$$x_1 = b_{12 \cdot 34 \cdots n} x_2 + b_{13 \cdot 24 \cdots n} x_3 + \cdots + b_{1n \cdot 23 \cdots n-1},$$

$$x_2 = b_{22 \cdot 34 \cdots n} x_1 + b_{23 \cdot 14 \cdots n} x_3 + \cdots + b_{2n \cdot 23 \cdots n-1}$$

are two regressions for the n variates [there are $(n-2)$ other regressions which may be obtained by proper interchange of indexes], Yule calls $b_{12 \cdot 34 \cdots n}$ the net or partial regression coefficient of x_1 on x_2 and defines

$$r_{12 \cdot 34 \cdots n} = \sqrt{b_{12 \cdot 34 \cdots n} b_{21 \cdot 34 \cdots n}} \quad (3 \cdot 13)$$

as the net or partial coefficient of correlation between x_1 and x_2 in a group associated with a single type $(x_3, x_4, \cdots, x_n)$. For distinction, Yule also calls r_{12} the gross coefficient of correlation and $r_{12 \cdot 3 \cdots n}$ the partial correlation coefficient.

3.6.3 Yule's Justification for Defining $\sum xy / N \sigma_x \sigma_y$ as the Correlation Coefficient

Yule demonstrates that the regression and Correlation Coefficients derived according to the criterion that the mean square deviations from the regression line shall be a minimum are identical to corresponding values for normal correlation.

The procedure he uses is first to derive a line of least squares and identify the regression coefficients with the values obtained by Bravais <u>on the assumption of normal correlation</u> for the regression of x on y, and the regression of y on x.

From this identification, (he then concludes) it follows that the Bravais values for regressions are simply those values of b_1 and b_2, which make the sums of the squared-deviations from the respective regression lines

$$S(x - b_{12}y)^2 \text{ and } S(y - b_{21}x)^2$$

minima, whatever be the form of the correlation between the two variables. The demonstration is simple. Let x, y be a pair of associated deviations from their respective means, let n be the number of observations in any x-array, and d be the horizontal distance of the mean of this array from the line RR', $x = a_1 + b_{12}y$

which is fitted to the curve of regression of x on y by imposing the condition that the sum of all quantities like nd^2 shall be a minimum, i.e., the condition of least squares; and let σ be the standard deviation of any array about its own mean. Then for any one array

$$S\{x - (a_1 + b_{12}y)\}^2 = n\sigma_{ax}^2 + nx^2.$$

Hence, extending the meaning of S to summation over the whole surface

$$S(nd^2) = S\{x - (a_1 + b_{12}y)\}^2 - Sn\sigma_{ax}^2.$$

But in this expression $S(n\sigma_{ax}^2)$ is independent of a and b, it is, in fact, a characteristic of the correlation surface. Therefore, making $S(nd^2)$ a minimum is equivalent to making

$$N\sigma_{2\cdot 1}^2 = S'[x - (a_1 + b_{12}y)]^2 = \min. \qquad (3\cdot 14)$$

That is to say, the method may be viewed in another light.

We may say that we form a single valued relation

$$x = a_1 + b_{12}y$$

between a pair of associated deviations, such that the sum of the squares of our errors in estimating any one x from its associated y by the relation is a minimum. This characteristic relation is simply the line of regression.

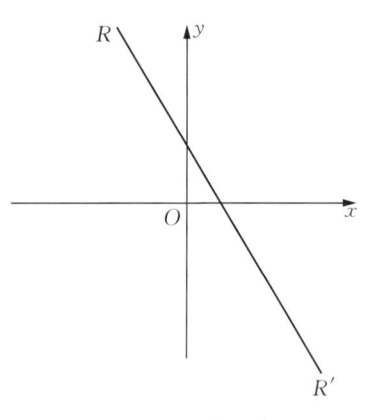

Figure Regression Curve

The normal equations for determining a_1 and b_1 so that

$$S[x - (a_1 + b_{12}y)]^2 = \min.$$

are

$$S(x) = Na_1 + b_{12}S(y)$$
$$S(xy) = a_1 S(y) + b_{12}S(xy),$$

N being the total number of correlated pairs.

Since $S(x) = 0$, $S(y) = 0$,

we have

$$a_1 = 0, \quad b_{12} = \frac{S(xy)}{S(y^2)}.$$

To simplify our notation, let us write

$$S(x^2) = N\sigma_1^2,$$

$$S(y^2) = N\sigma_2^2$$

$$S(xy) = Nr\sigma_1\sigma_2, \qquad (3 \cdot 15)$$

r is Bravais' value of the coefficient of correlation. Rewriting b_{12} in terms of these symbols, we have

$$b_{12} = r\frac{\sigma_1}{\sigma_2}, \qquad (3 \cdot 16a)$$

similarly, the parameters in the regression equation of y on x:

$$y = a_2 + b_{21}x$$

are

$$a_2 = 0,$$

$$b_{21} = r\frac{\sigma_2}{\sigma_1}. \qquad (3 \cdot 16b)$$

But the expressions on the right side of $(3 \cdot 16a)$ and $(3 \cdot 16b)$ are the values obtained by Bravais on the assumption of normal correlation for the regression of x on y and y on x. That is to say, Bravais' values for the regression coefficients and correlation coefficient may be obtained by simply fitting a linear regression equation by a generalized method of least squares which does not assume any definite form for the frequency distribution. "In any case, then, where the regression appears to be linear, Bravais' formula may be used at once without troubling to investigate the normality of the distribution. The exponential character of the surface appears to have nothing whatever to do with the result." (p.481)

The meaning of the above expressions $(3 \cdot 14)$ to $(3 \cdot 16b)$ when the array means do not lie exactly on straight lines is easily obtained. Giving b_{12} and b_{21} their values from $(3 \cdot 16a)$ and $(3 \cdot 16b)$, then we have

$$N\sigma_{2\cdot 1}^2 = S(x - b_{12}y)^2 = N\sigma_1^2(1 - r^2) = \min.$$

$$N\sigma_{1\cdot 2}^2 = S(y - b_{21}x)^2 = N\sigma_2^2(1 - r^2) = \min. \qquad (3 \cdot 17)$$

It means that the equations $x = b_{12}y$ and $y = b_{21}x$ are equations for estimating respectively the mean of the x's associated with a given type of y and the mean of the y's associated with a type of x in such a way as to make the standard error of estimating the least possible, or equations for estimating the mean of x's associated with a given type of y and the mean of the y's associated with a given type of x in such a way as to make the correlation coefficient, r, the largest possible, since the standard error of estimate is a minimum when the correlation coefficient is maximum, and maximum when the correlation coefficient is minimum, and conversely (see equation $3 \cdot 17$).

Moreover, from equations of ($3 \cdot 17$), it is seen that the numerical values of r cannot exceed ± 1, for the sum of the series of squares (in equation $3 \cdot 17$) is then zero and the sum of a series of the squares cannot be negative. If $r = \pm 1$, it follows that all the observed pairs of deviations are subject to the relation $\dfrac{x}{y} = \dfrac{\sigma_1}{\sigma_2}$ and it is said that there is a perfect correlation between x and y.

In the case of normal correlation, $\sigma_1 \sqrt{1 - r^2}$ is the standard deviation of any array of the x variate, corresponding to a single type of y. In the non-normal distribution, this expression is, however, no longer the standard deviation of an array of x's, but may be regarded as the weighted mean standard deviations of all the y-arrays of x's from the regression line. Or it may be regarded as the standard error made in estimating x from the regression equation: $x = b_{21}x$. This interpretation is independent of the form of correlation. In other words, "the use of normal regression formula is quite legitimate in all cases, so long as the necessary limitations of interpretation are recognized. Bravais' r always remains a coefficient of correlation" (p.489).

Yule also gave a similar detailed demonstration for the case of three variables and then extends the method to the general case of n variates in the following manner.

Let $x_1, x_2, \cdots, x_n$ be a group of associated variates measured from their means. Let n be the number of observations in an array of x_1's associated with fixed types x_2, x_3, $\cdots$, x_n of the remaining variates, let σ_{1a} be the standard deviation of this array, and let d be the difference of its mean from the value given by a regression equation

$$x_1 = b_{10} + b_{12}x_2 + b_{13}x_3 + \cdots + b_{1n}x_n,$$

then as before, the coefficients b_{12}, b_{13}, $\cdots$ are to be determined so as to make $\sum(nd^2)$ a minimum. But this is again equivalent to making

$$\sum(x_{1\cdot23\ldots n}^2) = \sum\{x_1 - (b_{10} + b_{12}x_2 + b_{13}x_3 + \cdots + b_{1n}x_n)\}^2$$

a minimum, for

$$\sum\{x_1 - (b_{10} + b_{12}x_2 + b_{13}x_3 + \cdots + b_{1n}x_n)\}^2 = \sum(n\sigma_{1a}^2) + \sum(nd^2).$$

This linear equation is termed the characteristic equation. It is evident that if there are n variates, n characteristic equations can be formed between them, expressing each one in turn in terms of the others. The magnitude and sign of the coefficients of x's on the right of such an equation show in what direction and to what extent the average of x_1 will be altered when x_2, x_3, $\cdots$, x_n undergo alterations of any given magnitude and sign.

Thus, it is fair to any that the whole problem of correlation to Yule lay in obtaining the characteristic equation and its interpretation; there is no reference to the form of frequency distribution and therefore the method is concerned, not with getting a "best fit"[1] to the correlation table or diagram, but rather with getting a fairly good approximation to the general trend of the rise and fall, directly or inversely together, of the variates.

3.6.4 Formulas for Correlation Coefficients

Yule also gives formulas for the regression and correlation coefficients, net and multiple, in terms of the gross correlation coefficients. These formulas for the general case of n variates are elegantly demonstrated[2] in a later article by making use of a new system of notation. They are:

---

[1] Pearson, K., "The History of Correlation", Op. Cit.
[2] Yule, "On the Theory of Correlation for any number of variables, treated by a new system of notations", Proc. Roy. Soc., Vol.79, p.182, 1907.

$$\sigma^2_{1\cdot 23 \cdots n} = \sigma_{1\cdot 23 \cdots (n-1)}\left[1 - r^2_{1n\cdot 23 \cdots (n-1)}\right], \qquad (3\cdot 18a)$$

or

$$\sigma^2_{1\cdot 23 \cdots n} = \sigma^2_1(1 - r^2_{1n})(1 - r^2_{13\cdot 2}) \cdots \left[1 - r^2_{1n\cdot 23 \cdots (n-1)}\right] \qquad (3\cdot 18b)$$

$$b_{12\cdot 345 \cdots n} = \frac{r_{12\cdot 34 \cdots (n-1)} - r_{1n\cdot 34 \cdots (n-1)} r_{2n\cdot 34 \cdots (n-1)}}{1 - r^2_{1n\cdot 34 \cdots (n-1)}} \cdot \frac{\sigma_{1\cdot 34 \cdots (n-1)}}{\sigma_{2\cdot 34 \cdots (n-1)}} \qquad (3\cdot 19)$$

$$r^2_{12\cdot 34 \cdots n} = \frac{r_{12\cdot 34 \cdots (n-1)} - r_{1n\cdot 34 \cdots (n-1)} r_{2n\cdot 34 \cdots (n-1)}}{\sqrt{1 - r^2_{1n\cdot 34 \cdots (n-1)}} \sqrt{1 - r^2_{2n\cdot 34 \cdots (n-1)}}} \qquad (3\cdot 20)$$

$$r^2_{1(23 \cdots n)} = (1 - 1 - r^2_{12})(1 - r^2_{13\cdot 2})(-r^2_{14\cdot 23}) \cdots \left[1 - r_{1n\cdot 23 \cdots (n-1)}\right] \qquad (3\cdot 21)$$

whence

$$1 - r^2_{1(23 \cdots n)} = \left[1 - r^2_{1(23 \cdots \overline{n-1})}\right]\left[1 - r^2_{1n\cdot 23 \cdots (n-1)}\right].$$

The number of subscripts after the period, i.e., the secondary subscripts, is the index of order. For example, $b_{12\cdot 34 \cdots n}$ denotes the partial regression of x_1 on x_2 of the $(n - 2)$-th order, b_{12} being regarded as of order zero. Here Yule introduces some additional concepts for the partial regression, and partial correlation coefficients.

Let

$$f(1\cdot 23 \cdots n) = b_{12\cdot 34 \cdots n} x_2 + \cdots + b_{1n\cdot 23 \cdots (n-1)} x_n \qquad (3\cdot 22)$$

be the linear regression function of x_1 on $(x_2, x_3, \cdots, x_n)$, and let $x_{1\cdot 34 \cdots n} = x_1 - f_1 - f(1\cdot 34 \cdots n)$ and $x_{2\cdot 34 \cdots n} = x_2 - f(2\cdot 34 \cdots n)$ be the deviations of x_1 and x_2 from their respective regression planes. Then the partial regression coefficient $b_{12\cdot 34 \cdots n}$ of the $(n - 2)$-th order as given by $(3\cdot 19)$ or directly solved from the normal equations is merely the simple regression between $x_{1\cdot 34 \cdots n}$ and $x_{2\cdot 34 \cdots n}$; that is to say, $b_{12\cdot 34 \cdots n}$ is the value that would have been obtained by taking a regression equation of the form

$$x_{1\cdot 34 \cdots n} = b_{12\cdot 34 \cdots n} x_{2\cdot 34 \cdots n} \qquad (3\cdot 23)$$

and determining $b_{12\cdot 34 \cdots n}$ by the method of least squares, which gives

$$b_{12\cdot 34 \cdots n} = \frac{\sum (x_{1\cdot 34 \cdots n} \cdot x_{2\cdot 34 \cdots n})}{\sum (x^2_{2\cdot 34 \cdots n})}. \qquad (3\cdot 24)$$

Being the geometrical mean of partial regression coefficient, the partial correlation coefficient of $(n - 2)$-th order is merely the gross correlation coefficient between $x_{1\cdot 34\cdots n}$ and $x_{2\cdot 34\cdots n}$ that

$$r_{12\cdot 34 \cdots n} = \frac{\sum (x_{1\cdot 34 \cdots n} \cdot x_{2\cdot 34 \cdots n})}{\sqrt{\sum (x_{1\cdot 34 \cdots n}^2) \sum (x_{2\cdot 34 \cdots n}^2)}}. \qquad (3\cdot 25)$$

Furthermore, Yule defines the multiple correlation coefficient of $(n - 1)$-th order as the gross correlation between x_1 and $f(1\cdot 23 \cdots n)$ so that

$$r_{1\cdot 23 \cdots n} = \frac{\sum x_1 f(1\cdot 23 \cdots n)}{\sqrt{\sum x_1^2 \sum f^2(1\cdot 23 \cdots n)}} = \sqrt{1 - \frac{\sum x_{1\cdot 23 \cdots n}^2}{\sum x_1^2}}. \qquad (3\cdot 26)$$

Evidently this definition can lend itself to extension to the case of a non-linear regression curve or surface; that is to say, if $f(1\cdot 23\cdots n)$ is a non-linear function of $x_2, x_3, \cdots, x_n$, then $r_{1\cdot 23 \cdots n}$ so determined from $(3\cdot 26)$ will be the non-linear correlation coefficient or the index of correlation as Mills[1] termed it when he elucidated this case.

In this circumstance, the gross correlation coefficient r_{12}, the partial or net correlation coefficient $r_{12\cdot 34 \cdots n}$, and the multiple correlation coefficient $r_{1(234 \cdots n)}$ are brought parallel to each other in the sense that

(i) r_{12} is an index to indicate how closely x_1 can be expressed in terms of a linear function of x_2 alone;

(ii) $r_{12\cdot 34 \cdots n}$ is an index to indicate how closely $x_{1\cdot 3 \cdots n}$ can be expressed in terms of a linear function of $x_{2\cdot 34 \cdots n}$ alone.

(iii) $r_{1(234 \cdots n)}$ is an index to indicate how closely x_1 can be expressed in terms of a linear function of $x_2, x_3, \cdots, x_n$.

Moreover, seeing that

$$\sigma_{1\cdot 23 \cdots n}^2 = \sigma_1^2 [1 - r_{1(23 \cdots n)}^2] \text{ (by equation } 3\cdot 11)$$

and that $\sigma_{1\cdot 23 \cdots n}$ in a minimum, we may, alternatively, regard the values of the

---

[1] Mills, F. C., The Measurement of Correlation and the Problem of Estimation, Jour. Amer. Stat. Ass., Vol.19, p.273, 1924. Cf. also M. Ezekiel, "A Method of handling curvilinear correlation for any number of variables", Quarterly Pub. Amer. Stat., Vol.19, pp.431−453, 1924.

regressions as determined by the condition that the correlation between x_1 and its regression value $f(1 \cdot 23 \cdots n)$, where n may take either value of 2, 3, $\cdots$, n according to the number of variates in the question, shall be a maximum.

Furthermore, by equations $(3 \cdot 10)$ and $(3 \cdot 21)$, Yule concludes:

(i) that $1 \geqslant r^2_{1(23\cdots n)} \geqslant r^2_{1i}$, $i = 2, 3, \cdots, n$;

(ii) that the necessary condition to makes a smaller standard error in estimating x_1 from $(n-1)$ associated variables $x_2, x_3, \cdots, x_n$ than in estimating it from $(n-2)$ associated variates $x_2, x_3, \cdots, x_{n-1}$, i.e., the necessary condition for profitably introducing a new variate x_n to control x_1, is

$$r^2_{1n \cdot 23 \cdots n-1} > 0; \qquad (3 \cdot 27)$$

(iii) and that, having obtained the $\dfrac{n(n-1)}{2}$ correlation coefficients between the n variates $x_1, x_2, \cdots, x_n$, equation $(3 \cdot 21)$ by the aid of $(3 \cdot 20)$ will determine the limits for one of the $\dfrac{n(n-1)}{2}$ correlation coefficients if the others are already known. Thus, in case of $n = 3$, if r_{12}, r_{13} are known, then r_{23} must lie between the limits

$$r_{12}r_{13} \pm (1 + r^2_{12}r^2_{13} - r^2_{12} - r^2_{13}).$$

3.6.5 In Practice, Yule Recommends Two Methods for Computing the Constants

3.6.5.1 The First Method

(i) Write down the normal equations which in the case of four variates (for purpose of simplicity and definiteness, the case of four variates may be regarded as a model for the general case of n variates) are:

$$\sum(x_1 x_2) = b_{12 \cdot 34} \sum(x_2^2) + b_{13 \cdot 24} \sum(x_2 x_3) + b_{14 \cdot 23} \sum(x_2 x_4)$$

$$\sum(x_1 x_3) = b_{12 \cdot 34} \sum(x_2 x_3) + b_{13 \cdot 24} \sum(x_3^2) + b_{14 \cdot 23} \sum(x_3 x_4)$$

$$\sum(x_1 x_4) = b_{12 \cdot 34} \sum(x_2 x_4) + b_{13 \cdot 24} \sum(x_3 x_4) + b_{14 \cdot 23} \sum(x_4^2) \quad (3 \cdot 28)$$

and solve them straightforwardly for the b's which are coefficients of the regression line:

$$x_1 = b_{12 \cdot 34} x_2 + b_{13 \cdot 24} x_3 + b_{14 \cdot 23} x_4.$$

And the other regression coefficients $b_{21\cdot34}$, $b_{23\cdot14}$, $\cdots$, $b_{43\cdot12}$ may be solved by similar procedure, if they are required.

(ii) Evaluate

$$N\sigma^2_{1\cdot234} = \sum(x_1^2) + b_{12\cdot34}\sum(x_2^2) + b_{13\cdot24}\sum(x_3^2) + b_{14\cdot23}\sum(x_4^2)$$
$$- 2b_{12\cdot34}\sum(x_1x_2) - 2b_{13\cdot24}\sum(x_1x_3) - 2b_{14}\sum(x_1x_4)$$
$$+ 2b_{12\cdot34}b_{13\cdot24}\sum(x_2x_3) + 2b_{12\cdot34}b_{14\cdot23}\sum(x_2x_4)$$
$$+ 2b_{13\cdot24}b_{14\cdot23}\sum(x_3x_4).$$

(iii) Compute

$$r_{1(234)} = \sqrt{1 - \frac{\sigma^2_{1\cdot234}}{\sigma^2_1}}.$$

(iv) The partial correlation coefficients, if required, are computed by

$$r_{12\cdot34} = \sqrt{b_{12\cdot34}\cdot b_{21\cdot34}}, \text{ etc.}$$

3.6.5.2 The Second Consists in Using the Recursion Formulas for the Net Correlation Coefficient

(i) Form the correlation tables for computing all the gross correlation coefficients r_{12}, r_{23}, $\cdots$.

(ii) By the use of equation (3·20), compute successively the net correlation coefficients of higher orders straightforwardly.

(iii) Compute the standard errors of higher orders by the use of equation (3·18b).

(iv) Compute the regression coefficients by aid of the formula:

$$b_{12\cdot34\cdots n} = r_{12\cdot34\cdots n}\frac{\sigma_{1\cdot34\cdots n}}{\sigma_{2\cdot34\cdots n}}.$$

(v) Compute the multiple correlation coefficient by use of either (3·11) or (3·21).

3.6.6 Yule's Suggestions with regard to Non-linear Correlation

Yule confines his treatment to the linear regression equation because it is the simplest possible form to calculate. Even in this form, Yule thinks, the amount of arithmetic involved in arriving at the linear characteristic equation for four or five variables will be quite sufficient to content the most enthusiastic statistician. Nevertheless, Yule did point the way of approach to the non-linear correlation in hie second memoir "On the Theory of Correlation". First, he suggested as the regression of x_1 on x_2, x_3, x_4, ⋯ a more general equation

$$\begin{aligned}f(1 \cdot 23 \cdots) = a_{11} &+ a_{12}x_2 + b_{12}x_2^2 + c_{12}x_2^3 + d_{12}x_2^4 + \cdots \\ &+ a_{13}x_3 + b_{13}x_3^2 + c_{13}x_3^3 + d_{13}x_3^4 + \cdots \\ &+ a_{14}x_4 + b_{14}x_4^2 + c_{14}x_4^3 + d_{14}x_4^4 + \cdots \\ &+ \cdots \end{aligned} \qquad (3 \cdot 29)$$

which could be solved on precisely the same principles, i.e., the method of least squares. After having determined $f(1 \cdot 23 \cdots n)$, the non-linear correlation may be computed according to $(3 \cdot 26)$.

By analogy, we may venture to add some new correlation coefficients such as

$$r(1^3 \cdot 2^3) = \sqrt{c_{12} \cdot c_{21}}, \; r(1^4 \cdot 2^4) = \sqrt{d_{14} \cdot d_{41}}, \; \text{etc.}$$

and call them the 3rd, 4th, etc. power correlation coefficient of $(n-2)$-th order.①

Second, Yule suggested a generalized correlation coefficient which seems to be identical to the correlation ratio. Yule says: "one seems almost to require a generalized correlation coefficient, measuring the approach of the distribution towards a single-valued law of any form, for the case of general correlation. It would be easy to get a limit to such a coefficient by finding the standard deviation from the actual line of means."② Let the standard deviation from the actual line of array means $\bar{x}_y$ be σ_{1a} and substitute it for $\sigma_{1 \cdot 2}$ in $(3 \cdot 10)$, the resulting generalized correlation coefficient, as Yule might have called it,

$$\sqrt{1 - \frac{\sigma_{1a}^2}{\sigma_1^2}} = n_{12} \qquad (3 \cdot 30a)$$

is seen to be identical to the correlation ratio of which the theory was fully

---

① Wicksell has defined some similar coefficients as described in Chapter II.
② "On the Theory of Correlation", Jour. Roy. Stat. Soc., Vol.60, p.821, footnote, 1897.

developed by Pearson① in 1905 in his famous memoir "Skew Correlation and Non-linear Regression" of which we shell presently give an account.

3.7 The Correlation Ratio (Pearson)

In this memoir, Pearson established a general theory of non-linear regression in the case of two correlated variates. He shows that regression ceases to be linear when the correlation ratio n differs sensibly from the correlation coefficient and establishes criteria for parabolic, cubic, and higher forms of regression.

Pearson's definition of correlation in this memoir is practically the same as he defined it 10 years② previously. Briefly speaking, if certain values of a given statistical character B are relatively more likely to occur with a given value of another statistical character A than others, these two characters A and B are said correlated.

The Correlation Ratio.

Let the N observed pairs of A and B be

$$x_1, x_2, \cdots, x_N$$

$$y_1, y_2, \cdots, y_N$$

and n_x of them have the character A = x. The distribution of B's associated with the given type A = x is termed an x-array of B's. This array, like any other frequency distribution, will have its mean, $\bar{y}_x$, and standard deviation σ_{n_x}. Let the grand mean of all the B characters be $\bar{y}$ and their variability given by the standard deviation σ_2. Similarly, $\bar{x}$, σ_1 will denote the mean and standard deviation of the A's, and n_x, $\bar{x}_y$, and σ_{n_y} the number of individuals, the mean, and the standard deviation for a y-array of A's.

The curve obtained by plotting $\bar{y}_x$ to x (or $\bar{x}_y$ to y) is termed the regression curve of y on x (or x on y). A curve, in which the ratio of σ_{n_x} to the standard

---

① "Skew Correlation and Non-linear Regression", Drapers' Company Research, Memoirs, Series II, 1905.

② "Regression, Heredity, etc.", Op. Cit.

deviation σ_2 is to plotted to x, will measure the scatter in the arrays and is termed a scedastic curve. The weighted mean array variance,

$$\sigma_{2a}^2 = \sum (n_x \sigma_{n_x}^2)/N = \frac{1}{N} \sum \sum \{n_{xy}(y - \bar{y}_x)^2\}, \quad (3 \cdot 30b)$$

corresponding to the square of Yule's standard error, will measure the average variability in B to be found associated with any given type x of A. Now, Pearson, in the manner of Yule's definition of correlation as given in equation $(3 \cdot 10)$ and $(3 \cdot 11)$, defines the η by

$$\eta^2 = 1 - \sigma_{2a}^2/\sigma_2^2.$$

Correlation ratio/ η must lie between ± 1, because σ_{2a}^2 cannot be negative, being the sum of a number positive squares. When $\eta = \pm 1$ (i.e., when $\sigma_{2a}^2 = 0$ and $\sigma_{n_x}^2 = 0$ and therefore the scedastic curve coincides with the x-axis), the correlation is prefect or we have causation.

Let the standard deviation of the array means $\bar{y}_x$ be σ_{M_2} defined by

$$\sigma_{M_2}^2 = \frac{1}{N} \sum \{n_x(\bar{y}_x - \bar{y})^2\}. \quad (3 \cdot 31)$$

By a well-known property of moments

$$\sigma_2^2 = \sigma_{2a}^2 + \sigma_{M_2}^2,$$

we obtain[①]

$$\eta_{21} = \frac{\sigma_{M_2}}{\sigma_2}. \quad (3 \cdot 32)$$

This shows that the correlation ratio is the ratio of the variability of the means of x-arrays to the variability of B's in general. If $\eta = 0$, it follows that σ_{M_2} is zero and therefore the regression line parallel to the x-axis, there is no correlation between A and B. Thus, the correlation ratio η, as defined by $(3 \cdot 30b)$ or $(3 \cdot 32)$, "is an excellent measure of the stringency of correlation, always lying numerically between the values 0 and 1, which mark absolute independence and complete causation respectively".

[①] As $\sigma_{M_2} \neq \sigma_{M_1}$, and $\sigma_2 \neq \sigma_1$, we cannot have $\eta_{12} = \eta_{21}$, though $r_{12} = r_{21}$.

The relation between correlation ratio and the correlation coefficient.

As the correlation coefficient r is (for ungrouped data $n_{xy} = 1$):

$$N\sigma_1\sigma_2 r = \sum \{n_{xy}(x - \bar{x})(y - \bar{y})\},$$
$$= \sum \{n_x(x - \bar{x})(y - \bar{y})\}, \qquad (3 \cdot 33)$$

we have, from $(3 \cdot 31)$ and $(3 \cdot 33)$,

$$N(\eta_{21}^2 - r^2)\sigma_2^2 = \sum \left\{n_x(\bar{y}_x - \bar{y})\left[\bar{y}_x - \bar{y} - \frac{r\sigma_2}{\sigma_1}(x - \bar{x})\right]\right\}.$$

Let

$$Y = \bar{y} + \frac{r\sigma_2}{\sigma_1}(x - \bar{x}),$$

we obtain, through simple reductions,

$$N(\eta_{21} - r^2)\sigma_2^2 = \sum \{n_x (\bar{y}_x - Y)^2\}. \qquad (3 \cdot 34)$$

This equation has two important meanings. First, as the right side cannot be negative, the correlation ratio is always greater than the correlation coefficient, except in the special case when the means of x-arrays of y's all fall on a straight line and then they are equal. Second, the right side is the weighted mean square deviation of the regression curve from the straight line which fits this curve most closely. As a consequence,

$$\eta^2 - r^2 = 0 \qquad (3 \cdot 35)$$

offers a necessary condition for linear regression.

Pearson finds the standard deviation of a correlation ratio to be given by

$$\sigma_{\eta_{21}}^2 = \frac{1}{N}\left\{(1 - \eta_{21}^2)^2 + \frac{\mu_4 - 3\mu_2^2}{4\mu_2^2}\eta_{21}^2 + \frac{\lambda_4 - 3\lambda_2^2}{4\lambda_2^2}\eta_{21}^2(1 - 2\eta_{21}^2) \right.$$
$$\left. + (x_1 - 1)(1 - \eta_{21}^2)\left(1 - \frac{5}{2}\eta_{21}^2\right) - x_2\eta_{21}(1 - \eta_{21}^2)^{3/2}\right\} \quad (3 \cdot 36)$$

where

$$\mu_s = \frac{1}{N}\sum \{(y - \bar{y})^s n_{xy}\}$$

$$\lambda_s = \frac{1}{N} \sum \{n_{x_p}(\bar{y}_{x_p} - \bar{y})^s\}$$

are the s-th moments of y's and of the x-array means about their mean, and

$$X_1 = \frac{\sum \{n_{x_p} \sigma^2_{x_p}(\bar{y}_{x_p} - \bar{y})^2\}}{N\sigma_2^2(1 - \eta_{21}^2)\sigma_{M_2}^2}$$

$$X_2 = \frac{\sum \{n_{x_p} m_s (\bar{y}_{x_p} - \bar{y})\}}{N\sigma_y(1 - \eta^2)^{3/2}\sigma_{M_2}}$$

where m_s is the s-th moment of y's in the x_p-array about the array mean:

$$m_s = \frac{1}{n_{x_p}} \sum (y_{x_p} - \bar{y}_{x_p})^s n_{x_p} y_{x_p}.$$

As X_2, $(X_1 - 1)$, $(\mu_4 - 3\mu_2^2)/\mu_2^2$, $(\lambda_4 - 3\lambda_2^2)/\lambda_2^2$ will probably be small, we have approximately

$$\sigma^2_{\eta_{21}} = \frac{1}{N}(1 - \eta_{21}^2). \quad (3 \cdot 37)$$

This will suffice for many practical cases. η is a biased quantity, since it always tends to exceed numerically its true value. For this reason, a correction is needed. When the true η is zero, the mean observed value of η is proven[①] to be

$$\bar{\eta}_\varepsilon = \sqrt{\frac{k-1}{N}} \quad \text{for true } \eta = 0 \quad (3 \cdot 38)$$

where k = no. of classes and N = no. of observations. Hence an observed value of η ought to be compared with

$$\bar{\eta}_\varepsilon + E_\eta = \bar{\eta}_\varepsilon + 0.674\,5 \frac{1 - \eta^2}{N} \quad (3 \cdot 39)$$

where $\bar{\eta}_\varepsilon$ is the mean value of η for zero correlation, and E_η the probable error of η. No observed value of η can be considered as significant if it is not sensibly greater than $\bar{\eta}_\varepsilon + 0.674\,5/N$.

[①] Pearson, K., "On a correction to be made to the correlation Ratio", Biom., Vol.8, p.254, 1911.

3.8 Partial and Multiple Correlation Ratio

For the same reason that the correlation ratio is introduced to describe non-linear regression of two variates, Isserlis[1] and Pearson[2] have introduced the multiple and partial correlation ratio corresponding to the multiple and partial correlation coefficient.

Parallel to (3·30b), the multiple correlation ratio $\eta_{z(xy)}$ of z on x and y is defined by

$$[1 - \eta^2_{z(xy)}]\sigma^2_z = \frac{\sum\sum\sum\{n_{xyz}(z - \bar{z}_{xy})^2\}}{N} \qquad (3\cdot 40)$$

where n_{xyz} is the frequency of the three correlated characters $A = x$, $B = y$, $C = z$. The triple sum in left side may be simplified in the following way:

$$\sum\sum\sum\{n_{xyz}(z - \bar{z} + \bar{z} - \bar{z}_{xy})^2\} = \sum\sum\{n_{xy}(\bar{z} - \bar{z}_{xy})^2\}$$
$$+ \{2\sum\sum(\bar{z} - \bar{z}_{xy})\}\cdot\{\sum[n_{xyz}(z - \bar{z})]\}$$
$$+ \sum\sum\sum[n_{xyz}(z - \bar{z})^2]$$
$$= \sum\sum\{n_{xy}(\bar{z} - \bar{z}_{xy})^2\} - 2\sum\sum\{n_{xy}(\bar{z} - \bar{z}_{xy})^2\} + N\sigma^2_z.$$

Hence

$$\eta^2_{z(xy)} = \frac{\sum\sum\{n_{xy}(\bar{z} - \bar{z}_{xy})^2\}}{N\sigma^2_z}, \qquad (3\cdot 41)$$

which is a form parallel to (3·32).

Further Isserlis in the manner that Pearson derived (3·34), has obtained its extended form for the three variates:

$$[\eta^2_{z(xy)} - r^2_{z(xy)}]N\sigma^2_z = \sum\sum\{n_{xy}(\bar{z}_{xy} - z)^2\} \qquad (3\cdot 42)$$

where $r_{z(xy)}$ is the multiple correlation coefficient of z on x and y and z represents the regression plane of z on x and y. This shows the similar properties of η, that is, $\eta^2_{z(xy)} > r^2_{z(xy)}$ except when the regression is strictly linear, and $\eta^2_{z(xy)} > 1$.

---

[1] Isserlis, L., "On the Partial Correlation Ratio", Biom., Vol.10, p.391, and Vol.11, p.60, 1914–1916.

[2] Pearson, K., "On the Partial Correlation Ratio", Proc. Roy. Soc. A, Vol.91, p.492, 1915.

The definition (3・33) and the properties (3・41) and (3・42) have been extended to the general case of m variates. Let $x_1, x_2, \cdots, x_m$ be the m variates, let $\bar{x}(1\cdot 23 \cdots m)$ be the mean of x_1 when $x_2, x_3, \cdots, x_m$ are given and let $\sum\limits_{1\cdots m}$ be a summation sign extending to the variates $x_1, x_2, \cdots, x_m$. Then the multiple correlation ratio of x_1 on $x_2, x_3, \cdots, x_m$ is defined by the equation:

$$N\sigma_1[1 - \eta^2_{1(23\cdots m)}] = \sum_{1\cdots m}\{[x_1 - \bar{x}(1\cdot 23 \cdots m)]^2 n_{12\cdots m}\} \quad (3\cdot 43)$$

and the formula parallel to (3・41) and (3・42) are given as

$$N\sigma_1^2 \eta^2_{1(23\cdots m)} = \sum_{2\cdots m}\{n_{2\cdots m}[\bar{x}_1 - \bar{x}_1(1\cdot 23 \cdots m)]^2\} \quad (3\cdot 44)$$

and

$$N\eta^2_{1(23\cdots m)} - r^2_{1(23\cdots m)} = \frac{\sum\limits_{2\cdots m}\{n_{2\cdots m}[\bar{x}_1(1\cdot 23 \cdots m) - X_1]^2\}}{N\sigma_1^2}.$$

$$(3\cdot 45)$$

Isserlis has also investigated some of the conditions under which the determination of the multiple correlation ratio $\eta_{z(xy)}$ may be based upon the simple correlation ratios $\eta_{zx}, \eta_{xz}, \eta_{zy}$, etc. Thus, if the regression in question may be approximately represented by an equation of the form:

$$\frac{z}{\sigma_z} = d + \frac{ax}{\sigma_x} + \frac{by}{\sigma_y} + \frac{cdy}{\sigma_x \sigma_y}.$$

Isserlis has succeeded in expressing the multiple correlation ratio in terms of the simple correlation ratios as follows:

$$[\eta^2_{z(xy)} - r^2_{z(xy)}]\frac{q_{x^2y^2} - 1}{q_{x^2y^2} - r^2} = \frac{r_{xy}q_{x^2y} - q_{xy^2}}{q_{x^2y}r_{xy} - q_{xy^2}r_{xy}}$$

$$- \frac{r_{yz} - r_{xz}r_{xy}}{1 - r^2_{xy}}\left\{(\eta^2_{zy} - r^2_{zy}) - \left(\frac{r_{yz}r_{xy} - r_{xz}}{1 - r^2_{xy}}\right)^2\right\}(\eta^2_{xy} - r^2_{xy})$$

$$+ \frac{r_{xy}q_{xy^2} - q_{x^2y}}{q_{xy^2}r_{yz} - q_{x^2y}r_{xz}} \cdot \frac{r_{xz}r_{xy}}{1 - r^2_{xy}}\left\{(\eta^2_{zx} - r^2_{zx}) - \left(\frac{r_{xz}r_{xy} - r_{yz}}{1 - r^2_{xy}}\right)^2(\eta^2_{yx} - r^2_{xy})\right\}.$$

$$(3\cdot 46)$$

Moreover, in case $q_{x^3} = q_{y^3} = 0$ and $\eta_{xy} = \eta_{yx} = r_{xy}$, Isserlis obtains approximately

$$\eta_{z(xy)}^2 - r_{z(xy)}^2 = \frac{2r_{xy}^2}{1 + r_{xy}^2}(\eta_{zy}^2 - r_{zy}^2) \qquad (3 \cdot 46a)$$

or

$$\eta_{z(xy)}^2 - r_{z(xy)}^2 = \frac{2r_{xy}^2}{1 + r_{xy}^2}(\eta_{zx}^2 - r_{zx}^2) \qquad (3 \cdot 46b)$$

where

$$q_{x^s y^t z^u} = \frac{\sum\sum\sum n_{xyz} x^s y^t z^u}{N \sigma_x^s \sigma_y^t \sigma_z^u}$$

with $\bar{x} = 0$, $\bar{y} = 0$, $\bar{z} = 0$, and $q_{x^s y^0 z^0} = q_{x^s}$, and $r_{z(xy)}$ denotes the multiple correlation coefficient of z with x and y when the regression is linear.

Brown, Greenwood, and Wood[1] used the multiple correlation ratio to deal with the distribution of births, deaths, and population in 1 000 Englishers, registration sub-districts, and also of the birth- and death-rates and population in these districts. The material is highly heterogeneous as shown in the high values of the standardized moments of the 3rd order, i.e., Pearsonian β_1 for deaths is 16.020 5 and for death rates is 61.539 2. The multiple correlation ratios obtained by direct calculation are:

$$\eta_{1 \cdot (23)} = 0.938\ 4 \text{ for 1 000 sub-districts},$$

$$\eta_{1 \cdot (23)} = 0.921\ 3 \text{ for 999 sub-districts},$$

where sub-index stands for deaths, and 2 and 3 for births and population respectively.

The approximation formula for Isserlis gives a pretty close value in the case of small β_1 values; that in the case where the β_1 value for population is 0.088 6 and that for birth is 0.337 2. The multiple correlation ratio $\eta_{1 \cdot 23}$ computed from Isserlis' approximation formula $(3 \cdot 46)$ is 0.938 8, or from the simpler formula $(3 \cdot 46a)$ is 0.933 8.

From this memoir[2], we also see that the multiple correlation ratio has been independently developed by Snow who thereby finds that for planar regression

$$\eta_{z(xy)}^2 - r_{z(xy)}^2 = 0$$

---

[1] "A Study of Index Correlation", J.R.S.S., Vol.77, p.317, 1914.
[2] Ibid., p.322.

which is also given by Isserlis as a necessary condition for linear regression in case of three variates.

The partial correlation ratio was introduced by Pearson. In a problem of three correlated variates, the values of x and y associated with a given type z_p constitutes a sub-population. In such a sub-population, the correlation ratio between x and y is $\eta_{yx} \cdot z_p$ defined by

$$1 - \eta^2_{yx \cdot z_p} = \frac{\sum_x \sum_y \{n_{xyz_p}(y - \bar{y}_{xz_p})^2\}}{n_{z_p} \sigma_{y \cdot z_p}}$$

where n_{z_p} is the total frequency of this sub-population and n_{xyz_p} is the cell frequency of (xy) in this sub-population, $\bar{y}_{xz_p}$ is the mean of an x-array of y's in this sub-population, and $\sigma_{y \cdot z_p}$ is the standard deviation of all y's in such a sub-population. Now the weighted mean of $\sigma_{y \cdot z_p}$ is

$$\frac{1}{N} \sum_{z_p} (n_{z_p} \sigma^2_{y \cdot z_p}) = \sigma^2_y (1 - \eta^2_{yz}).$$

Pearson defines the partial correlation ratio $\eta_{yx \cdot z}$ by

$$1 - \eta^2_{yx \cdot z} = \frac{\sum_x \sum_y \sum_z n_{xyz}(y - \bar{y}_{xz})}{N \sigma^2_y (1 - \eta^2_{yz})}. \qquad (3 \cdot 47)$$

Hence, by $(3 \cdot 40)$,

$$(1 - \eta^2_{yx \cdot z})(1 - \eta^2_{yz}) = [1 - \eta^2_{y(xz)}] \qquad (3 \cdot 48)$$

which is parallel to a formula of $(3 \cdot 21)$ when $n = 3$.

The identical relation $(3 \cdot 21)$ for the general case has also been demonstrated by Pearson to hold connecting the partial correlation ratio with the multiple correlation ratio; namely,

$$1 - \eta^2_{12 \cdot 34 \cdots m} = \frac{1 - \eta^2_{1(23 \cdots m)}}{1 - \eta^2_{1(34 \cdots m)}}.$$

3.9 The Partial Multiple Correlation Coefficient

In 1927, Tappan[1] introduced a partial multiple correlation coefficient. It is

---

[1] "On Partial Multiple Correlation Coefficient", Biom., V.19, p.39, 1927.

a multiple correlation coefficient of a sub-universe obtained by giving a constant value to each of some variates of the whole universe in question.

Let subscripts $123\cdots nuv\cdots w$ denote the manifold of correlated characteristics. In a sub-universe where the characteristics $1\cdots n$ vary but $uv\cdots w$ are constant, the multiple correlation coefficient of the characteristic 1 with the characteristics $23\cdots n$ is a partial multiple correlation coefficient, denoted by $R_{1\cdot 23\cdots n| uv\cdots w|}$. By equation (3 · 21), Tappan obtains

$$1 - R^2_{1\cdot 23\cdots n| uv\cdots w|} = (1 - r^2_{12\cdot 34\cdots n| uv\cdots w|})(1 - r^2_{13\cdot 45\cdots n| uv\cdots w|})$$
$$\cdot (1 - r^2_{14\cdot 5\cdots n| nv\cdots w|})\cdots(1 - r^2_{1\cdot n| uv\cdots w|}) \qquad (3 \cdot 49)$$

where $r_{15\cdot 2\cdots n| u\cdots w|}$ is a partial correlation coefficient between the characteristics 1 and S in the sub-universe defined above and which is evidently identical to $r_{12\cdot 34\cdots nuv\cdots w}$.

Let $\Delta = |r_{st}|$ be the determinant formed of all the correlation coefficients of the manifold with r_{st} as its st-element, let Δ_{st} the first minor corresponding to the element r_{st} and Δ_{stuv} denote the second minor after the rows and columns corresponding to the elements r_{st} and r_{uv} are deleted. Then

$$r_{12\cdot 34\cdots nuv\cdots w} = -\frac{\Delta_{12}}{\sqrt{\Delta_{11}\Delta_{22}}}$$

or

$$1 - r^2_{12\cdot 34\cdots nu\cdots w} = \frac{\Delta_{11}\Delta_{22} - \Delta^2_{12}}{\Delta_{11}\Delta_{22}} = \frac{\Delta\Delta_{11\,22}}{\Delta_{11}\Delta_{22}}.$$

Similarly,

$$1 - r^2_{13\cdot 4\cdots n\cdots w} = \frac{\Delta_{22}\Delta_{11\,22\,33}}{\Delta_{11\,22}\Delta_{22\,33}},$$

$$1 - r^2_{14\cdot 5\cdots n\cdots w} = \frac{\Delta_{22\,33}\Delta_{22\,33\,11\,44}}{\Delta_{22\,33\,11}\Delta_{22\,33\,44}}, \text{ etc.}$$

Substituting in (3 · 49),

$$1 - R^2_{1\cdot 23\cdots n| uv\cdots w|} = \frac{\Delta\Delta_{11\,22\cdots nn}}{\Delta_{11}\Delta_{22\,33\cdots nn}}. \qquad (3 \cdot 50)$$

But
$$\frac{\Delta}{\Delta_{11}} = 1 - R^2_{1\cdot 23\cdots nu\cdots w},$$

$$\frac{\Delta_{11\cdots nn}}{\Delta_{22\cdots nn}} = 1 - R^2_{1\cdot uv\cdots w}.$$

Accordingly,

$$1 - R^2_{1\cdot 23\cdots nu\cdots w} = \frac{1 - R^2_{1\cdot 23\cdots n|\ uv\cdots w|}}{1 - R^2_{1\cdot uv\cdots w}}. \qquad (3\cdot 51)$$

Thus, any partial multiple correlation coefficient may be expressed in terms of the correlation determinant and its minors, (3 · 50) or in terms of the ordinary multiple correlation coefficients as in (3 · 51).

A suggested application in economics is the problem: What is the total influence on the London-Berlin rate or exchange of the London-Amsterdam and Berlin-Amsterdam rates if we make the New York rates on London, Berlin, and Amsterdam constant?

3.10 The Criticisms of the Regression Method

As a criticism of the regression method, we quote Wicksell's statement[①]:

"The regression method suffers many disadvantages. Theoretically there is no means of making sure of the convergency of the developments; practically there is no means of determining the probability of an individual deviation within assigned limits from the regression curves. Thus, while the theory gives the mean of the one variate for any fixed value of the other. It does not give any adequate measure of the extent to which the first variate clusters about this mean, that is of the strength of correlation. The reason for this lies in the fact that the method makes no assumptions as to the mathematical form of the correlation function. Thus, while the method may be extended so as to give the standard deviation (scedasticity) and skewness(clisy) of the distribution of the one variate for any fixed value of the other, it cannot give the form of this distribution since it is not certain, in the general case, that these two characteristics are sufficient to describe that distribution."

---

① "The Correlation Function of Type A", Op. Cit.

To this we may add that there is no criterion for selecting a type of curve to describe the regression. As a consequence, the multiple regression curve and (or surface in more than two dimensions) may happen to be inconsistent with total regression curves as Camp has pointed out. Moreover, the correlation coefficient so determined does not measure the strength of correlation in the correlated system unless the frequency distribution is normal. Indeed, Yule himself has said that the vanishing of the correlation coefficient does not mean zero correlation. Yule's statement may, in a sense, be considered to mean that the correlation coefficient is not an exact measure of the strength of correlation even though there is no error resulting from random sampling.

Moreover, the formula for multiple and partial correlation ratios are very complicated, cumbersome, and biased. In case of two variates, if we use a parabolic polynomial to represent the regression, the cubic form requires the employment of moments up to the 6th order. As the probable error of the moments higher than the 4th order is very great as Pearson has pointed in his memoir on "Skew Correlation and Non-linear Regression", the quartic regression and perhaps to certain extent the cubic regression is of doubtful utility.

Finally, we will quote the comment on the regression method made by Pearson[1]: "... Theoretically therefore, to have justification for using the method of least squares to fit a line or place to a swam of points we must assume the arrays to follow a normal distribution (as the proof Gauss gave of his method of least squares is based on the assumption that the distribution of y for a given x follows the normal law of error). If they do not, we may defend least squares as likely to give a fairly good result but we cannot demonstrate its accuracy. Hence in disregarding normal distributions and claiming great generality for our correlation by merely using the principle of least squares, we are really depriving that principle of the basis of its theoretical accuracy, and the apparent generalization has been gained merely at the expense of theoretical validity. Take other distributions of deviations for the arrays end the method of least squares is not the one which will naturally arise for making the combined probability a maximum. It is by no means certain, therefore, that Mr. Yule's generalization

---

[1] "Historical Note", Biom., Vol.13, p.44.

indicates the real line of future advance."

3.11 The Fitting of Regression Curves

So far, we have described the main developments, in the theory of the regression method of correlation and the criticisms of it. There are many other minor developments which are essentially concerned with the employment of one or the other mathematical curve or a free-hand curve, to represent the regression of the correlation system. By the nature of the fundamental theory of the regression method as we have seen in the foregoing analysis, almost any mathematical curve or even a free hand curve may be employed for the representation of the regression curve, if it seems to be appropriate for some theoretical or practical reasons to the problem in consideration. After having the regression curve, the correlation coefficient can easily be determined according to (3 · 26).

To fit a theoretical curve is not a problem of selecting a type of theoretical curves[①], but a problem of finding the arbitrary constants in a function of known form which is assumed for certain reasons or experiences to be the right type of curve for the question in consideration.

We will not recount the various developments in fitting various types of curves or surfaces by mathematical or graphic methods except one or two cases where the technique has been quite well developed.

3.12 The Fitting of Orthogonal Polynomials

In the use or mathematical formula for the representation of regression

---

① To make a choice among the formulae which may be proposed to represent regression in general, we may borrow Edgeworth's criteria respecting frequency curves as a guide for our present problem:

(1) A priori validity,

(2) Correspondence with the observations,

(3) Adaptation to a special purpose,

(4) Descriptive neatness,

(5) Arithmetical ease—the values the function may easily be computed.

Cf. Edgeworth, F. Y., "On the Representation of Statistics by Mathematical Formula", J. R. S. S., Vol.61, p.670. The second criterion among the five is by far the most important, since in statistical method, we have to assume the data are typical samples of the universe in consideration, and this criterion may be tested objectively by some measure of goodness of fit.

curve, the polynomial form

$$P_r = a_0 + a_1 x + \cdots + a_k x^k + \cdots + a_r x^r \tag{3·52}$$

is of special interest, since this expression may be considered as the Taylor's expansion of the unknown true regression function $f(x)$ and since it is possible to determine the general expression for the difference

$$Q_k = P_k - P_{k-1}, \quad k = 0, 1, 2, \cdots, r \tag{3·53}$$

where Q_k is seen to be a polynomial of k-th degree:

$$Q_k = b_{k0} + b_{k1} x + \cdots + b_{kk} x^k \tag{3·54}$$

or, putting

$$c_{kj} = \frac{b_{kj}}{b_{kk}} (j = 0, 1, 2, \cdots, k-1),$$

$$A_k = b_{kk},$$

and

$$\xi_k = c_{k0} + c_{k1} x + \cdots + c_{k(k-1)} x^{k-1} + x^k,$$

we may write

$$\begin{aligned} P_r &= Q_0 + Q_1 + \cdots + Q_r \\ &= A_0 + A_1 \xi_1 + A_2 \xi_2 + \cdots + A_r \xi_r, \end{aligned} \tag{3·55}$$

so that the regression formula of 1st, 2nd, 3rd, $\cdots$, r-th degree may be built successively, each being obtained from the last by adding a new term which is calculated by carrying a single process of computation through a new stage without affecting the preceding terms already obtained.

This method is generally called the fitting of regression by orthogonal polynomials. But, as Neyman[①] has demonstrated, the theory may also be built up without any appeal to the orthogonal conditions:

$$\sum (Q_k Q_h) = \sum A_h A_k \xi_h \xi_k = 0, \quad h \neq k, \tag{3·56}$$

where the summation $\sum$ is taken over all the observed values of x.

---

① Neyman. J., "Further Notes on Non-linear Regression", Biom., Vol.18, p.257, 1926.

The principles involved in the fitting of curves by orthogonal polynomials were first considered by Tchebycheff[1] who found for the simplified case where the intervals of x are equal and can be taken as unity, the general expression for Q_k. The method has latter been treated by Gram,[2] Esscher,[3] Pearson[4] who also gives by aid of the correlation ratio the conditions for linear, parabolic, and cubic regression curves, Jordan,[5] Fisher[6] and Allan.[7]

The general principle may be summarized as follows:

The regression formula is fitted to the array means so that we may write

$$\bar{y} = Y = P_r = SA_k \xi_k, \ \xi_0 = 1. \qquad (3 \cdot 57)$$

Since the polynomials ξ_k are subject to the orthogonal conditions,

$$\sum \xi_k \xi_h = 0,$$

we have[8]

$$\sum (n\bar{y}) \xi_k = \sum y \xi_k = A_k \sum \xi_k^2 \qquad (3 \cdot 58)$$

---

[1] Tchebycheff, P. L., Memoires de l'Academie de St. Petersbourg, 1854, 1859, or, Oeuvres, 1899, Tome I. A resume by R. Radau, Bulletin Astronomique, Tome VIII, Paris, p.350 et seq., 1891. See also Lionville's Journal, 2nd series, Tome III, p.289 et seq., 1858.

[2] Gram, J. P., Thesis, 1879.

[3] Esscher, F., "Uber die Sterblichkeit in Schweden", Lunds Astro. Ob., 1920.

[4] Pearson, K., "On a General Method of Determining the Successive Terms in a Skew Regression Line, Biom., Vol.13, 1921.

[5] Jordan, C., Proceedings, Lond. Math. Soc., Series 2, Vol.20, pp.297–325, 1921.

[6] Fisher, R.A., "Studies in Crop Variation. I", Jour. Agr. Science, Vol.11, pp.107–135, 1921.

[7] Allan, F. E., The General Form of the Orthogonal Polynomials for Simple Series, Proc. Roy. Soc. Edin., Vol.50, p.310, 1930.

[8] It is easy to see that if the coefficients A's are determined by the criterion of least squares, i.e., by making

$$\sum (y - Y)^2 = \text{minimum},$$

we shall reach the same solution $(3 \cdot 58)$. Differentiating with respect to A_h and putting the result to zero, we have

$$\sum \{(y - SA_k \xi_k) \xi_p\} = 0, \ p = 0, 1, 2, \ldots, r,$$

which is equivalent to

$$\sum y_k - A_k \sum \xi_k^2 = 0$$

on account of the orthogonal conditions as given in $(3 \cdot 56)$.

or,

$$A_k = \frac{\sum y\xi_k}{\sum \xi^2}.$$

The polynomials ξ's may now be determined in terms of the moments of the x-distribution by means of the orthogonal conditions.① Writing

$$\xi_r = \sum_{s=0}^{r-1} c_{rs} x^s, \ c_{rr} = 1, \tag{3·59}$$

for the polynomial of degree r. The orthogonal condition

$$\sum (\xi_s \xi_r) = 0 \ (\text{summing over all } x\text{-values})$$

is equivalent to

$$\sum (\xi_s x^s) = 0 \ (\sum = \text{summation over all } x\text{'s})$$

for all integral values of s from 0 to $r-1$. As s takes successively the values from 0 to $r-1$, we obtain the $r+1$ equation in the unknows $c_{r0}, c_{r1}, \cdots, c_{r(r-1)}$:

$$c_{r0} + c_{r1}x + \cdots + c_{r(r-1)}x^{r-1} + x^r - \xi_r = 0, \tag{3·60}$$
$$c_{r0} + c_{r1}\mu_1 + \cdots + c_{r(r-1)}\mu_{r-1} + \mu_r = 0, \text{ etc.}$$

whence we deduce the equation for ξ_r in the form:

$$\begin{vmatrix} 1 & x & \cdots & x^{r-1} & x^r - \xi_r \\ 1 & \mu_1 & \cdots & \mu_{r-1} & \mu_r \\ \mu_1 & \mu_2 & \cdots & \mu_r & \mu_{r+1} \\ \cdots & \cdots & \cdots & \cdots & \cdots \\ \mu_{r-1} & \mu_r & \cdots & \mu_{2r-2} & \mu_{2r-1} \end{vmatrix} = 0 \tag{3·61}$$

where

$$\mu_r = \frac{1}{n}\sum x^r, \ n = \text{no. of observations}$$

---

① Pearson determines the first four polynomials by the criterion of least squares and gives the same solution, as is given here in the manner of Allan's proof, loc. cit.

is the r-th moment of the x-distribution. In this way, the coefficients c's in ξ_r are each given as the ratio of two moment determinants. Thus, if the variates x and y are measured from their means so that

$$\mu_{hk} = \frac{1}{n}\sum x^h y^k,$$

$$\lambda_{hk} = \frac{\mu_{hk}}{\sqrt{\mu_{20}\mu_{02}}},$$

$$\mu_{20} = \sigma_x^2,$$

$$\mu_{02} = \sigma_y^2,$$

then, for a regression of 3rd degree, we have

$$\frac{\bar{y}}{\sigma_y} = Y = P_3 = A_0 + A_1\xi_1 + A_2\xi_2 + A_3\xi_3,$$

where

$$A_0 = 0,$$

$$A_1 = \lambda_{11} = r,$$

$$A_2 = (\lambda_{12} - r\lambda_{30})/(\lambda_{40} - \lambda_{30}^2 - 1),$$

$$A_3 = \left\{\lambda_{13} - \lambda_{40}r - \frac{(\lambda_{50} - \lambda_{40} - \lambda_{30})(\lambda_{12} - r\lambda_{30})}{\lambda_{40} - \lambda_{30} - 1}\right\}$$

$$\div \left\{\lambda_6 - \lambda_{40}^2 - \lambda_{30}^2 - \frac{(\lambda_{50} - \lambda_{40} - \lambda_{30})^2}{(\lambda_{40} - \lambda_{30}^2 - 1)}\right\}.$$

$$\xi_1 = \frac{x}{\sigma_x},$$

$$\xi_2 = c_{20} + c_{21}x/\sigma_x + x^2/\sigma_x^2 = x^2/\sigma_x^2 - \lambda\xi_1 - 1,$$

$$\xi_3 = \frac{x^3}{\sigma_x^3} - \frac{\lambda_{50} - \lambda_{30}\lambda_{40} - \lambda_{30}}{(\lambda_{40} - \lambda_{30}^2 - 1)}\xi_2 - \lambda_{40}\xi_1 - \lambda_{30}.$$

Nor,

$$\frac{S(n_x \bar{y}_x^2)}{n\sigma_y^2} = \eta_{yx}^2 = \sum (n_x Y^2)/n = \sum \{n_x(SA_k\xi_k)^2\}/n$$

$$= r^2 + \frac{(\lambda_{12} - r\lambda_{30})^2}{\lambda_{40} - \lambda_{30}^2 - 1} + \cdots \qquad (3 \cdot 62)$$

It is seen therefore that the conditions for linear regression are $\lambda_{12} - r\lambda_{30} = 0$, and the following terms vanish. Likewise, for the second-degree regress, all the terms after the same in the right side of (3·62) must vanish, and so on. In this way Pearson has obtained the conditions for the 1st, 2nd, and 3rd order regression. As Pearson[1] pointed out, these conditions, especially with regard to their probable errors, become less and less manageable as we proceed up to higher and higher order parabola. Neyman[2] has, however, generalized in a determinant form for the general case.

The orthogonal polynomials can be used with great advantage in problems relating to time series where the increments of time are equal and fixed forms, for the polynomial ξ_r may be constructed in such a way that the coefficients of x in ξ_r are certain functions of n, the number of observations. Fisher has given such expressions for the first 5 polynomials[3], differing from Tchebycheff's form by a numerical factor; the coefficient of x^r in ξ_r being $(2r)!/r!$ in Tchebycheff's system, is absorbed in the coefficient A_r and therefore becomes unity in Fisher's system.

The proof given by Tchebycheff is quite lengthy and complicated while the proof for Fisher's system as given by Allan, making use of the interpolation formulas for finite differences, is much simpler. But we will not reproduce either of them.

A rapid method for calculating such polynomials may be found in a paper by Birge and Shea.[4]

The fitness of such a regression formula has been considered by Pearson,[5] Fisher,[6] and Schultz.[7] Indeed as Fisher has pointed out, it may be regarded as

---

[1][2] Pearson determines the first four polynomials by the criterion of least squares and gives the same solution, as is given here in the manner of Allan's proof, loc. cit.

[3] Statistical Method for Research Works, p.125, 3rd ed., 1930.

[4] "A Rapid method for calculating the least square solution of a polynomial of any degree", Uni. of Calif. Publications in Math., Vol.2, No.5, pp.67–118.

[5] Pearson, K., "On the application of Goodness of Fit Table to Test Regression curves and Theoretical curves used to describe observational data", Biom., Vol.11, pp, 239–261, 1916.

[6] Fisher, R. A., "The Goodness of Fit of Regression Formula, and the Distribution of Regression Coefficients", Jour. Roy. Stat. Soc., Vol.85, pp.597–612.

[7] Schultz, H., "The standard error of a forecast from a curve", Jour. Amer. Stat. Soc., pp.139–185, 1930.

a special case of a multivariate regression surface by treating $\xi_1, \xi_2, \cdots, \xi_r$ as r independent variates, and thereby the method can easily lend itself to extension to such a formula as is given by equation $(3 \cdot 29)$. The test of goodness of fit will be considered in Chapter IV.

3.13 The Graphical Method of Determining Regression

In the use of the freehand curve for the representation of the regression curve or surface, the result is dominated by personal subjective valuation or "taste". On this question, we may quote Wilson's[①] discussion of freehand curves. "There is no way in which the work can be checked. Of course, a dozen persons may be given the same sequence of points and be required each to fit the curve according to his taste; the results of those different fittings may then be compared to determine how much and in what way the solutions differ. I am not averse to this aesthetic procedure. When the curve to be fitted is a straight line, it has been found by experiment that the solutions obtained do not, on the average, depart from the 'least squares' solution by more than two or three times the probable error of the least squares solution, provided the drawing be made on an adequate scale. In cases where it is not important to check the work and where the precise least squares solution is unnecessary, the graphical method is often the best because the easiest to follow." In short, the graphic method, giving as the approximate representation that freehand or empirical curve which best suits a given set of actual observations in appearance, is convenient and simple in practice; yet the result cannot be viewed as satisfactory for many statistical purposes, particularly for purposes of comparison.

The Successive Approximation Method (Ezekiel).

The determination of a curvilinear regression by freehand or graphical method has, however, been advocated by several authors.[②] Ezekiel's successive

---

[①] Wilson, E. B., "Mathematics and Statistics", J.A.S.A., Vol.25, pp.1 – 8, 1930.

[②] Otis, A. S., "The reliability of Spelling Scales, including a deviation formula for correlation", School and Society, Vol.4, Nos.96 – 99, 1916.

Ritter, W. E., "A Step Forward in the Methodology of Natural Science (The Functional Relation of one Variable to Each of a Number of Correlated Variables Determined by a Method of Successive Approximation to Group Averages; A contribution to Statistical Methods. By George F. McEwen and Ellis L. Michael)", Proc. of the American Acad. of Arts and Science, Vol.55, No.2, pp.91 – 133, 1919.

approximation method is of special interest, since it employs apparently the criterion of least squares and thereby is freed, at least to certain extent, of the dangers of arbitrariness or bias. The approximation process① may be summarized as follows:

(1) Determine the linear regression equation by the method of least squares:

$$X'_1 = a + b_2 X_2 + b_3 X_3 + \cdots + b_n X_n.$$

(2) Compute residuals; i.e., the difference between estimated and observed values of the essential variate X_1:

$$e = X_1 - X'_1 = X_1 - (a + b_2 X_2 + b_3 X_3 + \cdots + b_n X_n).$$

(3) Plot these residuals, as deviations from the net or partial regressions determined from (1), successively against each of the associate variates. Thus, if M_1, M_2, $\cdots$, M_n are the means of X_1, X_2, $\cdots$, X_n respectively, then the partial regression of X_1 on X_2 is obtained by merely substituting M_3, M_4, $\cdots$, M_n for X_3, X_4, $\cdots$, X_n in the linear multiple regression:

$$X'_{12\cdot 3\cdots n} = (a + b_3 M_3 + \cdots + b_n M_n) + b_2 X_2. \qquad (3\cdot 63)$$

Now the residuals e determined in (2) are plotted against X_2 as deviations from this partial regression equation; that is, to plot the points ($e + X'_{12\cdot 3\cdots n}$, X_2) with X_2 as abscissa and $e + X'_{12\cdot 3\cdots n}$ as ordinates to form a correlation scatter diagram. Using this scatter diagram to indicate where a connection for non-linearity is required, draw a freehand curve as the partial regression of X_1 on X_2. This curve is called a first approximation to the true partial regression of X_1 on X_2. To facilitate this procedure, the residuals e may be arrayed with regard to X_2 and averaged for each array. Let the average of the residuals in such an array be $\bar{e}_2$. Then the scatter diagram constructed between $\bar{e}_2 + X'_{12\cdot 3\cdots n}$ and its type value X_2

---

① Ezekiel, M., "A Method of Handling Curve-linear Correlation for any Number of Variables", Jour. Amer. Stat. Ass., Vol. 19, p. 431, 1924. Here Ezekiel says: "Otis (Op. Cit.) has suggested computing a coefficient of curvilinear correlation by the use of a curvilinear regression graphically determined. His coefficient, however, uses median deviations rather than standard deviations, and hence is not directly comparable with Pearsonian Coefficients. The following method is similar to that of Otis; but yields a coefficient directly comparable to the Pearsonian coefficient of correlation."

will provide the basis for drawing in the first approximation curve for the partial regression of X_1 on X_2. Applying the same process to each associate variate, all the partial regressions of X_1 on X_2, on X_3, and finally on X_n are obtained.

(4) To determine from the partial regression curves so determined the first approximation multiple regression surface:

$$x''_1 = K' + f'(X_2) + f'(X_3) + \cdots + f'(X_n), \qquad (3 \cdot 64)$$

where $f'(X_j)$ represents the first approximation partial regression of X_1 on X_j and K' is constant to be determined so as to make

$$\sum (e'^2) = \sum (X_1 - X''_1)^2$$

a minimum.

(5) Now apply the whole process to the new multiple regression curve; i.e., compute the new residuals $e' = X_1 - X''_1$ as in Step (2), plot these new residuals, as deviations from the new partial regressions determined from (3·64) as in Step (3), to indicate where additional connections are necessary and draw freehand curves as the second approximation partial regression curves, and then determine the second approximation multiple regression curve from these partial regression curves as in Step (4).

(6) Repeat until the residuals, when averaged and plotted as deviations from the last set of partial regression curves, will indicate that no further modifications are necessary in the curves.①

(7) Compute the standard error of estimate, if $f(X_2, X_3, \cdots, X_n)$ be the final approximation of the multiple regression of X_1 on $X_2, \cdots, X_n$, by the

---

① "So long as the standard deviation of each new set of residuals is smaller than that of the previous set, the approximation curves may be regarded approaching closer and closer to the underlying true curves. When, however, the curves have been determined as closely as is possible from the given data, the standard deviation of the residuals will show no further decrease, and may even increase slightly. In such case the set of curves showing the lowest standard deviation of residuals may be regarded as the final curves determined by the process", Methods of Correlation Analysis, pp.211 - 212. To this criterion, attention may be called to the fact that the standard error will be minimum when the partial regressions pass through the array mean residuals. In this circumstance the personal taste holds sway whether the smooth freehand curve shall pass as closely as possible to these array mean residuals and, as a consequence, the least square criterion becomes idle, since if this criterion enters into play, the regressions should pass through all the array mean residuals.

formula:

$$s_{1\cdot 23\cdots n}^2 = \frac{\sum \{X_1 - f(X_2, \cdots, X_n)\}^2}{N - m}$$

where N = number of observations and m = the estimated number of constants in the regression equation.

(8) Compute the index of correlation

$$\rho_{1\cdot 2\cdots n}^2 = 1 - \frac{s_{1\cdot 23\cdots n}^2}{s_1^2}.$$

In 1929, Bean[1] modified Ezekiel's method by omitting the computation of linear multiple regression as in Step (1) and, in its stead, he draws freehand curves as the first approximation curves and then plots residuals as deviations from approximation curves to connect them as Ezekiel does.

As to the theoretical basis, it is explained by Ezekiel that the values of X_1 estimated from the linear regression equation would differ from the observed values, in general, for three causes:

(i) "The effects on X_1 of factors other than those taken into account in the regression equation."

(ii) "Difference between the true curvilinear effect of X_2 on X_1 and the linear effect estimated."

(iii) "The inability of the several linear regressions to represent the curvilinear relations."

Thus, "if the observations were arrayed with regard to X_2, and means of residuals taken for each array, the part of the residuals due to (i) would tend to average out, and the means would be the average of the part or the differences due to (ii). Besides the failure of the net linear regression of X_1 on X_2, the means of residuals arrayed with regard to X_2, would also reflect failure of the other net regressions to account for curvilinear regression of X_1 on the other variables. The extent to which these latter components would mark the difference due solely to curvilinearity in the regression of X_1 on X_2 would depend upon the

---

[1] Bean, L. H., "A Simplified Method of Graphic Curvilinear Correlation", Jour. Amer. Stat. Ass., Vol.24, p.386, 1929.

inter-correlation of X_2 with X_3 to X_n, and the similarity of the curves of regression".

"It seems probable that in most cases elements due to variables other than the one upon which the residuals were arrayed would be sufficiently diverse so that the means of residuals arrayed according to X_2 would tend to show the curve-linearity of the relation of X_1 on X_2, even though somewhat marked by the other components..."①

The advantages claimed for the approximation method are twofold:

(i) It does not require assumptions as to the specific type of each curve, but instead permits each regression to be indicated by the observations themselves.

(ii) It requires less computation than a mathematical curve or surface does.

But, in our judgment, the approximation method requires, in no less degree than the fitting of mathematical curves does, assumptions as to the type or form of a freehand curve drawn to fit the data. Undoubtedly, it is a matter of "taste" whether one assigns one set of weights or another to the various points and it is also a matter of "taste" whether he drew a freehand curve passing through or nearby certain points, which means to decide how many inflections② the freehand curve is allowed to have, and which is equivalent to judging whether certain mathematical curves or surfaces are appropriate to the problem in hand. Moreover, the successive approximation process, involving plotting in an adequate scale, reading the numerical values from the freehand curve, and so on, does not, in general, seem to be any easier and shorter work.

The graphic method suffers, however, a serious disadvantage when compared with the mathematical method owing to the fact that the member of constants which reduce the effective number of observations, cannot be exactly known. Since the degree of freedom or the effective number of observations

---

① "A Method of Handling Curvilinear Correlation", Op. Cit., pp.439 – 440.

② Ezekiel is not ignorant of this fact as he says: "...Spuriously high correlation could be obtained by drawing curves with many inflections so as to pass through as many of the individual observations or averages as possible. In most cases, however, some reasonably smooth curve would seem to be indicated, and this should be borne in mind in smoothing the line of average residuals." "Curvilinear Correlation", Ibid., p.449.

which is a parameter used in the test of significance, can only be estimated in a more or less arbitrary way, the confidence in the result of the significance test will be much diminished. The importance of knowing the reliability of the net regression curves or of the index of correlation has recently been recognized by Ezekiel[①] and an attempt has been made to determine the sampling error of multiple regression curves and the index of correlation obtained by the successive approximation process by means of the experimental method. "The results, however, are not fully consistent, and the error formulae are not completely satisfactory."[②]

3.14 "Joint" Correlation

Ezekiel has extended the successive approximation method to the determination of regression functions of the form:

$$X_1 = f(X_2, X_3, \cdots)$$

which cannot be expressed in the form:

$$X_1 = A + f_1(X_2) + f_2(X_2) + \text{etc.} \qquad (3 \cdot 65)$$

and called by Ezekiel the "joint" functional regression.

If $w(X_1, X_2, \cdots, X_n)$ be the frequency surface of $X_1, X_2, \cdots, X_n$, then the regression of X_1 on $X_2, X_3, \cdots, X_n$ is given by

---

① Ezekiel, M., "Application of the Theory of Error to Multiple and Curvilinear Correlation", Jour. Amer. Stat. Ass. Supp., Vol.24, pp.99 – 104, 1929; and also "The Sampling Variability of Linear and Curvilinear Regressions", Annals of Math. Stat., Vol.I, pp.275 – 333, 1930.

② The quotation is from "The Sampling Variability of Regression", Op. Cit., p.276. The tentative error formula for the correlation index is the same as that given by Fisher for the linear correlation coefficient; namely

$$\sigma_\rho = \frac{(1 - \rho^2)}{n' - m}$$

where n' is the number of observations and m, the number of constants in the regression equation. And in the case of the error of net regression curves, the error formulae, concludes Ezekiel, "are such a poor approximation that much work remains to be done before the results of such analysis can be used with anything like the degree or confidence that can be felt in older and more well-established statistical procedures".

$$f(X_2, \cdots, X_n) = \int_{-\infty}^{\infty} w(X_1, X_2, \cdots, X_n) X_1 dX_1 \div \int_{-\infty}^{\infty} w(X_1, X_2, \cdots, X_n) dX_1$$

$$(3 \cdot 66)$$

which, if expressible in the form of (3 · 65), may be interpreted in such a way that the net influence exerted by each of the associate variates upon the essential (or dependent) variate is independent of the values assumed by the other associate variates, that is to say, for any change in the values of an associate variate X_i, there is a definite associated effect upon the essential variate X_1 no matter what the values of the other associate variates are at the same observation. Such a correlation is often found in price analysis work.[1] However, if the regression function in (3 · 66) cannot be expressed in the form of (3 · 65), then the change in the essential variate due to a change in one of the associate variates depends upon the magnitudes of the other associate variates and the associate variates are said to have a "joint" relationship with the essential variate. Farm management data furnish many examples of this type of correlation.

As Camp[2] has demonstrated, the regression function (3 · 66) is often not an integral function of the associate variates. Furthermore, the regression surface or curve directly determined by the regression method may be different or inconsistent with that found by the correlation surface method. For instance, the illustrations given by K. Pearson in his "General Theory of Skew Correlation" have been fitted with Correlation A-functions by S. D. Wicksell[3] and given regression functions entirely different from those obtained by Pearson. It is therefore to be observed that, on the one hand, the regression method as we have shown in Chapter I, may be said to be related to the correlation surface method, but, on the other hand, it has been developed by Yule and Pearson on a quite different basis and, in a sense, may be called a theory of similarity.[4] In this connection we may call attention to Warren's[5] discussion with regard to

---

[1] Warren, S. W., "Multiple Correlation Analysis as Applied to Farm Management Research", Memoir 141 of the Cornell University Agricultural Experimental Station, 1931.
[2] "Mutually Consistent Multiple Regression Surface", Op. Cit.
[3] "The Correlation Function of Type A and etc.", Op. Cit.
[4] Cf. the discussions on Yule's contributions.
[5] Op. Cit., p.4.

some of the precautions that should be taken in using correlation methods of analysis:

"Independent variables which have a causal relationship to one another should not be included in the same multiple correlation problem, whether it be linear, curvilinear, or joint. In multiple linear and curvilinear correlation analyses, the factors should be chosen so that the effect on the dependent variable due to a change in one independent variable does not depend on the magnitude of another independent variable. These limitations to be observed in the selection of variables to be included in the correlation problem have been overlooked in many cases." These considerations do not, however, concern the correlation surface method, so soon as the correlation surface is rightly determined, the regression function, whatever (joint or not joint) it may be, is always given by (3·66).

3.14.1 The Determination of Joint Correlation by the Successive Approximation Method

For determining the joint regression surface in the case of two associate variates, the successive approximation method[①] may be summarized as follows:

(1) Classify the observations according to one independent variable, sub-classify according to the other, and determine the averages of X_1, X_2, and X_3 for each group.

(2) For various given values of X_2, plot the changes in X_1 with changes in X_3 and draw in freehand curves as the first approximation partial regression curves of X_1 on X_3. "In drawing such curves, it is desirable to keep them as nearly of the same shape as the data will permit, and to change the shape only gradually from the next."

(3) Smooth the estimated values of X_1 from the freehand curves for specified values of X_3 with respect to X_2. To do this, the estimated values of X_1 for specified values (at convenient intervals) of X_3 are now plotted with varying values of X_2 and freehand curves are then drawn in as the partial regression

---

① Ezekiel, M., "The Determination of Curvilinear Regression Surface", Jour. Amer. Stat. Ass., Vol.21, pp.310-320, 1926; and also, The Methods of Correlation Analysis, Chapter 20 and 21, 1930.

curves of X_1 on X_2.

(4) The readings from the new partial regression curve of X_1 on X_2 are again smoothed with respect to X_3. To do this, the estimated values of X_1 for specified values of X_2 are plotted with varying values of X_3 and freehand curves are drawn in to represent the partial regression curves of X_1 on X_3. These curves are the final approximations, and are taken as defining functional relation between X_1 and X_2, X_3 because estimates of X_1 for any combination of values of X_2 and X_3 may be made directly from these curves.

(5) Let X'_1 be the estimated values of X_1 from the regression surface as represented by several curves obtained in Step (3). The standard error of estimate is then

$$s^2_{1\cdot 23} = \frac{1}{n' - m} \sum (X_1 - X'_1)^2$$

where n' is the number of observations and m, the estimated number of constants in the regression surface.

(6) The index of correlation is given by

$$p^2 = 1 - \frac{s^2_{1\cdot 23}}{s^2_1}.$$

3.14.2 Waugh's Method

The procedure just described was simplified, in 1929, by Waugh[1] to the following steps:

(1) The averages of the subgroups are plotted on a two-variable diagram, with one independent variable as ordinate, the other as abscissa.

(2) The average of the dependent variable is written in next to the dot which designates the subgroup.

(3) Contours of isotropic lines are drawn in so that the averages of the dependent variable having approximately the same values are enclosed.

(4) The standard error and the index of correlation may be computed as in Ezekiel's method.

---

[1] Waugh, F. V., "The Use of Isotropic Lines in Determining Regression Surfaces", Jour. Amer. Stat. Ass., Vol.24, pp.144 – 151, 1929.

3.14.3 Court's Method

In 1930, A. Court[1] proposed two empirical equations for fitting "joint" regression surfaces. These equations are:

$$x_1 = ax_2 + bx_3 + c^{x_2} + d^{x_3} + ex_2^{x_3} + k$$

and

$$x_1 = ax_2 + bx_3 + cx_2^2 + dx_3^2 + ex_2x_3 + f(x_2x_3)^2 + k, \quad (3\cdot 67)$$

the coefficients of which may be determined by the method of least squares. But the second form seems to be easier for computation. The joint action in this equation is provided by the compound elements $(x_2 x_3)$ and $(x_2 x_3)^2$. "The first of these $(x_2 x_3)$ is of peculiar value, for when used in combination with the linear and squared values of the individual independents, it is capable of setting up parabolic bending moments at any or all directions not parallel to the axes. This possibility of bending at many angles provides a degree of flexibility and warp ability which enables the surface to define relationships which show joint causation."

The method can easily lend itself to extension to the case of more than three variables by merely including in addition to $f(x_2 x_3)$ such compound elements as $f(x_2 x_4)$, $f(x_3 x_4)$, and $f(x_2 x_3 x_4)$. Even where the relation is incapable of any spatial representation, it is possible to proceed under routine arithmetic procedure with but little skilled direction.

The choice between the mathematical and the graphic methods would, in general, depend upon the nature of the problem, the particular purpose of analysis, and the personal taste with the various techniques.

3.15 The Degrees of Freedom

The number of conditions imposed upon the data for the determination of the constants reduces the number of effective observations. This fact is important when we are dealing with finite or small[2] samples. But it had been neglected in

---

[1] A. Court, "Measuring Joint Causation", Jour. Amer. Stat. Ass., vol.25, pp.245–254, 1930.

[2] When the sample is large, the number of conditions is negligible as compared to the total number of observations.

the correlation analysis until in 1922 when R. A. Fisher[①] recognized the importance, in the interpretation of statistical results, of the number of degrees of freedom which may be defined as the number of observations less the number of restrictions imposed upon the observations. For example, in a sample of n observations x_1, x_2, $\cdots$, x_n so restricted that their mean value is zero, the number of degrees of freedom is $n - 1$, since the n-th value is fixed as soon as the first $n - 1$ values are known. Thus, allowing for the fact that we have used up one degree of freedom in determining the mean, the best estimate of the standard deviation from a sample is obtained by dividing the sum of square deviations by the number of degrees of freedom, i.e.,

$$\hat{s}_x^2 = \frac{1}{n - 1} \sum (x^2). \qquad (3 \cdot 68)$$

So if the standard deviation is calculated by the usual formula

$$s_x^2 = \frac{1}{n} \sum (x^2),$$

it ought to be adjusted by the formula:

$$\hat{s}_x^2 = \frac{n}{n - 1} s^2.$$

likewise, the optimum value of the standard error of estimate from a regression equation containing p constants is obtained by the use of the formula:[②]

$$\hat{\varepsilon}^2 = \frac{1}{n - p} \sum (y - Y)^2 \qquad (3 \cdot 69)$$

where n is the number of observation, and $(y - Y)$, the deviation of observation from the regression curve of surface. So if the standard error of estimate is

---

① "On the Interpretation of X^2 from Contingency Tables", Jour. Roy. Stat. Soc., Vol.85, p.87, 1922; "The Goodness of Fit of Regression Formulae", loc. cit.; "The Influence of Rainfall on the Yield of Wheat at Rothamsted", Phil. trans. Roy. Soc., London, B., Vol.213, pp.89 - 142, 1924; and "On a Distribution Yielding the Error Functions of Several Well-known Statistics", Proc. Int'l. Math. Congress, Toronto, pp.805 - 813, 1924. The least square theory seems, however, to have always recognized this fact. See Wright, I. W. and Hayford, J. F., *Adjustments of Observations*, pp.24 - 40, 132 - 133, 1905, and Merriman, M., *Method of Least Squares*, pp.80 - 82, 1911.

② Ibid. or Cf. Sec. 5, Chap. IV.

calculated by the usual formula:

$$\varepsilon^2 = \frac{1}{n}\sum (y - Y)^2,$$

it ought to be adjusted by the formula:

$$\hat{\varepsilon}^2 = \frac{n}{n - p}\varepsilon^2.$$

The formula (see Formula 3·11) for the computation of the correlation coefficient now becomes

$$\hat{R}^2 = 1 - \frac{\hat{\varepsilon}^2}{\hat{s}_y^2} = 1 - \frac{(n - 1)\sum (y - Y)^2}{(n - p)\sum (y^2)}. \quad (3 \cdot 70)$$

So if such a correlation coefficient is computed by the usual formula:

$$R^2 = 1 - \frac{\sum (y - Y)^2}{\sum (y^2)} = 1 - \frac{\varepsilon^2}{s_y^2},$$

it ought to be adjusted by the formula:

$$1 - \hat{R}^2 = \frac{n - 1}{n - p}(1 - R^2).$$

This adjustment formula was introduced by Fisher[①] in 1924. Thus, if the linear correlation coefficient of zero order is computed by the usual formula:

$$r = \frac{\sum xy}{\sqrt{\sum (x^2) \cdot \sum (y^2)}},$$

it ought to be adjusted by the use of the formula:

---

① "On the Interpretation of X^2 from Contingency Tables", Jour. Roy. Stat. Soc., Vol.85, p.87, 1922; "The Goodness of Fit of Regression Formulae", loc. cit.; "The Influence of Rainfall on the Yield of Wheat at Rothamsted", Phil. trans. Roy. Soc., London, B., Vol.213, pp.89 – 142, 1924; and "On a Distribution Yielding the Error Functions of Several Well-known Statistics", Proc. Int'l. Math. Congress, Toronto, pp.805 – 813, 1924. The least square theory seems, however, to have always recognized this fact. See Wright, I. W. and Hayford, J. F., *Adjustments of Observations*, pp.24 – 40, 132 – 133, 1905, and Merriman, M., *Method of Least Squares*, pp.80 – 82, 1911.

$$1 - \hat{r}^2 = \frac{n-1}{n-2}(1 - r^2).$$

In 1925, B. B. Smith[1] gave a similar correction formula which is:

$$1 - \bar{R}^2 = \frac{n}{n-p+1}(1 - R^2)$$

where $\bar{R}$ is the adjusted correlation coefficient. And, in 1929, Ezekiel[2] modified Smith's formula to the following form:

$$1 - \bar{R}^2 = \frac{n}{n-p}(1 - R^2).$$

To decide which one of the three forms of adjustment is most satisfactory for practical uses, Ezekiel[3] made a study of the relation of the adjusted values to the distribution of simple linear correlation coefficients when computed from random samples of various sizes dram from universes with specified correlations. This study is based upon the tables given by Soper and others in their cooperative study.[4] The tables given in this cooperative study show the theoretical distributions for the linear simple correlation coefficients computed from 3 to 25, and 50, 100, and 400 observations, for true correlation coefficients ranging from 0 to 0.9 by tenths. Ordinates of the distributions of observed correlations are given for each value from $r = -1.00$ to $+1.00$ by 0.05 steps. With the frequency curve thus defined by as many as 41 ordinates, a rough integral of the curve was constructed by a cumulative summary of the ordinates. Then dividing by the total area, the proportion below any particular value was then determined. By applying Fisher's formula, which becomes for the case of the simple linear correlation coefficient:

---

[1] Smith, B. B., "Forecasting the Acreage of Cotton", Jour. Amer. Stat. Ass., Vol.20, p.41, 1925.

[2] Ezekiel, M., "Application of the Theory of Error to Multiple and Curvilinear Correlation", Jour. Amer. Stat. Ass., Supp., Vol.24, pp.99 – 104, 1929.

[3] Ezekiel, M., "The Sampling Variability of Linear and Curvilinear Regressions", Annals of Math. Stat., Vol.1, pp.275 – 333, 1930.

[4] Soper, H. E., Young, A. W., Cave, B. M., Lee, A., and Pearson, K., "On the Distribution of Correlation Coefficient in Small Samples. A Cooperative study", Biom., Vol.11, pp.352 – 359, 1917.

$$\hat{r}^2 = 1 - \frac{n-1}{n-2}(1-r^2),$$

the distributions for $\hat{r}$ may be obtained from the corresponding distribution for r, and thereby the proportion of relative frequency of the samples which show adjusted correlations exceeding the true value may be determined. The following tabulation shows the results so obtained by Ezekiel:

Size of Sample (n)	When Correlation in Sample is					
	0.0	0.2	0.4	0.6	0.8	0.9
4	0.42	0.29	0.36	0.42	0.49	0.51
5	0.39	0.29	0.37	0.43	0.48	0.50
9	0.35	0.30	0.38	0.44	0.48	0.49
17	0.33	0.32	0.40	0.45	0.48	0.49
25	0.32	0.34	0.42	0.46	0.48	0.49
50	0.31	0.37	0.44	0.47	0.48	0.50
100	0.31	0.40	0.46	0.48	0.49	0.50

Proportion of samples, of specified sizes, drawn from universes of specified correlations, which show correlations in excess of the value in the universe, even after adjusting the observed correlation by the formula:

$$\hat{r}^2 = 1 - \frac{n-1}{n-2}(1-r^2).$$

Taken from Ezekiel, M., "The Sampling Variability of Linear and Curvilinear Regressions", Annals Math. Stat. Vol.1, p.282.

Applying the same process to Smith's and Ezekiel's formula, similar tables may be obtained for comparison with that given above. From the results of such a study, Ezekiel concludes that Fisher's correction formula "gives the most satisfactory simple method for adjusting coefficients of simple or multiple correlation to remove the positive bias" which exists in the computed correlation on account of not allowing for the reduction of the number of degrees of freedom used up in the determination of the constants in the regression equation.

However, it may be observed that, in the case of high correlation, practically 50% of the samples will give values larger than the true value, and that, in the case of low correlation, the adjustment as given by Fisher seems too severe, since only about 40% of the samples will give values larger than the true correlation.

3.16 The Correlation Coefficient VS. Coefficient of Determination

It is customary to regard r as being in some way a measure of the number of common causes[1] which underlie the variations of the two quantities considered.

Let the variations of x and y be due respectively to a number $m + n$ and $m + n'$ of elementary errors, m of these causes being common to both x and y, while the remaining n and n' errors are independent. Then we may write

$$x = A_1\alpha_1 + A_2\alpha_2 + \cdots + A_m\alpha_m + B_1\beta_1 + B_2\beta_2 + \cdots + B_n\beta_n$$
$$y = D_1\alpha_1 + D_2\alpha_2 + \cdots + D_m\alpha_m + C_1\gamma_1 + C_2\gamma_2 + \cdots + C_n\gamma_n'$$

(3 · 71)

where $\alpha_1, \alpha_2, \ldots, \beta_1, \beta_2, \ldots, \gamma_1, \gamma_2\ldots$ are all independent of one another. We shall further simplify the problem by supposing that the M. N. S. introduced in x and y by any one of the independent elementary causes are equal. Then

$$x = \sum_1^m \alpha_s + \sum_1^n \beta_s$$
$$y = \sum_1^m \alpha_s + \sum_1^{n'} \gamma_s$$

where the M. S. E. of each variable α, β, or γ are equal and denoted as σ^2. Then if ε_x, ε_y be the M. S. E. of x and y respectively,

$$\varepsilon_x^2 = (m+n)\sigma^2, \quad \varepsilon_y^2 = (m+n')\sigma^2 \qquad (3 \cdot 72)$$

$$x + y = 2\sum_1^m \alpha_s + \sum_1^n \beta_s + \sum_1^{n'} \gamma_s$$

$$(x+y)^2 = 4\sum_1^m \alpha_s^2 + \sum_1^n \beta_s^2 + \sum_1^{n'} \gamma_s^2 + 4\sum \alpha_s\alpha_t + 2\sum \beta_s\beta_t + 2\sum \gamma_s\gamma_t$$
$$+ 4\sum \alpha_s\beta_t + 4\alpha_s\gamma_t + 2\sum \beta_s\gamma_t.$$

---

[1] Brunt, David, The Combination of Observation, London, 1917.

If ε_{x+y} be M. S. E. of $x + y$, then

$$\varepsilon_{x+y}^2 = 4\sum_1^m \bar{\alpha}_s^2 + \sum_1^n \bar{\beta}_s^2 + \sum_1^{n'} \bar{\beta}_s^2$$
$$= (4m + n + n')\sigma^2. \qquad (3\cdot 73)$$

The product terms all vanishing. But if

$$F = ax + by + cz + \cdots$$
$$F^2 = a^2x^2 + b^2y^2 + c^2z^2 + 2abxy + 2acxz + 2bcyz + \cdots$$
$$\sigma_F^2 = a^2\sigma_x^2 + b^2\sigma_y^2 + 2abr_{xy}\sigma_x\sigma_y + 2acr_{xz} + c^2\sigma_z^2 + 2bcr_{yz}\sigma_y\sigma_z + \cdots$$
$$(3\cdot 74)$$

A special case is

$$\sigma_{x+y}^2 = \sigma_x^2 + \sigma_y^2 + 2r_{xy}\sigma_x\sigma_y \qquad (3\cdot 75)$$

and

$$\sigma_{x-y}^2 = \sigma_x^2 + \sigma_y^2 - 2r_{xy}\sigma_x\sigma_y. \qquad (3\cdot 76)$$

This affords a method of evaluating r_{xy} by evaluating σ_x, σ_y, σ_{x-y}.

From $(3\cdot 75)$,

$$\varepsilon_{x+y}^2 = (4m + n + n')\sigma^2$$
$$= \varepsilon_x^2 + \varepsilon_y^2 + 2r_{xy}\varepsilon_x\varepsilon_y$$
$$= (2m + n + n')\sigma^2 + 2r\sqrt{(m+n)(m+n')}\,\sigma^2$$

$$\therefore r = \frac{m}{\sqrt{(m+n)(m+n')}}$$

If $n = n'$,
$$r = \frac{m}{m+n}.$$

Thus, in this particular case, r measures the proportion of elementary causes of variation which the two variables have in common. Moreover, if $(n - n')$ is small compared to $(m + n)$, (that is, if x and y have approximately the same total number of causes), then $(m + n)(m + n') \to (m + n)^2$ and r may be considered as a measure of causes common to x and y.

The assumptions that the variations of the elementary errors, being very small, are equal and that the number of elementary errors as the causes of deviations in variates are approximately equal, are reasonable. It is simply a modified form of Laplacean-Charlier hypothesis① in explaining the phenomena of variation in a heterograde of continuous series.

Mr. Ezekiel's interpretation or contention that the coefficient of determination② but not the correlation coefficient measures the percentage of common causes in the independent and dependent variables is not satisfactory in view of the fact that he assumes the variation of the independent variable to be due only to causes or elementary errors which are also present in the dependent variable. It is very likely that the variation of x is due to causes of which some are and the rest are not present in y. If this is true—which is at least a more reasonable assumption, then, as we have demonstrated above,

$$r^2 = \frac{m^2}{(m+n)(m+n')}$$

does not measure the proportion of the variance in y determined by x. Hence, Ezekiel's use of r^2 is misleading.

On account of the sampling fluctuation of r, a correlation coefficient estimated from a particular sample may be more satisfactorily interpreted, as will be explained in Chapter IV; by proceeding to transform the correlation coefficient into another parameter z, introduced by Fisher, and thereby to determine the optimum value of the correlation coefficient, which may be considered as measuring approximately the proportion of the contributory causes in the variation of y common to x.

---

① The hypothesis may be stated that every variate of individual deviation from a certain normal is generated as the sum of a mass of small and unknown quantities, generally infinite in number, which are known as elementary errors. Cf. Chap. II, section 13 and 24.

② Ezekiel says: "Where both X and Y are assumed to be built up of simple elements of equal variability, all of which are present in Y but some of which are lacking in X, it can be proved mathematically that r^2 measured that proportion of all the elements in Y which are also present in X. For that reason, in cases where the dependent variable is known to be causally related to the independent variable, r^2 may be called the coefficient of determination. It may be said to measure the per cent to which the variance in Y is determined by X, since it measures that proportion of all the elements of variance in Y which are also present in X ..." p.120, and also pp.169, 177 – 178, 376. Ezekiel, M., *Methods of Correlation Analysis*, John Wiley and Sons, N. Y., 1930. Mills, F. C., also used the coefficient of determination in Behavior of Prices, National Bureau of Economic Research, N. Y.

3.17 Spurious Correlation

In respect to problems of correlation between index numbers, Pearson called attention to the possible introduction of a "spurious correlation".[①] If x_1, x_2, x_3, x_4 be the absolute sizes of any four correlated subjects and v_1, v_2, v_3, v_4 their coefficients of variation, the correlation between x_1/x_3 and x_2/x_4, neglecting cubes of v^3, is:

$$\rho = \frac{v_1 v_2 r_{12} - v_1 v_4 r_{14} - v_2 v_3 r_{23} + v_3 v_4 r_{34}}{\sqrt{v_1^2 + v_3^2 - 2 v_1 v_3 r_{13}} \sqrt{v_2^2 + v_4^2 - 2 v_2 v_4 r_{24}}}. \tag{3·77}$$

Suppose $r_{12} = r_{14} = r_{23} = r_{34} = 0$, then $\rho = 0$. That is, if the absolute values are uncorrelated, the indices formed from those values are uncorrelated.

But if any two of the absolute values are identical, say $x_3 = x_4$, then $r_{3r} = 1$, $v_3 = v_4$, and

$$\rho = \frac{v_1 v_2 r_{12} - v_1 v_3 r_{13} - v_2 v_3 r_{23} + v_3^2}{\sqrt{v_1^2 + v_3^2 - 2 v_1 v_3 r_{13}} \sqrt{v_2^2 + v_3^2 - 2 v_2 v_3 r_{23}}}. \tag{3·78}$$

Again, if $r_{12} = r_{13} = r_{23} = 0$, we have

$$\rho = \frac{v_3^2}{\sqrt{v_1^2 + v_3^2} \sqrt{v_2^2 + v_3^2}}. \tag{3·79}$$

This is the measure of purely spurious correlation, due to merely to the common base in the two indices, or that which results simply from the algebraic processes involved.

In special case when $v_1 = v_2 = v_3$, $\rho = 0.5$.

In 1921, Wicksell gave an exact formula for spurious correlation:

$$\rho = \frac{v_3^2}{\sqrt{v_1^2 + v_3^2 + v_1^2 v_3^2} \sqrt{v_2^2 + v_3^2 + v_2^2 v_3^2}},$$

where v denotes the coefficient of variation of $x_3 = \dfrac{1}{x_3}$ while v_1 and v_2 the coefficients of variation of x_1 and x_2, and demonstrated that Pearson's formula is a

---

[①] K. Pearson, "On a form of spurious correlation that may arise when indices are used in the measurement of organs", Proc. Roy. Soc., Vol.60, p.489, 1897.

first approximation of this exact formula.

Moreover, from equation (3 · 77) it is seen:

$$\rho_{\frac{x_1 x_2}{x_3 x_4}} = - \rho_{\frac{x_3 x_2}{x_1 x_4}}$$

$$\left| \rho_{\frac{x_1 x_2}{x_3 x_4}} \right| \neq \left| \rho_{\frac{x_1 x_3}{x_2 x_4}} \right|,$$

all the combinations can be grouped[1] into three according as x_1 appears in the ratio containing x_2, x_3, or x_4. There are 4 possible cases in each group; say in the group which contains the ratio x_3 to x_1:

$$\rho_{\frac{x_1 x_2}{x_3 x_4}},\ \rho_{\frac{x_1 x_4}{x_3 x_2}},\ \rho_{\frac{x_3 x_2}{x_1 x_4}},\ \rho_{\frac{x_3 x_4}{x_1 x_2}}.$$

These 4 indices (coefficients of correlation) are equal in absolute value.

From (3 · 77) it will be seen that spurious correlation is positive when the denominators or numerators of both ratios are equal; negative when the numerator of either ratio and the denominator of the other are equal. Examples are found in correlation between indices with other fixed base or changing base.

Professor Pearson suggested a formula for the correlation of this spurious correlation. The partial correlation formula:

$$\rho_{\frac{x_1 x_2}{x_3 x_3} \cdot x_3} = \frac{r_{\frac{x_1 x_2}{x_3 x_3}} - r_{\frac{x_1}{x_3} \cdot x_3} r_{\frac{x_2}{x_3} \cdot x_3}}{\sqrt{1 - r_{\frac{x_1}{x_3} \cdot x_3}^2} \sqrt{1 - r_{\frac{x_2}{x_3} \cdot x_3}^2}}$$

has also been suggested for patriating out the effect of a common factor.

But Yule[2] thinks that "there is no special reason for supposing that correlations between indices are more likely to be misleading than correlations between any other measures of shape or size". So Yule distinguishes 3 cases as regard the use of indices in correlation:

First, "if the causes, the nature of which we wish to elucidate, influence directly the absolute magnitudes of the variables x_1 and x_2, or the mode in which

---

[1] Neefeeld, M. R., "A Study of Spurious Correlation", Jour. Amer. Stat., pp.331–338, 1927.
[2] Yule, G. U., "On the Interpretation of Correlations between Indices or Ratios", Jour. Roy. Stat. Soc., Vol.73, p.644, 1910.

their values are combined, the correlation between the two indices or ratios x_1/x_3 and x_2/x_4 will be misleading; the correlation should be worked out between the absolute magnitudes of the variables x_1 and x_2".

Second, "if the causes, the nature of which we wish to elucidate, influence directly the ratios of indices, x_1/x_3 and x_2/x_3, or the mode in which these ratios are combined, the correlation between the absolute values of the variables x_1 and x_2, will be misleading: the correlation should be worked out between x_1/x_3 and x_2/x_3".

"This is the case of death-rates. All the causes in which we are interested—the nature of which we wish to elucidate—determine directly the death-rate, not the number of deaths. The number of deaths is determined mainly by the population of the district. It is clearly the ratio of deaths to population which is directly influenced by the sanitary character of the district and the physical character of the individuals living therein."

"This case is, in fact, precisely the converse of the first; the correlation between the absolute values of the variables has become the spurious or misleading correlation."

Yule thinks "the process of correction suggested by Pearson is unnecessary"; and he says his "view is supported by the result of his (Pearson's) investigation in Dr. Maynard's case, so far as a single result goes".

Third, "if we have no knowledge of the mode of operation of the causes in the case under consideration, either the correlation between the indices z_1 and z_2 or the correlation between the absolute values of the variables x_1 and x_2, or both, may be misleading".

Moreover, there is another source of spurious correlation, for instance, two variables may be uncorrelated in each of two sets, but show correlation in mixed sets.① This would be the case whenever the relative magnitudes of v_1^2 and v_2^2 chance as the two sets are mixed. The correlation r is zero when $v_1^2 = v_2^2$. It is very unlikely for v_1^2 and v_2^2 to remain equal after two sets of observations with unequal means (i.e., $\bar{x}_1 \neq \bar{x}_2$, $\bar{y}_1 \neq \bar{y}_2$ where $\bar{x}_1$, $\bar{y}_1$ are arithmetic means of the first set of N_1 pairs of observations and $\bar{x}_2$, $\bar{y}_2$ the means of the second set) are mixed.

---

① K. Pearson, Phil. Trans., Vol.192, p.257, 1899; Cf. G. U. Yule, Introduction to the Theory of Stat., p.219, 1929.

For if we consider the following expressions:

$$\sum (x_1 - \bar{x}_1)^2 = \sum (x_1 - x)^2 + \sum (x_1 - \bar{x}_1)^2$$
$$= (N_1 - 2)v_{2x_1}^2 \text{ for the 1st set;}$$

$$\sum (x_2 - \bar{x}_2)^2 = \sum (x_2 - x_2)^2 + \sum (x_2 - \bar{x}_2)^2$$
$$= (N_2 - 2)v_{1x_2}^2 + v_{2x_2}^2 \text{ for the 2nd set;}$$

$$\sum (x - \bar{x})^2 = \sum (x - x)^2 + \sum (x - \bar{x})^2$$
$$= (N - 2)v_{1x}^2 + v_{1x}^2 \text{ for the mixed set.}$$

$\sum (x - \bar{x})^2$ is likely greater than $\sum (x_1 - \bar{x}_1)^2$ or $\sum (x_2 - \bar{x}_2)^2$ because the largest deviation of $(x - \bar{x})$, both positive and negative, shall be equal to the larger one of $(x_1 - \bar{x}_1)$ and $(x_2 - \bar{x}_2)$. So $v_{2 \cdot x}^2 > v_{2 \cdot x_1}^2$, $v_{2 \cdot x}^2 > v_{2 \cdot x_2}^2$. Moreover, v_{1x}^2 would likely not differ from $v_{1x_1}^2$ or $v_{1x_2}^2$. Hence $z = \dfrac{1}{2} \log \dfrac{v_{1x}^2}{v_{2x}^2}$ would probably not be zero and so is r.

There have been introduced recently some additional coefficients, called the coefficient of part correlation[1] and the coefficient of separate determination.[2] No attempt will be made here to explain these concepts. Any service which can be rendered by them may be obtained from those coefficients which we have already discussed.

CHAPTER IV ON RANDOM SAMPLING DISTRIBUTION AND THE ANALYSIS OF VARIANCE

The existence of correlation between variates under consideration must be sought from statistical evidence. The correlation analysis is designed to give certain quantities for describing adequately the evidence discoverable from statistical data. There are, as we have seen, many quantities or measures

---

[1] Ezekiel, M., Methods of Correlation Analysis, Chapter 13.

[2] Wright, S., "Correlation and Causation", Jour. Agr. Research, Vol.20, pp.557 – 575; Elliott, F. F., "Adjusting Hog Production to Market Demand", Univ. Ill. Agr. Expt. Sta. Bul. 293, 1927; and Ezekiel, M., Correlation Analysis, pp.380 – 383.

devised for this purpose. In calculating such a quantity or measure from the available statistical data, we are really making an estimate of its true value in the theoretical infinite population of which the data at hand is considered as a sample. Such an estimate from a sample which, for particular cases, may be small on account of difficulty in obtaining a sufficient number of observations, cannot be expected to be identical with the true value sought. The immediate problem before us is thus: What is the precision of such an estimate from a given sample? Moreover, we may need to know whether a given sample of observations is or is not in agreement with specified hypotheses. Each of the two circumstances requires a knowledge of the sampling distribution of the estimated quantity. The sampling distribution of an estimate may render us some other services as we have seen in part I(a theory of correlation), chapter II.

A theory of sampling distribution is a mathematical method of obtaining the theoretical frequency distribution with respect to the number or the relative frequency of an estimated quantity having a certain amount of error. The distributions of each of the correlation coefficients and of the correlation ratio, computed from samples taken at random from a normal population, are now available for use. But little is known about the distributions of a coefficient if it is computed from samples, either taken not at random from a normal population, or taken at random from a non-normal population.

We shall now trace the development of sampling distributions.

4.1 The Three Classical Distributions

There were three classical distributions known before the time when Galton realized that the normal bivariate surface may be used to express the correlation between the two organs under consideration, the statures of the mid parent and its offspring. These are: the binomial distribution, due to Bernoulli,

$$P_r = \frac{n'}{r!(n-r)!} p^r q^{(n-r)}, \qquad (4 \cdot 1)$$

the normal distribution, due to Laplace and Gauss,

$$P_r = \frac{1}{\sigma \sqrt{2x}} e^{-\frac{x_r}{2\sigma}} dx, \qquad (4 \cdot 2)$$

and the Poisson series, due to Poisson,

$$P_r = \frac{m^r e^{-m}}{r!}. \qquad (4 \cdot 3)$$

All three of these distributions possess the property that the mean or the aggregate of the values of a sample is itself distributed in a distribution of the same type. An account of these three distributions with respect to the experimental conditions under which they occur and the statistical methods of recognizing their occurrence may be found In R. A. Fisher's *Statistical Method for Research Workers*, Chapter III. The distribution of the regression coefficient, being a weighted mean, may be determined from Laplace's work as already pointed out in chapter II. But this fact has evidently not been mentioned by writers on statistics.

4.2 The T-distribution, due to Student

In 1908, Student[①] empirically found the distribution of the variance s^2 of a sample of n observations from a normal population:

$$d_{F(s^2)} = c(s^2)^{\frac{n-3}{2}} e^{-\frac{ns^2}{2\sigma^2}} d(s^2) \qquad (4 \cdot 4)$$

where
$$\sigma = \frac{1}{\left(\frac{n-3}{2}\right)!} \cdot 2^{-\frac{n-3}{2}} \left(\frac{n}{\sigma^2}\right)^{\frac{n-1}{2}}.$$

Since the x deviations are subject to the restriction $\sum_{i=1}^{n} x_i = 0$, there are only $(n-1)$ degrees of foredoom [that is, only $(n-1)$ deviations are variable, the n-th is determined when $(n-1)$ are known]. Using the number of degrees of freedom, denoted by n_1, as the parameter in the formula for the frequency

---

① "Student", "The Probable Error of a Mean", Biom., Vol. 6, pp. 1 – 25, 1908. It may be appropriate to point out that Pearson says, in "Historical Note on the Distribution of the Standard Deviations of Samples of any Size Drawn from an Indefinitely Large Normal Parent Population", Biom., Vol. 23, pp. 416 – 418, that the original discoverer of the distribution of the standard deviation was C. F. Helmert and in 1876 and that the method of deduction differs considerably from more recent investigation and has been reproduced by Czuber in Beohachlungsfehler, Sec. 147. Pearson reproduced Helmert's deduction in this paper.

distribution of the estimated variance, we have①

$$d_{F(s^2)} = c(s^2)^{\frac{n_1-2}{2}} e^{-\frac{n_1 s^2}{2\sigma^2}} d(s^2)$$

or, putting $\dfrac{n_1 s^2}{\sigma^2} = v^2$,

$$dF(v^2) = \frac{1}{\left(\dfrac{n_1-2}{2}\right)!}\left(\frac{v^2}{2}\right)^{\frac{n_1-2}{2}} e^{-\frac{v^2}{2}} d\left(\frac{v^2}{2}\right). \tag{4·5}$$

From (4·4) Student was able to derive the exact distribution of t which is the mean of a sample in terms of the standard deviation of the sample.

If x is a value with normal distribution (in this case it stands for the mean of a sample) and σ is its true standard error, then $\tau = \dfrac{x\sqrt{n_1}}{\sigma}$ follows the normal distribution:

$$\frac{\sqrt{n_1}}{\sqrt{2x}} e^{-\frac{n_1 x^2}{2\sigma^2}} d\left(\frac{x}{\sigma}\right). \tag{4·6}$$

But in general, we do not know σ and have to use an estimate s in its place. This is equivalent to dividing the true value by a factor s/σ, which introduces an error. Now if $t = \dfrac{\tau}{v} = \dfrac{x}{s}$, the equation (4·6) may be written in the following form:

$$\frac{\sqrt{n_1}}{\sqrt{2x}} e^{-\frac{n_1 s^2 x^2}{2\sigma^2 s^2}} d\left(\frac{x}{\sigma}\right) = \frac{1}{\sqrt{2x}} e^{-\frac{v^2 t^2}{2}} v dt.$$

Since the variation of $\dfrac{x}{\sigma}$ is independent of that of $\dfrac{s}{\sigma}$, the simultaneous distribution of t and v^2 is

---

① R. A. Fisher, "The General Sampling Distribution of the Multiple Correlation Coefficient", Proc. Roy. Soc., London, Series A., Vol.12, p.654, 1928.

$$df = \frac{1}{\left(\frac{n_1-2}{2}\right)!}\left(\frac{v^2}{2}\right)^{\frac{n_1-2}{2}} e^{-\frac{v^2}{2}} d\left(\frac{v^2}{2}\right) \cdot \frac{1}{\sqrt{2x}} e^{-\frac{v^2 t^2}{2}} v dt$$

$$= \frac{1}{\sqrt{x}} \frac{1}{\left(\frac{n_1-2}{2}\right)!}\left(\frac{v^2}{2}\right)^{\frac{n_1-1}{2}} e^{-\frac{(1+t^2)v^2}{2}} d\left(\frac{v^2}{2}\right) dt. \qquad (4\cdot 7)$$

Integrating with respect to v^2 from 0 to ∞, we obtain the distribution of t:

$$d_{F(t)} = \frac{1}{\sqrt{x}} \frac{\left(\frac{n_1-1}{2}\right)!}{\left(\frac{n_1-2}{2}\right)!}(1+t^2)^{-\frac{n_1+1}{2}} dt. \qquad (4\cdot 8)$$

This is a Pearsonian Type VII curve. It was first found by Student and then rigorously obtained by Fisher[1] by a method in which a sample in represented by a point in Euclidian hyperspace, the separate measurements being the coordinates of the point.

Tables of the probability integral of the above Type VII distribution have been prepared by "Student"[2] for values of n_1 from 0 to 30.

It was further shown by Fisher[3] that the distributions of regression coefficients, whether total or partial, and whether employed in a linear or a non-linear formula, are equivalent to Student's distribution.

In a simple linear regression formula

$$Y = a + b(x - \bar{x})$$

of which the coefficients a and b are calculated by the equations

$$a = \frac{1}{n}, \ S(y) = \bar{y}, \ b = \frac{S\{y(x-\bar{x})\}}{S(x-\bar{x})^2},$$

---

[1] Fisher, R. A., "Frequency distribution of the values of the correlation coefficient in samples from an indefinitely large population", Biom., Vol.10, p.507, 1915.

[2] "Student", "Tables for estimating the probability that the mean of a unique sample of observations lies between $-\infty$ and any given distance from the mean of the population from which the sample is drawn", Biom., Vol.11, pp.414–417, 1917.

[3] Fisher, R. A., "The Goodness of Fit of Regression Formulae", Jour. Roy. Stat. Soc., Vol.85, pp.597–612, 1922.

it is noted first that a and b are orthogonal functions, in that given the observed values of x, their sampling variation is independent.

Now, a, being a sample mean, is normally distributed so that, if α be the population value of a, σ be the population standard deviation of y for a given x, and $\tau = \dfrac{a - \alpha}{\sigma} \sqrt{n}$, then τ is normally distributed about zero with standard deviation unity. If σ^2 is unknown, the best estimate that can be made of it from the sample is

$$s^2 = \frac{1}{n-2} S(y - Y)^2 \qquad (4 \cdot 9)$$

where the sum is divided by the number of degrees of freedom which is $n_1 = n - 2$ to allow for the two constants, used in fitting the regression line. Then the distribution of s^2 is, if $v^2 = n_1 \dfrac{s^2}{\sigma^2}$, given by equation $(4 \cdot 5)$.

Observing that the distribution of a and s are wholly independent, and putting

$$t = \frac{\tau}{v} = \frac{(a - \alpha) \sqrt{n}}{\sqrt{S(y - Y)^2}} = \frac{a - \alpha}{s_a}, \qquad (4 \cdot 10)$$

we have the same form for the simultaneous distribution of t and v as given in equation $(4 \cdot 7)$. Likewise, the distribution of t is given by equation $(4 \cdot 8)$ after integrating for v^2 over its entire range. If we replace n_1 by $n - 2$, it is of the form:

$$\frac{1}{\sqrt{\pi}} \frac{\dfrac{n-3}{2}!}{\left(\dfrac{n-4}{2}\right)!} (1 + t^2)^{-\frac{n-1}{2}} dt.$$

Similarly, for b,

$$\sigma_b^2 = \frac{\sigma^2}{S(x - \bar{x})^2}, \quad \tau = \frac{b - \beta}{\sigma_b},$$

$$v^2 = (n - 2) \frac{s^2}{\sigma^2},$$

and if
$$t = \frac{\tau}{v} = \frac{(b-\beta)\sqrt{S(x-\bar{x})^2}}{\sqrt{S(y-Y)^2}}, \qquad (4\cdot 11)$$

we arrive, as before, at the same distribution (4.8) for t, with β denoting the population value of the regression coefficient.

The above argument immediately extends itself to regression lines of any form and involving any number of coefficients. For, suppose the regression equation is of the form
$$Y = a + bX_1 + cX_2 + \ldots + kX_p,$$
where $X_1, X_2, \ldots, X_p$ are orthogonal functions of x for the observed values, so that
$$S(X_i X_j) = 0.$$
If X_j is a polynomial of $(x-\bar{x})$ of j-th degree, then[①]
$$k = \frac{S(yX_p)}{S(X_p^2)}$$
and
$$\sigma_k^2 = \frac{\sigma^2}{S(X_p^2)}.$$

Since $p+1$ constants have been fitted, there are $n_1 = n - p - 1$ degrees of freedom so that the best estimate for s^2 is
$$s^2 = \frac{1}{n_1} S(y-Y)^2 = \frac{1}{n-p-1} S(y-Y)^2.$$

As before, let
$$\tau = \frac{(k-K)}{\sigma_k},$$

[①] See Chapter III, or Allan, F. E., "The General Form of the Orthogonal Polynomial for Simple Series", Proc. Roy. Soc., Edin, Vol.50, pp.310–320, 1930; and J. Neyman, "Further Notes on Non-linear Regression", Biom., Vol.18, p.257, 1926.

$$v^2 = n_1 \frac{s^2}{\sigma^2} = (n - p - 1) \frac{s^2}{\sigma^2};$$

and, if

$$t = \frac{\tau}{v} = \frac{(k - K)\sqrt{S(X_p^2)}}{\sqrt{S(y - Y)^2}}, \qquad (4 \cdot 12)$$

the distribution of t is likewise given by $(4 \cdot 8)$. After replacing n_1 by $n - p - 1$, it becomes

$$\frac{1}{\sqrt{x}} \frac{\left(\frac{n-p-2}{2}\right)!}{\left(\frac{n-p-3}{2}\right)!} (1 + t^2)^{-\frac{n-p}{2}} dt.$$

Of course, all the other regression coefficients will be distributed in like manner, only substituting the corresponding subscript for p.

For the case of the multiple regression plane, let the regression of y on its associated variates $x_1, x_2, \ldots, x_p$ be

$$Y = b_1 x_1 + b_2 x_2 + \ldots + b_p x_p.$$

After allowing for the $p + 1$ constants used in fitting this regression plane, we have $n_1 = n - p - 1$ degrees of freedom. The accuracy of the regression coefficients is only affected by the correlations which appear in the sample, so that if

$$\Delta = |S(X_i X_j)|, \quad i, j = 1, 2, \ldots, p$$

be the determinant with $S(X_i X_j)$ as its ij-th element and Δ_{11} be the cofactor of $S(X_1^2)$, then

$$\sigma_{b_1}^2 = \frac{\sigma^2 \Delta_{11}}{\Delta}.$$

As before, let

$$\tau = \frac{b_1 - \beta}{\sigma_{b_1}}, \quad v^2 = n_1 \frac{s^2}{\sigma^2} = \frac{\sum (y - Y)^2}{\sigma^2}$$

$$t = \frac{\tau}{v} = \frac{(b_1 - \beta_1)\sqrt{\Delta}}{\sqrt{S(y-Y)^2 \sqrt{\Delta_{11}}}}, \qquad (4 \cdot 13)$$

then t will be distributed according to $(4 \cdot 8)$. If we put $n - p - 1$ for n_1, the distribution is

$$dF(t) = \frac{1}{\sqrt{x}} \frac{\left(\dfrac{n-p-2}{2}\right)!}{\left(\dfrac{n-p-3}{2}\right)!} \cdot (1+t^2)^{-\frac{n-p}{2}} dt.$$

In 1931, Hotelling[1] generalized the statistical coefficient t for samples from n-variate normal population and found the distribution of T which is the product of the generalized t and the number of degrees of freedom in the sample, by means of the property of the invariance of T under all homogeneous linear transformations of the n variates in the population. The same distribution was also obtained by S. S. Wilks[2] by making use of the solution of a certain type of integral equations. The result may be stated as follows:

In a sample of N observations from an n-variate normal population, let

$$N\bar{x}_i = \sum_{i=1}^{N} x_i$$

$$a_{ij} = a_{ji} = \frac{1}{N} \sum_{i=1}^{N} (x_i - \bar{x}_i)(x_j - \bar{x}) = r_{ij} s_i s_j,$$

$A = |a_{ij}|$, the determinant with a_{ij} as its ij-th element.
$A_{ij} =$ the cofactor of a_{ij} in $|a_{ij}|$,

$$\frac{T^2}{n_1} = \frac{T^2}{N-1} = \sum_{i,j=1}^{n} \frac{A_{ij}}{A}(\bar{x}_i - m_i)(\bar{x}_j - m_j) \qquad (4 \cdot 14)$$

where m_i is the population mean of x_i. The distribution of T is found to be

---

[1] H. Hotelling, "The Generalization of 'Student's' Ratio", Annals of Mathematical Statistics, Amer. Stat. Ass., Vol.II, pp.359–378, 1931.
[2] S. S. Wilks, "Certain Generalizations on the Analysis of Variance", Biom., Vol.24, p.471, 1932.

$$\frac{2\Gamma\left(\dfrac{N}{2}\right)}{\Gamma\left(\dfrac{N-n}{2}\right)\Gamma\left(\dfrac{n}{2}\right)(N-1)^{n/2}} \frac{T^{n-1}dT}{\left(1+\dfrac{T^2}{N-1}\right)^{\frac{N}{2}}}. \qquad (4\cdot 15)$$

4.3 The Distribution of X^2

In 1900, Pearson① devised the X^2-test of goodness of Fit. If $x_0 + m_0$, $x_1 + m_1$, ..., $x_n + m_n$ are the observed frequencies in a series of $n+1$ classes, and $m_0, m_1, ..., m_n$ the corresponding expectations or the theoretical frequencies, then the discrepancy between observation and expectation may be measured by calculating

$$X^2 = s\left(\frac{x}{m}\right)^2. \qquad (4\cdot 16)$$

The discrepancy as measured between a random sample and its theoretical population is significant if X^2 has a value much greater than usually occurs. The judgment of this requires a knowledge or the distribution of X^2. Pearson found it to be of the Pearsonian Type III curve:

$$dF(X^2) = Je^{-\frac{1}{2}X^2}X^{n-2}d(X^2), \qquad (4\cdot 17)$$

where n, as shown later by Fisher②, should be interpreted, not as the number of classes or cells, but as the number of the degrees of freedom. Consequently, in using Elderton's tables③ of Goodness of Fit, the value of n' with which the table should be entered, is not now equal to the number of classes or cells but to one more than the number of degrees of freedom. Moreover, it is then seen that this distribution is really equivalent to that of the estimated variance found by Student (Cf. eq. 4·5).

The significance of a discrepancy may now be expressed in terms of the chance that a system of deviations between observation and expectation would

---

① Pearson, K., "On the Criterion, etc.", Phil. Meg. Ser. V, Vol.50, pp.157–175, 1900.

② R.A. Fisher, "On the Interpretation of X^2 from Contingency Tables", Jour. Roy. Stat. Soc., Vol.85, p.87, 1922.

③ K. Pearson, *Tables for Statisticians and Biometricians*, Cambridge University Press, 1914.

yield a X^2 value as great or greater than that observed; that is,

$$P = \frac{\int_x^\infty e^{-\frac{1}{2}X^2} X^{n_1-2} \mathrm{d}(X^2)}{\int_0^\infty e^{-\frac{1}{2}X^2} X^{n_1-2} \mathrm{d}(X^2)}. \tag{4·18}$$

This test is an essential means of justifying a posteriori the description of observational data by a theoretical curve or surface.

Pearson[1] has further used X^2 to test whether two independent distributions are likely to be random samples from the sane population. This method was later shown by Fisher[2] to be exactly the same as the direct application of X^2 to the contingency tables.

The application of X^2 test to the contingency table was considered by Pearson,[3] and also by Yule and Greenwood.[4] But they were then in error because they took, for a contingency table of r rows and c columns, $n' = rc$ in applying Elderton's Table of Goodness of Fit. However, Yule and Greenwood did point out the discrepancy between the results given by the X^2 method, as then ordinarily applied to the fourfold table for estimating the probability that any given divergence from independence might have arisen by random sampling, and the results given by the more elementary test afforded, if $p_1 = \dfrac{(AB)}{(B)}$ and $p_2 = \dfrac{(A\beta)}{(\beta)}$, by

Attribute	Attribute		Total
	(not attached)	(attached)	
A (inoculated)	$(AB) = a$	$(A-) = b$	$(A) = a+b$
(not inoculated)	$(\alpha B) = c$	$(\alpha\beta) = d$	$(\alpha) = c+d$
Total	$(B) = a+c$	$(\beta) = b+d$	$N = a+b+c+d$

---

[1] Pearson, K., "On the Probability that two independent distributions are really samples of the same population", Biom., Vol.8, p.250, 1911.

[2] Fisher, "On the Interpretation of X^2", Op. Cit.

[3] Pearson, K., "On the Theories of Multiple and Partial Contingency Tables", Biom., Vol.11, p.145, 1915.

[4] Yule, G. U. and Greenwood, M., "The Statistics of Antityphoid and Antichorela Inoculations", Proc. Roy. Soc. of Medicine, Section of Epidemiology and State Medicine, Vol.8, p.113, 1915.

comparing $p_1 - p_2$ with its probable error; they found that deviations which judged by the X^2 method are not improbable, seem much less probable to occur when judged by the other test. The source of the discrepancy has been demonstrated by Fisher to be in the misinterpretation of the parameter n in the distribution of X^2.

Fisher's proof① consists in representing the values of x (following the same notation given above, i.e., $x + m$ be the observation, and m the corresponding expectation) as independent coordinates in generalized space; then owing to the linear relations by which the deviations are restricted, for example the marginal totals of the population should be equal to those observed, all possible sets of observations will lie relative to the center of the distribution, specified by the assumed population, in a plane space, of the same number of dimensions as there are degrees of freedom. The frequency density at any point in this space is proportional to

$$e^{-\frac{1}{2}s\left(\frac{x^2}{\sigma^2}\right)}$$

when the sample is sufficiently great for the distribution of x to be regarded as normal, and where σ_1, σ_2, ... represent the standard deviations of x_1, x_2, ... To determine what values have to be assigned to the σ's when the x's is entirely independent, we must take account of the variation in the total number,

$$S(m + x) = N.$$

Since the different values of x are independent,

$$\sigma_N^2 = s(\sigma^2).$$

The variation of x may be regarded as due to two independent causes, namely, the variation of N, and the variation of the proportion, which falls into any one compartment; we have therefore the series of equations,

$$\sigma_1^2 = p_1 q_1 \overline{N} + p_1^2 \sigma_N^2$$

---

① "On the Interpretation of X^2", Op. Cit. For experimental illustrations, see Yule, "On the Application of the Method to Association and Contingency Tables, with Experimental Illustrations", J. R. S. S., Vol.85, p.95. For a rejoinder to the criticisms of Fisher and Yule, see Pearson, "On the Test of Goodness of Fit", Biom., Vol.14, p.186.

$$\sigma_2^2 = p_2 q_2 \overline{N} + p_2^2 \sigma_N^2 \qquad (4 \cdot 19)$$

....

where p_1 is the chance of any observation falling in the cell (1).

Summing these, we find

$$\sigma_N^2 = \overline{N} S(pq) + \sigma_N^2 S(p^2),$$

whence, since $S(p) = 1$ and $p - p^2 = pq$,

$$\sigma_N^2 = \overline{N}.$$

Substituting in (4 · 19),

$$\sigma_1^2 = (p_1 q_1 + p_1^2) \overline{N} = p_1 \overline{N} = m_1,$$

$$\sigma_2^2 = (p_2 q_2 + p_2^2) \overline{N} = p_2 \overline{N} = m_2,$$

whence

$$s\left(\frac{x^2}{\sigma^2}\right) = s\left(\frac{x^2}{m}\right) = X^2, \qquad (4 \cdot 20)$$

and the frequency density at any point in generalized space is

$$e^{-\frac{1}{2}X^2}.$$

The surfaces of equal density are therefore the series of similar end coaxial ellipsoids, X = constant, and since X measures the linear dimensions of the corresponding ellipsoid, which by a homogeneous strain passes into a sphere, and since the plane space in which the observations lie passes through the point $X = 0$, the total frequency in the range of X must be proportional to

$$X^{n_1 - 1} e^{-\frac{1}{2}X^2} dX \qquad (4 \cdot 21)$$

where n_1 is the number of the degrees of freedom.

In the fourfold table, when the marginal totals are fixed, there remains only one[①] degree of freedom and consequently X is normally distributed with unit standard deviation over the positive half of a normal curve:

$$df = \frac{2}{\sqrt{2x}} e^{-\frac{1}{2}X^2} dX. \qquad (4 \cdot 22)$$

---

① Cf. Yule, G.U., *The Theory of Statistics*, 9 th Ed., Chapter III, especially, p.36, 1929.

And for a contingency table of r rows and c columns when the marginal totals are fixed, there are $n_1 = (r-1)(c-1)$ degrees of freedom and we must take $n' = (r-1)(c-1) + 1$ in applying Elderton's table.

When the parameter in the X distribution is rightly interpreted, the difficulty observed by Yule and Greenwood in applying X^2 method to a contingency table disappears; for the standard error of p_1 is

$$\sigma_{p_1} = \sqrt{\frac{(a+c)(b+d)}{(a+b+c+d)^2(a+b)}},$$

and that of p_2 is

$$\sigma_{p_2} = \sqrt{\frac{(a+c)(b+d)}{(a+b+c+d)^2(c+d)}},$$

so that if

$$x = p_1 - p_2 = \frac{ad - bc}{(a+b)(c+d)},$$

then

$$\frac{x^2}{\sigma_x^2} = \frac{(ad-bc)^2(a+b+c+d)}{(a+b)(c+d)(a+c)(b+d)} = X^2,$$

and X is distributed according to $(4 \cdot 22)$. Therefore, the two tests, used by Yule and Greenwood, are in reality identical.

In applying X^2 to test whether two independent distributions are likely to be random samples from the same population, we may simply treat the two samples as a contingency table of two rows and s columns:

1st sample	f_1	f_2	...	f_s	N
2nd sample	f'_1	f'_2		f'_s	N'

so that

$$= S \left\{ \frac{\left(f - \frac{f+f'}{N+N'}N\right)^2}{\frac{f+f'}{N+N'}N} + \frac{\left(f' - \frac{f+f'}{N+N'}N'\right)^2}{\frac{f+f'}{N+N'}N'} \right\}$$

$$= S \left\{ \frac{NN'}{f+f'} \left(\frac{f}{N} - \frac{f'}{N'}\right)^2 \right\};$$

the summation taken over all the columns. In this case, there are $n_1 = s - 1$ degrees of freedom.

4.4 The General z Distribution

The recognition of the fundamental importance of the parameter n_1 which, specifying the number of degrees of freedom, is used in applying the X^2-test and by means of which the distribution or X^2 is recognized as equivalent to that of the variance, has led Fisher[①] to arrive at his z-distribution, which is the general form of a family of distributions, including the normal distribution, t-distribution, X^2-distributions, the distributions of correlation coefficients, etc.

Let s_1^2 and s_2^2 be the independent estimates of the variances σ_1^2 and σ_2^2 from two samples, based respectively upon n_1 and n_2 degrees or freedom. Now Fisher introduces the quantity z defined by

$$e^{2z} = \frac{s_1^2}{s_2^2} = \frac{n_3 \sum_1 (x_1^2)}{n_1 z_3 (x_2^2)}, \text{ or } z = \frac{1}{2}(\log_e s_1^2 - \log_e s_2^2) \qquad (4 \cdot 23)$$

where the summations are taken over all the values in the respective samples. If we put

$$e^{2\xi} = \frac{\sigma_1^2}{\sigma_2^2}, \text{ or } \xi = \frac{1}{2}(\log_e \sigma_1^2 - \log_e \sigma_2^2), \qquad (4 \cdot 24)$$

then

$$e^{2(z-\xi)} = \frac{\sigma_2^2}{\sigma_1^2} \frac{n_2 \sum_1 (x_1^2)}{n_1 \sum (x_2^2)}. \qquad (4 \cdot 25)$$

The distribution of the quantity $(z - \xi)$ may be derived ae follows:

Since the distribution of s_1^2 is independent of that of s_2^2, we have the simultaneous distribution of s_1^2 and s_2^2

$$df = \frac{1}{\left(\frac{n_1 - 2}{2}\right)!} \times \left(\frac{v_1^2}{2}\right)^{\frac{n_1-2}{2}} \times e^{-\frac{v_1^2}{2}} \times d\left(\frac{v_1^2}{2}\right) \times \frac{1}{\left(\frac{n_2 - 2}{2}\right)!} \times \left(\frac{v_2^2}{2}\right)^{\frac{n_2-2}{2}} \times e^{-\frac{v_2^2}{2}} \times d\left(\frac{v_2^2}{2}\right)$$

[①] Fisher, R. A., "On a Distribution Yielding the Error Functions of Several Well-known Statistics", Proc. of International Congress, Toronto, 1924. Fisher, R. A., "Distribution of Multiple Correlation Coefficient", Proc. Roy. Soc. A., Vol.121, p.654. 1928.

where
$$v_1^2 = \frac{n_1 s_1^2}{\sigma_1^2}, \quad v_2^2 = \frac{n_2 s_2^2}{\sigma_2^2}.$$

Substituting
$$v_1^2 = \frac{n_1}{n_2} e^{2(z-\xi)} v_2^2,$$

we obtain the simultaneous distribution of $z - \xi$ and v_2^2,

$$df = \frac{1}{\left[\frac{1}{2}(n_1 - 2)\right]! \left[\frac{1}{2}(n_2 - 2)\right]!} \left[\frac{n_1}{n_2} e^{2(z-\xi)}\right]^{\frac{n_1}{2}} \left(\frac{v_2^2}{2}\right)^{\frac{1}{2}(n_1+n_2-2)}$$
$$\cdot e^{-\frac{v_2^2}{2}\left[1+\frac{n_1}{n_2}e^{2(z-\xi)}\right]} d\left(\frac{v_2^2}{2}\right) d(z - \xi).$$

This expression may be integrated with respect to v^2 to yield the distribution of $(z - \xi)$ in the form

$$df = \frac{2 \cdot \left[\frac{1}{2}(n_1 + n_2 - 2)\right]!}{\left(\frac{n_1 - 2}{2}\right)! \left(\frac{n_2 - 2}{2}\right)!} \cdot \frac{n_2^{\frac{n_2}{2}} n_1^{\frac{n_1}{2}} e^{n_1(z-\xi)}}{\left[n_2 + n_1 e^{2(z-\xi)}\right]^{\frac{1}{2}(n_1+n_2)}} d(z - \xi). \quad (4 \cdot 26)$$

Knowing this distribution, we can tell at once if an observed value of z is or is not consistent with any theoretical value of the ratio $\xi = \frac{\sigma_1}{\sigma_2}$.

The two integers n_1 and n_2 involved in the distribution are symmetrical, in the sense that if we interchange n_1 and n_2, we change the sign of $(z - \xi)$. In more detail, if P is the probability of exceeding any value $(z - \xi)$, then, after interchanging n_1 and n_2, the probability of exceeding $(z - \xi)$ will now be $1 - P$.

If two samples be taken from the same population, we have
$$\sigma_1 = \sigma_2 = \sigma$$
$$\xi = 0,$$

and the equation $(4 \cdot 26)$ becomes the distribution of z

$$df = \frac{2 \cdot \left(\frac{n_1 + n_2 - 2}{2}\right)!}{\left(\frac{n_1 - 2}{2}\right)! \left(\frac{n_2 - 2}{2}\right)!} \cdot \frac{n_2^{\frac{1}{2}n_2} n_1^{\frac{1}{2}n_1} e^{n_1 z}}{(n_2 + n_1 e^{2z})^{\frac{1}{2}(n_1+n_2)}} dz, \quad (4 \cdot 27)$$

completely independent of the unknown variance of which s_1^2 and s_2^2 are two independent estimates. By the insertion of the appropriate values of n_1 and n_2, the probability P of exceeding any value of z may be obtained and tabulated. Fisher gives a table[①] corresponding to $P = 0.05$ and $P = 0.01$ for some values of n_1 and n_2 which may satisfy quite sufficiently the pretorial needs. This table is used in the analysis of variance of which the correlation method may be considered as one instance.

Values of special interest for n_1 and n_2 are ∞ and 1:

Case i. If $n_2 \to \infty$, the z-distribution degenerates into X^2 distribution; since

$$\frac{\sum_2 (X^2)}{n_2} = \sigma^2 \qquad (4 \cdot 28)$$

$$e^{2z} = \frac{1}{n_1} \frac{\sum_1 (X^2)}{\sigma^2} = \frac{1}{n_1} X^2.$$

Case ii. When $n_1 = 1$, the z-distribution becomes the t-distribution of Student; since

$$e^{2z} = \frac{n_2 x^2}{\sum_2 (x^2)} = t^2. \qquad (4 \cdot 29)$$

Case iii. When $n_1 = 1$, $n_2 = \infty$, the z-distribution reduces to the normal distribution; since

$$e^{2z} = \frac{x^2}{\sigma^2}. \qquad (4 \cdot 30)$$

Further, if x be any value of a sample from the Poisson series and $\bar{x}$ the mean of the sample, then

$$X^2 = \frac{S(x - \bar{x})}{\bar{x}}$$

is distributed according to X^2 and belongs to the system of z-distribution.

Defining as the generalized sample variance, the moment determinant $|a_{ij}| =$

---

① Fisher, R.A., Statistical Methods for Research Workers.

ξ, where

$$a_{ij} = \frac{1}{N} \sum_{t=1}^{N} x_{it} x_{jt} = a_{ji},$$

for the reason that this quantity for n variate samples and the ordinary variance for samples of one variate are similar in the manner in which they enter the distribution of their component parts, Wilks[1] has found the distribution of the generalized variance ξ of a normal population. Likewise, he regards the ratio of two estimates ξ_1 and ξ_2 of the generalized variance from two samples of an n-variate population as a generalization of Fisher's z. By the same method, Wilks has found the distribution of this quantity. Indeed, several other distributions, including the distribution of the multiple correlation coefficient, generalized correlation ratio, the correlation determinant $R = |\ r_{ij}\ |$, and the ratio of this determinant to the product of its principal minors, have cropped up at the same time in the study of the solutions of two integral equations.

4.5 The Goodness of Fit of Regression Formulae

E. Slusky[2] in the 1913 and K. Pearson[3] in 1916 extended the X^2 test to apply to the fitness of regression formulae, Pearson's correlation ratio having also been employed for this purpose. Because they did not make allowance for the number of the constants fitted to the regression curve or surface and because they assumed the distribution of $\dfrac{\sum x^2}{\sigma^2}$ is equivalent to that of $\dfrac{\sum x^2}{\sigma^2}$, where s^2 is an estimate of σ^2 from a sample (it has been noted in the account of Student's t-distribution that, if x is normally distributed and σ its true standard derivation, $\tau = \dfrac{x}{\sigma}$ is normally distributed, but the substitution for σ of its estimate s changes the form of distribution. Similarly, a change in the distribution of $\dfrac{\sum x^2}{\sigma^2}$ takes

---

[1] Wilks, S. S., "Certain Generalizations in the Analysis of Variance", Op. Cit.

[2] Slusky, E., "On the Criterion of the Goodness of Fit of the Regression Lines, etc.", J. R. S. S., Vol.77, pp.78 – 84, 1913.

[3] Pearson, K., "On the Application of Goodness of Fit Tables to Test Regression Curves, etc.", Biom. Vol.11, pp.239 – 261, 1916.

place when σ^2 is substituted by its estimate), their results require a modification as shown by Fisher[①] who has obtained a solution of the exact distribution of $X^2 = \dfrac{\sum x^2}{s^2}$, appropriate to test the goodness of fit of the regression formulae. His solution may be stated in the following way.

Let x and y be two variates of normal distribution. In a sample of N observations, let the cell frequency of $x_p y_q$ be n_{pq} and the frequency of an x_p-array of y's be n_p. Let $\bar{y}$ and s_p be the array mean and variance in the sample and m_p and σ_p be their expected values, then

$$z_p = \sqrt{n_p}(\bar{y}_p - m_p) \qquad (4 \cdot 31)$$

is normally distributed with a standard deviation σ_p and this distribution is independent of the size of the array. Now an x_p-array of y's may be regarded as a random sample from a population in which x is constant; but the value of y varies freely about the mean m_p with a standard deviation σ_p. Hence the quantity

$$X^2 = \dfrac{\sum\limits^{a} z_p^2}{\sigma_p^2} \qquad (4 \cdot 32)$$

is the sum of the squares of a (if there are a arrays) independent, normally, and equally variable quantities and will be distributed as is the Pearsonian measure of goodness of Fit, so long as σ_p is assumed known. Nevertheless, σ_p must, in general, be estimated from the data, and errors will be introduced from this source which necessarily influence the distribution of X^2, especially when the data are not numerous.

The best estimate of σ_p is by the method of maximum likelihood. The frequency with which the variance s_p^2 of an array in a normal sample falls in the specified range $d(s_p^2)$ is proportional to

$$\sigma_p^{-(n_p-1)} (s_p^2)^{\frac{n_p-3}{2}} e^{-\frac{n_p s_p^2}{2\sigma_p^2}} d(s_p^2);$$

[①] Fisher, R. A., "The Goodness of Fit of Regression Formulae", J. R. S. S., Vol.85, p.597, 1922.

the chance that all the observed values of s_p^2 fall in assigned ranges is the product of such quantities, for all are distributed independently. Taking logarithms and maximizing with respect to the variation of σ_p, we have

$$\frac{\partial L}{\partial \sigma_p} = \frac{\sum^a (n_p s_p^2)}{\sigma_p^3} - \frac{\sum^a (n_p - 1)}{\sigma_p}$$

whence the optimum value of σ_p^2 is

$$s^2 = \frac{1}{(N-a)} \sum^a (n_p s_p^2) = \frac{1}{N-a} \sum^N (y - \bar{y})^2. \quad (4\cdot 33)$$

Since the y's is subject to a linear restrictions of the form:

$$s_p(y) = n_p \bar{y},$$

there are $N - a$ degrees of freedom; and s^2 is distributed in the following form:

$$df_1 = C t^{\frac{1}{2}(N-a-2)} e^{-\frac{t}{2\sigma_p^2}} dt,$$

where $t = s^2(N - a)$. Similarly, if

$$\tau = X^2 s^2 = \sum^a (z_p^2), \quad (4\cdot 34)$$

and if $p + 1$ constants have been used in fitting,

$$df_1 = C' \tau^{\frac{1}{2}(a-p-3)} \cdot e^{-\frac{\tau}{2\sigma_p^2}} d\tau.$$

These two distributions are independent of each other; for t depends only on the deviations from the means of normal sample and τ only on the means. The simultaneous distribution of t and τ will be the product $df_1 df_2$.

Now,

$$X^2 = (N-a)\frac{\tau}{t} = \frac{\sum(z_p^2)}{s^2}, \quad (4\cdot 35)$$

we may obtain the simultaneous distribution for t and X by substituting $\tau = \frac{X^2 t}{N-a}$ in the product $df_1 df_2$:

$$(X^2)^{(a-p-3)} t^{\frac{N-p-3}{2}} e^{-\frac{t}{2\sigma^2}\left(1+\frac{X^2}{N-a}\right)} dt d(X^2).$$

The integration from 0 to ∞ with respect to t give the distribution of X^2

$$df(X^2) = \frac{(N-a)^{-\frac{a-p-1}{2}}\left(\frac{N-p-3}{2}\right)!}{\left(\frac{N-a-2}{2}\right)!\left(\frac{a-p-3}{2}\right)!}(X^2)^{\frac{a-p-3}{2}}\left(1+\frac{X^2}{N-a}\right)^{-\frac{N-p-1}{2}}dX^2$$

(4·36)

which is a Pearsonian Type VI curve and approximates a Type III curve as $N \to \infty$.

$$df = \frac{2^{-\frac{a-p-1}{2}}}{\left(\frac{a-p-3}{2}\right)!}(X^2)^{\frac{a-p-3}{2}}e^{-\frac{1}{2}X^2}dX^2 \qquad (4\cdot 37)$$

The ratio of the coordinates of (4·36) to the corresponding ones when expanded as far as the terms in $\frac{1}{N}$, is

$$1 + \frac{1}{4N}\{x^4 - 2(n'-1)X^2 + (n'-1)(n'-3)\}. \qquad (4\cdot 38)$$

In order to make use of Elderton's table of X^2 distribution which is based upon the Pearsonian Type III curve, Fisher gives the correction in P read from that table

$$C = \frac{n'-1}{4N}\{(n'+1)P_{n'+4} - 2(n'-1)P_{n'+2} + (n'-3)P_{n'}\} \qquad (4\cdot 39)$$

where $n' = a - p$ with which Elderton's table is entered.

Knowing the distribution (4·36) or applying Elderton's table of X^2 distribution together with the correction (4·39), the correlation ratio may be accurately used to test the fitness of a chosen regression formula.

Let Y be the function of x used as the regression formula, and fitted to the data by the method of least squares so that

$$S[n_p(\bar{y}_p - Y_p)^2]$$

is a minimum, then

$$N(1-R^2)s_y^2 = SS[n_{pq}(y-Y_p)^2] \qquad (4\cdot 40)$$

when R is the correlation coefficient, s_y^2 is the sample variance of y, but the correlation ratio is given by the parallel formula,

$$N(1 - \eta^2)a_y^2 = SS\{n_{pq}(y - \bar{y}_p)^2\} = (N - a)s^2, \qquad (4 \cdot 41)$$

hence, by subtraction,

$$N(\eta^2 - R^2)s_y^2 = S\{n_p(\bar{y}_p - Y_p)^2\} = X^2 s^2$$
$$= X^2 \frac{N}{N - a}(1 - \eta^2)s_y^2.$$

In other words,

$$X = (N - a)\frac{\eta^2 - R^2}{1 - \eta^2}. \qquad (4 \cdot 42)$$

To test the significance of $\eta^2 - R^2$, we may compute from the distribution $(4 \cdot 36)$ the probability P of a greater discrepancy occurring by chance, or we may enter Elderton's table with $n' = a - p$, where $p + 1$ is the number of constants fitted to the regression line, and then apply the correction given in $(4 \cdot 39)$. Thus, for a linear regression formula,

$$Y = a + bx,$$

we have
$$X^2 = (N - a)\frac{\eta^2 - r^2}{1 - \eta^2}$$

$$n' = a - 1.$$

With these values we read from Elderton's table the preliminary P' and then add to it the correction factor c computed according to $(4 \cdot 39)$ to obtain the final P. If P is greater than 0.05, it is inferred that the regression is likely to be linear.

Since in practice η is usually employed to test the validity of a linear or other regression formula, it is not the distribution of η but of the more variable quantity $\dfrac{(n^2 - R^2)}{(1 - \eta^2)}$ that is required for this purpose.

Moreover, we may regard m_p in the formula $(4 \cdot 31)$ as the value of a theoretical curve representing the trend of a time series and y_p as an index of the time series and take $n_p - 1$, for there is usually one index at one time in a time series, so that

$$X^2 = \frac{\sum (z_p^2)}{s^2} = \frac{\sum (y_p - m_p)^2}{s^2}$$

may be used to test the fitness of a theoretical curve to the available time series. For practical purposes, it seems to be a useful means to justify a posteriori the free use which is made of empirical trend curves, although we are theoretically not justified to say so because z_p can not be shown to fulfill the conditions assumed in the derivation of (4・36).

4.6 Distribution of Correlation Coefficient

In 1915, R. A. Fisher[1] deduced the formula for the simultaneous distribution of the three quadratic statistical derivates, namely, the two variances and the covariance (the product moment coefficient), by interpreting the individual values of either variate appearing in the sample as the coordinates of a point in Euclidean space of n dimensions. Thus, let $x_1, x_2, \cdots, x_n$ represent the sample values of the x-variate, and $y_1, y_2, \cdots, y_n$ the corresponding values of the y-variate, let σ_1 and σ_2 be the standard deviations of the sampled population and ρ the correlation coefficient of the population. We then calculate the following statistical derivatives from the sample:

$$N\bar{x} = \sum_1^N (x), \; N\bar{y} = \sum_1^N (y),$$
$$Ns_1^2 = \sum_1^N (x - \bar{x})^2, \; Ns_2^2 = \sum_1^N (y - \bar{y})^2,$$
$$Nrs_1s_2 = \sum_1^N (x - \bar{x})(y - \bar{y}).$$

If we put

---

[1] "Frequency Distribution of the Values of the Correlation Coefficient in Samples from an Indefinitely Large Population", Biom., Vol.10, pp. 507 – 521, 1915. The distribution of r has been investigated experimentally by several authors before and after Fisher's work. See: "Student", "The Probable Error of the Correlation Coefficient", Biom., Vol.6, pp.302 – 310, 1909; G. A. Baker, "The Significance of the Product-Moment Coefficient of Correlation with Special Reference to the Character the Marginal Distribution", Jour. Am. Stat. Ass., Vol.25, pp.537 – 596, 1930; and also see footnote in p.277 of this book.

$$A = \frac{N}{2\sigma_1^2(1-\rho^2)}, \quad B = \frac{N}{2\sigma_2^2(1-\rho^2)}, \quad H = \frac{N\rho}{2\sigma_1\sigma_2(1-\rho^2)}$$

$$a = s_1^2, \quad b = s_2^2, \quad h = s_1 s_2 r,$$

then Fisher's result, for the simultaneous distribution of a, b, and h, may be put in the symmetrical form:[①]

$$dp = \frac{1}{\sqrt{x}\,\Gamma\!\left(\dfrac{N-1}{2}\right)\Gamma\!\left(\dfrac{N-2}{2}\right)} \left|\begin{array}{cc} A & H \\ H & B \end{array}\right|^{\frac{N-1}{2}} \cdot e^{-Aa-Bb-2Hh} \cdot \left|\begin{array}{cc} a & h \\ h & b \end{array}\right|^{\frac{N-4}{2}} \cdot da\,db\,dh.$$

$$(4 \cdot 43)$$

The distribution of the correlation coefficient was deduced by direct integration from this result and is of the form:

$$df = \frac{n-2}{x}(1-\rho^2)^{\frac{1}{2}(n-1)}(1-r^2)^{\frac{1}{2}(n-4)} \int_0^\infty \frac{dt}{(\cosh t - pr)^{n-1}} dr.$$

$$(4 \cdot 44)$$

This expression may be written with advantage

$$df = \frac{\left(\dfrac{n-3}{2}\right)!}{\left(\dfrac{n-4}{2}\right)!\sqrt{x}} (1-r^2)^{\frac{1}{2}(n-4)} dr \times \frac{\left(\dfrac{n-2}{2}\right)!}{\left(\dfrac{n-3}{2}\right)!\sqrt{x}} (1-\rho^2)^{\frac{n-1}{2}} \int_{-\infty}^{\infty} \frac{dt}{(\cosh t - pr)^{n-1}},$$

whence it is seen that, with zero correlation in the population, the distribution of r is given by

$$df = \frac{\left(\dfrac{n-3}{2}\right)!}{\left(\dfrac{n-4}{2}\right)!\sqrt{x}} (1-r^2)^{\frac{1}{2}(n-4)} dr. \qquad (4 \cdot 45)$$

This distribution $(4 \cdot 45)$, being a symmetrical curve centered at $r = 0$, may be used to test whether an observed correlation coefficient is likely to have arisen from random sampling.

The formula $(4 \cdot 44)$ reveals a very interesting fact that in the

---

[①] Romanovsky, Comptes Rendus, Tome 180, p.1897, 1925.

neighborhood of ±1, the curves of distribution become extremely skew, even for large samples, and change their form so rapidly that the ordinary statement of the probable error is practically valueless. Fisher then introduces the transformation

$$\rho = \tanh \zeta,$$

$$r = \tanh z, \text{ or, } z = \frac{1}{2} \{ \log_e (1 + r) - \log_e (1 - r) \}$$

to reduce the distributions to approximate normality and to approximate constant variance. The frequency curves so transformed are

$$df = \frac{n-2}{2} \operatorname{sech}^{n-1} \zeta \operatorname{sech}^{n-2} z \int_0^\infty \frac{dt}{(\cosh t - \rho r)^{n-1}} dz \quad (4 \cdot 46)$$

which may be expanded in power of $(z - \zeta)$, writing x for $z - \zeta$; then

$$\frac{n-2}{\sqrt{2x(n-1)}} e^{-\frac{n-1}{2}x^2} \left\{ 1 + \frac{1}{2}\rho x + \frac{2+\rho}{8(n-1)} + \frac{4-\rho^2}{8}x^2 + \frac{n-1}{12}x^4 \right.$$

$$+ \rho x \left[\frac{4-\rho^2}{16(n-1)} + \frac{4+3\rho^2}{48}x^2 + \frac{n-1}{24}x^4 \right]$$

$$+ \frac{4 + 12\rho^2 + 9\rho^4}{128(n-1)^2} + \frac{8 - 2\rho^2 + 3\rho^4}{64(n-1)}x^2 + \frac{8 + 4\rho^2 - 5\rho^4}{128}x^4$$

$$+ \frac{28 - 15\rho^2}{1\,440}x^6(n-1) + \frac{(n-1)^2}{288}x^8 + \cdots \right\}.$$

The form of the transformed curve involves ρ and is thus not absolutely constant in shape. Taking the 1st moment about $x = z - \zeta = 0$, we have

$$\bar{z} - \rho = \mu_1' = \frac{\rho}{2(n-1)} \left\{ 1 + \frac{1+\rho^2}{8(n+1)} + \cdots \right\}. \quad (4 \cdot 47)$$

This shows that the mean value of z does not agree with the population value; the estimate is always slightly exaggerated, whether positive or negative. In order to correct this bias, we ought to subtract from the value of z the correction

$$c_z = \frac{r}{2(n-1)}. \quad (4 \cdot 48)$$

The moments about the mean $z - \zeta = \mu_1'$ are found to be:

$$\mu_2 = \frac{1}{n-1} \left\{ 1 + \frac{4-\rho^2}{2(n-1)} + \frac{176 - 21\rho^2 - 21\rho^4}{48(n-1)^2} + \cdots \right\}$$

$$\mu_3 = \frac{\rho\left(\rho^2 - \frac{9}{16}\right)}{(n-1)^3} + \cdots$$

$$\mu_4 = \frac{1}{(n-1)^2}\left\{3 + \frac{224 - 48\rho^2 - 3\rho^4}{16(n-1)} + \frac{1\,472 - 228\rho^2 - 141\rho^4 - 3\rho^2}{32(n-1)^2} + \cdots\right\}$$

whence

$$\beta_1 = \frac{\rho^2}{(n-1)^3}\left(\rho^2 - \frac{9}{16}\right)^2 + \cdots$$

$$\beta_2 = 3 + \frac{32 - 3\rho^4}{16(n-1)} + \frac{128 + 112\rho^2 - 57\rho^4 - 9\rho^6}{32(n-1)^2} + \cdots$$

The curve therefore becomes symmetrical with extreme rapidity, remains slightly leptokurtic, but is sensibly normal for all but very small samples.

The standard deviation is practically independent of ρ and very nearly agrees with the formula

$$\sigma_{z-\zeta} = \frac{1}{\sqrt{n-3}}; \qquad (4\cdot 49)$$

the probable error may therefore be read off as X, in Table V of Tables for Statisticians compiled by Pearson, 1914.

To facilitate the transformation of r into z, Fisher gives a table[1] for the

---

[1] Fisher, R. A., Statistical Methods, Table V. B, p.177. Fisher discussed this transformation in his paper "On the Probable Error of a coefficient of correlation deduced from a small sample", Op. Cit. And, E. S., Pearson has investigated experimentally the sensitiveness of the distribution of r to changes in the form of the population and the degree of approximation of the optimum value for ρ (the population value in the following illustration), found from using Fisher's z transformation with special reference to the size of samples and to the form of the sampled population and concluded (tentatively) that "the distribution is not very sensitive to changes in population form"; "the observed (i.e., the values of r estimated from samples from non-normal population) and theoretical (i.e., the values taken from the tables given in 'A Cooperative Study', Biom., Vol.11, pp.379 – 404, which give the frequencies computed on the basis of equation $(4\cdot 44)$ and also the means and standard deviations of r for various sizes of samples) values for mean r are in quite close agreement, but the observed σ_r is always less, and sometimes considerably less than the theoretical" and that "the agreement between observation and normal theory increases as the size of sample increases", until the sample size $n = 20$, the agreement "is really very good". "Some Notes on Sampling Tests with Two Variables", Biom., Vol.21, pp.356 – 360, which suggests that the distribution of ratios (of which correlation coefficient is one) even in very small samples is remarkably insensitive to changes in the form of the population; "The Test of Significance for the Correlation Coefficient", Jour. Am. Stat. Ass., Vol. 26, p.123; and "Further Experiments on the Sampling Distribution of the Correlation Coefficient", Jour. Am. Stat. Ass., Vol.27, p.121.

values of r corresponding to values of z, proceeding by intervals of 0.01, from 0 to 3.

The application of the methods is illustrated by the following examples:

In a sample of 25 pairs only of parent and child, the correlation for a certain character was found to be 0.600 0. What is the most reasonable value to assign to ρ in the sampled population, and what is its probable error?

Using the transformation $r = \tanh z$, we have

	r	z
calculated value	0.600 0	0.693 0
correction $\dfrac{r}{2(n-1)}$		-0.012 5
population value ρ	0.591 8	0.680 5
probable error of z for given ζ		±0.143 8
lower quartile	0.490 5	0.536 7
higher quartile	0.677 4	0.824 3

Now, a second sample of 13 from a similar population gives a correlation 0.7, what is the weighted mean of these two values? This weighted mean is the estimate of the correlation in the population. The two values of z must be given weight inversely proportional to their variance. Thus

	r	z	weight	$z \times$ weight
first sample	0.60	0.693 0		
correction		-0.012 5		
		0.680 5	22	14.971
second sample	0.70	0.867 3		
correction		-0.029 2		
		0.838 1	10	8.381
mean	0.622 9	0.729 7	32	23.352

The corresponding distribution of the intra-class correlation was found by Fisher[1] in 1921, the formulae have been given in Chapter II. This distribution, as Fisher[2] pointed out in 1928, is really the general distribution of the analysis

---

[1] Fisher, R. A., "On the Probable Error of a Coefficient of Correlation Deduced from a Small Sample", Op. Cit.

[2] Fisher, R. A., "The General Distribution of the Multiple Correlation Coefficient", Op. Cit.

of variance as given in equation (4·27). In 1924, Fisher① demonstrated by the use of geometrical representation in hyperspace that the distribution of partial correlation coefficients is exactly the same as that primarily found for the total correlation, provided that unity is deducted from the sample number for each variate eliminated.

4.7 The Distribution of the Multiple Correlation Coefficient

Finally, the distribution of the multiple correlation coefficient was solved② in 1928 by the same method as used in obtaining the distribution of the simple correlation coefficient. The general expression is of the form:

$$\mathrm{d}f = \frac{\left(\dfrac{n_1 + n_2 - 2}{2}\right)!}{\left(\dfrac{n_2 - 2}{2}\right)!\left(\dfrac{n_1 - 3}{2}\right)!}(R^2)^{\frac{n_1-2}{2}}(1 - R^2)^{\frac{n_1-2}{2}}\mathrm{d}(R^2) \times \frac{(1 - \rho^2)^{\frac{1}{2}(n_1+n_2)}}{x}$$

(4·50)

$$\int_0^z \mathrm{d}\psi \int_{-\infty}^{\infty} \frac{\sin^{n_1-2}\psi \, \mathrm{d}t}{(\cosh t - \rho R \cos \psi)^{n_1+n_2}}$$

where n_1 is the number of the associated variates, $n_1 + n_2 + 1 =$ the number of observations in the sample, and R and ρ are the multiple correlation coefficients respectively in the sample and in the population. It reduces to (4·44) when $n_1 = 1$, with $r = R\cos\psi$ according to the assumption in the process of solution; and the second factor becomes 1 when $\rho = 0$.

Completing the integral and expressing in hypergeometric form, the general form (4·50) reduces to

$$\mathrm{d}f = \frac{\left(\dfrac{n_1 + n_2 - 2}{2}\right)!}{\left(\dfrac{n_1 - 2}{2}\right)!\left(\dfrac{n_2 - 2}{2}\right)!}(1 - \rho^2)^{\frac{n_1+n_2}{2}} \cdot F\left[\frac{n_1 + n_2}{2}, \frac{1}{2}(n_1 + n_2), \frac{n}{2}, \rho^2 R^2\right]$$

$$\times (R^2)^{\frac{n_1-2}{2}}(1 - R^2)^{\frac{n_2-2}{2}}\mathrm{d}(R^2).$$

(4·51a)

---

① Fisher, R. A., "The Distribution of the Partial Correlation Coefficients", Metron, Vol.3, pt.3, p.329, 1924.

② Fisher, R. A., "The General Distribution of Multiple Correlation Coefficient", Proc. Roy. Soc., A.121, Vol.222, 1928.

This expression is called the distribution form a.

The approximate distribution appropriate to the theory of large samples, for different values of $p\sqrt{n_2}$, may be obtained by allowing n_2 to increase indefinitely. Let, $n_2\rho^2 = \beta^2$, $n_2R^2 = B^2$ and allow n_2 to increase indefinitely, the limiting form taken by the general distribution is

$$df = \frac{\left(\frac{1}{2}B^2\right)^{\frac{n_1-2}{2}}}{\left[\frac{1}{2}(n_1-2)\right]!} e^{-\frac{B^2}{2}-\frac{\beta^2}{2}} \left\{1 + \frac{1}{n_1}\frac{\beta^2 B^2}{2} + \frac{1}{n_1(n_1+2)}\frac{\beta^2}{2}\frac{B^2}{4} + \cdots\right\} d\left(\frac{B^2}{2}\right)$$

(4·51b)

which is called the distribution form b and may be expressed in terms of a Bessel function as

$$\left(\frac{B}{i\beta}\right)^{\frac{n_1-2}{2}} e^{-\frac{B^2-\beta^2}{2}} \cdot J_{\frac{1}{2}(n_1-2)}(i\beta B) \cdot d\left(\frac{B^2}{2}\right).$$

Fisher gives a table for values of β from 0 to 5 and of n_1 from 1 to 7, corresponding to the values of B which will be exceeded by chance in 5 per cent of random trials, and which therefore give a presumption that β is really greater than the value postulated.

Further, Fisher in this memoir has shown how the distribution of the multiple correlation coefficient is coherently connected with that of the analysis of variance. The solution of the distribution of the multiple correlation coefficient has indeed introduced an extensive group of distributions which in their generality underlie the analysis of variance and which in their mere mathematical structure provide an extension of the analysis of variance in a new direction (i.e., to the cases of non-central deviations; for instance, in the X^2-distribution, the n_1 independent variates all have zero means while in this case the n_1 independent variates are normally distributed with equal variance, but not with zero means).

To show this, Fisher has proved that a quantity τ^2, defined by

$$\tau^2 = \frac{1}{\sigma^2}\sum_{p=1}^{n_1}(x_p - a_p)^2 = \frac{n_1 s_1^2}{\sigma^2} \qquad (4\cdot52)$$

in which $x_1, x_2, \cdots, x_{n_1}$ are variates distributed normally and independently about zero with the common variance σ and a_p is an arbitrary constant, follows the distribution form b as given in equation (4·51b); that is, distribution of τ^2 is obtained by merely substituting τ^2 for B^2 in (4·51b).

From this result it follows that the distribution from b may be interpreted as the distribution of the sum of the squares of n_1 variates normally distributed with equal variance, but not with zero means, and may thus be regarded as a generalization of the X^2-distribution; it is used to replace the X^2-distribution in the analysis of variance for cases in which the sum of squares corresponding to n_1 degrees of freedom is derived theoretically for "non-central deviations".

If we replace the theoretical variance σ^2 in τ^2 by its estimate s_2^2 based upon n_2 degrees of freedom, the distribution will change its form. Let $t^2 = \dfrac{n_2 s_2^2}{\sigma^2}$, and

$$X^2 = \frac{\tau}{t} = \frac{\sum (x_p - a_p)^2}{s_2^2},$$

the distribution of X^2 may be found by the same process as we did in Section 5, for X^2 defined by (4·35). However, we are not here interested in this. Now if the regression of an essential variate y on $x_1, x_2, \cdots, x_{n_1}$ is expressed by the equation

$$Y = b_1 x_1 + b_2 x_2 + \cdots + b_{n_1} x_{n_1}$$

such that the correlation of y with Y is R which is, by definition, the multiple correlation coefficient of y with $x_1, x_2, \cdots, x_{n_1}$, then the variance of y may be analyzed into two parts, representing that within and that between the classes of which the data is composed of, in the following form:

variance	degrees of freedom	sum of squares
of regression formula	n_1	$n_1 s_1^2 = \sum (Y^2) = (n_1 + n_2 + 1) R^2 s_2^2$
deviations from regression formula	n_2	$n_2 s_2^2 = \sum (y - Y)^2 = (n_1 + n_2 + 1)(1 - R^2) s_2^2$
total	$n_1 + n_2$	$\sum (y^2) = (n_1 + n_2 + 1) s^2$

Hence, $\dfrac{\tau}{t}$ may be expressed in terms of R,

$$\frac{\tau^2}{t^2} = \frac{n_1}{n_2}\frac{s_1^2}{s_2^2} = \frac{n_1}{n_2}e^{2z} = \frac{R^2}{1-R^2}. \qquad (4 \cdot 53)$$

The simultaneous distribution of t and τ is the product of that for t, as given in equation $(4 \cdot 5)$, i.e.,

$$df(t) = \frac{1}{\left(\frac{n_2-2}{2}\right)!}\left(\frac{t^2}{2}\right)^{\frac{n_2-2}{2}} e^{-\frac{t^2}{2}} d\left(\frac{t^2}{2}\right),$$

and that for τ as given in equation $(4 \cdot 51b)$ with B^2 replaced by τ^2, making the following changes of variables:

$$t^2 = \frac{1-R^2}{R^2}\tau^2, \quad dt = -\frac{\tau^2 dR^2}{R^4}, \quad t^2 + \tau^2 = \frac{\tau^2}{R^2}.$$

In the simultaneous distribution of t and τ, we obtain the simultaneous distribution of τ and R

$$\frac{1}{\left(\frac{n_2-2}{2}\right)!}e^{-\frac{\beta^2}{2}}e^{-\frac{\tau^2}{R^2}}\left(\frac{1-R^2}{R^2}\right)^{\frac{n_2}{2}}\frac{dR^2}{R^2(1-R^2)}\sum_{p=0}^{\infty}\frac{\tau^{\frac{1}{2}(n_1+n_2+2p-2)}\beta^{2p}}{\left(\frac{n_1+2p-2}{2}\right)!2^p p!}d\tau^2,$$

the integration of which with respect to τ^2 from 0 to ∞ yields the distribution of R:

$$df = \frac{\left(\frac{n_1+n_2-2}{2}\right)!}{\left(\frac{n_1-2}{2}\right)!\left(\frac{n_2-2}{2}\right)!}(R^2)^{\frac{n_1-2}{2}}(1-R^2)^{\frac{n_2-2}{2}}e^{-\frac{\beta^2}{2}}\times\left\{1+\frac{n_1+n_2}{n_1\cdot 1!}\frac{R^2\beta^2}{2}\right.$$

$$\left. + \frac{(n_1+n_2)(n_1+n_2+2)}{n_1(n_1+2)n\cdot 2!}\left(\frac{R^2\beta^2}{2}\right)^2 + \cdots\right\}dR^2. \qquad (4 \cdot 54c)$$

This is called by Fisher the distribution from c for R. From the above demonstration, it is seen that there is a coherent connection between the distribution of multiple correlation coefficient and that of the analysis of variance.

4.8 The Distribution of the Correlation Ratio

The solution of distribution of the multiple correlation coefficient really includes that of the correlation ratio. If, corresponding to any value of the associated variate, a number of values n_x of the essential variate y are observed, then the correlation ratio E (let us reserve η for the population value of the correlation ratio) of y on x is defined by the relation

$$\frac{E^2}{1-E^2} = \frac{S\{n_x(\bar{y}_x - \bar{y})\}}{S(y - \bar{y}_x)^2}$$

in which $\bar{y}_x$ is the mean of y in any array, and $\bar{y}$ is the general mean; the variance in all arrays is supposed equal, and the summation in the numerator is applied to the several arrays, while that in the denominator is applied to the whole of the individual observations. In most practical cases, the idea of a sampling distribution of E^2 can only be given a definite meaning by supposing the number n_x in each array to be the same for all samples. In such a case, the distribution of E^2 will be that of R^2 in the distribution form (c), writing

$$R^2 = E^2, \ \beta^2 = N\frac{\eta^2}{1-\eta^2},$$

and with n_1 equal to one less than the number of arrays, and $n_1 + n_2 + 1$ equal to the total number of observations.

If, however, the array totals vary from sample to sample, the sampling distribution is then given by distribution form (a) by writing $R^2 = E^2$, $\rho^2 = \eta^2$, and will be exact if the expectations of y for the values of x in the sampled population are normally distributed.

This distribution (c), of which Fisher did not study the properties though he did for the distribution from (a), has been further investigated by Wishart[1] who obtained the probability integral. It is shown that the results obtained from the (a) and (c) distributions equally tend in the limit to the corresponding parameters of the (b) distribution, i.e.,

$$n_2\eta^2 = \beta^2, \ nE^2 = B^2.$$

4.9 The Analysis of Variance[2]

From the above discussion, it is seen that all the distributions of the

---

[1] Wishart, John, "a note on the distribution of the correlation ratio", Biom., Vol. 24, p. 441, 1932.

[2] "The term 'variance' has recently been introduced by Student as a useful term for the squared standard deviation", Karl Pearson, "notes on skew frequency surface", Biom., Vol. 15, p. 222, footnote.

statistical coefficients used in the correlation analysis have grouped themselves in a single system; all may be reduced to an equivalent problem of the distribution of half the difference of the logarithms of two independent estimates of variance, based respectively upon n_1 and n_2 degrees of freedom, i.e.,

$$z = \frac{1}{2}(\log s_1 - \log s_2), \text{ or, } e^{2z} = \frac{s_1^2}{s_2^2},$$

and they are all amenable to the same technical procedure known as the analysis of variance. This procedure developed in full detail may be found in R. A. Fisher's Statistical Methods For Research Workers.①

The simple arithmetical procedure with which the correlation when considered as an analysis of variance is treated, may be summarized as follows.

In the analysis of variance, the variance is analyzed into two parts representing that within and that between the classes of which the data are composed. Thus, with two variates x and y of normal distribution, if N_{it} be the cell frequency of $(x_i y_t)$ and N_i the x-array frequency of Y's so that

$$N_i m_i = \sum_t N_{it} y_t$$

$$m \sum_i \sum_t N_{it} = \sum_i N_i m_i = \sum_i \sum_t (N_{it} y_t),$$

then,

$$\sum_i \sum_t N_{it}(y_t - m)^2 = \sum_i \sum_t N_{it}(y - m_i)^2 + \sum_i N_i(m_i - m)^2.$$

The term in the left side of the equation is the sum of squares of deviations of individual values from the grand mean, the first term in the right side of the equation is the sum of squares of deviations from the array means and therefore represents the total variability within arrays or the intra-array aggregate variance, and the second term is the sum of squared deviations of the array means from the grand mean and therefore represents the total variability between arrays or the inter-array aggregate variance. The sum of squared deviations divided by the degrees of freedom is called the mean variance, and the resultant variance will be denoted by σ_y, σ_2, σ_1.

---

① Op. Cit.

Now suppose a sample of n observations, taken from such a population, be arranged in k arrays so that the cell frequency of (x_i, y_t) is f_{it} and the frequency in an x-array of y's is f_i, and let

$$f_i \bar{y}_i = \sum_t f_{it} y_t$$

$$n \bar{y} = \sum_i f_i \bar{y}_i = \sum_i \sum_t f_{it} y_t,$$

then

$$\sum_i \sum_t f_{it}(y_t - \bar{y})^2 = \sum_i \sum_t f_{it}(y_t - \bar{y}_i)^2 + \sum_i f_i(\bar{y}_i - \bar{y}),$$

whence we may obtain, by dividing each term by the corresponding number of degrees of freedom, the estimates of the three variances mentioned above:

source of variation	sum of square deviations	degrees of freedom	mean variance
inter-array	$\sum_i f_i(\bar{y}_i - \bar{y})^2$	$n_1 = k - 1$	s_1^2
intra-array	$\sum_i \sum_t f_{it}(y - \bar{y}_i)^2$	$n_2 = \sum_i (f_i - 1)$	s_2^2
total	$\sum_i \sum_t f_{it}(y_t - \bar{y})^2$	$n_1 + n_2 = \sum (f_i - 1)$ $= n - 1$	

If now there are equal number of observations in each array, then

$$\sum f_i = k f_a,$$

if the constant array frequency be f_a, and

$$\sum_i f_i(\bar{y}_i - \bar{y})^2 = f_a \sum (\bar{y}_i - \bar{y})^2 = n_1 s_1^2.$$

Moreover, as the y's in an x_i-array may be regarded as a random sample from a population in which the value of x is constant while the value of y varies freely about the array mean m_i with the standard deviation $\sigma_i = \sigma_2$, the array mean of the sample, $\bar{y}_i$, for arrays of any given size n_i, has a standard error equal to $\sigma_2/\sqrt{f_i}$. It is then easy to see that this variation, due to random sampling, increases the estimated inter-array variance; for

$$\sum f_i(\bar{y}_i - \bar{y})^2 = \sum f_i(\bar{y}_i - m)^2 = \sum f_i(\bar{y}_i - m_i)^2 + \sum f_i(m_i - m)^2$$

which may be written in the following form, if f_a is the same for all the arrays:

$$f_i \sum (\bar{y}_i - m)^2 = f_i \sum (\bar{y} - m_i)^2 + f_i \sum (m_i - m)^2$$

where $f_i \sum (m_i - m) \to f_i n_1 \sigma_1^2$ as f_a and n increase. Hence in calculating the inter-array variance s_1^2 and the intra-array variance s_2^2, we are really making estimates respectively for $f_a \sigma_1^2 + \sigma_2^2$ and σ_2^2; that is to say,

$$s_1^2 = f_a \sigma_1^2 + \sigma_2^2$$
$$s_2^2 = \sigma_2^2.$$

Now, if x and y are independent of each other, then $\sigma_1 = 0$, $\sigma_2 = \sigma_y$, and s_1^2 and s_2^2 are really two independent estimates of the same variance, σ_2^2, based upon n_1 and n_2 degrees of freedom respectively. Hence a material aberration between s_1^2 and s_2^2 which could not be regarded as likely to have arisen by random sampling, must mean that the hypothesis respecting the independence between x and y cannot be true and that there is a considerable inter-array variance, i.e., the array means of y vary as x varies. In other words, the inter-array variance exists when the variates are not independent, and the test of the existence of the inter-array variance reduces itself to a test if there is a significant aberration between the two independent estimates, s_1^2 and s_2^2.

The aberration between s_1^2 and s_2^2 may be expressed in terms of z; namely,

$$e^{2z} = \frac{s_1^2}{s_2^2}, \text{ or, } z = \frac{1}{2} (\log s_1^2 - \log s_2^2),$$

and if P is the probability of exceeding any value of z by chance, it is possible to compute the value of z corresponding to different values of P, n_1, and n_2. If the convention that an aberration between s_1^2 and s_2^2 is considered as significant when P is less than 0.05 and highly significant when P is less than 0.01, is agreed upon, then Fisher's table (Table IV, Statistical Methods for Research Workers) which gives values of z for the important regions $P = 0.05$ and $P = 0.01$, and for a number of combinations of n_1 and n_2 sufficient to indicate the values for other combinations, will suffice for the practical requirements of a test for significance.

In case where the frequency f_i is not the same for all arrays, the above theory still holds so long as the true value of the inter-array variance is zero and therefore the same test may be applied.

It is thus seen that the method of correlation reduces itself to an analysis of the inter-array and the intra-array variance, and the z test amounts to test whether the hypothesis that x and y are uncorrelated be true. If it is true, then s_1^2 and s_2^2, being two independent estimates of a same variance, will be expected not to differ significantly, i.e., the value of z corresponding to the estimates s_1^2 and s_2^2 will be expected not likely to be exceeded by more than 5 per cent of random samples. If the expectation is not realized, then it is inferred that the hypothesis will not likely hold, and therefore there is correlation between the variates.

Since the regression curve is fitted to array means, the inter-array variance in this case will be the variance of the regression formula and intra-array variance will be the variance about the regression formula, and therefore the practical working of correlation considered as an analysis of variances is of the form shown in the preceding section. Moreover, for samples from uncorrelated material, the distribution of R may be inferred from that of z. Thus, substituting

$$\frac{n_1}{n_2}e^{2z} = \frac{\sum(Y^2)}{\sum(y-Y)^2} = \frac{R^2}{(1-R^2)}, \quad dz = \frac{1}{R(1-R^2)}dR,$$

we obtain for the multiple correlation of an essential variate y with the associate variates $x_1, x_2, \cdots, x_{n_1}$ in $n = n_1 + n_2 + 1$ observations

$$df = \frac{\left(\frac{n_1+n_2-2}{2}\right)!}{\left(\frac{n_1-2}{2}\right)!\left(\frac{n_2-2}{2}\right)!}(R^2)^{\frac{n_1-2}{2}}(1-R^2)^{\frac{n_2-2}{2}}d(R^2),$$

which degenerates when $n_1 = 1$, into the distribution of the simple correlation coefficient

$$df = \frac{2\cdot\left(\frac{n_2-1}{2}\right)!}{\left(\frac{n_2-2}{2}\right)!\sqrt{x}}(1-R^2)^{\frac{n_2-2}{2}}dR$$

When the method is applied to the problem of the significance of the correlation ratio, the ingredients of the analysis of variance are as follows:

variance	degrees of freedom	sum of squares
inter-array	$n_1 = k - 1$	$\sum_i f_i(\bar{y}_i - \bar{y})^2 = n\eta^2 s_y^2$
intra-array	$n_2 = \sum (f_i - 1)$	$\sum_i \sum_t f_{it}(y - \bar{y}_i)^2 = n(1 - \eta^2)s_y^2$
total	$(\sum_i f_i) - 1 = n - 1$	$\sum_{i,t} f_{it}(y_t - \bar{y})^2 = ns_y^2$

The distribution of the correlation ratio for uncorrelated material is thus identical to that of R. The transformation is

$$\frac{\eta^2}{1 - \eta^2} = \frac{\sum_i f_i(\bar{y}_i - \bar{y})^2}{\sum \sum f_{it}(y - \bar{y}_i)^2} = \frac{n_1}{n_2}e^{2z}$$

and therefore, the significance of a correlation ratio may be tested by entering Fisher's table of the z-distribution with the value of z computed from the above relation. Clearly, this procedure can lend itself to extension to the case of multiple correlation ratios although Fisher did not mention this possibility.

Moreover, it is observed that, if the observations are increased so that $n_2 \to \infty$, then

$$n_2 \frac{\eta^2}{1 - \eta^2}$$

tends to be distributed in the X^2-distribution corresponding to $(k - 1)$ degrees of freedom, while for the multiple correlation with n_1 associate variates

$$n_2 \frac{R^2}{1 - R^2}$$

tends to be distributed in the X^2-distribution with n_1 degrees of freedom. These are two examples of statistical derivates not tending to the normal distribution for large samples.

Analysis of variance may be considered from another point of view. Suppose we are concerned with the variation of y and required to ascertain if the variation is random, or, more specifically to ascertain if the variation is to some extent due to a certain cause factor x. If the contribution of x to the variation of y varies from group to group, it will be effective to restrict y through the control of x if the latter is controllable. That is to say, if y be the t-th observation in the x-group or array, we suppose

$$y_{t;\,x} = a_x + V_{t;\,x}$$

where $V_{t;\,x}$ is a random variation, and a_x is a constant for all individuals in the x-array. And the method consists in testing if the hypothesis that a_x does not vary with x, be true.

In the more complex problems, it is supposed that y is subject to a random variation and to the aggregate variation, if any, of a number of terms due to the factors x_1, x_2, x_3, etc., so that

$$y_{t;\,x_1 x_2 x_3 \cdots} = a_{x_1} + b_{x_2} + c_{x_3} + \cdots + V_{t;\,x_1 x_2 x_3 \cdots}$$

As long as the variation of the residual terms $V_{t;\,x_1 x_2 x_3 \cdots}$ is normal and independent of the factors x_1, x_2, x_3, etc., the two estimates of variance, one from the terms of $a_{x_1} + b_{x_2} + \cdots$ and the other from the random term $V_{t;\,x_1 x_2 x_3 \cdots}$ are independent, and each is distributed according to a Pearsonian Type III, giving a Pearsonian Type VI curve for the sampling distribution of their ratio (cf. Section 4, on the distribution of the test of the fitness of the regression formula), or giving Fisher's z-distribution with z equal to the half of the difference of their natural logarithms.

There are a variety of problems to which the analysis of variance may be applied. In addition to those in agricultural plot experimentation in connection with which the technique was first developed by R. A. Fisher, the method has, for instance, been applied to problems of textile research by Tippett[1] and to problems of time series by Shultz.[2] The process of analysis is to group the observations in such a way that it is possible to test separately for the presence of an x_1 factor, an x_2 factor, etc. This is done by obtaining in each case the inter-array and the intra-array variance which would differ only through chance fluctuations if that particular factor were either without influence or made the

---

[1] L. H. O. Tippett, "Statistical Methods in Textile Research", Shirley Institute Memoirs, Vol.8, 1929.

[2] Schultz, T. W. and Snedecor, G. W., "Analysis of Variance as an Effective Method of Handling the Time Series in Certain Economic Statistics", Jour. Amer. Stat. Ass., Vol.28, pp.14−30, 1933.

same contribution to every array or group.

It is to be noted, however, that all the proofs of the sampling distributions mentioned in this chapter are based upon the assumption that the samples are drawn from normal population. If the population is not normal, the theory will not be exactly true. Little work has yet been done as to the validity of the application of the method to the non-normal distributions. With respect to the z-distribution or the distribution of the ratio of the two independent estimates of a variance, E. S. Pearson has made an investigation and concluded that "the distribution of such a ratio" "may not be very sensitive to changes in population form".① But how far the approximation will really represent the situation is, according to his results, not possible to say as yet.

CHAPTER V CORRELATION OF TIME SERIES

A sequence of values of a variate defined for selected units of time (such as day, week, month, or year) and therefore "ordered in time"② is called a

---

① Pearson, E. S., "Analysis of Variance in case of Non-normal Variation", Biom., Vol.23, 114, 1931. And also see footnote in p.277 of this book.

② This usage was introduced by Pearsons. Cf. "An Index of General Business Conditions", Rev. Eco. Stat., Vol.1, p.132, 1919. Here we will also quote in length his statement of the essential differences between measurements of "organs" (any measurable characteristics) and the items of times series.

(a) "The items of time series must be defined for a selected time unit; they measure one form of activity of industry society, whereas biological measurements are individual observations of objects whose measurements are independent of time."

(b) "Because they are defined for units of time, the items of time series are ordered in time; each item has a definite position with respect to the other items. The way to compare the items of two such series is to set up a relationship in time; that is, to pair concurrent items, or those definitely related in time. When we are correlating pig-iron production and interest rates, for instance, we wish to know not only the degree of correlation for one set of pairs, but the degree of correlation for various sets. There are various options possible in pairing items. On the other hand, when we are considering the correlation between measurements of organs, such as the stature and weight of the same individuals, or statures of fathers and sons, there is a unique pairing of items determined by the problem. The questions, does weight vary directly with stature, and do tall fathers have tall sons, obviously cannot be answered by pairing the stature of one individual with the weight of another or the stature of a father with the stature of his neighbor's son. The concept of lag is thus peculiar to time series."

(c) "Because they are ordered in time, the adjacent items in time series may be determined by overlapping or persistent causes; a succession of items of similar sizes is the rule rather than the exception.

time series. In the field of economics, the data (such as prices, physical production in units of number, weight, length, area, value or energy, interest rates, etc.) which "are utilized in problems relating to wealth getting or wealth consuming activities of men"① are largely in the form of time series. The time series have many forms — price, aggregate money values, percentage of a total. ratios to some other quantity, and so on.

In a non-time series, the order of the items in a sample or population has no significance while in a time series each of the successive items holds its position in relation to the others. For this reason, the items in a time series may be spoken of as being "conditioned", or simply called a conditioned series in the sense that the successive items are not random but correlated, i. e., $\sum x_p x_{p+k} = 0$, where x_{p+k} denotes the $(p + k)$-th item of a time series measured from the mean. On account of this special characteristic, the measurement of correlation in time series demands special methods.

5.1 The Fluctuations of Any Time Series

"Occur as the result of the operation or various forces that affect the

---

(footnote continued) Adjacent measurements of organs, on the other hand, are not so connected. Expressed in other words, the items of time series, even though corrected for secular trend and seasonal variation, are apt to show a high degree of correlation when paired with succeeding items of the same series, whereas the items of biological series show only nominal degree of correlation when so paired. Thus, the coefficient of correlation for the cycles of pig-iron production of one month and that of two months following is +0.84."
"In the preceding paragraph 'overlapping causes' were mentioned. The manifestation of such causes, it was stated, is similarity between contiguous items of a series. Since we have eliminated secular trend and seasonal variation from each series to secure the 'cycles', we have, presumably, eliminated the effect of two classes of overlapping causes before we correlated the cycles of any series. The coefficient of correlation for two series of economic statistics will frequently be larger than it otherwise would be, however, because of the influence of the same set of overlapping causes operating upon both series during the business cycle. It does not appear legitimate, therefore, to compare coefficients of correlation obtained from times series of economic data with those obtained from biological measurements. Each set of coefficients measures a type of correlation peculiar to the data utilized. A coefficient of correlation computed from economic data is not significant merely because of its absolute size; it is significant because of its size as compared with the size of other coefficients computed for the same two series but for other pairings of the items."

① Pearsons, W. M., "Statistics and Economic Theory", <u>Rev. Eco. Stat.</u>, vol. 7, p.187.

phenomena observed.①These forces may sometimes operate in the same direction and sometimes at cross-purposes; some of them may be more potent and significant than others; and, finally, some may be recurring and regular while others are occasional and accidental (the respective manifestations of which are the wave-like movements and the irregular fluctuations). That several kinds of fluctuations appear in any time series is obvious. For example, we expect pig-iron production to be vastly greater in 1910 than in 1890, because of the growth of the industry in the interval. On the other hand, we know from experience that there are periods of prosperity and depression, and are not surprised notwithstanding the large increase for the whole period, to find considerable ups and downs in the production of pig-iron during the period. Irregular or accidental occurrences, likewise, cause fluctuations — a strike, a court decision, the outbreak of war. Within any given year, also, there are typical fluctuations. The round of the seasons is known to produce changes in the volume of production or of sales, as well as other related changes (indications of such seasonal variations can be traced in a monthly plot of many time series). Moreover, all of these forces may be at work simultaneously; and all of them play a part in determining

---

① In theoretical statistics, the concept that a deviation or fluctuation is the resultant of a large number of contributory causes is almost a universally accepted hypothesis which cannot, however, be proved: Laplace, Edgeworth, Pearson, Charlier, Wicksell(cf. the description of the contributions of these authors in chapters II and III), Yule (who defines statistics as quantitative data affected to a marked extent by a multiplicity of causes. Theory of Statistics, 6th ed., p.5), Mitchell (who says: "A few of the series which such an investigator uses report the variations in factors which are indivisible units in the business situation. For example, the official minimum discount rate or the Bank of England is single figure, known with precision for every week through long years. Many different matters have been weighed by the bank's directors in deciding upon the rate announced each Thursday: but once announced there is no analyzing the rate into constituent parts. Most time series, however, are aggregates, or averages, which the investigator can, and frequently should, analyze. For example, if bank clearings in the United States fall five per cent between July and August, it may be that in a majority of the clearings houses transactions increased; and in the minority of towns where transactions shrank, the declines may have varied from a fraction of one per cent to half the July volume. Similarly, an index number of wholesale prices shows for each date merely the net resultant of most diverse changes in the prices of individual commodities — changes which nearly always run the gamut from a considerable decline to a considerable rise... It is true that an investigator often writes of series like bank clearings or price indexes as if they represented magnitudes not less definite than the Bank of England rate. Doubtless there are problems which justify the practice — problems in which the one matter of significance is the net resultant of a complicated mass of movements..."(Business Cycles, pp.206 – 208,1927), and Persons(see the above quotation) all have assumed this hypothesis in their work.

the fluctuations which occur in statistical series. Those fluctuations are thus a confused conglomerate growing out of numerous causes which overlie and obscure one another."①

In view of this complexity the simple comparison of items within time series, in what may be termed their crude state, is of but little significance. A survey of the graphs of such fundamental monthly series as bank clearings, iron production, commodity prices, and new building permits led Persons to the following work hypothesis, namely:

"Each series is a composite consisting of four types of fluctuations. The four types are:

(i) A long-time tendency or secular trend; in many series, such as bank clearings or production of commodities, this may be termed the growth element.

(ii) A wave-like or cyclical movement superimposed upon the secular trend; these waves appear to reach their crests during periods of industrial prosperity and their troughs during periods of industrial depression, their rise and fall constituting the business cycle.

(iii) A seasonal movement within the year with a characteristic shape for each series.

(iv) Residual variations due to developments which affect individual series, or to momentous occurrences, such as wars or national catastrophes, which affect a number of series simultaneously."②

Although these four types of fluctuations occur in all series, they are by no means uniform in different series. The trend, the seasonal movement, and the irregular variations of each series are peculiar to itself and the cyclical (wave-like) fluctuations③ of the various series which appear more alike to each other, are neither synchronous nor of the same intensity. However, if the cycles may be considered as the results of underlying business conditions affecting industry and

---

① Persons, "Indices of Business Conditions", Rev. Eco. Stat., Vol.1, pp.7 – 8.
② Persons, "Indices of Business Conditions", Ibid., p.8.
③ A valuable discussion of the methods of eliminating and measuring the secular trend and the seasonal variations, so that the cyclical-irregular fluctuations may be isolated for study, and of the effects of the fitness of the lines or curves representing the trends on the correlation coefficient of the cyclical-irregular fluctuations may be found in Mitchell's Business Cycles, pp.212 – 280, 1927.

trade generally, they must be related to each other.

Since the pairing of items of two time series is made possible by the position of those items in time either because they occur in the same time interval (concurrent) or in definitely related intervals (lag), the problem may be not only to determine the correlation but to find what pairings give the maximum correlation of the cyclical fluctuations. Hence, the first type of problems which may make use of correlation analysis is that of ascertaining the sequence① of phenomena in the various economic processes.

In this manner, the time series representing the various economic process may be sorted into groups so that each group is composed of series having cyclical fluctuations which are similar and simultaneous. The synchronous items in each group are then combined so that a number of synthetic indices② are obtained. Since each series of the index numbers epitomizes the general situations of a certain specified field, the relations between the several series of indices specify the inter-relation of the various economic phenomena. After the inter-relations between the several series have been so established, the series having fluctuations preceding those of the other, say, business barometer, may be used in forecasting business cycles.③ For this reason, the primary function of correlation analysis of economic statistics is to describe more or less completely and, at the same time, more or less simply the fluctuations of the general economic conditions and the inter-relations of the various economic phenomena.

---

① The technique of determining the "lag" or time sequence of phenomena wan developed by Hooker. Cf. Section 5.8. Moore used this technique to detect the period of critical relation between yield and rainfall, that in to ascertain, for each crop, the month of combination of months, within the interval between planting and harvesting, whose rainfall gives the highest correlation with the ultimate yield per acre of the crop. Economic Cycles, p.42, 1914. See also A. A. Young's discussion of the interpretation of correlation coefficients in hie introduction to Social Consequences of Business Cycles, by M.B. Hexter, Boston and New York, 1925. According to Young, the chief use of the coefficient of correlation in business cycle work has been to determine the lag of one series in relation to another.

② Persons, "An Index of General Business Conditions", Op. Cit., p.111.

③ Persons, "Construction of a Business Barometer", Amer. Eco. Rev., Vol.6, p.739. The paper discusses: "First, what statistical series should logically be combined to secure a barometer of general business conditions for the United States? Second, what series have variations precedent to the variations in the business barometer thus obtained and, therefore, offer a reliable basis for forecasting business conditions?" Cf. also Section 5.8.

It is sometimes desired to study the correlation between the residuals of times series after the influence of the time element has been eliminated.① Thus, as Greenwood has pointed out:

"Let me suppose, purely for the sake of argument, that the death-rate in any country is substantially modified by two factors and that these factors operate to a greater or smaller degree upon all the constituent items of the death-rate. Let the first be a more or less regularly progressive improvement of the general conditions of life, the second, quasi-periodic oscillations, perhaps consequences of the greater or lesser activities of public health services under the pressure of recurring waves of opinion, political or social. By hypothesis, there will be a general downward trend of the death-rate and more or less considerable quasi-periodic fluctuations imposed upon this trend. Both these phenomena are intrinsically important, but if we seek to learn whether the fatalities of two diseases, A and B, are more intimately related one to another than those of C and D or of B with C or D, admitting that all four are influenced by the two changes mentioned, we do desire to eliminate both secular and oscillatory effects, and, if those effects can be eliminated, what remains is surely of the greatest importance…"②

A number of different methods have been developed for eliminating the influence of the progressive, quasi-periodic, and irregular changes which take place as time goes on, but no one may be said to be entirely adequate to deal with the difficulties which arise from the inherent complexity of this type of problem.

It is observed that, for example, the effect of cotton price on acreage is only from one cropping to another. In such a case the correlation desired is between the changes of the cotton price from one year to the succeeding year, and accordingly we should correlate the first differences, or the link relatives, or

---

① Fisher, "The Influence of Rainfall on the Yield of Wheat", Phil. Trans. Roy. Soc., B., Vol. 213, p.99.

② Greenwood's discussion of Yule's paper "On the Time Correlation Problem", J.R.S.S., Vol.84, pp.528 – 529.

the rates of change① in order to obtain appropriate information of the relationship.

"Anything is a cause which antedates or accompanies a phenomenon."② The effects follow the causes as instant sequences in some cases and, in others, spread over long or short periods. Thus, the relation between two phenomena may be not only sequential but also "distributed" sequential. For instance, Fisher③ devised a technique of determining the "distributed lag" of the influence of the changes in prices on the volume of trade.

5.2 Considerations in Applying Correlation Analysis to Time Series

The correlation analysis, as we have seen in Chapters II and III, has been primarily developed by the astronomers and biometricians. Its adaptation to the problems of economic statistics needs further considerations with respect to the assumptions underlying the theory so that we may see whether the results obtained from time series can be compared and interpreted in the same manner as those obtained from non-time series for which the correlation analysis was originally developed.

In general, the formulas have been deduced upon the assumptions:④

---

① Cf. Sections 5.9, 5.12, and 5.13.

② Pearson, Grammar of Science, 3rd ed., pp.113 – 175. Here Pearson discusses beautifully the concepts of correlation and of causation. In the present text, the expression that one phenomenon is the effect of or depends upon another, is meant to include the alternative that both are actually influenced by a third set of causes.

③ Fisher, I., "Our Unstable Dollar and the So-called Business Cycle", J.A.S.A., Vol.20, pp.179 – 202.

④ Galton's original concept and Yule's theory of correlation (see descriptions of the contributions of Galton and Yule, Chapter III), primarily stress similarity or conformity, but neglect the distribution (whatever the form may be) or the variations of the variates, and, accordingly, do not involve these assumptions. For this reason, the theory of correlation as expounded by them is merely a theory of similarity in variations of variates, and the magnitude of the coefficient so computed is, not a measure of correlation in the sense explained in section 16 of Chapter III, but merely a relative expression for the degree of similarity, which cannot be given a probability interpretation and whose significance should be judged in the light of reason and other evidence, but not on the basis of the probable error which is deduced upon assumptions with respect to the form of distribution, to which no consideration has been given, by Yule, in the derivation of the formulas for the correlation coefficient. See also Gressens and Mouzon, "The Validity of the Correlation Coefficient and a New Coefficient of Similarity", J.A.S.A., Vol.22, pp.483 – 492.

(i) There are an indefinitely great number of contributory causes.

(ii) Each cause is itself equally likely to give rise to a contributory (or elementary) deviation or the same magnitude in excess and defect.

(iii) A statistical deviation (i.e., a direct or indirect observation measured from the mean) is the resultant of the numerous contributory deviations from the contributory causes (which are assumed independent, or correlated in a specified manner in the generalized hypothesis of elementary errors. Cf. Chapters II and III) and the contributory deviations are negligibly small when compared to the resultant deviation.

The assumptions are not fulfilled or not exactly fulfilled in many cases, especially in economics. A cause such as war, or strike, or development of new technique, etc., may give rise to a great change, say, of a certain price (or the installation of safety devices reduces the accident ratio in a given industry), and that change in price is evidently dominated by that cause. Thus, in economic statistics, we can no longer say that the contributory deviations arising from contributory causes are negligibly mall in comparison with the resultant deviation. Furthermore, the contributory causes likely operate① in a manner not as assumed.

In judging the significance of a correlation coefficient of time series, the test of significance or the probable error will no longer have the usual meaning,② since some, at least, of the assumptions upon which the theory of

---

① Cf. footnote 2 in p.290 of this book.

② The point that the usual formula for the standard error or probable error simply does not apply when we are dealing with correlations between time-series was made by Persons in 1924: "The probable error of coefficients of correlation (or other constants) computed from time series of economic statistics do not have the usual meaning. The theory or probability does not apply to our data because, first any past period that we select for study is, in fact, a special period with characteristics distinguishing it from other periods, and so cannot be considered a 'random' selection; second, the individual items of the series are not chosen independently, but they constitute a <u>group</u> of successive items with a characteristic conformation. Consequently, the probable error of 0.03 in the coefficient of correlation quoted above (i.e., the correlation coefficient between the cycles of pig-iron and interest rate with a lag of 6 months for 1903-1914 is +0.72) does not indicate, as one would conclude from the theory of probability, that if we compute a coefficient from 'any' other actual period, the chances are equal that it will be between +0.72 and +0.78. In fact, the significant of the probable error of a constant computed from time series is not known." (Handbook of Math. Stat., edited by Rietz, pp.162 – 163) It is therefore not surprising when we actually find that the correlation coefficient between the cycles of pig-iron production and of interest rates, with a lag of 6 months,

sampling distribution is built, do not hold. As Yule has pointed out:

"In obtaining the formula for the standard error (or the sampling distribution) we assume, to speak... in terms of drawing cards from a record: (1) that we are drawing throughout from the same aggregate and not taking one sample from one aggregate, a second sample from another aggregate, and so on; (2) that every card in each sample is also drawn from the same aggregate, in such a way that the 1st, 2nd,..., n-th card in any sample are each equally likely to be drawn from any part of the aggregate, not the first card from one batch, the second from another, and so on; (3) that the magnitude of x drawn on, say, the second card of the sample is quite independent of that on the first card, and so on for all other pairs in the sample; and similarly for y; there must be no tendency for a high value of x on the first card drawn to imply that the value of x on the second card will also probably be high; (4) in order to reduce the formula to the very simple form given, we have also to make certain assumptions as to the form of the frequency distribution in the correlation table for the aggregate from which the samples are taken (the

---

(footnote continued) for the period 1915-1918 is only +0.38 in comparison with +0.75 for 1903-1914. "We find sufficient explanation of this result, which is almost impossible and really astounding when viewed from the standpoint of random sampling, in the war demands for pig-iron, the tremendous imports of gold, government financing, and the inauguration of the Federal Reserve system during the period in question. As another illustration, "suppose we are considering the probability that 1924 will be a year of business depression and that we have the record of business conditions for the past 100 years in which there were 40 years of depression and 60 years of non-depression. Then, according to the statistical record, the probability that a year taken at random would be depressed in 4/10. But this probability cannot refer to 1924 unless that year is a random year, that is, unless we have no specific information that differentiates it from other years. In fact, we do have specific information about the economic conditions in 1923 and about the relation of economic conditions in consecutive years, which we cannot reasonably ignore, so that we cannot view 1924 as 'any' year taken at random. Every item of knowledge which we obtain bearing upon the situation in 1923 removes not only that year, but also 1924 one step further from its classification as 'random'. Such items of knowledge do not lead merely to continued revisions of the numerical probability that next year will be a year of depression; rather, they render inapplicable the method of mathematical probability, to the problem of making a rational forecast. Moreover, the actual statistical data utilized as a basis for forecasting economic conditions, such as a given time series of statistics for a selected period in the past, cannot be considered a random sample except in an unreal, hypothetical sense; that is to say, unless assumptions be made concerning our material which cannot be retained in actual practice. Any past period that we select for study is, in fact, a special period with characteristics distinguishing it from other periods, and in not 'random' with respect to the present. We must, therefore, discard statistical probability and arrive at a forecast for 1924 on another basis. Some Fundamental Concepts of Statistics", Op. Cit., pp.6-7.

sampling distributions have all been derived on the assumption that the parent population is of normal distribution)."①

Time series do not in the least resemble a random series, since the data necessarily refer to a continuous series of months or years, and the changes in both variables are more or less continuous.② However, in practical application, we need not confine ourselves to cases where these assumptions are strictly valid. Indeed, there is no other way available in practice. According to Mark H. Ingraham,③ the situation with respect to the reliability or dispersion of the correlation coefficient may be akin to that with respect to the Bernoulli, Poisson, and Lexis dispersions for one variable; under different assumptions for the distribution about a regression plane or surface, the results might well be even more precise than for random sampling from a constant universe. For this reason, he suggests that until more accurate formulas are developed, the reliability of a statistical derivate from times series may be assumed the same as it would be if the assumption of random sampling did apply.

5.3 Suggestions for Interpreting the Correlation Results

Although it is expedient to use the standard error or the sampling distribution as our initial basis for judging the significance of a correlation coefficient, the conclusion drawn from such basis does not command complete confidence as an accurate statement of probability, on account of the fact that the conditions justifying the use of the probable error or the sampling distribution, are far from being justified. In order to guard ourselves from any greet error, we must interpret the results in the light of experience, reason, and other statistical results. The stability④ of statistical results and agreement with

---

① Yule, "Why do We Sometimes Get Non-sense Correlations between Time Series", J. R. S. S., Vol.89, p.5.

② A price of a commodity, or the volume of production, or the income, etc., is not, at the time, a random item or sample from any larger homogeneous population. It is perhaps on this account that a method of similarity has been developed. But the theoretical reasons are nothing more than those given by Yule, and, moreover, no formula for the standard error sampling distribution is given. See Gressens and Mouzon, "A New Coefficient of Similarity", J. A. S. A., Vol,22, pp.483 – 492.

③ Discussions on Ezekiel's paper "The Application of the Theory Error", Proc. J.A.S.A., Vol.24, p.115, 1929.

④ "A stable empirical statistical result persisting over the entire range of our experience is precisely the same as a law of nature." Persons, "Some Fundamental Concepts of Stat.", Op. cit., p.5.

non-statistical evidence greatly increase the confidence in the conclusions drawn from the particular results of a statistical investigation. The following considerations may serve as some standards for this purpose: "first, if similar or consistent statistical results obtain for sub-periods; second, if similar or consistent statistical results obtain for other periods and under different circumstances; and third, if all of the statistical results agree with, are supported by, or can set in the framework of, related knowledge of a statistical or non-statistical nature."① Furthermore, just as the representative value of a mean must be judged by the form of the frequency distribution from which it is computed, so the representative value of a correlation coefficient must be judged by critical study of the materials, represented in a chart, combined in getting it.

5.4 Rational Hypotheses for Guiding the Search for Inter-relationship

The search for some hidden relationships between time series is likely to prosper, as suggested by Mitchell, if guided by rational hypotheses.

"These hypotheses usually occur to our minds in terms of cause and effect. What we know from non-statistical sources about business processes may suggest that the activities represented by one time series lead to consequences shown by one or more other series. Before plunging into the computations which such a notion suggests, it is wise to think out the hypotheses with care. Precisely what feature of the first series (regarded as being the cause) is causally important — the actual magnitudes as reported, the (absolute or relative) changes in these magnitudes from date to date, the percentage rates of change, the accumulated changes, the excess beyond some critical range, the ratio of the causal factor to some other variable, or what? Similarly: upon what feature of the series regarded as showing effects is the casual effect exercised? The suggestions just listed are possible answers to this question also. Is the relationship direct, or inverse? If the effect immediate or postponed? Is the effect cumulative? Does the effect change with the phases of business cycles? All these matters, and in many cases others, should be considered. often it is only by trial computations that one

---

① "A stable empirical statistical result persisting over the entire range of our experience is precisely the same as a law of nature." Persons, "Some Fundamental Concepts of Stat.", Op. cit., p.5.

can decide the issues raided; but they are best raised before computations are begun, and then thought out again in the light of what the computations suggest."①

5.5　Introduction to the History of the Applications of Correlation to Time Series

In order to make this chapter parallel in form and in substance to the preceding chapters, we now, survey the work that has been done in the adaptation of the correlation analysis to time series, with special emphasis on the new techniques of application. Inasmuch as the literature dealing with correlation of time series is very voluminous, I may have overlooked some of the contributions that should have found a place in thin treatise.

5.6　The First Application

An account of the early history of the application of correlation analysis to time series may be found in Yule's "The Applications of the Method of Correlation to Social and Economic Statistics". ② In this memoir, we see that the first application of the correlation analysis to time series was made by Yule in his investigations of pauperism. ③ Here we also find the first use of link relatives and the rates of change④ during a given period, instead of the values at a given time, as the quantities correlated. The investigation consists in finding the relation of changes in pauperism in each district to three other variates, viz., changes in (1) the ratio of out-relief to indoor relief, (2) the proportion of the aged (over 65 years of age) in the population, (3) the population itself. The

---

① Mitchell, Op. cit., p.269.

② J. R. S. S., Vol.72, pp.721 – 730, 1909.

③ "On the Correlation of Total Pauperism with Population of Out-Relief," Econ. Jour., Vol.5, p.603, and Vol.6, p.613, 1895.

④ "The changes in all these quantities were invariable measured as percentages. Thus, for example, let P_1 be the pauperism of any union in 1871, P_2 be its pauperism in 1881, then by the change in the pauperism during the decade I mean 100 ($P_2/P_1 - 1$) percent. To avoid dealing, however, with positive and negative signs, I have frequently used not the percentage change, but simply the percentage ratio, 100 P_2/P_1, e.g.: the value of the pauperism in the later year, taking the earlier year as 100." Yule, "The Causes of Changes in Pauperism", Op. Cit., p.254.

changes in each of these variables were tabulated for all the unions of England for the two inter-censual decades 1871 – 1881, and 1881 – 1891, and the correlations worked out for four separate groups of unions, classified by density of population. The results were discussed by means of the regression equations in four variables, the partial correlations not being used.

5.7 The Correlation between Deviations from Trends

In the investigation of correlation between marriage rate and trade, Hooker[①] noted that the changes in time series are of two distinct kinds; namely:

(i) Slow secular movements.

(ii) More or less rapid changes of sensible magnitude from year to year, and that the slow movements may be quite unrelated while the short period changes, are of extra-ordinarily close correspondence. He introduced, then, the "instantaneous average" (moving average), called by him the trend, so that the correlation coefficient was computed from the deviations of the two variates from the instantaneous average of each, instead of from the average of the whole period. In his problem, he regards it as being sufficient for practical purposes to take an average of nine years round a given year as the instantaneous average, and calculate the correlation coefficients between the oscillations accordingly.

Four years later in a paper "On the Correlation of Successive Observations",[②] Hooker gave an illuminating discussion of the necessity for illuminating the secular trend when correlation between short period changes only is to be expected. Thus, he says that the correlation coefficient " affords a test of similarity of the two phenomena as influenced by the totality of the causes affecting each of them. When, however, the observations extend over a considerable period of time, certain difficulties arise in discussing the relations between the two variables. These difficulties, which find no precise parallel in the case where the whole of the observations refer to the same moment or time, are due to the fact that outside conditions, i.e., those affecting the variables unequally — may be very different after a certain period, so that the values of

---

① "Correlation of the Marriage Rate with Trade", J. R. S. S., Vol.64, p.485.
② J. R. S. S., Vol. 68, p.696.

the two variables may have been considerably and unequally modified by them. If a diagram be drawn, illustrating by 'curves' the changes of the two variables during the period under investigation, some relation will often be apparent (or suggested) between the usually smaller and more rapid alterations between successive observations, while the slower 'secular' changes may or may not exhibit any similarity. If, then, the correlation coefficient be formed in the ordinary way, we shall obtain (a) a value that is very high if the 'secular' changes are similar (the value being almost entirely independent of the similarity or otherwise of the more rapid changes), (b) a value approximating to 0 if the 'secular' changes are of quite dissimilar character, even although the similarity of the smaller rapid changes may be extremely marked. The 'secular', in fact, may entirely mask the other changes, and deductions drawn from the ordinary correlation coefficient as to the interdependence of the two phenomena may in such cases be erroneous. What is required is to eliminate in some way the changing influences which affect the two variables unequally". ①

Hooker's method of correlating the deviations from the trends, represented by moving averages or mathematical curves fitted by the method of least squares, has since been extensively used. The most convenient type of mathematical curves for this purpose is the orthogonal polynomials. ② Thus, if y and y' are the two quantities, whose values are ordered in time at equal intervals, to be correlated, and an orthogonal polynomial of t is fitted to each of them so that

$$Y = A + BT_1 + CT_2 + \text{etc.}$$
$$Y' = A' + B'T_1 + C'T_2 + \text{etc.}$$

where T_r is an orthogonal polynomial in t of r-th degree, then

$$A = \bar{y} = \frac{1}{N} \sum (y)$$
$$B = \frac{12}{N(N^2 - 1)} \sum (yT_1)$$
$$C = \frac{180}{N(N^2 - 1)(N^2 - 4)} \sum (yT_2)$$

---

① J. R. S. S., Vol. 68, p.696.
② Cf. Chap. III, or Fisher, Statistical Methods, p.126.

and, in general, the coefficient of the term of the r-th degree is

$$\frac{(2r)!\,(2r+1)!}{(r!)^4 N(N^2-1)\cdots(N^2-r^2)}\sum(yT_r).$$

And A', B', C', etc. have the same meaning, that is to substitute y' for y in the formulas.

Now the correlation coefficient between y and y' may be directly calculated from the coefficients of the equations given above. Thus, the sum of the squares of the deviations of the variates from the equations representing the trends are given by the following formulas:

$$(y-Y)^2 = \sum(y^2) - NA^2 - \frac{N(N^2-1)}{12}B^2 - \cdots,$$

$$(y'-Y')^2 = \sum(y'^2) - NA'^2 - \frac{N(N^2-1)}{12}B'^2 - \cdots,$$

while the sum of the products may be obtained from the similar equation

$$\sum\{(y-Y)(y'-Y')\} = S(yy') - NAA' - \frac{N(N^2-1)}{12}BB' - \cdots.$$

The required (partial) correlation is then

$$r_{yy't} = \frac{\sum\{(y-Y)(y'-Y')\}}{\sqrt{\sum(y-Y)^2\cdot\sum(y'-Y)^2}}.$$

"In this process it will be understood that both variates must be fitted to the same degree, even if one of them is capable of adequate representation by a curve of lower degree than is the other."①

If the trend exhibited in the two-time series could be represented effectively by a straight line, it would be sufficient, as has been demonstrated by Crum②, to consider time as a third variate and eliminate it by calculating the corresponding partial correlation coefficient:

$$r_{yy'\cdot t} = \frac{r_{yy'} - r_{yt}r_{y't}}{\sqrt{1-r_{yt}^2}\sqrt{1-r_{y't}^2}}.$$

---

① Fisher, Statistical Methods, p.175.
② Crum, "A Special Application of Partial Correlation", J. A. S. A., Vol.17, p.949.

5.8 Determination of the Temporal Order of the Occurrence of Fluctuations

If variations (or fluctuations) of one time series appear to precede or follow the corresponding variations of certain other time series by intervals of time, which are fairly constant, the average length of the intervals is called the lead or lag. The use of correlation method for determining the lag or one phenomenon behind certain other phenomenon was first made by Hooker in 1901 in his investigation of the correlation of the marriage rate with trade. He was led to the lag by the following question: Does the marriage-rate respond immediately to general property? "To answer this question, I have worked out the correlation coefficients of the marriage-rate with the trade of the same year, the previous year, and the following year, of half a year earlier, and half a year later (the trade of half a year earlier is taken as the mean of the trade of the year and the previous year). It at once appears that these coefficients, when plotted on a diagram, lie on a more or less smooth curve, in which a maximum is clearly indicated. And in this way, we can obtain, I think, a measure of the lag of one phenomenon behind another upon which it is in some way dependent. In the case of exports and the marriage-rate, for instance, it appears that a maximum coefficient (+0.86) is obtained by correlating the marriages with the exports of half a year earlier. Hence I conclude that, on the average of the thirty-five years, the marriage-rate follows the exports at an interval of half a year."①

This technique has since come into common use among economic statisticians.② Thus, by means of this technique, Persons was able to sort the several time series representing the various economic processes into groups so

---

① Hooker, "Correlation of the Marriage-rate with Trade", Jour. Roy. Stat. Soc., Vol.64, pp.487 – 489.

② Moore, "Economic cycles", p. 42, and cf. footnote 1 in p. 294 of this book. Persons, "Construction of a Business Barometer", American Economic Review, Vol.6, pp.740 – 769, 1916; "An Index of General Business Conditions", R. E. S., Vol.1, pp.111 – 151, 1919; "Correlation of Time Series", Handbook of Math. Statistics, edited by Rietz, Boston, pp.160 – 165, 1924. Hansen, Cycles of Prosperity and Depression, Madison, Wisconsin, p.38, 56, 60, 1920.

that after the secular trend and seasonal variation are eliminated, the series, in each group have similar and synchronous fluctuations and are combined into a synthetic index to epitomize certain business situations. Indeed, as Mitchell has pointed out: "it has been a leading aim of statistical research to determine the time sequence in which important series pass through the successive phases of business cycles, to find cases in which this sequence is fairly regular, and in such cases to measure the average intervals by which certain series or groups of series lead or lag behind others."①

The feature of the temporal order in the fluctuations of time series has been taken advantage of in business forecasting, but does not afford a basis for prediction with invariable accuracy.

"If certain changes in banking operations regularly preceded certain other changes in discount rate by a regular interval, the latter changes could be foretold as soon as the former changes had been reported. Further, if an invariable series of such time relations between the cyclical fluctuations of different economic processes could be discovered, and if this series returned upon itself in the sense that the last set of changes in one cycle preceded the first set of changes in the next cycle by a regular interval, then business forecasting could be raised to a quasi-mechanical level. No such chain of events with links of unchanging length has been discovered. Perhaps no statistician has expected to find such a chain."②

Thus, for the period 1879 – 1913, the cycles of price and pig iron production are concurrent. For the period 1879 – 1896, the pig-iron cycles precede price cycles by a year. For the period 1897 – 1913, the cycles of the two series are strongly concurrent.

Forecasting by means of the time-sequence feature is different from forecasting by means of a regression equation. The latter is a classical procedure

---

① Jerome, Migration and Business Cycles, pp. 83 – 88, 82 – 188; Mitchell, W. C., Business Cycles, p.281.

② Mitchell, W.C., Business Cycles, p.281.

of correlation analysis, ① adapted to time series, and the prediction is estimated quantitatively; while the former was developed in studies of time series representing economic processes② and the precision is made primarily of the time and direction, rather than the amount of the expected change. Examples of forecasting by means of a regression equation are numerous. ③ Works attempting to determine the factors affecting the price of a certain commodity④ or to determine the interrelationships of supply and price, ⑤ also belong to this class. For an illustration of forecasting by means of time sequence, we may mention the well-known "Harvard Business Index". ⑥

5.9 Correlation between First Differences

The method of correlating the first differences between the consecutive items of time series was first⑦ suggested by Hooker, in 1901, on "The

---

① See contributions of Yule, Chap. III.

② Persons' "Construction of a Business Barometer", 1916, seems to be the first in combining the method of determining the sequence by means of the correlation analysis, of which Hooker was the originator, with the method of forecasting by means of time sequence, which was an old idea since as early as 1875, Berner (Book of Prophecies. Brookmire says: "In extenuation it may be said that Berner deserves to be given prominence as the pioneer in the work of systematically forecasting business conditions in this country... His methods although crude, are not without points of resemblance to some at present in use." "Methods of Business Forecasting", Amer. Eco. Rev., Vol.3, p.41, footnote) used the pig-iron prices to forecast the business conditions and then, in 1911, a French commission appointed by the government prepared 8 indices of business conditions and said, by comparison of maxima and minima of the various indices with each other and with the dates of crises, "certain of these indices appear to precede crises and in some measure to forecast them. Others are concurrent" (Rapors sur les Indices des Crises économiques et sur Measures financières propre à atténuer les Chômages résultant de ces Crises, 1911). Persons' method has subsequently been extensive.

③ Moore's forecasting of the yield ratio of cotton, in Georgia, from the rainfall ratio for May and the temperature ratio for June is a typical example. Forecasting the Yield of Cotton from Weather Reports, 1917.

④ Hass and Ezekiel, Factors Affecting the Price of Hogs, Bul. 1440, U. S. Dept. of Ag., 1926. Working, Factors Affecting the Price of Minnesota Potatoes, Uni. Minn. Ag. Exp. Stat., Bul. 29, 1925.

⑤ Warren and Pearson, Interrelationships of Supply and Price, Cornell Uni. Ag. Exp. Stat., Bul. 466, 1928.

⑥ Harvard Eco. Rev., and Karsten, "The Harvard Business Index — A New Interpretation", J. A. S. A., Vol.21, p.409.

⑦ Yule, "On the Time Correlation Problem", J. R. S. S., Vol.48, p.499. Compare Pearson's statement in "Further Evidence of Natural Selection in Man", Biom., Vol.10. p.489.

Suspension of the Berlin Produce Exchange". ① In this memoir, Hooker worked out the correlations between the daily corn prices at Berlin, Liverpool, and Chicago for the years between 1892 and 1900, in order to see whether the Berlin market was as intimately connected with the rest of the world during the period 1807 – 1899, while the exchange was suspended, as previously. The results were irregular and unsatisfactory; and Hooker suggested in the conclusion that it would be better to "correlate the differences between prices on consecutive days, instead of the differences from the average prices". ②

The new method with illustrations was published in 1905. ③ The results obtained by the use of the first difference method were more consistent than the former results obtained by correlating the deviations from the trends, and on the whole it seemed that Berlin prices were not less dependent upon quotations at other markets while the produce exchange was suspended than they were before.

It is also of interest to note that, in the concluding paragraph of this article, Hooker laid down tentatively rules as to choice of methods of correlating the deviations from the average, the deviations from the trend, and the first differences. Thus, he says:

---

① J. R. S. S., Vol.64, p.574.

② It is of interest to note how the "mean daily movement" or a "measure of steadiness" (freedom from rapid changes) from day to day led Hooker to the conception of the first difference method. The mean daily movement is defined as

$$\text{M.D.M.} = \sum (x_1 \sim x_2)/n$$

where x_1 is the price on any one day, and x_2 that on the following day. "It is the measure adopted by Herr Mancke, except that he uses the total daily movement, i.e., $\sum (x_1 \sim x_2)$, instead of the mean and it certainly seems the most satisfactory." (p.592) In conclusion of this memoir, Hooker suggested the first difference method in the following manner: "With some hesitation I submit that, in a comparison of prices at different market, correlation may be a measure of the difference between the effect of world-wide influences (common to both markets) and local influences upon the price. But, bearing in mind what has been said on p.592 (i.e., the advantages of using M.D.M. as a measure of variability over the usual measure σ in the case of time series with a considerable trend) as to the greater suitability of the M.D.M., rather than the σ, as a measure of stability in such inquiries, I would suggest that the problem — to what extent do the fluctuations at one market follow those at another? — requires to be attacked by the use of some formula which should correlate the differences between the prices on consecutive days, instead of the differences from the average price." Hooker, "The Suspension of the Berlin Produce Exchange", J. R. S. S., Vol.64, pp.592 – 593 and 604.

③ Hooker, "On the Correlation of Successive Observations", Op. Cit.

"In conclusion, it hardly seems possible to lay down definite rules as to the particular values most desirable to use in forming the correlation coefficient in any particular inquiry. Perhaps it may be suggested that, speaking generally, in examining the relationship between two series of observations extending over a considerable period of time, correlation of absolute values (deviations from the arithmetic mean) is the most suitable test of 'secular' interdependence, and may also be the best guide when the observations tend to deviate from an average that may be regarded as constant. Correlation of the deviations from an instantaneous average (or trend) may be adopted to test the similarity of more or less marked periodic influences. Correlation of the difference between successive values will probably prove most useful in cases where the similarity of the shorter rapid changes (with no apparent periodicity) is the subject of investigation, or where the normal level of one or both series of observations does not remain constant. It may even, in certain cases, be desirable to combine the two methods, and to correlate the deviations from the mean in the one series with the successive changes of the other." ①

In 1904, Miss Cave② correlated the corresponding differences of the successive (daily) readings of the barometric heights at two stations and therefore may be said to have reached the first difference method independently.③ Miss Cave did not give any reason for the choice of the daily rise or fall as the variable to be correlated. In a later paper④ by Cave and Pearson, it is stated, however, in the introductory paragraph, that Miss Cave "endeavored to get rid of seasonal change by correlating first differences of daily reading at two stations". This then assigns the same reason as is given by Hooker for the use of the first difference method: the use of first difference represents an attempt to get at the correlation of short period, as against long period, changes.

---

① Hooker, "On the Correlation of Successive Observations", Op. Cit., p.703.

② "The Time Factor in the Correlation in the Barometric Heights", Proc. Roy. Soc., Vol. 74, p.403.

③ "The method was used by Miss Cave in Proc. Roy. Soc., Vol.74, p.407 et seq., that is in 1904, but being used incidentally in the course of a paper, it attracted less attention than Hooker's paper which was devoted to describing the method. The papers were no doubt quite independent." "Student", "The Elimination of Spurious Correlation due to Position in Time or Space", Biom., Vol.10, p.179, footnote.

④ "Numerical Illustrations of the Variate Difference Correlation Method", Biom., Vol.10, p.340.

Furthermore, in 1905, March① dealt with the same method, and generally speaking, his ideas seem very similar to those of Hooker. According to Yule②, his work is independent of those by Cave and Hooker.

As Persons has demonstrated, the coefficient of correlation between the first differences of the successive items of the original data and that between the first differences of the deviations from straight lines representing secular trends are identical. ③ "Significant coefficients of correlation for first differences indicate that the cyclical fluctuations (i. e., fluctuations about the secular trend for annual series) synchronize, if there be cyclical fluctuations. Evidence of such cycles may be secured by plotting the deviations from the assumed secular trend."④

5.10 Correlation between Higher Differences

In 1915, "Student"⑤ generalized the "variate difference correlation method"⑥ by showing: (i) that, if $X_1, X_2, \cdots, X_n$ and $Y_1, Y_2, \cdots, Y_n$ be corresponding values of the variates X and Y, such that they are randomly distributed in time or space, the correlation between the corresponding n-th differences is the same as that between X and Y; and (ii) that, if $x_1, x_2, \cdots, x_n$ and $y_1, y_2, \cdots, y_n$ are corresponding values of the variates x and y such that

$$x_i = X_i + bt_i + ct_i^2 + \cdots + kt_i^n$$
$$y_i = Y_i + b't_i + c_i t_i^2 + \cdots + k't_i^n \qquad (5 \cdot 1)$$

where $i = 1, 2, \cdots, N$ and X_i and Y_i are independent of time or space [i. e., have the same meaning as in (i)], and since each differencing reduces one

---

①   Op. Cit.
②   "The paper by Monsieur March... reviews the whole problem, evidently independently", "On the Time Cor.", Op. Cit., p.500.
③   Persons, "Correlation Method and Curve Fitting", Jour. Amer. Stat. Ass., Vol.15, p.602.
④   Persons, ibid., p.622.
⑤   "Student", "The Elimination of Spurious Correlation due to Time or Space", Biom., Vol.10, p.179.
⑥   The term was introduced by Cave and Pearson, "Illustrations of the Variate Difference Correlation Method", Biom., Vol.10, p.340.

degree of the polynomials in t (equation 5 · 1) and therefore x_i and y_i in the n-th difference will be independent of t, the correlation between the n-th differences of x and y is the same as that between X and Y and is also, by (i), the same as that between the differences of $(n + 1)$-th, $(n + 2)$-th, etc., differences of x and y. Thus "Student" concludes that "if we wish to eliminate variability due to position in time or space and to determine whether there is any correlation between the residual variations, all that has to be done is to correlate the 1st, 2nd, 3rd, $\cdots$, n-th differences between successive values of our variable with the 1st, 2nd, 3rd $\cdots$ n-th differences between successive values of the other variable. When the correlation between the two n-th differences is equal to that between the two $(n + 1)$-th differences, this value gives the correlation required".① The meaning of "Student" is that the correlation required is indicated by the ultimate steadiness of values of the correlation coefficient for higher multiple differences of the item. ②

In the same year, Anderson provided the probable errors of the successive difference correlations, when they become steady, of a system of variates:

$$X_1, X_2, X_3, \cdots, X_N,$$
$$Y_1, Y_2, Y_3, \cdots, Y_N,$$

where the correlations of random pairs of values in each series of values are zero.

Anderson further gave the values of the standard deviations of the successive differences, i. e.,

$$\sigma_{\delta^m X} \text{ and } \sigma_{\delta^m Y}$$

which represent the ultimate values of $\sigma_{\delta^m X}$ and $\sigma_{\delta^m Y}$ when we have carried to the m-th difference so that the series has become steady.

Moreover, Cave and Pearson gave numerical illustrations of the variate difference correlation method by applying it to fifteen Italian indexes.

The nature and the utility of the variate difference method has been more

---

① Op. Cit., p.180.
② Pearson and Cave, "The Variate Difference Method", Biom., Vol.10, p.340, footnote.

clearly brought out by the criticisms and rejoinders to the criticisms of the method by Persons①, Yule②, Greenwood③, Pearson④, Anderson⑤ and Fisher⑥.

According to Fisher, the repeated differencing of the observed data belongs to the same class of procedure as computing deviations from smoothed values determined by:

(i) Fitting a polynomial or other curve to the whole of the data.

(ii) Using the "smooth" values obtained by compounding a number of neighboring terms such as moving averages; and the main draw of this class of methods is reduced to minimum by the use of polynomials fitted to the whole series. The exposition of this proposition is well stated in the following extensive extract from Fisher. ⑦

"In all these cases the resulting residuals designed for use as correlation variates may be successfully freed of any slow progressive trend which vitiates the original series; but in all cases this is achieved by entangling together to some extent the successive values. This effect is inevitable, for we must judge of the smooth value from which our residual is measured by the values at neighboring epochs."

"It might appear that simple differencing should be placed in a separate class, since here no smooth value objectively appears. There is no essential difference however; for if $2r$ is any even integer, we can construct a function,

$$v = u - (-1)^r k \delta^{2r} u,$$

which is in effect the smooth value, the deviations from which are proportional to the $(2r)$-th differences; to make $\bar{v}^2$ a minimum for a series of equally variable quantities in random order we require

---

① "On the Variate Difference Correlation Method", Pub. Amer. Stat. Ass., Vol.15, p.602.
②③ "On the Time Correlation Problem", J. R. S. S., p.497.
④ Pearson and Elderton "On the Variate Difference Method", Biom., Vol.14, p.281.
⑤ Anderson, "Nochmals uber 'The Elimination of Spurious Correlation due to Position in Time or Space", Biom., Vol.10, p.269, Biom., Vol.15, p.134; and Biom., Vol.18, p.293.
⑥ Fisher, "The Influence of the Rainfall on the Yield of Wheat at Rothamsted", Phil. Trans. Roy. Soc., B. Vol.213, p.89.
⑦ "The Influence of Rainfall on the Yield of Wheat at Rothamsted", Op. Cit., pp.103–107.

$$k = \frac{(2r!)^3}{(r!)^2 4r!}.$$

Thus, the smooth value corresponding to 6th difference is

$$v_0 = u_0 + \frac{5}{231}\delta^6 u_0$$

$$= \frac{1}{231}\{131 u_0 + 75(u_1 + u_{-1}) - 30(u_2 + u_{-2}) + 5(u_3 + u_{-3})\}.$$

The formula so obtained is identical with that given by Sheppard (15, p.31), for 7 point smoothing, using a polynomial of the 5th degree. The variate difference method is therefore only an extreme form of the use of Sheppard's smoothing formula — the extreme in which the number of terms is a minimum for given degree of the slow change eliminated — while the other extreme is represented by the process of fitting a polynomial of the required degree to the whole of the series."

"In treating these three processes as special forms of Sheppard's smoothing process one distinction must be made. In fitting a polynomial to the whole of the series we wish to use not only the residual of the middle term, but the whole series of residuals. So in using smooth values from (say) a 15 point formula, the first and last seven residuals may be obtained from the curves fitted to the first and last sets of 15 points. In the applications which have been made of the Variate Difference Method, only the residuals of the middle terms have been used. The number in the series has been diminished by one with each differencing; if however, we wish to add the missing terms, this is easily done by means of binomial coefficients; for example if a, b, c are the sixth differences of a series, the three missing residuals prior to a are as follows: $-\frac{a}{20}$, $+\frac{6}{20}a$, $-\frac{15}{20}a$, a, b, c, ..."

"The effects of such processes in entangling the neighboring terms may best be seen by considering the effect of applying them to an unchanging series (i.e., random with respect to time) of equally variable quantities. If u stands for such a quantity, then, for example, the sixth difference may be written

$$v = -20u_0 + 15(u_1 + u_{-1}) - 6(u_2 + u_{-2}) + (u_3 + u_{-3}),$$

hence evidently,

$$\overline{v^2} = +924\,\overline{u^2},$$

$$\overline{v_p v_{p+1}} = -792\,\overline{u^2},$$

$$\overline{v_p v_{p+2}} = +496\,\overline{u^2},$$

and so on, the numerical coefficients being those of the expansion $(1+x)^{12}$. Consequently, the correlations between neighboring values of v will be

$$r_1 = -\frac{6}{7} = -0.857\,1,\quad r_2 = \frac{5}{8}\cdot\frac{6}{7} = +0.535\,7,$$

$$r_3 = -\frac{4}{9}\cdot\frac{5}{8}\cdot\frac{6}{7} = -0.238\,1,\quad r_4 = +0.071\,4,$$

$$r_5 = -0.013\,0,\quad r_6 = +0.001\,1."$$

"If such high correlations as these are produced in an originally uncorrelated series, it is clear that they cannot be used without drastic correction in an examination into such correlations between neighboring terms as exist in the original series. Equally large are the effects when two separate series are correlated. If we take, for example, a second series u', and obtain

$$v' = \delta^6 u',$$

then if the original two series were correlated so that

$$\overline{u_p u'_{p+R}} = \rho_R \sqrt{\overline{u^2}\cdot\overline{u'^2}},$$

it is easy to see that the correlations obtained from the 6th differences will be expressible in terms of the ρ series, in the form

$$r_R = \frac{1}{924}(\delta')^2 \rho_R."$$

"By such a method there we shall not obtain the true values ρ, but quantities proportional to the 12th differences of the series. Only if all values of ρ, except one, vanish, and we correlate the corresponding values of u and u', will we obtain an estimate of the correlation unaffected by gross inaccuracy. This constitutes a fatal objection to the applications which have been made of the variate difference method in its original form."

"The same source of error still persists in more moderate degree when smoothing formulae involving more terms are used. Let us take for example Sheppard's formula for fitting a polynomial of the δ-th degree to sets of 18 points. The smoothed middle point is

$$\left(1 - \frac{50}{11}\delta^6 + \frac{75}{13}\delta^8 + \frac{36}{13}\delta^{10} + \frac{10}{17}\delta^{12} + \frac{15}{373}\delta^{14}\right) u;$$

whence we have the residual

$$v = \frac{1}{11 \cdot 13 \cdot 17 \cdot 19} \{35\ 126 u_0 - 10\ 125(u_1 + u_{-1}) - 7\ 500(u_2 + u_{-2})$$
$$- 3\ 755(u_3 + u_{-3}) + 165(u_4 + u_{-4}) - 2\ 937(u_5 + u_{-5})$$
$$+ 2\ 860(u_6 + u_{-6}) - 2\ 145(u_7 + u_{-7})\}.$$

The correlations between neighboring terms of an originally uncorrelated series now become

$$r_1 = -0.307\ 5, \quad r_6 = +0.122\ 1, \quad r_{11} = +0.009\ 9,$$
$$r_2 = -0.237\ 0, \quad r_7 = -0.156\ 5, \quad r_{12} = -0.002\ 7,$$
$$r_3 = -0.111\ 9, \quad r_8 = -0.013\ 2, \quad r_{13} = -0.007\ 6,$$
$$r_4 = +0.035\ 5, \quad r_9 = +0.007\ 2, \quad r_{14} = +0.002\ 8.$$
$$r_5 = +0.144\ 0, \quad r_{10} = +0.015\ 8,$$

The correlations are now much more moderate. Their alterations are less violent, and since their sum is compelled to be -0.5, their actual values are permitted to be considerably smaller. Such values are, however, sufficiently large to show that great inaccuracy will be introduced if we ascertain the mutual correlations of members of a series from those of the residuals from smooth values obtained from 15 adjacent points."

"It is evident also that, apart from the question of the correlation of successive values, the correlations between two series will be vitiated in the same manner as by the variate difference method, though to a less degree; the correlations obtained may be expressed in terms of high differences of the true correlations, for if we write

$$\varphi(\delta^2) = \frac{50}{11}\delta^6 + \frac{75}{13}\delta^8 + \frac{36}{13}\delta^{10} + \frac{10}{17}\delta^{12} + \frac{15}{323}\delta^{14},$$

and $\varphi^2(\delta^2)$ for $\{\varphi(\delta^2)\}^2$,

then we have
$$r_k = \frac{\varphi^2(\delta^2)\rho_k}{\varphi^2(\delta^2)\rho_0}.\text{''}$$

"The general problem of eliminating the cross correlations from a pair of series showing slow changes is extremely complex; in the simplest case each value of the one series is correlated with only two adjacent values of the second series. To this case probably belongs the relation of wheat crop to weather, for the crop is admittedly much affected by the weather in the harvest year, and may to a much less extent be influenced, through the condition of the seed, or of the soil, by the weather of the previous year …"

"The two series of infantile death rates in the first and second years of life, are probably connected principally, if not wholly, by the fact that the mortality, in any one year, of children in the second year of life, refers to nearly the same group of children as the mortality in the previous year of children in the first year of life; and by the second fact that mortality in the two age groups during the same year will be conditioned by the same meteorological and epidemiological conditions. If the first effect is the main object of study, the latter will appear as a cross correlation introducing errors into our estimate of the first effect, according to the method of estimation employed."

"In 1918 Elderton and Pearson found, using the variate difference method, the value -0.688 for the correlation between t the mortalities of the same group of children (males) in the two years. In 1923 the same authors using Sheppard's 15-point smoothing formula find the value -0.463. The discrepancy is very great and suggests that the neglect of the correlation between the mortalities of the two groups of children in the same year has produced a large negative bias, which is more pronounced in the earlier estimate. Fitting a polynomial to the whole series further diminishes, though it does not eliminate, the error; for the polynomials of the 4th, 5th, and 6th degrees we find the values -0.308, -0.311, -0.377."

"Now, assuming that only two correlations are really operative, these values may be corrected by calculating in a similar manner the apparent correlations in mortality for the two groups of children in the same year. These values are +0.470 6, +0.545 6 and +0.521 7; taking, then, the correlation between successive residuals of a series of n terms fitted by a polynomial of degree r to be $-(r + 1) / (n - 1)$, we have the equations

4th degree	$\rho_0 - 0.087\,7\rho_1 = -0.308\,3$	$\rho_0 = -0.269\,1$
	$-0.087\,7\rho_0 + \rho_1 = +0.470\,6$	
5th degree	$\rho_0 - 0.105\,3\rho_1 = -0.310\,9$	$\rho_0 = -0.256\,3$
	$-0.105\,3\rho_0 + \rho_1 = +0.545\,6$	
6th degree	$\rho_0 - 0.122\,8\rho_1 = -0.376\,8$	$\rho_0 = -0.317\,5$
	$-0.122\,8\rho_0 + \rho_1 = +0.521\,7$	

The values of ρ_0 obtained from these equations are unbiased estimates of the correlation required; they agree in indicating a correlation about -0.3. This value may be confirmed from the figures given by Pearson and Elderton for their 15-point smooth curve, which lead to the equations

$\rho_0 - 0.307\,5\rho_1 = -0.454\,8$	$\rho_0 = -0.280\,8$
$-0.307\,5\rho_0 + \rho_1 = +0.652\,1$	

The concordance of these results indicates that whereas the variate difference method has exaggerated the value of this correlation to the extent of more than doubling it, the correlation of residuals from the 15-point smooth curve has reduced the error to about 50 percent, and is moreover capable of correction provided only a few important correlations are present. The method of polynomial fitting has introduced errors of about 20 percent only, and the correction applied to it may be expected to be for this reason all the more precise."

On the whole, the method of correlating the higher differences theoretically suffers great defects and practically is laborious. It is not commonly used.

5.11 Adaptation of the Analysis of Variance to Ascertaining Correlation of Time Series

In connection with the investigation of crop variation, Fisher[1] developed

---

[1] Fisher, "Crop Variation", Jour. Ag. Sc., Vol.11, pp.107 – 135; Vol.13, pp.311 – 320. And "The Influence of Rainfall on the Yield of Wheat", Op. Cit.

the technique of applying the analysis of variance method to ascertain the correlation of time series. This technique has since been used by other statisticians.① For a full discussion of the technique, reference must be made to the original papers, since the principle of the method has been given in Chapter IV and the detail of the technique of applying to a particular problem is too lengthy for inclusion here.

5.12 Correlation between Link Relatives

Correlation between the links or the rates of changes of the successive values of the variates in consideration is quite similar to that between the first differences, in the sense that the correlation so determined signifies the relationship between changes in the variates from time to time. There is, however, an essential difference which should be observed in making the choice between them, that the former process automatically eliminates at the same time a progressive change exhibiting in the series which may be effectively represented by an exponential or compound interest curve while the latter eliminates a progressive change which may be represented by a straight line.②

As we have seen above, Yule was the first to use link relatives as the variates to be correlated. In 1911, Irving Fisher correlated the link relatives of the actual price level (denoted by P) and the estimated price level denoted by P', computed from the other quantities in his equation of exchange, i. e., P' is computed from the equation

$$P' = \frac{MV + M'V'}{T}$$

so as to show the goodness of the representation of the relationship between the price level or purchasing power of money and the quantity of money. Fisher's choice of the link relatives as the variates to be correlated is explained in the following manner:

"The proper method of applying a coefficient of correlation to successive date appears to be to calculate the coefficient, not for the raw figures, but for

---

① See section 9 of Chapter IV.
② For further discussion on the rates of change, see a later section.

their successive year-to-year ratios. In other words, we tabulate and compare the ratios of each year's P to the preceding year's P and of each year's $(MV + M'V')/T$ to the preceding year's $(MV + M'V')/T$. If the two sets of ratios should rise or fall together, the curves would show a close parallelism or agreement in their successive changes of direction.

In short, the choice of the particular form in which the series should be expressed depends upon the object of the correlation sought and the nature of the data.

5.13 Correlation between Rates of Change

Link relatives for items equally spaced in time are a form of rates of change, but the correlation analysis has also been applied to rates of change expressed in other forms. The rate of change for any given period of time, as originally used by Yule① was measured by subtracting the item for the preceding period from that for the given period and reducing the result to a percentage of the given period, but its recent form② as modified by Irving Fisher is measured by subtracting the item for the preceding period from that for the succeeding (instead of the given) period and reducing the result to percentage of the intervening (i.e., the given) period.

According to Fisher,③ rising but not high prices temporarily stimulate trade and falling but not low prices depress trade. For this reason, he correlated, in an endeavor to show that wherever the dollar suffers wide fluctuations in purchasing power, those fluctuations largely predetermine or, at any rate, precede closely related fluctuations in trade, the rate or change, or the slope P', of the price level P with the volume of trade T. Furthermore, Fisher says that to eliminate the secular trend from the price level is almost an useless procedure,

---

① See section 5.6 and footnote 4 in p.301 of this book.

② Fisher, "Our Unstable Dollar and the So-called Business Cycle", J. A. S. A., Vol.20, pp.181 – 182, and The Theory of Interest, Chap. XIX. See also Sasuly, "The Simplest Symmetrical Expression for Rate of Change", J. A. S. A., Vol.25, p.72. If x_i be the item for the i-th period of time and x_{i-1} and x_{i+1} be respectively the item for the preceding and succeeding periods, then Fisher's expression for the rate of change for the given period is: the rate change for the i-th period = $(\dfrac{x_{i+1} - x_{i-1}}{x_i}) \times 100$.

③ Fisher, "Our Unstable Dollar and the So-called Business Cycle", J. A. S. A., Vol.20, p.179.

not only because the price level cannot properly be said to have any secular trend, or long time tendency in one direction, but also because, to eliminate any such supposed trend is to throw away a part of the rise or fall, which is the very important factor, and that the rate of change, P', "supplies an oscillating barometer without requiring any of the corrections for secular trend and seasonal variation found necessary in most 'cycle' data".

5.14 Distributed Lag

In an endeavor to obtain the maximum correlation between fluctuations of the dollar (i.e., the rate of change of the price level) and the volume of trade, Fisher[1] used the correlation analysis to determine a "distributed lag" in place of the fixed lag determined according to the usual method. As Fisher explains:

"The reason for distributing the lag is that the full effect of each P' (P' is the rate of change of the price level, P. For the definition of the rate of change, see section 13), item is extremely unlikely to be felt at only one instant, such as seven months later, and not felt at any other time either earlier or later than seven months. Can we imagine that the sharp rise of prices in April 1917, did not begin to affect trade until November, 1917, and that then the whole effect suddenly exploded, as it were? It is far more probable that the influence began at once, showing itself in the very next month, May, and that it then gradually increased to a maximum a few months later and thereafter tapered off indefinitely according to the probability distribution. It stands to reason that some industries respond more promptly than others and that even the same industry feels the influence not as a sudden jolt but in a graduated crescendo and diminuendo."

The type of probability curve according to which the lag is assumed to be distributed, is selected so that it "most nearly accounts for the behavior of T (the volume of trade)". In other words, he selects the type of probability curve, by an elaborate set of experiments, such that the correlation coefficient for P' and T, with the lag so distributed according to that type of probability curve is practically the highest. In his problem, Fisher found as the appropriate type the normal curve with the abscissa in logarithmic scale,

---

[1] Fisher, "Our Unstable Dollar and the So-called Business Cycle", J. A. S. A., Vol.20, p.179.

i. e., the trans-formed normal curve by substituting for each abscissa of the ordinary normal curve its logarithm, and obtained a correlation coefficient equal to 0.941, in comparison with 0.727 for a fixed lag of seven months in volume of trade.

Thus, Fisher developed a more realistic concept of lag and applied the correlation analysis to the determination of how the lag is likely distributed, although the method of procedure, by trial and error, is laborious.

5.15 Further Methods of Determining Correlation

We must teat content with mere mention of a number of special methods of correlation analysis.① We have not touched on the methods② of dealing with correlation of charterers which do not seem to admit of exact measurement, but of classification. Thus, we classify a given population into a twofold classification according to the presence or absence of a certain attribute or charterer such as the blind and seeing or the dumb and speaking, or into a manifold classification according to the intensity of a certain attribute or character such as the division of the eye-colours under the three headings: "blue", "grey and green", and "brown". The correlation between such characters has been dealt with in some cases by the method of tetrachoric correlation, ③ in other cases by the method of contingency④ and in cases, where the items are ordered but not measured, by

---

① In economic statistics, we deal usually not with the original observations, but with average values—index numbers of prices, production, trade, bank clearings, etc. Such averages cannot be regarded as discrete values because, owing to the operation of taking the means, a continuous transition of these extreme values into the intermediate values must be assumed. This is one reason why we have confined this treatise to the correlation theory with respect to continuous variates.

② A good exposition of the various methods may be found in Kelley's Statistical Methods, and Yule's An Introduction to the Theory of Statistics, 9th ed.

③ Pearson, "On the Correlation of Characters not Quantitatively Measurable", Phil. Trans. Roy. Soc., A., Vol.195, p.1. For a criticism, see Yule, "On the Methods of Measuring the Association between Two Attributes", J. R. S. S., Vol. 75, p.579; and for a rejoinder to the criticism, see Pearson and Heron, "On Theories of Association", Biom., Vol.9, p.159.

④ Pearson, "On the Theory of Contingency", Drapers' Co. Research Memoirs, Biom., Series, 1, Lipps, "Die Bestimmung der Abhangigkeit zwischen den Merkmalen eines Gegenstandes", Berrichte der math. phys. Klasse der kgl. Sachsischen Gesellschafte der Wissenschaften, and Pearson, "On a Coef. Class Heterogeneity or Divergence", Biom. Vol.5, p.198.

the method of the correlation in ranks.① Gini's② methods of connection for dealing with correlation, the work of Tschuprow③ on correlation which has taken an important step toward connecting the regression method of dealing with correlation more closely with the theory of probability, and Bachelier's④ treatment of continuous probabilities of two or more variables have also been omitted.

Although the many omissions make it fairly obvious that this history is not at all complete, it is hoped that the foregoing chapter will suffice to indicate the stages the correlation theory has passed through and that the correlation analysis as methodology of science should be further improved and extended.

5.16 Conclusion

In conclusion we may well quote a remark given by Zizek in the introduction of his Statistical Averages with regard to the use of Averages; since this remark is equally applicable to correlation coefficients:

"... The application of averages has, as is well known, given rise to controversies of various kinds, which fill a considerable part of statistical literature. Not infrequently the incorrect use of averages has also led to erroneous conclusions and to contradictions which have shaken our confidence in statistics. Averages, indeed, are only applicable under strictly defined conditions, and conclusions based on averages are likewise permissible only within well-defined limits. It is the task of statistical science to investigate the application and use of averages from the general methodological standpoint, and to determine the part which averages should play in statistical methods."

---

① Pearson, "On further Methods of Determining Correlation", Drapers' Co. Research Memoirs, Biom., series, IV., p.10.

② Gini, "Nouvi Contributi alla Teoria delle Relazioni Statistiche", Atti del R. Instituts Veneto de S. L. A., Tome 74, p.II, and "Some Contributions of Italy to Modern Statistical Methods", J. R. S. S., Vol.89, p.703.

③ Tschuprow, Grundbegriffe und Grundproblame der Korrelations-theorie.

④ Bachelier, Calcul des probabilities.

CHAPTER VI   SUMMARY

6.1 Introduction

This thesis is an exposition of the basic concepts and methods in correlation analysis, with especial attention to their applications to economic statistics, in conjunction with a survey of their historical development.

Correlation analysis is designed to determine the existence, the type, and the intensity of relationship between two or more directly or indirectly observed variates.

There are four problems in correlation analysis:

(1) The choice of mathematical formulas for describing the correlation in question, for example, the choice between a normal surface or Charlier A-function, etc., in the correlation surface method; or between a straight line or parabola, etc., in the regression method.

An objective and efficient criterion for testing the fitness of the selected formula for the data is needed in order to remove dangers of empiricism or personal "taste" in making choice of formula.

(2) Estimation of the parameters, in the formulas for the description of correlation, from a given sample of observations on the variates.

Among the three methods of estimation, namely, (i) the method of least squares, (ii) the method of moments, (iii) the method of maximum likelihood, the method of maximum likelihood is theoretically the best.

(3) Determination of the Sampling Distribution of the estimated parameters.

A knowledge of such distributions makes it possible to infer, from the evidence of a sample the probable nature or the sampled population and of further samples and to test whether a given body of available observations is or is not in agreement with any suggested hypothesis.

(4) Application.

The Application of correlation analysis is an entirely different art from the development or the elaboration of a system of concepts, logical and mathematical, of the principles of correlation analysis. It involves the interpretation of the statistical results in light of the special characteristics and circumstances of the particular field in which the problem belongs.

Four methods of correlation analysis have been developed. They are: (i) the correlation surface method, (ii) the regression method, (iii) the analysis of variance method, and (iv) the matrix method. These four methods are related in certain respects, as we have pointed out in Chapter I. In the case of normal distributions, each method will lead to identical results; but in non-normal distributions, the descriptive information yielded is not the same for all four methods.

6.2 The Essential Features of the Four Methods of Determining Correlation

The correlation between a set of variates, say, x_1, x_2, $\cdots$, x_n, is completely known if the probability for the occurrence of any value of a variate, say, x_n, can be determined after each of the other $n - 1$ variates is known to have taken a specified value. This probability can be determined only when the law of frequency distribution of the n variates is known. The correlation surface method will yield complete information about correlation between variates, since the correlation surface represents the law or frequency distribution.

A correlation surface is equivalent to a scientific law stated in general terms as follows:

If each of certain conditions is known to exist, then a specified event has a definite probability of occurrence.

If the correlation function of n variates is geometrically represented in a rectangular system of coordinates in space of $n + 1$ dimensions so that the variates are reckoned along the n axes and the frequency, $w = F(x_1, x_2, \cdots, x_n)$, of any system of values of the variates is reckoned along the $(n + 1)$-th axis (or the w-axis), the correlation surface of the n variates is obtained. If contours are cut out of the correlation surface by planes parallel to, say, $(x_n w)$-plane, we obtain the partial frequency curves, representing the array distribution of the variate x_n of the $(x_1 x_2 \cdots x_{n-1})$-type. A correlation surface may be considered as the continuum or locus of these partial frequency curves, so its form must depend upon their characteristics. A partial frequency curve, just as an ordinary frequency curve, depends in its position on the mean, and in its form on the variance, the skewness, and the kurtosis. The loci of the mean, variance, skewness, and kurtosis of the partial frequency curves are respectively called the regression, scedastic, clitic, and kurtic curves. These curves are characteristic properties of a correlation surface. Furthermore, if the contours cut out of the correlation surface by planes parallel to $(x_1 \, x_2 \cdots x_n)$ -hyperplane are projected on that plane we obtain the curves of equal frequency. These curves may be considered as the fifth characteristic property of correlation surface.

The regression curve of x_n on $x_1, x_2, \ldots, x_{n-1}$ is given by

$$\frac{\int x_n w(x_1, x_2, \ldots, x_n) \, \mathrm{d}x_n}{\int w(x_1, x_2, \ldots, x_n) \, \mathrm{d}x_n} = f(x_1, x_2, \ldots, x_{n-1})$$

which may in some cases, but may not in others, be written in the form: $a + f_1(x_1) + f_2(x_2) + \cdots + f_{n-1}(x_{n-1})$.

Camp has shown that the total and partial regression curves must be mutually consistent.

At the present time, methods have not been developed except in the case of normal distribution, for determining the correlation surface from a knowledge of these characteristics. However, if we agree that the mean, variance, skewness, and kurtosis are quite competent for describing a frequency distribution, then the four curves may be regarded as a quite competent description of relationship between variates.

The regression method, as commonly used, amounts to taking the first two characteristics (i.e., the regression curve, representing the type, linear, or non-linear of relationship, and the scedastic curve in units of standard deviation, σ_n, of the essential or dependent variate, measuring the lack of perfection in the correlation as represented by the regression curve) of a correlation surface for describing correlation and is therefore not adequate.

The method of the analysis of variance, developed by R. A. Fisher, divides the variance in the essential variate into parts representing the variances ascribable to the respective associate variates considered as causes of variations, and to the "residual random error", in order to test whether the variation in each of the associate variates is significantly accompanied by variation in the essential variate. The analysis of variance method is developed on the assumption of a normal population and is thus not applicable, strictly speaking, to cases of non-normal distributions.

The matrix method, developed by Ragnar Frisch, studies correlation by means of a matrix which specifies the characteristics of the linear dependence of the variates and the determinant value of which represent the intensity of the correlation. The matrix method is limited to the linear type of correlation.

6.3 Development of the Correlation Surface Method

The normal bivariate function was first derived on a genetic basis by Laplace. In the 1870s, Galton came to the conception of correlation from his inquiry into the inheritance of men and then sought a formula to express the result of his statistical data. In 1886, with the assistance of Dickson, Galton found the normal bivariate surface to be the required formula. Since then, the correlation analysis has been rapidly developed for studying observational data where we can observe the occurrence of the various possible contributory causes of a phenomenon or quantity, but cannot control them.

The correlation surface method has been mainly developed by Laplace, Bravais, Galton, Edgeworth, Pearson, Charlier, Wicksell, and others.

Proofs for normal multi-variate correlation surface has been given by Gauss, Bravais (tri-variate), Edgeworth, and Pearson. To deal with skew correlation by the correlation surface method, we have only the Charlier A-function and the method of transformation.

Bravais was the first to study the properties of normal bivariate and tri-variate correlation surfaces. Edgeworth was the first to study a skew correlation surface by transforming it by the method of translation into a normal surface. This method has since been developed by Wicksell, who gave a generalized theory of elementary errors as the basis of the method of transformation and provided a method of logarithmic transformation, and by Van Uven who devised a graphic method of transforming a skew frequency surface into a normal surface.

Pearson endeavored to determine, in the manner that he determined his famous system of frequency curves, a system of surfaces from two differential equations to a certain hypergeometric series; but failed in this attempt since the integration of these differential equations has hitherto proven, and still proves, impossible. The special forms obtained by Filon, Isserlis, and Rhodes are of little value on account of restrictions upon the marginal distributions.

The use of hypergeometric series for the representation of a correlation surface has been studied by Isserlis, Pearson, and Wicksell. Wicksell proved that the regression of a solid hypergeometric series is strictly linear and thus concluded that, had Pearson's differential equations admitted a general solution, its application must be limited to cases where the regression is linear.

Pearson has also given a formula for the representation of non-skew correlation.

In order to free the arrays from restrictions by allowing more constants for the frequency function, Pearson has given a fifteen constants surface which is the same in form as the Charlier A-function.

The Charlier A-function as a means of representing correlation surfaces was first deduced by Charlier and Edgeworth and then considered by Wicksell, Esscher, and others. They have been deduced from three different types of hypotheses; namely:

(i) A probability problem of which the solution is a hypergeometric or multinomial series (Wicksell).

(ii) The theory of elementary errors (Charlier and Edgeworth).

(iii) Certain premises with respect to the frequency function and the range of the observed distribution (Van der Stoke).

This three-fold origin provides a wider basis for practical uses of the Charlier A-function. It may be applied to cases of moderate skew correlation.

The regression, scedastic, clitic, and the kurtic curves of the Charlier A-function has been studied and the necessary formulas for determining their parameters developed by Wicksell and Esscher. The equal frequency curves of the Charlier A-function in the case of two variates have been constructed by Wicksell.

Steffensen has contributed a surface to represent a slight degree of correlation.

(The objective of the correlation surface method is to specify the frequency distribution of any number of variates, whereby can be found the probability for the occurrence of any possible set of values of the variates.) The correlation surface method is closely related to the classical theory of probability and theoretically more adequate than the other methods of correlation analysis. Its use, however, is limited by (1) the requirement of large sample, (2) the great amount of labor required for the computation of the parameters, (3) the lack, as yet of formulas for adequate representation of some types of distributions. Furthermore, it cannot be legitimately applied to time series because the item in such series is ordered.

6.4 Development of the Regression Method

The regression method was Galton's ingenious discovery in the 1880s. The manner in which Galton arrived at the result was empirical. His creative mind led him to see that there was a partial causal relation between the characters of parents and of their offspring, that the simultaneous variation of such characters as revealed from the statistical data was an evidence of the existence of such relationship, and that the regression line representing the average variation of one character relative to the other was a measure of correlation, with the regression coefficient measuring the intensity of the correlation. Next, he came to recognize that this method was equally applicable to cases where the variates were not necessarily causally related and had different variabilities, provided each character was measured in units of its own variability. Finally, he expressed the correlation table by the normal bivariate surface and thereby gave the regression method a sound theoretical basis.

Pearson's contribution to the theory of the regression method consists mainly in giving a proof (in 1896) for the normal n-variate surface so as to provide a theoretical basis for the extension of Galton's method of correlation analysis to the case of any number of variates normally distributed; in giving an interpretation of correlation in terms of restriction of variability; and in deriving the correlation ratio (in 1905) for the description of non-linear correlation.

In 1897, Yule demonstrated that the correlation coefficients and the regression coefficients obtained through a generalized application of the method of least squares are the same as those are afforded by the normal theory, provided the regression may be reasonably assumed to be linear. This demonstration, he urged, provides the justification for defining $\sum(xy)/N\sigma_x\sigma_y$ as the linear correlation coefficient whether the distribution is skew or otherwise. In the case of non-linear correlation, the use of this formula as the definition of the correlation coefficient is merely by analogy. In this sense, Yule generalized the theory of regression approach to the theory of correlation.

Defining the multiple correlation coefficient of $(n-2)$-th order by $\sqrt{1-\sigma_{n\cdot123\cdots n-1}^2/\sigma_n^2}$ and the partial correlation coefficient between x_n and x_i of $(n-2)$-th order by $\sqrt{b_{n\cdot123\cdots n-1}b_{n\cdot123\cdots n-1}}$, Yule gave a series of formulas connecting the correlation coefficients, the regression coefficients, and the standard errors of estimate, with the aid of which we are able to compute a coefficient of higher order from those of lower orders.

Yule suggested the parabolic polynomials for the representation of curvilinear regression and the actual line of array means as the limit of the curvilinear regression. These seem to be the forerunners, respectively of curvilinear correlation and of the correlation ratio.

In 1914, Isserlis developed the multiple correlation ratio. In 1915, Pearson developed the partial correlation ratio. Both are simple in principle, but complicated in computation. In 1927, Tappan introduced a partial-multiple correlation coefficient.

Wicksell in 1917 and Pearson in 1921 both pointed out the weakness of the regression method in neglecting the form of distribution of the observed data.

The theory of fitting orthogonal polynomials for the representation of regression curves has been developed by Tchebycheff, Pearson, Fisher, and others. A graphic method of determining regression line was developed by Ezekiel and modified by Bean in the case of disjoint correlation, and by Waugh in the case of joint correlation. Court proposed two empirical equations for fitting the joint regression surfaces.

In 1922 – 1924, Fisher recognized the necessity of subtracting the number of degrees of freedom used up for the determination of the constants in the computation of the correlation coefficients from finite data, and accordingly modified the formulas given by Yule.

According to Brunt's development in 1917, r, but not r^2, may be regarded as a measure of the relative number of common causes which underlie the variations of the two variates in question.

The problem of spurious correlation has been considered by Pearson, Yule, and Wicksell.

6.5 Development of the Sampling Distributions of Parameters and the Method of the Analysis of Variance

The importance of knowing the exact distribution of statistical derivates was first recognized by "Student" in 1908 when he arrived at the exact distribution of t which is the mean of a sample in terms of the standard deviation of the sample. Before that time three classical types of frequency distributions were known. They are (i) the Bernoullian binomial distribution, (ii) the Laplacian normal distribution, and (iii) the Poisson series. The distribution of the variance was then not known to statisticians, although it had been derived by Helmert in 1876. The same distribution was also derived with different methods by "Student" in 1908 and by Fisher in 1915.

In 1900, Pearson derived the X^2-distribution for testing the goodness of fit. The same author arrived at this result again in 1915, if linear restrictions are imposed upon the variates. In 1922, Fisher demonstrated that it is the number of degrees of freedom, not the number of observations, which should be used in applying the X^2-test.

In 1924, Fisher derived the z-distribution, z being equal to half the difference of the natural logarithms of two independently estimated variances. This distribution is the basis of the analysis of variance. The distributions of any one of the correlation coefficients (simple, multiple, or partial) and of the correlation ratio when its population value is zero, may be derived from the z-distribution. On account of this coherent connection between the z-distribution and the distributions of correlation coefficients and of the correlation ratio, correlation analysis may be considered as analysis of variance, and accordingly the arithmetical procedure of correlation analysis is reduced to a routine of computing the parameter z and then testing its significance.

Furthermore, the normal distribution, the t-distribution and the X^2-distribution were shown in the same year (1924) by Fisher to be special cases of the z-distribution and therefore brought together to form a single system.

Fisher found the exact distribution, by a use of the geometrical representation in hyperspace, of the simple correlation coefficient in 1915, of the intra-class correlation coefficient in 1921, of the partial correlation coefficient in 1924, and of the multiple correlation coefficient and the correlation ratio in 1928.

The distribution of the regression coefficients was given by Fisher in 1922. It is the Pearsonian Type IV.

Distributions are thus available for testing the significance of all kinds of correlation coefficients computed from samples taken at random from a normal population. But little is known about the distributions of parameters computed from samples drawn from a non-normal population.

6.6 The Application of Correlation Analysis to Time Series

The correlation analysis was developed in connection with astronomical and biological studies. Most of the data with which economics deals are of a different type. There are a great variety of data which economics deals. Economic data which may be defined as those which are utllized in problems relating to the wealth getting or wealth consuming activities of men, consists largely of aggregates, or percentage ratios defined for selected time units and these items, being "ordered in time", have a characteristic conformation. On account of their special characteristics, the measurement of correlation between time series demands special methods.

The problem of the correlation of time series of economic statistics leads directly to the investigation of the various types of variations (secular, seasonal, cyclical, irregular) which time series exhibit. The method of determining the correlation between time series is, therefore, usually (i) to isolate and compare the secular trends and the seasonal variations, (ii) to correct the original data for the trends and the seasonal variations and then determine the lag or the temporal order of the fluctuations in the corrected series. The resultant correlation coefficient, with the allowance of the lag so determined, is a relative index of the intensity of correlation. Its significance must be judged, primarily in the light of other evidence, not merely on the basis of the sampling distribution, which has been developed on assumptions not retained in the time series.

The correlation desired may be in the changes from one period to the following period of time or in the residuals freed of time influence. Each case demands a special technique.

The first application of correlation analysis to time series was made by Yule in 1896 in his study of pauperism.

The necessity of eliminating the trends in times series was first recognized and explained by Hooker in 1901.

The use of the correlation coefficient for determining the lag was made by Hooker in 1901 and has since come into common practice. A technique for determining the distributed lag by means of correlation coefficients was devised by Irving Fisher in 1925.

The first difference correlation method was first suggested by Hooker in 1901 and then developed independently by Cave (1904), Hooker (1905), and March (1905).

The method of correlation between higher differences for eliminating the tine-influence was developed by "Student" (1915). The method was further considered by Anderson, Pearson, Persons, Yule, Greenwood, and R. A. Fisher. Fisher has shown, in 1925, that the method belongs to the same class as correlating deviations from fitted curves or from moving averages, and that the defect of this class of methods is reduced to a minimum by correlating deviations from appropriate curves fitted to the whole data.

The adaptation of the analysis of variance to determining the correlation of time series was developed by R. A. Fisher in connection with his studies of crop variation at Romthamsted.

Correlation between link relatives was first suggested by Yule in 1899 and then used by Irving Fisher in 1911 for showing the correlation between the quantity of money and the price level.

Correlation between rates of change was introduced by Yule in his studies of pauperism and then used in a modified form by I. Fisher in 1925.

BIBLIOGRAPHY

In the bibliography the names of many journals are abbreviated, but it is believed that the abbreviations require no explanation except possibly as follows:

Biom. Biometrika; Cambridge, England, The University Press.

J. A. S. A. Journal of the American Statistical Association, prior to June 1922, it was known under several other titles, but we have used this abbreviation to include all the previous titles.

J. R. S. S. Journal of the Royal Statistical Society, England.

Ark. for Math. etc. Arkiv for Matematik, Astronomi, och Fysik, Sweden.

Med. Lund. Astro. Obs. Meddelanden fran Lunds Astronomiska Observatorium.

Sv. Ak. Tid. Svenska Aktuarieföreningens Tidskrift.

Kun. Sv. Vet. Handl. Kungliga Svenska Vetenskapsakedmein Handlingar.

Kon. Ak. V. Wet. Konunklyke Akademie van Wetenschappen, Amsterdam.

Allan, F. E. (1930), "The General Form of the Orthogonal Polynomial for Simple Series", Proc. Roy. Soc. Edin., Vol.50, pp.310–320.

Anderson, O. (1914), "Nochmals über 'The Elimination of Spurious Correlation due to Position in Time or Space'", Biom., Vol.10, p.269.

Anderson, O. (1923), "Uber ein neues Verfahren bei Anwendung der 'Variate-Difference' Methode", Biom., Vol.15, p.134.

Anderson, O. (1926), "Uber die Anwendung der Differenzan Methode (Variate Difference Method) bei Reihenausgleichungen, Stabilitasuntersuchungen, und Korrelations messungen", Biom., Vol.18, p.293.

Bachelier, L. (1912), Caleul des Probabilitiés, Chapters 18 and 19, Paris.

Baker, G. A. (1930), "The Significance of the Product-Moment Coefficient of Correlation with Special Reference to the Character the Marginal Distribution", J. A. S. A., Vol.25, pp.387–396.

Bean, L. H. (1929), "A Simplified Method of Graphic Curvilinear Correlation", J. A. S. A., Vol.24, p.386.

Birge and Shea, "A Rapid Method for Calculating the least square solution of a polynomial of any degree", Uni. of Calif. Publications in Math., Vol.2, no.5, pp.67-118.

Boas, F. (1909), "Determination of the Coefficient of Correlation", Science, N. S., Vol. 29, p.823.

Bocher, M. and Duval, E. P. R. (1924), Introduction to Higher Algebra, 1st ed., Macmillan Co. New York.

Bowley, A. L. (1901), Elements of Statistics (now 5th ed.), P. S. King and Son, London, 1st ed., 1901.

Bravais, A. (1846), "Analyses Mathématique sur les probabilités des erreurs de situation d'um point", Hémoires présentes par divers Savants a l'Académie Royale des Science De l'Institut de France, 2nd series, Vol.9, pp.255-332.

Brookmire, J. H. (1914), "Methods of Business Forecasting Based on Fundamental Statistics", Amer. Eco. Rev., Vol.III, p.41.

Brown, J. W., Greenwood, M. and Wood, F. (1914), "A Study of Indeed Correlations", J. R. S. S., Vol.77, p.317.

Brunt, David (1917), The Combinations of Observations, Cambridge Uni. Press, London.

Camp, B. H. (1925), "Mutually Consistent Multiple Regression Surface", Biom. 17, p.443.

Camp, B. H. (1933), "Karl Pearson and Mathematical Statistics", Jour. Am. Stat. Ass., Vol.28, p.395.

Cave-Browne-Cave, F. E. (1904), "On the influence of the time Factor in the Correlation between the Barometric heights at station more than 1,000 miles apart", Proc. Roy. Soc., A., Vol.74, p.403.

Cave, B. M., and Pearson, K. (1914), "Numerical Illustrations of the Variate Difference Correlation Method", Biom., Vol.10, 1914, p.340.

Charlier, C. L. (1905), Researches on the Theory of Probability.

Charlier, C. V. L. (1905), "Uber das Fehlergesetz", Meddelanden fran Lunds Astronomiska Observatorium.

Charlier, C. V. L. (1915), "On Multiplle Correlation", Sv. Ak. Tid., p.18.

Charlier, C. V. L. (1909), Die Strange Form des Bernoullis' chen Theorems, Meddelanden fran Lunds Astronomiska Observatorium, Nr. 43; or, Arkiv for Matematik, Astronomi, och Fysik, Bd. 5., Nr. 15.

Charlier, C. V. L. (1914), "Contributions to the Mathematical Theory of Statistics. 6. The Correlation Function of Type A", Arkiv for Mat., Astr., och Fysik, Bd. 9, No. 26, pp.1 – 18.

Charlier, C. V. L. (1915), "Convergence of the Development in Series of Type A", Med. Lund. Astro. Obs., No.71.

Charlier, C. V. L. (1905 – 1915), "Contribution to the Mathematical Theory of Statistics" and the articles relating to thin subject, Meddelanden fran Lunds Astronomiska Observatorium (Contributions from the Astronomiscal Observatorium), Series I, Nos. 25, 26, 27, 34, 43, 49, 50, 51, 52, 58, 61, 66, 71, and Series II, Nos. 4, 8, 9, 14, Lund.

Cheshire, L., Oldis, E., and Pearson, E. S. (1932), "Further Experiments on the Sampling Distribution of the Coorel. Coef.", J. A. S. A., Vol.27, pp.121 – 128.

Coolidge, Julian. L. (1925), Mathematical Probability, Oxford Uni. Press, England.

Court, A. (1930), "Measuring Joint Causation", J. A. S. A., Vol. 25, pp.245 – 254.

Crum, W. L. (1921), "A Special Application of Partial Correlation", Quar. Pub. Am. Stat. Ass., pp.949 – 952.

Czuber, E. (1891), Theorie der Beobachtungsfehler, Leipzig.

Darmois, G. (1929), Analyse et Comparison der Series Statistique que se developpent dans le temps (The Time Correlation Problem), Metron, Vol. 8, pp.211 – 250.

Day, E. E. (1920), "An Index of the Physical Volume of Production", Rev. Eco. Stat., and Vol.3, 1921.

Day, E. E. (1922), "The Volume of Production of Basic Raw Materials in U. S.", Rev. Eco. Stat., Vol.4, 1922.

Edgeworth, F. Y. (1892), "Correlated Average", Philosophical Magazine, Vol.34, 5th Series, pp.190 – 201, 429 – 438, 518 – 526.

Edgeworth, F. Y. (1896), "Asymmetrical Prob. Curve", Phil. Mag., Vol.51, 5th Series, pp.90 – 99.

Edgeworth, F. Y. (1896), "The Compound Law of Error", Phil. Mag., Vol.41, pp.207 – 215.

Edgeworth, F. Y. (1898), "On the Representation of Statistics by Mathematical Formula", J. R. S. A., Vol.61, p.670.

Edgeworth, F. Y. (1898), "Method of Translation", J. R. S. A., and 1899, 1900.

Edgeworth, F. Y. (1905), "The Law of Error", Camb. Phil. Trans., Vol.20, pp.36 - 65, 113 - 141.

Edgeworth, F. Y. (1914), "On the Use of Analytic Geometry to Represent Certain Kinds of Statistics", J. R. S. S., Vol.77.

Edgeworth, F. Y. (1916), "On the Mathematical Representation of Statistical Data", J. R. S. S., Vols. 79 and 80.

Edgeworth, F. Y. (1906), "The Generalized Law of Error or Law of Great Numbers", J. R. S. S., Vol.69.

Edgeworth, F. Y., "Law of Error" in 10th ed., and "Probability" in 11th ed., Encycl. Brit.

Elderton, E., and Pearson, K. (1915), "On Further Evidence of Natural Selection in Man", Biom., Vol. 10, p. 488 (A paper using variate difference method).

Elderton, E. M., and Pearson, K. (1923), "On the Variate Difference Method", Biom., Vol.14, p.281.

Elliot, F. F., "Adjusting Hog Production to Market Demand", Univ. Ill. Agr. Exp. Sta. Bul. 293.

Esscher, F. (1920), "Uber die Sterblichkeit in Schweden 1886 - 1914", Meddelanden fran Lunds Astronomiska Observatorium.

Esscher, K. S. F. (1920), Some General Formulae in the Theory of Multiple Correlation, Arkiv for Matematik, Astr., och Fysik, Bd. 15, Nr. 19.

Ezekiel, M. (1924), "A Method of Handling Curvilinear Correlation for Any Number of Variables", J. A. S. A., Vol.19, pp.431 - 453.

Ezekiel, M. (1926), "The Determination of Curvilinear Regression Surfaces in the Presence of Other Variables", J. A. S. A., Vol.21, p.310.

Ezekiel, M. (1929), "The Application of the Theory of Error to Multiple and Curvilinear Correlation", Proc. A. S. A., Vol.24, pp.99 - 104.

Ezekiel, M. (1930), "A First Approximation to the Sampling Reliability of Multiple and Curvilinear Correlations", Annals of Math. Stat., Vol. 1, p.275.

Ezekiel, M. (1930), Methods of Correlation Analysis, John Wiley and Sons, New York.

Filon, L. N. G., See Pearson and Filon.

Fisher, I. (1911), "The Purchasing Power of Money" (Now 2nd ed.), The Macmillan Co., New York, either 1st or 2nd ed., pp.294 - 296.

Fisher, I. (1925), "Our Unstable Dollar and the So-called Business Cycle", Jour. Amer. Stat. Ass., Vol.20, pp.179 - 202.

Fisher, I. (1930), The Theory of Interest, New York.

Fisher, R. A. (1912), "On an absolute criterion for fitting frequency curves", Messenger of Math., pp.155 - 160.

Fisher, R. A. (1915), "Frequency distribution of the values of the correlation coefficient in samples from an indefinitely large population", Biom., pp.507 - 521.

Fisher, R. A. (1921), "Some remarks on the methods formulated in a recent article on 'the quantitative analysis of plant growth'", Annals of Applied Biology, Vol.vii, pp.367 - 372.

Fisher, R. A. (1921), "On the mathematical foundations of theoretical statistics", Phil. Trans. of Roy. Soc., of London, A, ccxxii., pp.309 - 368.

Fisher, R. A. (1921), "Studies in crop variation. I. An examination of the yield of dressed grain from Broadbalk", Jour. of Agr. Science, xi, pp.107 - 135.

Fisher, R. A. (1921), "On the 'probable error' of a coefficient of correlation deduced from a small sample", Metron, i. pt. 4, pp.1 - 32.

Fisher, R. A. (1922), "On the interpretation of X^2 from contingency tables, and the calculation of P", Jour. of Roy. Stat. Soc., pp.87 - 94.

Fisher, R. A. (1922), "The goodness of fit of regression formulae, and the distribution of regression coefficients", Jour. of Roy. Stat. Soc., pp.597 - 612.

Fisher, R. A. (1922), with W. A. Mackenzie, "The correlation of weekly rainfall", Quarterly Jour. of Roy. Met. Soc., pp.234 - 245.

Fisher, R. A. (1923), with W. A. Mackenzie. "Studies in crop variation. II.

The manurial response of different potato varieties", Jour. of Agr. Science, pp.311 – 320.

Fisher, R. A. (1924), "The distribution of the partial correlation coefficient", Metron, pp.329 – 332.

Fisher, R. A. (1924), The influence of rainfall on the yield of wheat at Rothamsted", Phil. Trans. of Roy. Soc., of London, B, pp.89 – 142.

Fisher, R. A. (1924), On a distribution yielding the error functions of several well-known statistics, Proceedings of the International Mathematical Congress, Toronto, pp.805 – 813.

Fisher, R. A. (1924), "The conditions under which X^2 measures the discrepancy between observation and hypothesis", Jour. of Roy. Stat. Soc., pp.442 – 449.

Fisher, R. A. (1925), Statistical Methods for Research Workers, Oliver and Boyd, Edinburgh (ed. 1925, 1928, 1930).

Fisher, R. A. (1925), Theory of Statistical Estimation, Proceedings of the Seabridge Phil. Soc., pp.700 – 725.

Fisher, R. A. (1926), "Applications of 'Student's' Distribution", Metron, V. pt. 3, pp.90 – 104.

Fisher, R. A. (1928), The general sampling distribution of the multiple correlation coefficient, Proceedings of the Roy. Soc., of London, A, pp. 654 – 673.

Frisch, R. (1928), "Correlation and Scatter in Statistical Variables", Nor. Stat. Tid., Bd. 8, pp.36 – 102.

Galton, Francis (1874), "Notes on the Marlborough School Statistics", Jour. Anthrop. Inst., Vol.4, pp.130 – 135.

Galton, Francis (1877), "Typical Laws of Heredity in Man", Roy. Inst. of Great Britain, Feb.9.

Galton, Francis (1885), "Address to Anthrop. Section, British Ass. at Aberdeen", Jour. British Ass., pp.1206 – 1214.

Galton, Francis (1885), "Regression towards Mediocrity in Heredity Stature", Miscellaneca Jour. Anthr. Inst., Vol.15, pp.246 – 263.

Galton, Francis (1886), "Presidential Address to the Anthr. Inst.", Jour. Anth. Inst., Vol.15, pp.489 – 499.

Galton, Francis (1886), "Family Likeness in Stature with an Appendix by J. D. Hamilton Dickson", Proc. Roy. Soc., Vol.40, pp.42–73.

Galton, Francis (1886), "Correlation and their Measurement", Proc. Roy. Soc., Vol.45, pp.135–145.

Galton, Francis (1889), Natural Inheritance, London.

Galton, Francis (1908), Memories of My Life, London.

Gauss, C. F. (1823), Theoria Combinationis Observationum Erroribus Minimis Obnoxiae, Gottingen.

Gauss, C. F. (1828), Supplementum Theoriae Combinationis Observationum Erroribus Minimis Obnoxiae, Gottingen.

Gini, C. (1914), "Nouvi Contribuli Alla Tooria della Relationi Statistiche", Atte del R. Instituts Veneto de S. L. A. Tome 74, p.II.

Gini, C. (1926), "Some Contributions of Italy to Modern Statistical Methods", J. R. S. S., Vol.89, p.702.

Gordon, C. (1921), Proc. London Math. Soc., Series II, Vol.20. pp.297–325.

Gram, J. P. (1879), Thesis "On Raekkeudviklinger bestemte ved Hjaelp af de Mindste Kradvaters Nethode", Kjobenhavn (for English Translation, see next reference).

Gram, J. P. (1879), "The Development of Series by Means of the Method of Least Squares", Doctor's Thesis Copenhagen.

Greenwood, M., See Brown and Yule.

Greiner, H. (1909), "Uber das Fehlersystem der Collectiv Masslehre", Zeitschrift fur Math. und Physik., Vol.57, p.227.

Gresseus, O. and Mouzon, E. D. (1927), "The Validity of Correlation in Time Sequences and a New Coefficient of Similarity", J. A. S. A., Vol.22, pp.483–492.

Hansen, A. H. (1921), Cycles of Prosperity and Depression in the United States, Great Britain, and Germany, A study of Monthly Data 1902–1908, Madison, Wis.

Harris, A., "On the Calculation of Intra-class and Inter-class Coefficient of Correlation from Class Momtns when the Number of Possible Combinations is Large", Biom., Vol.9, pp.456–472.

Harris, A. (1909), "A Short Method of Calculating the Coefficient of Correlation in the Case of Integral Variates", Biom., Vol.7, p.214.

Harvard University Committee on Economic Research, Rev. Eco. Stat., Camb. Mass.

Hass, G. C., and Ezekiel, M. (1926), Factors Affecting the Price of Hogs, U. S. Dept. Agr. Dept. Bul. 1440, Washington D. C.

Helmert, C. F. (1875), "Uber die Wahrscheinlichkeit der Potenzsummen der Beobachtungsfehler und uber einige damit in Zusammenhang stehende Fragen", Zeitschrift fur Math. und Physik, Vol. 20, S. 303; and Astromische Nachrichten, Vol.88, No.2096, 1876.

Hexter, M. B. (1925), Social Consequences of Business Cycles, Boston and New York.

Hooker, R. H. (1901), "On the Correlation of the Marriage-rate with Trade", J. R. S. S., Vol.64, p.485.

Hooker, R. H. (1901), "The suspension of the Berlin Produce Exchange and its Effect upon Corn Prices", J. R. S. S., Vol.64, p.574.

Hooker, R. H. (1905), "On the Correlation of Successive Observations Illustrated by Corn-prices", J. R. S. S., Vol.68, p.696.

Hooker, R. H. (1907), "Correlation of the Weather and Crops", Jour. Roy. Stat. Soc., Vol.70, p.1042.

Hooker, R. H. (1918), "An Elementary Explanation of Correlation", Quar. Jour. Roy. Met. Soc., Oct., p.285.

Hotelling, H. (1925), "The Distribution of Correlation Ratio Calculated from Random Data", Proc. National Academy of Science, Vol. 11, No. 10, pp.657 – 662.

Hotelling, H. (1931), "The Generalization of 'Student's' Ratio", Annals of Math. Stat. Amer. Stat. Ass., Vol.2, pp.359 – 378.

Ingraham, M. H. (1929), "Discussion of Ezekiel's Paper 'The Application of the Theory of Error to Multiple and Curvilinear Correlation'", J. A. S. A., Vol.24, pp.105 – 107.

Isserlis, L. (1914), "The Application of Solid Hypergeometrical Series to Frequency Distribution in Space", Phill. Mag., Vol.28, pp.379 – 403.

Isserlis, L. (1914), "On the Partial Correlation Ratio", Pt. I, Biom., Vol.10, p.391, and Pt. II, Vol.11, p.60.

Jerome, H. (1924), Statistical Method, Harper and Brothers Pub., New York.

Jerome, H. (1926), Migration and Business Cycles, Nat. Bureau of Eco. Research, New York.

Jordan, C. (1921), Proc. Lond. Math. Soc., Ser. 2, Vol.20, pp.297 – 325.

Jorgenson, N. R. (1914), "Note sur la fonction de repartition de Type B de M. Charlier", Ark. f. Mat., Astr. och Fysik, Bd.10, No.15.

Jorgenson, N. R. (1916), "Undersogelser over Frequensflader og Korrelation", Arnold Busek, Kobenhavn.

Kapteyn, J. C. (1903), "Skew Frequency Curves in Biology and Statistics", Astronomical Lab. at Groningen.

Kapteyn, J. C., Van Uven, M. G. (1916), "Skew Frequency Curves in Biology and Statistics", Hoitsema Bros., Groningen.

Karsten, K. G. (1926), "The Harvard Business Index—A New Interpretation", J. A. S. A., Vol.21, p.409.

Kelley, E. Lowell (1929), "The Relationship between the technique of partial correlation and Path. Coef.", J. Edu. Psychol., Vol.20(2), pp.119 – 124.

Kelley, T. L. (1919), "Tables to Facilitate the Calculation of Partial Coefficients of Cor. and Regr. Eq.", Bulletin of the Uni. Of Texas.

Kelley, T. L. (1923), Statistical Method, The Macmillan Co. N. Y.

Koren, John (1918), The history of statistics, their development and progress in many countries, in memoirs to commemorate the 75th anniversary of A. S. A.

Laplace, P. S. (1810), "Memoir sur les Integrales Definies et leur Application aux Probabilites", Memoire de l'Institute Imperiale de France, pp.279 – 347.

Laplace, P. S. (1812), Theorie Analytique des Probabilites, or cf. Vol.VII of Oeuvre de Laplace, National 4th ed., Ch. 4.

Leavens, D. H. (1931), "Frequency Distributions Corresponding to Time Series", J. A. S. A., Vol.26, p.409.

Lee, Alice (1908), "On the manner in which the percentage of employed workmen in this country is related to the import of articles wholly or mainly manufactured", Eco. Jour., Vol.18, p.96.

Lipps, G. F. (1905), "Die Bestimmung der Abhangegkeit zweischen den Merkmalen eines Gegenstandes", Berichte der Math. Phys. Klasse der Kgl. Sachsischen Gesellschaft der Wissenschaften, Leipzig.

Lorenz, Paul (1931), "Hobe Korrelations Koefficienten", Allgemeine Statistisches Archiv. Band 21, pp.415－421; and Band 22, pp.293－298 (A discussion of the influence of the time variable on the multiple correlation. A reply by Henry Schlitz. Band 22, 1932, pp.293－298).

March, L. (1905), "Comparaison numerique de combes Statistiques", Jl. de la Societe de Statistique de Paris, p.255 and 306.

Meitzen, A. (1891), History, Theory to Technique of Statistics, Trans. by R. F. Falkner, Phil., Am. Acad. Pol. soc. Sci.

Merriman, Mansfield (1877－1882), "A list of writings relating to the method of least squares, with a historical and critical note", Trans. of the Connecticut Academy of Arts and Sciences, Vol.4, New Haven, pp.151－232.

Merriman, M. (1910), Method of Least Squares, Wiley, New York.

Mills, F. C. (1924), "The measurement of correlation and the problem of estimation", J. A. S. A., Vol.19, p.273.

Mills, F. C. (1924), Statistical Methods Applied to Economics and Business, Henry Holt and Co., New York.

Mills, F. C. (1927), Behavior of Prices, National Bureau of Economic Research, Washington, D. C., pp.313－323, p.341, 349, 385.

Mitchell, W. C. (1921), The making and using of index numbers, Bul. 284, U. S. B. L. S.

Mitchell, W. C. (1921), The making and using of index numbers, Bul. 284, U. S. Bur. Labor. Stat.

Mitchell, W. C. (1927), Business Cycles, the Problem and Its Setting, National Bureau of Economic Research, New York.

Moore, H. L. (1914), Economic Cycles: Their Law and Cause, N. Y.

Moore, H. L. (1917), Forecasting the yield and the price of cotton, New York.

Narumi, Seimatsu (1923), "On the general forms of bivariate frequency distributions which are mathematically possible when regression and variation are subjected to limiting conditions", Biom., Vol.15, pp.77－

88, 209-221, 222-244.

Neifield, M. R. (1927), "A study of spurious correlation", J. A. S. A., Vol.22, p.331.

Neyman, J. (1926), "Further notes on non-linear regression", Biom., Vol.18, p.257.

Otis, A. S. (1916), "The Reliability of Spelling Scales, Including a Deviation Formula for Correlation", School and Society, Vol.4, Nos. 96-99.

Otis, A. S. (1923), "The Otis Correlation Chart", Jour. Educ. Research, Vol.8, p.440.

Otis, A. S. (1925), Statistical Method in Educational Measurement, Yonkers-on-Hudson.

Pareto, Vilfredo (1911), "Economie Mathematique", in the Encyclopedie des Sciences Mathematique, Tome I, Vol.IV, Fascicule 4, 1911, pp.611-613.

Pearson, E. S. (1929), "Some Notes on Sampling Tests with Two Variables", Biom., Vol.21, pp.356-360.

Pearson, E. S. (1931), "Analysis of Variance in Case of Non-normal Variation", Biom., Vol.23, p.114.

Pearson, E. S. (1931), "The Test of Significance for the Correlation Coefficient", Jour. Am. Stat. Ass., Vol.26, pp.128-134.

Pearson, E. S. (1932), "Further Experiments on the Sampling Distribution of the Correlation Coefficient", Jour. Am. Stat. Ass., Vol.27, pp.121-128.

Pearson, K. (1896), "Contributions to the Mathematical Theory of Evolution III. Regression, Heredity, Panmixia", Phill. Trans. Roy. Soc., Series A, Vol.187, pp.253-318.

Pearson, K. (1897), "On a Form of Spurious Correlation", Proc. Roy. Soc., Vol.60.

Pearson, K., Lee, A., and Bramley-Moore, L. (1899), "Genetic (reproductive) Selection: Inheritance of Fertility in Man and of Fecundity in Thoroughbred Racehorses", Phil. Trans. Roy. Soc., Series A, Vol.192, p.257.

Pearson, K. (1900), "On the criterion that a given system of deviations from the probable, in the case of a correlated system of variables, is such that it can be reasonably supposed to have arisen from random sampling", Phil.

Mag., 5th Series, Vol.50, p.157.

Pearson, K. (1900), "On the correlation of characters not quantitatively measurable", Phil. Trans. Roy. Soc., A., Vol.195, p.1.

Pearson, K. (1901), "On lines and planes of closest fit to systems of points in space", Phil. Mag., 6th Series, Vol.2, p.559.

Pearson, K. (1901), "On the systematic fitting of curves to observations and measurements", Biom., Vol.1, pp.265–303, Vol.2, pp.1–23.

Pearson, K. (1903), "On the mathematical theory of errors of judgment, with special reference to the personal equation", Phil. Trans. Roy. Soc., A, Vol.198.

Pearson, K. (1904), "On the theory of contingency and its relation to association and normal correlation", Drapers' Co., Research Memoirs, Biom., Series 1, Dulau and Co. London.

Pearson, K. (Editorial) (1904), "On an elementary proof of Sheppard's formula for correcting raw moments, and on other allied points", Biom., Vol.3, p.308.

Pearson, K. (1905), "On the General Theory of Skew Correlation and Non-linear Regression", "Drapers' Co., Research Memoirs: Biometric Series", II; Dulau and Co. London (The Correlation Ratio).

Pearson, K. (1905), "'Das Fehlergesetz und seine Verallgemeinerungen durch Techner und Pearson', A Rejoinder", Biom., Vol.4, pp.169–212.

Pearson, K. (1906), "On a coefficient of class heterogeneity or divergence", Biom., Vol.5, p.198.

Pearson, K. (1906), "Skew frequency curves, a rejoinder to professor Kapteyn", Biom., Vol.5, pp.168–171.

Pearson, K. (1906), Biography of Walter Frank Raphael Weldon (1860–1906), Biom., pp.1–52.

Pearson, K. (1907), "On further methods of determining correlation", Drapers' Co., Research Memoirs, Biom., Series. IV, p.10.

Pearson, K. (1911), "On a correction to be made to the correlation ratio", Biom., Vol.8, pp.254–255.

Pearson, K. (1911), Grammar of Science, 3rd. ed., pp.113–175.

Pearson, K. (1911), "On the Probability that two Independent Distributions are Really Samples of the Same Population", Biom., Vol.8, p.250.

Pearson, K. (1913), "On the theories of association", Biom., Vol.9, p.159.

Pearson, K. (1913), "On the influence of 'Broad Categories' on correlation", Biom., Vol.9, pp.116 - 139.

Pearson, K. (1914), Tables for Statisticians and Biometricians, Camb. Uni. Press, London.

Pearson, K. (1915), "On the general theory of multiple contingency, with special reference to partial contingency", Biom., Vol.11, p.145.

Pearson, K. (1915), "On the partial correlation ratio", Proc. of Roy. Soc., A. 91, p.492.

Pearson, K. (1915), "On certain errors with regard to multiple correlation occasionally made those who have not adequately studied the subject", Biom., Vol.10, p.181.

Pearson, K. (1916), "On the application of goodness of fit table to test regression curves and theoretical curves used to describe observational data", Biom., Vol.11, p.239.

Pearson, K. (1921), "Note on history of correlation", Biom., Vol. 13, pp.25 - 45.

Pearson, K. (1921), "On a general method of determining the successive terms in a skew regression line", Biom., Vol.13, pp.113 - 132.

Pearson, K. (1922), Francis Galton, 1822 - 1922: A Centenary Appreciation, No. 11 in the series questions of the day and of the fray.

Pearson, K. (1922), "On the X^2 test of goodness of fit", Biom., Vol. 14, p.186.

Pearson, K. (1923), "Further note on the X^2 of goodness of fit", Biom., Vol.14, p.418.

Pearson, K. (1923), "On non-skew frequency surfaces", Biom., Vol. 15, p.231.

Pearson, K. (1923), "Notes on skew frequency sufaces", Biom., Vol. 15, pp.222 - 244.

Pearson, K., and ELderton, E. M. (1923), "On the variate difference method", Biom., Vol.14, p.281.

Pearson, K. (1924), "Historical note on the origin of the normal curve of errors", Biom., Vol.16, p.402.

Pearson, K. (1924), "On a certain double hypergeometrical series and its representation by continuous freq. surfaces", Biom., Vol.16, p.172.

Pearson, K. (1925), "The 15-ocnstant bivariate frequency surface", Biom., Vol.17, p.268.

Pearson, K. (1925), James Bernoulli's Theorems, Biom., Vol.17, p.201.

Pearson, K. (1931), "Historical note on the distribution of the standard deviations of samples of any size drawn from an indefinitely large normal parent population", Biom., Vol.23, pp.16 – 18 (it is a reproduction of Helmert's original method of deducing the law of σ. The method differs considerably from more recent investigations. It has also been reproduced by Czuber. Beobachlungsfehler, s. 147).

Pearson, K. (1931), "Some properties of Student's z: Correlation, regression and scedasticity of z with the mean and standard deviation of the sample", Biom., Vol.23, p.109, pp.408 – 415.

Pearson, K. (1931), "Experimental discussion of (X^2, P) test for goodness of fit", Biom., Vol.24, p.351.

Perozzo (1881 – 1882), "Nuove Applicazioni de Calcolo delle Probabilila", Acta, Reale Accademia dei Lincei, pp.1 – 33.

Persons, W. M. (1916), "Construction of a Business Barometer", Am. Eco. Rev., p.755.

Persons, W. M. (1917), "On the Variate Difference Correlation Method and Curve-fitting", Publications Amer. Stat. Ass., Vol.15, pp.602 – 642.

Persons, W. M. (1919), "Indices of business conditions", Rev. Eco. Stat., Vol.1, p.5.

Persons, W. M. (1919), "An index of general business conditions", Rev. Eco. Stat., Vol.1, p.111.

Persons, W. M. (1924), "Some fundamental concepts of statistics", J. A. S. A., Vol.19, pp.1 – 8.

Persons, W. M. (1924), Ch. X., Correlation of Time Series, Handbook of Mathematical Statistics, edited by H. L. Rietz.

Persons, W. M. (1925), "Statistics and Economic Theory", Rev. Eco. Stat., Vol.7, p.185.

Plana, G. A. A., "Memoire sur divers Problèmes de Probabilité", Mémeires de l'Académie Imperiale de Turin, pour les Années 1811 – 1812, Vol.20, pp.355 – 498.

Pretorius, S. J. (1931), "Skew Bivariate Frequency Surfaces", Biom., Vol.22, p.121.

Rhodes, E. C. (1923), "On a certain skew correlation surface", Biom., Vol.14, pp.355 – 377.

Rider, Paul R. (1932), "On the distribution of the Cor. Coef. in small samples", Biom., Vol.24, pp.382 – 403.

Rietz, H. L. (1924), Handbook of Mathematical Statistics, Houghton Mifflin Co., Boston and New York, 1927, Mathematical Statistics, The University of Chicago Press, Chicago.

Ritter, W. E. (1919), "A step forward in the methodology of natural science", Proc. of the Am. Academy of Arts and Science., Vol.55, no. 2, pp.91 – 133.

Roy. Stat. Soc.(1928), Edgeworth's Contributions to Mathematical Statistics, London.

Sasuly, M. (1930), "The simplest symmetrical expression for rate of change of time series data", Jour. Amer. Stat. Ass., Vol.25, pp.72 – 75.

Sasuly, M. (1930), "Generalized multiple correlation analysis of Eco. Statistical Series", J. A. S. A., Vol.25, proc., pp.146 – 152.

Schultz, H. (1930), "The Standard Error of a Forecast from a Curve", J. A. S. A., Vol.25, pp.139 – 185.

Schultz, T. W., Snedecor, G. W. (1933), Analysis of V. as an effective method of handling the time series in certain eco. stat., J. A. S. A., Vol.28, pp.14 – 30.

Sheppard, W. F. (1898), "On the application of the theory of error to cases of normal distribution and normal correlation", Phil. Trans. Roy. Soc., A. Vol.192, pp.101 – 167.

Sheppard, W. F. (1912), "Reduction of errors by means of negligible differences", Fifth International Congress of Maths., Camb., pp.348 – 384.

Slutsky, E. (1913), "On the criterion of goodness of fit of regression lines and the best method of fitting them to the data", J. A. S. S., Vol.77, pp.78 – 84.

Smith, B. B. (1926), "Combining the advantages of first difference and deviation from trend methods of correlating time series", J. A. S. A., Vol.21, p.55.

Snow, E. C. (1911), "On restricted lines and planes of closest fit to systems of points in any number of dimensions", Phil. Mag., 6th series, Vol.21, p.367.

Soper, H. E., Young, A. W., Cave, B. M., Lee, A., and Pearson, K. (1916), "A cooperative study", "On the distribution of the correlation coefficient in small samples", Biom., Vol.11, pp.328 – 413.

Steffensen, G. F. (1917), "Note sur la fonction de type B de Charlier", Sv. Ak. Tid., Nos. 4 – 5.

Steffensen, G. F. (1922), "A Correlation Formula", Sk. Akt. Tidskr.

Steffensen, G. F. (1923), "Matematisk Iagllagelselaere", G. K. C. Gads, Kobenhavn.

Steffensen, G. F. (1924), "On Charlier's Generalized Frequency Function", Sk. Akt. Tidskr.

"Student" (1908), "The probable error of a mean", Biom., Vol.6, pp.1 – 25.

"Student" (1909), "Probable error of a correl", Coefficient, Vol.6, pp.302 – 310.

"Student" (1914), "The elimination of spurious correlation due to position in time or space", Biom., Vol.10, p.179.

"Student" (1917), "Tables for estimating the probability that the mean of a unique sample of observations lies between $-\infty$ and any given distance from the mean of the population from which the sample is drawn", Biom., Vol.11, pp.414 – 417.

"Student" (1925), "New tables for testing the significance of observations", Metron, Vol.3, no.3, pp.105—120.

"Student" (1931), "On the z Test", Biom., Vol.23, p.407.

Tappan, M. (1927), "On partial multiple Cor. Coefs. in a universe of manifold characteristics", Biom., Vol.19, p.39.

Tchebycheff, P. L. (1854), Memoires de l'academie de Saint Pétersbourg, 1854, 1859. A résumé by R. Radau, Bulletin Astronomique, Tome VIII,

Paris, 1891, p.350 et seq. See also Liouville's Journal, 2nd Series, Tome III, 1858, p.289 et seq. and Oeuvres, 1899, Tome 1.

Thorndike, E. L. (1913), An Introduction to the Theory of Mental and Social Measurements, New York.

Tiele, T. N. (1897), A general theory of observations. 1903 (An elementary abstract of the 1889 Danish edition "Almindelig Iagttagelseslaere" and a translation of a work in Danish issued in 1897).

Tippett, L. H. C. (1929), "Statistical Methods in Textile Research", Shirley Institute Memoirs., Vol.8, pp.175 – 196.

Tschuprow, A. A. (on Prob. and Con.) (1925), Grundbegriffe und Grund problem der Korrelations theorie, Leipzig.

Tschuprow, A. A. (1928), tr. by Isserlis, "The Math. Theory of the statistical method employed in the study of correlation in the case of three variables", Trans. Camb. Phil. Soc., Vol.23, pp.337 – 382.

Van der Stoke, J. P. (1908), "On the Analysis of Frequency Curves According to a General Method", Kon. Ak. Wet Amst. Proc., Sec. of Sc., p.10.

Van Uven, M. G. (1925), "On treating skew correlation", Proc. Kon. Ak. v. Wet., Amsterdam, Vol.28, pp.797 – 811, 919 – 935; and Vol.29, pp.580 – 590; Vol.32, pp.408 – 413.

Van Uven, M. G. (1929), "Skew Correlation between three and more variables", Proc. Kon. Ak. v. Wet., Vol.32, pp.793 – 807, 995 – 1007, 1085 – 1103.

Walker, H. M. (1928), "The relation of Plana and Bravais to correlation theory", Isis., Vol.10, p.466.

Walker, Helen M. (1929), The History of Statistical Method, The Williams and Wilkins Co., Biltimore, U. S. A.

Warren, G. F., Pearson, F. A. (1928), Interrelationships of Supply and Price, Cornell Uni. Agr. Exp. Stat., Bul. 466, Ithaca, N. Y.

Warren, S. W. (1931), "Multiple correlation analysis as applied to farm management research", Memoir 141 of the Cornell Uni. Agr. Exp. Stat., New York.

Waugh, F. V. (1929), "The use of isotropic lines in determining regression surface", J. A. S. A., Vol.24, pp.144 – 151.

Weldon, W. F. R. (1890), "The variations occurring in certain decapod crustacea. I. Crangon Vulgaris", Proc. Roy. Soc., Vol.47, pp.445 – 453.

Weldon, W. F. R. (1892), "Certain correlated variations in Crangon Vulgaris", Proc. Roy. Soc., Vol.51, pp.2 – 21.

Weldon, W. F. R. (1893), "Correlated Variations in Naples and Plymouth Shore Crabs", Proc. Roy. Soc., Vol.54, pp.318 – 329.

Westergaard (1916), "Scope and method of statistics", Quarterly Publications Am. Stat. Ass. Sept.

Westergaard, W. F. R. (1916), "On the future of statistics", Jour. Roy. Stat. Soc., Vol.81, p.499.

Wicksell, S. D. (1916), "Some theorems in the theory of probability with special reference to their importance in the theory of homograde correlation", Sv. Ak. Tid., p.12.

Wicksell, S. D. (1917), "The application of solid hypergeometrical series to frequency distributions in shape", Phil. Mag., Vol.34, pp.389 – 394.

Wicksell, S. D. (1917), "On logarithmic correlation with an application to the distribution of ages at first marriage", Sv. Akt. Tid., Haft. 4, pp.1 – 21.

Wicksell, S. D. (1917), "The correlation function of type A and the regression of its characteristics", Kungl. Sv. Vet. Akad. Handl., Bd. 58, pp.1 – 49.

Wicksell, S. D. (1917), "The construction of the curves of equal frequency in case of type A correlation", Sv. Akt. Tidskr., Haft. 2 – 3, pp.1 – 17.

Wicksell, S. D. (1917), "On the Genetic Theory of Frequency", Ark. for Math., Astro., och Fysik, Bd. 12, no. 20.

Wicksell, S. D. (Written in English) (1925), "Contributions to the analytic theory of sampling", Arkiv for Mathematik, Astronomi, och Fysik, Vol.17, pp.1 – 46.

Wilks, S. S. (1932), "Certain generalizations in the analysis of variance", Biom., Vol.24, p.471.

Wilson, Edwin B. (1929), "Probable error of correlation results", Proc. of Amer. S. Ass., Vol.24, (165 A-Suppl.), pp.90 – 93.

Wilson, E. B. (1930), "Mathematics and Statistics", J. A. S. A., Vol.25, pp.1 – 8.

Wishart, John (1928), "Table of Significant Values of the Multiple Correlation

Coefficient", Quar. Jour. Roy. Meteor. Soc., pp.258 – 259.

Wishart, John (1931), "The mean and second moment coefficient of the multiple correlation coefficient in samples from a normal population", Biom., Vol.24.

Wishart, John (1932), "A Note on the Distribution of the Correlation Ratio", Biom., Vol.24, p.441.

Wood, F., See Brown.

Working, H. (1921), "A Use for Trigonometric Tables in Correlation", Jour. Am. Stat. A., Vol.17, p.765.

Working, H. (1925), Factors Affecting the Prices of Minnesota Potatoes, Uni. Minn. Ag. Exp. Stat. Tech., Bul. 29.

Working, H., Hotelling, H. (1929), "Applications of the theory of error to the interpretation of trends", Jour. Am. Stat. Ass. Proc., Vol.24, 165A, pp. 73 – 85.

Wright, S., "Correlations and Causation", Jour. Agr. Research, Vol. 20, pp.557 – 575.

Wright, T. W., Hayford, J. F. (1905), Adjustment of Observations, pp.24 – 40, 132 – 133.

Yule, G. U. (1895 – 1896), "On the Cor. of Total Pauperism with Population of Out-relief", Eco. Jour., Vol.5, p.603, and Vol.6, p.613.

Yule, G. U. (1897), "On the Significance of Bravais' Formula for Regression, etc., in the Case of Skew Correlation", Proc. Roy. Soc., Vol.60, p.477.

Yule, G. U. (1897), "On the Theory of Correlation", Jour. Roy. Stat. Soc., Vol.69, p.812.

Yule, G. U. (1899), "An Investigation into the Causes of Changes in Pauperism in England during the last two inter-causal decades", Jour. Roy. Stat. Soc., Vol.62, p.249.

Yule, G. U. (1907), "On the Theory of Correlation for Any Number of Variables, Treated by a New System of Notations", Proc. Roy. Soc., Vol.79, p.182.

Yule, G. U. (1909), "The Applications of the Method of Correlation to Social and Economic Statistics", Jour. Roy. Stat. Soc., Vol.72, pp.721 – 729.

Yule, G. U. (1910), An introduction to the theory of statistics, 1st ed.,

Charles Griffin and Co., London.

Yule, G. U. (1910), "On the Interpretation of Correlation between Ratios", J. R. S. S., Vol.77, p.644.

Yule, G. U. (1912), "On the Methods of Measuring the Association between Two Attributes", Jour. R. S. S., Vol.75, p.579.

Yule, G. U., Greenwood, M. (1915), "The Statistics of Antityphoid and Antichorela Inoculations", Proc. Roy. Soc. Med., Sec. Epidem. and State Med., Vol.8, p.113.

Yule, G. U. (1921), "On the Time Correlation Problem", J. R. S. S., Vol.84, p.497.

Yule, G. U. (1926), "Why do We Sometimes Get Nonsense Correlations between Time Series? A Study in Sampling and the Nature of Time Series", J. R. S. S., Vol.89, p.1.

Yule, G. U. (1923), "On the Application of X^2 Method to Association and Contingency Tables, with Experimental Illustrations", J. R. S. S., Vol.85, pp.95–104.

Zizek, F. (1913), Statistical Averages, tr. by W. M. Persons, New York.

(本文第二章部分内容曾以"A Theory of Correlation"为题发表于《国立中央大学科学研究录》1936年第2卷第2期)

算学在统计学上之任务*

统计的对象,有时为一个事象,有时为二个或多个事象,譬如我们要统计 1934 年中央大学投考生的成绩,成绩便是问题里的事象,因为各人所得的成绩不等,所以这事象非是齐一不变的。因之统计事象,可称之为变量或变数(Variate)。在这投考生成绩问题,各人所得的成绩,便是变数所能取的各值,此等数值,均有一个通性(Common characteristic,本题的通性,即是 1934 年中央大学投考生的成绩),自成集团(Aggregate of individuals)。换言之,凡具有一通性的众数,自成集团,这集团谓之宇宙(Population or universe)。统计学是研究此种宇宙的方法(Statistics is the study of aggregates or populations of individuals rather than of individuals),此与研究集团中个体的本身有别,读者宜细辨之。物理学里气体运动学说(Kenetic theory of gases)及化学的质量反应学说(Theory of mass action),都是讨论集团的性质,而非研究集团中个体的例子。

集团中个体,为数甚多,故吾人颇难即刻明悉其通性,统计方法,即是简化集团中大众数量,综合为一个或数个示数(Statistical measures or parameters),以为集团通性的代表的手续(Methods of reduction)。

集团中个体,各不相同。若是相同,则此集团可以其中任何一个及其总数表之。于是故统计亦可谓研究集团中变化情形的方法(Statistics is the study of variation)。此种变化情形,可用频数分配(Frequency distribution)表之。例如中央大学投考生中三百人的成绩,分配如次:

---

* 本文大意,曾于四月十一日,在国立中央大学算学系讲演。

表 I

国立中央大学投考生的国算英平均成绩

（A）组　限	（B）实得人数（f_o）	（C）依正态分配的人数（f_t）
0—5	4	7.05
5—10	15	9.68
10—15	17	17.67
15—20	29	26.85
20—25	37	36.39
25—30	43	42.42
30—35	41	42.96
35—40	36	38.78
40—45	28	30.67
45—50	28	21.07
50—55	13	13.09
55—60	5	7.30
60—65	2	3.46
65—70	1	1.34
70—75	0	0.48
75—80	1	0.21
分总频数	300	300

平均数 $m=31$；标准差 $\sigma=13.4$

以总频数除各组的频数即得相对频数，文中所言频数分配，可作相对频数分配看。

由表吾人可知投考生程度的变化情形，所以统计的最大目的，在于求得变数的频数分配（Frequency distribution）。

此种分配表仍甚繁杂，记忆既难，了解尤艰，为欲求一简便法则，以归纳之，则惟算学是赖。例如上列例题，其频数分配情形，可以简明算式名正态曲线者表之：

$$\frac{1}{\sigma\sqrt{2\pi}}e^{-\frac{(x-\bar{x})^2}{2\sigma}}\delta x \tag{1}$$

式中 δx 为组距。而 $\bar{x}$ 与 σ 为参变数，足代表该分配的特性（Characteristics），故欲知一宇宙的分配情形，须知其分配式，亦即须知式中参变数，今若两变数 xy 的分配式为：

$$\frac{\delta_x \delta_y}{2\pi\sigma_1\sigma_2\sqrt{1-r^2}} e^{-\frac{1}{2(1-r^2)}\left\{\frac{(x-\bar{x})^2}{\sigma_1^2}+2r\frac{(x-\bar{x})(y-\bar{y})}{\sigma_1\sigma_2}+\frac{(y-\bar{y})^2}{\sigma_2^2}\right\}} \tag{2}$$

则其共变情形 Covariation,由 $\bar{x}$, $\bar{y}$, σ_1, σ_2, r 定之,倘测量时,各以其平均数 $\bar{x}$, $\bar{y}$ 为原点,且各以其标准差 $\sigma_1\sigma_2$ 为单位,则其共变情形,由 r 定之。此 r 谓之相关系数①(Correlation coefficient)一般论相关者,表面上,似仅言 r;实质上, r 之所以为讨论之中心者,因能代表共变情形也,故言 r 实无异于言(2)式。

一个宇宙里的变数,可为连续(Continuous),例如物价指数,可为不连续(Discontinuous),例如一家的人口数,一个宇宙所含的数量,可为有限(Finite),可为无限(Infinite)。但一般统计问题的变数,往往可假定为连续,且为无限。各种宇宙,因变数不同,其分配情形,亦互异,倘宇宙的频数分配为已知,则不难以算学方法,求得其真实的(True)或近似的(Approximate)算式,以综括之,但在事实上,我人所有的资料(Data),仅为宇宙的一部分,谓之样本(Sample),此种样本,不一定能充分地代表其宇宙;通常含有一种错误(Error),谓之偶错(Chance or sample error)。因统计资料含有此种偶错,其分配不必与原宇宙的分配完全相符合。所以统计是要根据一个样本的智识,推求全宇宙的情形;并不是预知宇宙的分配情形而求定任一样本的分配情形。例如表Ⅰ第二行为大学投考生的国算英平均成绩的一个样本,第三行若用总频数除之,为根据于此样本而求得的原宇宙(或消去偶错后的样本)的分配情形。

由是足见统计问题,约有三种:

1. 思考统计对象的性质,选定算式,用以表示其分配情形(Problems of specification)。

2. 求定算式中之参变数。

算式既经选定,则须根据样本的智识,求定算式中参变数之值,如是求定之参变数值,谓之统计示数(Estimated statistical constants),此种示数,常因算法不同而异其值。故算法之选定,为本问题之重要部分。

3. 考察算式之合宜性(Fitness)及统计示数之准确度(Precision or reliablity)。

第一种,选定算式须有算学智识,以为根据,其选择之手续:(a)我人可观察统计资料之分配,然后依其形状,选一合宜算式以配合之,其配合情形,

---

① 欲明相关的完全意义,请读作者之博士论文:"The Development of Correlation Theory and Its Application to Economic Statistics", University of Wis., Madison, Wisconsin, U.S.A., 1934。

再用别法试探之,关于一个变数的算式,现有贝尔逊氏之曲线组(Pearsonian system of curves),足供一般之需要。惟于二个或多个变数的问题,尚未有此种便利,有待于理论统计学家的供献①。(b)吾人可依照算式之出处(Derivation on the basis of certain hypotheses)与性质,考查统计变数,是否与其前提(by potheses)相符合,例如有一变数,为无穷个同级微量(Infinitely small quantities of the same order)所合成,其分配情形,必如正态曲线(Normal curve),已由Laplace-Hagen②证明之。于是任何统计事象,例如成年人的体高,为遗传与环境的结果,遗传又为父系母系无数个祖宗的结果,而环境方面,亦可分析为食物、气候、操作等因素。若再将因素继续分析之,则环境亦为恒河沙数个同级微量所合成。于是其分配情形,可以正态曲线表之,但财富的分配,必不为正态;盖财富可受遗传及所经营事业的影响。而此等因素(例如所经营的事业,为与军用品有关系者,则可因欧战而致富)不与其他因素为同级,故财富之成因,不与正态曲线之前提相符合。

第二种,算式既经选定,则算式中之参变数,可用下列三法中任一法求得之:

(a)旋力法(Method of moments)。

此法之原理甚简,计算亦易,惟其武断的性质(Arbitrary nature)甚强。

令 y 为 x 在 $(x, x+\mathrm{d}x)$ 间之实得频数(Frequency),并令 f 为所选定之算式,中含有 $k_1, k_2, \cdots, k_n$ 等 n 个变数,今如 y 之频数分配,可以 f 代表之,则必

$$\int_{-\infty}^{\infty} x^a f \mathrm{d}x = \int_{-\infty}^{\infty} x^a y \mathrm{d}x \tag{3}$$

或,如 f 为非连续函数,

$$\sum x^a f = \sum x^a y$$

式中 $a = 0, 1, 2, \cdots, (n-1)$。如将此 n 个方程式解之,可得 $k_1, k_2, \cdots, k_n$ 等参变数之值。

(b)最小二乘方法(The method of least squares)。

令 $f, y,$ 及 x 之意义,一如前节所设。则依最小二乘方原理,得

---

① 读者欲知理论统计学家在这一方面努力的结果,请参考作者所著 The Development of Correlation Theory and Its Application to Economic Statistics, University of Wisconsin, U.S.A., ch.II, 1934。

② 请参考作者所著之《二项展开式与正态曲线》,《计政学报》1935年第1卷第4期。

$$\int_{-\infty}^{\infty} (f-y)^2 \mathrm{d}x = \text{minimum} \qquad (4)$$

若为不连续,则该式可书为

$$\sum (f-y)^2 = \min$$

今若将此式对于 $k_1, k_2, \cdots, k_n$ 先后取微分,并令之为零,可得 n 个方程式,以求定 $k_1, k_2, \cdots, k_n$ 之值。但在实际问题中,由上式微分而得的 n 个方程式,往往为不可解。即使可解,由是求得之参变数值,是否为最佳,尚须视乎 $(f-y)=z$ 之是否为正态分配,盖最小二乘方之原理,固根据于此种假定推演得来者,请说明之:

设 $z_1, z_2, \cdots, z_n$ 为 n 个独立变数,各自依照正态分配,则欲此 n 个变数之值同时各在 $(z_1, z_1+\mathrm{d}z_1)$,$(z_2, z_2+\mathrm{d}z_2)$,……间隔内出见之机率为:

$$P_n = C_e^{-\frac{1}{2}\left\{\frac{(z_1-\bar{z}_1)^2}{\sigma_1^2}+(z_2-\bar{z}_2)^2+\cdots\right\}}$$

此机率最大之时,即 $\sum \dfrac{(z_i-\bar{z}_i)^2}{\sigma_i^2}$ 最小之时,此即高斯(Gauss)推求最小二乘方原理的方法,由是观之,应用最小二乘方原理,以求参变数,其值不必为最佳,倘若推求此原理的前提,不能使之满足。

(c) 最象法(Method of maximum likelihood)。

欲 x 之值,在 $(x, x+\mathrm{d}x)$ 之间,其机会为

$$f(x, k_1, k_2, \cdots, k_n)\mathrm{d}x$$

欲样本中之 x 值,有 n_1 次在 $(x_1, x_1+\mathrm{d}x_1)$ 之间,n_2 次在 $(x_2, x_2+\mathrm{d}x_2)$ 之间,等等,则其机率为

$$P = \frac{n_i!}{\prod(n_i!)} \prod \{f(x, k_1, k_2, \cdots, k_n)\mathrm{d}x_i\}^{n_i}$$

式中 $\sum n_i = n$,$\prod$ 为累乘之符号

欲此机率为最大,必须 P 之值为最大,亦即须

$$\sum n_i \log f = \text{极大} \qquad (5)$$

今若将此式对 $k_1, k_2, \cdots, k_n$ 取微分,可得 n 个方程式,以解 k_i 之值。但此等方程式有时为不可解,如为可解,则如是求得之参变数值,具有如

次之意义①。若宇宙之参变数,果为此等数值,则类此之样本的出现机率,必为最大。

第三种,算式既经求定,则其合宜性之检定,须根据于某统计示数之分配,以为论断之根据,此统计示数谓之 χ^2(读如 K_i)。

设 $x_0 + m_0, x_1 + m_1, \cdots, x_n + m_n$ 为实得之各组频数,$m_0, m_1, m_2, \cdots, m_n$ 为各组的理论频数,并设 $x_0, x_1, x_2, \cdots, x_n$ 之分配,各为正态,则欲一组数值 $x_0, x_1, x_2, \cdots, x$ 同时出现之机率为②

$$P = K e^{\frac{1}{2}\chi^2} \chi^{n-2} d\chi$$

式中 $\chi^2 = \chi_0^2 + \chi_1^2 + \chi_2^2 + \cdots + \chi_n^2$。由是欲实得频数与理论频数之差误,较之现在者更大,其机率为

$$\int_\chi^\infty K e^{-\frac{1}{2}\chi^2} \chi^{n-2} d\chi^2 \tag{6}$$

此积分式,已由 Eiderton 氏计算成表,以供统计学者之用。

设如表 I,中大投考生的国算英平均成绩,其各组之次数用 f_o 表之,今以正态曲线配合之,令此正态曲线为 f_t:

$$f_t dz = \frac{1}{\sqrt{2\pi}} e^{-\frac{z^2}{2}} dz \tag{7}$$

并令

$$\chi^2 = \sum \frac{(f_o - f_t)^2}{f_t} \tag{8}$$

则此量代表实得频数与理论频数分配的标准差。如原宇宙果为正态分配,则一样本的分配与理论的频数分配之差误,较此 χ^2 值为大者,其出见的机率,必不为甚小。倘为甚小,例如小于5%,则吾人将疑此差误 χ^2,非全由于抽样的偶错(Sampling error),而另有其成因在。换言之,吾人将疑算式(7)不足代表该样本的宇宙。亦即谓该样本的宇宙,非属于正态分配者。

---

① 请参考:R. A. Fisher, "Mathematical Foundations of Statistics", International Mathematical Congress, 1923; Also, Statistical Methods for Research Workers。
② 请参考:Pearson, K., "On the Criterion that a given system of Deviations from the probable etc.", Phil. Mag. 5th series, Vol.50, p.157, 1900; Also, R. A. Fisher, "On the Interpretation of χ^2", Jour. Roy. Stat. Soc., Vol.85, p.87, 1922。

又如第一节所述,一个变数的变化情形,可以算式表之,亦可以该算式中之参变数代表,今样本既含有抽样错误(Sampling error),则由此样本求得之参变数值即示数,亦必含有偶错。欲知此偶错之性质,必先求得此等示数之分配情形。试举例以明之:

设有一样本,计有 n 项,已知其来自正态分配的宇宙(Normal population):

$$\frac{N}{\sigma\sqrt{2\pi}}e^{-\frac{(x-m)^2}{2\sigma^2}}$$

则其分配情形,由下式定之:

$$\left.\begin{array}{l} m = \bar{x} = \dfrac{\sum x}{n} \\[2mm] \sigma^2 = s^2 = \dfrac{\sum(x-\bar{x})^2}{n} \end{array}\right\} \quad (9)$$

式中 $\bar{x}$ 名曰平均数(Mean),s 名曰标准差(Standard deviation)。

今若有似此之样本 n 个,则由此等样本求出来的平均数与标准差之值,必不相同,其变化情形,即为 $\bar{x}$ 与 s 所含的偶错的外表行为。盖若 $\bar{x}$ 与 s 不含有偶错,则必彼此相等而无所谓变化。于是故欲知 $\bar{x}$ 与 s 之可恃程度,必先知 $\bar{x}$ 与 s 的分配情形。故我人之问题可述之如次:

设已知宇宙的分配形状,试求其样本的变化情形。

如上所述,设宇宙为正态分配,并设由此宇宙任取 n 项之样本为 $x_1, x_2, \cdots, x_n$,则欲此样本在 $(x_1, x_1+\delta x_1), (x_2, x_2+\delta x_2), \cdots, (x_n, x_n+\delta x_n)$ 之间,其机率为

$$\begin{aligned}\delta P &= \frac{N^n}{\sigma^n\sqrt{(2\pi)^n}}e^{-\frac{1}{2}\sum\frac{(x_1-m)^2}{\sigma^2}} \\ &= Ke^{-\frac{1}{2}\sum(x_1-\bar{x})^2+n(\bar{x}-m)^2}\delta x_1\cdots\delta x_n\end{aligned}$$

今若变换坐标制,而以 $\bar{x}, s$ 为坐标,则

$$\delta P = K'e^{-\frac{1}{2}\frac{ns^2}{\sigma^2}-\frac{n(\bar{x}-m)^2}{\sigma^2}}s^{n-2}\delta\bar{x}\delta s$$

将此式对 s 积分之,有

$$f(\bar{x})\delta\bar{x} = K'e^{-\frac{1}{2}\frac{n(\bar{x}-m)^2}{\sigma^2}}\delta\bar{x} \quad (10)$$

此即平均数 $\bar{x}$ 之分配式,属于正态曲线;以 m 为其平均数,$\sigma/\sqrt{n}$ 为其标

准差①。换言之,若从一正态宇宙,任取若干个样本,每个样本含有 n 项,则由此等样本所求得的平均数,各有差异,其频数分配,谓之抽样分配(Sampling distribution)。其式恰为正态曲线。

今

$$e(\bar{x}) = e\left(\frac{\sum x_i}{n}\right) = e\left\{\frac{\sum(m+\delta_i)}{n}\right\}$$

$$= e\left(m + \frac{\sum \delta_i}{n}\right) = e(m).$$

足见 $\bar{x}$ 的理想值(Expected value)或平均数(Mean),即真确数(True value)。

又在实际问题,宇宙的标准差 σ 为不知,仅能由样本推算之,其法如次:

$$e(s^2) = e\left\{\frac{\sum\left(x_i - \frac{\sum x_i}{n}\right)^2}{n}\right\} = \frac{1}{n}e\left\{\sum x_i^2 - \frac{(\sum x_i)^2}{n}\right\}$$

$$= \frac{1}{n}e\left\{\sum(m+\delta_i)^2 - \frac{(\sum \overline{m+\delta_i})^2}{n}\right\}$$

$$= \frac{1}{n}e\left\{nm^2 + 2m\sum \delta_i + \sum \delta_i^2 - \frac{(\sum m)^2}{n} - \frac{2m\sum \delta_i}{n} - \frac{\sum \delta_i}{n}\right\}$$

$$= \frac{1}{n}e\left\{nm^2 + \sum \delta_i^2 - \frac{\sum \delta_i}{n} - nm^2\right\}$$

$$= \frac{1}{n}e\left(\frac{n-1}{n}\sum \delta_i^2\right) = \frac{n-1}{n}e\left(\frac{\sum \delta_i^2}{n}\right)$$

$$= \frac{n-1}{n}\sigma^2$$

于是故 σ^2 可以 $\frac{n}{n-1}s^2$ 代之。

---

① 平均数与标准差之求法如此:

$$\int_{-\infty}^{\infty} \bar{x} f(\bar{x}) d\bar{x} = m,$$

$$\int_{-\infty}^{\infty} \bar{x}^2 f(\bar{x}) d\bar{x} = \frac{\sigma^2}{n}$$

由上所论,我人对于平均数的可恃性,能有相当的了解:即 $\bar{x}$ 有一标准差等于 $\sqrt{\dfrac{n}{n-1}}s$;且在普通情形下,其与真确值之差,不至超过 $2s\sqrt{\dfrac{n}{n-1}}$。即偶或超过之,其机率仅为 0.045 5。

由上所论,如知统计示数(Estimated parameters)的可恃程度(Reliability)或准确性(Precision),必须求得该示数的分配式。而求此分配式的方法,往往含有艰深的数理,且在今日,统计示数的分配之为已知者,尚限于样本之来自正态宇宙者,至于样本之来自非正态分配的宇宙者,其示数的分配情形,多属未知,尚有赖于理论统计学家的努力。

(原载《国立中央大学社会科学丛刊》1935 年第 2 卷第 1 期)

二项展开式与正态曲线

1. 引　言

统计的对象,有时为一个事象,有时为二个或多个事象。譬如我们要统计中国财富的分配(或某种工人的工资,或成年男子的体高,或大学生的国英算的成绩),财富便是问题里的事象。因为各人所有的财富不等,所以这事象非是齐一不变的。因之统计问题里的事象,可称之为变量或变数(Variate)。这财富问题,各人所有的财富,便是变数所能取的各值。此等数值,均具有一个通性(Common Characteristic,本题的通性,即是中国个人的财富),自成集团(Aggregate of Individuals)。换言之,凡具有一个通性的众数,自成集团,这集团谓之宇宙(Population or Universe)。统计学是研究此种宇宙的方法(Statistics is the Study of the Aggregates of Individuals rather than of Individuals)。此与研究集团中个体的本身有别,读者不可不辨。物理学里气体运动学说(Kenetic Theory of Gases),以及化学里的质量反应学说(Theory of Mass Action),都是讨论集团的通性而非研究集团中个体的例子。

集团中个体,为数正多,故吾人颇难即刻明悉其通性。统计方法,即是简化集团中大众数量,综合为一个或数个示数(Statistical Measures or Parameters),以为集团通性的代表的手续(Method of Reduction)。

集团中个体,各不相同。若是相同,则此集团可以其中任一个及其总数表之。于是故统计亦可谓研究集团中变化情形的方法(Statistics is the Study of Variation)。此种变化情形,可用频数分配表(Frequency Distribution)表示之。

2. 次数与机率(Frequency and Probability)

设吾人观察某事象,共 n 次,计有 f 次为成功,则 f 谓之某事象出现之频数(Frequency)。下列任一项均为频数：

南京市人口，在 1934 年，675 504 人中，有 413 245 人为男子。

又某某三百个学生，在 1934 年，投考中央大学的国英算平均成绩为：

表 I

在 0 与 5 之间者有	2 人
在 5—10 之间者有	9 人
在 10—15 之间者有	16 人
在 15—20 之间者有	24 人
在 20—25 之间者有	35 人
在 25—30 之间者有	41 人
在 30—35 之间者有	46 人
在 35—40 之间者有	47 人
在 40—45 之间者有	36 人
在 45—50 之间者有	21 人
在 50—55 之间者有	9 人
在 55—60 之间者有	9 人
在 60—65 之间者有	3 人
在 65—70 之间者有	2 人
总频数	300

用总频数，除其成功的频数，所得的商数谓之相对次数(Relative Frequency)。在实用统计中，此相对次数，亦称机率(Probability)。但在理论统计学，此二者有别。试举例以明之。

设有形质完全相同的球一袋，共计 N 个，中有 F 个为白球，则此白球数 F 对于白球和黑球总数 N 之比，谓之取得一白球的机率。假如我人事先不知白黑球的个数，试自袋中连续取球，每次取一个，记载该球的颜色毕，返还袋中和匀后，再取第二球。如是继续行之，则每次取球时，袋中黑白球之比不变。设先后取球 n 次，中有 f 次为白球，则 f 与 n 之比，谓之白球出现的相对频数。今若 n 之值甚大，则 $\dfrac{f}{n}$ 之值，必与 $\dfrac{F}{N}$ 相差甚微。并且 n 之值愈大，则 $d = \dfrac{f}{n} - \dfrac{F}{N}$ 愈小。于是机率之意义，可定如下：

设在同一环境中，观察某事象 n 次，计有 f 次为成功。今若将观察次数 n 增至无限大时，$\dfrac{f}{n}$ 能趋于一定限 p，则此限 p 谓之机率。

本定义包含有二种假设：(1)相对频数，可有一定限(Limit)；(2)观察事象的环境,须是完全相同。此二假设,在实务统计上,有时不能满足,故本定义,尚不得谓为完美。惟较一般定义为近理且适用耳。为欲表示上列含义起见,统计学家,用下列符号记之：

$$E\left(\frac{f}{n}\right) = p$$

意谓 $\frac{f}{n}$ 之希望值或理想值(Expected Value),即是机率。

一事象出现的机率,有时可为预知。譬有一袋,中有形质完全相同的白球 7 个,黑球 3 个,则此十球的出见机会均等,故若从袋中任取一球,其为白球的机率为 $\frac{7}{10}$。此机率固亦可用统计法求得之。即按前节所述方法,自袋中取球多次,则白球出见之频数,与取球次数的比,即为白球出见的机率之近似值(Approximate Value)。当取球次数增至甚大时,此近似值与真值之差,必甚微小,可弃而不论。

一事象出见的机率,属于预知者,谓之先知机率(A Priori Probability)。其不为预知而必须根据于统计事实,以求得近似值者,谓之后知机率(A Posteriori Probability)。

3. 次数分配表

在统计,我人往往须将观察得的资料,分成组数。例如表 I 所示,中大投考生的成绩,分为十四组,在每组中,登记其人数,此种表格,谓之频数分配表(Frequency Distribution)。故频数分配表,实为表示变数的各值出见次数的一种计划(The frequency distribution specifies how frequently the variate takes each of its possible values)。

设有一变数 x ,可为 x_1, x_2, x_3, $\cdots$, x_n 等任一值,并设其取得各值的机率为 p_1, p_2, p_3, $\cdots$, p_n,则下表谓之理论的频数分配表：

x	x_1	x_2	x_3	$\cdots$	x_n
p	p_1	p_2	p_3	$\cdots$	p_n

$x_1 < x_2, \cdots < x_n$

今若有一函数 $f(x)$,能合于下列条件：

$$\int_{x_i}^{x_{i+1}} f(x)\,\mathrm{d}x;\ \int_{x_1}^{x_n} f(x)\,\mathrm{d}x = p_i$$

则此函数 $f(x)$，谓之 x 之频数分配函数。其所代表之曲线，谓之 x 之频数分配线。今中大投考生的国算英平均成绩，可用函数

$$f(x)\mathrm{d}x = \frac{1}{\sqrt{2\pi}\sigma}\mathrm{e}^{-\frac{(x-m)^2}{2\sigma^2}}\mathrm{d}x$$

表之，则此函数，谓之中大投考生的国算英平均成绩的频数分配线。但此曲线的形式，由参变数 m 及 σ 定之，故其成绩的变化情形，可以 m 及 σ 表之，毋须详记繁琐的次数分配。

由经验所示，统计事象的分配情形，可以上列函数表之者甚众，且严密的统计理论，可以说是根据于本函数[1]。于此足见其重要，爰请详论之。

4. 二项式与正态曲线

此曲线之命名不一，有名之为正态曲线者，因事象的分配情形，颇多类此；有名之为机率曲线者，因变数 x 出见的机率，等于该函数之值；有名之为高斯氏差误定律者（Gaussian Law of Error），因彼等认此曲线为高斯（Gauss）所发明者[2]；又称为钟状曲线者，因其形状，观之如钟故也。

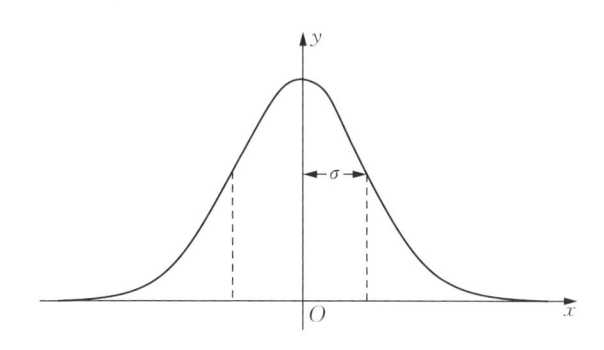

图 1　正态曲线

---

[1]　关于此问题，作者于去秋过伦敦时，曾访见 R. A. Fisher，略作商讨。彼之意见，可于最近将出版的 *Statistical Logics* 一书中见之。惟读者此时可深记算术平均数标准差，及相关系数等之理论根据，均在于此函数。且各种统计示数（Estimates of Statistical Constants）之抽样分配（Sampling Distribution），其求注亦均以此为出发点。请参考作者之博士论文 The Development of Correlation Theory, University of Wisconsin 的第四章。

[2]　关于正态曲线之发明史，请参考 Karl Pearson, "Historical Note on the Origin of the Normal Curve of Errors", Biom., Vol.16, p.402, 1924; James Bernoulli Theorem, Biometrika, Vol.17, p.201, 1925。

此曲线之函数,为二项展开式公项的限极,故其性质,多可由二项式得之,为欲明了此式与二项式的关系起见,请证明之。

A. 综合机率的定律①

设 Q, R 为二事象,其出见时,用 Q, R 表之;其不出见时,各以 $\bar{Q}, \bar{R}$ 记之。今若对于 $\bar{Q}\bar{R}$ 观察 n 次,其出见结果如下:

A, B 出见的情形	频 数
$Q \quad R$	a
$Q \quad \bar{R}$	b
$\bar{Q} \quad R$	c
$\bar{Q} \quad \bar{R}$	d

$$a + b + c + d = n.$$

则 Q, R 同时出见的机率为 a/n;或用符号表之:

$$P_{QR} = \frac{a}{n} \tag{1}$$

同样,

$$P_{Q\bar{R}} = \frac{b}{n} \tag{2}$$

$$P_Q = \frac{a+b}{n} \tag{3}$$

$$P_R = \frac{a+c}{n} \tag{4}$$

设 Q 已出见,而欲 R 出见,其机率为 $a/a+b$,用符号表之:

$$P_{R(如Q)} = \frac{a}{a+b} \tag{5}$$

由(1)(5)二式,可得下列关系:

---

① 本节证法,为 Poincaré 所发明,A. Fisher 曾引用之,见 Mathematical Theory of Probability。

$$P_{QR} = \frac{a}{n} = \frac{a+b}{n} \cdot \frac{a}{a+b}$$
$$= P_{R(如Q)} \cdot P_Q \tag{6}$$

由此足见 QR 同时出见的机率,等于 Q 出见的机率,乘 Q 已出见而欲 R 亦出见的机率之积。

又 Q 与 R 中有一出见的机率,为

$$P_{Q或R} = \frac{a+b+c}{n} = \frac{a+b}{n} + \frac{a+c}{n} - \frac{a}{n} = P_Q + P_R - P_{QR} \tag{7}$$

由此足见 Q, R 有一出见的机率,等于 Q, R 各自出见的机率的总和,减去 Q, R 同时出见的机率。

定义:如 Q 的出见,对于 R 的出见,不生任何影响,则 Q, R 二事象,谓之互相独立,或不相倚(Independent)。

定理 1:设 Q, R 为互相独立的事象,则

$$P_{RQ} = P_Q P_R \tag{8}$$

因 $P_R = P_{R(如Q)}$ 故也。

定义:如 Q 已出见,则 R 不能出见,反之亦然,则 Q, R 二事象,谓之互不相容(Exclusive)。

定理 2:设 Q, R 为互不相容的二事象,则

$$P_{Q或R} = P_Q + P_R \tag{9}$$

故 $P_{QR} = 0$ 故也。

B. 二项式分配(Binomial Distribution)

问题:设有形质完全相同的黑白球一袋①,由此袋中,陆续取球 n 个,自成一组(Set)。并设取第二球时,须先将第一球返还袋中和匀之,俾取得白球的机率,始终不变。若此机率为 p,并令 $1 - p = q$ 为取得非白球的机率。则含有 r 个白球的一组,其选法可有 ${}_nC_r$ 种。依定理一,每种出见的机率为 $p^r q^{n-r}$,于是 r 个白球的一组之出见率为

---

① 白球数与总球数之比,如为极小时,本问题之答案,为 Poisson's Law,请参考 Poisson, Recherches sur la. Probabilité de Jugements, Paris, p.205 ff, 1837。

$$B_r = {}_nC_r p^r q^{n-r} \qquad (10)$$

由是可知含有 0，或 1，或 2，…，或 n 个白球的一组的出见机率，依定理二，为：

$$\sum_{r=0}^{n} B_r = \sum_{r=0}^{n} {}_nC_r p^r q^{n-r} = (p+q)^n \qquad (11)$$

此式代表变数 r 之变化情形；盖由此式，吾人可知 r 任取一值（$r \leq n$）的机率也。兹求其平均数与标准差如次。

C. 二项式分配的平均数（Arithmetic Mean）

令 m 为平均数，则依定义，

$$m = \sum_{r=0}^{n} r \, {}_nC_r p^r q^{n-r} = \sum_{r=0}^{n} r \frac{n!}{(n-r)!r!}$$

此式之第一项为零。又其余各项，均有公因子 np，故将第一项去消，并将 np 括出，则

$$m = np \sum_{r=1}^{n} r \frac{(n-1)!}{(n-r)!r!} p^{r-1} q^{n-r}$$

$$= np \sum_{r=1}^{n} \frac{(n-1)!}{(n-r)!(r-1)!} p^{r-1} q^{n-r}$$

令 $s = r - 1$，则

$$m = np \sum_{s=0}^{n-1} \frac{(n-1)!}{(n-1-s)!s!} p^s q^{n-1-s}$$

$$= np(p+q)^{n-1} = np \qquad (12)$$

因 $p + q = 1$ 故也。

D. 二项式分配的平均差（Average Deviation）

令 δ 为平均差，依定义，即

$$\delta = \sum_{r=0}^{n} (r - np) \, {}_nC_r p^r q^{n-r}$$

$$= \sum_{r=0}^{n} r \, {}_nC_r p^r q^{n-r} - np \sum_{r=0}^{n} {}_nC_r p^r q^{n-r} = np - np = 0 \qquad (13)$$

故算术平均差为零。

E. 二项式分配之标准差(Standard Deviation)或变异量(Variance)

令 σ^2 为变异量,其平方根之正值为标准差,则依定义,

$$\sigma^2 = \sum_{r=0}^{n}(r-np)^2{}_nC_r p^r q^{n-r} = \sum_{r=0}^{n}(r^2 - 2npr + n^2p^2){}_nC_r p^r q^{n-r} \quad (14)$$

欲求左边第一式之值,令 $r^2 = r(r-1) + r$。于是

$$\sum_{r=0}^{n} r^2{}_nC_r p^r q^{n-r} = \sum_{r=0}^{n} r(r-1){}_nC_r p^r q^{n-r} + \sum_{r=0}^{n} r{}_nC_r p^r q^{n-r}$$

左边第二式之值,依(12)为 np;其第一式之第一与第二项皆为零,故可书为

$$\sum_{r=2}^{n} r(r-1){}_nC_r p^r q^{n-r} + np$$

若将第一式各项中公因数 $n(n-1)p^2$ 括出,并消去分子分母中之公因子 $r(r-1)$,则为

$$n(n-1)p^2 \sum_{r=2}^{n} \frac{(n-2)!}{(n-r)!(r-2)!} p^{r-2} q^{n-r} + np$$

令 $s = (r-2)$,则

$$n(n-1)p^2 \sum_{s=0}^{n-2} \frac{(n-2)!}{(n-2-s)!s!} p^s q^{n-s} + np = n(n-1)p^2(p+q)^{n-2} + np$$
$$= n(n-1)p^2 + np \quad (15)$$

今将此式及(12)之值,代入(14),则

$$\sigma^2 = \{n(n-1)p^2 + np\} - 2n^2p^2 + n^2p^2 = npq \quad (16)$$

因之,

$$\sigma = \sqrt{npq}$$

变数 r 之分配式(11),含有参变数 n 与 p,但 n, p 可由(12)及(16)求得之。于是故 r 之变化情形,可用平均数 m 与标准差或变异量 σ^2 表之。

F. 正态曲线(Normal Curve)

二项展开式,各项之值,恒为正数,并无有为零者。当 $r = np$ 时,其

项为最大①。又因二项式之总和恒为一,故 n 愈大,则各项之值愈小。若令 $B_r = {}_nC_r p^r q^{n-r}$, $\Delta r = \left(r + \dfrac{1}{2}\right) - \left(r - \dfrac{1}{2}\right)$,则各项之面积,可用正长方形之面积 $B_r \Delta r$ 表之,所成之条图,恒以 $r = np$ 为对称轴;且随 n 之增加而低平:

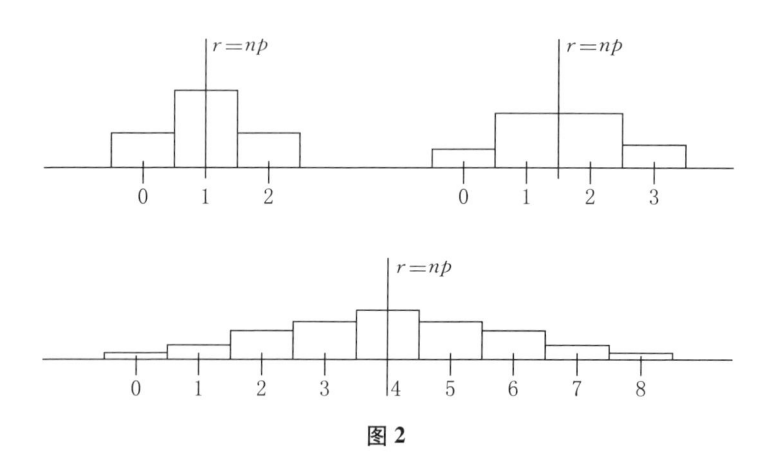

图 2

又于 n 增至甚大时,则计算任一项之值 $B_r \Delta r$,其法极繁,故为实用便利计,宜求简便式,以应需要。

欲将原点移至平均数,并欲以标准差为度量之单位,而免去度量单位之影响,可令

$$x = \frac{r - np}{\sqrt{npq}}, \quad y = \sqrt{npq}\, {}_nC_r p^r q^{n-r} \tag{17}$$

如是则每条之面积不变,亦即 r 出见之概率,等于 x 出见之机率:

$$B_r \Delta r = y \Delta x = {}_nC_r p^r q^{n-r}$$

令

$$\Delta x = \frac{r + \dfrac{1}{2} - np}{\sqrt{npq}} - \frac{r - \dfrac{1}{2} - np}{\sqrt{npq}} = \frac{1}{\sqrt{npq}} \tag{18}$$

---

① 严格言之,当 $np - p \leqslant r \leqslant np + p$ 时,其相当项为最大,但若将颇小之分数弃去不计,则当 $r = np$ 时,其频数为最大。请参考:Rietz, Math, Statistics, Chicago, p.25, 1929。

$$\frac{d}{dx}(\log y) = \frac{dy}{y dx}$$

$$= \operatorname*{Lim}_{n\to\infty} \frac{\sqrt{npq}\,({}_nC_{r+1}p^{r+1}q^{n-r-1} - {}_nC_r p^r q^{n-r})}{\sqrt{npq}\,{}_nC_r p^r q^{n-r} \dfrac{1}{\sqrt{npq}}}$$

$$= \operatorname*{Lim}_{n\to\infty}\left(\frac{n-r}{r+1}\frac{p}{q} - 1\right)\sqrt{npq} = \operatorname*{Lim}_{n\to\infty}\frac{(np-r-q)\sqrt{npq}}{(r+1)q}$$

$$= -\operatorname*{Lim}_{n\to\infty}\left\{\frac{r-np}{\sqrt{npq}} - \frac{npq}{(r+1)q} - \frac{q}{\sqrt{npq}} - \frac{npq}{(r+1)q}\right\}$$

但 $r = x\sqrt{npq} + np$，且 $\operatorname*{Lim}_{n\to\infty}xq\sqrt{npq} + q$ 之值；较之 $\operatorname*{Lim}_{n\to\infty}npq$ 为甚小，故

$$\operatorname*{Lim}_{n\to\infty}\frac{npq}{(r+1)q} = \operatorname*{Lim}_{n\to\infty}\frac{npq}{xq\sqrt{npq} + npq + q} \approx 1$$

$$\operatorname*{Lim}_{n\to\infty}\frac{q}{\sqrt{npq}} \approx 0 \tag{19}$$

故

$$\frac{d}{dx}(\log y) = -x \tag{20}$$

将(20)求积分，得

$$\log y = -\frac{x^2}{2} + c$$

或

$$y = Ke^{-\frac{x^2}{2}} \tag{21}$$

$$= Ke^{-\frac{(r-np)^2}{2npq}} \tag{21a}$$

今 ydx 为 x 在 $(x, x+dx)$ 内出见之机率，且 x 之值，必限于 $-\infty$ 及 $+\infty$ 之间，故 K 之值，可由下式定之：

$$\int_{-\infty}^{+\infty} ydx = 1 = 2\int_{-\infty}^{+\infty} Ke^{-\frac{x^2}{2}}dx \tag{22}$$

欲求(22)之值,请先求

$$I = \int_0^\infty e^{-u^2} du$$

令 $u = at$, $du = adt$, 则

$$I^2 = I\int_0^\infty e^{-a^2} da = \int_{t=0}^{t=\infty} \int_{a=0}^{a=\infty} e^{-a^2(1+t^2)} adadt$$

$$= \int_{t=0}^{t=\infty} dt \left[\frac{-1}{2(1+t^2)} e^{-a^2(1+t^2)}\right]_0^\infty$$

$$= \int_0^{t=\infty} \frac{dt}{2(1+t^2)} = \frac{1}{2} \arctan t \Big|_0^\infty$$

$$= \frac{\pi}{4}$$

$$\therefore \quad I = \int_0^\infty e^{-u^2} du = \frac{\sqrt{\pi}}{2}$$

令 $u = \dfrac{x}{\sqrt{2}}$, $du = \dfrac{dx}{\sqrt{2}}$, 则

$$\frac{\sqrt{\pi}}{2} = \int_0^\infty e^{-u^2} du = \frac{1}{\sqrt{2}} \int_0^\infty e^{-\frac{x^2}{2}} dx$$

$$\therefore \quad \int_0^\infty e^{-\frac{x^2}{2}} dx = \frac{\sqrt{\pi}}{\sqrt{2}} \tag{23}$$

将此代入(22),得

$$2K = \frac{\sqrt{\pi}}{\sqrt{2}} = 1$$

$$\therefore \quad K = \frac{1}{\sqrt{2\pi}}$$

$$y = \frac{1}{\sqrt{2\pi}} e^{-\frac{x^2}{2}} \tag{24}$$

$$ydx = \frac{1}{\sqrt{2\pi}} e^{-\frac{x^2}{2}} dx \tag{25}$$

或 $$_nC_rp^rq^{n-r} = \frac{y}{\sqrt{npq}} = \frac{1}{\sqrt{2\pi npq}}e^{-\frac{(r-np)^2}{2npq}}dr \qquad (25a)$$

例题：将 12 个银元掷之，试求五个至八个头出见之机率。

依定理 2，欲求之机率等于五，六，七，八个头各自出见之机率之和。今 $p = q = \frac{1}{2}$，$n = 12$，故

$$P = {}_{12}C_5\left(\frac{1}{2}\right)^{12} + {}_{12}C_6\left(\frac{1}{2}\right)^{12} + {}_{12}C_7\left(\frac{1}{2}\right)^{12} + {}_{12}C_8\left(\frac{1}{2}\right)^{12} = 0.733$$

但若用(25)式求之，如图所示，此机率等于自 $r_1 = 4.5$ 至 $r_2 = 8.5$ 间之面积。今

$$np = 6, \sqrt{npq} = 1.732$$

$$x_1 = \frac{r_1 - np}{\sqrt{npq}} = \frac{4.5 - 6}{1.732} = -0.866$$

$$x_2 = \frac{r_2 - np}{\sqrt{npq}} = \frac{8.5 - 6}{1.732} = 1.443$$

$$P' = \int_{x_1}^{x_2} ydx = \int_0^{x_1} ydx + \int_0^{x_2} ydx = 0.307 + 0.425 = 0.732$$

由此足见，当 $n = 12$ 时，用正态曲线求得之结果，已准确至第二位小数（差误恒小于百分之一），若 n 增至 30 以上，其准确程度，已足一切统计实务之用矣。(25)式的积分，为用既夥，遂有数学家计算其结果，列成表式①，以应实用，名曰正态曲线积分表。

G. 正态曲线之性质

正态曲线，形状如钟，均在 x 轴之上（即 y 之值，恒为正数，其总面积为 1），而以 x 轴为其几近线；对于 y 轴成对称，有一极大值，在 $x = 0$（即是平均数），盖

---

① 正态曲线的积分表，种类甚多，但下列数书，为此种表式之重要源流：
(i) J. Burgess, Trans. Roy. Soc. Edin., Vol.39, pp.257 - 321, 1895；
(ii) G. W. L. Glaisher, Phil. Mag. Series IV., Vol.42, p.436, 1871；
(iii) F. Galton and W. F. Shedrpnd., Biom., Vol.6, p.405, 1907；
(iv) T. L. Kelley, Statistical Methods, pp.373 - 385。

$$y' = \frac{dy}{dx} = \frac{1}{\sqrt{2\pi}} e^{-\frac{x^2}{2}}(-x) = 0, 即 x = 0$$

且于 $x = 0$ 时, y'' 为负数:

$$y'' = \frac{1}{\sqrt{2\pi}} e^{-\frac{x^2}{2}}(x^2 - 1) = 0, 当 q = 0$$

又 $y'' = 0$, 当 $x = \pm 1$, 故正态曲线,有二变向点在 $x = \pm 1$,亦即在变数等于标准差处。

正态曲线之平均差为零;盖

$$D = \int_{-\infty}^{\infty} xy dx = -\frac{1}{\sqrt{2\pi}} e^{-\frac{x^2}{2}} \Big|_{-\infty}^{\infty} = 0 \tag{26}$$

正态曲线之标准差为 1;盖原以标准差为度量之单位也[①]。

$$\sigma^2 = \int_{-\infty}^{\infty} x^2 y dx = \int_{-\infty}^{\infty} (y + y'') dx$$
$$= \int_{-\infty}^{\infty} y dx + \int_{-\infty}^{\infty} y'' dx = 1 + y' \Big|_{-\infty}^{\infty} = 1 \tag{27}$$

又

$$\int_{-1}^{+1} y dx = 0.682\,68; \int_{-2}^{+2} y dx = 95.45\%$$
$$\int_{-1.939\,64}^{+1.959\,64} y dx = 95\%, 或 2\int_{1.959\,64}^{\infty} y dx = 5\%$$
$$2\int_{2.575\,829}^{\infty} y dx = 1\%$$

故自 -1 至 +1 间所包含之面积,约占全面积百分之六八;自 -2 至 +2 间约占全面积百分之 95。因之,变数 x 在 -2 与 +2 间出现之机率,约为百分之九五。换言之,自正态分配的宇宙中,任取一项,其值与平均数之差,普通不至

---

① 见(18)式。如测量之单位,非足标准差,则正态曲线之公式为(25a)。若将此式依(27)之步法求之,其结果为 $\sigma^2 = npq$:

$$y' = -\frac{r - np}{npq} y, \quad y'' = -\frac{y}{npq} + \frac{(r - np)^2}{npq} y$$
$$\sigma^2 = \int_{-\infty}^{\infty} (r^2 - np) y dx = npq \int_{-\infty}^{\infty} (y + y'') dx = npq$$

超过标准差之二倍;其超过之机会仅为百分之五弱。在实用统计,可假定此点为分界点,意谓凡事象出见之机率小于5%者,在通常平均环境中,不得出见。故若有一项,设自正态分配的宇宙中取来者,则是项与平均数之差,不得超过标准差之二倍。倘若超过之,则吾人认为有注意之必要,而予以考究;或且怀疑原假设为不合理①。例如样本的算术平均数 $\bar{Z}$,属于正态分配,且样本的平均数的理想值(The Expected Value of an Arithmetic Mean of a Sample),为宇宙的平均数或真确值 Z_0(True Value):

$$e\left(\frac{\sum Z_i}{n}\right) = e\left(\frac{\sum (Z_o + \delta_i)}{n}\right) = e(Z_o) \tag{28}$$

又宇宙的标准差,可以

$$S^2 = \frac{\sum (Z - \bar{Z})^2}{n-1}$$

代之。如是可见样本的平均数与宇宙的平均数之差,不得超过 $2s$,亦即谓宇宙的平均数,当在 $\bar{Z}-2s$ 与 $\bar{Z}+2s$ 之间也。由此,吾人对于平均数的准确性,可有一明确的概念矣。

设有一数 p,其意义由下式定之:

$$\int_{-p}^{+p} y \mathrm{d}x = \frac{1}{2}, \text{即 } p = 0.6745$$

此数 p 谓之机差或偶差(Probable Error)。故机差为标准差之 0.674 5 倍,其数值与四分位差(Quartile Deviation)相等。故变数之值,在机差(-0.6747,$+0.6745$)间出见,与在机差 ± 0.6745 外出见之机率相等。

在实务统计,其资料恒为宇宙的一部分,谓之样本。此种样本,往往呈现不规则形状,因其含有偶错故也。倘若吾人有相当理由,假定此样本,以为原宇宙分配情形的代表,并借此以消去样本的偶错(Sampling Error)。

配合正态曲线样本,其法可简述之如次:

1. 将样本列成频数分配表,令 i 为其组距。

2. 求其平均数 m 及准差 σ,各以组距为单位,即 $\frac{m}{i}$ 及 $\frac{\sigma}{i}$。

---

① 请参考 R. A. Fisher, Statistical Methods for Research Workers, Chs.III and V。

3. 令 r 为各组的下限,求 $\frac{(r-m)}{i}$。

4. 求 $\frac{(r-m)}{i} \div \frac{\sigma}{i} = \frac{(r-m)}{\sigma}$。

5. 用正态曲线积分表,求自 o 至 x 之面积,再求其二相邻数之差,即得各组之相对频数。

6. 求 $\frac{N_i}{\sigma}$ 之值中 N 为样本之总频数。

7. 将(5)与(6)之结果相乘,即得理想的绝对频数 y。

8. 配合此理想的频数于实测的频数 y' 之上,以视其适合否。其适合的程度,普通须求得

$$\sum \frac{(y-y')^2}{y'} = x^2 \tag{29}$$

及组频数(Class Frequency)的独立变化的程度数(The Number of Degrees of Freedom),而后用 $x^2(x_i)$ 的积分表,求得机率,以为论断之根据①。

由是足见正态分曲线之效用有三:第一,用以描摹某种事象的分配情形;第二,用示某种示数(Estimated Statistical Parameters)[例如算术平均数]的准确程度或可恃性(Precision or Reliability);第三,用作推求示数的分配式(Frequency Distribution of Estimated Parameters)的根据②。

5. 正态曲线的一般求法

戴穆佛③(Demoivre)为求得正态曲线的第一人,时为 1733 年,其法即将斯德邻(Sterling)公式 $n! = n^n e^{-n} \sqrt{2n\pi}$ 代入二项展式之公项,简化之即得正态曲线。此后算学家兼物理学家赖拍拉史④(Laplace)及高斯⑤(Gauss),

---

① 请参考 R. A. Fisher, Statistical Methods, Ch. IV。
② 请参考 p.365 注 1。
③ K. Pearson, "Historical Note on the Origin of the Normal Curve of Errors", Biono., Vol.16, p.402; Also, "Games Bernoulli's Theorem", Biono., Vol.17, p.201, 1925.
④ "Memoir sur les Integrales Définices et Leur Application aux Probabilités, etc.", Memoires de l'Institute Imperial de France for 1810, pp.279–347.
⑤ Theoria Combinations Observationum Erroribus Minimis Obnoxiae, 1823, and the Supplementum, 1826.

先后因研究天文之需要,根据于不相同的假设,求得正态曲线,高氏名此线曰"差误分配定律"。意谓测量某量 X 所得之数值 x,恒受测量人的性格,仪器,及影响于测量人及仪器的环境的影响,而有偶差(Accidental Error)。此差误 $z = X - x$ 在 z 与 $z + dz$ 间出见之机率,等于下式之值:

$$\frac{h}{\sqrt{\pi}}e^{-h^2z^2} \tag{30}$$

式中 h 相当于(25a)之 $1/\sqrt{2npq}$,谓之准确程度(Precision)。盖在同一情况下,测量 X 所得之一组数值 x_1, x_2, …, x(x 为其中之任一项),其准确程度愈高,则 h 之值愈大,其准确程度愈低,则 h 之值愈小故也。继赖高二人而研究此式者,颇不乏人,其求得之方法,亦甚不一致,要可归纳为二大派:第一派根据于逆机率的理论(Theory of Inverse Probability)及平均数之原理;第二派的论证,根据于一个假设,即凡一个差误 $z = X - x$,为恒河沙数个微小差误之总和(The Error Committed in a Measurement is Assumed to be the Sum of Elementary Errors)。兹各举一例,以为表率。

(i)应用逆机率与平均数的原理,以求得正态曲线法。

包恩赉①(Poincaré)根据下列二个假设:

(a) x 为测量所得之值,其在 x 与 $x + dx$ 间之机率,为其偶差的函数 $\varphi(X - x)$,且 $\varphi(X - x)$ 的第一第二次纪数(Derivatives)为连续函数。

(b) 设 x_1, x_2, x_3, …, x_n 为测量 X 所得的一组数值,其"极大机率值"(The Most Probable Value),依据逆机率的理论,应为该组数值的平均数。

能证明任一量的真值 X,在 X 与 $X + dX$ 之间的先知机率(A Priori Probability) $H(X)dX$,与 X 无涉(Independent)。然后本此推演,求得差误 $Z = X - x$ 的分配定律,其式恰为(30)。

上列假设(a),实无异于柯立芝(Coolidge)②的假设:函数 $\varphi(X, x)$ 为

---

① Poincaré, Calcul des Probabilites, pp.174-176, 1912.
② Coolidge, Probability, p.114, 1925.

与原点无涉。至于假设 b,曾有许多学者,加以解释,旧派的分析,可于戚伯(Czuber)著的观测事象的差误理论①一书中见之。此书诚为近世机率论或偶差论所常引证者也②。较新的解释,可以薛巴雷利(Schiaparelli)为例。对于一组实测数 $x_1, x_2, x_3, \cdots, x_n$ 的最佳值,薛氏作下列假设:

(c) $\dfrac{\partial \beta}{\partial x_i}$ 能存在,式中 β 为最佳值, $i = 1, 2, 3, \cdots, n$。

(d) $\beta(kx_1, kx_2, \cdots, kx_n) = k\beta(x_1, x_2, \cdots, x_n)$。无论 k 之值为何,此关系式,恒能存在。此假定实表示最佳值与测量的单位无涉。

(e) $\beta(x_1, x_2, x_3, \cdots, x_n)$ 为 $x_1, x_2, \cdots, x_n$ 之对称式(Symmetric Function)。意谓 β 与测量的原点(Zero Reading)无涉。

(f) 如一组实测值 $x_1, x_2, \cdots, x_n$ 是同样的准确或可恃(Equally Trustworthy),则 $\beta(x_1, x_2, \cdots, x_n)$ 为 $x_1, x_2, \cdots, x_n$ 之对称式。

根据于上列假设,薛氏能证明最佳值,即是算术平均数(Arithmetic Mean)。由是观之,假设(b)实等于(c)(d)(e)(f)等四个假设。

此外包恩赉氏根据于下列一假设:

一组实测值 $x_1, x_2, \cdots, x_n$ 的平均数,应为 X 的理想值;即

$$e(X) = \int_{-\infty}^{\infty} XP(X)\,dX \tag{31}$$

求得下式

$$\varphi(X, x) = Ⓗ(X)\,e^{-k^2 \int Ⓗ(X)(X-x)\,dX} \tag{32}$$

式中 Ⓗ(X) 为 x 的一个任意函数,至于 $\varphi(X, x)$ 的形式,本于下列假设而决定:即先知机率(A Priori Probability 等于极小常数)。严格言之,此假设尚不能认为满意。

设实测值 $x_1, x_2, \cdots, x_n$,服从正态分配的定律,则 X 的理想值,可证为未来的无数个实测值的平均数,即

---

① Czuber, Theorie der Beobachtungsfehler, 1891.
② Mathematical Encyclopedia Article on Probability and on Theory of Errors; the Corresponding Articles in the Enclocypedia Brittanica; and Coolidge's Mathematical Theory of Probabitity.

$$e(x) = \int_{-\infty}^{\infty} xP(x)\mathrm{d}x = \int_{-\infty}^{\infty} XP(X)\mathrm{d}X = e(X) \tag{33}$$

此即吾人用平均数代表一组正态分配的实测值的根据。

(ⅱ) 设一差误,为无数个微小差误之和,试求定该差误之分配定律。

哈根①(Hagen)氏的证法,可为此派的代表。设一差误为 n 个微小差误之和,并设此等微小差误 ϵ 各自相等,为正或为负的机会均等,则如 n 个微小差误中,有 m 个为负,$(n-m)$ 个为正,其结果的差误(Resultant Error)之大小等于 $(n-2m)\epsilon$。但此差误可说是由 n 个差误中,选取 m 个为负,其余 $(n-m)$ 个为正所合成者,故其产生之方法,共有 $_nC_m$ 种。

设 $x-\epsilon$ 为如是产生之一差误,即

$$x - \epsilon = (n-2m)\epsilon,\text{或 } x = (n-2m+1)\epsilon \tag{34}$$

并设 $f(x-\epsilon)$ 为产生此差误的可能频数,即

$$f(x-\epsilon) = {_nC_m} = \frac{n!}{(n-m)!m!} \tag{35}$$

又差误 $x+\epsilon = (n-2m+2)\epsilon$,可说是由 n 个微小差误中,选取 $(m-1)$ 个为负,$(n-m+1)$ 个为正所合成者,故其出现之频数为

$$f(x+\epsilon) = {_nC_{m-1}} = \frac{n!}{(n-m+1)!(m-1)!}$$

因之,

$$\frac{f(x+\epsilon)}{f(x-\epsilon)} = \frac{m}{n-m+1}$$

微小差误 ϵ,依假设,本为极小之量,故实测差误 x,可视为 $-n\epsilon$ 与 $+n\epsilon$ 间之连续变数。若 $n\epsilon$ 为无限大,则 $x = \pm n\epsilon$ 出见之相对频数,必为极小。今令 $\varphi(x)$ 为 x 之一连续函数,且 $\varphi(x)\mathrm{d}x$ 为 x 在 $(x, x+\mathrm{d}x)$ 间隔内出见之频数,则因 $f(x)$ 为 x 在 $(x-\epsilon, x+\epsilon)$ 间出见之频数,吾人可得

$$f(x) = C\varphi(x)2\epsilon$$

$$\frac{\varphi(x+\epsilon)}{\varphi(x-\epsilon)} = \frac{f(x+\epsilon)}{f(x-\epsilon)} = \frac{m}{n-m+1}$$

---

① Hagen, Grundzuge der Wahrscheinlichkeitsrechnung, Berlin, 1837.

$$\frac{\varphi(x+\epsilon)-\varphi(x-\epsilon)}{\varphi(x+\epsilon)+\varphi(x-\epsilon)}=\frac{-(n-2m+1)}{n+1}$$

但 ϵ^2 较之 ϵ 为极小,故可弃之而不计,于是

$$\varphi(x+\epsilon)=\varphi(x)+\epsilon\frac{\mathrm{d}\varphi}{\mathrm{d}x}$$

$$\varphi(x-\epsilon)=\varphi(x)-\epsilon\frac{\mathrm{d}\varphi}{\mathrm{d}x}$$

将此式代入(36),得

$$\frac{2\epsilon\frac{\mathrm{d}\varphi}{\mathrm{d}x}}{2\varphi(x)}=-\frac{n-2m+1}{n+1}=-\frac{x}{(n+1)\epsilon}$$

或

$$\frac{1}{\varphi}\frac{\mathrm{d}\varphi}{\mathrm{d}x}=-\frac{x}{(n+1)\epsilon}$$

令

$$\frac{1}{(n+1)\epsilon^2}=h^2,$$

则

$$\frac{\mathrm{d}\log\varphi(x)}{\mathrm{d}x}=-h^2x$$

积分之,得

$$\varphi(x)=K\mathrm{e}^{-h^2x^2}$$

K 之值,如前所述,由下关系定之:

$$1=\int_{-\infty}^{\infty}\varphi(x)\mathrm{d}x=K\int_{-\infty}^{\infty}\mathrm{e}^{-h^2x^2}\mathrm{d}x=K\frac{\sqrt{\pi}}{h}$$

$$\therefore\quad K=\frac{h}{\sqrt{\pi}}$$

故

$$\varphi(x)=\frac{h}{\sqrt{\pi}}\mathrm{e}^{-h^2x^2}$$

对于此种证明,亦有可批评之处。即在事实上,有无所谓微小差误者,颇是疑问。

又在实务统计,其差误(Deviation)非为实测值(Observations)与其真确值(True Value)之差,而为实测值与其平均数之差。此种差误之成因[或各数值间差误(Differences between Individual Observations)之成因],是否同于偶差(Accidental Errors)者,吾人须先加考究。如考究之结果,足令吾人认为相同时,方得引用正态曲线,以为其变化情形之代表。否则必须设法——如 X^2 test——试验实测值的分配情形,是否与理想的正态分配相密合,以减免引用者的武断。

附积分表如次:

积分表 1

Area of Normal Curve from Mean to Indicated Deviation from Mean *

x/σ	Final Digit of x/σ									
	0	1	2	3	4	5	6	7	8	9
0.0	0.000 0	0.004 0	0.008 0	0.012 0	0.016 0	0.019 9	0.023 9	0.027 9	0.031 9	0.035 9
0.1	0.039 8	0.043 8	0.047 8	0.051 7	0.055 7	0.059 6	0.063 6	0.067 5	0.071 4	0.075 3
0.2	0.079 3	0.083 2	0.087 1	0.091 0	0.094 8	0.098 7	0.102 6	0.106 4	0.110 3	0.114 1
0.3	0.117 9	0.121 7	0.125 5	0.129 3	0.133 1	0.136 8	0.140 6	0.144 3	0.148 0	0.151 7
0.4	0.155 4	0.159 1	0.162 8	0.166 4	0.170 0	0.173 6	0.177 2	0.180 8	0.184 4	0.187 9
0.5	0.191 5	0.195 0	0.198 5	0.201 9	0.205 4	0.208 8	0.212 3	0.215 7	0.219 0	0.222 4
0.6	0.225 7	0.229 1	0.232 4	0.235 7	0.238 9	0.242 2	0.245 4	0.248 6	0.251 7	0.254 9
0.7	0.258 0	0.261 1	0.264 2	0.267 3	0.270 3	0.273 4	0.276 4	0.279 4	0.282 3	0.285 2
0.8	0.288 1	0.291 0	0.293 9	0.296 7	0.299 5	0.302 3	0.305 1	0.307 8	0.310 6	0.313 3
0.9	0.315 9	0.318 6	0.321 2	0.323 8	0.326 4	0.328 9	0.331 5	0.334 0	0.336 5	0.338 9
1.0	0.341 3	0.343 8	0.346 1	0.348 5	0.350 3	0.353 1	0.355 4	0.357 7	0.359 9	0.362 1
1.1	0.364 3	0.366 5	0.368 6	0.370 8	0.372 9	0.374 9	0.377 0	0.379 0	0.361 0	0.383 0
1.2	0.384 9	0.386 9	0.388 8	0.390 7	0.392 5	0.394 4	0.396 2	0.398 0	0.399 7	0.401 5
1.3	0.403 2	0.404 9	0.406 6	0.408 2	0.409 9	0.411 5	0.413 1	0.414 7	0.416 2	0.417 7
1.4	0.419 2	0.420 7	0.422 2	0.423 6	0.425 1	0.426 5	0.427 9	0.429 2	0.430 6	0.431 9
1.5	0.433 2	0.434 5	0.435 7	0.437 0	0.438 2	0.439 4	0.440 6	0.441 8	0.442 9	0.444 1
1.6	0.445 2	0.446 3	0.447 4	0.448 4	0.449 5	0.450 5	0.451 5	0.452 5	0.453 5	0.454 5

续表

x/σ	Final Digit of x/σ									
	0	1	2	3	4	5	6	7	8	9
1.7	0.455 4	0.456 4	0.457 3	0.458 2	0.459 1	0.459 9	0.460 8	0.461 6	0.462 5	0.463 3
1.8	0.464 1	0.464 9	0.465 6	0.466 4	0.467 1	0.467 8	0.468 6	0.469 3	0.469 9	0.470 6
1.9	0.471 3	0.471 9	0.472 6	0.473 2	0.473 3	0.474 4	0.475 0	0.475 6	0.476 1	0.476 7
2.0	0.477 2	0.477 8	0.478 3	0.478 8	0.479 3	0.479 8	0.480 3	0.480 8	0.481 2	0.481 7
2.1	0.482 1	0.482 6	0.483 0	0.483 4	0.483 8	0.484 2	0.484 6	0.485 0	0.485 4	0.485 7
2.2	0.486 1	0.486 4	0.486 8	0.487 1	0.487 5	0.487 8	0.488 1	0.488 4	0.488 7	0.489 0
2.3	0.489 3	0.489 6	0.489 8	0.490 1	0.490 4	0.490 6	0.490 9	0.491 1	0.491 3	0.491 6
2.4	0.491 8	0.492 0	0.492 2	0.492 5	0.492 7	0.492 9	0.493 1	0.493 2	0.493 4	0.493 6
2.5	0.493 8	0.494 0	0.494 1	0.494 3	0.494 5	0.494 6	0.494 8	0.494 9	0.495 1	0.495 2
2.6	0.495 3	0.495 5	0.495 6	0.495 7	0.495 9	0.496 0	0.496 1	0.496 2	0.496 3	0.496 4
2.7	0.496 5	0.496 6	0.496 7	0.496 8	0.496 9	0.497 0	0.497 1	0.497 2	0.497 3	0.497 4
2.8	0.497 4	0.497 5	0.497 6	0.497 7	0.497 7	0.497 8	0.497 9	0.497 9	0.498 0	0.498 1
2.9	0.498 1	0.498 2	0.498 2	0.498 3	0.498 4	0.498 4	0.498 5	0.498 5	0.498 6	0.498 6
3.0	0.498 7	0.498 7	0.498 7	0.498 8	0.498 8	0.498 9	0.498 9	0.498 9	0.499 0	0.499 0
3.1	0.499 0	0.499 1	0.499 1	0.499 1	0.499 2	0.499 2	0.499 2	0.499 2	0.499 3	0.499 3
3.2	0.499 3	0.499 3	0.499 4	0.499 4	0.499 4	0.499 4	0.499 4	0.499 5	0.499 5	0.499 5
3.3	0.499 5	0.499 5	0.499 5	0.499 6	0.499 6	0.499 6	0.499 6	0.499 6	0.499 6	0.499 7
3.4	0.499 7	0.499 7	0.499 7	0.499 7	0.499 7	0.499 7	0.499 7	0.499 7	0.499 7	0.499 8
3.5	0.499 8	0.499 8	0.499 8	0.499 8	0.499 8	0.499 8	0.499 8	0.499 8	0.499 8	0.499 8
3.6	0.499 8	0.499 8	0.499 9	0.499 9	0.499 9	0.499 9	0.499 9	0.499 9	0.499 9	0.499 9
3.7	0.499 9	0.499 9	0.499 9	0.499 9	0.499 9	0.499 9	0.499 9	0.499 9	0.499 9	0.499 9
3.8	0.499 9	0.499 9	0.499 9	0.499 9	0.499 9	0.499 9	0.499 9	0.499 9	0.499 9	0.499 9
3.9	0.500 0	0.500 0	0.500 0	0.500 0	0.500 0	0.500 0	0.500 0	0.500 0	0.500 0	0.500 0

* Arranged from Raymond Pearl, Introduction to Medical Biometry and Statistics, pp.362-367.

Example of use of above table: between ordinate erected at the mean and one erected 0.59 o from the mean is included 0.222 4 of the total area.

积分表 2
机率表 (Table of X)
The Deviation in the Normal Distribution in Terms of the Standard Deviation

	0.01	0.02	0.03	0.04	0.05	0.06	0.07	0.08	0.09	0.10
0.00	2.575 829	2.326 348	2.170 090	2.053 749	1.959 964	1.880 794	1.811 911	1.750 686	1.695 398	1.644 854
0.10	1.598 193	1.554 774	1.514 102	1.475 791	1.439 521	1.405 072	1.372 204	1.340 755	1.310 579	1.281 552
0.20	1.253 565	1.226 528	1.200 359	1.174 987	1.150 349	1.126 391	1.103 063	1.080 319	1.058 122	1.036 433
0.30	1.015 222	0.994 458	0.974 114	0.954 165	0.934 589	0.915 365	0.896 473	0.877 896	0.859 617	0.841 621
0.40	0.823 894	0.806 421	0.789 192	0.772 193	0.755 415	0.738 847	0.722 479	0.706 303	0.690 309	0.674 490
0.50	0.658 838	0.643 345	0.628 006	0.612 813	0.597 760	0.582 841	0.568 051	0.553 385	0.538 836	0.524 401
0.60	0.510 073	0.495 850	0.481 727	0.467 699	0.453 762	0.439 913	0.426 148	0.412 463	0.398 855	0.385 320
0.70	0.371 856	0.358 459	0.345 125	0.331 853	0.318 639	0.305 481	0.292 375	0.279 319	0.266 311	0.253 347
0.80	0.240 426	0.227 545	0.214 702	0.201 893	0.189 118	0.176 374	0.163 658	0.150 969	0.138 304	0.125 661
0.90	0.113 039	0.100 434	0.087 845	0.075 270	0.062 707	0.050 154	0.037 608	0.025 069	0.012 533	0

The value of P for each entry is found by adding the column heading to the value in the left-hand margin. The corresponding value of x is the deviation such that the probability of an observation falling outside the range from $-x$ to $+x$ is P. For example, $P = 0.03$ for $x = 2.170\,090$; so that 3 per cent. of normally distributed values will have positive or negative deviations exceeding the standard deviation in the ratio 2.170 090 at least.

积分表 3
Values of x for Small Values of P

P ..	0.001	0.000 1	0.000 01	0.000 001	0.000 000 1	0.000 000 01	0.000 000 001
x ..	3.290 53	3.890 59	4.417 17	4.891 64	5.326 72	5.730 73	6.109 41

Taken from R.A. Fisher, Statistical Methods for Research Workers.

This table gives the normal deviations corresponding to very high odds. In the use of this table, it should be remembered that even slight departures from the normal distribution will much effect these very small probabilities, and that we seldom can be certain in any particular case, that these high odds will accurate. The table illustrates the general fact that the significance in the normal distribution of deviations exceeding four times the standard deviation is extremely pronounced.

(原载《计政学报》1935 年第 1 卷第 4 期)

相关方法与变量之分析及其在智慧分析上之应用

相关方法为近世研究生物及社会科学之利器。自初倡以至今日,因其所根据之假设不同,其理论亦异。于此足见相关方法之难处,不在于推求一公式,以供统计实务之用,而在于求得此公式之前提,是否能与统计事象正相符合,以及用此公式所求得之相关,其可恃程度(Reliability)是否可知。

相关方法之算学的理论[①],肇始于赖拍拉斯(Laplace),经高尔登氏(Galton)之阐明而自成一科学。自后皮尔生(Pearson)、于尔(Yule)、薛理霭(Charlier)、费雪(Fisher)及弗理胥(R. Frish)辈统计学者,继起研究,使其学理益臻完善,其方法益臻严密。按其理论之不同,相关方法,可别之为下列四种:

(1) 相关曲面法(Correlation surface method)
(2) 回应线法(Regression method)[②]
(3) 矩阵法(Matrix method)
(4) 变异量的分析法(The analysis of variance method)

1. 相关曲面法

一个统计事象的变化情形,通常可以次数分配表(Frequency distribution)表之,为谋理论上之便利,并为减除抽样错误(Sampling error)计,吾人往往用一算学式代表一个次数分配,如一个统计事象的次数,呈现钟状分配者,可以算式

$$\varphi(x) = \frac{1}{\sigma_x \sqrt{2\pi}} e^{-\frac{x^2}{2\sigma^2}} \qquad (\text{I})$$

[①] 关于相关理论之演进,请参考作者著:"The Development of Correlation Theory", Univ. of Wis., Madison Wis., U.S.A。

[②] Regression method 今译为回归分析法。——编者注

表之。此式所代表之曲线,谓之次数分配曲线。今如将上法推广,则依正态分配之二个或 n 个事象,则依同理,其分配情形可以算式

$$\varphi(x, y) = \frac{1}{2\pi\sigma_1\sigma_2\sqrt{1-r^2}} e \times p^{-\left\{\frac{x^2}{\sigma_1^2} + \frac{y^2}{\sigma_2^2} - 2r\frac{xy}{\sigma_1\sigma_2}\right\}} \quad (\text{II})$$

或

$$\varphi(x_1, x_2, \cdots, x_n) = \frac{1}{\sigma_1\sigma_2\cdots\sigma_n\sqrt{(2\pi)^n \Delta}} e^{\frac{\delta}{2\Delta}} \quad (\text{III})$$

表之,式中

$$\Delta = \begin{vmatrix} 1 & r_{12} & r_{13} & \cdots & r_{1n} \\ r_{12} & 1 & r_{23} & \cdots & r_{2n} \\ r_{13} & r_{23} & 1 & \cdots & r_{3n} \\ \cdots & & & & \\ \cdots & & & & \\ r_{1n} & r_{2n} & & & 1 \end{vmatrix} ? \quad \delta = \begin{vmatrix} 0 & \frac{x_1}{\sigma_1} & \frac{x_2}{\sigma_2} & \cdots & \frac{x_n}{\sigma_n} \\ \frac{x_1}{\sigma_1} & & r & \cdots & \cdots \\ \frac{x_2}{\sigma_2} & & & \vdots & \\ \vdots & & \vdots & \Delta & \\ \frac{x_n}{\sigma_n} & & \vdots & & \end{vmatrix} \quad (\text{IV})$$

算式(II)与(III)谓之相关曲面(Correlation surface)。任一组数值,依正态分配 $x_1, x_2, x_3, \cdots, x_n$ 在 $(x_1; x_1 + \mathrm{d}x_1), (x_2; x_2 + \mathrm{d}x_2), \cdots, (x_n; x_n + \mathrm{d}x_n)$ 间出见之概率,等于

$$P(x_1, x_2, \cdots, x_n) = \frac{1}{\sigma_1\sigma_2\cdots\sigma_n\sqrt{(2\pi)^n \Delta}} e^{\frac{\delta}{2\Delta}} \mathrm{d}x_1 \mathrm{d}x_2 \cdots \mathrm{d}x_n \quad (\text{V})$$

今若另有一组统计事象 $x_1, x_2, \cdots, x_n$,各不相倚(Independent),则其分配,可以下式表之:

$$\varphi(x_1)\varphi(x_2)\cdots\varphi(x_n) = \frac{1}{\sigma_1\sigma_2\cdots\sigma_n\sqrt{(2\pi)^n}} e^{-\frac{1}{2}\Sigma\left(\frac{x_i}{\sigma_i}\right)} \quad (\text{VI})$$

其任一组值在 $(x_1, x_1 + \mathrm{d}x_1), (x_2, x_2 + \mathrm{d}x_2), \cdots, (x_n, x_n + \mathrm{d}x_n)$ 间出见之机率,等于

$$P_0(x_1, x_2, \cdots, x_n) = \varphi(x_1)\varphi(x_2)\cdots\varphi(x_n)\mathrm{d}x_1\mathrm{d}x_2\cdots\mathrm{d}x_n \quad (\text{VII})$$

于是

$$P(x_1, x_2, \cdots, x_n) - P_0(x_1, x_2, \cdots, x_n) = R \quad (\text{VIII})$$

为 $(x_1, x_2, \cdots, x_n)$ 间相关之程度(Strength of correlation)。如 $(x_1, x_2, \cdots, x_n)$ 各不相关,则 R 等于零。故 R 之值愈大,其相关程度愈强。

今若统计事象仅有二个,则

$$P(x,y) - P_0(x,y) = \left[\frac{1}{2\sigma_1\sigma_2\pi\sqrt{1-\gamma^2}}e^{-\frac{1}{2(1-\gamma^2)}\left\{\frac{x^2}{\sigma_1^2}+\frac{y^2}{\sigma_2^2}-2\gamma\frac{xy}{\sigma_1\sigma_2}\right\}}\right.$$

$$\left. - \frac{1}{2\pi\sigma_1\sigma_2}e^{-\frac{1}{2}\left(\frac{x^2}{\sigma_1^2}+\frac{y^2}{\sigma_2^2}\right)}\right]\mathrm{d}x\mathrm{d}y$$

故 P 与 P_0 之差数,因 r 之存在而存在,如 r 为零,则此差数亦为零,于是 r 可称之为相关系数。

2. 回应线法(Regression Method)

依定义,x_1 对于 $x_2, x_3, \cdots, x_n$ 之回应线,为 x 在各组之平均数的轨迹(The loci of the array means of the type)——$(x_2, x_3, \cdots, x_n)$。用最小二乘方法,将一线配合于此等组平均数,其所得之回应线为

$$x_{10} = -\sigma_1 \sum_{q=2}^{q=n} \frac{\Delta_{1q}}{\Delta_{11}} \cdot \frac{x_q}{\sigma_q} \quad (\text{IX})$$

此式亦可命 V 之值为极大,即将 V 之指数微分而令其结果为零得之。

根据于(IX)式,可用 $x_2, x_3, \cdots, x_n$ 以估计 x_1 之值。今如实得之 x_1 值,完全与估计者 x_{1c} 相等,则

$$S^2 = \frac{1}{N}\sum(x_1\cdots x_{1c})^2 = 0 \text{ 或 } R = \sqrt{1-\frac{s^2}{\sigma_1^2}} = 1$$

此时 x_1 与 $x_2, x_3, \cdots, x_n$ 有完全关系。如 S^2 不为零,则 x_1 之值,不能由(IX)确定之。S 之值愈大,则由(IX)式以测 x_1 之值,其错误愈大,而 R 之值愈小,亦即谓 x_1 与 $x_2, x_3, \cdots, x_n$ 之关系亦愈弱,故 R 之值之大小,足表示 x_1 与 $x_2, x_3, \cdots, x_n$ 之关系之强弱,因名曰相关系数。

用上述方法求得之相关系数,谓之回应线法。

3. 矩阵法(Matrix Method[①])

统计事象间之相关情形,用向量(Vector)或矩阵(Matrix)研究者,其法名曰矩阵法,为弗理胥(Frisch)氏所阐明。

n 个事象或变数之一组值,在 n 度空间可确定一点,由原点引至此点之量,谓之向量。如此之 n 个向量或 n 点,可定一 n 度空间角度(Solid angle in n-dimensional space)。今如 n 个向量或 n 点均在一平面上,则此角度为零。故此角度之大小,可用以测量各点离开该平面的趋势。设统计资料(Statistical data)共有 N 组值,则由此 N 组值中,任取 n 组,可在空间确定一个空间角度。计可成 $_NC_n$ 个角度,其平均大小可以下式表之。

$$\sigma^2 = \frac{1}{n!N^n} \sum_{t_1, t_2, \cdots, t_n} \begin{vmatrix} x_1(t_1) & \cdots & \cdots & x_1(t_n) \\ x_2(t_2) & & & x_2(t_n) \\ \vdots & \vdots & \vdots & \vdots \\ x_n(t_1) & & & x_n(t_n) \end{vmatrix}^2 \quad (\text{X})$$

式中 $t_1, t_2, \cdots, t_n = 1, 2, \cdots, N$。

令 $m_{ij} = \frac{1}{N}\sum x_i x_j$,则上式(X)等于

$$\sigma^2 = |m_{ij}| = \begin{vmatrix} m_{11} & \cdots & m_{1n} \\ & \cdots & \\ m_{n1} & \cdots & m_{nn} \end{vmatrix}$$

令

$$\Delta = \frac{|m_{ij}|}{m_{11}m_{22}\cdots m_{nn}} = |r_{ij}|$$

则 $+\sqrt{\Delta}$ 谓之综合差。而

$$R = \sqrt{1-\Delta} \quad (\text{XI})$$

谓之复相关或综合相关(Collective correlation)。盖依代数学原理,当 σ 或 Δ 等于零时,$x_1, x_2, x_3, \cdots, x_n$ 谓之直线相倚(linear dependence),亦即谓 x_1,

---

[①] R. Frisch, "Correlation and Scatter in Statistical Variables", *Nordisk Stal. Tid*, Bd. 8, pp.36-102, 1928.

$x_2, \cdots, x_n$ 能合于一个一次方程式,当 Δ 之值异于零,而命之逐渐加大,则 R 之值由 1 而减小,终至为零;而 $x_1, x_2, \cdots, x_n$ 之关系,愈不能以一次方程式代表之,故 R 之值,足代表 $x_1, x_2, \cdots, x_n$ 间之关系渐近于一次方程式之程度。因直线相倚可以矩阵法研究之,而 R 之性质,多可由矩阵理推得之,故名此为矩阵法。

4. 变异量之分析法

标准差之平方(Squared standard deviation)谓之变异量(Variance)。

配合一曲线或直线于各班平均数(Array-means),其线谓之回应线(Regression curve)。令 y 对于 $x_1, x_2, \cdots, x_n$ 之回应线为

$$Y = f(x_1, x_2, \cdots, x_n) \tag{XII}$$

则
$$y = Y + v, \quad \sum y^2 = \sum Y^2 + \sum v \tag{XIII}$$

$$\sigma_y^2 = \sigma_r^2 + \sigma_s^2 \tag{XIIIa}$$

上列三个变异量,可作成一直角三角形(Right triangle)。

令

$$R = \sqrt{1 - \frac{\sigma_s^2}{\sigma_y^2}} = \frac{\sigma_r}{\sigma_y} = \sin\theta$$

则 R 谓之 y 与 $x_1, x_2, \cdots, x_n$ 之复相关。

但在此种相关问题中,其重要之事,乃为此等变异量的相对大小,故相当于三角函数中之任一比,皆可用为相关系数,今正切函数较之正弦函数,颇多便利之处,故吾人宜以

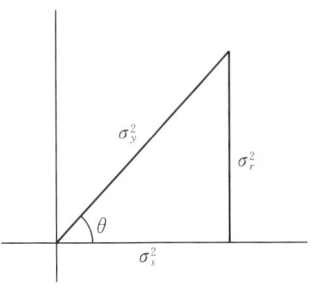

$$\tan\theta = \frac{\sigma_r}{\sigma_s}$$

代表相关系数。

由(XIII)足见一个变异量 σ_y,可分为二个变异量 σ_r 及 σ_s。若将如此分得之二个变异量,比较之以得其相关程度,其法谓之变异量之分析法。

在分析变异量时,吾人须注意变数之自由变化度数(Degrees of freedom)。例如 y, $Y = f(x_1, x_2, \cdots, x_n)$ 及 $v = y - Y$ 之平均变异量,等于其

平方和除以自由度数之商①。

变异量	自由度数	平方和
回应线	n	$ns_r^2 = \sum (Y) = (n + n' + 1)R^2 s^2$
与回应线之差距	n'	$n' s_s^2 = \sum (y - Y)^2 = (n + n' + 1)(1 - R^2)s^2$
总值	$n + n'$	$\sum y^2 = (n_1 + n_2 + 1)s^2$

故

$$\frac{ns_r^2}{n' s_s^2} = \frac{R^2}{1 - R^2} \qquad (\text{XIV})$$

今若令

$$e^{2z} = \frac{s_r^2}{s_s^2} \qquad (\text{XV})$$

则 Z 之分配式为

$$df(2) = 2 \frac{\left[\frac{1}{2}(n + n' - 2)\right]!}{\left[\frac{1}{2}(n - 2)\right]! \left[\frac{1}{2}(n' - 2)\right]!} \frac{n'^{\frac{1}{2}n'} n^{\frac{1}{2}n} e^{nz}}{(n' + ne^{2z})^{\frac{1}{2}(n+n')}} dz \qquad (\text{XVI})$$

此式之分配形状,近似于正态曲线(Normal curve),故其可恃性,可以通常方法表之。

令

$$\frac{n}{n'} e^{2z} = \frac{\sum Y}{\sum (y - Y)^2} = \frac{R^2}{1 - R^2} \qquad (\text{XVII})$$

代入(XIX)式,即为各不相倚的变数间之相关系数 R 的分配式,其形状不同于正态,故通常之用 R 的标准差 $\sigma_R = \frac{1 - R^2}{\sqrt{N}}$ 或 $\sigma_R = \frac{1 - R^2}{\sqrt{N - n}}$,以表 R 之可恃程度,实不足取法。为真确计,吾人宜用下关系变换之:$z = \frac{1}{2} \{\log(1 + r) - $

---

① Tehyin Y. Li, "The Development of Correlation Theory", Ch.4, 1934.

$\log(1-r)\}$, $\sigma_2 = \dfrac{1}{\sqrt{N-n-1}}$

由上所论,相关方法可视为变异量之分析法的一种,其相关程度可用Z表之：

$$Z = \dfrac{1}{2}(\log S_r^2 - \log S_s^2)$$

而Z之标准差,可由(XIX)求得之,其值为

$$\sigma_z = \sqrt{\dfrac{1}{2}\left(\dfrac{1}{n} + \dfrac{1}{n'}\right)} \tag{XVIII}$$

5. 变异量之分析法的其他用途

变异量之分析法,为用甚宏。除能解决相关问题外,且可用于农业试验场中以为解决关于选种施肥之问题(R.A.Fisher, "Studies of Crop Variation. I", Jour. of Agr. Sci., 1923),可用于工业品之研究(L. H. C. Tippett, "Statistical Methods in Textile Research", Shirley Institute Memoirs, Vol. 8; E.S. Pearson, "Analysis of Variance in Case of Non-normal Variation", J.A.S.A., Vol. 23, 1931),且可用于时间数列研究(Shultz et Als, "Analysis of Variance as an effective method of handling the time series in certain economic statistics", J.A.S.A., Vol. 28, 1933)。今试将此法,用于中央大学投考生成绩的研究。

本题之研究,先假定国英算之平均成绩,足代表学生的天赋能力与其所受之训练(如其所受之训练为相同,足视为天赋能力的代表)。一个学生的国英算成绩之差异,足代表其天赋能力对于各种科学反应能力之差异,故研究之目的,在欲知各人的天赋能力的差别。是否较每人所赋予的天赋才智,对于各种科学的,反应能力的差别为大。如其为然,则国文成绩佳者其英算之成绩亦必佳,否则国文成绩佳者,其对于英算之成绩未必亦佳,即谓一人的天赋才能恒有所偏,长于此者,不必长于彼。

今投考生成绩的变化,既由于二种原因:(1)天赋才能的差别,(2)其才能对于各种科学的反应的差别。故成绩的变异量可分析为二部分,第一部分代表各人才能的差别;第二部分代表各人才能对于各种科学的反应的差别。

令 a, b, c 各代表国英算之成绩,x 代表国英算之平均成绩,并令 $\bar{x}$ 代表 x 之平均数,则

$$\sum\{(a-\bar{x})^2 + (b-\bar{x})^2 + (c-\bar{x})^2\}$$
$$= \sum\{(a-x)^2 + (b-x)^2 + (c-x)^2 + 3(x-\bar{x})^2\}$$

今自 2 400 投考生中,任取 100 人分析之,其结果如下:

$$\sum\{(a-\bar{x})^2 + (b-\bar{x})^2 + (c-\bar{x})^2\} = 36\,210.298\,0 + 62\,202.486\,0$$
$$+ 25\,842.062\,5 = 124\,254.846\,5$$
$$\sum\{(a-x)^2 + (b-x)^2 + (c-x)^2\} = 28\,126.617\,1 + 23\,068.820\,8$$
$$+ 17\,344.880\,9 = 77\,871.878\,8$$
$$\sum(x-\bar{x})^2 = 14\,693.788\,0$$

由此可得下表:

变异量	自由度数	平方差之和	平均变异量
天赋才能的差别	99	14 693.788 0	148.422
天赋才能对于各种科学的反应的差别	200	77 871.878 8	389.359
总　量	299		

$$Z = \frac{1}{2}(\log_e 389.359 - \log_e 148.422) = \frac{1}{2 \times 0.434\,29}\{2.590\,35 - 2.171\,49\}$$

$$= \frac{0.418\,86}{0.868\,58} = 0.482\,25$$

$$\sigma_z = \sqrt{\frac{1}{2}\left(\frac{1}{99} + \frac{1}{200}\right)} = 0.03$$

于此足见各人天赋能力的差别,不如每人天赋能力对于各种科学反应的差别之大。故人之天赋才能,恒有偏专长于此者,不必善于彼,学者宜择其有所专长之工作而服务,庶几乎于社会于个人两受其利。

人的天赋能力,足视为各不相倚(Independent),其变异量既小于每人对于各种科学的反应能力之变异量,则各人的国算英成绩,亦必为各不相倚。今用回应线相关法,求得其结果如下:

(1) 国算英平均分数在 40—50 之间者,国文与算学成绩之相关系数等

于-0.39,所用之人数为50。

（2）英文分数在30—40之间者,国文与算学成绩之相关系数等于0.067,所用之人数为50。

（3）国文成绩在20—30之间者,算学与英文成绩之相关系数等于0.29,所用之人数为51。

若用下列关系

$$Z = \frac{1}{2}\{\log(1+r) - \log_e(1-r)\}$$

将 r 变为 Z,则以(1)为例,可求之如下：

$$r = -0.39 \quad Z = -0.41$$

$$\sigma_z = \frac{1}{\sqrt{n-3}} = 0.15$$

$$r + \sigma_r = -0.63 \quad z + \sigma_z = -0.56$$

$$z - \sigma_z = -0.26$$

由此观之,国算英间有极微之相关度。

本文中之例题,一部分为作者学生余捷琼君代为计算。借此机会敬向余君道谢,又此结果算出后,曾告朱师君毅,始悉朱师曾于民国十一年研究留美中国学生的国文与英文成绩之关系,其结果为 $r = -0.024$（见朱君之博士论文第51页）,故作者之结果,又为朱师之续,亦可为作朱师结论之复证。

（原载《科学》1936年第20卷第6期）

新货币政策之史的背景及其将来

一 导 言

货币管理,在世界经济恐慌爆发以后,成为世界各国挽救危机之中心政策,竞以膨胀的方式,贬低币值,冀对内抬高物价,对外实行汇兑倾销,争夺国际市场,避免恐慌袭击。英国首即采取此种政策,于一九三一年九月二十一日停止金本位,其他各国,相继步其后尘。同年日本于十二月十三日停止金本位,实行外汇管理。一九三三年六月,美国亦以停止金本位,管理外汇闻矣,实行以来,成效卓著。其他德意等国,虽未离去金本位,然已先后实行外汇管理,统制金融,故仍能在世界经济恐慌袭击之下,勉强挣扎,反观法国领导下之金集团国家,则日呈崩溃之象,良以潮流所趋,已不能不用国家统制力量,应付于国际舞台上。在此竞争日益尖锐化之巨涛中,我金融基础薄弱产业落后国家,亦被迫不能不走同样之途径,于本年十一月四日,财政部遂公布通货管理之紧急法令,惟此时宣布虽嫌其过晚,然以时机未成熟,准备不完善,不能为有效之措施。当一九二九年世界经济恐慌发生时,我国因银价跌落,外汇较低,尚不受若何影响,惟自民二十以还,外因各国货币贬值,汇兑倾销,内受天灾战祸影响,农村破产,工商业不振,经济恐慌发生,去岁美国更抬高银价,白银外流,致使我国金融紧缩,加紧经济恐慌。我国固应早宣布此政策,以救此危机,惟我国货币制度,向极紊乱,即银本位制亦不健全,中央银行不巩固,不足以控制金融与管理通货,且外汇控制权操于外人之手,若突然废银用纸,势必发生重大之纷扰,益增经济恐慌,无补于实际。吾人试考察近年来政府关于币政之措施,即可了然于此次政策之宣布,由于年来之改革,与时势所促成之结果,故在未讨论此政策以前,势有一考察年来币政措施之必要。

二 币制改革之史的发展

民元以还,时局在飘摇动荡情况之下,军阀割据,战祸频年,币制紊乱,达于已极,自无若何重大改进之可言,仅民三公布国币条例于一元银币留点成绩,至革命军北伐全国统一完成后,财政部认为有整顿币制之必要,于十七年六月二十日,召开全国经济会议于上海,对于币制改革,多所擘划。在会议中通过了"国币条例草案""国币条例施行细则草案""造币厂条例草案"以及"废两改元案",是为筹划币制改革之开始。同年十月五日国民政府公布中央银行条例,力谋币制统一,自兹以后,种种计划,次第实现。兹将后来各种重要措施,分述于下。

1. 中央造币厂之成立

我国之有造币局厂,始于前清末年,各省分立。迨民国以后,分立各处者,计天津、南京、武昌、成都、广州、云南、奉天、长沙、重庆、杭州、安庆、口北、上海等十三处,以天津为总厂,余为分厂。实则天津徒拥总厂之名,难收统制之效,厂数既多,益以时局日非,各省为余利所动,各自鼓铸滥发,银元各种形色不一,币厂系统,日渐紊乱。至十七年财政部认为有整理各厂与统一铸币机关之必要,斟酌结果,乃于十月中改上海造币厂为中央造币厂统一铸币,并设监理委员会,督促进行,积极准备开铸。经数年之整理与筹备,至二十二年废两改元之议决定后,该厂乃于三月一日开始铸币,新银元产生。三日立法院并通过银本位币铸造条例,规定银本位币之铸造权,专属于中央造币厂,统一银本位之铸币,遂告完成。

2. 废两改元

以前银两之用为商场计算单位,具有很大势力。各地商家之来往记账,多以两来表示与支付,单位复杂,各地有各地之单位,如上海之规元、汉口之洋例、天津之行化,所含纯银与成色各不相同,各地间之交易往来,则按其单位间之比率升水计算之,繁难自不待言,诚为商业上交易之最大障碍。今既有银元以为全国共同之单位,则此银两之废除,当为必要,按废两改元之议,倡于民国六年,其后屡经讨论不果,至十七年在全国经济会议中,即通过此案。迄至二十一年七月间,财政部以世界经济状况,衰落日甚,为安定国内金融,自以统一银币入手,且时值上海厘价过贱,金认为实行废两改元之机会,乃决定步骤,先后施行,先从上海着手,规定上海市面通用银两,与银本位币一元或旧有一元银币之合原定重量成色者,以规元七钱一分五厘折合银币一元,为一定之换算率,即自二十二年三月十日起实施。所有上海市及江苏省内公私款项之收付、债权债务之清算、交易税收,均自该日起,按照前项定率,折合银币收付,各商店之货物市价,概以银币计算,不得再用银两,此项通令实行之后,情形颇称顺利,财政部乃宣布定于四月六日实行全国废两,改用银币。自兹改革以后,立见成效,凡公私款项之收付与订立契约票据,及一切交易均已改用银币。银两之中,势力最大之上海规元,汉口洋例,天津行化,自沪津汉三地,由中央银行与中交两行努力进行废两之后,其向以银两为表示申汇行市者,亦一律改用银元,其余如国外汇兑行市洋商银亦继华商之后,而改用银元计算矣,银元统一通货遂告成功,新银本位制因是确立。

3. 银出口税之征收

白银为我国本位币之币材,在世界各国,已视为一种普通商品,其价格之涨跌对于他国之影响尚小,若影响于我国金融则甚大。银自欧战以后,因需要之减少,生产之激增,在国际市场中,已呈显著存底增高现象。在一九二四年七月间国际重要市场存底总额,约不过 35 300 万盎斯。到一九三三年十月,则增加到 76 000 万盎斯之巨。银既觅不着出路,其价格遂不断惨跌。美国一方面为拥护其国内银矿业者之利益,另方面为扩张其远东市场,抬高远东人民购买力起见,则势有以人为力量提高银价之必要。美国毕特门(Pitman)氏遂于一九三三年六月伦敦世界经济会议席上,提出白银协定计划,取得墨西哥、加拿大、秘鲁、澳大利亚、中国、西班牙、印度七国同意,于七月二十二日订立正式协定,嗣于二十六日又成立补充协定,根据此协定,产银国必须于一九三四年四月一日以后,四年之内,按照下列数量,收买本国白银。

美国	97 685 640 盎斯
墨西哥	28 636 432 盎斯
加拿大	6 687 208 盎斯
秘鲁	4 381 300 盎斯
澳大利亚	2 609 420 盎斯

其次是四年之间,印度卖出之白银,以 140 000 000 盎士为限,西班牙以二千万盎斯为限,中国则只认不熔毁银币以卖给市场。从大体观察,伦敦协定之根本目的,即在提高银价而挽回美国在远东市场,至少为限制银之生产,使银价不再下落。白银协定既经签字,美总统罗斯福于一九三三年十二月二十一日,批准协定,并宣布购银计划,令造币厂随时收买国内银块,每盎斯现银官价,实值为一元二角九分。但宣言中规定铸币等费,须扣除 50%,

则持银者所得,仅为官价之半数,即六角四分半是也。若按一元二角九分,以现金给付,则金银比价成为十六与一。但此时造币厂所付者为银币,美国既已放弃金本位,美币价值久已跌落,其一元二角九分之官价,实际只值金币八角左右。于此更扣去一半为铸币费,故净银价格,不过金币四角。以此计之,金银比价仅为五十一与一。然较当时市场中七十五与一之比价,固已高多矣。至一九三四年五月,罗斯福总统为促进一九三三年之白银协定与购银方案实现起见,乃提购银法案于国会,经国会加以修正,于六月十一日经参议院通过,十三日亦经众议院通过,至十九日由罗斯福总统签字后,遂成为法令矣。即由政府在国内外购买现银,使货币准备中白银占25%,即维持金三银一之比例,八月更宣布白银国有政策,自是伦敦纽约银价涨风日炽。我国为银本位制国家,所受影响最大。我国市场银价与国外银价相差愈离愈远。即我国对外货币汇兑率同时发生极巨之差额。此时如由上海运大洋到港,每千元即可得利183.89元。大利所在,一般投机者遂将国内现金大量输出。尤其外国银行银存底,大半运出。自是年七月起至十月止,共出口银二亿零七百余万元之巨。如此急急外流,国内白银,大有竭尽之趋势,金融恐慌,因而发生。政府对此严重问题,力谋阻遏。特于十月十五日有征收白银出口税之施行,以阻止白银之输出。当时银出口税税率规定,(1)银本位币征出口税10%,减去铸费2.25%,净值7.75%,(2)其他银类征出口税10%,如伦敦银价折合上海汇兑之比价,相差之数,除缴上述出口税而仍不足时,应按其不足之数,并行加征平衡税。即自本月15日起一律实行。白银税征收之后,我国银价即与世界银价脱离关系,国内银价远低于国外银价,严格言之,我国已离去银本位制矣。惟差价愈大,则私运之利愈厚,我国主权不完整,偷运自所不免,难阻白银之继续外流。据美国商务部之统计,自十一月三日起至十六日止之两星期中,由华输美之现银,总额已达4 524 556美金之巨。(十一月二十八日《中华日报》)又据江海关统计,自十月十九日起至十一月二十二日止,五周之间,现银出口达375万元,于此可见加征出口税后,白银流出,报运似有减少,但由奸商私运流出者,为量颇大。是白银出口税不过可阻止明目张胆之运出,而非为根本办法矣。

4. 限制外汇及标金买卖

财政部为阻止白银外流,增强中央银行对于金融外汇统制力,乃于去年九月八日训令上海银行公会,交易所监理员,并致函中央银行限制外汇买卖,取缔标金投机。训令内容关于限制外汇买卖者,令各银行今后对于外国汇兑买卖交易,限于(1)合法及通常营业所必需者。(2)本年九月八日以前订有契约者。(3)旅行费用及其他私人需要者。除上三项以外,一律即日暂行停止。关于取缔标金投机者,令交易所监理员,转饬上海金业交易所,所有新做交易,应用现金交割,不得再用外汇结价,以免投机者造谣操纵。盖因白银输出,投机者大肆活动,套取厚利,实为重要原因。此种办法规定后,实给与买空卖空之投机者一个致命的打击,外汇投机行为减少,白银输出自然缓和。又我国外汇以每年巨额入超关系,汇兑之权,悉操于外商银行之手,尤其是汇丰银行之每日挂牌行市,向为贸易上汇兑的标准,全国市场均听命于彼,自兹规定后,即以中央银行关金行市,而代汇丰挂牌,为全国国际汇兑之标准。因此规定汇兑行市之权,由外商银行移转于中央银行之手,我中央银行开始控制外汇矣。至十月十五日,白银出口税征收确定后,为避免汇市激烈变化起见,乃由金融界商请财政当局,设立外汇平市委员会,由中央中国交通三行合组,各派代表一人为委员,共筹集基金一万万元,于十月十九日正式成立。该会之任务,则为视市面之需要,平衡国外汇兑市价,如国外汇兑只有卖出,以致市价暴落,则由该会买进,如只有买进,以致市价暴涨,则由该会卖出,以资平衡,由此奠定了统制外汇之基础。

5. 中交两行增加官股

我国之有新式银行,肇于前清光绪二十二年,民国以还,银行业日见发达,近年来尤突飞猛进,外商银行不计,银行所能支配之资力为二十六万万余元,占全国金融市场总资力90%以上。其中央银行为国家银行,中国银行系政府特许之国际汇兑银行,交通银行系政府特许发展全国实业银行,三行能支配之资力,共为十二万三千八百余万元,约占银行总资力43%。最近三行之总发行额,为三万一千八百余万元。总行虽在上海,其分支行遍及全国,资金之运用,遍于各地,足以操纵全国金融。三行中,中国交通两行尤具有悠久历史与巩固之信用。中央银行历史不久,不过在政府法令维持之下,增加其势力,人民对于中央钞票信用远不逮于中交两行。政府为统制全国金融,势非先将两行完全置于其控制之下不可。中交两行,本有官股,然商股居大半,是商办性质较多,政府难收指挥自如之效。因此财政部为增加中央中交三行金融实力,以调剂金融起见,乃于今年三月发行一万万元金融公债,以充实三行资本,除拨民国二十四年金融公债三千万元以补充中央银行资本总额为一万万元外,并拨是项公债以增加中交两行官股。按中国银行原有资本总额为国币二千五百万元,其中官股为五百万元,商股为二千万元,此次拨付民国二十四年金融公债二千五百万元,增加资本总共为五千万元,官股占3/5。并修改中国银行条例,在实际上中国银行已成为国家银行矣。其次交通银行原有资本总额为一千万元,官股为二百万元,商股为八百万元,此次拨民国二十四年金融公债一千万元,增加资本总共为二千万元,官股亦占3/5,是大权亦操在政府手中矣。两行既已实际变为国家银行,则以三行在金融上卓越之势力,而改革金融,固可应付自如也。

由以上种种改革,铸币之统一,银本位之确定,银价之脱离,外汇之控制,国家银行势力之巩固,固已为新政策之准备。此次突然改革,实施统制而不发生纷乱现象,且进行颇顺利者,即可豁然洞悉矣。时机已成熟,势不能不为有效之措施也。

三　新货币政策之意义

今年十一月四日财政部所公布之货币政策紧急法令,大要内容有下列五点,(1)定中央中国交通三行钞票为法币,禁止行使硬币。(2)其他银行钞票,仍准照旧使用,惟以后不得增发,并应逐渐收回,代以法币,其发行之准备金,须交由发行准备管理委员会保管之。(3)设立发行准备管理委员会,办理法币准备金之保管,及其发行收换事宜。(4)持有银币及其他银类者,应即兑换法币使用,其有债务以银币订立者,到期应以法币偿还。(5)中央中国交通三行应无限制买卖,以稳定对外汇价。

此种重大之改革,诚开吾国货币史上之新纪元,不惟为金融上之伟大改革,且关系于国计民生,至重且大,值得吾人最大之注意与讨论者也。兹由其本质与作用,分析之可得下列各点。

1. 停止银本位,实行通货管理

此次改革,既禁止使用银币,以三行钞票代替,定为法币。则我国币值与银价从此脱离关系,自由处分与自由移动之特性既失,银本位制显然离开矣。本来自去年征收白银出口税与平衡税限制白银移动后,即已脱离银本位,此次停止使用现金,不过明显的划开银价与币价关系,即货币制度脱离了白银之束缚。良以在今日世界上,仅我国与中美各小国仍保留着银本位制,我国为白银最大之尾闾,白银增多,足以造成我国之通货膨胀,白银外流,亦足以造成通货紧缩现象。在我金融基础薄弱,产业落后国家,其价格之涨跌,均不能得着如何利益,仅足以扰乱金融与货币制度,而造成经济恐慌,今后即脱离此种束缚。以纸币代替银币来衡量物价,似乎采用纸本位制来代替银本位制。惟纸本位应为纯粹的无准备的发行。若此次改革,则设立了发行准备管理委员会,来集中准备。政府且宣布有百分之百以上准备,似乎未脱离准备关系,是此次公布之法令,即暂置本位问题之不问,而为通货管理政策。以政府的法令,三行控制金融的力量,来稳定币值。对内安定物价,由伸缩钞票发行的数额,来衡量物价水准。对外稳定外汇,由三行无限制买卖外汇,以避免汇价激烈之变动。以购买力平价来决定外汇,今后即在此统制管理之下,进行于币价之安定。

2. 白银国有以保存现金

国内现银,自去年美国购银政策实行后,急急外流,致国家命脉所系之准备金,大有竭尽之趋势,金融恐慌发生。良以我国现银多散存于民间,存于政府手中者微乎其微,移动甚易。值此国际风云日急之秋,若任此尚未流尽之准备金,分散流动,小之则零星偷运,漏卮堪虞,大则紧急之来,集中不易。若乘此时机集中保存,在平时可赖以谋金融之安定,在非常时期,更可赖以为挹注之资源,关系于对内对外国策上,至重且大。是以此次法令颁布,禁止行使现金,违者全数没收,如有故存隐匿意图偷漏者,应准照危害民国紧急治罪法处治。持有银币与其他银类者应即兑换法币使用,至十一月十五日,并续布兑换法币办法,严密规定,除工艺原料用银、古币、稀币,或有关文化之银质古物及旧有银质器具装饰品外,各地银钱行号商店及其他公共团体或个人持有银币厂条、生银、银锭、银块及其他银类者,应于民国二十四年十一月四日起,三个月内就近交各地兑换机关换取法币。此办法规定后,兑换者尚踊跃。财政部并训令银钱两业公会"除发行部分现金,应全数交由中、中、交,三行接收外,其营业部分已封存之现金准备及兑换法币收入之现金,均准由各该行庄按照原有领券办法,以现金六成,加配政府债券四成,向中、中、交三行换取法币,或照章领用法币"。此种规定,诚为集中现银之进一步有效办法。新政策公布后,国内银价与海外银价相差更大,故当公布之日,平衡税为 57.25%,外加出口税 7.75%,纳税总额即达 65%,事实上报关运银出口自难获利,白银出口即可阻止。惟偷运之风,自不可免,不过停止兑现后,各行现银收归国有,当难入于偷运者之手,偷运者只有向民间零星收集,偷运之风自可稍杀也。不过人民用银已成传统习惯,窖藏现金观念,牢不可破,此次突然以钞代现,势必引起惊愕,窖藏之风,或将更盛。此当有待于法币信用之巩固,不足以收尽民间藏银。据一般估计,我国所有白银全数大致合值二十万万元左右,除东三省外,只有十五万万元左右。其中在金融界准备即可集中者,约有五万万元左右,散藏于民间者,约有十万万元左右。如能全部集中,则于将来金融上不惟可以安定,即在国策上亦能为有效之措施也。

3. 统一发行,以伸缩纸币之流通

法令既定中央中国交通三行钞票为法币,自兹以后,三行钞票即具有无限法币资格,为债权债务者之通用工具。三行以外钞票,虽准照常行使,惟限制以后不得增发,并应逐渐收回,代以法币。即中国交通二行之钞票发行权,亦限制两年,今后专由发行准备管理委员会办理发行事宜,由中央银行发行钞票。是钞票之发行,由分散制而变为集中制,将来可由该委员会视市面需要法币之多寡,而伸缩法币之供给,以安定物价,不致因散发漫无统计,而使通货膨胀或紧缩。除限制各商业银行纸币外,各省市立银行所发行纸币,为数亦多,且较复杂,则省市钞之整理,当不容缓。惟据十二月一日报载"各省市政府设立之省市银行,或用其他银行名义而有省市银行性质者,其所发各种钞券,亦已截止发行。并已将已印未发,已发收回新旧各券,先行封存,连同现在流通券额所有之准备数目,查明呈报财部。所有冀、陕、晋、甘、湘、鄂等省银行。河南农工,及杭州浙江地方,天津大中、边业,汉口中国农民,北平北洋保商等各银行,所发流通市面钞券之准备,连同已印未发,已发收回新旧各券,已先由当地三行会同或单独接收完竣"。由此则统一发行已收相当之效果,其他各地因政治上之关系,为地方当局所把持者,整理自感困难。今后当有待于政治上统一,以达到完全统一发行之目的。

4. 贬低币值以救济经济恐慌

我国经济恐慌开始于民国二十年,原因固多,然感于外国汇兑倾销与国币价值提高之苦,实为重要之原因。去秋美国实行购银政策后,白银急急外流,我银本位制国家,筹码紧缩。由是币价更高,国内物价惨跌,对外汇市日见放长,致工商衰败,百业不振,国际收支不利,国民经济日呈衰落之象。势非贬低币值,压低外汇,以抵制外来之倾销,提高国内物价,不足以消灭此种危机。减低币值,必先脱离银价关系,才能为适当之措施,故当宣布此政策后,外汇平价,即已减低。如对美外汇,在今年五月为40多元,此时则为29元半左右。又如对日外汇,在五月时为142元,此时则为103元。实已减低了27%,就是外货价格增高了27%。价格既涨,当难畅销,即可减少外货之

输入,同时币值下落,在国内物价上涨,可以刺激工商业之发展。但物价虽涨,若折成外币,则已减低,即可促进国货之输出,入超可以减少,国际收支可望平衡,经济上可望有繁荣之机。

5. 金融扩张使财政得以整理

我国财政收支向难适合,尤其在数年来通货紧缩期中,其弱点暴露无遗。在今日政府支出不惟难于减少,且日有增加趋势情况之下,另方面经济紧缩,百业不振,税收当无法增加,收支自不易平衡,无已只有发公债借外款以填补亏空,然在经济紧缩期中,公债难于发出,由是公债价格跌落,于财政收入当不丰裕。整理财政,自较困难。故当此政策宣布后,财政当局即有于十八个月内,谋财政上收支适合之表示。是整理财政,亦为此次重大之作用。良以在币制改革后,税收即可望增加,如关税标准为金单位,当外汇上涨时,金单位价格就落,外汇跌时就涨。今年五月外汇上涨时,国币一百元合美金四十元多,金单位一枚合中国一元六角,现在汇价贬低到美金二十九元七角五分,金单位即合中国二元二毛七分,增加了六角七分。是海关上金单位数目未增,但是财政收入增加。至于统税印花税,因经济转趋向于扩张,税收不久可望增加。当金融扩张时,发公债亦较容易,如目前公债市价,即已平均升高20%以上。良以在货币恢复平衡后,可藉公开市场运用以抬高债券价格,压低市场利息,是政府债务之支出,可望减少。其次白银国有,政府即可乘此银价高涨时卖出,可获利数万万元之巨,保存国库,可作种种基金,以及其他正当用途。值此局势紧急之秋,为支付未来维持民族生命费用,则整理财政,诚为刻不容缓之图。

6. 以钞代现养成人民用钞习惯

我国之用银,由来已久,内地人民扭于用银习惯,对于钞票之信用,尚未臻浓厚。平时银纸并用,尚无若何轩轻,都市中且以用钞为便,若至紧急非常时期,辄有挤兑风潮发生,银行准备不能照兑时,势必纸币价格打折。银纸之差价既大,则引起金融紊乱,社会纷扰,以前之经验甚多。在时局飘摇动荡情况之下,集中现金,维持纸币价值,自为不可能之事。值此压迫日急,瞻望我国前途时有亡国之虞,势非一战不足以谋我民族之出路,为预防国内未来之纠纷,在现在时局安定情况之下,政府足以运用法令来集中现金,稳定纸币价值,扩大纸币信用,增加人民对于政府信任。在平时现金既已相继集中,人民用钞之习惯亦复养成,遇到非常时期,金融之纷扰,当可减除。此于未来之准备,含有深远之意义也。

上述各点,为此次改革之重大意义,在目前我国情势日非,当为必要之措施,而影响于社会经济生活,极为密切,应为举国上下一致之拥护与督促者也。

四　今后之种种问题

此次法令之宣布,不过为改革之开端,而如何促其实现,能收良好之效果,尚有待于继续之努力。改革后之种种问题,自然很多,兹略举几种如下。

1. 健全组织问题

通货管理,当然需要健全之组织来担负管理责任。发行管理委员会既因是而产生,改中央银行为中央准备银行,亦在筹划之中,使成为银行之银行。将来调剂金融之周转,控制信用之紧弛,伸缩法币之发行,维持外汇之稳定,确定银行系统,促进经济之发展,责任何等重大,足以操纵整个国民经济,必需其组织健全,才能发挥其重大之功用。据报载孔氏宣言中,将来之中央准备银行,所有股本应由各银行认出,并许人民购买,使成为超然机关。此当然为必要之措施。吾人更希望其地位为社会公有之成分居多,政府不过处于指导地位,以决定其方针,且不以营利为目的,应在发展国民经济上努力。其利用特殊地位所得之赢利,应贡献政府整理财政与发展经济之用。今后新政策之实行是否圆满,健全此种组织,实为重大之关键。闻政府以中国银行为国际汇兑银行,交通银行为实业银行,将来拟设普通汇兑、储蓄、信托等国家银行,使各负专责,又拟筹设各地县乡银行,以发展各地信用,吾不禁馨香祷祝此种计划之早期实现也。

2. 膨胀通货问题

管理通货之最大目的,当为稳定币值,以衡量物价,不使其过高过低,以致物价涨落不定,人们感受生活不安之苦。往时在银本位制下,发行钞票,须有60%现金准备限制,纸币不过代表现金流通于市面。除非采取纸币政策,通货膨胀,自不容易。今既定不兑换纸币为法币,则其发行数额之多寡,可无须现金准备。今后货币仅有其为交易媒介之职务价值,而其价值之若何,乃由社会需要之多寡,与其供给之数量来决定。其价值之总量,即等于物物交换时不经济的费用之总量焉。其膨胀或紧缩,皆可在任意决定,即可影响于物价起伏不定,社会经济生活动荡不宁矣。此次币价既脱离了银价,币值相当贬低,物价亦相当上涨。若过分上涨,固可刺激工商业之发展,形成繁荣现象;然一般以一定收入为生活者,即感受购买力渐减,生活日困之苦。工人之工资,虽因物价上涨,而谋增加;然其增加之速度,不弱物价上涨之快,未免受相当之痛苦。负有一定债务者,当然因币值下落而减轻其负担,另方面债权者即受无形之损失。此于社会财富有无形重新支配力量,而失去了分配平衡原则。为调整社会经济生活,则稳定币值,当为要图。是以今后货币发行,应按货币数量学说之理,因社会经济上之需要,伸缩货币之供给,使物价自然安定于一水准上,如社会经济发展,需要膨胀通货,当然增加货币以应之。此后对于物价指数之编制,宜精确普遍的统计,作为发行货币之标准,方不致蹈通货膨胀之危机。按各国通货膨胀,每在非常时期,因财政上之需要,而滥发纸币。战后卢布马克价值之等于零,即为显例。我国此次改革币制,既有整理财政作用,谋收支之平衡,则自应力加整顿,以准备于未来非常时期。惟原则上此后谋财政上之收支适合,应在财政上开源节流想办法,幸勿以滥发纸币蹈通货膨胀之危机,为理财之手段也。故今后谋经济上之通货膨胀则可,谋财政上之通货膨胀则不可。

3. 稳定外汇问题

外汇贬低,为此次改革之特色,亦为目前重大之问题。外汇此次平均贬低了40%左右,如对美平价定为29.5元左右,对英平价为一先令二便士半左右,对日平价为103元左右。据称为近五年来之平均汇价,此固可作为相当标准汇率,不过此种汇率是否高或低,尚有待于以后实际上之决定,应以何种汇率,才能对于国际收入为有利,减少外货之输入,促进国货之输出,而得一适当标准率,即稳定于此汇率上。至外汇之涨落,今既由三行无限制买卖外汇,使汇率不致有剧烈之变化,然此非有巨额基金不足以维持汇价之安足,英以三万万余金镑,美以二十万万美金,作为平衡外汇之基金,即为防止外汇之变动。我国国际贸易固远不若彼等之巨量与频繁,然需要相当巨额之基金,则为不可否认之事。原有外汇平市委员会之基金固有一万万元,恐不足以应付自如,骤涨骤落之风险,即可促进国际贸易之发达。外人以我国利率较高,亦乐于投资于我国,不虑有意外之损失。此时利用外资发展国内经济,当为良好之机会。

4. 平衡国际贸易问题

我国国际收支最大之致命伤,为贸易入超之过巨。往时外汇高涨时,固感外货倾销之苦,国货难于输出,国际支出过巨。此次我国亦贬低外汇,在理当然可以减少外货之输入,增加国货之输出,而收汇兑倾销之利,谋国际收支之平衡。但在事实上我国产业落后,农村破产,不但工业品仰赖于国外,即农产品亦不能自给,如米麦每年尚大批输入。若长此依赖于海外供给,则外货之输入并不一定因外汇之贬低,而阻止其输入,且国人反感高价购货之苦。反之我国输出品不加改进,有组织对外贸易,则亦不能利用汇兑倾销而扩大国际市场。不过因此次外汇贬低,可以稍减外货倾销之威力,刺激国货之输出,入超可望减少,然于国际收支仍不能得到平衡。是以今后当力从发展产业与振兴农业着手,以谋国际贸易之平衡。本来我国工业幼稚,资力薄弱,在近年来内外经济恐慌袭击之下,已不胜其摧残而崩折矣。旧有产业,纵不停工或倒闭,亦只能在现况之下,勉强挣扎,遑云新兴产业。不过此次币值跌落,物价上涨,可以刺激产业复兴,更因金融活动,企业家可赖以发展其产业。此时固赖政府督促金融界来扶持产业之发展,更须要产业界大规模组织起来,以促进生产效率,节省生产成本,改良生产品。庶几一方面不致因稍有恐慌之袭击而倒闭,另方面因价廉物美,在国内市场,即可与外货抗衡,减少工业品之输入,将来并谋工业品之输出。至于我国本以农立国,农产品可以自足自给,只因年来天灾人祸影响,致农村破产,粮食生产不足,引起大批的输入。且交通不便,不能懋迁有无,有的地方谷贱伤农,有的地方发生粮食恐慌,内地米之输于各沿海口岸者,不惟品质较洋米劣,且价格亦较洋米高,一般人遂乐于食洋米,致洋米年年大批输入,为入口之大宗。以农立国者尚以粮食为输入大宗,岂不为世间最可耻之事,是以救济农村,便利交通,为目前刻不容缓之企图,所谓农村复兴委员会以及种种改良农产机关,应名副其实,积极于农村中工作,而尤要者为县乡银行应速谋成立,内地农民之痛苦,诚为都市中人梦想所不到,他们完全凭其劳力牛马式的终年工作,以挣得其一年糊口的粮米,诚有"谁知盘中餐粒粒皆辛苦"之慨。他们在高利贷盘剥之下,谈不到利用资本,来施肥换种,改良土地,更谈不到改良生产方法,来大规模生产,当然不能自足自给。益以年来水旱频仍,匪祸骚扰,农村已不能生产,而粮食为一日所不能缺乏,自仰赖于海外大批供给。是以今后恢复农村,则活动农村金融,为最切要之图,使农人得利用资本,来改良其生产方法,发展其生产。如能完成农村之金融网,则农村金融可与都市金融密接,农村经济才可繁荣起来,将来纵不能大批粮食输出,至少能做到自足自给地步。其次关于对外贸易,最大之出口货,如生丝、茶叶、桐油之类,向由人民自谋出路,且因经营方法不良,致年来遭极大之惨败。丝茶年来输出已锐减,桐油反为出口之大宗。长此衰落下去,当不堪设想,是以今后欲谋出口之增加,应对于出口货加以改良,其品质形色格度应求标准化,其品质劣者,应限制出口,庶不致失信任于国际市场,而遭受排击。其次对于国外贸易,应有完美之组织,成立对外贸易推销机关,预先在海外各地调查市场上之需要,各地中国领事馆应加以协助,而后有组织大规模输出,同时与国内有力银行联络起来,给与金融上之协助。政府之奖励与扶助,自为必要,庶几对外贸易可望发展,国际收支可望平衡。此次贬低外汇,由买卖外汇当中而寓有统制贸易之意,固可减少入超,然求国际贸易平衡,自非努力于上述之准备与发展不可。

5. 辅币整理问题

我国各地情形之复杂,在辅币方面,实足可以表现出来,可谓极紊乱之情事。各地有各地之辅币,省有省辅币,市有市辅币,县有县辅币,种类庞杂,式样纷奇。据去年财政部币制研究委员会调查,全国现行辅币计有二十余种之多,他如各地发行之辅币券,惟于统计,各有其流行区域,有甲省通行而乙省不能用者,亦有一省之中分界行使者。如旅行各地,首先须熟悉各地使用辅币情形,此就种类复杂而言。铜元银角各省以有利可图,积年滥铸伪造,质量日劣,数量愈多,辅币限制之特性完全消失,十进制早已破坏矣。辅币价值遂日渐跌落,如上海铜元在光绪三十年以前,银元一元仅可换得铜元80枚左右,至今年则跌到345枚左右,且市价早晚涨落不定,影响于物价变迁。一般投机者即藉此营利,往往利用时会,尽操纵之能事。富者稍受损失,尚不为虑,至大多数劳工阶级,因此而时受意外之损失,则于其生活上压迫,影响甚大。辅币问题之严重,自无可否认者也。现在乘此改革主币之后,即应积极整理各地辅币,严令各地方政府,按各地辅币近来对于主币之平均价值,规定一法定比率,如十二毫银角兑换主币一元,三百枚铜元兑主币一元,毋使时有变迁,以便将来以新辅币来代替旧辅币,并严禁奸商操纵辅币价格。阅报载政府现已筹划开铸银镍铜新辅币,以便流通于市面。此时对于单位种类形式质量自应有精密统一之规定,采取十进原则,当然合乎我国习惯。名目种类不宜繁多,形式应与旧辅币有显然区分之规定,较为新奇。成分重量宜规定中庸,不使过高过低以免有销毁与伪造之弊发生。所铸数量,当视市面需要之多寡,而有一定之限制,以表现辅币之特性。由铸造辅币所得之余利,应另作为调节辅币之基金,竭力免去以往有利可图而滥铸之弊也。立即以新辅币来代替旧辅币,当为不可能之事,自应假以时日,赶工铸造,各地需要辅币甚多,当然逐步推行。当开铸新币之时,须即颁布旧辅币收回法币与旧币,准许通用之期限,均应有明确之规定,俾数年后得到统一辅币之效果,此固赖中央积极推行,更须地方政府之竭力协助也。

五　结论

兹篇首在阐明新货币政策之历史性,由一步一步地改革,而产生此次重大之变迁。由国际之潮流,与国内环境之急迫,而造成货币管理之结果,新政策既因是而成长,则其价值之重大,与含意之深远,诚为吾人所不能忽视。然法令宣布后,所待解决之问题甚多,要在当局之努力积极进行与及全国上下一致之赞助,方能达到圆满之结果。否则徒多此一举耳。不过任何改革,皆有其重大之阻力,何况我国金融基础薄弱,货币制度紊乱,政治不统一,主权不完整,其阻力之大,当远甚于其他国家。实行以后,虽尚称顺利,英国领事即有禁止英侨行使银币严令之宣布,同情于我。然惟恐我国不乱之所谓邻邦,虽高唱其经济合作口号,乃在极力反对中,且庇护白银之私运出口,与制止日籍银行之交出白银,以破坏我新货币政策之进行。其次美国虽不反对我国新政策,但运用其购银政策,即可破坏我新政策之发展,如近来美国变更购银地点,使世界银市场之伦敦银价跌落,且其购银政策有变更之趋势。设银价一如以前惨跌,则我国此次改革殊无意义,收不到若何效果,国际局势之险恶,殊难以应付。其次我国表面,似乎为统一国家,其实各地各自为政,中央政令难及之地,新政策即不能为有效之措施,如此次白银,即难集中。北平一带白银即集中于北平,两广白银则集中于两广,四川白银集中于四川。一旦非常时期发生,各地即把持其集中白银,中央即难为集中准备之总动员。其次各地情形复杂,统一发行,即难成功。总之新货币政策障碍丛丛,今后之能否得到圆满效果,要在谋政治上之统一,与国际情势之应付如何耳。

(原载《时事月报》1936年第14卷第24期)

改进中国国际贸易拟议

国际贸易为本国货物对外之运销以及外国货物之购进。凡有利于上列事宜且能促进国民经济建设者，皆在设计改良之范围内。故下列问题为计划之中心。

（一）贸易政策之抉择。

（二）贸易机能之改进。

（一）贸易政策

贸易政策者，乃一国政府所采取之手段，用以调节本国对于外国之经济关系也。此种手段，要可归纳之为课税（Duties）、津贴（Bounties）、限额（Limitation），以及管理汇兑（Controling Exchange）与国营。

中国国际贸易，应以发展国民经济为立场。则凡能增进国民经济生产力之政策，均有妥当性。但中国经济落后，实业基础未固，难与工业先进国自由竞争。故自由贸易或放任政策，必不可用。统制贸易政策，为当今盛行于世之贸易政策。有刚性柔性之别。如苏俄之国营，为统制贸易政策中之最刚性者；德国之统制汇兑而行其以货易货之道，为刚性统制贸易政策中之其次者，法国之限定进口额，为刚性统制贸易中之又其次者；美英之课税津贴与互惠商约政策，可为统制贸易政策中之柔性者。统制性质与程度，虽有差别，然其作用则一，均在调节本国对外之经济关系也。

中国之欲行统制贸易政策，必须考虑本国所处之政治地位与经济环境。就经济环境言，中国为经济落后的国家，能力薄弱，若骤施急剧改革，恐难胜任，故以缓进为宜。就政治地位言，则刚性的统制贸易政策，如贸易全部国营，德国式的汇兑管理，定比制或特许制，或物物交换的商业协定制度，均有困难在。即关税率，在事实上，尚受强邻之挟制。但就刚柔难易言，只得参考英美贸易政策之旨趣，谋一柔性的统制贸易政策。

（1）逐渐并分别提高关税，以保育重要工业之发展；修改通商条约，达到实际的互惠,以通畅本国货物之出路,并废除出口税,以利外销。待政治地位容许时,斟行特许限额制。

（2）由政府与工商界合力改善贸易机能,以利进口与出口。

（二）贸易机能之改进

贸易机能,包含货物之买卖、运输、保险、金融、贮藏,以及输出物品之改良等。

(1) 改进贸易机构

欲求贸易机能之改进,必设一完备之管理机构。盖一切计划,均赖以逐步推行也。

本此前提,政府宜与人民合组国际贸易公司（就现有之国际贸易局改组成立,其法律上之地位,正如中国银行,扩大其范围,增进其功能,使成为一名实相符的对外然）贸易总揽机关。兹拟定组织纲领如次：

（甲）国际贸易公司,为政府与人民合组之独立公司,政府的指定董事若干人,参与行政与监督权。各同业公会由本公司请派代表组织顾问委员会（Advisory Council）。

（乙）总经理以专门人员任之。下设二部：一为技术委员会,一为管理委员会。前者为研究设计机关,后者为实际推动机关。

（丙）技术委员会之下,分设二部：

(i) 商情测报处,担任征集,分析及报告关于国内外商情（包括消费风尚式样等变动趋势）变动等工作。驻外领事改由外交部会同实业部委派之,负有调查驻在国商业状况之责任。

(ii) 商品改良技术处。担任研究（可与其他技术机关如中央研究院工程研究所中央农事试验场植物油料厂等合作）出入口商品之性质及促进国内商品改良与农产销售合作社等工作。

（丁）管理委员会之下,分设下列六组：

(i) 商品出入口信托处,按即代办出入口商品之意。代理本国商人向外国定货运货或外国商人向国内定货运货等事。

(ii) 贸易信用处。凡商人向国外办货或本国商品出口,一时缺乏信用调剂,可依法定手续,请求本处予以信用上之援助或保证,而谋对外贸易之便利。

以上两处，系为扶助业务较小，信用较弱之商民，其目的在改善贸易之一部而非全部。待实施者有成效，逐渐扩充其范围。

（iii）特种商品经营处，按此即对于特种商品之独占管理之意。贸易全部国营，就现状论，不能实行。但可选择若干特殊商品，试行独占方式的贸易，嗣有经验成效，逐渐推广，以进于大多数商品对外贸易的独占地步。本处工作即专任管理此种商品之出入口。

（iv）商品检验处。现在各口岸商品检验局，均令改组并隶属于本处。

（v）仓库业务处。本公司为便利商品之储藏，调剂产销之盈虚起见，附设巨大仓库若干所。

（vi）推广处，凡外国有需要之商品。设法介绍并采访事宜；中外商人旅行考察之指导事宜，国际博览会之征品参加事宜，以及进出商品纳税之指导事宜等，皆由本处担任之。

上述组织，若以图表之，其系统如下：

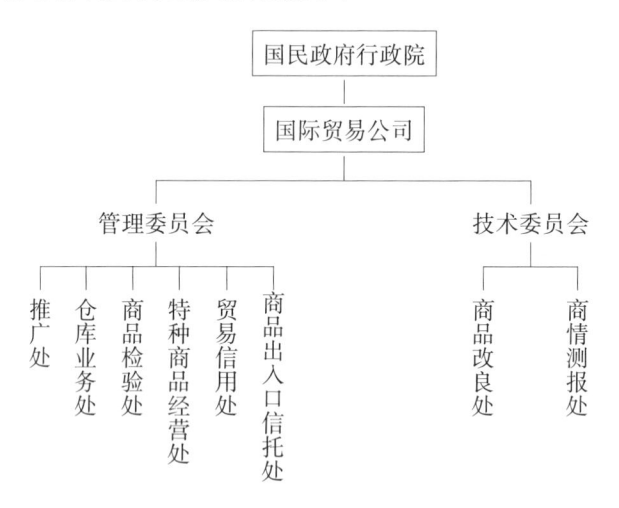

```
           国民政府行政院
                │
           国际贸易公司
          ┌─────┴─────┐
       管理委员会    技术委员会
    ┌──┬──┬──┬──┬──┐  ┌──┬──┐
   推 仓 商 特 贸 商   商 商
   广 库 品 种 易 品   品 情
   处 业 检 商 信 出   改 测
      务 验 品 用 入   良 报
      处 处 经 处 口   处 处
            营    信
            处    托
                  处
```

国际贸易公司对于政府之地位，约如中央银行，属于公私合营性质。

国际贸易公司在国内各埠如天津、青岛、连云港、广州等酌设分所。在国外如新加坡、伦敦、纽约、大阪等酌设支行或代理处。

国际贸易公司，因负有信用担保或暂时的部分垫款责任，应与负有国际汇兑专业责任的中国银行签订合同，由中国银行随时给予信用的便利。

进出口货物之海运保险，可委托中央信托局办理之。

国际贸易公司，对于若干特产商品有权独占经营。此种商品之价格，在可能范围内，应由该处评定并维持之。其经营之利得，除提出一定成数作为股息与基金外，余入国库。但所需之活动资金与信用，由中、中、交三行予以便利。

贸易公司之信托处,受私人或公司之委托,代为进口或出口。对于信托出口之货款,由本处保证,向中国银行贴现,以为对外输出之鼓励。

(2) 贸易信托处的组织

贸易信托处,系代理国内外商人办货之机关,故为国内外进口商之代办,与本国制造业之推销员。宜设下列数组,分任其事:

(甲)购买部,专任访求货物之来源及移转所有权于买主等事务。

(乙)销售部,专任对于外国进口商行及其他经理进口的买主,接洽售卖事宜。故其工作应包含激励需要的任务。凡以广告、陈列样本或其他兜售方面,足引起预期买主(Prospective Buyer)对于该商品之注意者,是为激励需要。

(丙)运输部,专办对外贸易的运输事宜。凡自生产地至出口岸的运输,出口岸的装卸,外洋运输,以及货物到达外国后的运输事务属之。

(丁)商险部。国际贸易中之商险,如

(i)货物运输时之损坏。

(ii)交易当事人中,有一方无能力或拒绝履行其债务。由本部办理之。

贸易信托处以代理进出口为原则。对于代办之事务,按定价表收佣金。

贸易信托之任务,在于扶助弱小商民及生产家。本处既代理国内各种工业向外推销,其运销之费用,将由各工业分担之。故每一工业所担负之费用必较独自出口时为廉,是有销售合作社之功能。换言之,生产者以较低之费用而达到更广的市场。此外如照顾货物的装运,分发货物于各买主,担负危险与融通货款,即皆由本处经理,可减除卖主的麻烦与成本。其影响所及,足以增加输出。再就进口言,本处既能与声望素著的厂家直接交洽,采购精良货物,且能以低廉手续费,代办运输、保险、装卸、存栈等繁琐之事。

(3) 特种商品之独占问题

上述为贸易机构问题,本节列举各种商品之适合于独占性质者,并略述施行独占经营的方法。

(甲)输出,出口商品之专营,先就下列商品试办之:(一)钨矿、(二)铁砂、(三)锑矿、(四)桐油、(五)茶叶。

（一）钨之出口，已由资源委员会独占，应由资源委员会转移于国际贸易公司接办。

（二）铁矿为国内工商发展所必需，年来多输往日本，吾人独占之目的，在保存资源以归本国利用。其办法：

（A）国际贸易公司，将全国铁矿收买之，收资之法，可由该公司发给股票于原矿主，使为股东维持其矿主的权利。否则以特种法令强制其产品只能售于国际贸易公司之特种商品管理处，由局标定价格输出。

（B）在有矿苗区域，由局商借资本，直接开发，标价输出。

（C）因铁为工业所必需，日人又甚缺乏，故标价可以从高（Charge the Price as the Tariff Canlbear），所得余利即可作为新资本。

（D）国际贸易公司有运铁出口之独占权，国府以命令禁止私人运铁出口。

（三）锑多产于湖南，现资源委员会将加以独占，此事应移归贸易公司接续办理，独占方法与资源委员会在江西之钨产独占相同——参照该会钨矿管理规程。

（四）关于桐油出口之管理，其方式略异于独占，盖美国植桐已有成效，深恐独占之后，反足以影响农民之植桐也。此时（一）应由国家策动植桐计划，在川、湘、鄂、皖、赣、浙等省，将未垦之公有土地，划为植桐区域，广栽桐苗。（二）由国际贸易公司与中央农事试验场合作，以研究桐种之改良，并辅导农民植桐方法。（三）促进桐户合作社，使与国际贸易公司特种商品管理处联络，以利运销，并谋物价之稳定。（四）同时国际贸易公司应筹集资金，设立炼油厂，将桐油按质以分级，使之标准化。（五）桐户可将桐子经由合作社转卖于贸易公司。（六）设立油漆研究处，改良油漆，以广利用。

（五）茶叶亦可由国际贸易公司独占之，其经营方式与上列四种各异，兹拟定办法如下。

（A）贸易公司商品独占经营处，先行划分茶区，登记茶号，指导茶农组织生产合作社，从事生产改良，转请中国农民银行与中国银行分别酌予贷款。

（B）由该处在每年春季茶期前，根据过去平均茶价，估计将来茶销情形，拟定标准品级的熟茶价格。

（C）由标准熟茶价格，按焙制加工费及耗费情形，并依毛茶品质拟定毛茶价格。

（D）茶农集中茶叶于合作社，转售于该处。暂依拟定价格七成收款。

余额俟茶叶脱售后,由实价扣除手续费补发之。

（E）毛茶由合作社或该处用新法焙制之。

（F）熟茶依品质市价全数售于国际贸易公司或零售商。

（G）商品独占经营处将所收之茶,验分等级,直接输出销售,私人可在国内买卖,但不得运售于国外,由政府以特种命令禁止之。

（乙）入口,入口之独占与出口之独占的用意不同,出口独占之目的,在求得较广市场与较多利益,入口独占在减少国外商品对国产工业之竞争,故其物品种类完全不同。

出口独占较易,于生产上市之时,即由公司直接收买,运出售卖。至入口商品因帝国主义势力关系,似甚困难。惟政府必需且需要大量之物品,如汽车、汽油、煤油等,可集中购买,由贸易公司信托处代办。如是买之,故可在价格上运输费上获得便宜。又米麦关系国计民生,宜由政府特许该公司独占经营,且俟施行经验丰富之后,可逐渐推广于糖、香烟、煤及棉布等。

中国之对外贸易,近年甚形衰落,非有大规模之推进计划,前途将更不堪设想,原则上当施以刚性的统制或国营,但揆之实际深觉困难繁多,故惟有采取缓进方法,逐步推行,上述管理机构之改造与若干产品之独占,为一种初步的计划。就中国实际情形论,若干基本产业尚有赖于关税之保护,故对外贸易政策,似应适应国内经济环境而逐渐改变。在目前,适当关税政策的运用,似仍重要也。

（原载《是非公论》1936年第34期）

中央银行改组为中央储备银行时应有之认识*

各位听众，今天敝人要讲的题目，是"中央银行改组为中央储备银行时应有之认识"。本题范围广大，当然不是短时间内所能讲完，只能择要来讲。前年十一月三日颁行新币制法令时，孔财长宣言中，即声明现在之中央银行，将改组为中央储备银行，以保持全国货币之稳定，且供给各银行以再贴现之便利；于此足见中央银行之改组为中央储备银行，实有极重大之意义。现在中央储备银行法，已由财政部依据中央颁发之原则，拟就草案，呈请行政院咨送立法院审议；在该法未通过以前，我人应有贡献意见之余地：据报所载，我们觉得中央储备银行，系抄袭资本主义国家银行制度的典型，不能适合于三民主义国家的政制的；我们中国有我们中国的民族文明、历史、习惯，更有我们立国的主义，任何政治经济的制度，都不能和这个主义相违背的；所以在倡立中央储备银行法时，对于这点，应该特别郑重考虑的。莫说政治经济的制度，不能随便抄袭，就是植物，亦因为时令地域的关系，不能任意移植。譬如美国棉花产量丰富，纤维很长，我们想把他移植到中国来，虽然经过了二十年的试验，到如今，依然不敢说有很好的结果。再引晏子的话来讲："江南有橘，移之江北，则化而为枳。"所以然者，地土不同也。

我们中国的经济政策，以节制资本、平均地权为最高原则，及今中央储备银行依草案规定将由官民合办，私股之存在就是违背节制资本之精神，何以言之？查考各国中央银行之营业经验，无不每年赚利累万，即就我们中国的中央银行营业经验看，自民国十七年成立以来获利甚厚，现在公积金计有四百万元，每年纯益约有一千四百万元，既无亏损之机会，凡是中央储备银行之股东，都可不劳而获，坐以致富，而我们民众，又不是都有做股东的机会，这不是违反了三民主义的精神吗？从客观的立场来说，中央储备银行若非完全国营，亦只能容许本国经营银行及钱庄业务的法人参与其中，万不可有私人股东。

---

* 六月二十四日在本处中央电台播讲。

依报所载,中央银行之所以定为官民合办,在欲保持中央银行之超然地位,换言之,可使中央银行勿受财政政策之支配。年来政府收支,不能切实平衡,未免有向中央银行透支借款过滥之事,当借款超过一定数额之后,则又发行新公债以抵偿之;中央银行即以公债为准备,增发纸币,通货既增,物价亦涨,物价愈涨,财政收支差额愈大。如是因果相循,可无限制,公债与纸币同时膨胀,其结果,一方面增加虚伪的购买力,他方面减少社会有效的资金,实足以扰乱社会经济,破坏币制,危险殊大。但此种弊端,不必以官民合营的方式来避免,假使这样做去,好比是因噎废食的办法。今试举一例以说明之,法兰西银行,居法国中央银行之地位,属于私营,且著成效者,然考其内幕,则该行实为少数金融巨头所操纵;依该行规例,凡股东握有八十万法郎以上之股权者,始有参加股东大会之选举权,因之,四万个股东中只不过二百个股东有选举权;在此二百个股东中,有一百五十个股东为六个银行家所操纵,即马雷奥丁格、米拉波、范尔内、邰暖佛里士、伏格是;于是此六巨头就独裁了法兰西银行,凭藉法兰西银行的势力,要挟政府,并操纵内阁的命运。例如一九二四年,赫里欧内阁的去职,一九二五年凯奥内阁的倾覆,继任之班乐卫内阁,在一个月内又被迫下台。一九二六年阁员罗尔潘勒之辞职,接着是白里安内阁的退休,赫里欧再度组阁,法兰西银行立刻加紧进攻,政府证券价格暴跌,外汇突涨,于是赫里欧内阁又倒下台来。这些事实,都是这六位金融巨头利用法兰西银行的势力来造成功的。今我国中央储备银行,定为官民合营,以私股占其十分之六,且总裁副总裁均由股东大会所推选,经国民政府任命,倘国民政府不同意时,又未明文规定重选,是则选任总裁之大权,操诸股东大会,其结果之恶,固不必如法兰西银行之甚,然而小银行将逐渐归并而成少数大银行。又民众股东必辗转而操诸少数银行家之手,此乃资本主义制度的自然趋势,可于欧洲各国金融史中见之。而此少数寡头必利用中央银行之势力,为私人集团谋利,又为人之天性使然。故谓一国中央银行必须超然,其所以超然之道及超然之程度,实有选择考虑之必要。

中央储备银行法之超然态度,似采取一九二二年日内瓦财政会议之原则,即谓中央发钞银行,应不受政治之压力,而自由执行其业务。要知此项原则,为当时非常环境的结晶品,不必适合于今日之时势,更不必适合于我国今日之国情。盖是时适欧战之后,各国经济组织,受战争之摧毁,工商凋敝,国库之收入,日益短绌,不得不向中央银行借款以为弥补,中央银行在战时为供应战费,已发出巨额之不换纸币,战后又因政府财政之支绌,无限制增发纸币,因之物价随通货之增加而腾贵。结果资金外逃,贷借关系失去平衡,非维有售于分配,抑且不利于生产经济。社会所受惨痛既深,反动亦剧,故于日内瓦财政会议时,一般人士都主张中央发钞银行,应当脱离政治压力,俾可自由执行其业务,并应恪守安全货币政策,以保持货币价值之稳定。然而时迁境易,一九三〇年经济恐慌弥漫全球,生产过剩,销售滞涩,工厂倒闭,工人失业,金融紧急,银行危殆;且当时计划经济及统制经济之思潮,应运而起,于是政府统制金融及管理中央银行之事,遂盛行于世:一九三六年七月法兰西银行的改组,规定总裁一人,副总裁二人,由内阁任命外,所有理事二十人,由股东大会选出二人,全国经济委员会储蓄银行最高委员会及法兰西银行职员等三团体,各选一人,财政部长就全国消费合作社联合会、全国经济委员会劳工总会、工匠联合会、全国商会会长联合会,及全国农会会长联合会等六机关中,各指定一人,财政部国民经济部及殖民部各派一人,其余六理事由财政部直辖机关指派之,很可以代表这种趋势。

其实银行为人民之金融机关,凡经济事业之发达及全民之幸福,都和其有休戚相关的联系。故属于公营经济之范围内,其业务之经营,自当以服务为目的,不可以牟利为目的。比如铁道,邮政等事业,宜以国营为原则;至于中央银行居银行之中心,享有发行钞券及保持存款准备之唯一特权,负有控制金融之责任,尤须以国营为原则,最低限度政府应握有管理权。盖钞票之发行,若任私营性质之银行自由经理,则将以自己之营利为第一目的,欲为经济社会的公正统制,怕不容易做到。

今日我国,正集中力量于国防建设及国民经济建设,以为抗敌之准备,在此共同目标之下,人民必须信任政府,予政府以必要之权力,设中央银行绝对超然,不受政府之指挥管理,无异于政府在国防建设上,失去指臂之助。故吾人主张,中央银行之政权应属于政府,换言之,中央银行之总裁及理事人等,应由国民政府就农工商学术金融团体中选任之,俾能代表社会中各种分子之利益,使其行政,随时随地顾到全民族之福利。——为防止中央银行受政府收支不平衡的不良影响起见,建议下列办法:

(一)中央银行总裁、副总裁及理事等人员,不得兼任政府官吏。

(二)政府向中央银行之借款由政府与中央银行理事会商定一最高限度,非得立法院之同意,任何时不得超过此限度。

(三)政府借款的归还期限,应明白规定。

(四)政府向中央银行借款的用途,应有一定限制,例如以之用于国防建设,或预算案中所有的用途为限。

（五）中央银行的资产中，政府证券所占的成数，应有一定之限制。

（六）中央银行对于政府之放款，应逐月送请立法院备案，并在中央日报及中央银行月刊上公布之，以防止政府向中央银行秘密通融之事，并受民间舆论之监督。

（七）中央银行对于商业银行之重贴现，应规定政府公债库券在贴现账中所占之一定成数或最高限额，如是中央银行可不因重贴现而获得巨额之政府公债库券，以致危及该行之准备金地位。

（原载《广播周报》1937年第145期）

维持外汇法价与黑市汇价

一 汇价之意义

货币之价值,有所谓对内价值,与对外价值之别。本国货币对于本国商品之购买力,谓之对内价值。故本国商品之平均价格涨,则其货币之价值跌。本国商品之平均价格跌,则其货币之价值涨。是故货币对内价值之变动,可以国内物价指数之倒数表示之。本国货币对于外国商品之购买力,谓之对外价值。故本国货币对外价值之变动,可以外国物价指数之倒数表示之。然本国货币在外国不能通用,故欲购买外国商品,必先将本国货币换成外国货币。本国货币与外国货币之交换比,谓之汇价,例如我国法币一元合美元三角,是为对美汇价。又国币一元合英币一先令二便士半,是为对英汇价。设中外商品(包括勤务)无互相交易之必要,则无对外汇兑之事,故对外汇兑因贸易而起。中国对美国货币之需求,实为该货币对美国商品有购买力之故。美国对中国货币之需求,实为中国货币对于中国商品有购买力之故。如是中美货币之交换比,应等于其购买力之比,即等于中美物价指数之反比。是为购买力平价。就汇价变动之长期趋势言,应与平价相符合,犹如影之随形,一步一趋,常相一致。然汇价可因汇兑市场上一时供需之失均衡,背离平价而自变。是为临时变动或短期变动。设平价未变,而外汇之需求,超过于外汇之供给,则汇价跌落。非至外汇之供给,足适应外汇之需求时,汇价不能恢复原有之高度。

我国货币,在一九三五年十一月四日实行新币制以前,以白银为基础。银在中国之购买力,即为中国货币之对内价值;银在美国之购买力,即为中国货币对美商品之购买力;银在英国之购买力,即为中国货币对英商品之购买力。而银在美国之价格,若将常数之倍数舍去不计[此常数为 1.04。盖银在美国之价格,为一英两纯银合美元若干之数值。但一英两等于四百八十格厘(Grains)。而中国对外汇价为上海规元一两合美币若干之谓。上海规元一两合纯银 499.201 Grains 又 499.201÷480 = 1.04。故上海规元一两,等于1.04英两。若上海银对于金之比价,等于纽约银对于金之比价,则中币对美币之汇价,为纽约银之1.04倍],即为中币对美币之汇价。银在英国之价格,亦即为中英之汇价。依前节所言,此汇价之变动,应与平价之变动相似。此可用统计证明之。据前实业部银价讨论委员会报告云:"各国对于白银之需要既日减,白银之购买力遂因之而跌,其跌风在英国约起自一八八五年。从是年至一九三一年间未曾稍杀(表I)。同时期内以银计算之中国物价亦上涨不得,而趸售物价指数之倒数之中国银购买力指数,与英国之银购买力指数正相符合。"①

欧战期间,英国禁银出口,银禁实行后,银价之涨风,较之趸售物价方面,颇见缓慢,以是英国之白银购买力,较之中国之白银购买力大为低落。此种低落状况,直至解禁后,始见消除。

自一八八五年左右起,至现在止,中国之银购买力与在美国者相仿佛(表II),欧战时美国未尝禁银出口,故于彼扰攘期间,中美两国之银购买力亦无甚分别。

今美(英)国之银购买力指数,等于美(英)国银价指数除以美(英)国趸售物价指数。故上段所云,实无异于证明中美(英)汇价之变动,与中美(英)货币购买力平价之变动相符合:

$$\frac{1}{中国趸售物价指数} \propto \frac{美(英)国银价指数}{美(英)国趸售物价指数}$$

$$中美货币购买力之平价 = \frac{美(英)国趸售物价指数}{中国趸售物价指数} \propto$$

美(英)国银价指数 = 中美汇价指数

表II为中美汇价与中美货币购买力平价之比价。设基期之年,平价与汇价相同,则汇价指数与平价指数,可望互相符合。一九二六年在美国经济状况虽属平和,但在中国,北伐军事正在进行之中,不能称为平和之时,中美经济关系,自非常态。故其汇价难望与平价相同。以是年为基期之指数,自亦不能互相符合。然其变动趋势,仍相一致。例如一九二六年至一九三二年,为中美汇价长期跌落之期。而中美趸售物价及生活费指数之平价,亦显示长期跌落之趋势。虽其程度较微,此盖受基期汇价不等于平价之影响。

---

① 《中国银价问题》第2页。

又自一九三二年至一九三五年(此后中国推行法币政策,中美汇价维持于中币1元合美币0.2975元之值上。此汇价之选定,无经济学理之根据,由财政当局任意指定,自不必与平价相合,因此平价发生适应变动,使中美物价恢复平衡之势),中美趸售物价及生活费指数之平价均涨,因之中美汇价亦向上涨。故中美汇价,可谓追随平价而变动。同理,他国之汇价亦同。

二 外汇黑市之由来

自一九三五年十一月四日实行法币政策之时起,至今年三月十四日实行统制外汇之时止,中国货币对外汇价,维持于一定之水准,未有变更,且人民得依法价买卖外汇,不受限制。法币信用稳固,金融安定,自无黑市存在之余地。三月十四日政府开始统制外汇之后,人民之需要外汇,必先依法请求政府核准,方得向中央银行购买,故不必要商品之进口,即无法请准购买外汇以作支付货款之需。贸易以外之不必要的外汇需要,更不能请准购买外汇。于是有私行购买外汇之需求。

统制外汇,原为维持法币信用安定金融之必要手段。其理由甚简,战时军需浩繁,有赖于外国之接济,尤以军需工业不发达之中国为甚,军需品输入愈多,外汇之需求愈增。如非将其他商品之输入减少,或将输出商品增加。以资抵销,则输入超过输出之数值,必须动用外汇基金,以为偿付。军需品之输入,为数极大,若无外债以资挹注,全赖外汇基金之应付,则外汇基金虽大,亦有用尽之日,而法币信用动摇矣。为求金融之稳定,当从增加输出及减少输入着手。但在战时,因人民入伍作战者增多,从事生产者减少之故,生产量有减少之倾向。且此铁路未修,水道只通木船,而公路交通工具以忙于军运故,运输亦不如平时之便利。欲求输出之增加,殊属不易。因之欲求入超之减少,应力求输入之减少。求输入之减少,其道多端。(例如按照过去三年之平均标准,一律减少若干成,进口或用进口许可制,或用偿付协定制,或用以货易货制等。)限制外汇之购买,亦是一法。且统制外汇后,输入货款以外的外汇需求,亦在统制之中,三月十四日公布之核准外汇办法,实为限制输入商品及购买外汇之一种有效手段。其法甚善,惜行之稍迟耳。

物价腾贵为战时不可避免之现象。盖在战争期间,军需浩繁,糜费至巨,货物之需要必大增。同时供给方面,以人民入伍作战者增加,从事于生产者减少之故,反而减少。供需失调,物价高涨,乃自然之趋势,且战时政府支出骤增,欲藉税收或举债以应付,每为事实所不许,只能增发纸币以济急。欧战时英德法诸国莫不于开战后一年之内,增发钞票至一倍左右。迨至一九一八欧战告终时,英德钞票流通额增至十倍,法国钞票流通额增至五倍有奇。(见表Ⅳ)通货增加,又足促进物价之上涨。故在一九一八年英国物价约增105,德国物价约增119,法国约增234。(见表Ⅴ)设使英、德、法各国当局,对于生活必需品之价格,不加管理,则其物价上涨之程度,当不止此数。总之,战时物价,以有上列两原因之存在,必然上涨,虽有种种管理之手段,亦不能完全阻止。今次中国之抗战期间,前种原因,以产业落伍之故,必较英德法诸国为深重。此可毋庸赘言。至于后者原因,有钞票发行额可考:

抗战以来法币发行数额及指数

1937	六月	七月	八月	九月	十月	十一月	十二月
发行额（单位百万元）	1 407	1 445	1 512	1 544	1 556	1 603	1 639
指数（1937年6月=100）	100	103	107	110	111	114	116
1938	一月	二月	三月	四月	五月	六月	
发行额（单位百万元）	1 678	1 697	1 679	1 694	1 705	1 727	
指数（1937年6月=100）	119	121	119	120	121	123	

于此足见我国抗战一年期间,钞票增加率为23%,远不如欧战时英德法诸国钞票增加率之速。此由于去年八月十七日财政部颁布安定金融法,以限制提取存款,及其补充办法,以同业汇划代替法币使用之故。待原有存款如数提完之后,则该法失去限制之效用,法币流通额之增加,将较前此为速,物价之上涨,亦将加快。就目前论,通货膨胀促使物价上涨之原因,较欧战时英法德诸国者为弱。然物价上涨之趋势(见表Ⅲ),则甚显著。自去年七月至今年六月,每月平均约增百分之二。国内物价继续上涨,而外汇价格不变(未随购买力平价之变动而变),则进口商获利之大,超于寻常。例如一先令二便士半之英国商品,除去运费关税等不计,在抗日战事发生之前,原售国币一元即可够本。现今以国内物价高涨故,可售至一元二角,则此二

角即为进口商之格外利润。换言之,进口商可因国内物价高涨而得20%的格外利润。且进口货以供给较少之故,其涨价之程度,每较国产涨价之程度为大。故进口商实得之额外利润,尚较物价指数增加之程度为高。例如前门牌香烟,在战前之售价为四角,今则售至一元三角。价格已增二倍有奇,就此例而论,进口商所得之额外利润,何至20%？由是观之,当国内物价上涨之时,外汇价格仍维持于固定之水准,徒足激励进口商之输入外货。输入既增,外汇之需求亦增。若不能依法请准购买外汇,必求之于黑市。故在外汇价格钉住及国内物价高涨之环境中,进口贸易自由私营实为外汇黑市之根由。

三　黑市外汇之供给来源

设外汇黑市无汇票之供给,则徒有黑市外汇之需要,亦不能使黑市存在。然则黑市外汇之供给来源如何？约有下列三种:(1)偷运出口之货款;(2)逃资;(3)华侨汇款。

(1)政府为集中外汇起见,颁布商人运货出口及售结外汇办法。兹录之如下:

一　凡运输货物出口,出口商应依照下列程序向交通部水陆运输联合办事处申请登记。

甲　应向中国银行或交通银行依照其规定,办理一切手续。并取得"承购外汇证明书"。

乙　将承购外汇证明书提交海关查验后,方允报关。

丙　向水陆运输联合办事处填具货物托运单时,应提交"承购外汇证明书""关单"及其他证件,经审核无误后,准予登记,并在"货物托运单"上加盖水陆运输联合办事处印章,该单收货人应为出给承购外汇证明书之中国银行或交通银行。

二　出口商接到水陆运输联合办事处派车通知后,即向运输机关接洽装运,惟提货单或货票之抬头,应为出给承购外汇证明书之中国银行或交通银行。

三　出口商取得提货单后,即应向发给承购外汇证明书之中国银行或交通银行办理一切手续。

四 出口商所售之货价,应以外币计算,此项外币,应售与约定之中国银行或交通银行,按其所规定之汇率,换取法币。

五 出口商向约定银行换取法币时应将承购外汇证明书缴还该行核销。

至于寄往国外之邮包,亦经颁布"邮政包裹售结外汇办法"。节录如次:

(二)寄包人须预先向中国银行交通银行或其委托行,依照其规定,取得"承购外汇证明书",将该证明书提交海关查验后,方得报关。

(三)邮局非经提验"承购外汇证明书"及"关单"后,不得邮递。

(四)中交两行,或其委托行,为邮包所发给之"承购外汇证明书",必须实数收得外汇或确能在以后收得外汇,方可发给。

如是出口货物,如无偷运,其货款将全数集中于中交两行。然自一月至七月出口货值,与中交两行在同期间承购外汇之数额相较(见表Ⅵ及表Ⅶ),相差悬殊。虽其数字所包括之地域不等,未能认定差额即系偷运之值。顾表中所列商埠汉口广州永嘉重庆长沙为出口货之重要集中地,且自海岸被敌封锁之后,惟永嘉、香港可以对外通商。汉口、广州、重庆、长沙等地之货,皆运往香港出口,浙赣及皖南之货,皆运经永嘉出口。至于经由昆明出口之货物,为数不大,以由内地至昆明及昆明经海防至香港出口,运费过大故也。据财政部贸易委员会之估计,由重庆贵阳经昆明至香港每公吨货物之运费如下:

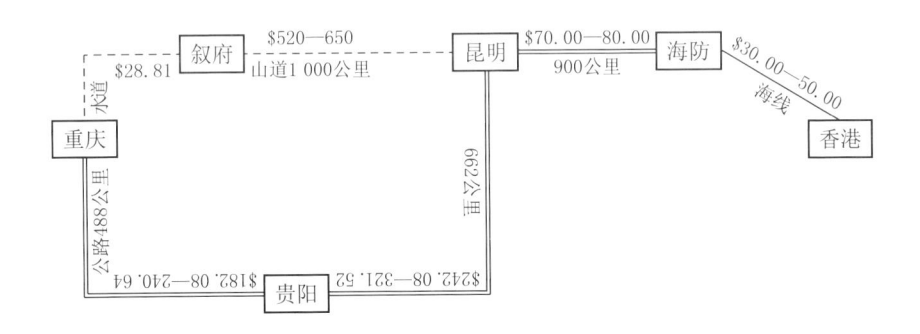

```
            $520—650              $70.00—80.00          $30.00—50.00
    叙府 ─────────────── 昆明 ─────────────── 海防 ─────────────── 香港
     │   山道1 000公里      │    900公里              海线
$28.81│                    │
水道  │                    │662公里
     │                    │
    重庆                   │
     │                    │
公路488公里                  │
     │  $242.08—321.52   │
     └──────── 贵阳 ───────┘
         $182.08—240.64
```

如此重大之运费,非价值昂而体积小或重量轻之货物,不堪负担。但中国之重要出口货,多属原料品,与此条件不符。又云南土产之出口贸易,向来不盛。故经昆明出口之货物,为量必小。是故表 VI 所列中交两行承购外汇之数额,大约可代表报关出口之货值。表 VII 所列之差额,大约可代表偷运及沦陷区域出口之货值。此项货款原为外币计算之外汇,既不结售于政府指定之中交两行,必直接出售于黑市中之需要外汇者,或经由银行转售于黑市。是为黑市外汇供给来源之一。

（2）自七七抗战发生,以至三月十四日统制外汇,相隔凡七月余。在此期间,拥有巨资者,或恐法币购买力之跌落或恐外汇之降低,有购买外汇逃避者。据外汇管理委员会之估计,此项逃资约合国币三万万元。设使此项逃资永留国外,则无可为黑市外汇供给之来源。然亦有不得已之故而归来者。例如避居香港之人,除非在当地获有职业,则日常衣食住行之所需,必动用所携之外汇。但香港所消费之衣食用品,大部分给于内地。故当香港商人向内地采购衣食用品时,必将港币兑换为内地货币。总此以观,逃资之一部分,为黑市外汇供给来源之一。

（3）华侨汇款,每年约可二万万元。我国贸易入超,向赖此项收入以为挹注。但居留外国之侨民,以粤籍为大多数,其汇款均经香港外国银行之手。当此法定汇价与暗盘汇价悬殊之时,经手之银行及汇款之人,均以利之所在,不愿依法价售与中国,理至显然。例如美国华侨汇款至其家属,若依法价结售于政府,则美币 29.75 元可换取法币 100 元。然若持售于黑市,则依八月份之汇价,可得法币 183.5 元,即

$$\frac{29.75}{16.19} \times 100 = 183.5$$

故自收款人视之,必欲出售其外汇于黑市,以得此 83.5 元之格外收入。遂为黑市外汇供给之又一来源。

四 外汇黑市对于法币之威胁

外汇黑市原为统制外汇制度之一种通病。例如苏俄德意诸国,内有统制经济以辅助统制外汇之行使,犹不能消弭黑市。但以统制严密之故,黑市亦未能使其币制崩溃。故黑市对于法币之压力,设使主管及有关当局,因时地以制宜,应付得法,亦不足为大害。试就外汇黑市对于法币之威胁,分别

言之,以供主持者热心者谋对症下药之道。

一 外汇因有黑市不能集中于政府或国家银行。外汇之收入,约有下列数款:输出货款,华侨汇款,外国使领人员及驻华军队之费用,外人在华旅费,对外投资之本息利润等。除第一款受政府统制部分之外汇,为中交两行承购外,其余各款以及第一款之偷运部分,均将成为黑市外汇之供给。是故收集于政府之外汇(见表VII);为数不多。计自一月至七月期间,共计仅约4 600万元。政府收集之外汇愈少,可用作购买军火及民生必须品(如药品,汽油,汽车,钢铁,机器等)之资源亦愈少。不得已而动用外汇基金。汇兑基金愈减,外汇价格愈不稳固。且如外汇仍为供不应求,一般人对于法币之信用相随而减弱,甚至恐慌。此时汇价之降落程度,必超过物价之上涨程度,且汇价先跌落,物价随之腾贵。当此种景象激烈化时,国内物价将以汇价上涨之程度作标准而提高之。又当汇价日跌物价日涨之时,货币所有者,以货币购买力涨落之故,皆争将所有之货币转化为商品,而商品所有者,以商品价格日贵之故,不欲出售,使市场商品之供给减少。即令出售,亦必要求异常高价。盖非如是,则此后物价更高时,今日售得之货币,不能购回原有之货物,以补充其货底。外汇价格与货币之安定,诚有密切之关连,是故欧战后,各国整理币制,皆从安定外汇始。

二 外汇之需求将因有黑市故而增加。核准外汇之分配如次:

(Ⅰ)军需65%　　(Ⅱ)建设事业15%　　(Ⅲ)文化事业4%
(Ⅳ)工商15%　　(Ⅴ)其他1%

据可靠消息,包括在(ii)至(v)款内之商品,约有四十种。除此四十种以外之商品,一律不准购买外汇,亦即本文中之所谓不必要的输入商品。核准外汇之每月平均值,虽不可知,然该款以包括军需在内,决不能视外汇收入之多寡,以为伸缩。由此吾人可断定外汇当局早已不犹豫地动用外汇基金,以弥补收支之差额。政府所能集中之外汇(即中交两行所承购之外汇)愈少,则动用外汇基金以弥补收支差额之数值必愈大。今以有黑市故,外汇不能集中,遂有外汇需求之相对增加。是为黑市对于外汇需求的间接影响。

当此战争之期,国内货物稀少,商人输入外国商品,每可居奇图利。设无外汇黑市,则不必要的输入品,将以无法购得外汇而偿付其货款故而停止输入。今以有黑市故,不虑外汇之不能购得,且输入之后,可抬高奇价出售以获大利。故商人争相输入。何怪乎三炮台、大前门香烟与口红、胭脂等奢侈品仍充斥市场。是故黑市之存在,足增加输入,因而增加外汇的需求。且外汇需求之增加,又足使外汇价格更跌。此所以黑市汇价犹低于购买力平价也。

三　输出将因黑市之存在而减少。其理由有二:

(i) 不必要的输入品,既须由黑市购入外汇,则成本贵而售价亦贵。间接足使国内产物成本提高,此为物价组织之定例。输出货物之价格既增高,则在国外之销售量有减少之趋势。

(ii) 输出货物按法定汇价销售,则每值美元 29.75 元之货款,可得 100 元。但在沦陷区域之商人,以同额之美元收入,可换得 183.5 元。故若有必要时,可减价出售,以谋输出之增加。但受政府统制之区域中商人,则不能。因此输出有减少之趋势。

总上以观,黑市之存在,足使外汇需求增加,外汇之供给减少,供不敷求,且其不敷之数,与时俱增。欲藉外汇基金以为弥补,则基金虽大,为数有限。以有限之数,不能填无限之差额,是为黑市对于外汇基金之压力。又黑市汇价与货币价值有直接之关系,汇价如不稳定,或造成继续下降之局势(如平价继续下降,汇价如无适当方法统制。此为必然之现象),则法币动摇矣。

五　维持汇价之出路

汇价之当维持,不待智者而后知之。就目前论,设使汇价继续下降,而逐渐趋于零,则人民对于法币之信用动摇。法币信用动摇,足使财政金融崩溃则抗战无法继续矣。今日中国人民与政府之一切活动,均以抗战建国为最高原则。违背此原则之任何政策,皆认为与国策不符。是故汇价必须维持。

维持汇价之问题,可别之为二:

(一)维持汇价于何等水准? 本问题又可分之为二:

(i) 维持旧法定汇价欤?

(ii) 抑依新经济环境重订法定汇价然后维持之? 简言之,维持新法定汇价欤?

(二)如何维持汇价?

维持旧法定汇价与维持新法定汇价之选择,要视何者比较能巩固法币之信用为断。欲使旧法定汇价之维持,名副其实,消去人民之疑窦,恢复人民对于法币之信用(或以人民对于法币之信用如故,未曾稍变相诘难,要知人民有逃资外国之倾向,即对于法币信用减弱之表征),要实行下列两事为前提:

(ⅰ)政府或中央银行明白规定简捷办法,以便人民获得"正当需要"之外汇。同时维持供给"正当需要"之外汇。

(ⅱ)维持货币购买力,勿使更往下跌。

今日中国外汇黑市,与苏俄德意诸国之外汇黑市,有不同之处。(a)中国黑市汇价之变动,约与购买力平价相符,而外国则不然。(b)中国黑市,自政府视之为黑市,自人民视之,实为惟一可得外汇之汇市,无异于公开自由汇市,政府不加查禁,亦无法禁止。但外国黑市为政府所严密查禁,只能秘密买卖外汇。(c)中国人民"正当需要"之外汇,有时亦不准购买。例如某公司所购买之机器已到香港,请购外汇,经二月之久,未得批准。仍向黑市如数购得外汇,始将货款提交。而外国人民可依规定章则请准购买。今中国欲维持旧法定汇价,并使黑市(实为公开汇市)不影响政府管辖区域(沦陷区域事实上管不着,未便作为对象)中人民对于法币之信用,必须一面明白列举"正当需要"之外汇及其请购办法,同时维持此种"正当需要外汇"之供给。一面查禁黑市,凡用黑市汇票购运之商品,如经查出,一律充公。设如不然,则凡有需外汇者,皆必仰给于黑市,则所谓维持旧法定汇价,徒有其名,何补于事?

黑市汇价之所以能停留于英币八便士美币一角六分左右,全赖货币购买力之支持。设使货币购买力,因国内货物稀少至无可出口,或因通货增加至过度,以致人民对法币,不复信用,而逐渐降落至于零。则黑市汇价,亦必趋于零,无可避免。此时人民对于法币之信用,亦将消失。故黑市汇价与法币信用有关。设欲支持黑市汇价,必须支持法币购买力。而影响货币购买力之二原素:商品量与通货量。前者虽因战事而减少,但其有限,故其危险性少。后者每因军政费之需要,不受人力之控制,例如欧战后之德奥,增加过度,以致货币购买力及汇价暴跌,不可制止。故其危险性大。欲维持法币购买力勿令下跌,法币之发行额(七月后法币发行额,未照常公布),应有相当限制。然法币购买力之维持,间接为黑市汇价之维持。

就目前论,黑市汇价,较购买力平价,约低二便士。其原因约有三种:(一)心理的原因。此由于人民恐惧汇价继续下跌。(二)基期平价与汇价,亦有差额,且为数颇大(见表I)。自一九二六年以来,平价与汇价之差额,以一九二八年为最小。设以一九二八年为基期,则平价与汇价之差距,可望减小。(三)供给不敷需要,引起汇价上涨。设货币之购买力,能维持于现有之水准而无急剧之变动,则黑市汇价亦必能相当安定。

欲谋"正当需要"之外汇,能维持供给于不匮,必须:

(i) 筹备充足之外汇基金。

(ii) 设法平衡对外收支。

在推行法币政策之时,原有充足之外汇准备金。然自抗战年余之后,对外收入不敷支出,因此动用外汇基金至若何程度,局外人无法臆断。设外汇基金仍极充足,则筹备外汇基金之问题,已不存在。今如外汇基金有补充之必要(据某方面消息,极感需要),筹措之方,约有二途:(a)举外债。此事政府正在进行中,闻有可能性,然未敢定也。(b)政府密令中央银行委托其他银行在黑市中,秘密收买外汇。迨购得相当数量,重订外汇法价并切实维持此新法价。若欲维持旧法价,但以缺乏外汇基金之故,未能实行,不妨采行此策。当此抗战期间,如能避免此途,自以避免为是。盖采行新汇价之利,在能筹措外汇基金,符合于新经济环境,以及外汇不至完全流入黑市,可为政府所集中。其弊足引起人民之误会。

平衡对外收支之法,须从下列诸事着手:

(i) 激励国内生产事业,增加生产量,以供消费,以供输出。

(ii) 开辟交通路线,尤须整理内河运输及修筑湘黔与川滇缅铁道,以利输出。

(iii) 征发逃资,以充实外汇基金。

(iv) 开辟川湘金矿以补充外汇基金。

(v) 限制法币发行额,以维持法币之购买力。

(vi) 统制国际贸易。贸易货款之收支,为国际收支之大宗。欲谋对外收支之平衡,必须统制贸易。至于统制贸易之方法,约可别之为七种:

(1) 贸易货款清算协定制。此制利用汇划方法以清理贸易商品及勤务之债款。其法可约言之如次:甲国进出口商人,将其所欠应收乙国商人之货款,交由该国清算机关清理收付。同样,乙国进出口商人,亦将其所欠应收甲国之货款,交由该国清算机关清理收付。甲、乙两国之清算机关,在规定时期,互相总算清结。清算之差额,或由短欠国支付外汇,或由债权国增加输入以平衡之。德国曾利用此法,先向南欧诸国增加输入,迫其扩充对德之输入。

（2）以贸易货制。此制以德国所推行者，为最完备。德国除与缔约国订有以货易货协定，以为贸易之准绳外。关于私人间之易货，亦有详细规程，列举准许易货之物品，及其交易之比例。除德国工业必需原料品外，易货比例，均须于德国有利。其差值必须以外汇支付。为推行以货易货之便利计，德国复创设国际贸易马克 Aski。外国商人对于德国之输出货款，可如数取得贸易马克以为代价，再转让与欲向德国购货之进口商人。此种马克之市场汇价，较普通马克为低，为德国向南美推进贸易之一种手段。

（3）偿债协定制。此制为输出业比较发达之国家，用以清偿债务之一种手段。两缔约国商人照常用汇票偿付货款。惟债务国按输出货值之一定成数，向债权国以输入。如是债务国对债权国之进出口，恒为出超。此出超之额，即用以偿付债务，或留一部分外汇自由处分。此制起源于一九三四年之英德偿付协定。德国以其成绩良好，曾推行于其他债权国。

（4）国营贸易制。如苏俄所推行者。朱祖晦先生曾在经济动员第十期作有详细之介绍，兹不赘。

（5）比例限额制，选定某年或某某年为标准时期，就此时期中各货进口量，一律减低若干成，以为进口之限度。

（6）购买外汇请核制。此制对于各种货物之进口，无一般之限制。惟进口商向外国采购货物，均须向主管机关请购外汇。所有外货，非经核准购买外汇，不能报关进口。德国自一九三四年秋以来，实行此制。购买外汇之核准，由外汇分配委员会（四年经济计划总理，财政部，经济部，铁道局，及国家银行组织之）主持之。该会就各期实收外汇总数，分配于各类进口货管理处，再由各处核售于请购外汇之进口商。我国今日所推行者与此制相似。

（7）进口许可证制。此制分商品为两类。第一类商品（大都为奢侈品及不重要之消费品）之输入，必先请得主管机关之进口许可证，方准购买外汇报关进口。其余商品为第二类（大都为生产工具，原料品及重要消费品），则不受此限制。

就目前中国情形论，以采行国营制为最理想。如是一面可增加输出，一面可尽量限制输入。至于国营之机构问题，将另文论之。至购买外汇请核制，其次者也。

表 I　上海对外汇价表 Jan. 1937 Aug. 2938

		英汇		美汇		港汇		日汇	
		国币一元值便士	指数 1929=100	国币百元合美金元	指数 1929=100	国币百元合港币元数	指数 1929=100	国币百元合日币元数	指数 1929=100
		实值		实值		实值		实值	
1929		20.712	100	41.901	100	88.8	100	90.8	100
1937	一月	14.202	69	29.302	70	95.67	108	102.625	113
	二月	14.375	69	29.375	70	96.75	109	102.625	113
	三月	14.375	69	29.375	70	96.75	109	102.625	113
	四月	14.375	69	29.375	70	97	109	102.625	113
	五月	14.375	69	29.375	70	97	109	102.625	113
	六月	14.375	69	29.375	70	96.5	109	101.75	112
	七月	14.25	69	29.25	70	96.5	109	101.5	112
	八月	14.25	69	29.25	70	94.25	109	101.5	112
	九月	14.25	69	29.25	70	94.25	107	101.5	112
	十月	14.25	69	29.25	70	94	107	101.5	112
	十一月	14.25	69	29.25	70	94	106	101.5	112
	十二月	14.25	69	29.25	70	94	106	101	111
1938	一月	14.25	69	29.25	70	93.875	106	100.875	110
	二月	14.25	69	29.25	70	93.875	106	100.875	110
	三月	13.937	67	28.625	68	91.0625	103	97.25	107
	四月	13.00	63	26.875	64	86.875	98	92.5625	102
	五月	11.313	55	23.4375	56	75.6875	97	80.875	89
	六月	9.00	43	13.5625	44	59.875	68	64.0625	71
	七月	8.813	43	73.1875	43	58.75	66	63.00	70
	八月	7.937	38	16.1675	39	52.875	60	56.6875	63

汇价转载国定税则委员会《物价月报》。指数系 1929 年为基期计算而得。

表 II 中美汇价与中美购买力平价 1926—1937

	（I）上海趸售物价指数 1926=100	（II）美国劳工局趸售物价指数 1926=100	（III）购买力平价即（II）÷（I）	（IV）中国一元之美元汇兑率	（V）中国一元之美元兑换指数 1926=100	（VI）上海生活费指数 1926=100	（VII）美国生活费指数 1926=100	（VIII）中美购买力平价（VII）÷（VI）1926=100	（IX）每一盎斯白银在纽约之美元价格（V）−（III）	（X）（V）−（VIII）
1926	100.0	100	100	48.7	100	100	100.0	100.0	0	0
27	104.4	95	90.9	43.4	89.8	106.7	98.0	91.8	−1.1	−2.0
28	101.7	97	96.5	45.8	94.1	102.5	97.0	94.6	−2.4	−0.5
29	104.5	95.3	90.8	41.901	86.0	107.9	97.0	89.9	−4.8	−3.9
30	114.8	86.4	75.3	29.917	61.2	121.8	94.0	77.2	−14.1	−16.0
31	126.7	73.0	57.6	22.437	45.9	125.9	86.3	68.5	−11.7	−22.6
32	112.4	64.8	57.7	21.736	44.5	119.1	77.6	65.1	−13.2	−20.6
33	103.8	65.9	63.6	**.598	58.6	107.2	73.7	68.6	−5.0	−10.0
34	97.1	74.9	77.2	34.094	70.0	106.2	76.6	72.1	−7.2	−2.1
35	96.4	80.0	83.0	36.571	75.0	106.6	78.5	73.1	−8.0	+1.3
36	108.5	80.8	74.6	29.751	61.0	113.3	79.5	70.0	−12.7	−8.1
37	129.1	86.3	66.5	29.606	70.6	131.8	81.5	61.8	−5.9	−1.2

1. 国定税则委员会，上海物价月刊。
2. 美国劳工局趸售物价指数，见《美国联邦准备局月报》一九三八年七月期。
3. 此系以美国趸售物价指数除以中国上海趸售物价再乘100。
4. 一九二九年至一九三七年录自《美国联邦准备局月报》一九三七年七月期。一九二六年至一九二八年根据《中国银价问题》108页第四五表换算而得。该表夹系规元一两值美金分数，作者误作华币一元。规元与国币之换算率为0.715，即国币一元等于规元0.715两。
5. 国定税则委员会《物价月报》各期。
6. 《美国联邦准备局月报》一九三七年七月期。
7. 中国生活费指数除美国生活费指数之百分数。

表III 中英美日蚕售物价指数及购买力平价指数 1929＝100

	中国上海物价	英国	美国	日本	中英购买力平价	中美购买力平价	中日购买力平价
1937	123.2	95.2	90.6	108.4	77	73	88
一月	116.2	90.1	90.1	106.1	77	77	91
二月	117.5	91.0	90.6	104.8	77	77	89
三月	117.8	94.0	92.1	109.1	80	78	93
四月	118.4	95.4	92.3	112.8	80	78	95
五月	119.7	96.9	91.7	109.8	81	77	92
六月	120.8	96.8	91.5	108.4	80	77	90
七月	120.2	97.6	92.2	108.7	81	77	90
八月	122.0	97.5	91.8	107.0	80	75	88
九月	124.1	97.4	91.7	108.5	78	73	87
十月	127.3	96.8	89.6	107.6	76	70	85
十一月	134.2	95.0	87.4	108.1	71	65	81
十二月	135.2	94.2	85.7	109.7	70	63	81
1938							
一月	133.5	94.3	84.9	111.6	70	63	84
二月	132.4	92.6	83.7	113.4	70	63	86
三月	133.1	91.2	83.6	114.4	68	63	86
四月	136.5	90.3	82.6	112.3	66	61	82
五月	135.7	89.3	82.0	113.3	67	61	84
六月	139.0	88.2	82.1	115.7	63	59	83
七月	146.7	88.1		115.7	55		79
八月	157.5						

上海物价系根据国定税则委员会指数换算而得。英美日三国蚕售物价指数转载国定税则委员会《物价月报》，中英汇率，根据上列平价指数，三四五六七月之汇价应为：14.09 13.68 13.86 13.03 10.88，较表II所列之实际汇价为高。平均相差约二便士许。此差额可由三种原因解释：一为心理的，由人民恐惧汇价之继续下跌；一为以基期；一为汇价之差异，以1928为最小。官用1928为基期。但以缺资料故，不得已采用1929为基期。一为供不敷求。

表 IV 欧战期间及战后四年间英美法德四国钞券流通额及指数 1913=100 流通钞券以年底为准 单位为百万

	英国 £	指数	美国 $	指数	德国 Mark	指数	法国 Franc	指数
1913	34.6	100	2 575	100	2 902	100	5 714	100
1914	79.6	176	2 680	127	5 862	202	10 043	176
1915	144.9	231	3 061	160	8 360	288	13 216	231
1916	196.8	289	3 032	206	11 438	394	16 580	289
1917	266.0	390	3 392	226	18 246	628	22 336	390
1918	399.2	530	4 368	242	33 069	1 139	30 250	530
1919	449.0	652	4 597	*295	50 064	1 723	37 275	652
1920	*486.4	662	*4 813	182	81 387	2 800	*37 902	662
1921	439.4	638	3 953	154	122 497	4 300	36 487	638
1922	404.2	635	3 997		*1 295 228	44 600	36 359	635

转载国联出版"Memorandum on Currency, 1913–1922", pp.60–69。
* 最高流通额

表 V 欧战期间及战后四年间英美德法四国趸售物价指数 1913=100

	英国 Statist	英国 Economist	美国 劳工局	德国 Official	法国 Official
1913	100	100	100	100	100
1914	100	98.7	98	106	102.9
1915	127	123.1	101	142	140.0
1916	160	160.5	127	153	188.6
1917	206	204.1	177	179	262.0
1918	226	224.9	194	219	333.8
1919	242	235.1	206	415	356.9
1920	*295	*283.2	*226	1 486	*510.3
1921	182	181.0	147	1 911	345.6
1922	154	159.5	149	34 182	327.2

转载国联出版"Memorandum on Currency, 1913–1922," pp.174–182。

表 VI 二十七年一月至七月承购外汇数额统计

		汉 口	重 庆	长 沙	广 州	永 嘉	总 计
	一月	338 000 (354 000)					338 000 (354 000)
	二月	412 000 (431 000)					412 000 (431 000)
	三月	1 400 400 (1 465 000)					1 400 400 (1 465 000)
	四月	3 216 687 (3 361 438)					3 216 687 (3 361 438)
	五月	1 279 572.50 (1 337 153)	2 818.70 (2 945)	922 983 (964 517)			2 205 374.20 (2 305 615)
	六月	1 391 472 (1 454 028)	42 772.50 (44 697)	238 818 (249 565)	1 508 832.65 (1 576 730)	22 507.18 (23 530)	3 204 402.33 (3 345 610)
	七月	1 294 112 (1 352 347)	467 424.91 (488 459)	1 597 286 (1 669 163)	1 577 355.12 (1 648 366)	*	4 936 178.03 (5 158 305)
港币	小计	9 332 243.50 (9 756 026)	513 016.11 (536 101)	2 759 087 (2 883 245)	3 086 187.77 (3 225 066)	22 507.18 (23 530)	15 713 041.56 (16 423 968)
美金	一月	47 400 (163 000)					47 400 (163 000)
	二月	244 000 (828 000)					244 000 (828 000)
	三月	229 900 (785 000)					229 900 (785 000)

续表

		汉 口	重 庆	长 沙	广 州	永 嘉	总 计
美金	四月	158 703.50 (533 456)					158 703.05 (533 456)
	五月	399 137.55 (1 341 638)					399 137.35 (1 341 638)
	六月	185 674 (624 114)	71 935 (241 798)				257 609 (865 912)
	七月	136 872 (410 073)	550 (1 848)				137 422 (461 921)
	小计	1 401 686.40 (4 735 281)	72 485 (243 646)				1 474 171.40 (4 978 927)
英镑	一月	22 980-0-0 (388 000)					22 980-0-0 (388 000)
	二月	40 300-0-0 (684 000)					40 300-0-0 (684 000)
	三月	102 770-0-0 (1 750 000)					120 770-0-0 (1 750 000)
	四月	212 541-9-10 (3 548 519)					212 541-9-10 (3 548 519)
	五月	228 020-15-0 (3 806 955)					228 020-15-0 (3 806 955)
	六月	132 730-7-3 (2 216 020)			214 987-10-0 (3 589 357)	7 656-16-1 (127 835)	355 374-13-4 (5 933 212)

续表

		汉 口	重 庆	长 沙	广 州	永 嘉	总 计
英镑	七月	73 911-6-5 (1 233 997)			154 074-7-6 (2 572 372)	*	227 985-13-11 (3 806 369)
	小计	813 253-18-6 (13 627 491)			369 061-17-6 (6 161 729)		1 189 972-12-1 (19 917 055)
法郎	五月	49 344 (46 280)					492 344 (46 280)
	六月	80 846.40 (7 607)					80 846.40 (7 607)
	小计	573 190.40 (53 887)					573 190.40 (53 887)
共计	港币	9 332 243.50 (9 756 026)	513 016.11 (536 101) 72 485 (243 646)	2 759 087 (2 883 245)	3 086 187.77 (3 225 066)	22 507.18 (23 530)	15 713 041.56 (16 423 968)
	美金	1 401 686.40 (4 735 281)					1 474 171.40 (4 978 927)
	英镑	813 253-18-6 (13 627 491)			369 061-17-6 (6 161 729)	7 656-16-1 (127 835)	1 189 972-12-1 (19 917 055)
	法郎	573 190.40 (53 887)					573 190.40 (53 887)
	折合国币	28 223 935	779 747	2 883 245	9 386 795	△616 016	41 889 738

附注：括弧内系折合国币数。
* 永嘉七月份港币英镑数字不详。
△ 包括七月份永嘉港币英镑合折国币数字在内。

表 VII 二十七年一月至七月中输出货值及中交两行承购外汇数额表

	全国输出值 单位千元 (I)	承购外汇值 单位千元 (II)	上海输出货值 单位千元 (III)	差　额 (即全国输出值减承购外汇值) 单位千元 (IV)=(I)-(II)
一月	43 098	905	10 681	42 193
二月	40 913	1 943	10 398	38 970
三月	50 152	4 000	12 553	46 152
四月	56 639	12 158	12 086	44 486
五月	57 417	7 500	11 956	49 917
六月	74 385	10 199	15 147	64 186
七月	77 263	9 426	20 068	77 837

(I) 及 (III) 录自《经济动员》第九期第 429—430 页。
(II) 由表 VI 计算得来。
(IV) 为 (I) 减 (II) 之差额。

（原载《时事月报》1938 年第 19 卷第 7 期）

隔离外汇黑市之建议

一、外汇黑市与法币信用

我国货币,自一九三五年十一月四日实行法币政策以后,即具备现代币制之条件。本位币与辅币有一定之兑换率,在国内各省区一律通用无阻。旧有杂钞均被代替而绝迹于市场。对外汇兑,则有充实之外汇准备基金,存储于世界金融中心——伦敦及纽约,以与英镑及美元联系,使无剧变,而利国际贸易与贷借。法币管理既善,人民信用,故基础巩固,自无所谓问题。迨后中日战争延长,我国乃于一九三八年三月十四日实行统制外汇,于是有外汇黑市之产生。而黑市汇率,因国内物价高涨,外汇之供给不敷需求,逐渐降落。五月以后,跌风尤烈,六月十四日对英汇率不过八便士二五①,约为法定汇率百分之五七。我国黑市实为明的公的自由市,与德俄等国之暗的私的黑市不同②,故黑市汇价之跌落,足影响法币之信用。去年五月以后,上海黑市汇率猛跌,引起一般人对于法币信用之忧虑,良以此也。今年六月七日及七月十八日外汇平准基金委员会停止出售外汇,黑市汇率再三猛跌③,法币信用又形动摇。故法币制度自一九三五年推行以来,只因黑市汇率之降落,而惹人注意与忧虑;不以他故而动摇或危险。故今日法币问题,实即外汇问题(有人以为法币之所以成为问题,由于准备金之低落,乃提议引用金银铜铁锡五金为准备,以求准备金之增加。设政府果采此说,不徒无补于实际,且足增多困难。)而外汇之所以成为问题,由于官市以外,又

---

① 见《从我国外汇问题说到贸易国营》之附表,《经济动员》第二卷第一期。
② 见《维持外汇法价与黑市汇价》第四节及附表,《时事月报》第十九卷第七期,廿七年十二月号。
③ 六月七日前后及七月十七日前后外汇黑市对英汇价如下表。

日/月	6/6	7/6	8/6	9/6	10/6	11/6	……	17/7	18/7	19/7	20/7	21/7
汇价（便士数）	$8\frac{1}{4}$	$7\frac{1}{4}$	$6\frac{1}{2}$	6.531	6.5	6.5	……	$6\frac{9}{16}$	$5\frac{1}{4}$	5	4.843 75	$4\frac{3}{8}$

有黑市。此黑市汇率之涨落,对于法币信用有直接影响。故今日欲谋巩固法币之信用,必须消除黑市汇价变动之威胁。

二、上海黑市能否禁绝

消除黑市汇价变动对于法币信用之威胁,其道有三:
(甲)邀请友邦协同根本禁绝黑市;
(乙)维持黑市汇价于一定之水准,使无甚变动;
(丙)隔离黑市,使黑市汇价之变动,不能影响法币之信用。
今请分别论之。

上海,香港,天津以及游击区域中之商埠都市,皆有外汇黑市,而上海为黑市之大本营。其他各处之黑市汇价,直接或间接取决于此,交易数额亦较小,故讨论黑市,可以上海为对象。

黑市既在租界内,非我主权之所能及。欲求禁绝,有下列两个前提条件:
(一)须获得英美法(即租界主权国)政府之诚心诚意合作;
(二)英美法政府须有充分勇气及决心,不受日本之威胁,坚持协助我政府严密查禁黑市,使之无法存在,或至消形匿迹。①

此等前提条件,能否完全达到,以目前形势度之,殊少成功之希望。香港现为英国领土,沪津租界以英国为最占势力,在华经济利益以英国较为重大;又外汇黑市之构成分子,亦以英商银行最富实力。故欲严格查禁黑市,必须英国能具备上列两个条件。

三、黑市汇价要否维持

黑市既不能禁绝,如能维持黑市汇价于一定高度之水准,使无激烈之变动,则黑市虽存在,亦不害于法币信用。故对黑市汇价,如力能维持,且其代

---

① 据东京十日路透电讯:日本各报所传日方要求于英方者,共有八项,其中关于经济方面者有:(一)改变英国在政治及经济上之政策。(二)禁止法币在租界内流通。(三)租界内各中国银行之存银,应移交日方。(四)日当局有权审查租界内之中国银行汇兑经纪人。若以此消息与七月廿八日重庆联合报所载英日初步协定之声明参看,似可窥见英国对日本接受之程度,并可知日方所称英国已接受日本要求之说,或非全属子虚。又据伦敦七月十八日路透电,英下院工党议员史特劳斯于十七日询问英政府谓现在上海设有分行之某英国银行与日方合作,企图削弱中国之对外汇兑基金,英政府对于该行是否已有表示?外次白特勒答曰未。又三月十四日我政府实行统制外汇,外商银行即于同月廿八日废止维持外汇法价的绅士协定。于此可见邀请友邦协助之难!

价或弊害不过大,自宜维持之,以坚定华北华中人民对于法币之信用,而巩固其向心力。并以法币汇价稳定之故,使英美等友邦得确保远东贸易的利益而予日圆在华封锁势力以打击。无如维持黑市汇价,直似以金沙填补无底洞,为不可能之事。盖日人以由人民收没之法币及海关之收入(依 John Ailen 的统计,自去年六月一日到今年五月底,总数已达国币二万万元,其中半数系江海关之收入),与用其他方法在日军占据区域内榨取之法币(如滥发"联银券"及"华兴券",在市场上收买法币①或以伪币及军用票强购民间货物,转为出售以吸收法币等),用向上海外汇黑市购取外汇②。而出卖外汇之银行,由卖出外汇所得之法币,不能封藏于库中,将因金融作用而归还于市场。况游击队饷需之供给,及后方工作人员对于住在游击区域中家属之接济,皆足使法币源源流往日军占据区域之内,任其没收与榨取。再以没收及榨取所得之法币,套取我之外汇。如此循环不已,无有终止。以有限之外汇平准基金,除非有继续不断的巨额外汇收入,足以应付此循环不已之套取,在短期间内,即可完全用罄③。然外汇收入之二种主要项目——出口贸易及华侨汇款——均已减缩。盖各海口被敌控制后,输出贸易,除经由西南各关如蒙自、思茅、腾越、龙州出口外,所有出口货物易得之外汇,皆为日本所攫去。故我政府所能集中之出口贸易外汇,为数已微。④ 又自去年十月广州失陷,潮汕、新会、中山、台山及开平,辄受威胁。其地之侨民家属,因皆纷纷外移。按以华侨汇款,除在抗战期间有一部分捐助政府及购买金公

---

① 据上海七月廿一日合众电,日人主持之华兴银行纸币,仍维持其六便士之比率(按东京十九日路透电称,日本兴亚院与伪华兴银行当局商洽后,决定华兴伪币应与英镑联系,其价值为华兴券一元合英币六便士。将来无论如何将维持此比率云),但交易极少。华兴银行以华兴券购买法币,若以此汇价为准,华兴券百元折合法币一百五十元。但华兴以华兴券百元合法币一百二十五元左右之价格收买法币。本月廿一日内已购进法币三百万元。其购价自一百廿元至一百四十元不等。伪联以联银券调得之法币数额虽未正式发表,但据日方估计,约为三千万元。

② 据日七月十九日广播宣传,法币此次跌价原因,第一为法币北方券五百万元大量流入上海,其次即系关于东京进行之英日谈判引起各种谣言云。又据七月十八日上海路透电,本市中国各银行,今日起一致拒收天津、汉口、山东及其他沦陷区域所发行之法币。战事发生以来之金融困难情形,因此更趋严重。中国银行家对此事之解释,谓政府虽无明令禁止接受该项法币,但津沪等地之法币外汇价格差异甚大,故为防止该数必走私起见,必须采取是项措置。闻上海各行已电各总行请示中。目前大多数兑换银钱商家,仅收印有上海字样之法币云。

③ 据七月廿二日某方讯,平准基金二千五百万镑已大量消耗,仅余一百余万镑。按外汇平准基金于廿八年三月十一日成立,至七月廿二日,先后凡一百三十五日,每日平均消耗外汇基金约十七万余镑。

④ 去年一月至七月期间,东南海口尚未为日人所控制,政府所能集中之外汇,约四万六千万元,尚不及出口总值八分之一。见拙作《维持外汇法价与黑市汇价》附表,《时事月报》第十九卷第七期。

债外,皆系接济家属之用费。今家属既已外移,毋庸汇款接济,故华侨汇款一项,自必较往年为小。由是观之,黑市汇价,欲由平准基金以无限制买卖之方法,以为支持,实为力所不能及。论者或认外汇黑市,宜由外汇平准基金委员会统制管理,审核外汇之用途,分别限制或拒绝卖出。果如是,则今日统制外汇黑市与去岁三月十四日实行统制外汇官市情形相似,黑市外将另有黑市之存在。此第二黑市对于法币信用之影响,同于前一黑市,今又何异于昔?况外汇平准基金委员会,原由中英合组而成,审核制度能否成功,尚须视英国之态度为如何耳。

黑市汇价,非但不能维持,且不应维持,其理由有三:

第一,与政府原先所采取之审核制度相反。设欲维持黑市汇价,必须无限制供给外汇,以应市场上之一切需要(包括非正当的外汇需要)。既予日人以套取外汇之便利,又与政府所采取之审核请购外汇制度相反。日人之进攻,固不以军事行动为限;今且侧重于攻击我法币制度。故我维持法币信用之安全,即所以维持抗战,其重要仅次于军事。日人套取外汇,原为破坏法币之一种手段。设我不维持黑市汇价,则彼失去套取外汇之便利,无所施其技矣。

第二,外汇平准基金被日利用。在华日军之军需,原须由日本向外国购入转运来战区者,今多利用我外汇平准基金,改在上海进口,据六月十七日《密勒氏评论》载称:"最近日本大规模利用中英外汇平准基金委员会之外汇,使中国政府及基金委员会,不再采用过去办法。"以基金委员会之外汇,所购进之进口货,几全为日本所利用故也。例如进口棉花已达空前巨额,几占进口货总值四分之一。在四月份进口之棉花,约有百分之七五,为驻沪之日本纱厂所购进。又如由沪进口之某国平滑油及液体燃料,亦系利用中英外汇平准基金之外汇所购得者。但此类平滑油及燃料,又皆为日本所购去,以为该国驻华之机械化部队及空军之使用。此种事实,我政府必已早鉴及。如本月十七日财部发言人对于外汇风潮之解释,其中有云:"又有非必需之物品,大批输入国内,其中大部均系运至沦陷区内,政府最近虽曾下令禁止此种物品入口,然而输入者仍源源不绝。其中且有一部分系转供日军需用者……"然既知之,当谋所以改之。否则徒使日人利用中国国力以攻击中国。故欲保卫自己国力,并集中之以争取抗战之最后胜利,当放弃维持黑市汇价政策。

第三,增大贸易入超。维持黑市汇价,固可安定法币信用,要亦在抵抗日圆封锁,以使友邦得确保对华贸易之利益。据海关报告所载,今年一月至四月全国对外贸易,洋货进口净值国币三万九千三百九十六万元,出口国货净值国币二万五千九百四十九万元,入超一万三千四百四十六万元(折合英镑八百余万镑),比较去年同期,入超增加二千九百二十九万元。且今年四个月中,每月均为入超,其中尤以四月份为最大,创开战以来之新纪录,计为五千六百五十四万元。入超愈大,对于外汇市场之压迫愈烈。设进口洋货皆为抗战建国之必需物,亦不为日人所利用,自当别论。但进口货之运往日军占据区域,为日利用者已多(如下表所示,天津、胶州二埠入超达九千万元,进口值升至一万三千万元以上)。而奢侈品之进口,亦颇不少,计自一月至四月期间,共值九百三十四万元,占进口总值百分之三左右。且在此巨额入超期间,日货输入激增,计为九千六百万元。除一小部分以日元支付外,余皆须以外汇支付。以外汇皆须仰给于黑市场,间接由外汇平准基金供给,是无异于以外汇资日。

表一　本年一月至四月及四月份对外贸易表(单位国币千元)

时　期	本年四月份	去年一月至四月	本年一月至四月
进口值	122 222	295 976	393 962
出口值	65 680	190 802	259 493
入　超	56 542	105 174	134 469
由日本输入值	98 538	(此外由关东租借地输入者尚有 32 322 千元系指一月至四月期言)	
奢侈品进口值	3 615	3 456	9 350

表二　游击区重要各关入超数额表(民国廿八年一月至四月)

关　别	进口货值	出口货值	入超额
上　海	185 633	113 347	72 316
天　津	108 809	34 502	74 307
胶　州	27 770	12 819	14 951
秦皇岛	14 525	11 639	2 886
烟　台	7 816	2 807	5 009

总上所论,法币黑市汇价,非但不能维持,且不应维持。但若任令黑市汇价自由变动,其变动必甚剧烈。对我有大量贸易关系之外国,将蒙受不利之影响。自我观之,则可减少不必要货物之进口,因而得以节省外汇之消耗,未可谓为不利。且我向外国购买军火军需及经济建设事业必要物所需

之外汇,自抗日战争发生以来,皆由外国借得信用或由外汇基金以应付之。是故黑市汇价之变动,对于抗战建国所需货物之输入,尚无若何不良影响之可言。若云黑市汇价之继续降落,将引起我后方人民对于法币信用之疑惧,则赖隔离黑市政策以安定之。

四、隔离黑市以巩固我后方法币之信用

自去年七月以来,依法价请购外汇,虽属正当需要,事实上极难照准。依朱祖晦先生根据金融商业报(Finance and Commerce)各期所载,估计我国统制外汇后各次外汇请求数额及核准数额如下表:①

表三　中国统制外汇后各次外汇请求数额及核准数额估计比较表

廿七年		请求金额估计数(£)	核准金额估计数(£)	核准额对请求额之百分比
月	日			
三	一七	900 000	150 000	50%
	二四	1 494 500	465 500	31.1%
	三一	1 544 500	428 500	27.7%
四	七	1 400 000	429 000	30.0%
	一四	1 800 000	350 000	19.4%
	二一	1 000 000	350 000	35.0%
	二八		220 000	
五	五	1 000 000	260 000	26.0%
	一二	1 000 000	235 000	23.5%
	一九		225 000	
	二六		200 000	
六	二	1 300 000	185 000	14.2%
	九		145 000	
	一六	1 100 000	95 000	8.6%
	二三	1 375 000	71 000	5.1%
	三〇	1 400 000	82 000	5.8%

---

① 见《经济动员》第二卷第一期第十八至十九页。

续表

廿七年 月	廿七年 日	请求金额估计数（£）	核准金额估计数（£）	核准额对请求额之百分比
七	七		60 000	
七	一四	1 150 000	55 000	4.7%
七	二一		72 000	
七	二八	1 500 000（一）	53 000	3.5%
八	四		30 000	
八	一一	800 000	53 000	6.6%
八	一八	900 000	38 000	4.2%
八	二五	880 000（一）	47 000	5.3%
九	一	800 000	40 000	5.0%
九	八		31 000	
九	一五		27 000	
九	二二		17 000	
九	二九		8 000	
一〇	六	880 000	11 200	1.2%
一〇	一三		—	
一〇	二〇		10 000	
一〇	二七		—	
一一	三		—	
一一	一〇		—	
一一	一七		6 000	约1.0%
一一	二四		5 000	
一二	一		5 000	
一二	八		—	此后核准数额极小
一二	一五		—	
一二	二二		—	
一二	二九		—	

由此表观之，自七月以后，每周核准数额，大都在五万镑以下，占请购数额百分之五弱。故外汇之需要，几全数仰给于黑市。则黑市汇价，成为法币

之有效汇价,亦即法币之真实汇价。法币信用之安危,足反映于黑市汇价之上;而黑市汇价之涨落,可影响人民对于法币之信心。原有之法定汇价,在人民心目中,早已等于虚设,不复注意。故上海黑市汇价跌风摇动法币信用之势力,未因法定汇价之不变而削弱。故黑市汇价与法币信用有密切之关联。黑市既不能禁绝,而黑市汇价又不应维持,惟有隔离黑市以断绝黑市所在之区域与内地之联系,使汇价之变动,不复能影响于法币信用,是为隔离黑市政策。

地域与其他各处之经济关系,因贸易汇兑之流通而存在。设若此一地域与其他各处不通贸易与汇兑,则其物价水准各自独立而不相影响;此地之货币价值(可以物价水准表示之),将不因他处货币价值之涨落而发生变动。若设喻以譬之,犹如两水柱中各盛以水,其间有水管接通,则两水柱中之水位必相等。今此地与其他各处之贸易与汇兑,犹如两水柱间之连通水管;此地之物价水准,因贸易与汇兑之流通,恒受他处物价水准涨落影响而发生调整变动,以趋于相等。犹如两水柱中之水位,因连通水管之流通而保持相等。今如此一地域统制其对他处之贸易与汇兑,则其物价水准可不因他处物价水准涨落而发生任何变动(例如一九三一年以后之德国,因厉行统制其对外全部贸易与汇兑,其物价水准与马克价值,已不因他国物价水准与货币价值涨落而发生若何变动。至于马克纸币准备金之多寡,更无论矣);犹如两水柱间之连通水管被阻塞之后,其水位将各自独立而不必相等。隔离黑市之用意,即欲使我后方各省区之物价水准,勿受黑市所在区域物价水准涨落之影响;即欲使我后方各省区内货币之对外价值弗受黑市所在区域内货币对外价值涨落之影响;亦即使我后方各省区法币对外汇价,勿受上海黑市汇价涨落之影响,因之我后方各省区之民众,对于法币之信用,可不因上海外汇黑市汇价之跌落而生疑虑或动摇。故隔离黑市之办法,只须厉行统制我后方各省区对外(包括上海、香港及游击区域在内)全部贸易与汇兑。凡我后方各省区输往港沪及游击区域之一切货物,如同输往外国,一律须结售外汇(或由国营),否则不得出口。又凡自我后方各省区汇款至港沪及游击区域,视若汇款至外国,必属正当需要而有充实证明,并经管理当局核准,方得汇出,否则不得汇出。自港沪及游击区域汇款至后方各省区者,亦同此办法。

为昭信守而安定民心起见,关于正当需要之范围及请购之手续,政府应厘订章则,以为管理之准绳。如是则请购外汇者,无幸冀之心,而主持审核之当局,以有章则足资遵循,可免除去年三月初行统制外汇时之流弊;或只参考入超而不注意正当需要,或故示宽大而不依据政策。果若上下同心,奉公守法,则信用确立。信用立,则投机之风,及社会不安之心理,皆可平定,而法币不可动摇矣。

　　隔离港沪及游击区域之后,我后方各省区内法币对外汇兑,只有官市,不容有黑市。如有私相买卖外汇,一经查出,按危害民国罪议处。查禁既严,黑市可望根绝。如是我后方各省区内法币对外汇价,只有官市法价,无所谓黑市汇价或自由市汇价。我后方之法币与上海及游击区域中之法币,如同两种不同之货币,上海黑市汇价之变动,如同他国币汇价之变动,不能影响于我后方各省区内法币之信用。此种情形,与一九三一年实行统制汇兑及贸易以后之德国相似。德国货币有自由马克、封锁马克、登记马克、证券马克、清算马克、阿斯奇马克等种类,在国外之价值皆不相等,但在国内均无差别。以能严密统制其对外汇兑及贸易之故,自由马克之法定汇价,始终未受其他各种马克汇价变动之影响。我后方各省区与上海及游击区隔离之后,则法币在上海黑市之汇价,不能影响于我后方法币之信用,可比如德国登记马克在伦敦市场之汇价,其涨落不能影响于自由马克之信用。

　　隔离黑市政策推行之后,游击区域内之法币,虽仍可被日伪所吸收,而日伪将无所利用。设使日伪将其所吸收之法币,偷运至我后方各省市内,若欲用以套取外汇,因请购外汇綦严,非属正当需要而有充实证件者,不得核准购买。故套取外汇之企图,必无法实现。若欲用以购运货物出口,因我厉行统制贸易,非先结售外汇,不得出口。(如我实行国营贸易,更无换取物资之可能。)故换取物资之企图,亦无法实现。

　　我后方各省市,自与港沪及游击区域隔离之后,法币对外汇兑,均须在官市买卖,则官市将采用原有之法定汇价为汇价乎？抑将重订一个更能切合中国实际现状而绝对有利的新汇价(时人皆以贬值名之)？关于此点,学者及商人曾有一番热烈之讨论。作者亦曾一再发表意见①,似毋庸多赘。惟此处有须指出者,隔离黑市政策之成功,有赖于对外汇兑之善良管理;而法定汇价距离现实经济状况愈远,则管理对外汇兑愈艰。又贬值若行于今年三月十一日中英外汇平准基金委员会成立以前,或能引起社会不安。然其严重性,据吾人之想象,决不至比今年六月七日重新调整黑市汇价水准或七月十八日黑市汇价猛跌所造成之恐慌情形为更恶。迨外汇平准基金委员会成立,黑市汇价,已变成半官式汇价,且在中外人士之心理中,视为实际上

---

① 《时事月报》第十九卷第七期及《中央日报》。

之法币汇价。若于此时期实行重订外汇法价,使能更切合于中国现实经济情形,将与一九三六年九月法国实行贬值之结果相似,非特无碍于人民对法币之信仰心,反足巩固法币之信用。至于重订新法价于何等水准,原属技术问题。购买力平价在理论上及技术上虽备受批评①,在实用上虽不无限制,然对于汇价问题之研究,总不失为主要准则②。果若我政府欲重订汇价,亦不能漠视购买力平价也。

有人或认隔离政策,足使政府可得利用之外汇减少,因而削弱我对外购买抗战建国所需要之洋货。其实日人早已采用霸占海关及统制贸易政策,以集中游击区域中之外汇,几无我方收购之余地。华北伪政权曾规定自三月十日起,凡输出其所规定之十二种重要商品者,必须以其所得外汇依照一先令二便士之汇率,结售予伪联合准备银行,否则不准报关出口。近据七月七日路透电称③华北伪政府又决定自七月十日起将华北全部输出货物,均置于伪联合准备银行汇兑管理之下,以图多得外汇。故华北方面出口货易得之外汇,已全部为日伪所攫去。至于华中方面,据第三战区来人报告:"日人统制海关,除上海一处英美人势力较大,日人尚不能为所欲为外,其他在日人支配下各海关,凡遇商品出口,须先经海关特许。其条件即商品出售以后,必在日方银行结售外汇,方得出口。"④又据中央社樊城一月十日电称:"上月底我某部查扣伪安徽警察处长金国木令和县警局文一件,其内容以'日本支那派遣军特务部通告'依军事之要求,在此时期内,所有民间之钢材,特殊钢材,铜及铜材,黄铜及黄铜材料,石炭,煤,麻,茧,棉,羊毛,皮革等物,除由'中支那派遣军经理部长'许可外,一概停止由日军占领区内,向上海方面移动。"故华中方面输出货物所得之外汇,亦多为日伪夺去。日伪统制外汇,原在增加外汇头寸。故输入商品者向伪联行请购外汇,总难得其允许。进口商既不能在伪联行购得外汇,不得不转求之于法币外汇黑市。因

---

① Keyner, A Tractor Monetary Reform, and A Treatise of Money, Zapolen, Q. J. E., 1931. Pigon, Essays in Applied Eco. Haberler, Theory of Int'l Trade; Viner, Studies in the Theory of Intl. Trade, A Report of the Royal Institute of Int'l affairs, Helfferish, Money,《经济动员》第二卷第六期,Gregory, Foreign Exchange, Cassel, Writtings.

② Hall, Ex, Equalization Account; Haberler, Op. Cit.

③ 七月十七日路透电称:伪临时政府顷公布自七月十日起,货物出口,除私人用品,船上用品,新鲜食物,书本,图书报章,包裹等十二种外,应一律于事前缴验购买外汇证明书,凡对日及"伪满"之出口货,其外汇依照一对一之比率,换作联银券。至于对其他各国之出口货,则其外汇依照十四便士合一元之比率换作"联银券"。同时复发表优惠进口货名单。惟其列举之货物,大体俱系日本所能供给或华北经济工业发展所需之物品云。

④ 《经济动员》第二卷第六期第二九六页。

之,黑市中只有进口商对外汇之需求,而无出口商向之供给,而无外汇,自无多余外汇以供我政府之收集与利用。故隔离黑市,非但无损于我政府外汇之供给来源,反能使之移用外汇黑市平准基金于正当用途。未可谓为不利也。

以上所论,为隔离黑市之一般原则。至于如何施行,宜由行政当局按此原则,详订办法,以为准绳。非属本文之范围,故略。

五、隔离黑市政策对于游击区法币生命之影响

隔离黑市并放弃以政府力量维持黑市汇率以后,黑市汇率之变动必大,且将呈现一种下跌之趋势,其影响或将及于游击区内法币之生命。最可注意者,乃沦陷区同胞对于法币之信用,或易发生动摇。因此,法币对日伪钞券及军用票之战斗能力,将被削弱,以至危及法币之生存;而"日圆集团"或"日满支经济协同体"之封锁势力,遂得乘机发展。且英美等国在游击区口岸进口贸易,将因法币黑市汇率变动过猛,感受严重之损失,以致影响英美等国商人对我之好感。凡此皆属事实问题,关系利害者甚大,不可不慎重考虑者也。

法币黑市汇价之稳定,对于法币信用,有极伟大之贡献,自系事实,为人所公认。然而时在今日,黑市汇率已不及法定汇率三分之一。一般乡间平民对于法币之信用,未尝用黑市汇率之涨落而发生变动。彼等既少使用外汇之需要,亦不过问法币黑市汇率之高下,惟有少数买办阶级,资本家及外汇投机者,稍感不安耳。其实彼辈在七七卢沟桥事变之后,八一三沪战爆发以前,对法币之信仰心业已动摇。或逃资国外,或利用汇率变化以为投机买卖而图利,罪在扰乱金融而摇动汇市,何须维持其人心。所谓支持黑市以维系人心,实乃维系少数特殊阶级之人心而已。故隔离黑市之后,法币在游击区内之信用,想不至完全动摇,而黑市汇率,以法币保有购买力故,其变动虽大,亦不至跌落为零。当此时机,设英美等国为谋确保在华贸易利益,并激于正义同情心,援去年八月至今年三月期间暗中支持上海黑市汇率之旧例,选定合于游击区内经济现状之汇率,在不消耗外汇基金之条件下,实行平准外汇黑市汇率,则有现行制度之利,而无现行制度之弊矣。

当我推行隔离黑市政策之时,设游击区内同胞,受日伪滥言宣传淆惑,以致失去对法币之信用心,则游击区内法币之生命危矣。游击区内之法币,原已备受日伪各种阴谋之攻击,已感防守之不易。就理论言,在日伪势力控制下之游击区内法币,如其信用优于伪币及军用票,则依古拉襄定律,劣币

驱逐良币于流通界之外,法币将被收藏,或受津贴而换成伪币。故在市场上流通之法币,将逐渐减少。若法币之信用劣于伪币及军用票,则诚恐法币价值跌落,将相率持出以换伪币。而法币亦终难持久生存。就事实言,自廿七年三月十日日伪在华北设立伪联合准备银行发行钞券以来,压迫法币之手段,层出不穷。同年六月十日起禁止华南地名法币钞票在华北流通,并规定华北地名法币,在一年内,得与伪币平价行使。同年八月七日起又改定华北地名法币对伪币九折通用。廿八年二月廿日起又改定华北地名法币对伪币六折通用。同年三月十一日起禁止法币在华北流通,以谋"华北通货一元化"而为"日圆集团"之一员。当华北伪政府明令抑低法币对伪币比价时,甚且于禁止法币通用以后,伪联合准备银行反以伪钞对法币升水之手段,收购法币。①藉此既可推行伪币,又可以收集之法币套取我外汇,其计良毒。在华南方面,自廿七年十一月起,日军即开始推行军用票,以吸收法币。嗣后又于今年五月十六日开设伪华兴银行发行伪华兴券,并抄袭伪联合准备银行之故技,以伪华兴券对法币升水之手段,收购法币。据上海七月廿一日合众电称,一日之内,已购进法币三百万元。然日伪计谋多端,事态之演变,尚不止于此。

日伪除统制占领区域输出贸易外(廿八年三月十一日起,日伪规定华北十二种重要出口商品,即蛋品、胡桃、花生油、落花生、烟草、杏仁、香芹、通心粉条、煤炭、毛毡、金丝草帽、盐等须向伪联合准备银行依照伪币一元合十四便士之汇率,结售外汇。后于七月十日改为统制全部出口贸易。在华南方面,日人以统制其占据海口之方法,统制由华中一带输出重要商品之贸易),复实行一种专卖制度。凡进口洋货及重要土货,皆由日人独占经营;华人除非得其特许,不得经理售卖。而日商售货时只收军用票及伪钞。故欲购买洋货者,必先以其法币向日人所特设之兑换所换成伪币或军用票。如此为之,非特法币将逐渐被日伪所收集转向港沪购买外汇,而伪钞及军用票亦将藉以推广流通矣。

此外华北对华南贸易之出超状态,及上海银号商帮之勾通津沪汇兑,亦有增长伪币通用势力。去年华北对华中及华南之土货转口贸易出超额,约有二千余万元。此种贸易货款之汇拨,通常均以上海金融机关为枢纽。②华北货商在华中及华南售货所得之法币头寸,除在华北直接出售其法币汇票

---

① 在四月底五月初期间,伪币易法币每百元升水三十余元。见朱偰《伪币贬值与日金跌价》,重庆各报联合版五月廿四日。
② 崔晓岑著《中央银行论》。

后,均交由上海金融机关汇至平津等地而在平津等地收进伪钞。平津等地之银行,为上海金融机关解出汇款以后,即在上海金融机关保有法币头寸,藉可接收伪钞汇沪支付法币。于是华北伪钞勾通申汇之现象发生。又近来上海各银行存款激增,而运用资金之途径甚狭,除用于地产投机,商品投机,及外汇投机外,多以低利(大率在七厘左右)放款于银号商帮。银号商帮为勾通津沪汇兑之主角。津沪汇兑业务,获利甚厚。银行商帮既能在上海调借头寸,遂在平津等地大量出售上海汇票,以图厚利。凡此事实非特便利日伪之套取外汇,且使伪钞得与使用法币区域通汇,以增加伪钞之用途而助长其推广流通,亦即削弱法币之流通势力,予游击区内法币生命以直接威胁。

游击区内法币生存问题,非仅与金融政策有密切关系,而外交、党政,及游击战之运用,亦有重大影响。设天津租界及北平东交民巷内存银,英国接受日本之要求而全数引渡于伪政府,以为伪"联银券"之发行准备金,或津沪租界内准许伪"联银券"通用,则伪"联银券"之信用增高,亦即法币之信用相对的减弱。自中日货币战之形势观之,日本所遭遇之最大问题,在求各国承认"联银券"及"华兴券"。否则"日圆集团"及"日满支经济协同体"之基础不稳,于此可见外交在中日货币战中之地位。故若隔离黑市政策,能与外交、党政,及游击战配合前进,游击区内法币对于伪钞之防卫战,尚可望持久。倘我政府当局对于日伪之进攻方策,不善谋应付,虽弗采用隔离黑市政策,游击区内法币之生命,亦殊危殆可虑。此不可不注意也。

六、结　论

政策本身原无所谓是非或优劣,且有利亦必有弊;要视吾人之目的如何,以定取舍。隔离黑市政策,以解决外汇黑市对法币信用之威胁为最大目的。此政策有自主性及独立性,毋庸乞怜于外国以求取其援助。且实行之后,以上所述种种弊害,皆可完全消去。则我后方各省市内法币信用,必将增强,安如泰山;而日伪有意攻击,亦无计可施。我后方各省市为抗战根据地。根据地之法币信用巩固,方可以退守或乘伪币之弱点以进攻。此军事战争原则之运用于货币战也。至于隔离黑市政策对游击区内法币生命之影响,要视我外交及党政军工作为何如耳。

一九三九,七,二九,于重庆南泉
(原载《财政评论》1939年第2卷第4期)

再论维持外汇与黑市汇价

我国法币对外汇兑,自去年三月由政府统制以后,便有"黑市"和"官市",或"统制市"和"自由市"的对立。当初黑价和官价无甚差别;且敌伪套取外汇的企图,因我实行统制,完全失败了。此时一般人士,都感觉到无限欣慰。五月以后,黑价步跌,黑价和官价的差异,逐渐地显著。在六月十四日(六月中汇价最低的一日),黑价为八便士又八分之一,只合官价百分之五七,这才使人们感到不安。报章杂志上发表了很多文字讨论这个外汇问题。有的主张重新厘订汇价,使合于经济现状,再设法切切实实地维持它;有的主张始终维持原定的汇价,就是有名无实地维持,亦认为必要的;有的主张支撑黑价,以免黑价的变动,摇惑人们对法币的信用;有的主张由政府把官价和黑价的差额发还或津贴出口商人。此外还有其他主张,不必零举。后来政府采取了一种两元政策,一方面坚持原定法价(合英币一先令二便士又四分之一),虽然平民已无法请准购买了。他方面举债一千万镑(由英商汇丰和麦加利银行贷出五百万镑,中交二行筹集五百万镑,按当时黑价折算,约合国币三万万元)成立平准外汇基金,来支持黑价,所以黑价就安定在八便士又四分之一的一点上。敌人见我外汇平衡基金管委会供给黑市外汇,以为吸收法币套取外汇的机会又到了,乃不惜牺牲"日元集团"的币制信用,于五月十九开始压低日元和伪币对法币的比价,收买法币,以便套取我外汇平衡基金的外汇准备。在这时期,我政府当局和一部分人士,不了解敌人的阴谋,误以为日元和伪币行将崩溃的潜兆,未筹对策,以为防范。到了六月初旬,敌伪抛出大批法币套取外汇,外汇市场一时供不应求,谣言四起,酿成挤兑风潮,不得不于六月九日限制供给黑市外汇,并重新"调整黑市汇价"。黑市汇价从此以后钉在六便士半的一点上;虽然实际交易的汇价,仍多变动,低的时候,一元只合五便士。所以外汇又为一般人士的注意中心。

通常管理或统制外汇的主要目的,原在不丧失黄金和外汇准备的条件下,维持比较自由市场汇价更高一点的汇率。现在我国统制外汇的主要目的,除了上述目的,还要防止敌伪吸收法币套取外汇。若只讲求第一目的,而置第二目的于不顾,那就等于让敌人利用我们的资金来打我们了。所以我们管理外汇的工作,一定要顾到这一点。去年三月开始管理或统制外汇的时候,政府发言人特别提到这一点。然而今年成立外汇平衡基金来支持黑价,给敌人以套取外汇的机会,把原先统制的目的忘了,不能不说是当局的疏忽。黑市原是黑的私的,为法所不许的,至少名义上是如此。外汇平衡基金委员会对于黑市供给外汇,事实上是等于承认了黑市,黑市便不能再说是黑的私的,只能说是明的公的了。并且人们买卖外汇,都在黑市交易。那么,黑价的变动,才能反映着法币价值的变动,黑价的变动,才能影响人们对于法币的信用。至于法定汇价的存在,已可说丧失作用了。所以支持黑市汇价,不是一种妥善的政策。

依外汇平衡基金管委会性质言,他的工作在于压制投机和调节季节变动。投机家抛出外汇,平衡管委会便买进来,投机家收买外汇,平衡管委会便卖出去,以免汇价受投机买卖的影响。又当外汇供不应求的季节,平衡管委会便卖出外汇,当外汇供过于求的季节,平衡管委会,便买进外汇,以避免汇价的季节变动。所以平衡管委会的工作,不像俄德意各国管理外汇机构,不能抬高或维持汇价比较自由市场的汇价高些;亦不能分别外汇需要的性质,限制或禁止购买额。所以黑价变动的长期趋势,一定和购买力平价相符合的;除非人们对于法币的信用发生动摇(现代币制通常都只有部分的正货准余为保证准备,保证准备的本身是一种信用,所以现代币制,都含有信用因素,因此含有心理因素,讨论货币问题的人们,都有形或无形的假定了这点)。购买力平价的变动,除非通货膨胀不止,不至于有跌无已。至少到现在为止的黑价,设使政府不出来撑持,亦不会跌到比现在的汇价更低。所以黑市汇价不必要平衡基金去撑持的。

新近财政部公布的《出口货物结汇领取汇价差额办法》第二条云:

> 前项依照法价结汇之出口货物于实际结清汇额后,得凭结算证件向结汇银行领取法价与该行挂牌价格之差额,结汇银行得向结汇人收取银行向例应得之手续费,但不得超过百分之三。

由此看来,法定汇价已在无形中贬值了。依法价请购外汇,事实上早已不行,所以需求外汇的人们只能依黑价购进。所以就购进外汇的交易看来,黑价就是法币的汇价。今依财部颁布的领取汇价差额办法,由输出贸易所得外汇,先依法价结售,再加领法价与市价差额。所以出口商人售出外汇的汇率,不是法价而是黑价。所以中交银行挂牌汇价,名义上是市价或黑价,实际上是法币的真实汇价。此黑价与法价的差额,便是贬值的程度。所谓法价仍是有效,是掩耳盗铃的话。这种做法,怕比径直了断的贬值更为不利些。今日的贬值,也不比早些时(例如去年开始统制汇兑时或今年开始支持黑价时)贬值为有利。

关于维持汇价,亦即所以维持法币信用,我们具有不同的见解,供献在下面,就正于高明,并备当局的参考。

（一）依据经济现状,重新厘订法币汇价,并照新定法价切实管理维持之。

（二）管理外汇以非陷敌区域为限,陷敌区域之外汇市场任其自由发展。

（三）对于陷敌区域之汇款和贸易,严加限制或课重税或禁止。

（四）中交总行之未迁渝者,由政府命令其立即迁入,使金融重心归宿于政府所在地,不得停留于港沪。

（五）设法增加并集中政府权力所及地域(陷敌区域除外)之外汇供给,同时惩罚逃资及在外国之资产。

（六）审核外汇需要之性质,分别限制或禁止外汇之购买。

（七）关于生产消费方面,对于有外国市场之货物(如桐油、红茶等)奖励生产并节约甚或禁止在国内消费,以增出口货物以换得外汇。

（八）关于财政者,增开新税并提高旧税之税率,以增加税收,而减少入不敷出之赤字财政差额,来缓和钞票发行额之增速。

（九）关于金融方面,依照廿六年九月颁布的办法,限制银行存户之提款,以减低流通量。

（十）由国库津贴华侨汇款千分之五,以资鼓励,使华侨汇款,得集中于政府之手。

如此做去,黑市场虽能存在,必须是黑的私的,一经查出,如其在政府权力区域内,必严惩不贷,使它在汇兑市场上,没甚影响。即在租界或陷敌区域内的黑价,犹如德俄等国之黑市,对于币制亦不能发生多大影响,则黑价自不用政府之撑持了。

贬值对于许多方面似乎是件可怕的事,要遭遇着猛烈地反对的,其实政府已悄悄地贬值了。我相信贬值不见得会有如他们所想象的那样不良影响。设使能引起社会的不安，一定是暂时的，等到人们懂了贬值是么一回事，便会安定下去的。反正我们对外购买军火，不是付现而是记账；价值的计算，不是国币而是外币，所以贬值不能影响到我们对外购买军火。关于进口货方面，不必要的奢侈品和半奢侈品，将国货价抬高而减少，可以节省一部分的外汇的供给，不能说是不利的。

上列第二条和第三条办法，竟在截断陷敌区域和非陷敌区域的联系，免使陷敌区域的外汇行市，影响到非陷敌区域的法币汇价。第四条在于补充第二条和第三条的不足，其余各条的用意，在于直接的或间接的增减外汇的供需，以缓和汇市的压力。

一九三九，七七，纪念日于南泉怡园
（原载《时事月报》1939年第21卷第1期）

树立平价行政机构议

前在四月间曾就平价问题提出意见,三月以来,物价问题迄未获得适当之解决,而其严重性亦未尝减少。中央七中全会对此深加注意,并决议于政府机构之中增设中央设计局以为全国政治经济之统筹计划机关,又复增设战时经济部担任战时经济行政工作,将平定后方物价之任务,包括在内,当此两机关尚在筹组之时,试就平价问题,再加检讨,一方面重申前说,他方面则对平价机构,略贡意见,以备参考。

吾人以为统制物价之实施,必须注意三项基本事实:第一,物价之变动,非但同地各物价间相关甚大,而异地之物价,亦常相互影响,譬如以盐价煤价而论,盐之生产成本中有百分之四十属于燃料费(据富荣场统计),倘煤价高涨百分之五十,则食盐生产成本,至少当增加百分之二十(假定其他因素未变),如是,而欲求盐价之单独平抑,舍亏本折利而外,殆不可能。又如渝市食米之主要来源为嘉陵长江两岸,倘两河沿岸,食米渐减,米价渐贵,而欲重庆米价不涨,亦属显然不可能之事。故平价办法宜求各地各种物价之平,而后可收预期之效。第二,现在我国经济社会,根本缺少基层组织,而物价之统制,必须普遍实施,方能有效,是则基层组织之从速建立,实为刻不容缓之事。欧战期中,各国竞施统制,讥之者云,统制虽严,亦不能每一牛设一警察,语虽近于滑稽,然颇能表示统制经济在实行上之症结所在。卢郁文先生谓:先进国统制经济之困难,在与大企业家争权力,后进国之困难则在克服零落散漫之组织使尽纳于纪纲。今我国统制物价之困难,此亦其一点。第三欲求物价之平定,在乎严密之执行与督导者半,在乎合理价格之规定者亦半。而合理价格之规定确非易事。月前渝市煤炭突感奇缺,煤业中人悉委之于官定价格太低,运销无利,故来货稀少,而管理者固不承认其规定价格之不当,但亦无以证明其确属适当,自信不深,执行难期贯彻。又譬如月前苦旱,渝市河米之供给日鲜,价格亦逐步上涨,以当时情势推之,徒抑米价恐不足以应需求;而月来甘霖普降,屯米多求脱手,米价亦落,使月前维持低价视为不可能者,变为可能。凡此种种天时人事之变换无常,既极复杂,又皆足影响政策之执行,苟非当事者考察周详,根据事实,确定合理价格,则在执行平价时,将必朝令夕废,于事无补,此又一基本事实也。

明了上述事实,则回忆已往办理平价之经过,将必深感于准备工作之不足矣。吾人过去平抑各项物价,固未尝将各项物价作通盘之考虑,非独昆明重庆间各项物价未尝平衡,即成都重庆物价何尝平衡？非独原料与产品之价格未尝平衡,即如棉花之与棉纱、棉纱之与棉布相互关系最为显明者又何尝平衡？再以简单之例言之:试问平价购销处自上海香港购运日用品时,对于后方日用品缺少之数量是否有所估计,日用品运到后可能发生之效力如何？社会上增加此一批货物之后,应维持其市价于何等水准方可谓平？又如农本局出售屯米后应压低米价至何种程度？凡此种种似应为厘定价格者所应熟知,而事实上绝难作到。此固不能归咎于任何一人,任何一机关,盖平素既少调查统计,可资参考,仓卒间又无事权集中之组织,从事周密之策划故也。至于基层经济组织之建立,吾人曾详细论述,虽非短期内嗟咄可办,但时至今日,尚未能迅速进行,欲求平价工作之顺利,亦未免近于奢望矣。

是以今日之问题宜在下层,建立以同业公会为中心之统制机构,在中央宜建立事权集中之统制机构,同时更树立一综合各项经济建设问题之设计机关,就全部经济现状综合观察,以国家经济政策为准绳,作平定物价之设计,然后在上层与下层之间造成合理之联系,以形成一完整之体系。兹略述此项机构之概略如下:

(一)设计机关　设计机关之组织,利在兼顾经济问题之各方面,恰如前段所举,平抑盐价,不能置煤价于不顾,平抑川省物价,不能置其他省分于不顾。他如重复之运输与逆转运输,以及工厂矿场不合理之地域分布,皆足以使物品之成本提高。凡此种种,必须有全盘计划,而后能求合理解决。是以物价设计机关宜设于统筹设计之机关内。今者中央七中全会已有设立中央设计局之决议,此诚一贤明之举措,吾人以为在中央设计局之中有关物价者,至少应设二个重要部分,一为统计处,一为物价委员会。

(1)统计处——统计处应为中央设计局中之经常组织,担负调查统计工作。其有关物价之调查事项包括物品之生产量、消费量、运输量、交易量及市场组织、商品价格等项。调查所得之各项经济资料,即加以整理分析。凡物品成本之计算,运输费用之计算,合理利润之计算等皆包括在内,并根据统计结果,提供改进计划。

(2)物价委员会——由于物价问题牵涉之广,关系之巨,有非单一部门所能决定者,故宜在中央设计局之中成立委员会,由各有关部会派遣代表参

加,以设计局中主要负责人员主持之,其工作内容约如下述:

① 根据调查统计之资料及统计处拟订之每期物价草案,议订全国各地之基价。

② 根据全国经济计划及物价涨落趋势,议订各种物资之开发收购屯储运输分配等事项。

③ 审议各级统制物价之组织及统制办法。

④ 审议或议订其他有关物价之重要设施或计划。

(二)执行机关 我国过去平价,偏重于按物品设机关,譬如燃料平价属于燃料管理局,粮食平价属于食粮管理局,他如平价购销处,仅能负平价工作中购销一部分工作,各省市政府又仅能就当地当时情形勉为应付。至专责统制物价之机关,迄今尚付阙如。此种机关究竟采取何种组织,论者亦少。伍启元先生在《新经济》三卷七期中曾有《平衡物价之组织》一文,其主张在沿袭现有之精神,于实际执行物价管理时,分门别类,利用现有政府机构,或半官方机关,加以管理。例如军需物品,及重要矿产之价格,可由兵工署及资源委员会等机关负执行责任,关于农产品价格,可由农本局负执行责任,又在农本局之下分设各种农产价格管理处,每处之中设有设计委员会,负设计之责任,并于处下设立分支处遍布各地。

吾人以为平价组织可分纵横两种关系:纵的关系为自中央以至各省市县区乡镇之一贯统属关系,横的关系为每级组织内各种物品统制部门之连络关系,试以图示如下:

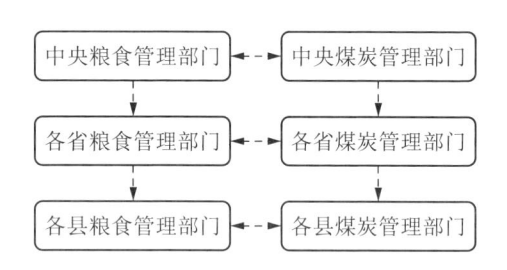

```
┌─────────────┐     ┌─────────────┐
│中央粮食管理部门│◄--►│中央煤炭管理部门│
└──────┬──────┘     └──────┬──────┘
       ▼                   ▼
┌─────────────┐     ┌─────────────┐
│各省粮食管理部门│◄--►│各省煤炭管理部门│
└──────┬──────┘     └──────┬──────┘
       ▼                   ▼
┌─────────────┐     ┌─────────────┐
│各县粮食管理部门│◄--►│各县煤炭管理部门│
└─────────────┘     └─────────────┘
```

分业统制,如伍氏所主张之机构,系加重纵的统属关系,即使每一物品自中央以至省县区乡,均由一个机关管理,其结果固可收指挥灵便之利,而其弊有二:一、为机关复杂,无论在中央或在地方,常有若干统制物价机关各行执权,互相独立,易使同一区域之内政出多门,系统紊乱。二、管理物价不仅在求各地物价之平衡,更宜求各类物品之平衡,此理已于篇首详述,今忽略统制物价机构内之横面连络关系,则不易求各类物品互相平衡之效。有此二种弊端,则行政上既感不便,平抑之效,亦复难望。

基层组织之中,实际监督交易市场之物价,必赖有分业之统制,是以吾人一贯之主张,认为应健全同业公会,使之成为深入社会之基层统制机构,但在同业公会之上,必须联系若干同业公会,加以组织,以期互相作技术上之联系,是则有赖地方统制机构之建立。循此以进,愈趋中央则有待于联系者愈殷,即其横面关系愈应逐渐加强,凡关于人事之调度训练,商品之运输经营,以及执行时之考核等工作,皆应由同一机关发号施令,以期各项物价得其平衡,不致有偏枯偏荣,顾此失彼之弊(至于决定方策拟定计划之工作,其牵涉尤广,虽顾及全部物价,犹感不足,是以物价之设计工作又必设于中央设计局内,冀与生产、交通、国际贸易等取得联系)。此皆根据经济现象之本质,不得不用此纵横联系之机构也。关于设计机关之组织已详前述,兹再分述执行机关之各级组织于下:

(1) 物价统制局 物价统制局,为全国最高统制物价之执行机关,应直隶于战时经济部之下,根据中央设计局之计划,受战时经济部之督导,办理全国平定物价工作,局中分设下列各处:

① 总务处 分下列四科:

(a) 文书科——其任务为文书收发拟稿及典守印信等事项。

(b) 统计科——其任务在执行本局内之行政考核,汇编局内工作报告,办理中央设计局委托之调查及本局必要之调查,整理统计资料,编制统计报告等项。

(c) 会计科——掌理本局一般会计事项,至公营商店等,应另立特别会计另设管理部门。

(d) 庶务科——掌理本局一般杂务。

② 组训处 依职务分设下列各科:

(a) 公会科——掌理同业公会之组织及其人员任免考核。

(b) 辅导科——掌理公卖处及合作社之辅设指导事项。

(c) 训练科——掌理平价人员之抽调训练事宜。

③ 营运处 依职务分设下列各科:

(a) 收购科——在生产有余之地收购或指挥分局收购商品。

(b) 仓储科——指导各区,或自行设立商品储存仓库,以储存收购科收购之商品。

(c) 运输科——依中央设计局之计划运输商品或监督分局运输商品。

(d) 公营科——指导各区设立公营处,销售购运商品以平抑市价。

④ 督查处　依职务分设下列各科：

（a）稽核科——掌理公私账册之稽核以审查有无囤积之事实，并为各公私商店记账之便利，及主管机关稽核之敏捷计，拟订简易会计规程，颁发各店援用。

（b）经济警察科——掌理经济警察之训练组织指挥调度事项。

（c）特务督查科——掌理特务人员调用指挥事项。

（d）控诉科——接受人民对于平价之意见，及对于平价人员之控诉，与市场非法活动之告发等事项。

（2）物价统制处　每省或市，应设物价统制处，秉承中央物价统制局之命令，执行平价政策。战时经济部成立之后应在后方各省成立战时经济委员会，恰如战区各省之设有战区经济委员会者然，有此统筹战时经济问题之委员会，则战时经济之各部门始得以同时推进，步伐整齐，而物价统制处应即直接隶属于此战时经济委员会之下，俾与其他部分相互联系。在经济委员会尚未成立前，应直接隶属省政府。其内部组织应分设总务、组训、营运、督查四科，分别执行各省平价工作，各科之职掌与中央物价统制局相似。

（3）物价统制分处　每县市，应设立物价统制支处，秉承各该省物价统制处之命令，执行平价政策，当战时经济委员会成立后，各县应设立战时经济科，统筹战时问题，而物价统制支处，应即直接隶属于战时经济科之下，在此种组织尚未建立之前，应直属于县政府，其内部组织应分下列四股：

① 总务股——掌理文书、统计、会计、庶务等事项。

② 组训股——辅设合作社及组织同业公会，训练平价人员等事项。

③ 营运股——直接收购商品，运输商品，设立公营商店及仓库，或委托私人团体经营购运销售等业务。

④ 督查股——稽核账册，接受控诉，指挥经济督察等事项。

（4）同业公会　同业公会，为人民团体，政府在执行平价政策时，必须先将每一同业公会（包括工业商业）加以调整，一面使之有执行政令之权力与能力，一面使之接受政府之指挥与命令。依吾人之主张首须使公会职员任免受政府之管理，即每一公会改组后应将选举结果，呈报县战时经济科，或省战时经济委员会，或战时经济部（各依其地域及组织之大小），由科会或部依选举情形圈定主席及秘书后，以政府命令加委。并派员参加于公会组织之内，政府对于公会职员有免职之权力，同时规定分门办事详细规程，以期切实担负其所负之使命。各个公会备全之后，应联合各地同业公会成立联合会；由县联合会以至于省，由省以至于全国，凡两县以上之同业公会联合会,应受省战时经济委员会直接指挥,凡两省以上之同业公会联合会,应受战时经济部之直接指挥。如是则公会逐渐加强,联合会逐渐扩大,战时经济部及省战时经济委员会之职责日增,经济统制权有逐渐集中之趋势;而完备之统制机构,亦可逐渐完成矣。至于同业公会在平价工作上所负之任务,已于前次撰文详述,其主要任务,盖在实现同业监督之理想也。

兹将上述平价机构图示于后:

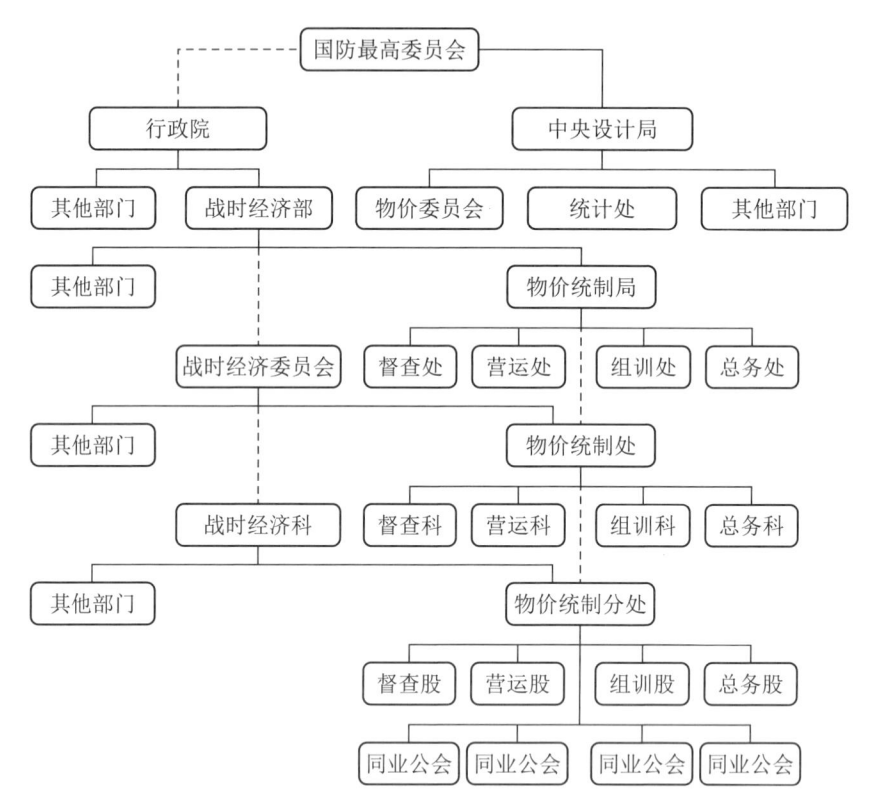

```
                    ┌─────────────┐
            ┌───────│国防最高委员会│───────┐
            │       └─────────────┘       │
       ┌────┴───┐                   ┌─────┴─────┐
       │ 行政院 │                   │ 中央设计局│
       └────┬───┘                   └─────┬─────┘
      ┌─────┴─────┐              ┌────────┼────────┬─────────┐
  ┌───┴──┐  ┌─────┴──┐      ┌────┴───┐ ┌──┴──┐  ┌──┴─────┐
  │其他部门│  │战时经济部│      │物价委员会│ │统计处│  │其他部门│
  └──────┘  └────┬───┘      └────────┘ └─────┘  └────────┘
       ┌────────┤
  ┌────┴───┐    │                      ┌──────────┐
  │其他部门│    │                      │物价统制局 │
  └────────┘    │                      └────┬─────┘
           ┌────┴─────────┐        ┌───┬────┼────┬────┐
           │战时经济委员会│        │督查处│营运处│组训处│总务处│
           └────┬─────────┘        └───┘  └───┘ └───┘ └───┘
       ┌───────┤
  ┌────┴───┐   │                        ┌──────────┐
  │其他部门│   │                        │物价统制处│
  └────────┘   │                        └────┬─────┘
          ┌────┴─────┐         ┌───┬────┼────┬────┐
          │战时经济科│         │督查科│营运科│组训科│总务科│
          └────┬─────┘         └───┘ └───┘ └───┘ └───┘
      ┌───────┤
  ┌───┴────┐  │                        ┌───────────┐
  │其他部门│  │                        │物价统制分处│
  └────────┘  │                        └────┬──────┘
                          ┌───┬────┼────┬────┐
                          │督查股│营运股│组训股│总务股│
                          └───┘  └───┘ └───┘ └───┘
                    ┌─────┬──────┬──────┬──────┐
                    │同业公会│同业公会│同业公会│同业公会│
                    └─────┘└─────┘└─────┘└─────┘
```

上述机构,系依各级原有行政组织增设,可以得行政上之便利,避免改组创制之繁。然就现有行政区划而论,省区之范围过大,县区之范围过小,以全省战时经济委员会直接指挥各地同业公会,则有鞭长莫及之弊,以各县战时经济科直接秉承中央之命令,则中央之职责过于繁重,故不得不采用三级制。然事实上此种组织稍嫌繁复,稍稍不慎,易使省经济委员会成为公文承转之机关,而丧失其效力。补救之法,应划分经济区域,由中央政府直接指挥各经济区,由各经济区直接指挥各同业公会。

变三级制为二级制,始较合理。兹分述理由如下:

（一）平抑物价办法之实施，应与经济建设计划相配合，而计划经济之实施，必须划分区域。据美国伊黎博士(Richard T. Ely)之意，认为工业区域之选定，应依下列七因素：一、原料的供给，二、劳工的供给，三、水力的供给，四、资金的供给，五、市场的接近，六、气候的适宜，七、提前开始的势头(Momentum of an early start)。吾人于考虑经济建设之分区问题，势不能不考虑此七种因素；而现有行政区域，殊不能与此尽合。是以今后经济建设，似宜重新划分区域，务使在每一经济区域之内，原料、劳工足敷本区之用，动力方面足以形成一完密之动力网，金融方面可以建立一适当之金融中心，而此金融中心又足以配合全国金融网之总计划，此外更须顾及本区自然环境、政治环境、社会习惯以及原有经济组织之实况。譬如区内交通是否便利，区界是否与行政区划相符合，风俗习惯是否相同，区内有无商品集散市场等等问题，皆须审慎考虑，然后经济建设，始迅速发展，而无甚流弊。此项区域划分之后，平价机关即可依经济区设立统制处以执行区内平抑物价办法，并能与其他生产、分配、消费等计划相互配合，故分区办法基于全部经济建设之需要，非仅为平定物价而作此主张也。

（二）工商业团体之合理发展，足以协助政府执行平价政策，故宜积极促进各地工商业同业公会组织联合会。而此种联合会之组织，往往按经济自然需要而成，譬如甲地与乙地交易频繁，自易联合。倘政府按经济实况，划分全国为若干经济区，则在每区之内，对于同业公会联合会之组织，较易倡导，故分区统制，不但指挥灵便，且适于促进工商业之自然组合，以树立牢固之基础。

（三）分划区域以后，每一区域内经济环境相似，则商品之收购运输储存较易办理，即在中央统制机关对于筹划指挥亦较方便，且公平价格之订定，尤应按经济区域划分，盖唯有经济环境相似而后能求其价格之一致也。他如合作社之辅设、公卖处之经营、平价人员之训练，罔不宜在经济区内，统筹办理。举例言之，某区之生产能力、储存物资、消费状况皆已经过调查，中央设计局可以按全国供求状况，决定该区应收购若干、存储若干、输出若干、本区内缺乏之物品，应订价若干，待输出之商品应订价若干，然后依交通状况，需要状况，决定本区内物品之分配办法，并于适当地点设立公卖处，辅设合作社，并派遣职员，从事严密之监督，凡此种种便利，似非按原有省区所能获得者矣。

故吾人对于平价机构虽曾提出中央、省、县三级制之办法，但并不认为完善，特在目前环境之下，不易遽尔改弦更张，尚不妨以此为过渡之桥梁，至于合理制度之完成则必待全国经济区域划定后，始克完全实现也。

（原载《时代精神》1939年第2卷第2期）

论对日经济制裁

一 对日经济制裁

日本军阀于一九三七年七月无端发兵侵略中国,各国人民与政府,既恶暴日之不守信义,破坏和平,又痛其残暴横蛮,激于义愤,有倡为抵制日货及经济制裁,以为纠正暴日之手段者。最著之事例,先有一九三七年十二月美国国会通过鲁易士—史高托之议案(Lewis-Scoatt Resolution)授权总统,俾与他国合作,运用经济财政的手段——包括对日进出口贸易之禁止(日本平常需要之食粮除外),与对华贷款及物品之供给——以阻止日本之侵略行动而援助中国之抵抗实力,冀求战争之早日结束而恢复公允之和平。后有一九三八年九月国联行政院接受中国政府之声请,引用盟约第十七条,决议对日实施盟约第十六条之制裁。最近日本成立所谓"兴亚院",图谋建立"东亚新秩序",排斥第三国在华之利益。美、英、法诸国又盛倡经济报复之议。然而时至今日,尤未见对日经济制裁之实施,论者以为有所顾忌也。据吾人之所知,此种顾虑,仅为反对者之借口,未有事实以为依据,请分论之。

(1)怀疑制裁办法者,以为制裁之实行,可引起日本对制裁者宣战。其实日本之人力、物力,经与中国作战二十个月,损失惨重,已不敢向第三国挑衅。果若与远东有关诸国(美、英、法、苏、荷),联合或平行制裁,日本见其实力之雄厚,精神被胁,不足以言战。观诸意大利被制裁时未敢对制裁国发动战争,更可使吾人相信日本之不敢挑战。退一步言,即使日本对制裁国发动战争,只须各国认定制裁之持久,必使日本崩溃,则可暂时退守南洋群岛及威夷岛等处,甚且退守新加坡及巴拿马运河等地,避与交锋,以逸待劳,使之自趋没落,然后收回原有之权益,则战祸亦可避免矣。此处尚有须注意者,徒然畏惧战争,往往不足以避免战争,维其不作侵略战而随时准备作正义战,方能消弭战争。故英、美、荷、法、苏诸国,应本此精神,以实行经济制裁暴日,则正义可伸、和平可保、人道可存。

(2)怀疑经济制裁办法者,以为国联制意之失败,足证经济制裁之威力有限,不足使日本就范。其实国联制意之结果,不得引为经济制裁失效之明证,盖国联制意所遭遇之缺陷,非皆属不可补救者,且日本与意大利所处之地位不同,易受制裁之打击。虽然可用以比较之资料不全,未能作严密之比较,而较日本依赖于外国资源及贸易之程度,意国为甚,似可断言者:第一,日本产业集中于纺织业,必须依赖外国市场以消纳其制品,故消纳其纺织品之外国市场,对于日本产业之影响,亦极强烈。意国产业则比较的分散于各部门。又日本之减小输入,亦较意国为难。日本粮食大约足以自给,若欲减小输入,不能从意国之例,可酌量减小粮食之输入,必须减小原料品之输入,其结果足使若干部工业之一部或全部停业。第二,日本对外贸易集中于少数国家,而意大利则比较的分散于多数国家。故对日制裁只须有少数国家联合或平行实施,即可发生效力。英、美两国合共供给日本之输入63.2%,又消纳其输出48.2%。若将法、荷两国加入计算,共占日本之输入68%,占其输出56.5%。德、意两国只占其输出入额之5.1%及1.4%。日本所需要之原料,太半仰给于英、美、荷、法四国,其成数约如下表:

第一表　英、美、荷、法、苏五国供给日本之原料额

原料种类	供给原料之国名	在日本进口额中所占之百分数
煤汽油	美、荷、英、苏	100%
橡胶	荷、英、法	100%
铸铁	美、英	50%
废铁	美	100%
铝	美、英	81%
铅	美、英	70%
锌	美、英	8%
铜	美	97%
锡	英	72%
棉花	英、美	86%
羊毛	英	91%
汽车	美	94%
机器	英、美(余自德国输入)	50%

日本自德国输入之物品,大都为机器、颜料、硫酸铵等,合共不过日本总输入之5%。假如美、英、荷、法、苏联合或平行制裁日本,即使日本能利用若干代替品,以为补充,亦不能持久抵抗。

（3）怀疑制裁办法者，以为制裁国实施对日制裁之后，其产业将遭受损失。其实制裁所引起之损失，为数必不甚大。盖据专家之估计，如得英、美、荷、法、苏合作实施对日制裁，则日本最多只能撑持九个月至一年。但以精神被胁之影响，或可于六个月内结束之。设就最长时限之一年而论，制裁国所遭受之损失，必非对日贸易全额之损失；其中一部分贸易，将移转于其他各国。此种移转贸易，即为制裁国因制裁而遭受损失之部分补偿。

今如美国发动对日经济制裁，则美国所遭受之损失将如何？此可根据美日进出口统计估计之：

美货输日，在一九三七年计为 288 378 000 美元，（较一九三六年增加 84 030 000 美元或 41%。以日本对华作战所需之军需，有赖于美国之供给故也）。在美国输出贸易总额中占 8.6%。日货输美共为 204 202 000 美元（超过于一九三六者为 32 458 000 美元或 18.5%。），估美国输入贸易总额 6.6%。于此可知美国如禁止日货进口及美货输出，其损失亦不过为其对外贸易 8% 弱。

美国输日及日本输美之重要商品，根据一九三七年之贸易统计，约如下表：

第二表　美日之贸易商品

美货输日之物品	价值（千美元）
棉花	61 724
废铁类	39 278
铜	17 997
电线、马口铁、铅、铝等金属	47 148
煤汽油、滑油及其他液体燃料	44 821
汽车及机器	34 202
杉木	2 555
木浆	14 312
日货输美	价值（千美元）
丝	99 572
漂白布、丝织品等纺织品	34 451
植物食粮及饮料（如棉籽油、黄豆、茶叶等）	11 949
其他植物品	6 674

美国输日之重要物品,均系军需必要品,当此各国扩军备战之期,在日本以外之各国,亦均在竞购,故如美国政府禁其输日,亦不至完全搁浅。其中以棉花一项为额最大,占美国输日贸易21.4%。今如全数禁止输日,而不另谋其他出路,必为美国南部产棉区农民所反对。但如美国政府果欲履行条约中之义务,以维护条约之尊严而保持世界之和平,则可利用农业调整条例(Agricultural Adjustment Act,简称 AAA)收购棉花,以救济棉业农民因制裁日本所蒙受之损失。关于日货输美者,以蚕丝一项为最重要,占日货输美总额51%(若就一九三六年而论,该项为55%)。此种生丝什九用于制造女袜。今如美国政府禁止全部日货进口,则丝织工业将因缺乏原料故,不能开业,发生失业现象。考美国丝织业共约有资本5万万元,直接雇用25万工人,间接依赖此业者,略同此数。丝织业之总生产价值(零售价值),约可5.8万万元(见 International Labor News Service, Jan.29, 1938)。此种停业失业为经济制裁必有之现象,此不过其中之一例,当尽量设法解决之,但解决之道,宜按问题之性质,各别解决,未能求得通用公式。就本题而论,依美国民族杂志之考察,此等丝织业之工人及机器,大半可移用于代替品之制造,故停业失业之问题,并不严重(见 The Nation, Aug.18, Nov.6, 1937各期)。亦有人主张利用特种失业保险金(Special Unemployment Insurance Fund)以救济失业工人(见 Haery F. Ward, The Social Questions Bulletin, 1937, Issued by the Methodist Federation for Social Service)。总之,参与制裁之各国政府,如能设计周详,按问题之性质,分别设法救济,当能解决除其困难之大部分。

总上所述,经济制裁实施之后,制裁国之产业及工人,将遭遇若干困难及损失。然其代价为国际条约之得维护,世界和平之得确保,人类方能安居乐业,文化与文明方能延续而向上发展。设使破坏公约而肆行侵略者,为所欲为,无有仗义之国,出而干涉,纠正其错误,则战祸犹传染病也,不啻将蔓延于全世界,世界人类欲安享太平生活,不可得矣。故今日各国所遇之问题,非选择于"制裁"与"和平"之间,而是选择于"战争"与"制裁"之间,世界强国果能实行经济制裁,以维护国际章约,使无有敢再犯者,则战争可永免,和平可永保。故谓制裁时所遭遇之损失,乃保持和平之代价。如是以观,则吾人所付之和平代价,固甚微也。

(4)怀疑经济制裁者,以为英美在中日两国之投资甚巨,而此种投资皆在日人势力控制之下,故对日经济制裁之实施,未免有投鼠忌器之感。其实此种意见否认经济制裁之效力。若认定经济制裁必能使日本就范,则制裁完成之后,其主权必仍为英美所有,盖其时日人已失其控制之能力矣。此点理由正与上列(一)节所述相同。反之,若英美等国不发动经济制裁日本,又不给予中国以经济财政上之援助,致使日本得势,则英美等国在华之投资,以及其他一切经济利益,诚有被暴日歧视甚或没收之可能。关于英美在华之投资,据莱茂氏(C. F. Remer)之估计,英国在华之投资为11.9万万美元,上海占75%。美国在华之投资为1.9万万美元,上海占64%。关于英美在日之投资,据国际事务皇家研究院在一九三七年出版之国际投资一书所载,美国在日投资,至一九三三年底共为4.4万万美元(大部分为政府债券);英国在日投资,至一九三〇年止,共为6 300万镑。又据寇德斯莱(Robert Kirder-sley)之统计,截至一九三六年底止,英国在日本之投资为5 300万镑(大部分为政府债券)。在中国之投资,为4 100万镑(见Economic Journal, Dec.1, 1937)。于此可见英美在中日之投资,为数不大。即使为和平奋斗而牺牲,在富于资本之英美视之,因值不得顾虑也。

二 经济制裁对日之压力

日本为资源缺乏之工业国。其经济基础建立于国际贸易之上,一方面借进口贸易以取得原料;他方面借出口贸易以销售其制品。出口贸易被封锁,所有制品不能在国外市场销售,无法获得外汇以购取所需要之原料,则大多数工业将以缺乏原料故,只有停业,其结果足引起经济总崩溃。盖如下表所载,出口贸易约占其工业总生产25%强,连带关系之重大,于此可见。

第三表 日本出口贸易值与全国总生产值之比较(单位百万日元)

年 份	农业生产	工业生产	矿林水及畜产	输 出	输出对工业生产之百分比
一九一九	4 220	8 700	440	2 218	25.5%

又如进口贸易被封锁,则大多数工业无法取得原料,将被迫停业,以至于引起经济总崩溃,其理同上。设使日本工业各部门平均发展,其所需要之原料,由多数国家均分供给,则可利用经济制裁国不易取得一致行动及严密实施之漏洞,借以逃避制裁之压力,无如日本产业如第四表所示,集中于纺织业,而输出集中于蚕丝及棉丝布二项。又如第一表所示,其所需要之原料,大都由英美荷法苏五国所供给。故其经济易被此等国家所控制,诚是大弱点。

第四表　日本各工业部门在一九二九年之生产额

单位百万日元（录自东亚贸易大观）

纺织	金属	机械	化学	印刷	食料	其他	共计
2 208	591	544	957	168	886	545	5 719
34%	10%	10%	16%	3%	16%	10%	100%

日本重要输出品之价值及其在总输出中所占之百分比

年份	输出总值 单位千日元	蚕丝 价值千元	百分比	棉布 价值千元	百分比	人造丝织品	
						价值千元	百分比
1929	2 103 726	781 040	37%	412 706	20%	—	—
1931	1 121 580	355 393	31%	198 731	18%	39 710	3%
1932	1 365 812	382 366	28%	288 712	21%	65 130	5%
1933	1 812 315	390 901	22%	383 215	21%	77 365	4%

  论者以为日本进口贸易如被封锁，可提倡节约运动，增加本国生产量，如铜，人造代替品（如人造汽油、羊毛、棉纱等），利用废旧材料（如橡皮及废铁等），及由非军需必要之用途，移作军需工业之用。再加贮囤之量（如一九三四年六月二十三日公布之煤汽油业法律，规定各煤油公司于一九三五年十月以前，须贮备供给半年之用。又海军军需库，据报亦贮存足供一年用之汽油），至少可支持若干时日。然究能支持几何时？在无确实统计资料以前，吾人不能武断假定。但贮藏充足军需品，以供长期之用，靡费至巨，负担深重，即使日本陆海军部能深谋远虑及之，若无巨款以备购置，亦属徒然。衡诸日本之经济能力——资本缺乏，而又财政困难——殊不易囤积一切军需品，以足供一年或半载之需，盖其量或能将军需上无大量需要之物，如镍、锑、水银及铅等，预作囤积，以供非常时之需要，尚在情理之中。据德维特氏之估计，日本在被制裁之环境下，足可维持半年至一年之期间（见 Foreign Policy Association Report for Dec.1, 1937）。此种估计，庶几近于事实。但德维尔特氏之估计，时在一九三七年末，距今一年又二月。日本在此期间之消耗，必有可观。大约言之，果若本被封锁，决不能再支持六个月之久，此亦殆近乎事实。

  论者以为日本进口贸易如被封锁，可利用现金由其友邦（如德、意）间接购入军需原料。此事诚属可能。然其可能输入数量，要视日本存金之多寡，及制裁国对于德意之购买量是否加以限制为断。关于后者，无从推断。

关于前者,有事实足资考证。原来日本在平时,已感维持固有输入之不易。盖近年来日本对外贸易,每年均有巨额入超:

第五表 日本之对外收支及存金表(单位百万日元)

年 份	商品贸易入超	勤务贸易出超	在满洲之投资
一九三五	14.7	144	373
一九三六	135.1	178	183
一九三七	636.0	120	—

本表录自德维尔特氏文,见前注。

其原因,一方面由于日元贬值过低及原料品价格回涨之结果,其在国外购买成本增高,又因日本经济随世界经济之复兴,需要更多原料之输入,故进口货量及货价同时增加;他方面日本输出贸易,因受各国增加关税之阻碍,无大增进。国际收支既不相抵,日元感受威胁,乃于一九三七年正月七日颁行购买外汇请核制,借以限制外汇之购买。同年九月临时国会开会复通过法律,授权政府限制或禁止若干种货物之进口,并调整此等进口货之分配及消费,以求输入之减少。但日元之威胁(日元汇率常在法定汇价一先令二便士之下),不以统制外汇及限制进口贸易之实施而能去除,不得不输出黄金以为维持。故有若干人士以为日本之准备金,几已用尽。据我们之估计,其情形约如下表:

第六表 日本政府及银行之存金与日本全国黄金产额
并附该国保有外国证券额(录自美国联邦局月刊,惟证券额一项系四月份估计值)
(录自美国 Foreign Policy Report, Dec.1, 1937)
(单位美元百万元)

年月	日本银行及政府之存金	日本保有之外国证券(系按旧平价两日之合一万元折成)	日本黄金产额	日本运往美国之金额
一九三七				
八月	261	443	4.0	37.7
九月			4.0	40.9
十月			3.9	19.9
十一月			4.4	37.1
十二月			4.7	18.8

续表

年月	日本银行及政府之存金	日本保有之外国证券（系按旧平价两日之合一万元折成）	日本黄金产额	日本运往美国之金额
一九三八				
一月			3.9	
二月			4.3	
三月			4.2	4.5
四月			4.5	23.3
总和			37.9	182.2
平均			4.0	26.0
一九三八年四月时之存金	116.7	443		

由此可见日本在一九三八年四月时，有现金 11 670 万美元及外国证券 44 300 万美元，可用作购买外货之需。惟此项证券是否能即时如数脱售，尚成问题。设能如数脱售，共可得 55 930 万美元，约合日本每年平均进口额六分之五。然自一九三八年四月以来，因向外国购买军需品及海运输船移作军用之故，商品及勤务之入超，较往年为大，故输出现金以为补偿之额亦大。据一九三八年八月十四日上海合众电，自三月八日至是日为止，日本黄金前后运往美国者，共为 35 280 万美元（一九三七年同期输美之黄金额约为 11 100 万美元，计增 24 100 万元）。若将原存之黄金及证券总额，再加五个月中之新产之黄金额 2 100 万元（每月产额以 450 万美元计算），减去上列输出额，得 22 750 万元。此即日本在一九三八年八月中旬所保有之黄金及外币之总额。若以全数用于购进外国货物（此属不可能之事。盖果如是，则币制动摇矣），如在平时，约足敷五个月之需。由此观之，日本被封锁，欲借现金（包括外国证券）托由第三国间接购进军需物品，最多只能维持五个月。

经济封锁，对于日本财政，亦有严重之打击，因其产业受封锁之后，或减少生产或倒闭。营业既少，缴税自减，此自然之理也。且年来日本锐意扩军，预算大增。民众一面受资本家之压迫（日本工人因国内经济复入繁荣状态，一九三七年每周工作时间延长，所得较一九三三年约高 7%，然生活费则增高 39%。故其生活情况，尚不如一九三二年之佳），他方面苦于重税,生活境况,已是苦楚,实不堪再加税之负担。因此日本财政极感苦难,自一九三一年来,均赖发行大量公债,以资弥补。历年公债发行数额如下表:

第七表　日本自一九三一年各年发行数额及其总额
（单位百万日元）

年　度	1931	1932	1933	1934	1935	1936	1937
公债发行额	123	6 596	7 531	7 425	6 784	7 038	8 225
总公债额	61 880	68 476	76 006	8 321	90 205	97 240	105 465

据一九三七年上期之统计,日本全国各银行购存公债约 50 万万元,约与其储蓄存款之总额相等,为各种存款总数(约 130 万万元)之 40%。故银行吸收公债之额,已超过于惯例 20% 之限度,而达与储蓄存款相等之最高限度矣。今后政府欲再发行公债,将有无法销售之苦闷。然而政府预算有增无减,由一九三一年度之 1 476 800 万元增至一九三六年度之 2 282 200 万元(内军费占 47.2%)。一九三七年度之预算为 2 892 800 万元。然国会已另指定 2 581 700 万元为中日战事费。两共约占全国总收入 40%。于此可见其负担之重。一九三七年度(至一九三八年三月止)约须发行 34 万万元之公债,方能平衡收支。如公债不能再发出,只得走入通货膨胀之一途。其结果将使民众困苦更加深重。

总上所论,美、英、荷、苏、法等国联合,或平行制裁日本,不出十个月,日本必将崩溃。故经济制裁应为对外宣传之目的、外交之方针。至于能否劝改各国实施制裁,在于外交运用之巧妙矣。

（原载《外交研究》1939 年第 1 卷第 2 期）

我国当前外汇问题的出路

一 抗战以来的外汇政策

自从卢沟桥事变发生以来,我国外汇政策已经遇几次转变。大概可分为下列六个阶段:

从七七事变起,至八一五财政部公布非常时期安定金融办法限制提现止,为第一阶段,是放任政策时期。在此期间,政府当局不因为抗战发生,而在金融上采取紧急措施,以防止资金外逃而保持法币准备金,对于外汇依旧以英币一先令二便士半或美币二九元七五的法价无限制地供给。一般缺乏民族意识的贪官,买办,商人,及资本家,深恐法币将来跌价,便乘机大批购买外汇,或投资国外,或待时牟利。所以在这四十日内,中央银行卖出的外汇达八百万镑,每日平均要占二十万镑,这是一个很大的数额,假如我们想念到向外国告借信用的不容易,例如向英国告借五十万镑信用贷款及五百万法币外汇平准基金,向美国订借二千五百美元的桐油贷款,向法国订借二百五十万镑信用借款,合共仅合一千二百五十万镑,是在抗战中二年期间费了很大努力才成功的。

从八一五至三一二财政部公布购买外汇请核规则统制汇兑止,为第二阶段,是以限制存款提现为阻碍逃资的手段,可称为半放任政策时期,这办法关了个人(除了贪污大吏,他们仍有捷径可通)逃资之门,并未断了金融界逃资国外之路,在防止资金外逃上,只有些微作用罢了。在非常时期安定金融办法颁布施行以后的八十日期间,中行卖出外汇数额,确实减少了,但这不能完全归功于非常时期安定金融办法,而上海战事比较的稳定,亦是一个重要原因。所以上海战事失利以后,又有大批资金外逃。当时个人资金以受提存之限制,不能随意购买外汇,惟金融界本身既不受该法之限制,运用大量资金购买外汇,以便从中牟利。所以十一月以后的逃资,都是金融界本身的资金,非常时期安定金融办法,未曾顾到此点,或许是政府当局的失察,也或许是故意留了方便之门。我不了解政府当局会那样信任银行界,对于他们的购买外汇,毫不加限制!银行界中难道不会有缺乏民族意识的人吗?

从三一二到八月中旬英商银行开始暗中设法支持黑市汇率止为第三阶段,是统制外汇官市而放任外汇黑市时期。自三一二及三一三财政部公布购买外汇请核规则及中央银行管理外汇办法以后,政府仍维持其原有汇率,但限制外汇之供给,非得政府核准,任何个人都无法依官价购得外汇,这样政府的外汇政策,才由放任转入统制之路。设使中央银行能完全依法办理(银行购取外汇后,中央银行总行或其香港通讯处,得向索外汇用途清单,以备稽考),绝无私心或徇情之事,非特私人无法逃资,即银行界逃资之门亦关闭了,敌伪企图套取外汇之阴谋,更无所施其技。然而事情决不如此顺利,要向购买外汇银行索核外汇用途清单,便不能很满意地做到,外商银行因为请购外汇数额不能如数核准,便于三月二十八日废止维持外汇法价的绅士协定;从此自由挂牌买卖外汇,我政府无法禁止,亦未设法解决,遂造成明的公的外汇黑市,这黑市非但是统制外汇的严重问题,亦是维持法币信用的难题,作者很早便如此主张,在二十七年十二月一日中国经济学社开年会时,曾发表过这样意见,且以明快的词句作结语:"假使外汇黑市无法解决,法定汇率以及法币信用是不能维持的。"这篇论文后来在《时事月报》第十九卷第七期(二十七年十二月号)披露出来,一面说明外汇黑市对于法币的威胁,同时指出解决黑市的途径:"今中国欲维持旧法定汇价,必使黑市(实为公开汇市)不影响政府管辖区域(沦陷区域事实上管不着,未便作为对象)内人民对于法币之信用;必须一面明白列举'正当需要'之外汇及其请购办法,同时维持此种'正当需要'之供给;一面查禁黑市,凡用黑市汇票购运之商品,如经查出,一律充公。"①换言之,要巩固法币的信用,必须推行隔离黑市政策,使我后方各省市和黑市所在区域隔离,以消去黑市汇率变动对于法币信用的影响,且统制我后方各省市对外汇兑和贸易,同时查禁我后方各省市内的黑市。可惜这点当时不能使政府当局采纳!

从去年八月中旬到今年三月九日中英合组外汇平准基金委员会止,为第四阶段,是为统制外汇官市而纵容外商银行支持外汇黑市时期。英国在华经营百年的主要利益是对华商业,设使对华商业被"日圆集团"或"日满支协同体"所摧毁,则上海租界以及其他特权,都要失了功能,终将消灭。为要保持对华商业利益,就要维持法币汇价以抵制"日圆集团"势力的扩

---

① 《时事月报》第十九卷第七期第十页。

张。所以在上海的英商银行,为保持他们自身的利益,暗中设法支持法币的汇率;因此汇价便无大变动。在第三阶段中,当市场上有大量外汇的需要,或有大量外汇的抛出时,汇价便立刻发生反应,这显然是由于任令其自由涨落变动的缘故。在这一阶段中,暗中设法支持汇价的英商,早已注意前一阶段中汇率自由变动的趋势而拟定了一个合理的汇价,作为平准的标准价:当黑市汇价高过于拟定的合理汇价时,便无限制地买进外汇,当市场汇率低过于拟定的平准汇率,便无限制地卖出外汇,如此汇率便稳定在八便士余,这事对于法币信用,在当时确有良好影响。第一,由于汇率的稳定,近远期汇价的差异趋于正常,外汇投机暂告平息,而有心逃资者,亦暂存观望态度了。第二,汇率的稳定可以坚定华北华中同胞对于法币的信心,使敌伪及收法币套取外汇的阴谋难于实现。后来财政部公开承认黑市场汇率,并继续设法维持,直到今日犹不欲更弦易辙,怕是受了这短期间小成功的影响。这不能不说是这一阶段所遗下的一粒恶种子!

从三月九日到七月一日财政部公布出口货物结汇领取汇价差额办法及进口物品申请购买外汇规则止,为第五阶段,是为政府在名义上保存旧法定汇价,而在事实上公开承认市场汇率,并以全力维持市场汇率时期。自三月九日中英合组外汇平准基金委员会,依照八便士二五之平准汇率,无限制地买卖外汇以后,市场汇率虽甚稳定,但平准基金之损失,大而且速。一千万镑外汇平准基金,在两个月内,业已耗去大半。不得已于五月中再增加外汇平准基金一千五百万镑,合前共计二千五百万镑。这虽是一个很大数额(以八便士二五之汇价折成法币,得七万二千七百万元),但总填补不了敌伪套取外汇、贸易入超、逃亡资本所合成的无底漏洞!所以外汇平准基金委员会在六月七日停止依八便士二五的汇率供给外汇,汇价自此便大跌落。六月九日外汇平准基金委员会又拟定六便士半为平准汇率,继续平准工作。前车之覆,后车不知借鉴,所以六便士半的汇率,只维持了四十天,又告失败了。此后财政当局依然只顾港沪少数商贾的利益,或别有苦衷,而忽略了民族利益,仍未放弃维持黑市场汇率的一贯政策!这一阶段的政策,实是大错。第一,耗损了二千余万镑的外汇,于事毫无补益,反在民众心理上引起不良反应。第二,就政策论,这是开倒车。抗战以后的金融政策,原是由第一阶段的放任而至第二阶段的限制,再进而至第三阶段的统制。设使再进一步加紧统制我后方各省市对外贸易并实行隔离黑市,非特统制之功效可冀,亦无违于抗战建国纲领所规定的经济政策。今财政部舍此前进坦道而硬要开倒车,不知何所为而出此?若曰为敌伪套取外汇开了方便之门,我不忍作如此想,若曰为自己利益造机会,我不能置信。若曰受了洋人的愚弄,我不欲作如此观。毕竟如何,只能让历史家去考证了。

从七月一日以来,为第六阶段,是为政府当局运用贬值政策,以冀恢复人民对于法币信心,而挽救黑市汇率下跌的殆势。依进口物品申请购买外汇规则:

(一)凡进口商经营之进口物品,不在禁止输入之列,而为国内所必需者,得依照本规向外汇审核委员会申请购买外汇。

(二)凡经核准购买之外汇,由指定之中国或交通银行,按照法价售给,但申请人须缴纳按法价与中交两行挂牌价格差额之平衡费。

此无异于废止旧法定汇价,而以中交两行挂牌价格为出售外汇的法价。例如八月九日中交两行挂牌汇价为三便士七五,则申请购买人以法币一元按法价购得十四便士半,除去缴纳平衡费十便士七五,实得三便士七五。实即中交银行挂牌价格。又依出口货物结汇领取汇价差额办法:

(一)所有出口货物应结外汇,除桐油、茶叶、猪鬃、矿产四类,因与易货偿债及储料有关,应由政府贸易机关,体察产销情形及国际市价,随时以优惠价格统筹收购运销外,其余货物,无论由政府贸易机关运销,或由商号自行贸易,概须依照法价将所得外汇售与中国或交通银行。其售价应得之法币,由中国或交通银行取得结汇人同意于指定之内地地点,以法币支付之。

(二)前项依照法价结汇之出口货物于实际结清汇额后,得凭结算证件,向结汇银行领取法价与该行挂牌价格之差额,结汇银行得向结汇人收取银行向例应得之手续费,但不得超过差额百分之三。

这个办法的真意,就在废弃旧法定汇价,①而采用中交两行挂牌汇价为购进外汇的价格,例如八月九日中交两行挂牌汇价为三便士七五,则出口商人以十四便士半之外汇,按法价售与中国银行计得法币一元,再加领回汇价差两元八角七分(当中交挂牌价格为三便士七五时,十便士七五合法币二元八角七分),共得三元八角七分,是即依中交银行挂牌价格出卖外汇所得之值。这个办法确是很巧妙,名义上保持法价,而实际上贬低了汇价,况且德匈诸国都已行之而有成效。不过我国情形特殊,此办法尚须有隔离黑市

---

① 《时事月报》第二十卷第七期二十八年七月号。

政策为之补充;否则无济于事。

在这阶段中,除了贬值以外,还在进行举借外资加强平准基金,以冀维持黑市汇率,只因借款没有成功,维持黑市汇率政策暂时搁浅;市场汇率抵不住种种压力,便由六便士半逐步下落:

日/月	6/6	7/6	8/6	9/6	10/6	11/6…17/7	18/7	19/7	20/7
英汇	8.25	7.25	6.5	6.531	6.5	6.5…6$\frac{9}{16}$	5.25	5.0	4.843 75
美汇									
港汇									

日/月	21/7…4/8	5/8	6/8	7/8	8/8	9/8	10/8
英汇	4$\frac{3}{8}$	4.093 75				3.75	3.50
美汇						7$\frac{1}{16}$	6.812 5
港汇	29.3	28.6	28.0	27.0	26.0		

在这样六个阶段中,政府当局的措施,似乎是很周到,除了上述种种办法外,去年四月曾颁布商人运货出口及售结外汇办法,继又公布维护生产促进外销办法,今年七月一日又公布非常时期禁止进口物品办法。这些办法,都在加强外汇管理,一方面要求促进输出及集中外汇,他方面要减少不必要货物之进口以节省外汇之消耗。但这些办法缺少了急要的一环——隔离黑市,而又失之迂回缓慢,所以维持汇价及巩固法币信用的目的,始终相距很远。这是由于财政当局没有认识法币问题的核心,所有一切设施皆落边际,时至今日,法币的市场汇价已不及法币四分之一,贤明的政府当局,再不应该彷徨歧途——把法币的问题重加考虑,认清了问题的核心,再作对症下药的措施,才能达到巩固法币信用的目的。

二 法币的中心问题及其解决之途径

法币的中心问题,在于外汇官市以外,有明的公的外汇黑市,而此黑市汇率呈现一种下跌的趋势。这可以事实来说明的。例如去年秋季有许多人对于法币信用抱着忧虑,是由于五六七月间上海黑市汇价的猛跌。今年六月以来,又有许多人在那里怀疑法币信用的不稳,亦是由于六月七日及七月十八日以后黑市汇价的下跌。

上海外汇黑市的性质,和其他统制外汇国家的外汇黑市不同[①]。它的组成,有外商银行,亦有华商银行,它的位置,是在租界内,中国政府既无权查禁,亦不曾设法解决。所以上海外汇黑市,在当初便是一个明的公的自由市,而不是暗的私的黑市。汇率的变动,足以影响法币信用。因此统制汇兑的作用,便失去了一部分的效能。自今年三月九日中英合组外汇平准基金委员会,进行平准外汇黑市汇率,这黑市便升了格,由明的公的自由市,进而为官方承认的自由市,或称半官式的汇市,惟半官或汇市的汇率,才是法币的真实汇率。原先一先令二便士半或美元二角九分七五的法定汇率,虽未经明令放弃,在事实上,已是等于虚设,不再为一般人所注意,这半官式汇市汇率的跌风摇动法币信用的势力,未尝因为法定汇率的不变而削弱。因此敌人破坏法币的宿谋,就有了鹄的:只向半官式的黑市进攻,对于法定汇率或正式官市,可不必去顾虑了。

今日法币之所以成为问题,既是由于半官式黑市的存在及其汇率的下跌,故欲谋巩固法币的信用,必先解决外汇黑市问题。解决之道,不外下列三种办法:

(甲) 根本禁绝黑市;

(乙) 维持黑市汇率,使无甚变动;

(丙) 隔离黑市,使黑市汇价的变动,不能影响到法币的信用。

假使要禁绝黑市,因为黑市的大本营在上海租界,其次在香港,必须获得香港政府及租界当局的诚意协助查禁,更须要英美法政府不怕敌国的威胁,坚决的来支援租界当局及香港政府的认真查禁黑市。然而这点困难很多。所以解决黑市问题的途径,只剩乙丙两种办法。

三 维持黑市汇率

设使黑市汇率能维持于一定高度的水准,则黑市虽存在,亦无损于法币的信用。例如从去年八月到今年五月,因为黑市汇率始终在八便士的水准上,人民对于法币的信心,亦能安定下去。所以维持黑市汇率,不失为巩固法币信用的一种办法。

维持黑市汇率的办法,约有下列二种:一为统制黑市,一为依照拟定的平准价无限制买卖外汇。

---

① 《时事月报》第十九卷第七期第九页。

今日如欲统制黑市,其情形不比去年三月中我政府实行统制外汇官市时为优。去年统制外汇之所以失败,只因外商银行或租界中银行不受我政府之统制,亦不与我以协助。知乎此就可料想到统制黑市的困难了。

依照拟定的平准价无限制买卖外汇,就是我财政当局所采行的一贯政策。到了今日,他们似乎尚无改弦易辙的决心。这个政策,除非我有无限量的外汇基金,取之不尽,用之不竭,才能把黑市汇率永远维持下去,否则直似金沙填补无底洞,是不可能之事。六月七日汇率的下跌,虽说是有计划的重新调整外汇水准,实是难以为继的表征。所以七月十八日以后,汇率毕竟崩溃下来,事实胜于雄辩,平准基金办法已告失败。

我们始终觉得平准基金办法,是不适宜于目前环境的。我们既要依照拟定的汇价无限制地买卖外汇,以冀稳定汇率,敌人便可用种种方法吸收法币,把法币在黑市中抛出来换取外汇,企图消耗我们的外汇平准基金,扰乱黑市汇率,以打破法币信用。敌人吸收法币的计谋多端,防不胜防,亦有不及防备者。所以敌伪所能收集之法币,非特数额巨大,且能继续不断。盐税统税及海关税等,每月皆有收入。其中海关税收一项,月可达法币一万六千余万元。此外敌伪或欲压低伪币对法币之比率,向市场收购法币;或规定洋货由日商专卖,而倭人售货时,只收伪钞或军用票。因此凡欲购买洋货者,必先以法币向日人特设的兑换局,把法币兑为伪钞,如是伪钞既藉以推行,而法币亦被敌伪所吸收;或利用勾通津沪汇兑之奸商,在津交给奸商银行以伪钞托其汇沪支付法币,如是伪钞既可利用对沪通汇之便利,增加一种用途,复可吸收我在沪之法币,用以套取外汇。凡此种种方法,皆可继续行之,无有限制。敌伪收得之法币,在黑市中换取外汇后,即归还于流通界,仍可为敌伪所吸收。如此轮回不已,无有终止。以有限的外汇平准基金,怎能应付此轮回不已之套取?及今日敌伪的套取外汇,是有计划的,有步骤的,其用意,在于打破黑市汇价,以摇动法币的信用。至于由套取外汇以获得利益,是其次要作用罢了。在这种环境之下,要想以无限制买卖外汇办法来维持黑市汇价,是不能成功的。假如说这事可以成功,那么金沙亦能填满无底洞了!

以无限制买卖方法维持黑市汇率,在目前情形下,固属不可能之事,即使能之,亦属害多利少:

第一,维持黑市汇率于一定之水准,适足便利敌伪套取外汇,无异于资敌以粮,实与去年统制外汇之原意相反。

第二,维持黑市汇率于一定的水准,适足帮助敌人实现其以战养战的计划。敌人所需要之洋货,原须在日本输入者,今皆改由上海进口。其支付进口货价之外汇,则向上海黑市收购。因我维持黑市汇率之故,间接由我外汇平准基金供给,是无异使敌人利用中国国力以打击中国!

第三,维持黑市汇率,适足便利敌货及其他外国货物进口,以致入超增大而加重黑市的压力。

如此看来,法币黑市汇价,非特不能维持,且亦不应维持。我们只有隔离黑市,使黑市汇率的变动,不能影响到我后方各省市的法币信用。

四 隔离黑市政策

我始终觉得要维持外汇及巩固法币信用,必须隔离黑市。这个主张,业已发表过三次。第一次是在去年十二月《时事月报》中《维持法定汇价与黑市汇价》一文,①第二次是在今年七月《时事月报》中《再论维持外汇与黑市汇价》一文。第三次是在今年八月二十三日《中央日报》中《如何消去外汇黑市对于法币信用之威胁》。今为便利读者计,再写在这里。

一地域和其他地域的经济关系,是随着贸易汇兑而存在。这是经济学中的一般原理。所以贸易和汇兑,犹如两水柱间的连通水管。两水柱中的水,藉连通水管之流通,常使两水柱中水位保持相等。同理,贸易和汇兑能使各地域的物价发生调整变动,恒趋于相等;其货币亦因此而有一定的平价。今如此一地域统制其对他处之贸易和汇兑,则其物价水准将不因他处物价水准涨落而发生相应变动,其货币价值之变动,因亦与他处货币价值的变动脱节。(例如一九三一年以后的德国,因厉行统制其对外全部贸易和汇兑,其物价水准与马克价值,不因他国物价水准和货币价值涨落而发生相应变动。遂与其他各国物价水准及货币价值脱节。至于发行准备金的多少,并不能影响到纸币的价值。俄国情形,亦是如此。)犹如两柱间的连通水管被阻塞以后,其水位各自独立而不必相等。隔离黑市的用意,就是要使我后方各省市的法币汇率和物价水准,勿受上海黑市汇率和物价水准的影响。因此我后方各省市的人民,对于法币的信用,可不因上海外汇黑市汇率的跌落而发生动摇。故隔离黑市的办法,只须严格统制我对外(包括上海、香港及游击区在内)的全部贸易和汇兑。凡我后方省市输往港沪及游击区域之一切货物,如同输往外国,一律须结售外汇(或由国营),否则不准报关

---

① 《时事月报》第十九卷第七期第十页。

出口。又凡自我后方各省区汇款至港沪及游击区内，视若汇款至外国，必属正当需要而有充实证明，并经管理当局核准，方得汇出，否则不得汇出。

为建立信用以安定人心起见，关于正当需要外汇的范围及请购外汇的手续，政府应厘订章则，用作管理标准。如是则请购外汇者，无幸冀之心，而主持审核的当局，以有章则可资遵循，可免去上年三月初行统制外汇时的错误：只求参考入超而不注意正当需要，或故示宽大而不依据政策。果若上下同心，奉公守法，则信用确立。信用立，则外汇投机之风，及社会不安之心理，皆可平定下去，而法币不可动摇了。

对于汇款至上海及游击区域，亦应明白规定，正当需要汇款的范围及请购汇款的手续。如是则无正当需要者，不得汇出汇款，有正当需要者，可依章随时汇出汇款，而毋庸缴纳高额汇水。现行制度，凡汇款至上海，不问其汇款是否属于正当需要，一律须缴纳百分四十之汇水。实可以说是一种盲目政策。经营申汇的私家银行，可从汇款业务获得过分利得；有正当需要而汇款至上海者，必须缴纳百分四十之汇水，无异于被剥夺了百分四十之价值。因此，在后方各省市工作人员，有时为接济留居沦陷区内家眷，深感汇水剥夺之痛苦。今如实行统制汇款制度，此种盲目政策的弱点，一定可以减免去的。

隔离港沪及游击区以后，我后方各省市内法币对外汇兑，只许有官市，不容有黑市。如有私相买卖，一经查出，定予严惩，务使黑市根本绝迹。如此则我后方各省市内法币对外汇价，只有官市法定汇率，无所谓黑市汇价或自由市汇价；我后方各省市内的法币，与上海及游击区内的法币，如同两种不同的货币，各有各的汇价；而上海黑市汇价的涨落，如同他国货币汇价的变动，不能影响到我后方各省市内法币的信用。这可与一九三一年九月实行统制贸易和汇兑以后的德国情形相比拟，德国货币有自由马克、封锁马克、登记马克、证券马克、清算马克、阿斯奇马克等种类。这些马克在国外的价值，各不相等，但在国内的购买力均无差别。且其自由马克之价值，并未受其他各种马克汇率变动的影响。这是由于德国严密统制其对外全部贸易与汇兑的结果。故若我政府严格统制我后方各省市对港、沪、游击区，及其他外国全部贸易与汇兑，则法币在上海黑市场的汇率，决不能影响到后方法币的信用，真如德国登记马克在伦敦市场的汇率，不能影响到自由马克的信用一样。上海黑市汇率，既不能影响到我后方各省市法币的信用，自可任其自由涨落，毋庸顾虑，而政府当局亦可安心放弃其维持黑市汇率的一贯政策矣。

隔离黑市政策推行以后,游击区内法币,依然可被敌伪所吸收,但彼将苦无所用。设使敌伪把收集得的法币,偷运至我后方各省市内,要想套取外汇,因请购外汇的法制綦严,非属正当需要而备有充实证件者,不得核准购买。故套取外汇的企图,无法实现。若要想用以购运货物出口,以谋间接换取外汇,又因我统制贸易,非先结售外汇,不得出口(若我实行国营国际贸易,则统制尤为严密),故换取物资的企图,亦无法实现。所可利用者,只能收买汉奸或间谍而已。

如此说来,隔离黑市政策的主旨,在巩固我后方各省市内法币的信用。其办法包括有三部分:

(甲)统制我后方各省市对外(包括港沪及游击区域在内)的全部贸易与汇兑。

(乙)明白规定正当需要外汇的范围及请购外汇的手续,并维持供给此正当需要的外汇。

(丙)严禁我后方各省内黑市。

这些办法,想不至有行不通的地方。果如财政当局决意为全民族着想,为抗战建国着想,我相信他将来一定会走上这条路,因为没有更好的第二条路可走。

五 隔离黑市政策对游击区内法币生命的影响

隔离黑市并放弃以政府力量维持黑市汇价以后,黑市汇率的变动必大,且将呈现一种下跌的趋势。但于游击区内法币,可不至发生若何重大影响。

游击区内法币,受敌伪种种方法的破坏与压迫,自不免有保存为难之感。在华北方面,敌军占领区内,自伪政府实行严禁通用以后,事实上极难存在。其流通境界,几限于我游击队驻管区及租界内。隔离黑市政策推行以后,在此等区域内的法币,以有游击队及租界当局之支持,必仍可通用,将不因黑市汇率的跌落而动摇。再就华中方面言,据可靠方面消息,华兴银行对于华兴券的流通地域问题,将以内地为发行之重心,以上海为其次要地点。这是因为内地人民很少需要外汇,故在内地发行的钞券,只须有少量的外汇准备,可以减轻筹措外汇基金的困难。设如伪政府为求伪钞之推行,实行禁止法币在其管领区域内流通,我亦无奈彼何。即使我能维持黑市汇率而不变,亦无补于事。法币在游击区内作孤军奋斗,不能凭藉爱国情绪或其他心理作用以为支援。维持黑市汇价,虽不失为维系游击区内民众对于法币信任心的一种手段,然亦抵不住政治压力——雷厉风行的禁止通用。所以要保持游击区内法币的流通,只有加强游击队的实力,以保持游击区内广大地域的政权。至于被占领区域,一定要到恢复政权以后,才能恢复法币的流通。如此说来,维持黑市汇价,决不可能保持敌占区域内法币的生命;而隔离黑市政策,亦不足为害了。再说得彻底一点,时在今日,未有政权沦亡而币制能独存之事。即使能之,亦惟苟延残喘于一时罢了。伪联合准备银行及伪华兴银行发行伪钞及强制通用,我们既无法阻止,敌伪便可增发伪钞用作用费或用以吸收沦陷区内的物资,或完成其他目的。在此情形下,即使法币能在敌占领区域勉强行使,亦不足妨碍其大计。反之,设使沦陷区内法币全被伪币代替了,只要法币不能用以套取外汇,敌人只是发出伪钞换进法币。此法币于彼既无甚用处,自不能加大他的好处,况且将来我获最后胜利时,币制将随政权同时恢复原来真面目。今日何必为沦陷区内少数法币的目前的短时流通事,而白耗费大量的外汇呢!

(原载《新政治》1939年第3卷第1期)

国际贸易之理论

一 绪 论

国际贸易之理论,通常皆以劳工价值论为依据,似欠完备。特自经济平衡普通理论,导出国际贸易理论,以补劳工价值论之缺陷。盖在现实经济社会,劳工只是生产因素之一;此外尚有土地、天然资源、厂屋、机器,及原料等,不能以其一,代表其他。故价值之大小,未可以劳工之多少为断。更有进者,生产因素,每以专门化之故,不能任意移用。设使移用,则其生产效力,必大减低。是故专门化之生产因素,除特殊情形外,实无有移用者,生产因素之专门化,或以运输费过高,或以技术上不适宜于第二种用途故,其理由不一。此种移转之阻碍,有永存者,有于相当时期之后能克服者,例如工人经过训练之后,即可移转使用是也。一国之生产因素,既以专门化之故,有不能任意移用者,则国际贸易所引起之国际分工运动,恐不如理想上之有利。盖生产成本比较劣势之工业,因舶来品之竞争而衰落,所有专门化之生产因素,既不能移转使用,遂成废物。此种损失,在以劳工价值论为根据之国际贸易论未尝计入。兹篇亦将论述之。

[**劳工价值论之经济平衡观**] 劳工价值论之引用,原为确定 A、B 两种商品在甲、乙两国中之比较价格。若从经济平衡之立场论之,可用图表之如次:

(i)设生产成本为恒量。令 A 商品每单位之劳工成本为一工,B 商品每单位之劳工成本为二工。如图 1,A 商品之生产量以横轴表之,B 商品之生产量以纵轴表之,则此两轴间任何一点 P,代表商品 A 与商品 B 之一种配比。若以劳工之全数,用于 A 商品之生产,则其生产量为 Oa。若将生产 A 之劳工,移转于 B 之生产,则每放弃 A 商品两单位,可得 B 商品一单位,如是所有之劳工,或生产 A 商品量为 Oa' 及 B 商品量为 Ob',或生产 A 商品量为 Oa'' 及 B 商品量为 Ob'',如是类推。而 P 点恒在一直线上①,是为替代曲线(Substitution Curve),意即 B 商品之 Ob' 量,替代 A 商品之 $a'a$ 量,B 商品之 $b'b''$ 量,替代 A 商品之 $a''a'$ 量,以生产也,故其交换比等于 2 比 1,即两个 A 交换一个 B。

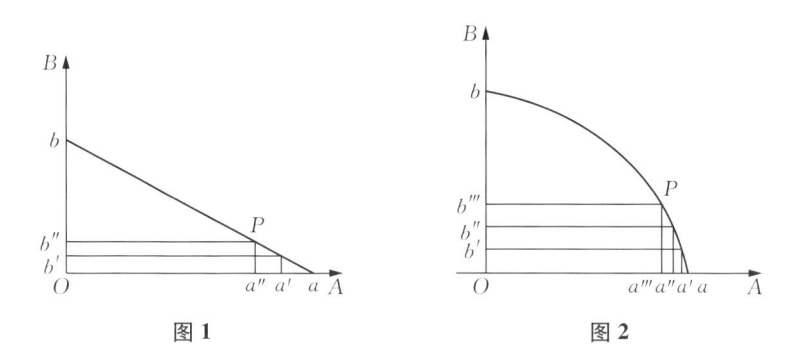

图 1

图 2

（ii）设生产成本为渐增,则替代曲线之形状如图 2,若将所有劳工以生产 A,可得 Oa。今欲生产 B 商品之 Ob' 量,必须放弃 A 商品之 $a'a$ 量。欲再生产 B 商品之 $b'b''$ 量,必须再放弃 A 商品之 $a''a'$ 量,如是类推。B 商品之生产量愈增多,则 B 之生产成本愈增大,A 之生产成本愈减小,每欲增多 B 商品一单位,必须放弃更大之 A 商品量以相替代。故若 $Ob'=b'b''=b''b'''$,则 $a'a<a''a'<a'''a''$,因之替代曲线必凹向原点 O,如图 2 所示(设图 2 之曲线为圆 $x^2+y^2=r^2$,则当 $y=0$,$x=r$,$y=1$,$x_1=\sqrt{r^2-1}$,$y=2$,$x^2=\sqrt{r^2-2^2}$,等等,$aa'=r-\sqrt{r^2-1}$,$a'a''=\sqrt{r^2-1}-\sqrt{r^2-4}$,$a''a'''=\sqrt{r^2-4}-\sqrt{r^2-9}$,故 $a<a'a''<a''a'''$)。

在生产成本为恒量之情形中,A 商品与 B 商品之交换比,完全由供给决定之;需求仅决定 A 生产量与 B 生产量的相对数。但在生产成本渐增之情形中,需求不仅决定 A 与 B 之相对的生产量,且亦影响 A 与 B 之交换比值。盖 A 与 B 之生产成本,随 A 与 B 之相对生产量而变,其交换比等于边际成本之比,而边际成本之比,又等于边际替代比。设如 A 与 B 之生产配比点为 P,则 A 与 B 之交换比(即替代比)为 $\dfrac{b'b''}{a'a''}$。此值是 $a'a''$ 趋于无限小时,为 P 点切线之斜度,故替代比亦可以切线表之,今欲增多 B 商品之 $b'b''$ 量,必须放弃 A 商品之 $a'a''$ 量。反之,如欲增多 A 商品之 $a'a''$ 量,必须放弃 B 商

---

① 此直线之方程式为 $y=-\dfrac{1}{2}x+\dfrac{1}{2}a$。

品量之 $b'b''$ 量,故 B 商品的 $b'b''$ 量所以替代 A 商品之 $a'a''$ 量而生产也。设 A 与 B 之交换比,不等于替代比,则为非平衡之状态,必有增多 A 生产及减少 B 生产之倾向;否则将有增多 B 生产及减少 A 生产之倾向。两者必居其一。

[多元成本价值论之经济平衡观] 上述理论,可应用于多元生产成本之情形,盖 A 与 B 两种商品相互替代生产之条件,可逐步求得之。此等条件可用曲线表示之,即为替代曲线,如需求为已知,则 A 与 B 之交换比,等于边际成本之比,在测量边际成本时,须以奥国学派之观念为根据。彼之所谓边际成本,非最后一单位之生产成本,乃是因生产此最后一单位商品而被放弃生产之替代物(Alternatives forgone)。例如 A 与 B 两种商品,当 A 之生产量,由 $(x-1)$ 增为 x,则 B 之生产量必须减少。所减少之量,即是 A 商品生产量为 x 时之边际成本。所谓 A 与 B 之交换价值,即此种意味上之边际成本之比。

生产因素之配合,要视 A 与 B 生产量之大小为转移。设欲增多而减少 A 与 B 之生产,则适用于 B 而不适用于 A 之生产工具,将增加使用而抬高其价值。至若适于 A 而不适于 B 之生产工具,将有一部分被废弃而无所用,其价值大减。是故专门化之生产因素,常因 A 与 B 生产量之消长,而变动其价值,因而影响所有权者之收入。此点将于后节再论及之。

[替代曲线之形状] 替代曲线之形状,与生产因素之专门化有关。设大多数生产因素能同时适用于 A 及 B 之生产,则替代曲线之曲度,较为圆直。如需求突有变动,对于 A 商品及 B 商品价格之影响,必甚微小。今如大多数生产因素为专门化,能适用于 A 之生产者,除非忍受甚大损失,不能移用于 B 之生产;能适于 B 之生产者,亦除非忍受甚大之损失,不能移用于 A 之生产,则替代曲线呈弯折形。此时需求如偶有变动,对于 A 及 B 价格之影响,必甚显著,例如 A 为农产物,B 为工业制品,则 A 及 B 之生产因素中,惟有劳工为可移转使用者,然在短时期内,此劳工亦殊少移转者。故其代替曲线,应有一曲折点。意即 A 之产量,不能因 B 之产量大减,而有所大增也。设如 A 及 B 之生产因素中,均为绝对不能通用者,则其替代曲线,当如 L 形,意即 A 之生产量,绝不能因 B 之生产量之减缩而有所增加也。在此情形下,需求如偶有变动,A 及 B 价格之相应变动,必极剧烈,盖生产事业,一时不能适应此新环境也。

生产因素之能否移用,不能脱离时间而言。在短时期内,大多数生产因素,如工厂、劳工及工厂设备等,几皆不能移转使用者,统称之为专门化之生产因素,亦无不可。但在长时期中,无论工厂与机器等资本货(Capital Goods)皆将变成老旧。其所代表之资本(Capital),此时可任意投资于新事业,以适应新环境之需要。工人亦能于长时期中,经过新训练而服务于新兴事业。假如时期极长,更有新时代之工人,起而替代原有之老工人,其能移转使用,自不待言。故就长时期论,所有生产因素,几无不可以移转使用者。是故替代曲线之形状,就长期言,大都为圆直形,就短时期言,大都为弯折形。

生产事业以有专门化之生产因素故,不能于短时期中,适应需要之减退而减少其生产量。盖自企业家言,若将生产量锐减,必有专门化生产工具之一部分,成为废物,或须忍受重大损失,移转于他业使用。为减少损失计,如其产业价格能支付主要成本,必照旧生产。是故需求减退之后,供给存旧,物价跌落。但经过相当时期之后,专门化生产因素,逐渐耗损,不复添置,其产量始渐减少,价格亦渐回复。反之,需求急增之产业,其工厂设备之添置,新工人之训练,及新工厂之创办,均须经过相当时期方能成功,故需求急增之后,产量不能于短时期中,相应增加,遂形成物价之膨涨。但经过相当期间,产业设备之扩张,逐渐成功,产量渐增,以应新增之需求,物价始告平复。故 A 与 B 之相对价格,在短期中,可因需求之消长而发生显著之变动,在长期中,不因需求之变动而生大变动。替代曲线之弯折形状,实即表示 A 与 B 相对价格之急剧变动,是故替代曲线之形状,一面能表示专门化生产因素之多寡,他方面足表示相对价格变动之大小。

上述现象,可于一国增收关税之情形中见之。进口货之需求必因关税之增高而减少。同时该国出口货之需求,以进口货减少故而减小,受关税保护之产业,以需要增加故而逐渐扩张。

[经济平衡学说在货币经济社会中之应用] 在货币经济社会中,商品间之替代关系非直接的而是间接的,其中介为货币。所有一切替代曲线,以有货币为共通中介故,皆变为成本曲线,而成本之计算单位为货币。故所谓成本,系指"货币成本"(Money Cost)而言。

上述经济平衡理论,在下列三个假定条件之下,能完全适用于货币经济社会。

(i)任何商品之价格,等于其边际生产成本,此生产成本,即用以生产最后一单位商品[即商品之生产量,由$(x-1)$增为x时]所需各生产因素之和。

(ii)任何生产因素之各单位,如能任意移动且可互相替代使用,则无论其用途如何,其价格相等。

（iii）每个生产因素（包括不能移动及专门化之生产因素在内）之价格,均等于其边际生产能力。故若生产因素之单位相同,且能互相替代使用,则无论其用途如何,均有相等之价格。反之,生产因素之价格相等者,得互相替代使用。

此等条件,因竞争之存在而确立。在现实社会中,工人、地主及资本家,将使用其劳工,土地及资本于报酬最高之途径。同时,企业家之运用此等生产因素也,必求最适当之配合,以达最高之生产效力,以得最大之收入（Incomes）,是故任何产业中如有一种生产因素之边际生产能力,不等于其价格,则企业家将减少此生产因素,以减低其成本,而此被裁减之生产因素,将移入于他种产业或他种用途,以提高其生产能力,使与价格相等。反之,如有一企业中,某生产因素之生产能力大于其价格时,则企业家将增用此种生产因素,以增加其收入,由是观之,自由竞争能使生产因素之价格与边际生产能力,在各种产业中,均能相等。

依上所论,任何生产因素之价格,总等于其边际生产量之价值,因此,等价之生产因素,在边际情形中,可互相替代（但此种替代,有时须全部生产因素,在各产业中重新配合后,方能成功）,又任何商品之价格,等于边际成本（即最后一单位商品所需各生产因素之价格之和）,故边际成本相等之两商品,其价格必相等。而价格相等之两商品,其边际成本必相等。是故 A 商品一单位,所可换取之 B 商品量,其边际成本必相等,亦即谓此 B 商品量所需之各生产因素之价格和,等于 A 商品一单位所需之各生产因素之价格和。换言之,A 商品与 B 商品之交换比,等于其替代比或边际货币成本之比。

二 基于经济平衡论的比较成本学说

前论比较成本学说,以劳工价值论为前提。今以经济平衡代替劳工成本之后,比较成本学说,能否继续成立,是为当前之问题,特证明其存在如下。

［建筑于替代比上之比较成本学说］　前论比较成本学说,以真实劳工成本为根据。在经济平衡中,交换比等于替代比。故其替代比与劳工价值论中之劳工成本相当,今比较成本学说,亦可建筑于替代比之上。设 A 与 B 之替代比,在甲国为 1 比 3,即 A 商品一单位,可换取 B 商品三单位;在乙国,为 1 比 2,即 A 商品一单位,可换取 B 商品二单位,则甲、乙两国通商之

结果,甲国将专力于 B 之生产而输入 A,同时乙国将从事于 A 之生产而输入 B。换言之,甲国将从事于生产成本比较优势之商品,乙国亦然。又分工之结果,足使甲乙两国之总生产量增加,亦可根据替代比以证明之。

(i) 设甲、乙两国各自生产 A 与 B 两种商品。

国　别	A	B	总量
甲	1	3	1A+3B
乙	1	2	1A+2B
总量	2A	5B	2A+5B

(ii) 设甲国专力于 B 之生产,则依替代比之意义,以生产 A 商品一单位之成本,移用于 B 之生产,可得 B 商品三单位。同理,乙国专力于 A 商品之生产,则原先用于生产 B 商品二单位之成本,移用于 A 之生产,可得 A 商品一单位。故两国之总生产量,以分工故,由两 A 加五 B,增为两 A 加六 B。

国别	A	B	总量
甲		6	6B
乙	2		2A
总量	2A	6B	2A+6B

是故比较成本学说之成立,不必以劳工价值论为前提,乃有普通理论为根据,因之建筑于比较成本学说上之国际贸易,遂成定论。

三　产业适应变动对于国际贸易利得之影响

[产业适应变动足破坏已存资本]　上述国际贸易之理论,包含有二种假设:

(i) 一国之内,所有生产因素,完全能任意移动;

(ii) 一国之产业,能依国际分工途径推进,而无损失。此等假设,以有专门化生产之因素之故,不能满足。而减轻关税所引起之产业变动,必使原先受关税保护之产业,遭受损失。盖此等产业中之专门化生产因素,如土地、房屋、机器半制品等,既不能移转于其他用途,只得减低价格,甚则弃为废物,因此其业主之收入大减。拥护关税论者,每持此以为反对减低关税之理由,其言曰减低关税所引起之产业适应变动,在于毁灭大量现存资本,以求将来生产量之增加,论其事,无异于此现存财富交换渺茫希望,论其代价,是牺牲今世之幸福,以增进后人之幸福,盖生产量之增加,必须产业适应变动(Adjustments and Adaptations)完成之后,方能实现故也。泛欧关税同盟之不能实现,此种论调与有力焉。

[产业适应变动对于专门化生产因素价格之影响] 产业适应变动所引起之资本损失,事实上不如上述之甚,且于国富之影响甚微。兹为简明计,举例说明之如次:

设某国有铁矿。其钢铁事业皆以此为基本。今因国外同业之竞争,使物价低落,以致该项工业之一部或全部停息,试追究其停业之过程与影响。

外国铁与钢价格之低落,可因下列原因之一而来:或因某国关税减低;或因运输费减轻;或因外国铁钢业技术突进而不为某国所知;或因外国政府津贴输出业;或因外国须长期对外付款(Unilateral Payments),以致成本降落。为说明便利计,兹假定外国铁钢价格之低落,非暂时现象,而有持久性。

某国铁钢业厂家之收支,或如下表:

收　　项	
出产品之销售收入	100
支　　项	
(1) 工资薪俸及原料等费及其利息	50
(2) 固定资本如厂屋,机器等之利息与折旧	20
(3) 地租包括铁矿在内	30
	100

第一项之 50,为对于可移动且非专门化之生产因素之支出。如果必要,此等因素可随时移用于其他用途。第二项为对于固定资本之支付,即马锡尔氏之所谓几似地租(Quasi-rent)。此等资本货物,非至老旧且其折旧准备金积至原额时,不能移转使用。第三项为对于完全专门化,生产因素之支付;绝对不能移转于其他业使用。

今设铁钢之价格降落,使该厂之收入减小 30,对于厂家言,此为甚大之损失。然该厂不因此而停业,盖如继续生产,地租虽不可收获;尚能获得固定资本与流动资本之利息,设使停业,即此固定资本之利息,亦不能得。两相比较,停业自不如继续生产之为愈。故某国之生产量,不减财富如旧。又消费者,以铁钢之价廉而获利,故厂家之损失,为消费者之利得所抵消。惟矿场之价值全消。今设铁钢之价格降落更甚,使该厂之收入又减小 10 或 15,此时厂家之损失更大。然以生产之结果,尚能支付流动资本及其利息(即第一项所包含之费用),并能为固定资本获得利息少许,该厂必继续生产而将固定资本之价值估低:能移用之资本货物,减至其他用途所有之价值,盖不能移用之物,减至材料(Scrap)所有之价值。至此阶段,几似地租及固定资本殆可谓完全消失,然生产犹未得减,因之国富仍旧不变。且厂家之损失,又为消费者之利得所抵消,是乃个人财富之重分配,非全国财富之有消长也。

设铁钢之价格低落更甚,使厂家之收入,非但无以支付第一项及第二项之费用,且不足支付第三项之费用;或该厂固定资本货物之一部分破旧须至修理或重置者,则该厂只得停业。在此情况之下,所有工人雇员及原料等,均可移转于其他有利产业,从事生产,自无所谓损失。惟固定资本货物,既因停业而全部废置,所有折旧准备金,如未积满原额,则所缺之数,即为损失之数。又以该厂停业之故,生产顿减,而移转他业以事生产之因素,足使该业之产品增加,彼方之所减与此处之所增,如能抵,则国富不变。否则变矣。工人之生产效力,非特与训练经验有关,且与配用之其他生产因素有关。改事他业,必不如原业之谙练,而配用之其他生产因素,是否早经充分准备等候新来工人之使用,亦属问题,故在该厂停业后之最短期内,亦即产业正在适应变更期间,生产量必减,国富因受损失。迨产业适应变动完成后,则生产因素均得从事于比较优势产业之生产,其生产效力,必较保留于原先产业者为佳,故生产量较前为大,国富因之增高。换言之,就将来言,以关税保护此种产业,使生产因素存留于该业,以事生产,乃全社会之一种损失。

各种工业,通常均有许多厂家。有经营得法者,获利甚丰;有经营比较的不得法者,获利较薄,有经营甚不得法者,非但利润毫无,且其收入不足支付地租。是为无地租之边际厂家。此种厂家,当其产品价格低落时,每以抵抗力薄弱之故而倒闭。所有可移转使用之生产因素,将转往比较优势之产业,以事生产。其影响于全国,财富之分配及消长,完全与上节所述者相同。一国之工业中,亦有边际厂家之收入,足能支付地租者。如是其产品价格之低落,一时不能使该厂倒闭。此种厂家,既将继续维持生产,所有可移转使用之生产因素,仍必保留于原有之产业中,而产业适应国际分工之变动,势必延期。在此特殊情形之下,该国政府如用关税保持此种工业产品之价格,对于产业之生产量,及生产因素在各产业之分配,不受直接影响(间接影响除外),所引起之惟一重要变动,为财富之分配。

四 不等工资率对于国际贸易利得之影响

国际贸易之理论,通常含有等工资率(Uniform)之假定。现时社会之工资率,与此假定不符。工资率不等之原因,约有下列三种:

(1)劳工品质之差别。工资率因劳工品质不同而有差别,一如土地品质不同而有地租之差异,其理相同。设工资率之差异,皆由此而起,则国际贸易,足使各国生产量增加之结论,不以工资率之不等而有所更变。

(2)劳工环境之殊异,工人之受业,除工资率外,对于工作性质之合意否,工作居住环境之良好否,必同时加以考量。设使工资率相同,则工人必选择工作性质合意,环境良好,并有保障者而就之。故工资率之差异,有时有对此等利益之报酬者,例如工人之接受工作性质不合意,或环境不好,或雇佣甚暂之职业,必须有较高之工资率,职是其故。今设国际贸易致使某国专业于工作性质及环境较佳(Relatively Attractive)之产业,因此其工资率较诸他业为低。今若该国在斯业所得比较成本利益之程度,较诸工资率之差异程度为小,又工资率恒等于工人之生产能力,则该国之财富,将因其专门化于生产效力较低之产业故,蒙受损失。然若职工性质及环境之美恶,亦作为财富之一种,即劳工报酬之厚薄,不仅以有形之薪金为计较之对象,凡工作性质之苦乐及环境之良劣等,皆包括在内,则该国之财富,仍必因国际分工故而增多,与前节所述之结论——各贸易国之生产量,因分工而增加——相符合。

(3)工会规例之约束。有种职业之工资,可因工会规例或因政府法令特别加以限制,以致该业之工资率超过于他业中同级工人之工资率。如是物价之比,不等于替代比,而国际贸易所引起之分工,有时足使生产量减少。兹举例说明之如次:

设 A 商品一单位及 B 商品一单位在甲国各须劳工一单位以生产之。[①] 但 B 业之工资,似有工会势力之维持,为 A 业之一倍。则:

物价之比 $\qquad A:B=1:2$

交换比 $\qquad A:B=1:\dfrac{1}{2}$

替代比 $\qquad A:B=1:1$

---

① 此处假定劳工成本,纯为说明便利计。若有其他生产因率与劳工配合以事生产,其所得结论仍同,惟较复杂而已。

又设 A 与 B 在其他各国之交换比与替代比为相等：

物价之比 $\qquad A:B=1:\dfrac{3}{2}$

交换比 $\qquad A:B=1:\dfrac{2}{3}$

如是甲国将专力于 A 之生产,而输入 B。今若替代比等于交换比,则贸易之结果,将使生产量增加。盖移转生产 B 商品一单位之成本,从事于 A 之生产,可得 A 商品二单位,再将 A 输出,而由外国输入 B,可得 B 商品 $1\dfrac{1}{2}$ 单位,故其利得为 $\dfrac{1}{3}B$。

然甲国之替代比为 1:1,不等于交换比。当 B 之产业紧缩之时,每减少 B 商品一单位,只能生产 A 商品一单位,以相替代,又依假设,每单位 A 只能换得 $\dfrac{2}{3}B$,故贸易之结果,甲国损失 $\dfrac{1}{3}B$。在此种情形之下,甲国如用关税手段保护 B 工业,有利而无弊。

上设事例,在现实经济社会中,殊不多见。盖如一种职业之工人,能维持特高之工资,则其工人成为独占群(Monopolistic Group)。此种独占群必具极坚强之团结力,以抵御外来之压迫,与其减低工资率,毋宁解雇。否则当外国商品输入压低该业产品价格之时,工资率必被减低,果如是,则国际贸易有打破"独占"(Monopoly)以终止其剥削消费人之威力矣。

五 递减成本对于国际贸易利得之影响

国际贸易之理论,如上所述,以下列假设为前提之一：

所有各种产业之生产成本,或为递增(Increasing Costs)或为固定(Constant Costs)。

现在产业之生产成本,如有递减者,则国际贸易之利得,是否存在,遂成问题。古拉亨[①]教授根据递减成本之假设,对于正统派国际贸易理论,严加批评。其批评之焦点,不在于比较成本学说,而在于比较成本学说之推论：

---

① Graham, Frank D., "Some Aspects of Protection Further Considered", Quarterly Journal of Economy, Vol. 37, p. 199 et seq., 1923. See also the Eriticism by Knight, "Some Fallacies in the Interpretation of Social Cost", Quar. Jour. Econ., Vol.38, p.582 et seq.,1924(now reprinted U1 Ethics of Competition, 1935); and Graham's reply and Knight's rejoinder, Q. J. E., Vol.39, p.324 et seq.; Viner, "The Doctrine of Comparative Cost", Wel sat schafiliches archiv, Vol.36, 1932.

即各国通商之后,各依比较成本原则,从事于生产成本比较优势产业之生产,造成国际分工之局,其结果为各国生产量之增加。古拉亨教授以为两贸易国之一,必然因分工而蒙受损失,特设例以说明之。

[(1)递减成本对于国际贸易利得之影响] 就古拉亨教授之例证言,贸易国之一方,设依比较成本情势之启示,放弃递减成本产业之发展,而专门从事于递增成本之扩充,将蒙受生产量减少之损失。依古氏之意,农业国家通常皆处于此种不利地位。例如十九世纪前半叶之欧陆诸国以及十九世纪后期之美国,对于英国之贸易言,其处境均系如是。反之,工业国家专门从事于递减成本产业之发展,则享受生产量增加之利益。

为说明古拉亨教授理论之便利计,特举古氏原例如次:

设麦代表农业产品,表代表工业产品,当国际贸易开始之前,麦与表之交换比,在英国为 40 个单位之麦交换 40 个表,在美国为 40 个单位麦交换 37 个表。按比较成本之情势言,美国以致力于麦之生产为有利,遂专门从事于麦之生产。同时英国以生产表为较有利,遂专门从事于表之生产。今设美国农产之生产成本为递增,其工业之生产成本为递减。又古氏为说明便利计,设英国工业之生产成本,不以生产量之增加,而发生显著之变动;其农业亦不以生产量之减少,而发生显著之变动。今如英美通商之条件,极有利于美国,40 个单位之麦,可换取 40 个表。前美国之劳工与资本,将由工业逐渐移至农业。盖美国之劳工与资本,用于工业时,可生产 37 个表者,若移转使用于农业,能得 37 余个单位之麦,则农业与工业相较,以农业能付较高之工资与利息故也。

设美国表业减少生产量,计为 37 000 个单位。其劳工与资金移转于农业,共增加麦之生产量 37 500 个单位。此数必较 40 000 为小,以美国农业之生产成本为递增故也。依假设,此 37 500 个单位之麦,可换得 37 500 个单位之表。今美国表业之生产成本,因生产量之减缩而递增,原先可生产 37 个表之成本,而今只能生产 36 个表。倘以此成本量移用于麦之生产,能得 36 余个单位之麦,则劳工与资本之由工业移转于农业之运动,将必继续进展。设表之生产量又减缩 36 000 个。其成本移转于麦之生产,计增 36 200 个单位。此数可换得英国之表 36 200 个。但美国因贸易而分工,因分工而减缩表之生产量,共为 74 000 个单位。其成本移转于麦之生产以输出,与英国之表相交易,计得 37 500+36 200＝73 700 个单位。两者相较,足见美国所受贸易之损失为 300 个表。上述情形,尚可继续进展,直至美国制表业完全为英国所代替。此时美国之损失更大。兹列表示之如次:

通商之前

美国：所需之麦与表，皆由本国自产之。麦与表之替代比 = 交换比 = 40∶37。麦之生产成本为递增，即麦之生产成本因生产量之增加而增高。表之生产成本为递减，即表之生产成本，因生产量之减小而增高。

英国：所需之麦与表，皆由本国生产之。麦与表之替代比 = 交换比 = 40∶40。麦之生产成本不变。表之生产成本不变。

通商之后

美国循比较利益之原则，逐步扩充表之生产。而减缩麦之生产。

放弃生产之表	替代比	替代表而生产之麦	麦与表之国际贸易比	由贸易而得之麦	发展表业以可能产表之获得之结果
37 000	37∶37	37 500	1∶1	37 500	37 000
36 000	36.2∶36	36 200	1∶1	36 200	37 000
73 000				37 700	74 000

损失 = 300

英国循比较利益之原则，逐步扩充表之生产。而减缩麦之生产。

放弃生产之麦	替代比	替代麦而生产之表	麦与表之国际贸易比	由贸易而得之麦	发展农业以产麦而能获表之结果
37 500	1∶1	37 500	1∶1	37 500	37 500
36 200	1∶1	36 200	1∶1	36 290	36 200
				73 700	73 700

损失或利得 = 0

任何国家,其处境同于上例中之美国者,所受国际分工之影响,为一般产业成本之向上增高。正在扩充之产业,皆为生产成本递增之产业,故其生产成本,因生产量之增大而增高。正在减缩之产业,皆为生产成本递减之产业,故其生产成本,因生产量之减少而增高。

古拉亨教授之理论,以递减成本(即生产成本,因生产量之逐渐增加而递减,又因生产量之减少而递增)为前提。故其结论能否确立,要视其假设与现实经济社会相合否以为断。欲知古氏之假设。在何等情形中方能存在,吾人必先研究成本学说。①

[(2) **成本减轻之意义**] 任何产业,如其平均成本或边际成本随生产量之扩充而减轻,是为成本递减产业。经济学者中,有认为如此意味上之成本递减产业,实不能存在;且以观念亦惟动态经济学中有之,在静态经济学中,无存在之余地。盖成本之减轻。必因生产方法之变更而来。所谓生产成本随生产量之增加而减轻之事,非改变生产方法不可。如是经济情形已非旧昔,当属于动态经济学之范围。

此种见解,实不确当。静态经济学只假定技术智识及应用能力不变,而未尝假定生产方法不变也。所用生产方法之变更,是由于生产量有增加之需要。至于技术智识及应用能力之变更,常为技术上新发明之结果。两种情形不同,不可不辨。关于前一种情形,新用之方法,在当初为已知;其所以未引用者,乃因生产量过小,用之反为不经济故也,关于后一种情形,新技术代表一种新智识;在当初为未知,或未实验,是新增进之文明。诚属于动态经济学之现象,设使成本之减轻,完全由于文明之进步,既非静态经济学说所能解释,亦不在本问题范围之内。盖本问题之重心,乃成本之减轻,纯由国际贸易而起故也。姑舍而不论。今只取前一种情形论之。

[(3) **经济理论中之递减成本**] 经济理论中之递减成本,常为生产量需要增加之结果,诚如上述。然其招致之道,有由于内围经济(Internal Economics)者,亦有由于外围经济(External Economics)者。内围经济由于

---

① On the problems of decreasing costs, see especially: Moogenstern, "Offene Problem der Kosten und Ertragacheonie", Zeitschrift für Nationalökonomie, Vol.2, p.481, 1931; Viner, "Cost Curves and Supply Curves", Zeitschrift für Nationalökonomie, Vol.3, p.23 et seq., 1931; Harrod, "Notes on Supply", Economie Journal, Vol.40, p.238 et seq., 1930; and "The Law of Decreasing Costs", Eco. Jour., Vol. 41, p. 566, 1931. See also Weiss Art "Abnehmender Ertrag" in Handworterbuch der Stadtswissenschaften, 4th ed.; Schuller, Schutzzol und Fneihandel, Absch; Marshall, Principles of Eco; Carver, Distribution of Wealth. The Exposition of These Problems is Particularly Good in Carver and Hausen, Principles of Economies, 1928; Robinson, The Economies of Imperfect Competition, 1933.

公司或工厂扩充内部而起；外围经济常伴随整个工业之发达（例如新工厂之兴起）而来。经济学家中［如宣配德（Schumpeter）］有以为成本递减之事不能存在者，其心目中颇以下列事实为重：任何产业，若因生产量需要增加而发达，其所需要之生产因素，将必涨价。生产因素之价格既涨高，则其生产品之成本，将随生产量之增加而增高矣。故成本递减之事，似属不可能。然如内围经济及外围经济所引起成本减轻之程度，超过于生产因素涨价所引起成本增高之程度，则成递减成本之现象矣。

　　[（4）递减成本之由于内围经济者]　产业规模之扩大，致使成本减轻者，其主要理由在于生产工具之不可分性（Indivisibility）。例如汽车工业中之搬运制度（Conveyor-system），或印刷工业中之铸字机（Linotype Machine），非至该产业发展至相当规模，不便引用。倘若引用，反为不经济。但经引用之后，则其他辅佐或合作生产工具，亦将发生更动，且其专门化程度，将更加深。盖生产方法已与原先者不同故也。其次，生产工具虽有大小不同之各种号码，大者备供大规模工厂之选用，中等或小号备供中等或小规模工厂之使用。然其价格之变动，不与生产效力规模同比例。例如发电能力大一倍之发电机，较之发电能力小一倍之发电机，所费仅增百分之三十而已。此外工厂中所有之生产因子（例如厂中职员及一切设备），尚可因生产量之扩充，而获得之更善之利用。由此观之，生产费用，虽必伴随产量之扩充而增大，然生产量之增加，每较生产成本之增加，为速且大，因之，每单位产品之平均成本，必较前此为轻。在工商业界中，规模较大之厂店，较规模小之厂店为有利，亦为习见不鲜之事。故内围经济似亦事理之极显明者。①

　　持反对论者，对于上述意见，不尽同情。设有工厂，能从扩充工厂之规模，以减轻生产成本者，其厂主（或企业家）必早已为之。减轻成本原为厂主之职务，亦为厂主之利益。盖惟成本减低，方能定价低廉。以低廉之价格。竞卖于市，方能压倒竞争对手。故在自由竞争（Free Competition）制度之下，各工厂均已发展至最适宜之程度。工厂扩充之进程，非至下列情景不止：(i)工厂之规模，业已达到最适宜之限度。如再事扩充，将有技术上或管理之困难，其生产成本非但不能因扩充而减轻，且将加重。(ii)有时市场过小，只能维持少数厂家，而此少数厂又为保持其本身利益与地位计，互相谅解，甚或成立协定，瓜分市场而垄断之。如是自由竞争已不复在。是故在自

---

① 读者如欲作详细之研讨，可参阅：Robinson, The Structure of Competitive Industry; Marshall, Principles of Economics and Industry and Trade。

由竞争制度之下,递减成本之事不能存在,以各工厂均已扩充至最适宜之限度,过此则为递减成本矣。今古拉亨教授之例证,设美国表业,尚在递减成本阶段中,从事于表之生产;因受英国表业之自由竞争压力,逐步减缩其生产量,以致成本渐次加重。其所假设者,为递减成本之美国表业,能存在于自由竞争制度之下,是与事实不符。设美国表业果在递减成本之阶段中,必已成为独占企业(Monopoly)。

独占企业,既无同业竞争,不必以减低成本及价格为务,其目的在于最大利润。故独占企业虽在递减成本之阶段中,亦无扩充生产量之动机,除非其生产品之需要弹性颇大,扩充生产量之结果,足增益其利润。一旦遭受外国商品进口之竞争,以致跌价,则独占企业家之利润被削,而独占之局破矣。然独占企业之生产,将不至逐步紧缩,一如古拉亨例证中所言者。盖独占企业家与自由竞争企业家不同,对于市场情形,能作统盘观察,以为生产之参考。设其工厂之生产情形,尚在递减成本之阶段中,必将增加生产,以求成本之减轻,竞卖于国内外市场中。设依市场价格出售其产品之收入,不敷成本之支出,则此独占企业家所处之境遇,与本文第三节所言者相同。其地租及几似地租(Quasi-rents)将跌落。设出售产品之收入,既无以支付地租及几似地租,且不足支付非专门化生产因素(Non-specific Factors)之费用,该厂倒闭矣。无论如何,此独占企业,必不至受外国同业之逐步压迫而逐次减少其生产量,一如古拉亨例证中之所言者然。

此种意见,是否与事实相符,尚有疑问。企业家虽有扩充其工厂至最适宜限度之动机与计划,然必赖充分资本以实现之。在资本缺乏之国家,企业家每不能罗致充分之资金,计划虽佳,亦属徒然。我国利率高于外国利率,是为缺乏资本之象征,而各工厂流动资产对于总资产之比,常较外国者为小,又足为我国工厂缺少资本之明证。至于小工厂林立及其出品成本过高等事实,又可为各工厂尚未发展至适宜限度之证据。倘有对本题发生兴趣者,选取若干工厂,作详密之研究,必能发见我国工厂大都缺乏资本,并以资本缺乏故,未得扩充至最适宜限度之病理。如是古拉亨教授之理论,自有其根据也。

[(5)递减成本之由于外国经济者[①]]　　马夏尔(Marshall)于其所著经

[①] 参考:Marshall, Principles of Economics and Industry and Trade; Taussig, Principles of Economics, Vol.1, chap. 14; Viner, "Cost Curves and Supply Curves", Zeitschrift für Nationalökonomie, Vol.3, 1931; Shove, "Increasing Returns and the Representative Firm", Eco. Jour., 1930。

济学原理及工业与商业两书中,曾说明一种商品之成本与生产量有双重关系:第一,成本伴随工厂之规模而变。如第(4)节所述,一个工厂可因扩充生产量而获得内围经济(Internal Economics),以减轻其成本。第二,任何部门工业之厂店,其生产成本,可因该种部门工业之扩充而减轻。范诺(Viner)教授曾于其所著《成本曲线与供给曲线》("Cost Curves and Supply Curves")一文中,证明各个厂店之生产成本,虽均为递增状态(即当生产量增加时,其成本随同增高),但于整个工业扩充之后,所有各个向上倾斜之成本曲线,均较前为低,是为外围经济(External Economics),促成递减成本之明证。故一个工厂之生产成本,非仅为本厂生产之函数(Function),且为该种部门工业总生产量之函数。

外围经济之意义,既如上述,兹再举数例以明之。(i)一种部门工业因新厂之兴起而扩充。而有训练且富于经验之工人又因该种部门工业之扩充而增多。此种良好工人之发展,为外围经济之一因。(ii)一种部门工业所需用之交通运输(Communication and Transportation),常伴随该种部门工业之扩充而发展。交通运输工具改善之结果,自能减轻使用者之负担,是为外围经济之一例。(iii)一种部门工业扩充之结果,每使该业所用机器及其他生产工具价格减低。盖此等机器及其他生产工具,必因该种工业之扩充而增加其需要,故可以较大规模之工厂生产之,其成本当较前此为低,因之其价格亦较前此为廉,是为外围经济又一例。

由此观之,一种工业,可因其产品需要之增加而扩充(通常为新厂之兴起);而该业所所用之工人、机器、交通运输,及其他一切生产工具,又可因该业之扩充而改进,则其产品之成本及价格,当能伴随该业之扩充而减低。是故外围经济促成递减成本之现象,自非不可能之事。

外围经济与内围经济有一根本不同之点,此处宜加说明。内围经济之利益,为工厂扩充之结果,厂主有设法实现之动机。故内围经济之事可任令企业家为之,毋须乎政府之促成。至于外围经济,为整个工业扩充之结果,其利益为同业各厂所共享。而任何企业家,罕有改进外围经济(例如改进技术工人之效能)之动机,以其成果,不必为改良者所占有享受,有时反为竞争对手所攫取故也。因此外围经济之事,不能任由企业家为之,而有待于政府之筹划扶植。

此点与古拉亨教授之理论颇有关系。今有工业发展至相当程度,同业各厂均能享受外围经济之相当利益。设此工业能再扩充,或由原有各厂增加生产,或由新厂兴起,则各厂所得外围经济之利益更大,但自受外国同业竞争之压力,此项工业不得扩充,且有被迫减缩之事,果如减缩,则各工厂原有之外围利益被削,其生产成本将较前此为高,处境益恶。若非政府暂用关税加以保护,使得充分发展,以便收获外围经济之利益,则该项工业不能与外国同业竞争也。

(原载《政治季刊》1939年第3卷第3期)

抗战以来之物价现象

价格制度是现代经济组织下支配生产分配与消费的工具,研究现代经济生活者,若置货币及物价于不顾,必无所获。盖有价格制度存在而后能表现现代生产之特质——分工与合作,有价格制度存在而后生产者知社会需要之商品为何种,及其需要之数量,如何于千百万种企业之中选择一最有效率之途径,如何于企业各部门中加以适当之管理。再推论全部经济活动之所以能继续进行,亦不过赖物价起伏波动之中常有差额,形成利润,企业者之企业动机即在于此。价格之变动足以激励或削减生产量或消费量。故物价之变动,实足以反映生产及消费之增减。于此可见物价机能之一斑。

各种物价之变动,骤视之似不相连属,然细加研究,则知现社会中实已完成一整个体系。各种物价、各时物价、各地物价,皆相互影响;其变动极为灵敏,密切尔(M.C.Mitchell)谓:"价格制度为许多部分所合成之一错综复杂制度,细析之,千变万化,富于伸缩性;约言之,条理井然,具有一定之关系,其组织恰如一有机体,对于循环变动,自具调整之功能。"[1]已能指出各个物价变动之特征,及一般物价现象之齐一性。经济学者自发现经济社会中有此伟大支配力量,并知其有此完善与统一之特性,于是有人应用统计方法分析物价行为[2]。即以简单数字表示一般物价水准之升降,或各种物价,各类物价在各时期之变动现象及其相互关系。于是"深奥、错综、复杂、相似、相异、相关"之物价现象,始得一比较明确之认识。

物价指数代表各时期之物价变动,故其应用极广,最普通之应用为测量一国生活程度、经济循环、货币价格,以及国际贸易条件之变动等。然所采用之物价指数,常随需用之目的而各异,例如以测量生活程度之变动为目的

---

[1] 密切尔《商业循环》一九一三年版第三十一页。在一九二七年重订版仍有同样之观念。
[2] 米尔氏《物价行为论》(Mills, *Behavior of Prices*)及其所引证之论文。

者,宜用消费物价指数;以测量经济循环为目的者,潘苏氏采用十种趸售物价指数;以测量货币价值之变动为目的,有采用趸售物价指数者(费雪),有采用消费物价指数者(开恩氏);以测量进出口贸易条件之变动为目的者,宜用进出口贸易货价。然如上所述,各种物价合成整个物价系统,其间有一定之关系,知其一而可测度其他。是以研究经济现象者多取趸售物价一种而研究之。然若欲于物价行为,作一详确之研究,则现有之物价资料,实不合用。为达此目的,吾人应搜集多种单纯物价数列,代表同种物品在各地域之价格,在生产及分配过程中之各阶段价格。所谓单纯价格,必须合于下列条件:

(1) 同用途同品级之物价。

(2) 单一市场之价格(非为数个市场之平均)。

(3) 同类或同条件之交易价格。

若有充过之单纯物价数列,代表各地域各阶段之价格,再用适当方法分析之,所得之结果,必能显示各物价之特征,物价系统之组织,各种各类物价间之关系,各物价之循环变动现象等。此种物价资料之充分收集,实有待于学术机关之激励,统计事业机关之努力。

抗战以来,我国经济遭逢巨大之变革。经济学者每据所见,各抒高论,而物价指数遂常被引用,尤以上海物价指数,以历史久远,又为全国主要商埠之指数,常为学者用作研究资料。通常引用之例,约有下列数种:

(1) 以物价指数研究货币对内价值。物价之高低可视为单位物品所值货币额之多少,反之如谓为单位货币所能购买之物品有多少,亦无不可。是故物价指数,固足以表示物价之高低,另一方面亦足以表示货币价值之涨落,经济学者大多承认此说,不过马夏尔(Marsshall)及凯恩斯(Keynes)则主张用消费物品物价指数表示货币购买力,与主张以一般物价指数计算者不同,其理由不能具述。总之研究货币现象者,舍以物价指数比较外实无他法以表示货币价值。我国抗战以来,研究法币价值之变动亦多用此法。

(2) 以物价指数研究货币价值之变动(外汇)。在金本位时代两国外汇汇率变动,可以金平价为基点;其涨落有现金输送点为界限。故汇价之变幅甚小。自停止金本位以来,各国相互间汇率之变动,已无固定标准,通常以两国货币在本国之购买力之比表示之,简称曰购买力平价(Purchasing Power Parities),凯赛尔(Gustar Cassl)氏曾用此法解释欧战以后汇价现象

(见凯氏著《一九一四年后之外汇》)。本文作者之一,曾用以解释我国黑市汇价现象(见《时事月报》第十九卷第七期及《中央日报》廿七年十二月十四日社论,廿八年元月六日诸论文)。当此抗战时期,外汇问题关系全国金融安危、商业兴替。论外汇平价时,不得不援用物价指数。我国尚无全国趸售物价指数,只能以一地域之物价指数为代表。于是上海物价指数,可以代表全国物价指数否?遂成一急待研究之问题。

(3)以物价指数研究国民生活程度。前次世界大战期中各国人民生活不安,论者每归咎于物价上涨引起生活程度提高,遂使定额收入者(如赖工资薪水生活者)之实际所得减少。盖工资等收入不可能随物价之上涨而即刻上涨,当其名义工资不足以维持生计时,社会必致不安,取其极端之例,如战后德国物价飞速上涨,一日所得竟不能购得一块面包,其困苦不言而喻。我国战时物价亦有上涨之趋势,其影响于生活程度者如何,固有待于各种生活费指数之编制,然零售物价常伴随趸售物价而变动,惟变幅较小。故趸售物价指数,亦得用以表示国民生活程度之大约情形也。

(4)以物价指数研究进出口贸易之条件。一国物价上涨足以鼓励输入,物价下落足以刺激输出,故两国物价之相对增减,足以表示进出口贸易之增减趋势。抗战时期输出贸易为获得外汇换取军需之重要手段。如何增进对外贸易,正有待于研究,而物价指数于此亦遂显示其功用。

(5)以物价指数判断经济循环趋势。经济循环为一般经济活动兴衰交替之现象,其影响及于农工商各业。如何预测经济循环变动,规避恐慌,为现代经济组织之一重要问题。据米切尔氏之研究,经济循环变动均反映于一般物价之上;潘荪氏且作一十种物价指数用以表示经济循环变动,并作为预测之一种工具。故若上海物价指数,可以代表全国物价指数,则其所有经济循环变动,即可视作我国经济循环变动之反映。

研究者既多引用上海物价,则上海物价之能否代表全国物价,实为急待研究之问题。兹取上海、重庆、广州等三处之物价,求其差距;更就其变动之方向,递增率比较之,以见上海物价与其他各地物价变动之同异情形。

一九三七年一月至一九三八年八月上海、广州、重庆物价指数①如

---

① 重庆物价指数为四川省政府建设厅驻渝办事处所管,广州、上海物价为财政部国定税则委员会所管。

下表：

表一　上海、广州、重庆三地趸售物价指数

月　份	上　海 （民 15 年 = 100）	广　州 （民 15 年 = 100）	重　庆 （民 26 年 = 100）
26 年 1	121.6	115.73	93.5
2	122.9	118.40	96.2
3	123.0	117.50	96.7
4	123.9	119.78	97.9
5	125.1	119.81	98.3
6	126.1	118.73	98.8
7	125.8	116.12	95.1
8	127.8	121.07	95.7
9	129.9	121.85	103.1
10	133.1	128.21	104.4
11	140.3	125.12	104.0
12	141.4	123.66	98.3
27 年 1	139.6	123.85	109.3
2	138.4	128.05	119.2
3	139.2	129.23	127.2
4	142.8	129.55	124.1
5	141.9	135.69	123.4
6	145.2	141.28	128.2
7	153.0	147.29	130.6
8	164.8		132.5

上列指数，以基期不同，不便比较。兹取二十六年上半年为基期以为比较之基础。此种基期不能认为完善，因半年之内或有季节变动影响在内也，然观此六月中各地物价甚为平稳，想以半年为基亦无大妨碍，变换基期后之三地指数如下表：

表二　上海、广州、重庆同基期物价指数

以 28 年上半期为基期

月　份	上　海	广　州	重　庆	平　均
26 年 1	98.3	97.9	96.5	97.5
2	99.3	99.8	99.3	99.5
3	99.4	99.4	99.8	99.5
4	100.1	101.3	101.0	100.8
5	101.1	101.3	101.4	101.3
6	101.9	100.4	102.0	101.4
7	101.7	98.2	98.1	99.3
8	103.3	102.4	98.8	101.5
9	105.0	103.0	160.4	104.8
10	107.5	108.4	107.7	107.9
11	113.4	105.8	107.3	108.8
12	114.3	104.6	101.4	106.8
27 年 1	112.8	104.7	112.8	110.1
2	111.8	108.3	123.0	114.4
3	112.5	109.3	131.3	117.7
4	115.4	109.5	128.1	117.7
5	114.7	114.7	127.3	118.9
6	117.3	119.5	132.3	123.0
7	123.6	124.5	134.8	127.6
8	133.2		136.7	

现即可据上表加以分析：

（1）三地物价指数之差距。三地之指数当然不能尽同，吾人应计算其不同之程度若何，其方法即先取各月间数值求其三地之平均值 m_i，得一数列，此平均值与各地指数相较之绝对差除以原平均值，即各地之差距，再将三地之差距平均之，所得数列即平均差距，代表三地指数变动所生之差异。

$$U_m = \frac{|m_i - I_1| + |m_i - I_2| + |m_i - I_3|}{3m_i}$$

表三　三地物价指数之差距计算表

月　次	（指数—三地平均数）÷三地平均数			
	上　海	广　州	重　庆	平　均
26年1	0.007 4	0.003 1	0.010 6	0.007 1
2	0.001 6	0.003 5	0.001 9	0.002 3
3	0.001 2	0.001 5	0.002 8	0.001 8
4	0.006 9	0.004 8	0.002 2	0.004 6
5	0.002 0	0.000 3	0.001 5	0.001 3
6	0.004 7	0.010 1	0.005 3	0.006 7
7	0.023 4	0.011 4	0.012 0	0.015 6
8	0.017 7	0.009 1	0.026 7	0.017 8
9	0.001 6	0.016 7	0.015 2	0.011 2
10	0.003 2	0.004 8	0.014 8	0.007 6
11	0.041 6	0.027 9	0.013 9	0.027 8
12	0.070 2	0.020 5	0.049 7	0.046 8
27年1	0.024 5	0.048 8	0.024 4	0.032 6
2	0.022 2	0.053 3	0.075 4	0.050 3
3	0.033 2	0.071 3	0.115 5	0.073 3
4	0.019 4	0.069 0	0.088 3	0.038 6
5	0.035 7	0.035 1	0.070 9	0.047 2
6	0.046 3	0.028 9	0.075 3	0.050 2
7	0.031 5	0.024 3	0.055 9	0.033 9
平　均	0.030 7	0.023 4	0.034 3	0.049 5

由表三可以看出三地物价指数之变动，未能完全一致，有0.18%至7.4%之差异，差异最小者在一九三七年五月，差异最大者在一九三八年三月。

（2）各地指数之变动方向。其法将全数列相邻两数字比较之，物价上升者记之为正，反之为负。凡由正变负或由负变正者，为变向一次。将变向之次数除以总项数减一,即得变向系数。此系数之最大值为一,即逐月变向之意,其最小值为零,即永升或永降之意也。

$$变向系数 = \frac{变向次数}{总项数 - 1}$$

表四　变向系数计算表

月次	1	2	3	4	5	6	7	8	9	10	11	12	13	14	15	16	17	18	19
上海指数		+	+	+	+	+	+	+	+	+	−	+	+	−	+	+	−	+	+
广州指数		+	−	+	+	−	+	+	+		−	−	+	+	+	+	+	+	+
重庆指数		+	+	+	+	−	+	+	+	−	−	+	+	+	−	−	+	+	+

在此表中,因广州指数未有八月份数字,且上海、重庆二指数之第二十项数字不影响变动方向,故三指数均取十九项。其变向系数完全相等即:

$$变向系数 = \frac{6}{19-1} = 0.33$$

若分别比较各数列间之变动,可知广州与其他二地之变动尚不若重庆、上海二地变动之吻合,重庆、上海二地物价几乎以同样形态上下波动,如以图示之,更为显著。

既已知变动方向有一致之趋势,而波动次数相同,又已知差距虽不能免,而最大不过7.4%,吾人将进而研究各地指数递增率之数异。

（3）三地物价递增率（Rate of change）。此地用递增率一词,取其意义显明也。实则物价变动有递减之趋势亦属可能。为明了递增率之意义计,可先举简单之例作为说明,譬某地物价以直线趋势上涨,各月之数值如下:

x（月份）	0	1	2	3	4	……
g（物价）	100	103	106	109	112	……

则此趋势可以简单之方程式表示之:

$$y = a + bx \quad 或$$
$$y = 100 + 3x \quad 此处 \quad b = 3$$

该地物价逐月递增,而增加量恒为3,此3即该地物价之递增率也。一般直线趋势之变动,皆可以此种形式之方程式表示之。

实际上物价变动未必尽能以直线式代表之,亦可改用他式。可以代表物价变动之曲线颇多,总以选择其与实际数字之变化趋势相似者为宜。欲稽核选定之曲线,与实际数字之配合情形如何?可将求出之曲线做成图形,绘于透明纸上,覆置于原数字图形之上,以观察其配合之程度,或求标准差(Standard Error),然后再用尤分配式(T-distribution)以判断之。然为比较计,各地指数必用同一形式之方程式以配合之。

观上海、广州、重庆三地物价变动情形,吾人选择下式:

$$y = ab^x, x \text{ 为时期}, y \text{ 为指数}, a \text{ 及 } b \text{ 为常数}。$$

换为对数以表示之,则可改为下式:

$$\log y = \log a + (\log b)x$$

以此与直线式

$$y = a + bx$$

相比较只不过以 $\log y$ 代 y,将直线式之递增率 b 用对数表示之而已。故 $y = ab^x$ 式中之 $\log b$ 与直线式中之 b 同义,易言之,$\log b$ 表示 $\log y$ 之递增率,即每当 x 增加一单位,$\log y$ 所有之相当变量也。

为求上海、广州、重庆三地物价指数之递增率,以上述曲线配合于各指数;而求出三个 $\log b$,此三数值之差异,即是三地物价变动速度大小之差异。

计算 $\log b$ 的方法,在本问题中因 x 之增加常为一,故为方便。盖

设 x_i 为第 i 月份,$i = 0$ 或 $1, 2, 3, 4, \cdots$

y_i 为该月份之指数。

则 x_{i+1},y_{i+1} 为后一月份及该月份之指数。

依方程式

(1) $y_{i+1} = ab^{x_{i+1}}$

(2) $y_i = ab^{x_i}$

故 (3) $\dfrac{y_{i+1}}{y_i} = \dfrac{ab^{x_{i+1}}}{ab^{x_i}} = b^{x_{i+1}-x_i} = b \quad (\because x_{i+1} - x_i = 1)$

如实际指数数值中果真相邻二指数皆有上述关系,则以 $y = ab^x$ 方程式配合之必绝对相符合,而 b 之值等于任何两相邻 y 值之比,但事实上,xy 等

数值绝难如此巧合,故必求平均数

(4) $\dfrac{1}{n}\sum \dfrac{y_{i+1}}{y_i} = \dfrac{1}{n}\sum b^{x_{i+1}-x_i} = b$

故 b 之值等于物价指数环比之平均值。由 b 可得 $\log b$。

兹列表如次:

表五 各地物价指数递增率计算表

月　次	上海环比	广州环比	重庆环比
0	0	0	0
1	1.010 6	1.018 7	1.028 9
2	1.000 1	0.995 4	1.005 1
3	1.007 3	1.019 4	1.012 4
4	1.009 6	1.000 3	1.004 1
5	1.008 0	0.990 9	1.005 0
6	0.997 6	0.978 0	0.962 5
7	1.015 4	1.042 5	1.006 3
8	1.016 4	1.006 4	1.077 3
9	1.024 6	1.052 2	1.012 6
10	1.054 1	0.975 9	0.996 2
11	1.007 1	0.998 2	0.945 2
12	0.987 3	1.001 5	1.111 9
13	0.991 4	1.033 9	1.090 5
14	1.005 8	1.009 2	1.079 1
15	0.025 8	1.002 5	0.975 5
16	0.993 6	1.047 4	0.994 5
17	1.023 1	1.041 1	1.038 9
18	1.053 8	1.042 5	1.018 3
19	1.077 1		1.014 7
平均	1.016 0	1.013 7	1.019 8

上海: $b = 1.016\,0$　递增率 $\log b = 0.006\,9$
广州: $b = 1.013\,7$　递增率 $\log b = 0.005\,9$
重庆: $b = 1.019\,8$　递增率 $\log b = 0.008\,1$

故从上述方法计算出三地变动率,相互比较,所差不过千分之二,于此又可获一证明,即三地物价变动之速度相差亦微。其中最稳定者为广州,其次为上海,变动较大,递增较速者为重庆,其所以如此者,盖因政府迁渝办公后,该地人口骤增,对于物品需求大增,而外地输入物品以运输不便故,供不敷求,以致物价腾贵之情形与沪广有别。

若欲得三地物价指数变动之曲线,可将全部方程式求出,其方法如下:

$y = ab^x$ 方程式内 b 已求出,现欲求者仅常数 a。

$a = \dfrac{y_i}{b^{x_i}}$ 可以依求下时之方法求 $\dfrac{y_i}{b^{x_i}}$ 之平均数。

但为便于计算,可改成对数即

$$\log a = \frac{1}{n} \sum \log y_i - \frac{1}{n} \sum x_i \log b$$

依此式求出结果如后(计算步骤从略)

上海:$\log a = 1.971\,83$　$a = 95.88$

广州:$\log a = 1.970\,68$　$a = 93.47$

重庆:$\log a = 1.966\,17$　$a = 92.51$

将 a、b 代入原式得三地物价指数曲线

上海:$y = (95.88)(1.016\,0)^x$

广州:$y = (93.47)(1.013\,7)^x$

重庆:$y = (92.51)(1.019\,8)^x$

上述三曲线可以代表上海、广州、重庆三地物价变动之趋势,其递增率为 b 之对数。

今 b 之意义,尚有可得而言者,上述公式与复利率式

$$本利和 = 本金 \times (1+利率)^{时期} 或$$
$$S = P \times (1 + r)^T$$

为同类,故 b 之小数部分,相当于复利率,此数值在上海为 0.016 0,在广州为 0.013 7,在重庆为 0.019 8,以利率作比喻,则重庆利率高于广州者为 0.005 1;而广州之利率高于上海者为 0.002 3,相差固甚微也。

以上用三种方法研究上海、广州、重庆三地物价,得其结果如下:

(一)变向系完全相同,三地物价变动起伏之次数相同。

(二)平均差距时有大小,最大时到 7.4%,以时间言,二十六年初本有渐趋一致(差距渐小)之势,抗战军兴,差距增加,但至十月稍稍恢复,十月

后差距增大,至二十七年三月时差距最大,此后则逐渐减少。

（三）各地物价变动皆有上涨之趋势,其速度虽不相同,所差尚小;比较言之,广州上涨速度最小,盖由于交通便利之故;其次为上海,盖亦因货运较便;比较速度较大者为重庆。

吾人根据此种事实之所昭示,可知自民国二十六年一月起至抗战一周年止,此一段时间内我国主要商埠之物价仍有一致之趋势,而以上海物价代表全国尚有相当的可靠性。以上所述为此三地物价之初步研究结果,至于较长时期之观察,较新材料之搜集,与更完密方法之应用,尚有待于进一步之研究,容有结果,再行发表。

（本文与范宝信合作,原载《政治季刊》1939 年第 3 卷第 2 期）

战时物价问题

物价之决定,恒受物品供求法则之支配,在常态经济之下,生产者可以在比较自由之环境下,从事生产以供需要,故常能自动决定于适当水准之上。而战时经济则不然,一因战争之破坏致生产力骤形减少;二因军用浩繁致物资之消耗增大,同时谋国者为求民族生存,不得不以争取胜利为目标以集中全社会之生产力于军用部门而限制一般民生用品之供给,在这种特殊环境之下,物价之上涨乃必然之趋势,殊无足异,遍观各国战时之先例盖莫不皆然也。

试以上海物价与英、德、法三国在第一次欧战时之物价相比,则上海自一九三六年至一九三九年增加134%,英国自一九一三年至一九一六年(战争之第三年)增加60%,德国在同期内增加53%,法国在同期内增加89%,①其趋势之缓急与我国不相上下。

惟自战事发生以后,全国各地物价增加之程度各有不同,其增加速度,各不相等;以昆明之涨率为最大,西安、重庆次之,上海又次之,广西各地为最缓和。若将上列各地物价总指数之每月涨率平均计之,则自二十六年六月至二十七年六月每月平均增加1.98%,自二十七年六月至二十八年六月每月平均增加5.45%,二十八年下半年每月增加18.39%,故其上涨之速度,有逐月递增之势。

各地物价上涨直接影响于民众之生活,于是专家学者,对于涨价之原因竞相探讨,以求解决之道。或谓物价之涨由于生产不足,或谓由于消费过度,或谓由于外汇日趋跌落,或谓由于运输不便。而其中最直接之原因盖莫过于市场紊乱,商人操纵,屯积居奇,致促成物价不合理之上涨。夫战时物资缺乏固足以诱致操纵屯积,造成商人之不当利得。若政府对于市场施以适当之统制,必有成效,尤以经济组织健全之国家为然,即如敌国于七七事变发生后即将前次欧战时公布之"暴利取缔令",加以修正,并扩充范围,虽

---

① 第十五届经济学社年会论文,厉德寅著《我国抗战以来物价动态及其安定办法》。

其统制之法,不足以掩其经济上之弱点,然对于不当利得之取缔,颇有成效。反观我国虽有种种平抑物价之法令,然以办法欠善,机构缺乏,且行之不力,殊少实效,试以重庆市之棉纱为例,而说明之:

1. 重庆棉纱之供给,大部分系来自上海,故其价格之上涨应等于上海纱价加以运费、杂费及关税等项费用之和,查棉纱自上海运至重庆,每包运费为400元,杂缴约为原价之74%。设自上海运至重庆,需时三月,则重庆纱价可估计之如下:

上海纱价 (廿支双马)	715.0 (廿八年十月)	651.5 (廿八年十一月)	720.0 (廿八年十二月)
运　　费	400.0	400.0	400.0
杂费7%	329.1	482.1	532.8
利息3%	21.5	19.5	21.6
小计	1 665.6	1 553.1	1 674.4
利润20%	333.1	310.6	334.9
重庆估计纱价	1 998.7 (廿九年一月)	1 863.7 (廿九年二月)	2 009.3 (廿九年三月)
重庆实际纱价	1 603.4	1 782.6	2 392.4

重庆棉纱之来自上海者实际上常有早期所购之纱在内,故实际价格应较估计价格为低,然就上表三月份之实际价格观之,已超过估计价格380余元,殊难以正当理由为之解释,显系由于商人操纵之故。

2. 经济部平价购销处成立之初,商人以为政府决心平价,故期现各货均形看松,政府统制颇有收效之可能,乃自二月二十六日评价委员会开始挂牌,规定廿支双马牌价格为1 776元,定价既失之过低,对于购纱又未严密规定,而取缔屯积亦未严格执行,遂为奸商所乘。

在此期内上海纱价颇为稳定,每包上涨不过百分之十,贵阳纱价初亦无涨势,故在此一周内重庆纱价之重大变动,绝非受上海纱价之影响,亦非运输困难来源骤减所致,又足为商人操纵之明证。

3. 棉纱与棉布棉花关系极为密切,前者与后者价格之变动应相一致,然自三月一日至二十七日四周之内,棉纱每包自1 874元,涨至3 420元,约占82%。而兰亭牌阴丹士林布,每匹价格仅自91元涨至142元,约占55%;梨花牌灰哈□呢,自76元增至118元,约占55%;冲哔叽自69元增至100

元,约占45%;标准布自83元增至126元,约占52%;棉花自207元增至310元,约占50%,其涨势颇不相侔,显然并非由于疋头之需要急迫,或棉花之供给缺乏致引纱价上涨之风,而为屯积操纵所致。

基于上述之理由可见屯积操纵之事实显然存在,虽曰生产与节约乃平抑物价根本解决之策,殊不知屯积操纵之现象亦不能视为细微末节,无足重轻,设若交易市场无合理之统制,则增加生产与节约消费之运动恐亦未必能收实效,盖现代经济,生产者与消费者已失直接联系,一切物品之供求罔不藉交易市场以达其分配之目的,若在平时生产者可以相互竞争,尽量以消费者所需之物品供给于交易市场之上,故购买者不虞物品之缺乏,生产者非有特殊势力绝不能存垄断之心,其结果物价可以维持于正常水准之上。战时经济则不然,一国自平时入于战时,必以大部生产能力尽量集中于军用部门,更有大量人力编入军队以发挥其最大战斗力,争取国家之胜利,故除军用以外,其他民用物品之供给,将因生产因素之移用而减少,供给既减,交易市场若无适当之统制,则物价自必上涨,一般商人阶级原以贱买贵卖为能事,今见货物缺少与价格步涨之势,将必利用时机,从事屯积,藉获高利。屯积之结果,可有三种影响:

一、物价愈涨,屯积愈甚,屯积愈甚,物价愈高,遂使消费者愈感购买力薄弱而陷于贫乏,同时屯积者获利既厚,资力愈充,益足以扰乱市场。

二、生产资金因用于屯积而减少,生产能力普遍下落,于是物品之供给渐减,物价之涨势愈甚。

三、民生日用品既因屯积而上涨,则此种生产者之利润较高,于是一般生产力虽减,反以此微弱之生产能力集中于可供屯积之物品上,此项生产者遂与军需工业争取物资与劳力,此与经济动员之本旨大相背离。

在现有经济制度之下既不能直接将生产品分配于消费者之手,同时在战时环境之中又不应对一切物品作无限制之供给,故在交易市场无适当之统制以前,徒欲增加生产,节制消费,实不足以求物价问题之彻底解决。

统制交易市场之问题有因,一曰下层统制机构之树立,二曰公平价格之厘定,三曰执行之方法,四在执行之程序,五曰中央统制机构之健全。兹分述如下:

商业社会繁复零碎,政府欲施行统制,势不能对于每一商店,每一交易,加以统制,而同时政府又必须有深入社会之机构,方能发挥力量,我国经济落后,旧有经济组织基础极弱,惟同业公会较有悠久之历史,组织亦较为完善,勉可用为下层统制机构,况自二十七年一月十三日同业公会法再经修正后,益臻完善。卢郁文先生曾指出四点,为旧法所不及:一、将工业商业及输出业分开,二、重要工商业经指定后必须加入公会,三、旧法公会之成立系由七家以上之发起,而新法则规定工业两家以上,商业三家以上,即应组织,四、旧法无任务之规定,而新法则有之。故卢先生亦主张建树工业经济商业经济统制之施行机构以应修正商会法商业工业及输出业三种同业公会法为基干①,惟欲普遍管理交易市场,抑制抬价屯积投机等活动,则对于全部交易不能有所遗漏,故依法应加入同业公会者固强迫应加入同业公会,即受法令限制不能参加同业公会者如资本在三百元以下之商店,或无动力及工人不及三十人之厂家,以及私人,社团等如有商品出售,则必须采取下列方式:(一)售与同业公会之会员,(二)报告同业公会取得特许证,并与会员厂商受同样之限制,(三)联合若干小企业成立预备组织再行加入同业公会,务使屯积者无自由出售之可能,而后能断其非法活动之念。至于同业公会与政府之关系,亦须加强。朱祖晦先生谓中国各同业公会之经费及会计仅由商人自动处理,殊不足以担负强大任务,主张按照全国各地之营业数量加以估计,将各公会分若干等级给以津贴,并由主管机关监督之,其会计员亦由地方主管机关派任之,②此固可加强公会与政府间之关系,但同业公会之人事,政府亦应加以统制。一、同业公会举行选举后应由政府圈定主席,二、政府有撤换公会职员之权,三、每一公会应由政府指定秘书专负平价之责任,四、由政府另派专员协助各地公会议定公价,五、秘书专员之俸薪应分别由公会及政府支给之。除上述调整外,各同类物品之工业公会应与商业工会成立联合会,以期密切联系,协议进行。

公平价格之厘定,非特足以影响于统制物价之执行,且可影响国民经济之发展,盖公价之规定过高,则无平抑之效,规定过低,则压抑厂商过甚,不易严格执行,其甚者,足以防碍生产,断壅经济基础,尤为不利。日本产业界与金融界为官定物价之高低发生政争③,已足见其关系之重大。且也,各地经济环境不同,物品之供需状况各异,设以中央之权力普遍规定全国各地之价格,则恐政府耳目未周,难期公允,故宜由中央以审慎之态度,规定各地之基价,再由当地主管机关邀同公会依此基价斟酌当地情形以为伸缩,而厘定公价,发布施行。同时中央更可予地方以相当限制,使在基价上下若干之限

---

① 卢郁文著:《新经济的三个原则》,《新经济》第一卷第二期。
② 朱祖晦著:《目下我国应采用之对外贸易国营方案》,《经济动员》第二卷第五期。
③ 中央国际宣传处在本年四月份发表《日本产业资本家与金融资本家的斗争》(标题或有错误)。

度以内,可以自由订定,但在限度以外则必须呈请中央核准,如此者一则可免中央统制之烦,一则可使公会适合地方之状况。至于基价之规定,以成本为依归,倘能管理得法,则中间商人之过分利得庶几可免,亦即日本所谓"行庄之手续费制度"①之本意可以实现。

执行之方法可分四种:

一、厂商呈报办法——为欲明了各厂商有无屯积之企图,市场上可能供给之数量,以及所订公价之是否适当,应责令各厂商,每月呈报各项物品之定购量、运送量、运到量,以及各厂之生产量,定出货物已交之数量、储存量以及上月底原料结存量,本月内原料之购进量等,传供主管机关之参考。

二、经济警察办法——考德日等国皆有经济警察之制度,盖政府为谋遂行其统制之计划,非但须有专责执行机关,且须有严密监督机构。以我国物价问题之严重、交易市场之紊乱,经济警察实属有设立之必要。至其任务,应在稽察市场有无下列违法情事:1.售价过高者,2.囤积不售者,3.假造发票或不作发票者,4.不受公会管辖私自发售者,5.私行进货不向公会发售者,6.其他扰乱市场之活动。

稽察工作进行时,经济警察并得请普通警察及特务机关协助之。

三、民众监督办法——物价抬高对于消费者有切身利害,故宜利用购买者随时监督。其办法首应使出售者将商品一一标明价格,置于显明之地位,使购买者得以相互比较,更应规定平价物品之交易,一律须开具发票,并备存根,其存根须按期汇呈公会,发票须交购买者,倘索价超过公价,则购买者得以发票为根据,请公会或法院依法处办,并获相当酬报,以示奖励告发之意。

四、限制购买限期出货办法——重要商品之便于统制者得以依据需要,按户发给购买证,以限制需要量,对于制造厂家更应在购买原料后若干日内必需出货若干,呈报公会(此法可称为原料与制品连锁制),藉以避免屯积原料之弊,同时政府可依此作适当之调度,以求分配之合理化。

统制交易市场,必须循序渐进,盖全国同时举办非但政府之人力、财力有所不及,即或发现错误亦不易纠正,故应择重要地点、重要物品,逐步实施,关于地点之选择应自较大之城市开始,同时对于各种日用品之主要集散市场亦应早日统制,关于物品之选择自应以民生日用品为主,而民生日用品

---

① 《中外经济拔萃·日本战时物价对策之发展过程》,原载《国际经济周报》第十九卷第十九期。

中以衣食二项最为主要,衣料之中可选棉纱、棉布二者,食物之中俗所谓"柴米油盐"皆不可或缺,柴可包括煤炭二种,米可包括米及面粉。故纱、布、煤、炭、米、面、油、盐八种应为着手统制之起点,然后逐渐扩充,或更易收实效也。

现时我国统制物价之工作系由经济部负责主持,惟物价问题关系国民生计之巨,又非短期内所能解决,就上述办法而言,工作已极繁重,而在全盘统制之时,尤必兼顾各地生产、消费运输、国际贸易、金融等状况,其范围之广,将必涉及内政、外交、交通、经济、财政各部之职司,而其权限又必有直接指挥各社团民众之活动,故各国平抑物价常直属于内阁,盖在行政上实有必要也。吾人以为我国平抑物价应在行政院之下成立全国物价总监部,由政府特派大员主持之,重要地点设立分监部、总监部及分监部内各以专家组织物价委员会,设任调查、设计、监督、审议等工作,庶可使全国统制物价机构臻于健全,而后能收指臂之效。

我国社会基础原甚薄弱,以言增产,则旧有产业尚无完备之调查;以言节约,则人口数量尚无翔实之统计;以言合理分配,则商业社会原无健全之机构。轻言彻底统制,实非易事。然在上述办法实行之后,则统制之机构可渐臻于健全,公务人员可渐获统制之经验,重要之商品可自各地厂商之呈报而得其数量,同时人民亦不以统制为苛虐,然后逐渐改进,将必水到渠成,无所滞凝矣。至于政府现有公营商店之应继续扩充,固属当然,盖此不独为将来彻底平价之阶梯,即在统制交易市场之时,亦往往有奸商以停止运货为要挟,政府必以公营为准备,然后能贯彻其平价之政策也。

(原载《中国青年》1940年第2卷第6期)

统制贸易之理论与办法

> 一、绪言
> 二、自由贸易理论之批评
> 　　(甲)个人主义或自私自利的假定
> 　　(乙)自由竞争的假定
> 　　(丙)自然调整的假定
> 　　(丁)生产成本为固定与递增的假定
> 　　(戊)国内每一单位货币之边际效用皆相等的假定
> 　　(己)纯经济观点的假定
> 　　(庚)贸易国经济发展程度相等的假定
> 三、统制贸易的理论
> 　　(甲)全体与个体或部分
> 　　(乙)国家得视为有机体
> 　　(丙)贸易政策之趋势
> 　　(丁)本于国情的贸易政策
> 四、统制贸易之办法
> 　　(甲)直接统制法
> 　　(乙)间接统制法
> 五、我国统制贸易的原则与办法
> 　　(甲)原则
> 　　(乙)办法

一、绪　言

国际贸易是经济学的一个部门,在十八世纪以前,就已有许多关于国际贸易理论与政策的讨论,但是也如同其他经济学的部门一样,没有完成一个系统严密的理论。自一七五二年休谟(Hume)的经济文集(*Political Discourses*)问世之后,便奠定了古典学派国际贸易理论的基础。嗣经斯密(Smith)、李加图(Ricardo)、穆勒(Mill)的引申,复经新古典学派马谢耳(Marshall)、巴士推波(Bostable)、屠斯格(Tanssig)和数理学派(经济平衡学派)柏赖图(Porets)等的修正和补充,放任主义的国际贸易理论,已是完整的学说①。从逻辑上说,确实四方周到,八面玲珑,无可訾议。不过,一种学说的健全,除了检讨学说逻辑的本身之外,还要看看学说有些什么假定(Hypotheses)? 这些假定是否完整? 是否切合实际? 我们检讨自由贸易的学说,便是本着这个准则。

二、自由贸易理论之批评

(甲) 个人主义或自私自利的假定

主张自由贸易的人们,认定国家是个人之和,国家利益是个人利益之和,所以个人利益最大时,便是国家利益最大时。所以个人的经济活动,应以自私自利的意志为意志,各自循着获取最大货币收入(Money Income)的途径,自由发展,使每个人的利益和幸福,都可以达到顶点,同时整个国家的利益和幸福,亦伴随着而登峰造极。这便是自由主义或放任主义的立场,亦是经济和谐的说法。这种主张,在资本主义的初期,对于资本的累积、实业的发展、科学的进步,以及其他物资文明都有很大的贡献,也许值得称道赞扬。然而时过境迁,个人利益与社会利益相冲突的现象,到处皆是,只要我们看看现今经济的情形,便可随口举出许多例子来。譬如握有经济权势的少数人常在剥削多数人的利益,又如在同一社会里,一方面有面黄肌瘦的饿莩,同时,在另一方面有生产过剩的大量食粮送到海里去的现象。又如经济落伍的国民在自由贸易制度之下,受了经济先进国民的压迫和剥削,永陷于农业和手工业的阶段,生产事业既不能发展,购买力薄弱,生活贫乏,文化水准亦难得提高,个人的福利既不能与全体相调和,个人主义的社会,既有这些弊病,我们再不能认同"放任"的主张,凡事听其自然了。我们要牺牲小我而保护大我,我们要用全体的智慧,来指挥社会的经济活动,我们再不能让自私自利的野马驰骋于我们田园之上了。

---

① 关于国际贸易学说之文献,请参考 Angell, *Theory of international prices* 及 Viner, *Theory of international trade* 两书中参考书目。

(乙) 自由竞争的假定

在自由竞争的假设下,任何商品之价格,等于其边际生产成本,任何生产因素之各单位,如能任意移动,且能互相替代使用,则无论其用途如何,其价格相等,每个生产因素之价格,均等于边际生产能力。因此,任一商品 A 与另一商品 B 之交换比,等于边际货币成本之比,①今若 A 与 B 之交换比,在甲国为一比三,在乙国为一比二,则甲、乙两国自由贸易之结果,甲国将专力于 B 之生产而输入 A,同时,乙国将从事于 A 之生产,而输入 B,换言之,甲国将从事于生产成本比较优势之商品,乙国亦然。交分工之结果,足使甲乙两国之总生产量增加,而贸易国之消费者,可以最低廉之价格,获得所需要的商品。然而现实社会里情形怎样?自由竞争的现象是否存在?

第一,从商品方面看来,因为下列两种力量的存在,使用(或购买)的习惯和商品的照牌(或信誉)、商品的价格,不一定等于其边际生产成本,常有享受独占利益趋势。

从国际贸易的立场,商品可别为三类:纯国际商品、准国际商品和非国际商品,例如土地、地上附着物(若房屋,公路,铁路)、公营事业(电灯电话、自来水等)和体大质重而价小的物品,都不能运销国外,是为非国际贸易品,与国际贸易无关,兹就前二者论之。

所谓纯国际商品,即是各国市场上有齐一或相当价格的物品,例如金银及棉麦羊毛等普通大宗原料品,都属于此一类。这一类商品的价格,只要质与量相等,决不因产地或销场的不同,而有差异。即使有之,也不会大于运输费用与关税之和。例如同一成色的黄金,无论在伦敦或纽约,或柏林,或上海,其价格总相等或相当。设若彼此之间发生差异,其差数大于关税与运输费用之和,则市场上会发生套买套卖作用(Arbitrage Obligation),使之齐一。所以这类商品,在国际上,只有一个价格。买卖的竞争可以说是完全自由的。

至于准国际商品(Quasi-international Goods),虽是国际贸易的商品,但与前述之纯国际贸易商品不同。这类商品,大都是工业复制品,即使功用名称相同,其质地、花样、结构等亦不一定相等。例如美国福特汽车、雪佛兰汽车和拍力卯(Plymouth)汽车,可以说是同等级的物品,具有同等功用。然其结构质料有别,花样亦各异。花样关系美观,而美观之重要性,较诸其他条件为如何?是一主观的问题,如何方称美观?其意义亦甚微妙。宣传广告

---

① 厉德寅著《国际贸易之理论》,中政校研究部《政治季刊》第三卷第三期第七十一页。

等,就在这个微妙处发生作用。凡此种种皆足使同名称的物品,更可微分细别而为多数种类,而异牌号的物品,有时或可归合为一类。是故工业制品在各国市场上没有一致的价格,可因当地购买人的嗜好或使用习惯以及厂家对于使用人的商誉之不同,造成价格的差异。这就是说,质地相同的物品,受了使用习惯和商标信誉的影响,不能互相自由竞争,反而形成"不相竞争群"(Non-competing Groups)了。厂家有鉴于使用习惯和商标信誉的惯性作用,常以低价倾销政策,把同业驱出市场,建立了自己的商誉,垄断市场而收获近乎独占企业的利益,同时消费人便要出高过于"自然价格"(Natural Price)的代价,才能购买到这种物品,这样建筑在使用习惯和商标信誉上的独占利益,自不如真正独占企业那样稳固,一旦使用习惯转变或商标信誉减退,这种独占利益便要被另一种商品所占有。然则商品虽有更迭,独占情形不变,所以自由竞争不能说是完全存在。

第二,从生产因素方面看来,因专门化生产因素不能自由移转使用之故,①每个生产因素之价格,不一定都等于边际生产能力,并可因用途之不同而有差别,此所以有准地租(Quasi-rent)情形之存在。

生产因素,可别之为劳工、土地及资本三种,主张自由贸易者,认为工人,地主及资本家,为自私自利心之所驱使,互相竞争使用其劳工、土地及资本于报酬最高的途径。同样,企业家的运用此等生产因素,亦必追求最适当的配合,使能达到最高的生产效力,以求最大的收入。因此,任何产业中,如有一种生产因素之边际生产能力,小于其价格,则企业家将减少此生产因素,以减低其成本,而此被裁减之生产因素将移入于他种用途,以提高其生产能力,使与价格相等。反之,如有一企业中,某生产因素之生产能力大于其价格时,则企业家将增用此种因素,以增加其收入,直至其生产能力等于价格时为止。如此看来,在自由竞争的条件下,果如各个生产因素能完全自由移转使用,则各部门实业的每个生产因素,其价格总等于边际生产能力。故可以说,在边际生产力上决定了生产因素的报酬,在边际成本上,决定了商品的价格,然而这个结论,因为专门化生产因素之不能自由移转使用,毁灭了他的真实性。

生产元素之能否移转,自然不能脱离时间而论,时期愈短,生产元素转移的可能性愈小。在短期间所可转移的,只有流动的资本。使用寿命(Length)短于生产过程的生产期,及不必训练的劳工,至于训练需时的劳工

---

① 厉德寅著《国际贸易之理论》,中政校研究部《政治季刊》第三卷第三期第六十九至七十页。

和其他一切固定的生产资产,就难于转移了。这些不能自由移转的生产元素,便是所谓专门化的生产元素(Specific Factors of Production)。只因为专门化生产元素的存在,有时某一种工业部门的利润率,可以超乎寻常而其他部门工业一时无法改换生产以加入竞争。该种工业,在此时期内,可以说享有独占利益。反之,处在不利地位的企业部门,虽然由于市场的价格低落,不能获得寻常的利润,或甚至不能支付他们间接成本(Secondary of Indirect Cost),仍未能立即减少生产量,只好忍受损失。这种道理,亦可适用于其他方面,例如工人企业家,生产工具,虽然他们的报酬过低,但也不能立刻转移他业,换言之,在这种情况之下,替代的法则,就未必尽然了;价格决定在边际成本的说法,就很不正确了。

在长期间,劳工技术可以训练完成,固定资本可以得到充分的折旧准备金,转移使用可以说是不成问题。有些企业部门固然可以在短期间得到适宜的调整,但是有些企业部门非经数十年工夫,不能完成其适应变动的途程。

从商品方面和生产元素方面看来,自由竞争的假定,可以说是与事实不符。况且现在世界各国中,究竟哪一国是确实奉行自由贸易呢?不是实行保护关税制,便是采取统制贸易制。即此而论,自由竞争的假定已无异空中楼阁了。

(丙)自然调整的假定

古典学派认为人类的一切经济活动,都应顺其自然的发展;惟其如此,平衡的状态(Equilibrium)才能达到;纵然可能发生扰乱平衡的势力(Disequilibrating Forces),但是随着扰乱势力之后,便产生一种或几种拨乱反正的势力(Equilibrating Forces),互相调整,于是又达到另一个新的平衡。这是所谓自然的调整或自动的调整(Natural Balance or Self Balance)。在国际经济里,物价、汇价和资金移动便是组成确保国际收支平衡的自然调整机构的三个元素。通常称为"物价汇价资金机构"(Price Exchange-special Mechanism)。至于扰乱国际收支平衡的势力很多,例如:一、关税的增减,二、输出业的津贴,三、国际生产技术的变动,四、国际需要(International Demand)的改变,五、货币贬值,六、倾销,七、国外单方付款(Unilateral Payments)等,皆可以影响国际收支平衡的失调。但是因为有了调整机构的作用,也可随即使之转入新的平衡。譬如其他情形不变,国外对于中国丝织品的需要,因为日本人造丝的竞争,骤然减少,以致中国出口额减少而引起外汇上升(即外币折合本国币之数额增加),并如上升之程度超过现金输出点(金币本位国间与金银本位国间,皆有现金输出入点。若在外汇本位国间,外汇上升而至某种限制以上,也可使国内外汇头寸或国外外汇存款减少),则现金外流。在国内发生通货紧缩现象,一面进口物价上升,进口减少,一面出口物价下降,出口增加,一减一加,于是国际收支又达到一个新的平衡。反之,亦然。

因为有了自然的调整机构,所以正统学派主张顺乎自然。然而这种自然的调整,只是说明一种趋势而已。至于这种趋势何时可以完成,没有人能给一个肯定的答复。这就是自然调整说的弊端。在人类社会里,趋势尽管可能,但是如果只是听其自然的期待着,那么趋势的实现,新平衡的达到,恐怕要在一个渺茫的将来,尤其在"承平为变态,战乱为常态"(关于这一点以后要详加说明)的现时代里,各国为了多多获取对外的购买力,为了刺激国内的生产,谁都要维持一个有利的国际收支差额,那个处在逆势差额下的国家,再不假手人力来挽回逆势,徒然坐待这个自然调整的来临,恐怕在自然调整的平衡尚未达到之前,国内的经济或许早已走到全部衰落的境界了。

(丁) 生产成本为固定与递增的假定

虽然古典学派对于生产成本分析至为详尽,却是在国际贸易上,似乎他们只假定了两种成本,固定与递增。因为我们如果根据递减成本来分析,并不能得到如他们所说的结果——自由贸易可使参加贸易的国家都得到最大的利益。

现在产业的成本,如有递减的,则国际自由贸易的利益,是否存在,是一个值得注意的问题。古拉亨教授(Professor Graham)①曾经根据递减成本的假设,对于自由贸易的古典学派,给予严格的批评。他批评的焦点,并不是比较成本学说(Theory of Comparative Costs)而是比较成本学说的推论,即是各国通商之后,各依比较成本的原则,从事于生产成本比较优势产业的生产,造成国际分工的局面,可使各国生产量增加,但是古拉亨教授以为两贸易国的一方亦许会因为分工而蒙受损失。

贸易的一方,如依比较成本情势的指示,放弃了递减成本产业的发展,而专门从事于递增成本的实业扩充,将蒙受生产量减少的损失。农业国家通常都是处在这种不利的地位。例如十九世纪前半期欧洲大陆的国家,以

---

① 厉德寅著《国际贸易之理论》,中政校研究部《政治季刊》第三卷第三期第六十九至七十页。

及十九世纪后半期的美国,对于英国的贸易而言,他们的处境都是如此。反之,工业国家专门从事于递减成本产业的发展,便可享受生产量增加的利益。故尔贸易国之一,可因贸易而蒙受损失。此与自由贸易论者之想象完全相反。今递减成本之事,可因内围经济或外围经济之故①确可在现实经济社会中存在,则自由贸易之理论自有其内在的缺陷,未可盲目援用。

(戊) 国内每一单位货币之边际效用皆相等的假定

自由主义认为对于进口应听其自由,不应加以人力的干涉,因为进口货之所以进口,是由于本国人民对于此等货物有需要,且此等货物,或为本国所不能生产,或能生产而成本过高。如果加以限制,便是限制了需要,或使国内人民不能以最小的代价,获得最大的满足,这个假定也是不对的。

我们知道,每一个人都有他自己的一个消费水准(Consumption Level),便是说,一个人所消费的各种物品的最后增加的最小单位,对于他所提供的效用,都有相等的趋势。这就是应用在消费方面的替代原则(Principle of Substitution Applied to Consumption),也叫作选择原则(Principle of Choose)。收入额(income)约略相等的人,或许因为消费习惯,或许因为社会地位等的不同,对于同一物品的消费量不一定相等,然其消费水准总相差不远。所以收入额的不等,可说是消费水准不等的主要原因。穷富之间,消费水准既有差异,则每一个单位的货币(购买力)在穷富之间的边际效用,可以相差很远。富有资财的人,可以消费很珍贵的物品,但生活在饥饿线的人们,即是一日三餐也觉不易。

在自由竞争的场合,价格便是各人竞争的核心,货币便是夺取物品的工具。谁的货币数量多,谁的货币边际效用小,谁的购买力使雄厚,就可以在市场取得他们所需要的一切物品。因此购买力贫弱的人们间接的便被购买力雄厚的人所压迫。因为在自由放任的战场里,一切生产事业,都顺随着价格的启示。厚利之所在,生产之所趋,这是自由资本主义制度社会下的特质。设如社会的生产力没有增加,只是奢侈品的需要增加了,则奢侈品的价格上升。这种物价的上升,表面上看来,似乎不会影响到购买力贫弱的人们,然而事实并不如此。当奢侈品的价格上升时,其生产元素的报酬,便会提高,因此从事于生产日常生活必需品的生产元素,可有移转于生产这种奢侈品的趋势。其结果足使必需品的生产量减少,使一般生活在饥饿线上的

---

① 厉德寅著《国际贸易之理论》,中政校研究部《政治季刊》第三卷第三期第六十九至七十页。

人们,感受物价之高的压迫,甚至于生存为难了!

因为财富的分配不平均,各人所有货币的边际效用并不一致。如果听其自由竞争,便可发生这样的悲剧。固然在国家主权之内,我们可以用政府的力量来限制奢侈品的生产;至于对于国外奢侈品的生产,我们只有用统制贸易限制进口的手段了。我们且看奢侈品的需要增加,对于国内的影响如何。

我们知道国际需要的增减,是决定贸易条件的力量,如果我们对洋货的需要增加,依自然的调节作用,起先是外汇上涨,随着便是本国出口货物价格降低和进口货物价格上涨。因此贸易的条件便向与我们不利的方向移动。换言之,便是同等质量的出口货,所购得的洋货数量减小了,今如上面所说的变动,是因为国内产业兴旺,引起了外国生产资产输入的增加,其变动虽有不利,但是为了发展国内的产业,也只好容忍。假如是因为奢侈品输入的增加而引起上述的变动,这种损失,便不应随便忍受的!

自由贸易学说,既假定每一单位货币的边际效用相等,而这个假定又不切合实际,反可招致不幸的结果,其有缺陷,毋庸多说了。

(己) 纯经济观点的假定

自由贸易学说的不切实际和缺乏,在前面已经大体说明。不过退一步来说,即使承认自由贸易的结果,可以使参加贸易的国家都能获得经济利益,我们也难苟同自由贸易的主张。

世界大同是人类理想中的至境,虽然这不是一个不可达到的理想!不过人类的行为,目前还是滞留在极端的国家主义的阶段里,纵然有些国家,在标榜世界主义,但是事实所昭示的,只是变相的帝国主义而已。直接的说,这个世界里,没有不吃人的狼,和平与共存,只是力的平衡,国家不求生存则已,欲求生存,第一着便是国力的强大,有了国家的力量,才能保障和取得经济的幸福。不然,纵然人民的购买力增加,生活程度提高,也不过老虎嘴里的肥羊而已!所以我们衡量国际贸易的各种政策,不能单凭经济的尺度。除了国民的所得和需要顾及之外,他如国力的培养、社会的分配,等等,都应置于考虑之列。为了应付战乱为常,承平为变的局面,即是处在不利的贸易条件之下,有时也得要维持国家的自给自足,或国防工业的发展。德国自希特勒登台之后,为了重整军备与建立重工业,虽然他们对外贸易的条件趋于不利,也值得忍受。

总之,民族的幸福,不能单以财富的增减为权衡的标准。所以要厘定一国的对外贸易政策,必须对于民族生存的安全(政治问题),生产分配的情形(经济问题)和社会生活的状况(社会问题)兼筹并顾,不可偏废。古典派的国际贸易学说,至多只能作为国际贸易的经济理由,至于政治社会的理由,当有待于其他学说经验和国策等的补充。

(庚) 贸易国经济发展程度相等的假定

正统派国际贸易学说,忽略了经济先进国家的实业,比较经济落伍国家的同业为有利的情形,这不可不注意。关于这点,李士德(Lest)曾有明确的说明:"英国之制造业建立已久,较之他国新兴之制造业,颇多特殊利益之处。例如前者能以极廉之工资,雇得多数具有技能且富经验的工人,以及最有训练的技师与工头,能以极贱的代价,购得良好机器;能于便宜的买卖中获得最大的利益;能以极廉的运输费,办理其所购置原料及出售商品的运输;能以低的利息,由银行及金融机关给予制造业以信用的便利。此外如可贵的商业经验、良好的工具、适宜的厂屋、合式的布置,均须经数世之尝试而成功者,亦为彼之擅长;且有广大的国内市场,以销纳其生产品。……凡此种种皆足以保障其事业之能继续存在,即使为欲统制外国市场,须至以长期信用赊卖者,亦有雄厚的资本为其后盾。"通常言之,"既成之业,求其扩充与改进,必较创立新业为易。世代相传的老成企业,其营业利益,恒较草创之同业为丰。欲于实业未兴之国,创办工业,必较同样性质的工业已盛之国为难;盖在此情形下,所需之技师、工头及工人等,皆须先经训练而后可用,非然者必须雇自外国,且该种企业之能否获利,未经证明,遂不足获得资本家之信任,而引起彼之投资决心"①。所以经济落伍的国家,不应该实行自由贸易;必须要用全体智慧实施合理的管理。

三、统制贸易的理论

(甲) 全体与个体或部分

自由贸易理论的错误和流弊,前面业已指出。我们再略略谈谈一点全体与个体的关系。

无论哪一种社会都有它的目的,这个目的是属于这个社会全体的,即所谓共善(Common Good or Common Interest),个人主义的正统学派,以为达到

---

① 李士德《国家经济学》(*The National System of Political Economy*),第 294 页及第 316 页。

这个目的的途径，便是全体中的个体，都顺着各自的利益。这就是个人主义的功利说。这种说法，很明显的犯了一种错误，即把个体与个体间的关系（Relationship）和个体对于全体的功能（Function）混为一谈。为供求律所支配的价格，只是表示个体与个体间的经济关系。某种价格上涨，即表示某种经济行为，对于其他个体的关系发生变动。价格下落，表示该个体对于其他个体的相对重要性低落了。价格上涨，即表示该个体对于其他个体的相对重要性增加了。但是这种经济行为对于社会全体的功能，是否变动？那就难说了。个体与个体关系的变动，并不能表示个体对于全体的功能的变动。关系与功能并不一致。譬如奢侈品的价格上涨，但是从事于生产奢侈品的经济行为，对于社会全体的功能，并不能增加。粮食价格下落，并不是说粮食对于社会全体的功能减少。

个体存在的价值，便是看看他对于全体的功能如何，不是看他对于个体的关系。

但是在自私自利的原则下，各个个体努力的趋向，是在寻求关系的重要，而不注重于个体对于社会全体的功能。关系是个体利益的来源，功能是社会全体利益基础，所以各个个体利益之和，并不是全体的利益。

为了全体的利益，为了完成全体的共善，我们应当伸出一双智慧的手，来统制个体的经济活动！

个体与全体是两个相对的名词。就家庭来说，家庭经济是全体；就地方来说，地方经济是全体；就国家来说，国家经济是全体；就世界来说，世界经济是全体。全体的范围越扩大，全体中的各个个体的经济幸福，愈可增加。但是人类的行为和谅解，迄今还滞留在国家经济的阶段上，即所谓国家至上，民族至上，一切活动，都要以国家的生存和繁荣为最大目的。凡事与国家经济相违反的一切个体的经济行为，都不容许它存在。

(乙) 国家得视为有机体

国家虽由个人所合成，然国家为全体，而个人只为其一细胞；且个人之和不等于国家，各个人财富之和，亦不等于国家之财富，犹如细胞之和，不等于有机体，其理由正同。国家自身有志愿与野心，使其经济组织，依政治的或文化的或军事的，或其他目标而发展。故个人之意志与利益，不必常与国家之意志及利益相符合。故国民之活动，宜兼顾个人与社会之双方利益，方能无大过失。近世各国皆以发展国内工业为职志。盖有鉴于制造业发达国家所有之特殊利益也。例如英国为制造业先进之国，所有之特殊利益，非仅生产量增加,足以提高人民之生活水准,且能促成教育之普及,民主政体之发展,以及国家威权之强盛。又个人经济活动,以赢利为目的,利润遂为一切个人经济活动之原动力。但有利润之经济活动,不必皆能增进众人之幸福。故国家政府为保护全体国民之幸福计,不能放任个人自由经营企业或贸易。生产、贸易及消费等事既在政治法律保护之下进行之,故国家为发展个人经济之中心。

(丙) 贸易政策之趋势

贸易为经济活动之一种,故贸易政策为经济政策之一部,经济政策已由重商主义经过自由主义而入于计划主义。今日为计划主义之时代。重商主义时代之贸易政策,为干涉贸易政策,其目的在使输出超过输入,以出超之额,换取各国之金银。自由主义时代为自由贸易政策时代,其目的在使各国能适应其经济环境,利用劳工资本等生产因素于生产成本比较优势之产业,以冀获得国际分工而增加生产量。计划主义时代为计划贸易政策或管理贸易政策,其目的在使对外贸易能适应国内之经济情形,以扶植国内产业之合理发展,并兼顾对外收支差额的状态,以保护币制之安定。

国际贸易为经济活动的一种,贸易政策就是国家经济政策的一个部门,在统制经济政策大前提下的国际贸易,自应实施统制贸易政策。

以人为的方法,来管理经济活动的方式,本来不只统制一端,重商政策、保护主义,都是以人为的方法管理经济活动,不过,这些方法与统制经济也有很大的区别。

重商主义的理论要点大致为:

1. 现金是重要的财富,而国家富庶是国威隆盛的基础。
2. 增加国家的现金,必先使对外的贸易取得有利差额。
3. 取得有利的差额,必定要管理贸易,以求输出的增加和输入的减少。

而统制贸易的意义,却在使对外贸易能适应国内产业的合理发展,使能达到下列的目的:

1. 增强国力,即发展国防经济。
2. 发展或保护国内的实业。
3. 促进全体的经济幸福。

至于保护主义,也是主张以人为的方法,来限制贸易的自然的活动。但与统制贸易不同,其最重要的区别,即是保护主义,以放任经济制度为背景,而以关税和津贴或奖金等手段,用来保护国内实业的发展,达到预期的目的。统制贸易则以计划经济制度为背景,而所用的办法较为径直,也可以说是比较的严格。

(丁) 本于国情的贸易政策

我国建国之至高原则为三民主义及孙总理遗教,而孙总理之经济政策为计划经济,《实业计划》一书,即为最具体的计划经济之典型,故抗战建国纲领之关于经济者,明白属定"经济建设以军事为中心,同时注意改善人民生活,本此目的以实行计划经济……管理进出口"。故我国目前之经济政策为计划经济,基于计划经济之贸易政策,为管理贸易或计划贸易。计划贸易之意义,当由政府设立专门机关,统筹办理进出口贸易,以适应国内政治经济情形,使本国需要的物品,有充裕之供给;使国内经济,获得合理的发展。

我国经营对外贸易之商人,漫无组织,既缺乏资本,又不谙世界市场情形。其负担之职务,只可谓为代洋商采购及运集土货于出洋口岸;或代向内地销售洋货,买卖价格,全受洋商操纵。故我之对外贸易,完全处于被动地位。输出物品与输入物品之交换条件,日益恶劣,下列统计,即其明证:

年 份	输出物价	输入物价	输出与输入之交换条件
一九二六	100.0	100.0	100.0
一九二七	106.1	107.3	101.1
一九二八	104.5	102.6	98.1
一九二九	105.2	107.7	102.3
一九三〇	108.3	126.7	117.0
一九三一	107.5	150.2	139.7
一九三二	90.4	140.2	155.1
一九三三	82.0	132.3	161.3
一九三四	71.7	132.1	184.2
一九三五	77.6	128.4	165.5
一九三六	96.1	141.7	147.4

观上表,在一九三六年欲得一九二六年之输入物品,必须增加47%之输出,以换得之。若在一九三四年更须增加输出物品84%,始能换得之。易言之,以更多之土货,交换更少之洋货。欲谋改进,必由政府统筹办理输出入,以达到贸易主动地位,并以统购统销之手段,获得最优之价格。

我国人口,以农民占大多数,约合全人口85%,可以说是典型的农业国家。农业国家与先进的工业国家自由贸易的结果,工业国家便发生了累积的优势,农业国家便发生累积的劣势,农业国家,欲使其产业由不利的农业,转到工业化,必定要一方面用人为的力量,削弱工业国家的制成品,在我国市场的优势,另一方面要用出口货换取国外机器和原料的进口,如此才有工业化的可能。

一切经济活动,都含有不可预测的原素,是为风险,贸易风险,约有下列三种:

(1) 国际汇率变动的风险。

(2) 损坏的风险。当货物从生产地点运至消费地点,须经水路长途运输,在此期间,可有全部或局部破损或腐坏的危险。时期愈长,此种风险愈大。

(3) 判断失误的危险,例如价格的不利变更,及需要减退,以致货物不能脱售的危险。

若由国家统制经营,可设驻外商务官传递市场消息,以减低判断错误的危险。若由国家统筹办理,则所有损坏危险,将由集体担负,较诸私人担负,其为害当可较小。

四、统制贸易之办法

(甲) 直接统制法

(1) 许可统制(License System)

此制之要义,在规定一切输出与输入,非经主管统制机关之许可,并给予输入许可证者,皆在被禁之列。又许可证之发给,尚可以遵守他种统制法规(如平定物价法规)为条件。例如美国参加第一次欧战期间,对于橡胶许可证的发给,曾规定输入商以遵守政府所定的市价为条件,又一九一七年美国羊毛市价大涨,除由政府自向外国输入羊毛以平抑市价外,对于私人输入羊毛,施行许可证制,而许可证之发给,以遵守战时实业委员会(Manufacturing Industrial Board)定章为条件,即输入之羊毛必须供给毛纺织业,或经其许可方得出售;且政府有权收买其未售尽之存货。①

(2) 限额制(Quota System)

此制之要义,在于对各种进货,皆规定以一定限额,限额数目,或由政府制定法律或命令规定之,或以协定方式订定之。②

---

① Clark, Hamilton and Moulton, Readings in the Economics of War, p.886.
② Haberler: Theory of International Trade, p.347.

(3) 物物交易制(Barter Trade)

贸易国以协定方式,规定输出入货物之种类,数量及交换条件,实行物物交易。现今全部中苏贸易,属于此种办法。

(4) 国营贸易制

政府机关或特设公司,自办输出输入之事务,是为国营制。当第一次欧战期间,美国于参战之后,即实行统制输出入贸易。因此,外国私人商行在美贸易诸多不便,英国政府乃派购买特使(Special Buying Mission)驻美,以向美国政府商购,或取得美政府之许可,按照规定官价与指定来源,自行收购。同时美政府亦因为英政府实行双重价格制(即政府收购可援用低价,而私人购买,则须依照高价),特由战时实业委员会派遣驻外经济使者,前往英国办理采购输出事宜。又英政府为统筹购买小麦起见,曾在国外设立小麦输出公司(Wheat Export Company)专办驻在国外采购输出等业务事宜。此等事实可谓政府机关专营制度,亦可谓为国营国际贸易国营制度是为全部国营对外贸易之滥觞。苏联于革命后,即于一九一八年以法律制定对外贸易之先例。苏俄的经济制度为计划经济,故其国营办法,与上述英美所实行者不同,其贸易业务,完全以各种经济计划为根据,务使对外贸易之变动,与经济建设发生密切的连锁关系,以使苏俄的幼稚工业获得适当的保护,免受外国同业之压迫伤害。其贸易机构,在行政方面,有对外贸易人民委员会,订定对外贸易的办法,并指导监督经营贸易的组织;其营业方面,有政府与外商联合投资的混合公司,及特种对外贸易有限公司,同在对外贸易人民委员会指导监督之下,办理输出入之业务。此外尚有驻外商务官担任购买进口商品及出售出口商品,更有附属机关分布于各联邦及各区域,担任基层执行及沟通的工作,诚计划经济制度下的一种好办法。①

(乙) 间接统制法

(1) 购买外汇请核制

这种办法对于各种货物的进口,无一般的限制。但进口商向外国采购货物时,须向主管机关请购外汇,所有外货,非经核准购买外汇,不能报关进口。德国自一九三四年开始施行"新计划"起,便实行这种办法。在此"新计划"之下,输入商品,分为二十七类,由二十七统制局(Control Bureau)分别负责统制其输入,而请购外汇之审核,由外汇分配委员会(四年经济计划

---

① 朱祖晦《苏俄对外贸易国营制度》,《经济动员》第一卷第十期。

总理财政部、经济部、铁道部及国家银行组织之)主持之。该会就各期实收的外汇总数,分配于各个进口商。我国自二十七年三月以后亦实行与此相仿的办法。

(2) 贸易货款清算协定制

即利用汇划方法清理贸易商品及勤务的债款。例如甲国进出口商人,将他所欠和应收乙国商人的货款,交由本国的清算机关清理收付。同样乙国进出口商人也将他所欠和应收甲国的货款,交由乙国清算机关清理收付。甲乙两国的清算机关,在规定时期,互相总清算一次,清算的差额,或由短欠国支付外汇,或由债权国增加输入,使之平衡。德国曾经利用此法,向东南欧诸国输入大批农产品,而东南欧诸国,为取得输出代价起见,迫不得已,乃向德国购买大批工业制造品。贸品货款清算制,既以汇划方法清算,实等于物物交易制,惟其物品不必经政府指定罢了。

(3) 优先制

这种办法,便是对于所有适合于国家计划的进出口货物,予以种种优先的方便例。如对于所要奖励输出的物品,优先供给生产者以原料及其他种种便利(如尽先供给运输工具,以及政府垫款等)近今日本对于棉纺织业等所需的原料,给以输入的便利,即是优先统制的一例。我国对于桐油、茶叶等出口货物,优先供给运输便利,亦是优先统制的一例。

(4) 外汇申水制

即是利用两种或几种不同的外汇率。如欲限制输入,可在供给进口商人外汇时,加征申水。反之如欲鼓励输出,可以在收买出口商人外汇时,加给申水。我国七月三日财政部公布施行的"进口物品申请购买外汇规则"及"出口货物结汇领取汇价差额办法"是加征附加费及加给申水的两种办法,故可说是申水制的一例。就原理言,申水制(Premium on Exchange)与津贴制(Bounty)相同。

间接法与直接法的区别,便是后者实行之后所有输出入货物的种类及数量,完全可以按照预定计划做到,而前者则伸缩性较大,常常不能完全达到预定的目的。

统制贸易方法虽然有以上各种制度,但是何者为优,就很难说。政策所以贵为政策的,便是要能适合国家的时间和空间的环境,所以我国采取统制贸易的办法,也不能一味抄袭别国的制度,因为别国有他自己的环境。

五、我国统制贸易的原则与办法

(甲) 原则

（一）国际贸易，须与国内实业相配合，使国防实业与民生实业，均能获得最善的发展。

（二）国际贸易以国家经济为单位，所有进出口贸易，由政府统筹办理之。

（三）进口贸易须尽先取得国防实业及军需物品之充分供给，次及于民生必需品。

（四）出口贸易在不违背国内实业计划之条件，尽量增加输出值。

（五）国际贸易须顾及国际收支之平衡。

（六）国际贸易依实际需要，由国家或特许之合作社及公司经营之。

（七）国际贸易金融保险，运输等分别由四行(中、中、交、农)、中央信托局及交通部中国运输公司优先供应之。

(乙) 办法①

（1）行政

为谋统筹办理进出口贸易事务，以增进效能，贸易行政应求集中，贸易机构务使健全，经营人员应加培育，行政院应设贸易部，统筹办理进出口贸易，其行政系统如次：

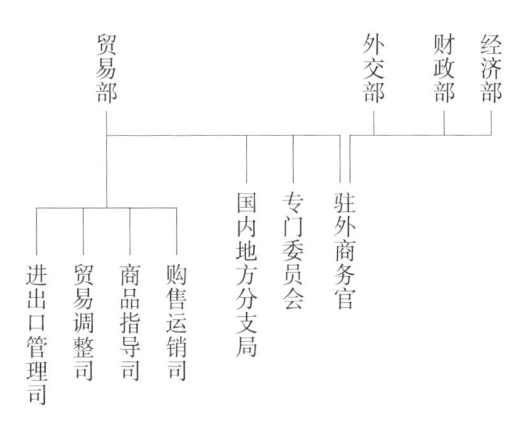

```
                    贸易部                        外交部  财政部  经济部
                      |                            |
  ┌────┬────┬────┬────┬────┐                  驻外商务官
进出口  贸易  商品  购售  国内   专门
管理司 调整司 指导司 运销司 地方  委员会
                          分支局
```

---

① 《中央日报》二十八年二月二十六日厉德寅《国营国际贸易议》。

国家政府为适应国内经济情势之需要,得宣布若干种进出口货物,为国营商品,并自设公司经营之。进出口管理司,为关于此方面之主管机关,其职掌拟定如下:

（一）关于国际贸易国营公司之指导监督。

（二）关于国外市场状况及需要情形之调查,为输出之参考。

（三）关于国内需要情形之调查,统计,以为输入之参考。

不在上列国际贸易国营公司经营范围内之物品,依国内产业情形及需要性质,得分别规定为特许贸易与自由贸易商品。对于前者,可采用许可证制,以限制其输出入之数额,一方面限制需要物品之输出及增加其输入,而维持国内之必要供给,他方面限制不必要物品之输入量而平衡分配于各种用途。对于后者任令特许之合作社及商管公司经营之。为担负此种工作,拟设贸易调整司主管之。其职掌如下:

（一）关于特许证之核发。

（二）关于一般关税率之制定,以限制自由贸易物品之进出口。

（三）关于输出入物品成本运费等之调查,及其价格之评定,以推行政府稳定输出入物价的政策。

（四）关于输入货物之合理分配。

商品指导司掌理下列事项:

（一）关于进出口商品之检验事项。

（二）关于出口商品之标准化及改良等事项之指导。

（三）关于外国市场需要情形变动之宣传,以引起产业家之注意,俾便改变产品之性质或式样,以适应之。

为谋集中购买与合力推销,国内应设出口商行及转运公司,并在国外设立分支处,代商人在国外采购或推销货物,及指洽运输保险报关等事宜。购售运销司为主管此等事务之机关,其职掌如下:

（一）关于进出口商行及转运公司之指挥监督等事项。

（二）关于外国洋行驻华经理处或代理处之调查登记及取缔等事宜。

国内各省县之分支处,直接秉承贸易部之命令而活动。

驻外商务官掌理下列事项:

（一）调查驻在国之商业市场状况,及对于我国输出品之需要情形,向国内报告。

（二）介绍我国经济现状重要输出品性质及通商情形于外国政府及实业界。

（三）研究通商条约之条件。

驻外领事，须由贸易部会同外交部派遣之，负责推进对外贸易及调查驻在国一般经济及商业状况。

驻外大使馆应增设秘书一人，专任研究驻在国经济、财政、金融、贸易情形。

专门委员会为贸易部之咨询机关，由有关国外贸易之政府机关暨实业界代表组织之，以审议及条陈有关对外贸易之计划及问题。

（2）贸易金融

一、国营公司之资本，由国库筹备。

二、国营公司之流动资金，由中中交农四行协助之。

三、输出物品之生产业，应由四行转予低利放款贴现之便利。

四、输出货物之货款，应集售于四行，而四行应垫款或放款于出口商人，使可尽量向生产者收买，以便运往外国销售，多得外汇。

（3）贸易保险

输出货物之保险，由中央信托局为之，其保险费暂准记账，待出口货脱售时补付。

（4）贸易运输

贸易运输由中国运输公司代理之，其费用亦准记账。

（5）贸易业务

一、贸易业务以增加输出而多得外汇为准则。国营贸易公司之盈亏损益由国库担负之。

二、为适应政治经济环境，依货物之性质，分别为国营、合作社经营及商营三类。经营对外贸易之合作社及公司，必先呈准主管政府登记注册方得营业。

二九，四，一一，于重庆纯阳洞

（原载《贸易月刊》1940年第2卷第3期）

三年来之农业金融及今后改进之途径

一、战前农业金融之略史

战前我国农业金融之演变,可以分为二期。自民国四年至民国十六年为第一期。我国新式农业金融机关之创设,以民国四年成立之通县农工银行为嚆矢,办理小工小农之贷款。继之成立者,有吴江震泽镇之江丰银行及华洋议赈会,皆系办理合作贷款。前者偏于养蚕贷款,并注意农业生产之技术与农民之组织,后者为一慈善性质之机关,除放赈救灾外,兼理农村合作贷款。此期贷款,数额微小。至十六年底,江丰银行之贷款总额为五十余万元,华洋议赈会仅六万余元,地域限于江苏河北之少数县份。在此农业金融发展之初期,有二点颇值得注意:

1. 以往对于农民只有消极之救灾恤贫,现在进而为积极之资金融通。
2. 我国之农业金融,系利用合作组织,不仅予农民以资金上之融通,且在组织上与技术上加以帮助。

自民国十七年至抗战开始时为第二期。此期由于政府之策动,舆论之倡导及环境之要求,农业金融机关逐渐成立,而一般金融机关亦多兼办农贷。如十七年有江苏农民银行之创设,二十年后有浙江各县农民银行之相继成立,二十二年四月豫鄂皖赣四省农民银行开幕于汉口,二十四年改组为中国农民银行,其以农民或农村命名者先后不下二十余家,其中以江苏省农民银行及中国农民银行资力最为雄厚,范围较广。各行放款之对象,皆以合作社为主题,间亦由其他农民团体或个人者。放款种类大多为中短期信用放款及抵押放款,而以短期信用放款为最多。此期中,除新成立之各种农民银行专门办理农贷外,其他银行亦先后参加,如民国二十年上海银行创设合作贷款办法。中国银行金城银行仿之。二十年初上海银行总行设立农业合作贷款部,后因放款兼及农业仓库,改称农业贷款部。同年中国银行在总管理处,亦置有农业放款委员五人,司理农业放款事宜。交通银行除积极办理仓库之农村储押外,并于二十四年与上海、金城、浙江兴业及四省农民银行等合组中华农业贷款银团,在山东、河南、陕西、河北、江苏、浙江等地办理棉麦合作贷款。嗣后各省省银行及各地邮政储金局亦多继起举办农村贷款。二十三年七月公布之储蓄银行法第八条,更规定储蓄银行对于农村合作社之质押放款,及以农产物为质之放款,不得少于存款总额五分之一,强制各储蓄银行必须向农村贷款。二十五年九月农本局成立,依组织章程之规定,其使命在调整农业产品,流通农业资金,藉谋全国农村之发达。故该局设立农业仓库及合作金库,以为推动其事业之中心组织,其金融业务着重于储押及合作贷款。截至战前为止,农村金融事业,颇呈欣欣向荣之态,根据估计,二十三年底资金流入农村者,约有一千五百万元,二十四年底约四千余万元。与前期相较,进展颇速。此期农业金融发展之特性约有四点颇值注意:

（1）政府由认识农业金融之重要,进而设立农业金融机关,如中国农民银行及农本局是。

（2）一般金融机关为谋资金之出路,并觉悟农业金融之重要性,发起参加农村放款。

（3）放款之主要对象为信用合作社,短期信用放款为农贷之主流。

（4）农业金融机构实际发展之程序,是由上而下,合作社大多由县合作金库辅导而成,省县合作金库又大多由中国农民银行及农本局辅导而成。

二、战时政府对农业金融之实施

抗战开始农业金融便负有新使命,增加农业生产,以供给军粮民食;并运输出口,使能换取外汇;调整农产运销,以免谷贱伤农,且可稳定谷价;防止高利贷之流行,以安定农村巩固后方;经营垦荒,以抚辑流亡,并可作为战后退伍及残废兵士预谋出路。农业金融之使命既如是重大,政府为完成其使命,乃有各种措施,兹择要叙述如下:

1. 中、中、交、农四行内地联合贴放办法:民国二十六年八月二十六日,财政部为谋内地金融、农矿、工商各业资金之流通起见,公布四行内地联合贴放办法,贴放之范围包括抵押转抵押、贴现及财政部命令对于铁道、交通、农贷、工贷等项之放款。贴放之押品,除工业品矿业品及中央政府发行之债券外,列有农产品一项,计包括米、麦、杂粮、面粉、棉花、植物油、花生、芝麻、大豆、丝、茧、茶、盐糖、药材、蚕种、木、纸、烟叶、猪鬃、牛羊皮等二十二种,目的在便利农产品之储押运销,而谋农村资金之活动。

2. 各省市办理合作贷款:前实业部于二十六年九月十日令发各省市办

理合作贷款要点五条,内分信用放款、储押放款、运输放款、设备放款、工程放款五种,信用放款应照现行之办法继续扩张办理,储押放款以物值百分之八十为准,押品得由合作社代管,以减少管理费用,运输放款应充分贷放以便周转,设备放款包括动力、挑水、加工等项,以设备为抵押。放款额以押品值百分之八十为准,工程放款由合作社建议申请,再由县政府呈请建厅核准,然后贷款,此办法之重要性,在扩大放款范围,提高放款成数。

3. 战时合作贷款调整办法:二十六年底军事委员会公布战时合作贷款调整办法四条,要点如下:

(1) 凡金融机关在战前所规定办理合作农贷之区域仍应继续负责办理,原定农贷合约仍应继续进行,并照历年放款数额,不得减少,或察酌情形,量予增加。

(2) 如所办放款,因兵灾蒙受损失,应由财政部及省政府妥订分别担保办法。

(3) 各种食粮生产储押放款,应由各主管机关拟具计划陈请农产调整委员会核定办理之。

(4) 由有关部会召集合作机关及办理农贷之机关,讨论彻底整理合作农贷之统一切实办法。此办法之意义至为重大,实已具有二十九年度农贷办法纲要之精神。战前办理农贷之区域及所订之合约继续维持,且酌予增加。为保障其安全,由财政部及省政府分别担保。最后尤注意农贷机关与农贷办法之调整。

4. 改善地方金融机构办法纲要:廿七年四月廿九日财部公布改善地方金融机构办法纲要十条,与农业金融有关者如下:

(1) 各地方金融机构领用一元券及辅币券者,除旧有业务外,应增营新业务,其有关农业金融者,计为农业仓库之经营、农产品之储押、种子肥料耕牛农具之贷款、农田水利事业之贷款、农产票据之承受或贴现,完成合法手续及有继续收益土地房产之抵押。

(2) 领用一元券及辅币券之准备,有关农业者,有完成合法手续应有继续性收益之土地房产、农产品,及附有提单仓库及保险单之农业票据,其期限不逾180日者。

(3) 凡地方金融机关关于农产之各种放款,得与中国农民银行及农本局合作,其单独放款受押之农业抵押品,亦得商向当地中国农民银行或农本局转抵押。此纲要对农业金融之意义,在使农产品资金化为活跃农业资金。

5. 扩大农村贷款范围办法:二十七年八月行政院核准,扩大农村贷款

范围办法六项,其要点如下:

(1) 各办理农贷之机关,对增加农业各种放款,应尽量利用各种合作社。在抗战期间,凡经放款机关承认之农民组织,亦得为贷款对象。

(2) 各农贷机关应比照历年贷出金额,在各该区内扩充放款数额。

(3) 各省合作事业,应有各该省合作主管机关积极推进,务期逐渐普遍发展。

(4) 同区域内,如有两个以上之机关办理农贷时,应互相协商调整,避免重复偏枯。此办法系补充并加强战时合作贷款调整办法之效用,目的在确定农贷对象,推进合作组织,扩充放款数额,调整农贷机构。

6. 农业金融处之设立:二十八年九月国府公布战时健全中央金融机构办法纲要,成立中中交农四银行联合办事总处,负责办理政府战时金融政策有关业务,设有战时经济金融两委员会,下设贴放处、发行处、汇兑处、平市处、特种投资处、特种储蓄处、物资处、收兑金银处八大处。二十八年底,西康有农本局与中国农民银行放款之争执,经行政院召集各有关机关会商,拟由四联总处添设农业金融处,以便随时督促联络。四联总处遂于第十三次理事会决议,添设农业金融处。农业金融处原有设计委员会之组织,除处长为当然委员外,由四行及农本局各派代表一人,另聘专家一人至三人负统筹督促联络之责。三月间四联总处理事会主席手令扩大原有农业金融设计委员会之组织,除本总处秘书长副秘书长,农业金融处长及四行各派代表一人为当然委员外,另聘陈委员果夫等十四人为委员。其职掌之要者有改进农业金融制度、筹划及改进农贷办法、调查农村经济、考核农贷工作等项。原有设计委员会改为农贷审核委员会,负草拟农贷规章,审核农贷合约之责。农业金融处之使命,要在调查全国农贷进行之步伐,使全国农贷渐趋于制度化。

7. 二十九年度中央信托局,中央、交通、农民三银行及农本局草拟农贷办法纲要:为适应抗战建国需要,改善农贷办法促进农业生产起见,本总处第二十次理事会通过二十九年度农贷办法纲要,四联总处徐秘书长对该办法纲要之基本精神和主要意义,曾有核要之阐发(见《中农月刊》第一卷第三期):

> 第一,农贷业务之设计与监督。各行局办理农贷均须依照农贷办法纲要进行。各行局与地方政府签订农贷合约,应由四联总处核定,办理之进度随时由四联总处考核。第二,各行局之分工合作。农贷分联

合办理及分区办理两种,各以其宜。如农田水利及推广事业关涉数省或数县者,如战区及边区农贷非一行一局所愿承办者,则由各行局联合办理。如某行局在某地已经办有成绩,或可以由一行局独自办理者,则分区办理。农贷款额由四联总处视各地事实需要,随时决定,由各行局按下列比例分担:中信局15・中国25・交通15・农民35・农本局10。第三,贷款力求直接普遍。贷款对象除农民团体外,兼及农民个人与农业改进机关,贷款区域务使规定举办之每一县份,按期有农贷机构之设立,每一农民有请求贷款之机会。第四,贷款数额之提高及手续之改善。鉴于过去贷款数额之不足及办理手续之细繁,农贷办法纲要乃有第八条乙丙二项之规定(贷款之数额应予提高,以适合当地农民之生产需要)及(贷款手续应力求简洁适应农时)。第五,贷款种类之增加。除过去已办有相当成绩之生产、供销、储押及农田水利等贷款外,更添有农村或运输工具、佃农购置耕地、农村副业及农业推广等贷款,其中以前二项有关农产运销及"耕者有其田"政策之实行,意义最为重大。第六,与地方党政机关之联系。办理农贷不仅为金融机关之业务,同时也是国家之政策,故行局应联络地方党政机关协同调查宣传倡导。

上述六点,已将二十九年度农贷办法纲要之精义,发挥无遗。农业金融处为使纲要中办理农贷之规定,更形具体化,乃制定《各种农贷暂行准则》,将八种农业放款之用途,贷款额度、期限、对象、保障及利率分别规定,以为各机关办理农贷之标准,使前时形形色色之现象,可不复再见。

以上所举七项,系抗战以来政府对农业金融实施之要者,他如最近边区农贷实施原则之订定、农业金融与合作管理局联接办法之成立、农村金融调查之进行等,限于篇幅,不能一一具列。

三、战时农贷之统计与分析

民二十五六年间,国内政治经济,无不有长足之进展,农业金融也呈欣欣向荣之态。迨抗战军兴,一切事业为求适应抗战建国之需要,无不积极调整,突飞猛进。农贷事业经政府之督促,环境之需求,及金融机关自身之觉悟,发展极为迅速。惟因我国经济组织落后,一切制度未臻完善,更加战事乍起,抗战建国需兼程并进,预备工作势难充分,一切事业大多有早熟之弊,于是优于量而拙于质,农贷事业自未能例外。因政府初无统盘之筹划,与一贯政策,以致机构复杂,放款之种类太狭,期限过短,款额不敷等缺点丛生。更因合作社素质不良之故,资金是否贷予最急需之农民,是否用于有关生产之途,亦属疑问。然三年来,农贷数额确有显著之进步,而一般盛赞抗战以来农贷之成绩者,亦多指此方面而言。兹就已收集之资料,加以分析,庶对抗战以来历年农贷数量之发展及其分配情形得一鸟瞰,并可窥见抗战以来农贷事业之利弊,以为将来改进之参考。

1. 民国二十六年底之农村合作放款情形。本年因战事爆发,十一月间淞沪失守,各机关西迁,十二月首都沦陷,情形紊乱,各地农村放款几呈停顿之势,农贷数额之缩小,自在意料之中。该年全国农村贷款数字,无法求全,兹依据二十六年中央农业实验所的调查,辅以其他已得之资料编成第一表。

第一表　二十六年底各农贷机关农村合作放款统计表

贷款机关	放款数额	百分数
中国农民银行	14 605 059.47	53.98
中国银行	3 149 420.00	11.64
江西合作金库	1 344 177.00	4.97
实业部合作事业处	1 252 936.00	4.60
广东省银行	1 117 751.00	4.01
福建省银行	994 440.00	3.85
农本局	671 836.24	2.48
其　他	3 920 328.76	14.50
总　计	27 055 948.47	100.00

资料来源:
1. 中国农民银行,系根据其二十六年度营业报告。
2. 农本局系根据其自开办时至二十六年十月之业务报告。
3. 其余悉系根据《财政评论》第三卷第五期朱通九《战时农业金融之缺陷及其改变》,该文中之资料又系根据经济部中央农业实验所之调查。

注:本表限于资料所列数字为各机关年底之结余数。其余各表,除累计数外,亦均系结余数,结余数受季节变动之影响甚大,当农民需款之季节,结余数增大,当农民还款之季节,结余数减少。再者值此农贷突飞猛进之时期,长期趋势之增加率甚大,年底之数字当远大于年初之数字,此二因素均足影响用年底结余额所作之说明,惟本文所作之说明,注重相对数字之比较,各机关同受季节变动之长期趋势之影响,故仍可代表一般农贷之情形。

二十六年底各机关之农村合作放款,仅有 2 700 余万元,较之二十四年农村贷款之估计,既未增加,反减少 1 200 余万元,思其原因,不外三端:

(1) 以农村合作放款未能包括全部农村放款;

(2) 二十六年战事爆发后,各农贷机关大多停止或减少农村放款以防损失;

(3) 中央农业实验所之调查,恐将沦陷区内之放款未能全部列入。即就中国农民银行之放款而论,据该所之调查为 11 491 635 元,但该行之营业报告,单纯合作放款一项已达 14 605 059.47 元,其余可以类推。

就本表所载之数字而论,农业金融机关放款之次第,首推中国农民银行,超过全体之半数,占总额 53.98%。次为中国银行,占总额 11.64%。当时农本局之地位,并不重要,放款额为 671 836.24 元仅占总额 2.48% 而已。

2. 民国二十七年底之农村合作放款情形。二十七年起社会情形稍微安定,政府深知抗战之经济基础及兵士来源,在广大之农村,非活泼农业资金,以谋复兴农村,不能作长期抗战,乃于二十七年四月间公布改善地方金融机构办法纲要,使农产品资金化以谋农业资金之活动。于八月间核准扩大农村贷款范围办法,使农贷对象确定,数额增加范围扩大,并调整农贷机关之业务。金融界上受政府之督促,自身使命之认识及资金出路之限制,乃发起向后方农村贷款,故本年农贷情形,一反上年之沉寂而呈蓬勃之气象,本年自八月份起,各农贷机关向经济部财政部按月呈报合作贷款数字①。(见第二表"二十七年底各农贷机关合作放款统计表")

第二表 二十七年底各农贷机关农村合作放款统计表

贷款机关	贷出累计数	收回累计数	放款结余数	结余数所占之百分数
农本局			*1 4 322 226.17	6.97
中国农民银行	58 205 637.84	28 754 291.94	29 451 345.90	47.50
中国银行	15 084 593.00	3 290 055.00	*2 11 794 538.00	19.02
交通银行	2 546 314.00	1 024 173.19	*3 1 522 141.00	2.46
湖南省银行	114 207.60		114 207.60	0.18

① 各机关所报告之合作贷款数字,偶有工资数字掺杂其间。

续表

贷款机关	贷出累计数	收回累计数	放款结余数	结余数所占之百分数
陕西省银行	253 116.00	36 066.00	217 050.00	0.35
广东省银行	1 784 896.67	282 571.57	1 502 325.10	2.42
福建省银行	3 242 079.66	1 688 603.72	1 553 475.94	2.51
广西农民银行	3 752 054.21	2 440 559.76	1 311 494.45	2.12
江西裕民银行	1 542 397.88	830 283.54	712 114.34	1.15
富滇新银行	132 617.10	37 389.20	95 227.90	0.15
河南农工银行	197 210.00	17 210.00	180 000.00	0.29
四川省合作金库	5 794 240.16	2 077 780.98	3 716 459.18	5.99
江西省合作金库	10 324 368.95	6 043 586.84	4 280 782.11	6.90
贵州省政府	452 475.10	324 852.91	127 622.19	0.21
湖南省建设厅	228 714.00	102 529.20	126 184.80	0.20
湖北省建设厅合作处	478 221.15	——	478 221.15	0.77
安徽省建设厅	8 000.00	——	8 000.00	0.01
陕西省合作委员会	1 613 692.04	1 226 099.61	387 592.43	0.63
河南省农村合作委员会	6 498.00	4 853.00	1 645.00	0
江西省农业工商调整委员会	202 956.36	107 264.55	95 691.81	0.15
合　计	105 964 289.91	48 288 171.01	61 998 345.07	100 00

资料来源：
（1）农本局系根据其二十七年度及二十八年度业务报告。
（2）广西农民银行系根据广西农民银行半月刊二卷二期。
（3）其余各机关悉系根据其向经济部财政部按月呈报之《合作事业贷款状况月报表》。
注：
＊1. 农本局之放款结余数包括合作金库放款 4 076 019.79 元及农会放款 246 206.38 元两项。
＊2. 中国银行之贷出累计数仅包括本年贷放总数；收回累计数也仅包括本年收回总数。
＊3. 交通银行之贷出累计数系以上年底之结余数加上半年之贷放总数，收回累计数系本年之收回总数。

本年之放款结余数增至 61 998 345.07 元，较上年度增加 34 942 396.60 元，约为上年度之 1.3 倍，自表中贷出累计数观之，可知我国过去办理之农村贷款至少当在 1.1 亿元以上，已收回之贷款当在 5 000 万元以上（因农本局之贷出及收回累计数未加入），本年之实贷数额为六千余万元。至各农贷机关个别贷款情形，本年度仍以中国农民银行居首，贷款额高达 3 000 万元，占总额 47.50%。以贷款之绝对数而论，本年超过上年一倍有奇，以百分数而论,则较上年度略减,此种绝对数增加相对数减低之现象,固足以显出中国农民银行在农贷中之相对低位不若去年之重要,然此正可以反映其他农贷机关之积极参加及全国农贷之突飞猛进者。次为中国银行绝对数与相对数均有增加,放款额约占全国总额百分之一。最堪注意者为农本局之贷款,放款额为4 322 226.19元,较上年度增加5.5倍,占总数6.97%,较上年度增加1.8倍。本年度各机关贷款额之增加率及占全体百分数之增加率均推农本局为最快,此为一新兴农贷机关初期发展应有之现象。在省地方银行及农民银行中,则以福建省银行居首,贷款额为1 553 475.94元,占总数2.51%。广东省银行略逊,贷款数为1 502 325.10元,占总数2.41%。省合作金库有报告数字者,仅有江西四川二省,以江西省合作金库之4 280 782.11居首,占总数6.90%。其贷款数额之等第与农本局相埒。至于合作机关及其他农贷机关,其放款额无超过总额百分之一者。其中湖北省建设厅合作处为最多,也只有487 221.15元,占总数0.77%而已。

上面只将各农贷机关的个别情形,比较说明,现在为明了各种性质不同的农贷机关之贷款情形,乃将第二表中之二十一个机关,分为四类编成第三表。

第三表 二十七年底各类农贷机关合作放款统计表

农贷机关类别	贷出累计数	收回累计数	放款结余数	结余数所占之百分数
农本局,中国农民银行,中国银行,交通银行	75 836 545.03	33 068 520.13	47 050 251.07	75.95
*1 各省地方银行及农民银行	11 018 579.12	5 332 683.79	5 685 895.33	9.17
*2 各省合作金库	16 118 609.11	8 121 367.82	7 997 241.29	12.90
*3 各省办理合作事务机关及其他	2 999 556.65	1 765 599.27	1 224 957.38	1.98
合　　计	105 764 289.91	48 288 171.01	61 998 345.01	100.00

资料来源:根据二十七年底各农贷机关合作放款统计表分类归并编制而成。因农本局无累计数字之资料,故贷出累计数与收回累计数之差未能等于放款结余数,若自61 998 345.07元中除去农本局之结余数;61 998 345.07-4 322 226.17=57 676 118.90元,则全表平衡。

注:
*1. 包括四个省银行、一个农民银行、三个地方银行。
*2. 包括四川及江西二个省合作金库。
*3. 包括贵州省政府等七个机关。

无论就累计数或结余数而言,均以农本局及中农、中国、交通三行居首,其结余数为 74 090 251.07 元,占总额的 75.97%。超过全体贷款额四分之三,可见目前农贷资金之供给,大部分来自农本局及中国、中农、交通三行,次为各省合作金库贷款额约 800 万,估占总数的 12.90%,其地位驾各省地方银行及农民银行而上之。省合作金库为现有农业金融机构之中层组织,一方面向各金融机关透支款项,一方面供给各县合作金库之资金,既可省去各金融机关直接对各县合作金库贷放手续之麻烦,而各县合作金库间资金之运用,省金库也可善为调剂,故其地位在全国农贷事业发展中,日见重要。各省地方银行及农民银行之贷款数为 5 685 895 33 元,占总数 9.17%,内中包含银行数计有八家之多,而数额竟如是不称,此固由于各行资力薄弱,大多未加注意或注意而未尽厥力,实为主因。至合作机关及其他办理农贷之机关,其本身原非金融组织,放款数额之微小实属必然。尚有一点须声明者,各省合作金库之贷放资金,其中一部系由农本局或中农行认购提倡股或由局行给予透支而来,省农民银行有时亦然,故实际上全国农贷之资金来自各行局者,约占总数 90% 左右。

3. 民国二十八年底之农村合作放款情形。自上年十一月间汉口沦陷,抗战第二期开始,为求建国与抗战同时完成,为求发展后方经济以支持长期抗战,融通农业资金,以增加农业生产为急待解决之问题,二十七年度全国性之农贷机关已经注意后方农贷之举办,但仍属创始期,本年度则进入发展期。就与农贷最有关之县合作金库及信用合作社而论,二十七年之县合作金库约在 100 个左右,二十八年底已成立者增至 224 个,在筹备中者有 112 个,二十七年底之信用合作社有 55 466 个,二十八年十月底已增至 74 610 个,此种农贷基层机构之发展,正可以反映全国农贷事业之活跃。兹将本年度参加办理农贷之二十八个机关贷款数字,列如第四表。

第四表　二十八年底各农贷机关合作放款统计表

贷款机关	贷出累计数	收回累计数	放款结余数	结余数所占百分数
农本局			*1 12 927 803.52	11.48
中国农民银行	106 044 304.83	58 256 391.59	47 787 913.24	42.52
中国银行	22 725 979.00	7 749 779.00	*2 14 976 200.00	13.30

续表

贷款机关	贷出累计数	收回累计数	放款结余数	结余数所占百分数
			＊3	
交通银行	1 676 582.88	510 179.79	1 166 403.09	1.04
			＊4	
湖南省银行	263 945.85	103 442.00	160 502.85	0.15
陕西省银行	772 188.80	282 053.00	490 153.80	0.44
广东省银行	2 334 627.92	713 509.27	1 621 118.65	1.44
福建省银行	5 271 994.46	3 880 516.64	1 391 477.76	1.24
			＊5	
四川省银行			400 000.00	0.36
甘肃省银行			628 523.95	0.56
广西农民银行	3 166 065.00	181 816.00	2 984 249.00	2.65
			＊6	
江苏农民银行			6 440 236.14	5.72
江西裕民银行	1 868 448.99	268 034.99	900 214.00	0.80
富滇新银行			592 742.80	0.53
河南农工银行	197 197 210.00	167 210.00	30 000.00	0.03
四川省合作金库	13 924 655.14	5 356 539.27	8 568 115.87	7.61
			＊7	
江西省合作金库	16 018 476.24	11 161 671.59	4 856 779.65	4.31
			＊8	
浙江省合作金库			2 425 660.63	2.15
			＊9	
经济部合管局			1 768 292.35	1.57
贵州省政府	467 640.60	339 810.70	127 820.40	0.11
			＊10	
湖南省建设厅	558 764.00	291 529.00	267 235.00	0.24
湖北省建设厅合作处	512 507.72	201 624.92	310 892.80	0.28
			＊11	
安徽省建设厅	8 000.00	5 845.00	2 155.00	0
陕西省合作事业管理处	1 809 571.77	1 487 534.12	322 057.65	0.29
河南省建设厅合作事业管理处	552 501.00	5 987.00	546 514.00	0.49
云南省合作事业委员会			610 441.00	0.54

续表

贷款机关	贷出累计数	收回累计数	放款结余数	结余数所占百分数
华洋义赈会川分会			*12 8 385.00	0.01
贵州农业生产贷款委员会	300 000.00		300 000.00	0.27
合计	178 473 484.20	91 663 698.88	112 611 898.15	100.00

资料来源：

1. 农本局系根据其二十八年度业务报告。
2. 有累积数字各机关系根据其向经济部、财政部按月呈报之《合作事业贷款状况月报表》。
3. 无累积数字各机关系根据其向四联总处呈报之《农贷统计调查表》。

注：

 * 1. 农本局之放款结余数包括合作金库放款10 826 752.04元,合作金库代理农本局放款349 216.94元及农会放款1 751 834.54元。
 * 2. 中国银行之贷出累计数,仅包括本年贷放总数;收回累计数也仅包括本年收回总数本表所列系十月份报告数字。
 * 3. 交通银行之贷出累计数系以上年底之结余数加上本年之贷放总数,收回累计数系本年之收回总数。
 * 4. 湖南省银行系八月份报告数字。
 * 5. 四川省银行系二十九年二月份报告数字。
 * 6. 江苏农民银行系六月份报告数字。
 * 7. 江西省合作金库系九月份报告数字。
 * 8. 浙江省合作金库系二十九年二月份报告数字。
 * 9. 经济部和管局系二十八年六月份到十二月数字。
 * 10. 湖南建设厅系十月份报告数字。
 * 11. 安徽省建设厅系十一月份报告数字。
 * 12. 华洋义赈会川分会系二十九年二月份报告数字。

本年底之贷出累计数达178 473 484.20元,较上年增加72 509 194.29元,收回累计数91 663 698.88元,较上年度增加43 375 527.87元,放款结余数为112 611 898.15元。较上年度增加50 613 553.04元,为上年度131.64%。本年度贷款总数约一万万元,就增加数及增加率而言,均不得谓为不速。上年度各农贷机关合作放款之等第及重要情形之变动,本年十九依然存在,仍以中农行居首,累计数超过一万万元,结余数为47 789 913.24元,占总数42.52%,绝对数虽较上年增加18 336 567.34元,对全国放款总数反减少5%。中国银行次之,因其结余数只较前增加300余万元,故所占之百分数乃由 19.02% 跌至 13.30%，贷款数额之重要性较上期减少三分之一。在全国农贷事业之猛晋中该行之发展，似乎落后。农本局仍占第三位，结余数为 12 927 803.52 元，较上年度年度增加二倍，占总数 11.48%，较上年度约增加 65%，本年度之绝对数及相对数虽同属增加，然其增加之速度已较上年度大为减退。第四为四川省合作金库，占总数 7.61%。第五为江苏省农民银行，占总数 5.72%。省银行及地方银行之放款无过总数 1.5% 者。在非金融机关之放款中，以经济部合作事业管理局居首，结余数为 1 768 292.25 元，占总数 1.57%，本年交通银行之合作放款，结余数由 1 522 141.00 元减为 1 166 403.09 元，所占总数之百分数由 2.46% 减至 1.04%。原因不明。

兹再将各农贷机关分类以比较其合作放款情形（见第五表）。

第五表　二十八年各类农贷机关合作放款统计表

贷款机关类别	贷出累计数	收回累计数	放款结余数	结余数所占之百分数
农本局，中国农民银行，中国银行，交通银行	130 446 866.71	66 516 350.38	76 858 319.85	68.25
*1 各省地方银行及农民银行	13 874 481.02	6 296 781.90	15 639 219.95	13.89
*2 各省省合作金库	29 943 131.38	16 518 235.86	15 850 556.15	14.08
*3 各省合作事业机关及其他	4 209 005.09	2 332 330.74	4 263 802.20	3.79
合　计	178 473 484.20	91 663 698.88	112 611 898.15	

资料来源：根据第四表二十八年底各农贷机关合作放款统计表，将各机关分类归并编织而成，因有数机关之累积数字无报告，故余数与贷出累计数减去收回累计数之差数不等。

注：
* 1. 包括六个省银行、二个农民银行、三个地方银行。
* 2. 包括四川、江西、浙江三个省合作金库。
* 3. 包括经济部合管局等十个机关。

上表四种数字之位次，均属一致，仍与上年度相同。农本局及中农、中国、交通三行居首，次为各种合作金库，次为各省地方银行及农民银行，最后为各省办理合作专业机关及其他各省办理农贷之机关。农本局及三行之放款结余额为 76 858 319.85 元，较上年度增加 29 768 068.78 元，大都系中农行及农本局所增加者，所占百分数为 68.25%，较上年度减少 7.7%，此大部分系中国、中农二行之相对放款贷额减少所致。各省合作金库与各省地方银行及农民银行二者之结余数及百分数大致相等,各省地方银行及农民银行之结余数能由 5 685 895.32 增至 15 639 319.95,十九由于省农民银行放款之增加,省地方银行之放款无甚显著之变动。至其他合作农贷机关之放款结余额及百分数均增加甚远,此因为政府合作机构积极倡办农贷之结果,但其数额微小,对于全国放款数额无重大之影响。

4. 各农贷机关放款之对象分配情形,现在农贷之放款对象形形色色不下数十,为易于比较起见,划分为七类。(一)合作社包括合作社互助社及联合社。(二)合作金库包括省及县合作金库。(三)农仓,包括自办农仓协办农仓及简易农仓。(四)农场。(五)其他农民借款团体,包括非合作社之农民贷款团体,如借款协会等。(六)农业指导改进机关包括农业改进机关及农事指导机关。(七)其他包括其余上列六种以外之贷款对象。七类之中,以前三类最为重要,兹将其性质及作用申述如下:

(1) 合作社:我国合作运动,开始于薛仙丹氏,垂今已有二十余年之历史。战后发展,极为迅速。农村贷款自始即以合作为对象。现在之合作社分为信用、供给、生产、运销、消费、公用六类,在农村放款中以信用合作社最为重要。我国农民既贫穷且散漫,仅凭一己之信用,绝不能获得银行之资金,故在贷款机关为求遵守费用经济,手续简单,保障安全之放款原则。在一般农民为求利用"群力"以取得贷款,均非借合作之组织无以收效。借合作社组织取得之贷款,因手续费用节省,保障较为安全,故利率可以减低。农民取得贷款之后,因彼此负有连带保证责任,对于资金之用途,可以自动彼此监督,必按其借款之目的使用,此对放款机关资金之安全,无形中又加一重保障,而农贷之效用,亦可由此真正实现。

(2) 合作金库:自二十四年即有江西与四川二者合作金库之成立,二十五年农本局成立后为谋合作金融制度之树立,乃辅设县合作金库为其基层机构,以合作社为骨干,发展之程序由下而上。初期因农民知识浅薄,资金缺乏,先由金融机关、政府机关及其他不以营利为目的之法团认购提倡股,选举金库之理监事,然不论合作社认股如何微小,至少必估监理事各一席,嗣后社股渐增,社员所选之理监事也按比例增加,各机关因所认之提倡股较少而派充之理监事也随之减少,最后达到自营、自有、自享之境界。合作金库较合作社为更进一步之放款对象,在金融机关对经济简单安全之原则,可以获得更大之满意,在农民因合作金库之信用系建筑在各个合作社之结合上,可以取得较大之信用,且各金融机关之放款经过合作金库之组织,可收其分歧之标准调整而超过一致,故金融机关在某县辅设金库后,即不再对合作社直接放款,目的在运用合作金库之机构。

(3) 农仓:农仓在我国有悠久之历史,自战国时即有常平仓之设立。近代农仓事业,则始于民国二十年左右,至其发展,则最近三数年之事也。农仓不仅为推进放款之工具,举凡作物脱离生产过程后之经济活动,几皆可纳入其营业范围,如农产之保管、加工、运销等,至于农产押款不过其业务之一而已,目前农仓之业务,多数限于储押经营,对前三种效能未见充分应用。

兹将各农贷机关对七种农贷对象放款之数额列表如下(见第六表)。

本表之资料,系包括各农贷机关一切与农业有关之贷款(农产品之贴放不在内),与前面之合作贷款不同,合作贷款往往只包括合作社、合作金库及农仓三项,此三项虽是农贷中之主要部分,但究非全部。而本表不仅可看出全国贷款对象分配之情形,且可对全国农贷总数及各机关在总数中所占之地位得一鸟瞰。

在廿八年底左近,全国各机关之农贷总数计 151 324 481.46 元,表中包括机关二十有八,重要之贷款机关,均已列入,除商业银行未具报外,可谓遗漏甚少。故表中所列之数字至少可表示全国农贷之大概情形,各种对象之放款,以合作社为最多,计 71 477 335.78 元,占总数 47.23%,足证国内农贷之发展,大多借合作社为推进之机构。次为合作金库计 41 172 197.74 元,占 27.21%。合作金库历史极短,为农业金融中之新兴机构,三年来能有如此成绩,可见各方对合作金库推行之努力。合作金库贷款之对象为信用合作社及各种合作联合社①,故亦可包括于合作社贷款中,所计 112 649 533.58 元,占总数 74.44%。合作社在我国农贷事业中之地位,睹此数字,可以思过半矣。农仓放款 100 余万元,估 5.43%,居第四位。以农场放款之 406 122.46 元为最少,估 0.27%。在此七种放款对象中,除其他一项中含有期限较长之农田水利贷款,垦殖贷款外,几全为一年以内之短期贷款,其成数当占全体 90% 以上。

各机关在全国合作放款中所占之地位与在全国农业贷款中所占之地位不同,因合作放款仅占总放款额 74.42%,各机关所居之位次从无变动,而重要程度则显有差别,就本表言,仍以中农行贷款额居首,估 42.61%,与在合作贷款中之地位无甚出入,此可说明中农行对合作贷款与其他贷款(非合作贷款)数额之比例,颇为匀称。农本局升居第二位,估 16.38%,大于合作

---

① 经济部于二十八年一月间,有训令发陕西省合作委员会及贵州省合作委员会,信用业务之外各种合作社,在试办期间,得暂准酌认股额。

第六表 各农贷机关放款对象统计表

自 28 年 6 月至 29 年 2 月

贷款机关	截止日期	合作社 *1	合作金库 *2	农会	农场	其他农民借款团体	农业生产改进机关	其他	合计	百分数
农本局	28年12月	8 863 713.19	(a) 7 286 153.12 (b) 3 289 815.86	1 751 834.54				2 995 389.40	24 786 906.11	16.38
中农行	28年12月	27 778 004.08	19 201 266.15	808 643.01	328 270.79	1 560 201.00		16 356 644.44	64 472 828.47	42.61
中国行	28年10月	15 802 869.00						2 031.00	17 365 101.00	11.48
交通行	29年1月	534 159.27					59 223.30	5 742 641.31	6 336 023.91	4.19
湖南省行	28年12月	246 334.79		30 774.21			11 036.84	32 300.00	320 445.84	0.21
陕西省行	29年2月	391 826.00		59 038.80			22 758.45	6 000.00	479 623.25	0.32
广东省行	28年12月	642 590.02		469 042.00		708 714.12		9 523.02	1 829 869.16	1.21
福建省行	28年12月	932 046.61		40 000.00		119 367.74	236 049.70	94 607.18	1 422 071.23	0.94
四川省行	29年2月		400 000.00						400 000.00	0.26
甘肃省行		100 892.00		527 631.95					628 523.95	0.42
广西农民行	28年12月	2 984 249.00							2 984 249.00	1.97
江苏农民行	28年6月	2 139 469.87		4 300 766.27	77 851.67		711 871.00	312 977.94	7 542 936.75	4.98

续表

贷款机关	截止日期	合作社	合作金库	农会	农场	其他农民借款团体	农业生产改进机关	其他	合计	百分数
江西裕民银行	29年2月		382 895.60	200 000.00				712 575.27	1 295 470.87	0.86
富滇新行	28年12月	589 892.50		2 850.30					592 742.80	0.39
河南农工行	29年2月	16 400.00	30 000.00						46 400.00	0.03
四川省合作金库	29年2月	106 779.24	(a) 1 787 338.73 (b) 6 990 000.00						8 884 117.97	5.87
江西省合作金库	28年9月	4 856 779.65							4 856 779.65	3.21
浙江省合作金库	29年2月	1 545 660.63	(a) 516 000.00					364 000.00	2 425 660.63	1.60
经济部合管局	28年6月至12月	1 755 320.69		12 971.66					1 768 292.35	1.17
贵州省政府	28年2月	92 632.59							92 632.59	0.00
湖南省建设厅	28年12月	267 235.00							267 235.00	0.18
湖北省建设厅合作处	28年12月	48 310.00	688 728.28						737 038.28	0.49
安徽省建设厅	28年11月	2 155.00							2 155.00	0.00
陕西省合作事业管理处	28年12月	322 057.65							322 057.65	0.21

续表

贷款机关	截止日期	合作社	合作金库	农 会	农 场	其他农民借款团体	农业生产改进机关	其 他	合 计	百分数
河南省建设厅合作事业管理处	29年1月	546 494.00							546 494.00	0.36
云南省合作事业委员会	28年12月	603 080.00		7 361.00					610 441.00	0.40
华洋义赈会四川分会	29年2月	8 385.00							8 385.00	0.01
贵州农业生产贷款委员会	28年12月	300 000.00							300 000.00	0.20
总 计		71 477 338.78	41 172 197.74	8 210 913.74	406 122.46	2 388 282.86	1 040 939.32	26 628 689.56	151 324 481.46	100.00
百分数		47.23	27.21	5.43	0.27	1.58	0.69	17.60	100.00	

资料来源：
1. 农本局系根据其二十八年度业务报告。
2. 中国农民银行系根据《中农月刊》卷三期林荣《七年来中国农民银行之农贷》。
3. 广西农民银行，江西省银行，贵州省合作金库，贵州省政府，湖南建设厅，安徽建设厅，陕西省合作事业管理处，河南省建设厅合作事业管理处，贵州省农业生产贷款委员会，江西省农贷款委员会等，系根据农业部、财政部按月呈报之《合作事业贷款状况月报表》。
4. 其余各农贷机关系根据其向四联总处呈报之《农贷统计调查表》。

注：
* 1. 农本局合作社一栏，包括食品生产贷款 4 376 481.31 元，经济作物生产贷款 1 044 040.29 元及战区农业生产贷款 3 443 191.59 元，该三项放款，虽非全部以合作社为对象，但大半为之。
* 2. 农本局各农贷金库一栏数字中包括有合作金库代理农本局放款 349 216 94 元，此项放款系放于金库业务区域之内互助社、邻里无尚未设立农会之农立及未设立农会地域备高备押农产之农民。

放款中所占11.48%,此系农本局对其他贷款颇为重视,在全国农贷中之地位重于在合作放款中之地位。中国银行之情形相反,由第二位降为第三位,此系中国银行对其他种类放款未加举办,故在全国农贷中之地位不及在合作放款中地位之重要。交通银行之情形与农本局大致相同,程度则过之。其余各机关之90%略形减少,此由于其他农贷机关大多只办理合作贷款所致。兹再将各贷款机构分类列成第七表(见第七表"各项农贷机关放款对象比较表")。

表中放款数额之位次,以农本局及中农、中国、交通三行居首,占74.65%,各省地方银行及农民银行次之,再次为各省省合作金库,各省合作事业机关及其他机关居末位。仅就第七表观察尚无多大意义,若以第七表之百分数一栏与第五表之百分数一栏互相比较,则意义极为显明:(1)在合作放款中各类机关放款集中之程度不若全国农贷集中之程度。农本局及中农、中国、交通三行之合作放款占68.25%,而其农业贷款占74.65%,可见农本局及三行在全国农贷中之地位比在合作放款中之地位尤为重要。(2)各省地方银行及农民银行,各省省合作金库及各省合作事业机关三类,在第七表中百分数一致降低,此可说明此三类机关(大多为非全国性之农贷机关)对合作放款以外之农业贷款,未能加以密切注意,此或由于资金、地域、人才之限制。(3)各省地方银行及农民银行之位次,在第五表中低于各省省合作金库,在第七表中则高于各省合作金库,此可说明省合作金库因受法令之限制,几全以合作放款为对象,故在合作放款中占较重要之位置,各省地方银行与农民银行对他种放款之办理,虽不如农本局及三行之重视,究比省合作金库注意多多,故全在国农贷中占较重要之位置。

5.各农贷机关放款之地域分配情形。我国各种经济发展在地域上分布之情形,战前皆集中于沿海各省及交通便利之区域,继而随战事之变动,二十七年集中于华中一带,二十八年则集中于西南后方各省,此种情形在农业金融部门之活动,大体未能例外。惟二十二年豫鄂皖赣一带迭遭灾患,政府为复兴农村,有豫鄂皖赣四省农民银行之成立,设总行于汉口,二十四年改名为中国农民银行。虽在战前,该行办理农贷之区域大多集中于华中一带,致使农业金融之发达,华中数省占有特殊地位,可惜因以往各年农贷区域分配资料之缺乏,不能一一列表,洞察全豹,兹将二十八年底左近之全国农贷地域分配情形列成第八表(见第八表"各农贷机关放款分省统计表")。

第七表　各类农贷机关放款对象统计表

农贷机关类别	合作社	合作金库	农会	农场	其他农民借款团体	农业指导改进机关	其他	合计	百分数
农本局,中国农民银行,中国银行,交通银行	52 978 745.54	30 377 235.13	2 560 477.15	328 270.79	1 560 201.00	59 223.33	25 096 706.15	112 960 859.49	74.65
*1 各省地方银行及农民银行	8 043 700.79	812 895.60	5 630 103.53	77 851.67	828 081.86	981 715.99	1 167 983.41	17 542 332.85	11.59
*2 各省省合作金库	6 509 219.52	9 293 338.73					364 000.00	16 166 558.25	10.68
*3 各省合作事业机关及其他	3 945 669.93	688 728.28	20 332.66					4 654 730.87	3.08
合　计	71 477 335.78	41 172 197.74	8 210 913.74	406 122.46	2 388 282.86	1 040 939.32	26 628 689.56	151 324 481.46	100.00

资料来源:根据第六表《各农贷机关放款对象统计表》将各机关分类相并总制而成。

注:
* 1. 包括六个省银行,二个农民银行,三个地方银行。
* 2. 包括四川,江西,浙江三个省合作金库。
* 3. 包括经济部合管局等十个机关。

第八表 各农贷机关分省统计表 自民国 28 年 6 月至 29 年 2 月

	农本局 28年12月	中农行 28年12月	中国行 28年10月	交通行 28年12月	湖南省行 28年12月	陕西省行 28年12月	广东省行 28年12月	福建省行 28年12月	四川省行 29年2月	甘肃省行
四川	8 388 311.27	17 607 027.10	3 844 428.00	3 363 600.00					400 000.00	
陕西	1 137 595.22	7 348 855.42	627 599.00	423 731.84		479 623.25				
云南	191 368.11	492 285.21	2 031.00							
贵州	3 075 371.67	6 412 883.50								
西康	209 015.60	296 260.08	18 695.00							
甘肃		4 775 046.83								628 523.95
湖南	3 756 545.93	1 870 129.09	575 944.00		320 445.84					
湖北	472 460.76	6 375 459.70	198 575.00							
广西	1 938 530.24	1 405 677.90	2 738 684.00	997 481.31						
江苏	2 352 167.02	249 372.19	1 604 695.00	78 070.53						
安徽	205 184.35	7 218 234.74	1 033 371.00							
江西	100 000.00	4 668 224.89	489 832.00	189 501.30						
河北			1 811 936.00							
山东	494 586.88		3 226 459.00	44 000.00						
广东		267 714.66	8 018.00				1 829 869.16			
绥远			6 650.00							
河南	1 060 503.31	2 610 215.64	295 882.00							
福建	26 629.53	1 968 524.37						1 422 071.23		
山西		1 638.00								
浙江	464 011.97	909 778.65	882 352.00	146 536.34						
其他	914 625.15			1 093 102.59						
合计	24 786 906.11	64 472 828.47	17 365 101.00	6 336 023.91	320 445.84	479 623.25	1 829 869.16	1 422 071.23	400 000.00	628 523.95

续第八表 各农贷机关放款分省统计表 自民国28年6月至29年2月

	广西农行 28年12月	江苏农行 28年6月	江西裕民银行 29年2月	富滇新银行 28年12月	河南农工银行 29年2月	四川省合库 29年2月	江西省合库 28年9月	浙江省合库 29年2月	经济部合管局 28年6月至12月	贵州省政府 28年2月
四川						8 884 117.97				
陕西										
云南				592 742.80						
贵州										92 632.59
西康										
甘肃										
湖南									471 988.46	
湖北									374 559.47	
广西	2 984 249.00									
江苏		7 542 936.75								
安徽			1 295 470.87							
江西							4 856 779.65		632 240.51	
河北									289 503.91	
山东										
广东										
绥远										
河南					46 400.00					
福建										
山西										
浙江								2 425 660.63		
其他										
合计	2 984 249.00	7 542 936.75	1 295 470.87	592 742.80	46 400.00	8 884 117.97	4 856 779.65	2 425 660.63	1 768 292.35	92 632.59

再续第八表　各农贷机关放款分省统计表　自民国28年6月至29年2月

	湖南建设厅 28年10月	湖北建设厅 28年10月	安徽建设厅 28年11月	陕西省合作事业管理处 29年1月	河南省合作事业管理处 29年1月	云南省省合会 28年12月	华洋义赈会川分会 29年2月	贵州农业生产贷款委员会 28年12月	总　计	百分数
四川							8 385.00		42 495 869.34	28.08
陕西				322 057.65					10 334 462.38	6.83
云南						610 441.00			1 888 868.12	1.25
贵州								300 000.00	9 880 887.76	6.53
西康									505 275.68	0.33
甘肃									5 422 265.78	3.58
湖南	267 235.00								7 262 288.32	4.80
湖北		737 038.28							8 158 093.21	5.39
广西									10 064 622.45	6.65
江苏									11 827 741.49	7.82
安徽			2 155.00						9 091 185.60	6.01
江西									11 885 312.62	7.80
河北									1 811 936.00	1.20
山东									3 721 045.88	2.46
广东									2 149 601.82	1.42
绥远									6 650.00	0
河南					546 494.00				4 559 444.95	3.01
福建									3 390 596.10	2.26
山西									28 267.53	0.02
浙江									4 828 338.69	3.19
其他									2 007 727.74	1.38
合计	267 235.00	737 038.28	2 155.00	322 057.65	546 494.00	610 441.00	8 385.00	300 000.00	151 324 481.46	100.00

资料来源：与第六表相同。

表中所列全国办理农贷之机关,凡廿有八,但大多属地方性者,现将全国性之农业金融机关之地域分布情形加以分析。农本局之放款区域,包括有十五省,在各省中所放之贷款,以四川省为最多,结余数为 8 388 311.27 元,占该局放款总额三分之一,次为湖南,计 3 756 545.93 元,第三位贵州,第四为江苏,第五为广西,此五省之放款总额计 19 500 926.13 元,占该局总数 79%,故其放款可称集中于该五省,最少者为山西,仅 26 000 余元,与最多之四川相较,悬殊远甚。中国农民银行放款辐员,最为辽阔,遍布十七省之多,在各省中所放之款项以四川为首,计 17 607 027.10 元,占该行放款数额 38%。次为陕西,计 7 343 855.42 元。第三为安徽,计 7 218 234.74 元。第四为贵州,第五为湖北,各占 600 余万元,此前列五省之放款总额计 44 967 480.26 元,占该行总数 70%,其集中程度较农本局略逊。中国银行放款之地域有十六省,其分布情形与前二者不同,虽仍以四川省之 3 844 428 元居首位,而以山东之 3 226 469 元居次,第三为广西,又以河北之 1 811 936 元居第四位,第五位为江苏,山东河北二省系农本局与中农行所未放或不甚注意者,中国银行之放款能偏重之,颇足收地域上补偿之效。至其放款集中之程度,前列五省放款额计 13 226 202 元,占该行总数 76%,其集中程度约介于农本局与中农行之间。交通银行之放款区域仅有七省,以四川之放款为最多,计 3 363 600 元,已占其总额 53%,次则为广西陕西等省,放款额均不足百万元。

现全国办理农贷之区域已遍及二十省,放款之多,首推四川,放款机关有农本局等七家,结余额为 42 495 869.34 元,占全国 28.08%,以一省之范围,放款数占全国四分之一以上,可见该省在农贷地位上之重要。江西次之,在该省办理农贷之机关亦有七家,结余额为 11 889 312.62 元,占全国 7.86%。第三为江苏,放款之机关有五家,结余额为 11 827 741.49 元,占全国百分之 7.82%。第四为陕西,放款之机关有六家,结余额为 10 334 426.28 元,占全国 6.83%。第五为广西,放款之机关有五家,结余额悉在 1 000 万元以上。各省放款在平均数以上者八省,除上述五省外,尚有贵州、安徽及湖北三省。放款最少者为绥远、山西、西康三省,合计仅占全国放款额 0.35%,在全国农贷事业繁荣中颇有偏枯之感,本年度之农贷已注意及之。

根据二十九年度农贷办法纲要第二条"本年度农贷暂就后方各省尽先办理,并以四川西康为首要区域",为明晰后方六省所已办理农贷之情形及在全国中之重要性,乃就第六表之资料另行改编为第九表"各农贷机关对后方六省与其他各省放款统计表"。

第九表　各农贷机关对后方六省与其他各省放款统计表

	后方省							其他各省 *1		总计
	四川	陕西	云南	贵州	西康	甘肃	合计	百分数	合计	百分数	
农本局	8 388 311.27	1 137 595.22	191 368.11	3 075 371.67	209 015.60		13 001 661.87	52.45	11 785 244.24	47.55	24 786 906.11
中国农民银行	17 607 027.10	7 343 855.42	492 285.21	6 412 883.50	296 260.08	4 775 044.83	36 927 358.14	57.28	27 545 470.32	42.72	64 472 828.47
中国银行	3 844 428.00	627 599.00	2 031.00			18 695.00	4 492 753.00	25.87	12 872 348.00	74.13	17 365 101.00
交通银行	3 363 600.00	423 731.84					3 787 331.84	59.77	2 548 692.07	40.23	6 336 023.91
其他各农贷机关 *2	9 292 502.97	801 680.90	1 203 183.80	392 632.59		628 523.95	12 318 524.21	32.11	26 045 097.76	67.89	38 363 621.97
合计	42 495 869.34	10 334 462.38	1 888 868.12	9 880 887.76	505 275.68	5 422 265.78	70 527 629.06	46.61	80 796 852.40	13.39	151 324 481.46
占后方省贷款总额百分数	60.25	14.65	2.68	14.01	0.72	7.69	100.00				
占全国贷款总额之百分数	28.08	6.83	1.25	6.53	0.33	3.58	46.61		53.39		100.00

资料来源：根据第八表"各农贷机关放款分省统计表"。

注：
* 1. 其他各省包括前表中湖南等十四省及其他。
* 2. 其他各农贷机关包括地方银行、农民银行、省合作金库及合作事业机关等二十四家。

在全国1.5亿元之农贷中,后方六省占70 527 629.06元,占全国总额的46.61%,显然超过其耕地面积或农村人口所占之百分比,此系由政府倡导及环境使然。再以各全国性金融机关对后方六省放款之个别情形加一观察,就相对注意之程度而论,以交通银行59.77%,占首位,此因交通银行之放款较少,而对四川一省放款已占其全体53%之故。次为中农行之57.28%。再次为农本局之52.45%。其他各机关多属地方性质,故其放款之分配,自不易有高度集中之现象,所以只占32.11%。中国银行之放款区域,偏于华北沿海及长江下游诸省,故所占比数最少,仅25.87%。就放款结余数额而论,仍以中农行之36 927 358.14元居首,农本局之13 001 661.87元次之,中国行及交通行均不居重要位置。

兹再分析四川、陕西、云南、贵州、西康、甘肃,在后方六省中之重要性。此六省在后方六省中位置之先后,亦如在全国中之次第,并无变动。四川居首,占60.25%。次为陕西占14.65%,与陕西相持者为贵州,占14.01%。再次为甘肃及云南,最后为西康,仅占0.72%。为四川省1/84,云南也只占四川1/22,可见六省彼此间之重要性,相差悬殊,此种现象除土地、人口之因素外,尚受交通及政治之影响。

四、改进农业金融之途径

根据上述之分析,吾人可得下列几点印象:

1. 农业金融之现阶段:考察各国农业金融之发展,莫不趋向于制度化之建立,其内容由简单而复杂,由复杂而调整,最后乃成为一完备之体系,此为一种制度长成所必经之过程。自农村有私人相互借贷、当典、合会及常平仓等金融方式起,至民国十六年有少数小规模之农业金融机关时止,属于第一期,即农业金融之简单时期。自十七年起,除新式农业机关纷纷成立,专办农业金融业务外,原有之金融机关如商业银行、地方银行等,亦多积极参加办理农贷,不相联络,时生摩擦。迨至抗日战争发生以后,此种现象,益趋尖锐化,业务冲突时有耳闻。其错综复杂之情形,至二十八年底可谓已达极点。于是四联总处乃设置农业金融处,订定二十九年度农贷办法纲要,实行农业金融制度及业务之调整,现正依此方向迈进中。

2. 农贷之对象:我国农村放款,向以合作社为对象。二十九年度农贷办法纲要稍有变更,贷款对象,除合作社外,尚有其他农民团体、农民个人及农业改进机关,此或系战时不及组社之权宜办法,亦可谓农贷办法之进步,但合作社仍为放款之主要对象。

3. 合作社之素质：年来放款对象之合作社，因量之发展过于迅速，徒具形式，无论在组织上与活动上，皆尚停留于幼稚阶段。辅导设社之机关应努力设法改善，务求合作社素质之健全，以利农贷之推进。

4. 农贷之期限：我国新式农业金融之起源，似以救济农村破产为主因，属于偶发性质。且我国未有如欧洲之农奴制度，至今尚无大地主资本家阶级，是以生产问题尚比分配问题更为重要。农民所最急需者，尚为农业生产资金，故我国目前所举办之农贷，大都属于短期贷款，只有极少一部分为中期放款，至长期之土地放款，现仅有中农行在南昌着手试办，为数甚微。

5. 农贷资金之来源：全国农贷资金之供给，大部分来自全国性之金融机关，占全部74.65%。各省地方银行及农民银行合占11.59%，似应设法增进。商业银行以业务性质关系，固不宜于举办农贷，但兼办储蓄业务之商业银行，似尚未能依照储蓄银行办法办理，此有待于改进者也。

6. 农贷之地域分配，放款之区域分配，大多集中于交通便利及农产丰富之各省。而一省之内，又大多集中于交通便利及农产富庶之各县，农民需款孔急之荒僻区域，虽有贷款，亦远不足应需要，此种缺陷，或与治安有关，不可不急求补救。

如上所述，我国农业金融，刻已进入调整时期，则如何调整，确为当前重要问题，吾人之希望，宜依照下列数事，实行调整，以确立农业金融之健全基础：

1. 确定制度之体系：吾人主张中国应采取合资合营国资国营之金融制度，农业金融为金融之一部门，其原则亦同。此种制度之组织体系，一方面以单位合作社为细胞，由下而上，次第组织区联合社、县联合社（县合作金库）、省联合社（省合作金库），及全国联合社（中央合作金库），成为合作社系之农业信用组织体系，负营业之责任。他方面为一个国家农业金融机关（名曰农业或农民银行），重在辅导设社及供给资金。每个合作社之业务，不以单营对人之信用放款为限制，可以兼营动产抵押放款及不动产抵押放款，亦即兼营长期中期短期各种放款①。盖合作社之基础，在社员间之相熟悉，相联合及监督信用，既可以用为对人信用放款之基层机构，自亦同时可

---

① 法国农业互助社、南斯拉夫之农业信用机关、罗马尼亚之信用合作社及农家信用银行，均兼做长期中期短期放款。且南斯拉夫农业信用合作社之组织体系，颇与我国合作金库体系相似，但其联合社不仅包括信用合作社，此为与我国合作金库体系不同之点，颇值吾人之参考。

用为对动产及不动产抵押放款之机构,毋庸另行组社。至供给资金之机构,因我国一般农民大都穷困,距资金自足之理想境界为期尚远,更因农贷资金之性质特殊,筹措非易,故必须由国家农业金融机关供给资金。又现代银行业务发展之趋势,借会计独立为手段,一银行常经营多种业务,故国家农业金融银行,可兼办长短中期业务以避免分期分办之困难:人才之缺乏,手续之繁杂,费用之浩巨。惟各种农贷之资本及会计,彼此独立。在此制度下,其他金融机关不得直接办理农贷业务,但可投资于国家农业金融机关,由其转放。国家农业金融机关在原则上不直接办理放款,专以供给各省合作金库,或县合作金库(如省合作金库尚未成立者)之资金为限。如金库尚未设立之地,或非合作机构所能举办之事业,则仍可由国家农业金融机关直接办理,合作金库则办理一切经常农贷业务。此种制度,系统完整,机构严密,供给资金与办理业务各自分开,借分工而收合作之效,一机关供给多种资金,一社办理多种借款,借集中而收兼筹之功,此有望于政府从速厘定细则,作为今后推进之南针,以期完备之体系早日实现。

2. 健全合作社之素质:合作社不仅为我国农贷之主要对象,又为合作金融制度之骨干。在兼营制度下,其使命尤为重大。在过去,因急于推广农贷,加紧组社,数量虽增而素质不良,此颇足影响合作金融制度之发展,故望政府实行普及教育,以提高农民教育之水准,同时扩大宣传,以灌输农民之合作知识。而合作指导员之扶助农民组社,尤须重视合作社之素质,务使基础健全,以利发展。

3. 农业金融机关之业务调整:我国现时国家设立之农业金融机关有二:一为属于财政部之中国农民银行,一为属于经济部之农本局。此二机关之金融使命,大致相同,业务亦几无别,似此重复组织,早应调整,而在新制度下,尤不容缓。吾人主张现有之中国农民银行,修改章程,增发资金,改组为唯一之国家农业金融机关,供给各种农贷资金。至于农本局之业务,原有农产及农资两部分,今后应将农资部分逐渐收缩,让渡于改组后之国家农业金融机关继续办理,而专营农产部分,并加强其业务,或且增营如美国生产信用公司之业务。如此既便利新制度之推行,又可使农本局集中力量,尽其调整农业产品之使命。现任参加办理农贷之中国、交通二专业银行,在新制度中,应将其所办之农贷业务逐渐收缩而让渡于改组后之国家农业金融机关办理,并以全力完成办理国际汇兑,发展实业之使命。如欲供给农贷资金,亦可以购买债票方式,投于国家农业金融机关,由其转放,不必直接参加办理。

4.农贷金额之分配标准:今后对各省农贷资金之分配,不能悉依各省当局之要求,订定数额,应参照各省可耕地之亩数,重要作物之产量,及以往各年农贷额,订定贷放款数额的标准,然后再斟酌国家政策及当时环境等主观因素,加以增减。如此虽未恰如所需,亦必相差不远,庶免偏枯之弊。

5.农贷资金之合理来源:农贷资金之来源,自应有整个之计划,惟对于兼营储蓄业务之商业银行及邮政储金汇业局,应特别注意。二十八年底我国之商业储蓄银行有七十家,合其他银行、兼理储蓄者,两计当近于百家,所吸收之储蓄存款数额甚巨,邮政储金汇业局之储蓄业务亦颇不小。已经施行之储蓄银行法,对银行之举办农贷,本有强制之规定,惜乎未尝严格执行,希望政府今后对于兼营储蓄业务之商业银行,应严加监督,务使办理储蓄业务之银行,将其应对农村合作社之质押放款,及以农产品为质之放款,购买国家农业金融机关所发行之债券,其数不得少于存款总数五分之一。此举不但使农贷资金获得可靠而丰富之泉源,且可减少一般不良银行滥用平民血汗之资金,经营投机事业。

6.农业金融之行政系统:为谋合资合营金库及国资国营银行在工作上之密切合作,中央应设农业金融总管理局,分设银行部金库部及合作社辅导管理部,每部设监督一人董其事。各省设分局或支局为省管理机关,并设国资国营银行分行及省金库,各设经理和副理一人,主掌业务。

(原载《经济汇报》1940年第2卷第1—2期)

我国农业金融制度之展望

甲、农贷现状之分析

一、二十九年以前之农业金融概况

我国自民国四年举办新式农业金融以来，垂今已有二十余年之历史。迄至二十八年底止，政府颁布有关农业金融之法令，虽已成册，然大多属于推广农贷调整放款办法之性质，至若1923年及1928年英国之农地信用法，1921年意国之农业信用法，美国1916年之联邦农业贷款法，1923年之农业信用法，及1933年之农地信用法，德国1926年之佃农信用法，及法国1920年之农业信用法等，关系各该国农业金融制度之建立与完成者，尚付阙如。因之，关于办理农贷机构者，缺乏完整之体系。属于全国性者：有中国农民银行、中国银行、交通银行、农本局，及其他商业银行等；属于省单位者：有省农民银行、省合作金库、省地方银行、合作机关专款及省农民贷款所等；属于县单位者：有县农民银行、市县合作金库、各县乡商业银行等；属于农民组织者：有合作社、互助社、农民借款协会、水利协会、农仓及农会等，各种机关，林立杂处，不相统率，步调各异。关于农贷机关业务者，无一贯之政策，放款种类太狭，几乎全系短期之信用贷款，其间较长之水利贷款，农本局虽曾举办，其数甚微，至于长期之农地贷款，则未与闻焉。贷款之区域，群趋于交通便利、物产富饶之地，荒乡僻野，则相率裹足不前。贷款之手续，颇为繁琐，未能顾及农民之教育程度。放款之数额常不能应农民之需要，或对其申请数额，任意削减，致失去原来之效用，他如放款之利率，申请之审核，还款之方式各机关自立准则，从无一致之规定。历来贷款最主要对象之信用合作社，其组织极不健全，流弊甚大，农贷实惠多未及于贫农，故当二十八年底时，农业金融情形之纷乱，已至极点，行局间业务之冲突，时有所闻，识者咸谓我国只有农贷，尚无农业金融制度，实非无因。（关于二十九年以前之农业金融概况，请参阅拙著《三年来之农业金融及今后改进之途径》，载《经济汇报》第二卷第一期。）

二、二十九年度政府对农业金融之调整及其概况

长期抗战,经济重于军事,而农业金融之任务,随战事之延长更加深重,盖自抗战以来,我政府深知抗战之经济基础及兵士来源在广大之农村,非活跃农业资金,增加粮食及经济作物之生产,以供给军粮民食及换取外汇,不能作长期抗战。且国内他种经济金融事业,抗战军兴后,无不积极调整,为求农业金融部门与其他部门相配合,以利抗战工作之进行,对于农业金融,实有调整之必要。当二十八年底时,适西康有农本局与中国农民银行放款之争执,政府为求解决此种争执,并防止以后之继起,乃于四联总处战时金融委员会之下,添设农业金融处,以便随时督促联络各行局之农贷业务,负责草拟农贷规章,审核农贷合约,以调整全国农业进行之步伐,使农业金融之发展,趋于制度化,是为调整农业金融之始,兹将一年来各种调整工作之情形,及农贷业务概况,叙述于后:

1. 农贷机构之调整

四联总处为改善农贷办法以发展农村经济,而适应抗战需要起见,乃订立二十九年度中央信托局中国交通农民三银行及农本局农贷办法纲要,统一农贷业务之设计与监督,并扩大贷款种类,提高贷款数额,统一贷款手续。其中关于贷款机构之调整者:有农贷对象之规定,与五行局经办农贷之方式两点,兹分别述之,

一、农贷对象:我国农贷自始即以合作社为对象,但因合作行政机关为经费及人力所限,辅导设社,一时难以普遍,在农贷力求直接普遍之前提下,自应扩大贷款对象,以适应实际之需要。对象分为三类:甲、农民团体:除合作社互助社外,举凡借款协会、农会以及供销代营等组织,均可为贷款之对象。乙、农民个人:凡佃农与自耕农均可直接请求贷款,不必经过任何中间机构。丙、农业改进机关:凡以改进农业为目的之机关团体学校均可向农贷机关直接申请贷款。此次贷款,对象之扩大范围,可以合作社为限,目的在使每一县份有农贷机构之设立,每一农民有请求贷款之机会,此种规定,不可视为合作社未普遍敷设前之权宜办法,实系农贷办法之进步。

二、办理方式:为使贷款区域普遍起见,纲要中规定联合办理及分区办理两种,各以其宜,如农田水利及农业推广事业,关涉数省或数县者,又如战区及边区农贷,非一行一局之力量所能或所愿单独承办者,则由各行局联合办理。后方各省农产丰富或交通便利之区,则由四联总处按各行局在当地经办情形,划定区域,分任办理。关于联合办理区域之农贷工作,由各行局推定代表行局办理,放款数额由各分局按下列比例分担:中信局15%,中国

25%,交通15%,农民35%,农本局10%,关于分区办理之农贷工作,各行局依照四联总处所订后方各省农贷区域表(在一省之内,各行局分配有一定之县数),在其分配区域内,推进贷款。贷款区域经指定后,如有其他行局已在该区办理农贷时,则采取下列方式之一,推由四联总处核定:(1)指定之行局接受办理,并尽量维持原有之机构;(2)由指定行局与原放款行局联合办理,其分担成分商定之;(3)由指定行局委托原放款行局继续办理,其业务及账目委托行局审核之。农贷纲要中所以采用联合办理及分区办理者,其目的有二,一方面在集中力量,分头并举,以求农贷之普遍;一方面在避免各行局在同一区域内业务之重复。此种办法,虽不免有流弊,但在农贷事业由复杂趋于调整之过程中,自不失为一种权宜之策。

2. 农贷办法之统一

以往各机关办理农贷,均各如其贷款办法,而各省合作主管机关,亦各有规章,分歧复杂,殊不一致。四联总处有鉴于此,乃判订各种规章准则,使各行局共同遵守,以齐一步伐,增加工作效能,兹将其要者列举如下:

(一)四联总处各种农贷暂行准则:本准则就农业生产、农业供销、农村副业、农产储押、农业推广、农村运输工具、农田水利及佃农购置耕地等八种贷款,用途之种类、贷款之成数、期限之长短、对象之范围、保障之方式及利率之高低等,均按照实情,有明确之规定,以为各行局办理农贷之标准。

(二)二十九年度五行局办理合作社农贷手续暂行办法:农贷暂行准则,只对于农业贷款之性质及其内容,加以规定,至于各行局贷款手续之分歧复杂,仍须调整划一,乃有本办法之规定,举凡申请借款之手续、申请书表之填具、承贷行局之调查及审核、贷放时之手续、还款之预先通知、利息之计算,及因不可抗力而引起之展期偿还等,均有明细之规定,使各行局办理农贷时,得有依据,此办法系以依法登记之合作社或联合社为贷款对象者,但其他农民团体借款时,得适用本办法,故本办法实为办理农贷手续最重要之规章。

(三)二十九年度各行局办理农贷改进机关借款手续暂行办法,及办理农贷个人借款手续暂行办法:农贷对象不同,借款手续各异,此二种借款手续实行办法之订定,在求适合各种借款之情形。关于办理农事改进机关贷款之手续,大体与合作社相同,惟因农业改进,事属专门技术,故其申请期间及审核期间,较对合作社者为长,且因放款数额较大,而机关本身又不如合作社社员间负有保证责任,故另需要担保品或承还保证人,以谋贷款之安全。本办法所称之农事改进机关范围颇广,凡依法设立之中央省农业改进及推广等机构,各地实验场所暨各级农业学校社团等,均属之,此可证明年来政府对农事改进机关之努力协助也。

关于农民个人借款手续之办法,亦大体与对合作社者相同。所异者,农民既系个人借款,必须有承还保证人始可,有时须附有担保品,借款之利率,仍以当地合作社对于社员贷款之利率为准(大多为一分二厘),贫农得酌予减低,但不得少于月息九厘,此项规定之用意,可于本办法关于贷款对象之限制中见之,本办法所谓农民个人,指佃农及自耕农,且须受下列之限制:(1)家主地位,(2)未加入合作社或其他团体者,(3)借款者须于一年内或债务清偿时,加入附近之合作社或农民团体,否则翌年或以后不得申请借款。盖我国合作组织及农民团体尚未普遍设立,为使无团体组织之农民,亦有获得借款之机会起见,特订有本办法,惟借款农民终以加入合作组织或农民团体为宜,使农民本身得有组织,使农民机关放款便利,故有"否则以后不得申请借款"之规定,此项限制,实寓有积极之意义。

（四）各种农贷合约蓝本:为统一同种性质农贷合约之内容,以避免因立约人之不同而有差异,四联总处乃厘订各种合约草约,计有:一、普通区农贷合约草约,此系五行局与各省所订包括各种放款之总合约,适用后方及非战区之地域,内容大体根据农贷纲要,约内订有各行局分区办理及联合办理二种,但90%为分区办理。二、战区农贷合约草约:战区情形特殊,非任何一行局所愿单独承办,故悉为联合办理。贷款对象选择较严,仅限于农民团体一项。放款种类也只以农业生产、农业供销、农村副业、农村运输工具等四项为限。必须由订约之行政机关,负保证偿还之责,战区合约所以有此等不同之规定,目的在保障放款之安全,利率为月息七厘,较普通农贷利率低一厘,此所以减轻战区农民之负担,寓有政治上之意义。三、边区农贷合约草约,边区之情形,大概介于普通区与战区之间,系一种特殊区域,贷放目的亦含有政治意义,全部系联合办理,贷款对象及贷款种类,以农贷纲要中规定者为准,此可见办理时尚有斟酌实情之余地。利率月息八厘,贷款订约之行政机关负保证偿还之责。四、农业推广贷款合同蓝本:农业推广种类甚多,机关亦异,需要厘订合约草约,以作实际订约时之蓝本,本约所指之农业推广,以生产或采购种子、肥料、农具、运输工具、副业工具、病虫害防止药剂等事业为限,贷款数额最高不得超过实际预算总额之八成,其余二成自行筹措。且推广经费不得列入预算,并需由省政府负承还保证之责。本约之条件,颇为严厉。五、农田水利贷款甲种合同草案,及乙种合同草案:农田水利贷款之用途,包括筑坝、开渠、汲水灌溉、建蓄水库排除农田积水等工程,甲种合约系由各行局与省政府合组农田水利贷款委员会经办,其下设立工程处,办理各项工程之设施,贷款总额由省政府与五行局按照二八成分担。农贷会设总工程师及会计课长各一人,由各行局派员充任。省政府对于各行局之贷款,负保证偿还之责,但各项工程倘因设计不同或施工不慎,致不能利用时,其贷款损失由双方平均负担。甲种合约之精神,系双方共同办理,故损失也共同负担。至于乙种合约,双方并不设立农贷会,仅由省政府设立工程处经办,贷款总额由双方分担成数不定,临时磋商。乙种合约系由省府独负实际办理之责,各行局之贷款仅为一种借放性质,故倘因设计不过或施工不慎致不能利用时,其贷款损失应全部由省府负担,以示权责分明。上述各种草约蓝本,各行局与各省有机关商订贷款时,即以之为根据,然后参酌当地实际情形,酌予修改,于统一中得兼顾个人之特殊情形。

3. 农贷合约之签订

四联总处自订立农贷办法纲要、农贷准则及各种合约蓝本后,迅即由各分支处邀集各行局与省府代表商订合约,总处对于推进农贷,虽甚积极,惟各省当局对二十九年之农贷办法,间有异议,几经磋商,始得陆续签订。

迄至目前止,已有十六省签订合约,贷款总额达 322 100 000 元,以四川省农贷合约之数额最巨,数为 136 600 000 元,今日四川为抗战建国之中心,农贷纲要中列为本年度贷款之首要区域,放款数额巨大,理固宜然。

在所签订之二十三个合约中,计边区贷款合约二起,占全体 1.9%,战区合约八起,占全体 8.5%,普通区域合约十三起,占全体 89.6%。

普通区之农贷,可大致分为十类,首推合作与普通货款(其数额为 12 900 万元),占全体 44.7%,生产贷款次之,农田水利贷款占 21.3%,得 9.0%,占第三位。可见年来政府及金融界于后方之水利工程颇为重视。佃农购地贷款与垦殖贷款其性质均极重要,但约订数额似嫌过小,尚待努力推进!

此外未签订合约省份,尚有贵州、江西、云南、青海四省,黔赣滇三省均由各行局按照以往办法贷放,以免因合约签订之迟延影响农贷工作进行,至青海省,以该省合作事业尚无基础,暂且从缓办理,由二十九年初迄最近止,各种农贷合约已签订者凡二十三起,此种持续艰巨之工作,实由于农业金融处之设立,负各行局农贷业务督促联络之责,有以致之。

4. 农贷业务之推进

二十九年度农贷业务,政府自始即具积极推进力求普遍之决心,放款数额初拟订为四万万元,后以数额固定,有时反足以阻碍业务之发展,乃于农贷纲要中规定二十九年度之农贷数额,由四联总处视各地事实需要,随时决定,此项规定富有弹性,易于适合实际情形。

二十九年底五行局农贷之结余额为 2.1 亿元,较二十八年底之贷款余额约增加一倍,虽与年初之拟订额相较,仅及半数,然农贷人员缺乏,放款机构尚未普遍,且中途曾受券料供应之牵掣,而能有如斯成绩。四联总处及五行局对于农贷事业可称已尽相当之努力,本年度各行局放款余额以中农行居首,占全体 46.11%,次为中国行,占全体 24.54%,再次为农本局与交通行,中信局之农贷业务,本年度尚属创始,故居末位。设以各行局二十九年度之贷款余额与二十八年底者相较,就数额多寡之位次而论,农行之首位屹然未变,中国行则由第三位进至第二位,超过农本局之放款余额,交通行之位次无变动,就所占百分比之位次而论,当然与余额之位次相同,然其程度上之增减,却大有出入。中农行之百分比由 57.37 退至 46.11,较上年减少 11.26%,而中国行之百分比则由 14.92% 进为 24.54%,较前增加 9.62%,个中道理,极为明显。中农行之结余额二十九年底仅较二十八年底增加半倍,而中国行同期增加三倍,可见中国行对二十九年度之农贷业务较以往重视。农本局所占百分比约减去 3%,大概为该局下半年来农贷资金不足所致。交通行几无变动,就两年中各行局所占之百分比看来,二十八年度之离差,远大于二十九年之离差,位次间之重要性有减少之趋势,此可说明两种现象,一是在农贷事业突飞猛晋期中,各行局之努力程度并不一致,一是在最近之将来,农贷业务尚无完全集中于一行一局之可能。

二十九年度各行局农贷之区域,分布极广,共达二十一省。各省之贷款数量,就全体言,以四川为最巨,约占全体 40%,其次为湖南,约占全体 9%,再次为贵州、广西、陕西、江西等省。设若以后方四川、西康、云南、贵州、陕西、甘肃等六省为一单位,以睹其在全国中之重要性,后方六省贷款总余额,占全国 60.75%。二十八年底各行局后方六省之贷款,仅占全国 38.5%,可见二十九年后方六省之贷款余额超过二十八年远甚,其重要性亦不能同日而语,此悉系政府提倡及环境需要之故。

此外尚有须注意者,战区各省,如湖南、江西、广西等省,其农贷余额皆超过 1 000 万元,位列前茅,此一方而表示政府对农贷事业固注意于后方各省,但对战区各省,尤其产粮丰富者,也同样积极推广,以充实经济斗争力量,一方面证明敌人对我之侵占,只是点与线之掠夺,而广大之乡村仍属我方。

最后尚有一点需要声明者,现在我国农贷事业十之八九由五行局统筹办理,其他省地方银行及商业银行虽偶有举办者,其数额甚微,就全国论,不居重要地位,且其资料不全,故将其情形略而不述。

5. 农业金融基层组织之概况

我国农村放款,自始即以合作社为主要对象,盖我国农民既贫穷且散漫,其信用地位,殊难调查清楚。农业金融机关,为求放款之费用经济,手续简单,保障安全,必须利用农民之团体组织,而此种团体组织,似以合作社为最适宜,于是合作社乃成为农业金融之基层组织。此为年来我国合作事业发展之主因,合作社之业务,原不以信用为限,但年来合作社数之增加,以信用社为最多。兹将最近几年合作社数与信用合作社社数之增加情形,列为第一表。

第一表 历年合作社数与信用合作社数比较表

年　别	总社数	各种合作社			
		信　用		其　他	
		社数	百分数	社数	百分数
民国二十一年	3 978	3 227	81.11	751	18.89
二十二年	3 087	2 423	78.49	664	21.51
二十三年	14 649	9 841	67.20	4 808	32.80
二十四年	26 224	15 429	58.80	10 795	41.20
二十五年	37 318	20 620	55.25	16 698	44.75
二十六年	28 449	20 952	73.60	7 497	26.40
二十七年	64 565	55 466	85.91	9 099	14.09
二十八年	78 671	69 534	88.37	9 137	11.63
二十九年	103 444	89 939	87.00	13 445	13.00

资料来源:《合作事业月刊》第3卷第1至4期。

二十一年时,全国仅有4 000社,嗣后因农贷事业渐趋发展,合作事业颇受影响,社数顿减,翌年,始恢复常态,社数又复与年俱增。二十九年底增至103 444社,九年间增加近10万社,不可谓之不速。至于各种合作社社数之分配,以信用合作社社数占绝对多数,超过其他各种社数之总和,所占全体社数之百分比,而在50%以上,近年来且有逐渐增长之趋势。二十六年约占74%,二十七年约86%,二十八年增至88%,二十九年底为87%,此因二十九年度生产及运销合作社社数增加颇速,信用合作社所占之百分比乃稍顿挫。现信用合作社已有9万社,较二十一年底增加约8.7万社,占全体社数增加额87%,故年来合作事业之蓬勃现象,直可谓为由农贷事业之发展所造成,亦不为过。此外尚有互助社,亦系农民取得信用之组织,创立手续较合作社为简单,一年后即可改为信用合作社,互助社年来组织颇多,二十九年底已有2.2万余社,约当信用合作社数1/4,同为农贷之主要对象。合作互助社数量增加迅速,原系适应扩大农贷普遍推进之要求,但因此却难顾及素质之健全,致一般合作社在组织上与活动上皆停留于幼稚阶段,此有待于亟急改进者。

合作金库为银行放款予合作社之中间机构,设立原意,一方面系为树立由下而上之合作金融制度,一方面系将各银行办理农贷之分歧情形,借此调整,使归一致。合作金库之使命重大,且能适合环境需要,故其历史虽仅五年,已成为我国农业金融之基础机构,业务发展甚为迅速,目前农贷数额有40%系由金库贷放者,且兼营汇兑存储等业务,成立之地域已遍及后方各省,兹将历年来金库成立数目,及其分布地域列表如下(见第二表)。

民国二十五年,仅四川设立省合作金库一所。二十六年有川、湘、赣等七省设库,其数尚少,仅22所。二七年仍只有七省设库,但偏重后方川、桂、黔诸省,库数增至113所,超过二十五年五倍有奇。二十八年度扩大至十省,增至208所。至二十九年底,全国省市县库数计达373所,设库区域扩展至十三省,内计省库5所、市库1所、县库367所。在二十六年时,县库以湖南、四川、江西二省最多。其后因四川居后方中心,地大物博,农贷业务亦列为首要之区,金融数目增加最速,二十六年仅有5所,二十七年为62所,二十九年增至113所,居各省之首,占全体30%强。贵州、广西两省自二十六年后,成立之库数增加亦速,二十九年底时,前者有59所,后有46所,仅亚于四川,居第二三位。再其次为浙江、湖南两省,虽系战区,但农产丰饶,故成立库数亦多。目前我国所成立之金库,全由银行或合作行政机关参加辅设而成,其中十分之九为中农行与农本局辅导者,自今春农本局农贷业务奉命移交中农行后,殆几全为中农行所辅设者。

我国农业金融之基层组织,在放款方面以合作金库为最重要,在对象方面以合作社为重要,其他尚有农民借款协会,农会等也有其意义存在,然其重要性则远不及合作组织也。

第二表　历年我国各省市县合作金库统计表

省或市	二十五年 省库	二十五年 县库	二十六年 省库	二十六年 县库	二十七年 省库	二十七年 县库	二十八年 省库	二十八年 县库	二十九年 省库	二十九年 县库
四川	1		1	5	1	62	1	77	1	113
西康								9		10
贵州						16		39		59
广西						17		33	1	46
湖南				6		11		15		27
浙江						1	1	15	1	32
江西			1	5	1	5	1	3	1	9
湖北				1		2		11		17
河南								3		5
陕西								3		13
河北				1						
山东				2						
安徽				2						
南京市			1							
甘肃										10
福建									1	2
云南										9
重庆市									1	
总计	1		3	22	2	113	3	208	6	367

资料来源：二十五年至二十八年之数字系根据《经济通讯》二十五期黄贻孙《我国合作金库发展概况》，二十九年之数字系根据各行局向农业金融处之报告。

乙、树立兼营式农业金融体系之建议

一、近世各国农业金融之趋势

吾人既已将二十八年底以前我国农业金融之复杂纷乱情形加以描述，二十九年度四联总处调整农业金融之经过一一列举，则对我国农业金融之简史及其现状，可以得一客观之认识。兹请言目前各国农业金融之共同趋势,以便进而论及我国农业金融制度之可能发展。

近世各国农业金融,经百年来之发展,虽因各国有其特殊之政治、经济、文化背景,致演成各种类型之农业金融制度,但仍有其发展之共同趋势,此可谓由农业金融之特殊性而演成之普遍性,亦是各国依据国情推进农业金融制度之困难过程中逐渐革新改良所累积而成之宝贵经验。吾人固不应呆板模仿任一国之农业金融制度,但应参照其经验,以供吾国建立农业金融制度借鉴。依吾人之观察,现在各国农业金融发展之共同趋势,其显著而重要者有四:

一、农业金融自成一种专门金融制度。农业之生产是一种有机性之生长,需时较长,工作既经开始,不能中途停止,在生产过程中,不能中途改变方向,其收获之丰歉,需要长期低利之资金,非一般银行所能担任者。因此近代国家无不为农业金融成立一种专门金融制度。惟各国所采之方式略有差异,有设立关于农业金融之中央行政机关,以谋农业金融之统制者,如美国1933年所设立之农业信用管理局是;有设立专属于农业金融之中央金融机关者,如德国于1925年设立之农业中央银行,及法国于1920年设立之国立农业信用金库是。

二、农业金融之基层组织大多为合作社。合作社系农民依照合作互助之原则,根据彼此间之熟悉了解,负担连带责任而组成之团体,为农村放款之良好对象。1937年,Lauis Tardy曾调查四十余国之农业金融制度,并依其组织分别之为四类,虽各类之中,上层机构各有特点,但其基层机构,实际上均属合作组织,或采取合作原则而组成之团体,其中以信用合作社为对人信用机关之现象尤为普遍。

三、农业金融为推进农业政策之重要工具。农业现仍为大多数国家,最大多数人民之基本职业,且为经济生产之重要部门,政府为谋农业之发展,并使之与一般经济发展相配合,乃有种种农业政策之推行,但农业系一种分散性职业,散布区域极为辽阔,督导管制皆非易事,因有运用农业金融力量,以推行农业政策者,如政府欲建立家庭农场以培植自耕农,或鼓励某种作物之栽培,或限制某种作物之种植,或稳定农产品在市场上之价格,凡此种种均可假借农业金融之机能,加以控制与推进达到预期目的。

四、政府对农业金融之特殊待遇或辅助。一般农民知识较低,散漫而贫穷,在金融上之地位,处于劣势,且农业金融其于业务性质之要求,数额零细,周转滞缓,放款期间须长,利率要低,欲在金融市场上与他种金融竞争资金,实属不可能,故必有赖于政府之特殊待遇或辅助。一般辅助之方式,或特许农业金融机关发行债券,由政府负保证之责,并免除债券之一切租税负担,或由政府供给免息或低息之资金,或特许农业票据向国家银行贴现,其债券得充银行之准备金,上述各种方式,美、德、法诸国均曾先后采行。

二、我国究应建立何种农业金融制度

理论是实践之根据。吾人欲调整农业金融,必须建立一个健全之农业金融制度,使已往之经营不致垂废,未来之设施有准则可循。国家生命恒长,地区辽阔,欲使先后有同一之系统,趋同一之目标,全国守同一之法则,用同一之机构,并使事业发展到伟大而合理之境界,非建立一完善之制度不可,国家一切活动部门如此,农业金融亦然。

农业金融为要适应农业之特殊性,应另外成立一种专门制度,诚如上述已为各国之共同趋势。但在我国应否树立专门之农业金融制度,议者之态度,似未一致。我国目前之金融,尚无明确之制度,民国十七年虽颁布中央银行条例,成立中央银行,并改中国银行为国际汇兑银行,交通银行为发展实业银行,后又成立中国农民银行,使中国、交通、农民各成为一种专业银行,各负一方面金融之专责,但因格于事实,各银行之业务多混合经营,举凡有价证券之买卖、国内外汇兑之经营、一般存放款及农村贷款之举办,甚至储蓄与信托,也一并兼营,商业银行亦复如是,故就现实状况言,我国银行业为混合经营制。廿三年政府鉴于储蓄与信托业务,与一般银行业务之性质不同,储户存放需要特殊之保障,投资需要特别安全,乃有储蓄银行法之公布施行,依该法第十二、十三条之规定,一般银行得兼办储信业务,但须资金独立、会计独立,不受一般业务之影响,于是各行纷纷成立储蓄部及信托部,以符合规定。今以农贷业务之性质,有别于普通银行业务,欲另成一专门系统,特立专门机构办理,并规定一般银行不得兼营,此或可引起若干方面之反对,且正可采用办理储蓄信托之例,另设农业金融部,会计独立,资金独立,专门办理农贷业务。在允许一般银行业务采取混合制之原则下,此种主张初视之不无理由,然若作进一步之分析,殊不妥当。盖银行之普遍业务,与储信业务之不同,非为基本性质上之差异,储信业务之主要使命,是吸收社会上一般平民之资金,为国家集聚生产资本,其资金之用途,须特别审慎,必投放于生产而可靠之事业,以保障储信户资金之安全,故使储信之资金与会计独立,并受政府之监督,即可达到上述之要求,但农业金融与一般金融有基本性质上之差异,放款之对象、手续、期间、利率均不相同,尤其关于资金来源一层,其条件不是一般之存款所能适合,而且数量亦远非一部分储蓄存款所可济事,故需要用特殊方法——发行债券,以吸取资金,此所以农业金融不能与储信业务相提并论,不可由普通银行兼营,而应独立自成系统。

此外尚有一种主张,名合作金融制度者,表面上虽未明白反对农业应独立自成系统,实际上无异根本取消农业金融制度,在此处亦有讨论之必要。依此主张,现有合作金库之名义仍可维持,但须变更其性质。盖此种主张之中心思想,认为各级合作金库为政府发展合作事业之金融机关,而不视为合作社联合社之一种。放弃合作金库应属于农民自有自营自享之理想,并否认合作事业之发展应由下而上之理论。合作金库既不视为金库,后由中央金库辅设省县合作金库。中央合作金库之资本,以由省合作金库及全国性之合作社联合社认购为原则。但初设时,应由国库及金融机关认购90%。中央合作金库之业务方针,必须与中央合作主管机关之合作政策相一致,库设理事会,由党政合作团体及有关部会、金融机关等派人担任理事,内部业务包括工业合作金融、各种农业金融、信托保险及其他一切银行业务。

其资金来源有二:甲、发行债券,由四行承受。乙、得以其票据向四行贴现,或再贴现。自上述合作金库之组织及业务观之,合作金融制度派主张以合作金融制度来改革或代替原有之金融制度,事关国家整个金融制度之体系,超出本篇之范围,兹不具论。姑就农业金融部分言之,中央合作金库,可经营农业合作、土地合作、供销合作、保险合作与动产抵押等业务,殆已占有农业金融之全部。合作金库虽占有全部农业金融,自应成立系统,独立经营,实欲与他种业务共同隶属于合作金融制度之下,混合经营,此点显然违背农业金融应立一种专门制度之潮流与经验,故为不可取。且近世主张农业金融制度应采取农业合作金融制度之学者,所用农业合作金融一词之涵意,似在以合作组织为融通农业资金之机构,并拟假借农业金融之运用,以团结并发展农民生活,此可见合作与农业金融之关系。至于合作为手段,而以推进农业金融为目的,而合作金融制度派所主张之农业合作金融,反认农业金融为手段,而以推进合作事业为目的。吾人就农业金融之立场,自不能同意,在事实上,现在中国农民银行除已有信用放款外,已筹设中期农业金融与土地金融处,正可利用该行之发展,以建立一种独立之农业金融制度,目前已有之县合作金库,大都为农行所辅设。当信用合作社及县合作金库尚未达到自有自营自享以前,暂以该行为农业合作金融体系之上层机关,似属平实可行。若坚欲另外设立中央合作金库,无异使现有中农行之全部业务,移交与中央合作金库,放弃原有之机构、人力、事业不用,而另起炉灶,从新办理,非独在事实上困难万端,无法进行,亦且多事更张,损耗国力,吾人实未敢赞同也。

在建立一个专门农业金融制度之前提下,仍有种种不同。其重要者则有分营制与兼营制之争论。主张分营制者,有提议以农本局,办理短期之合作金融,中国农民银行办理中期农业金融,另设土地银行办理土地金融。亦有提议改组农本局为中央合作银行,放款于合作社及合作社联合社,中国农民银行暂时兼营长期及中期放款,将来另设中国农业银行以专营中期放款。虽其内容互有差异,然其基本精神,则在于农业金融之长、中、短三期放款,应由三个独立之农业金融机关分别经营。主张兼业制者,提议由政府设立一个国家农业金融机关,经营一切农贷业务,内分长期金融处、中期金融处、短期金融处等三部,分掌长、中、短三种农业信用业务。故其基本精神在于农业金融之长、中、短三期放款,由一个农业金融机关统筹办理,分部经营;各部之基金、会计独立(见拙作《三年来之农业金融及今后改进之途径》,载《经济汇报》第二卷第一、二期)。此二种主张各有立论,现从理论上及事业上来检讨其优劣得失,指出吾国未来之农业金融制度,应采取何种体系。

现代银行业务发展之趋势,在同一特殊部门之内,借会计独立为手段,一银行可以经营多种业务。目前国内各商业银行多兼营信托储蓄业务,惟其资本与会计各自独立,正足表示此种潮流,在农业金融方面,亦在演进中。南非联邦之农业金融制度即其一例[①]。南非联邦之农业信用,大半由土地农业银行供给,土地农业银行在各省设立分支行,供给下列三种农业信用:(1)短期农业信用借款:借款期间仅一年,其目的在帮助农民购置牲畜及偿付流动农业费用之用。(2)中期农业信用借款,借款期间最高不得超过十年,其目的在帮助农民改良土地性质、修理篱笆围墙、建筑水池、装置水管之用。(3)长期农业信用借款,年限最高为三十八年。其目的在帮助农民购得土地。南非联邦土地农业银行所经营之三种放款,是否会计独立分部经营,尚不知悉。但由一银行兼办三种农贷,则为南非农业金融制度之特色。此外尚有美国之农业金融制度,正向分部合营之方向演进中。美制设立农业信用局于华盛顿,局设总裁一人,对大总统负责,下置四司:土地金融司,中期信用司,合作银行司,生产信用司,分别掌管十二个联邦土地银行、十二个联邦中期信用银行、一个中央合作银行及十二个地方合作银行与生产信用公司。此制在行政上是集中管理,由一个农业信用管理机关,监督全国各

[①] 见《中农月刊》一卷六期,周鸿绪译《政府统制下的农业信用制度》。该文译自一九三八年十月《国联农业信用与农业制度报告》。

种农业金融机关。在形式上是各种农业金融机关,各自独立,自成系统,分别经营。故一般人士多认美制为分营制,其实,在农业信用总局方面系由一个行政管理机构,分司监管,虽不能即以四种金融机关为一行之四部,在实质上与一行分为四部兼营各种农贷极为接近,此种精神在区农业信用局(地方机关)表现最为明显。按美制划分全国为十二区,每区设一农业信用分局,为行政监督机关,下设有一联邦土地银行中期信用银行、合作银行及生产信用公司。此四种组织,虽营业之目的与对象,各不相同,但在同一地点办公,并由中央代表与各行经历共同组织顾问委员会,讨论一切有关事宜,而与农业信用局取得密切联络。故区农业信用局几无异为一个农业金融机关之分行分部,此吾人所以确认美制为兼营制也。美人李氏(V. P. Lee)为彼邦研究农业信用之权威。李氏于其大作《农业信用之原理》中,曾申论美制之精神:"明白说来,中期信用银行系根据联邦农业借款法而成立,受联邦农地借款局之监督(彼时尚未改为农业信用局),十二个联邦土地银行之理事,亦是中期信用银行之理事,其情形不啻每区之联邦农民银行设有两部:一为长期信用部,一为中期信用部(其实合作银行尚未成立)。"①李氏此段议论,已将美国农业金融制度之真相,阐述明白,美制在形式上似乎为一种分营制,实际上已具有兼营制之精神,此吾人研究美制所不可不察者也。

农业金融自成一种专门体系,且其业务由分营趋向于兼营,则必有其优劣得失之处,兹请略述之:

农贷制度。若采取分期分办之方式,困难殊多。就办理农贷之机关言,一农村生产事业,同时需要短期中期长期资金,倘因期间之限制,而由三机关分别办理,放款步骤既难一致,稽核监督尤多不便,纵令担任长中短各期之放款机关,一致贷放,而往返协商,多费时日反足以延误农时,阻碍农事之进行。就农民借款之手续言,农民需向三种农贷机关分别接洽,非独往返费时,且人事多二种麻烦。就对农民放款之根据,举凡农民之性格、嗜好、家属人口、所有田亩、房屋、不动产等之数量及其价值,负债情形,每年之收入及其支出情形,如此始可决定其农民之是否需要资金?数量几何?偿还能力如何?在分期分办之情形下,各行格于费用,其调查常略而不详,致失依据。就机关设立之费用言,机关鼎立,费用浩大,经营成本随之提高,必借利率之方式转嫁于农民,致增加农民之负担。就分期之困难言,所谓长、中、短之分

---

① 见 V. P. Lee: The Principle of Agricultural, p.52。

期,学者聚讼纷纭,莫衷一是,有以用途为准,有以年月之多少为准,有以抵押种类为准,而各国之实际划分也不一致,如由三机关分别贷放,介于二期中间之放款,或则重复相争,或则相率不放,此种情形在我国尤易发生。总上以观,分营制困难殊多,效率不强,兼营制则无此等弊端也。

合营制尚有三大优点:一、农业金融行政机关可以免设。农业金融情形特殊,性质重要,在分营制之下,政府必需设立一专门机关以负营理监督之责。但在兼营制之下,可以免设。盖全国只有一个国家农业金融机关,该机关之理事会原为决定政策及管理业务之组织,若由政府指派有关部会长官及专家等为理事,则理事会一方秉承政府意旨,执行国策;他方面指挥所属,推进业务,使行政监督与业务执行,融成一片,可收指臂之效。二、易于获得资金,既将三种农业金融由一行监管,则此一行可得有三行之资本,其实力运用自较三行分别运用为巨,雄厚之资本,易于博得社会之信用,信用既立,则其所发行之债券易于销售,是故兼营制必较分营制易于获得资金来源。三、有补偿作用。今若农业金融分期分办,各行以所做业务性质不同,风险程度互异,且投资者常避难趋易,于是各行之资金将有过与不足之弊。但若三种农业信用由一行兼办,则可以互相调剂。分营制各行之损益,各自负担,投资人之保障范围较狭,易遭危险,兼营制则各部农贷之损益,可以彼此补偿,危险较小。

基于上述各种论断,吾人主张我国建立一种兼营制之农业金融制度。

三、兼营式农业金融制度内容之建议及其推进办法

关于兼营式农业金融制度之内容,其纲要如下:

1. 体系方面:政府设立国家农业银行,受财部之监督,负责统筹办理全国农贷业务,设总行于首都,各省省会设分行,各重要农贷区域之中心得设分行之办事处,各县成立合作金库,由国家农业银行负责、辅导设立,其下为各种合作社及联合社。此种体系以农行为上中级主干,而以信用合作社合作金库为基层组织,形成一种政府扶助式之农业合作金融制度。

2. 组织方面:国家农业银行设理事会,为全国农业金融之决策及管理机构。理事由政府就农林、财政、社会、经济等有关部会及农业金融专家中指派之。总分行及合作金库在业务上之组织均分设三部:分掌合作金融、中期金融及土地金融,各部之资金及会计独立,俨若三行,此种组织三部虽分别独立,但在同一系统之下,步调一致,绝无重复纠纷之弊,行或库可用行务会议或库务会议之方式,三部彼此交换意见,分工合作,以期业务得最大之发展。

3. 资本方面:国家农业银行之资本,由政府认股60%,其余由合作金库摊认,合作金库摊认国家农业银行之资本有优先权,如合作社认股超过40%时,政府应逐渐退出让予合作金库承受。合作金库之资本优先由合作社认股,不足之数再由国家农业银行全部凑齐。嗣后,合作社认股增加时,由农行让予之。金库之管理权初由农行派员主持,以后农行按股金之减少,逐渐将管理权移转于合作社,其方式可以双方派充理监事人数之增减为之。合作金库应以合作社认购之股款,向国家农业银行认购股本,变成国家农业银行之股东。迨合作社认足国家农业银行全部股金时,农民之知识已经增高,农民之资金已经充裕,政府可以退居管制监督地位。由农民运用合作组织经营之,此时国家农业银行与中央合作金库合为一体。

4. 资金来源:国家农业银行之资金来源有四:

（1）政府特许国家农业银行发行农业债券,农业债券除直接向市场销售外,并得请求国家银行承受,国家银行可以农业债券为发行之保证准备。

（2）国家农业银行,得以其农业票据向国家银行贴现或再贴现。

（3）政府规定办理,储蓄、信托、保险等业务机关及基金保管机关,应以其所收受资金之一定成熟,购买农业银行之债券。

（4）国家农业银行之资本公积金及社员储金。

农业资金需要长期低利,自由筹措,极为困难,且亦非一般存款性质之资金所可应付,必须赖国家赋予种种特权,以发行债券之方式获取资金或强制特定之机关必须购买,同时政府为使农业债券易于推销起见,当牺牲财政上之收入,特许农业债券为免税债券。至于公积金及储金一项,在初期其数必甚细少,但须加以提倡奖励,日积月累,与时俱增,相当时期之后,应成为农业资金之重要来源。

5. 业务方面:国家农业银行之业务,以与农业有关者为限。统筹兼营长中短三期农贷,不得兼营他种银行之业务。他种银行亦不得办理农行重复之业务。订定国家农业银行之条例时,营业范围一项,应采列举制,以免含混不清,其内容可参照二十九年度五行局办理农贷纲要第四条农贷种类之规定,再添列农业保险及家畜保险等项。国家农业银行三部分业务之划分,应以经办便利为宜,其细则另订之。

6. 放款对象:国家农业银行之放款对象,包括各种合作社,农民团体。现行合作金库之放款对象,原以信用合作社,及各种联合社为限,后虽经修改,信用业务以外之合作社亦得为社员,但仍系以合作社为限,此种规定似欠妥善,目前我国之合作社一时决难普遍设立,且其素质,因成立过速,并不较他种农民组织为健全,故不应以合作社为唯一之农贷对象,已有之农民团体,如农会、借款协会及其他社会团体如农场、农业改进机关、农业生产促进机关等,应同视为放款之对象。

兼营制之农业金融制度,就目前之现状观之,似未能立即付诸施行,国内整个金融制度尚待调整,农业金融制度为整个金融制度之一部门,自不能脱离一般之影响,而独善其身。且抗战期间,一切设施应以配合抗战需要为前提,凡非当务之急者,亦不宜多事更张,但制度关系国家百年大计,其内容体系应早日确定。订立各种有效步骤,以期逐渐调整,逐渐推动,向所订标的迈进。兹草拟过渡期间推行之步骤如下:

1. 利用原有农行之机构。中国农民银行已有十余年之历史,分支行处将近百所,办事人员、社会信用,均已有相当规模,根据创建新机构究不若利用原有机构事半功倍之原则,可即改组董事会,加入有关部会长官,以便农贷业务与经济社会政策相配合,扩充资本,增厚中农行之实力,使能胜任其新使命,以作他日改组为国家农业银行之准备。至于改组之事,须待其他客观条件,如他行不得直接办理农贷、农业银行不得兼营他种业务等,均已具备,方可实行。

2. 应即发行农业债券。将来国家农业银行资金之来源须大部依赖农业债券之发行。现在国家纸币发行权尚未完全集中时,农行固可借发行纸币以筹得农贷资金,而毋庸借助于农业债券。然亦不妨乘此时机发行农业债券,以训练社会,而使社会投资家及银行家对其性质,逐渐认识,养成良好之印象,而树立信用基础。

3. 筹设中期信用部及土地金融部。目前中国农民银行之农贷业务,放款数额虽大,但几全部为短期信用放款,只有少数为中期之水利贷款,至佃农购地贷款尚在试办。中农行为负担改组后统筹兼营之新使命,应即着手筹备设立中期信用部与土地金融部。闻中农行土地金融处已于今年三月开始筹备组织,或可于最短期内成立,以便开始经营土地贷款。至于中期信用,传闻该行有农田水利会之设立。中期信用在他国诚然以农田水利放款为最重,但不应以农田水利放款为限,尚有机械、农具及家畜林业等。为求其与合作金融配合平衡发展起见,似以成立中期信用处为宜。

4. 业务之调整。现在因值战时,农行接受政府命令与中中交三行联合办理一般金融业务。同时中中交三行及一般商业银行也兼办农贷业务,使农贷业务机关益形复杂纷歧,而为推行新制度之最大障碍。自本年农本局奉令停办农贷业务,复杂程度固已减轻甚多,但为求实行新制度起见,此种现象仍需继续设法调整。中农行现有农贷数额仅及全部业务 1/10,就全国农业放款言,农行约占半数,今后农行对一般业务应避免或减少参加,而以其全部资力人力发展农贷业务,使在全国农贷业务中占绝对优势。至于现在办理农贷之其他各行骤令停止固有困难,而农行立时全部接受办理,力亦未逮,故调整之道,必经缜密考虑,以防流弊,兹提出下列三种办法以供采择:

(1) 各行局自动缩减农贷而让由农行接办。如中国银行办理农贷历史悠久且数额庞大者,自动逐渐收缩。至于其他行局办理不久而数额微小者,可即停办,各以其全力发展其固有之使命。

(2) 采用比数增减制。例如三十年度各行局分担农贷款额之比数为中信局15%、中国25%、交通15%、农民45%(按农民二十九年度为35%、农本局10%,现农本局停办农贷其业务由农行接受,故其应分担之成数,亦并入农行),以后可先将中信局之15%,并由农行分担。因中信局原系按四行联合办理战时金融业务之原则,代替中央行办理,二十九年度开始举办,该局办理农贷之人员及机构,两感缺乏,大部委托农行代放,故此项业务之移转,当无困难。中国、交通二行所分担之比例,可以逐年递减,最后全部农贷业务归于中农行之日,即国家农业银行改组成立之时,其因银行法规上之限制,必须为农村放款者,可以购债券之方式,投资农贷,不必直接参加办理。

(3) 今后贴放与内汇业务,各按专业性质分别担任。例如属于农业贴放者,责由农行担负之;属于交通公用事业之贴放者,责由交行担负之;属于工矿实业之贴放者,责由中国银行担负之;属于重贴现转抵押性质责者,责由中央银行担负之。至于内汇业务,亦可依汇款性质划分担任,以树立专业分营之基础。

5. 下级机构之充实。现有之合作金库,自农本局农贷业务由中农行接受后,不啻全部由中农行辅设而成。就一般情况论之,银行所辅设之合作金库,其营业管理监督之权,几悉操于银行之手,合作金库实已形成银行办理农贷业务之基层机构。现农行之分支行处仅有84所,还不如县合作金库数目之多(目前县合作金库共有360余所)。故农行为谋基层机构之充实,似应积极辅设新库,并加强旧库之组织,而扩大其业务。至于省金库,在新制度中根本无此组织,在目前似亦无此中间组织存在之必要,今后应即停止设立,其已经成立者,由中农行负责接收。

三十年四月一日

(原载《经济汇报》1940 年第 3 卷第 9 期)

法币与抗战

一、我国施行法币制度之起源

我国于法币政策实施前,采用银本位币制。银本位币制弊端甚多,举其要者:(一)世界各国多采用金本位而我国仍沿用银本位,对外汇价随金银市价之变动而涨落不定,非特对外贸易带有浓厚之投机性与冒险性,不易发达,国内经济之进展亦受其阻碍;(二)我国原非产银国家,国内存银数量亦仅占世界存银之一小部分,对于银价之涨落无控制之力。因此银币价值之变动,须完全听命于伦敦、纽约二大银市。如银价暴跌,则金汇高涨,进口商品腾贵,而在生活必需品有一部分须仰赖外国供给,吾国人民生活必受重大压迫;如银价暴涨,则金汇下落,进口货低廉,国内物价连带下落,非特产业之发展受其阻碍,且酿成不景气之衰落现象。故银价之暴涨暴跌,皆足使我国经济蒙受不利之影响。一九三三年美国提高银价,我国白银源源外流,物价继续低落,造成金融经济恐慌,其程度与时俱增;虽征收银出口税与平衡税,亦未能阻止白银外流而引起物价回涨。况白银走私偷运之风,有增无已,经济恐慌,日益严重。政府鉴于银本位不可再继续维持,乃毅然于民国廿四年十一月四日宣布改革币制,施行法币。是为我国施行法币制度之起源。

法币译自西文。英文原名为 Legal Tender,意即一国之合法通币。就史实言,法币可谓由法律规定有强制通用资格之不兑现纸币。用于交易或清偿债务,均属合法而债权人不得拒绝。我国法币制度创始于二十四年十一月四日之紧急法令,其要点为:(一)自廿四年十一月四日起,中央、中国、交通三银行所发之钞票,定为法币。所有完粮纳税及一切公私款项之收付,概以法币为限,不得行使现金,违者全数没收;(二)凡银钱行号商店及其他公私机关或个人,有银本位币或其他银币生银等类者,应自十一月四日起交由发行准备管理委员会,或其指定之银行兑换法币;(三)法币准备金之保管及其发行收换事宜,设发行准备管理委员会办理之;(四)旧有银币单位订立之契约,应各照原定数额于到期日概以法币结算收付之;(五)中央、中国、交通三银行以外,虽经财政部核准发行之银行钞票现在流通者,准其照常行使。其发行数额,即以截至十一月三日止流通之总额为限,不得增加。由财政部酌定期限,逐渐以中央银行钞票换回;(六)为使法币对外汇兑按照目前价格稳定起见,应由中央、中国、交通三银行无限制买卖外汇。自此项法令公布施行后,中中交三行所发行之纸币,皆为我国之合法通币(农民银行纸币于廿四年底始由政府规定为法币)。以前之银本位币,即停止使用,而银本位制下之自由兑现、自由输出、自由铸造等条件,一律废止,至对外兑付则以法币购买外汇充之,此法币意义之大要也。

法币政策实施后,上海金融市场因白银外流所引起之紧张情形,渐归平复,利率水准,逐步低落,而外汇稳定,物价回涨,工商各业亦渐呈活跃之象。廿五年已入于经济繁荣之时代矣。

二、法币对于抗战之贡献

法币政策之实施,不但削除银本位之弊端,完成其稳定币值安定金融及发展经济之使命,且为此次抗战经济奠定坚固不拔之金融基础。兹从消极方面(或反面)与积极方面(或正面)分述法币对抗战之贡献如下。

甲、从消极方面(或反面)观察法币对抗战之贡献。

(1) 设如我国仍沿用银币,则抗日战事一起,各银行必发生挤兑风潮,影响所及,足使金融混乱,人心浮动。

银本位之必要条件之一,即自由兑现,持银行钞票者,可根据条例向银行兑取一定成色重量之银本位币。我国战前银币之成分为银八八铜一二,总重 26.697 1 公分,含纯银 23.493 448 公分,故持银行钞票向银行要求兑现者,银行必须无限制付与此种成色重量之银币,用以维持钞票与本位币之等价关系。倘纸币停止兑现,则钞票与本位币之关系消灭,人民必起疑虑,钞票之价值,势将脱离本位币而自行下跌,故如我们仍用银本位,即必须维持自由兑现。

惟战时人心浮动,人民不愿保存钞票,而欲保存银币。盖银币除其通币价值外,尚有其商品价值。钞票则一经停止兑现,即将摇动其信用,以致价值惨跌。故我国于抗战之初,若仍沿用银本位币制,则人民必纷纷以钞票持向银行要求兑换银币,而发生挤兑风潮。银行平素既不能保持十足准备,一时又难集中银币以资应付(此时各行均同时遭遇挤兑之困难),则挤兑风潮必愈演愈烈,而陷金融市场于混乱状态,终至于不可收拾。一切正常之金融业务,将因此而无从进行。一切工商业之活动,亦将因此而停顿。其影响战时金融经济者,莫此为甚。若竟因挤兑风潮而银行倒闭或停止兑现,则纸币价值惨跌,金融经济更无法维持矣。

今我国于战前即废除银本位,禁止银币流通,而使用法币,人民既习用法币而深信之,故战事发生后,无挤兑之事,金融安定,人心平稳,一如平常,此皆法币之赐也。

(2) 倘未施行法币,而仍沿用银币,则金银不能集中。金银不能集中,则第一发行准备无法充实,第二调换外汇与外国物资之工具必感缺乏。

在银本位币制下,银币既流通于国内充作一般交易中介,自不能使之集中。而在战时因人心浮动,使窖藏现银生金者必较平时为多,更无法使之集中。金银既不能集中,则发行准备无法充实;发行准备既不能充实,则钞票之发行必大受限制,而一切战时财政运用与经济设施将皆无法推进。倘竟不顾准备而增加发行,因挤兑之事,又将无法应付,而金融必陷混乱。

其次,金银为国际支付之工具。战时对外国军火与物资之需要弥殷,故对于国际支付工具之金银,其需要自异常迫切。在银本位下,金银既无法集中,且须留备兑现,即不能大量运往外国,以换取军火与物资。

然我国在战前即已废除银本位而施行法币,一切交易悉用法币,行使金银列入禁例,并规定凡银钱行号商店及其他公私机关或个人有银本位币或其他银币生银等类,应交由发行准备管理委员会或其指定之银行兑换法币,其后政府又实行收兑黄金,从此金银均为国有,集中于政府,可以充发行准备,或换取国外物资。是亦法币之赐也。

(3) 倘未施行法币,而仍沿用银币,则在沦陷区之银币,将为敌伪搜集利用。

在银本位制度下,银币流通于市面充一般交易工具而为市场上所不可少者。故如我国战时仍沿用银币,则战区转移之时,银币则难随之撤退,而必仍留存于沦陷区里。则敌伪正可利用种种方法尽量搜集,充作敌人之发行准备,或运往外国换取物资,以供敌人利用。观乎法币政策实施前,敌人暗中主持之白银走私,其风之盛,即一明证也。

然事实上我国下战,既已施行法币,禁止银币流通,收白银为国有,故虽战区转移,地区沦陷,但因无银币流通,敌人遂亦无法搜集利用。

(4) 倘未施行法币,而仍沿用银币,则我国将失去抢购物资之利器。

物资争夺为经济战之主要任务,倘沦陷区之物资为我购得,则一面可供应我方,一面可防止资敌。若为敌伪抢夺以去,则我方既不能利用,而敌伪之经济力量反因而增强。故物资之抢购,关系抗战经济者至大。然抢购物资,必须持有购买工具,若我国仍沿用银币,则第一银币之运输不便,且易为敌伪劫夺;第二以银币购取物资,则银币流入战区,易为敌伪搜括,流币至多。幸我国于战前既已废除银币,施行法币,故此等困难,减轻不少(法币虽亦有为敌伪调换套取外汇之可能,但因我统制外汇,敌人殊难消耗我外汇基金,且反坐受汇价跌落之损失)。故若无法币,实等于失去一抢购物资之利器。

乙、从积极方面(或正面)观察法币对抗战之贡献。

(1)战事发生后,金融市场稳定如常。法币原非银本位制下之纸币,故发行银行无兑付银币之义务。且法币行使已久,人民习之,故虽战事发生,人心浮动,而人民无意且亦无从请求兑现,因此挤兑风潮,不致发生,金融市场得以稳定。惟法币虽无兑换银币之义务,但有无限制购买外汇之规定,一般无国家民族意识之大资产家,仍可借此以逃避资金。政府有鉴于此,乃于八一三沪战爆发后,即毅然下令银行休业二日,同时即颁布《安定金融办法》,限制银行提取存款,规定自八月十六日起,银行钱庄各种活期存款,每户只能照其存款余额每星期提取5%,每户每星期至多以提取法币150元为限。嗣又应上海银钱业之请求后,核定《安定金融补充办法》,规定活期存款因商业上之需要,可得以同业汇划付给。惟此种汇划不能调现,亦不能购买外汇。查此两办法之主旨,皆在防止资金逃避,维护外汇市场,并减轻银行付现之频繁。实行以后,银行即赖以应付裕如,金融市场亦赖以安定如常。故以法币制度下之战时金融,与银本位制度下者相较,实不可同日而语,而法币对战时金融之贡献,于此亦可见诸一般矣。

(2)金银集中于国家银行,可(一)用作发行准备,增强法币信用;(二)输往外国,调换外汇,加强外汇基金,或换取物资,购买军火。

法币政策实施时,白银定为国有,一切银币生银等类,均应交由发行准备管理委员会或其指定之银行兑换法币。除银本位币按照面额兑换法币外,其余银类各依其实含存银数量兑换,故法币政策之实施,已确立集中白银之基础。

至于黄金之集中,政府则于二十七年九月廿八日公布《金类兑换法币办法》,责成中、中、交、农四行,邮政储金汇业局,各地邮政局为收兑机关,其收金价格以中央银行逐日挂牌行市为标准。但以金类请兑法币的给手续费,最少3%,最多5%,至以金类交由四行换算作法币存款者,则除加给手续费外,并照银行规定利息,加给周息二厘,用资鼓励。其后又先后公布《金类兑换法币办法施行细则》《实施收兑金类办法》《限制私运黄金出口及运往沦陷区域办法》及《监督银楼业收兑金类办法》等,系对私议金价,加以禁止,运金外出,加以限制;同时委托各地银楼业代收黄金,并监督其营业,以加强政府之黄金集中政策。

抗战后,关于银类之兑兑,仍照战前公布之兑换办法与《收兑杂银杂币简则》等规定进行,廿八年一月七日为统一各种收兑办法,另颁《收兑金银通则》。其中关于收兑银类者,规定廿四年十一月四日以前十足通用之银币厂条一元兑给法币一元;以前江南各省通用之银角每十二角兑换法币一元;其他生银杂银及成色较差之银币银角,均按其所含纯银23.493 448公分兑换法币一元;凡以一切银币兑换法币,概给手续费5%。

综上观之,举凡收兑金银之工具,以及各种奖励办法之实施,无不惟法币是赖。计至廿九年六月底止,所收生金之价值折合国币已不下1.6亿元,所收银类价值折合国币,不下1 600万元。此项收集来之大量金银,当有一部分用作发行准备,以增强法币信用;而另一部分则输往外国,以换取外汇,充实外汇基金,或换取物资,购买军火。其对抗战之贡献,至为巨大。而饮水思源,实法币之伟大功效,有以致之也。

(3) 法币能在沦陷区域继续流通,故能以之维持沦陷区之军政工作人员,维系沦陷区人民之向内心理。

法币自施行以来,准备充实,信用巩固,价值稳定,人民乐用,已成为我国唯一的合法的一般交易中介。故虽在沦陷区域,我军政势力不能达到之处,仍可继续流通,购物雇工,无不接受。故我仍可以法币接济游击队,以及其他在沦陷区域内之军政工作人员,从事对敌工作。

又法币为我国家政权之代表,沦陷区人民之习用法币,即无异于沾濡我国权。且沦陷区内人民手中既皆保有法币,则无不希望法币之后盾坚强,亦即无不希望我政府之地位坚强,获得军事胜利,俾其得免因法币之跌价,而遭受损失。日人曾谓:"中国人民爱惜法币,故亦爱护国民政府,故欲打倒国民政府,必须先打倒法币。"由此可见法币具有维系沦陷区人民向内心理之作用,而为日寇统制沦陷区域之一大障碍也。

(4) 法币可用作抢购物资之利器。

利用我国沦陷区物资,乃敌人实行其"以战养战"政策之手段。我国防止资敌计,必须与敌进行物资争夺战,争取沦陷区之物资,为我利用。但我为保护人民之利益起见,于争取物资时,又不能任意向人民征发,而必须付以代价,此种代价,即为法币。法币既能在沦陷区内继续流通使用,则我即可利用法币以抢购物资。

（5）法币体小质轻，便于运输，战时军饷之接济，与通货之调剂，均可赖以顺利进行。

战时饷需巨大，动须运现接济，若我未施行法币，而仍沿用银币，则运现之困难，与运费之高昂，实难想象。甚至使战区军饷之接济，时有断绝之虞，亦未可知。今法币体小质轻，运输便利，较诸银币每一卡车可多运 500 倍之数额（每卡车载重一公吨，若以运输银币，可运 4 万元，若以运钞票，可运 2 000 万元），战时军饷之接济无缺，实利赖焉。

又战时资金之流动性较大，各地内汇之需要亦较殷，通货之多少，头寸之松紧，最后皆赖输现予以调剂。若我未行法币，而仍沿用银币，则因现币运费之高昂，内汇汇水必更较今日为高。甚至可因运现之困难，而造成某地之通币过度膨胀，而他地之通币则过度紧缩，其影响于物价与金融者，亦必更有甚于今日。而今日之所以能免于斯者，法币之功效也。

（6）可以增加发行，以筹措特种投资与放款之经费。

战时生产事业之投资，不能专靠人民资金，而必须由国家金融机关积极贷放，始克有济。益以我国民间资金素感贫乏，金融统制基础未立，生产事业之投资，依赖于国家金融机关者尤多。抗战发生之利，政府即行设立农产工矿贸易三调整委员会，拨定巨额资金，以供扶助生产之用。同时又由四联总处办理贴放，融通农工商各业之资金。廿八年底该处之专案贴放已达 5.35 亿元，普通贴放已达 22 200 万元，廿九年九月专案贴放已达 66 700 万元。此项巨额资金，对于战时农矿工商各业帮助之大，可以想见。

最近四联总处又订定廿九年度农贷办法纲要，规定由中信局中交农三行及农本局办理农业生产、农产供销、农产储押、农田水利、农村运输工具以及佃农购买耕地等贷款。在经济三年计划中，亦规定特种性质之工矿交通农林水利贸易等业之投资与贷款，应由国库筹拨，或四行投资或贷款。

上述种种之特种投资与贷款，均动需巨资，绝非嗟咄可济，而其唯一出路，即为增加法币发行，以资应付。或谓法币增发，易引起通货膨胀，殊不知增发之法币，若以之投资于正常产业，不但无通货膨胀之弊，且反可促进生产，繁荣经济，斯即法币之巧妙运用也。

三、敌伪破坏法币之阴谋

法币对抗战之贡献既如是之大，故敌伪不惜用尽各种阴谋以破坏法币，企图借此以削弱我抗战力量。兹概述其破坏法币之阴谋如下：

(1) 伪造法币,以扰乱法币。

据中央社去年三月十九日梧州电云:"敌人伪制我法币千万元,已运抵华南使用,图扰乱我金融。该项伪钞花纹较粗,四周白边较阔。"又据廿八年三月二日报载:"敌大藏省近来伪造我国法币五千万元,装运至上海,在吴淞日商永山钱庄发出,专在京沪各地使用。"此类赝造我中、中、交、农四行钞票,行使于沦陷区之消息,时有所闻,且战时经济研究所及四行均得有样本。查敌人此种阴谋之目的,乃在增多我法币之流通数量,以降低法币之价值一也。使人民莫辨真伪,惧于使用,以破坏法币之信用二也。法币紊乱,信用动摇之后,敌伪可趁势推行伪钞,三也。

(2) 排除法币于沦陷区流通界之外。

敌人在内蒙假伪"蒙疆自治委员会"之手,禁止法币流通,限定于二十六年十月二十日以前收回我法币及其他地方钞票,过期一律不准流通。在华北又假伪"中国临时政府"之手,于廿七年六月下令禁止中央无地名券及中国交通两行之南方券在华北流通。八月八日又强令将华北法币减值一成,使法币照伪币九折流通。廿八年一月三日又公布旧通货第二次减价布告,规定中国交通两行纸币依票面金额按伪"联银券"六成相当之价格流通。同年一月十八日又公布禁用法币令,规定自三月十一日起,绝对不准法币与"联银券"对换,嗣后亦不准流通。凡此措施,其用意皆在消灭我沦陷区之法币,断绝我沦陷区之金融势力。如此,则沦陷区内游击队饷糈之接济,物资抢购经费之供应,皆将失去凭依,其策略固极毒辣也。

(3) 设立伪银行,发行伪钞票,并推行军用票,以代替法币之流通。

敌伪于内蒙设有伪"蒙疆银行",发行一种伪"蒙疆法币"流通于内蒙;于华北设有伪"中国联合准备银行",发行一种伪"联准银行券"流通于华北;于华中设有伪"华兴商业银行"发行一种伪"华兴券"流通于华中。此外又推行一种军用票,行使于华中华南。同时运用各种政治力量金融手段,以维持并推行伪钞,截至廿九年六月底止,各种伪钞及军用票之发行数额如下(单位千元):

伪"蒙疆法币"	61 000
伪"联银券"*	458 000
伪"华兴券"	5 600
敌"军用票"	100 301

＊伪"联银券"系廿八年底发行额。

查敌人此项发行伪钞之阴谋,除用以兑换法币套取外汇外,其作用尚有(一)用以榨取沦陷区域之物资与劳力,(二)造成"日圆集团",便利敌伪物资交流,吸收我沦陷区之重要物资,倾销其本国过剩产品。

(4)套取外汇,以扰乱外汇市场,而破坏法币信用。

禁用法币之另一面,即为吸收法币,套取外汇。在伪"蒙疆"敌伪规定由伪"蒙疆银行"限期收回法币。在华北由伪"中国联合准备银行"发行伪"联银券"以调换法币,同时强迫人民及华商银行交出法币。在华中则一方面规定伪"华兴券"为关税收入之合法通币,但得以法币代替之,他方面不限制伪"华兴券"之发行数量,以便借关税收入,吸收法币。凡此种种措施,其目的皆在获得法币,以持向我国家银行或上海黑市购买外汇。如是可以削弱我外汇基金,使法币法定汇价无法维持,黑市汇价逐渐低落,以扰乱外汇市场,破坏法币信用。

(5)统制沦陷区经济,以推行伪币。

为推行伪"蒙疆法币",伪"蒙疆自治委员会"除与伪"满"政府缔结货币等价兑换协定、与伪"满"中央银行及朝鲜银行等缔结汇兑协定外,又统制伪"蒙疆"之外汇与重要物资之输出。规定:(一)汇往"蒙疆"以外千元以上之汇款,须得"蒙疆委员会"之许可;(二)金银铅铁煤油类、种籽、蛋类、毛皮等货物之输出,须得"蒙疆委员会"之许可,并须结售外汇于"蒙疆银行"。

为推行伪"联银券",敌伪除禁用法币外,又以统制华北汇兑与贸易办法,以集中外汇,支持伪券。廿八年三月伪"联合准备银行"公布管理汇兑办法,规定蛋类、花生、杏仁、棉花、烟叶、煤、盐等十二种货物出口所得之外汇,均须按一先令二便士之价格,售给伪"联合准备银行"。同年七月又规定所有出口货物其价值在一百元以上者,须一律结售外汇,用以取得外汇,维持伪券之信用。

为推行伪"华兴券"起见,敌伪规定"华兴券"为缴纳关税合法之币,为推行敌军用票起见,敌人曾在华中华南各地设立物资交换所,统制日用品如糖盐棉布棉纱等之交易,并限定以军用票购买。

上述种种阴谋,其目的皆在利用各种汇兑、贸易以及物资之统制,以推行敌票伪钞,遂行其榨取政策。

四、我方之对策

针对上述敌伪各种金融侵略之阴谋,我政府曾施行各种对策以防止之,兹分述如下：

（1）防止伪造法币之行使。

为防止敌人在沦陷区行使伪造之法币,四行在沦陷区域内不发新券而用旧券,以便易于识别,使假造法币无法混入市场行使,于是敌人伪造法币以扰乱我金融之阴谋,不能遂行。

（2）防止伪钞敌票之行使。

为防止伪钞敌票之行使,我政府规定：（一）全国人民应一律拒绝行使敌伪钞票,违者以汉奸论罪；（二）凡以敌伪钞票成立之契约一律无效。又令游击队检查伪钞之行使,遇有违犯者,除没收其敌伪钞票外,并予以惩罚。此外又联络外商银行,使不接收伪钞作为存款或汇款,今日伪钞敌票尚不能在沦陷区内普遍推行,职是其故。

（3）统制外汇,以抵制敌伪套取外汇之阴谋。

敌伪之发行伪钞,套取外汇,肇端于伪"中国联合准备银行"之成立。但此种阴谋,立即为我发觉,该伪行于二十七年三月十日成立,我则于同月十二日即公布《购买外汇请核办法》及《申请外汇规则》,从此不再无限制供给外汇,并指定中央银行办理外汇请核事宜,凡非正当用途者,概不核准购买,同时又与外商银行成立绅士协定,不供给外汇与投机者,敌人套取外汇之技术,遂无从施展矣。

嗣我为集中外汇起见,更实施进一步之外汇统制。廿七年四月公布《商人运货出口及结售外汇办法》及《出口货物应结外汇之种类及其办法》,实行出口贸易之统制,以集中出口贸易所得之外汇。廿八年七月又公布《出口货物结汇领取汇价差额办法》,对于出口贸易之统制与结汇办法予以调整。规定除桐油、茶叶、猪鬃、矿产四种由政府统购统销外,其余一切出口货物概须依照法价,将所得外汇售与中交两行。惟结汇后,尚可领取法价与该行牌价之差额,借以鼓励出口贸易,集中出口外汇。同时又公布《非常时期禁止进口物品办法》,规定凡非抗战建国及人生必需之进口物品皆在禁止之列。其目的则在平衡贸易,以减少外汇之需要。七月三日又公布《进口物品申请购买外汇规则》,规定凡进口商人申请购买外汇,须按法价与牌价差额,缴纳平衡费,以减少政府按法价出售外汇之损失。

上述种种统制外汇办法,对于增加外汇供给,减少外汇需要,颇有实效,而敌伪套取外汇之路,亦因此大多闭塞。

（4）暗中维持外汇黑市,以巩固币信。

自廿七年三月我政府施行外汇请核制以限制外汇之供给后,因核准外汇数额未能满足市场需要,遂有外汇黑市之发生。嗣以资金逃避,外汇投机,入超增大之故,黑市汇兑遂逐步跌落。七月间已破入十便士大关,八月初又下落至八便士。此时法币法定汇价虽仍定为一先令二便士半,但依法价而核准购买外汇者,为数有限,而黑市外汇供求逐增,反成为有力的汇市,影响法币价值者至大。政府为稳定法币价值,巩固法币信用起见,乃于廿七年八月中准中国、交通及汇丰三银行暗中维持法币黑市汇价于八便士水准,直至次年二月,法币黑市汇价始终稳定于八便士与八便士半之间。逃避之资金,一时颇有回笼者。廿八年三月成立外汇平衡基金,总额定为1 000万镑,中英合作共设委员会专司运用之责,其运用方策为以无限制买卖外汇方法,公开维持八便士四分之一之汇率。于是敌伪有机可乘,大肆搜集法币,积极套取外汇。我方有鉴于此,乃于二十八年六月七日突然放弃维持政策,黑市汇价于是大跌,而敌伪方面所握有之法币,以外币价值计之,乃亏折甚大,损失不赀。此后我方时而维持,时而放弃,相机运用,旨在一方面防止敌伪套取外汇基金,一方面维持汇价之相当稳定,以极小外汇基金之牺牲,求法币信用之巩固。

(5) 准战区各省银行发钞,以减少法币在沦陷区之流通量,免被敌伪吸收,套取外汇。

沦陷区及接近沦陷区之战区,因有敌伪调取法币之顾虑,四行未便充裕发行,但抢购战区物资,供应战地筹码,在在需要增加发行,势不能不利用省地方银行钞票代替一部分法币行使。爰于廿八年三月,财政部召集第二次地方金融会议,议定各省地方银行得酌发一元券及辅币券,以应战地需要,此项议案经呈准财部核定施行后,各省地方银行类多遵照办理。省银行钞票发行后,战区之法币流通量随之减少,敌伪之吸收法币套取外汇之计,遂不得售。

(6) 加强金融机构,执行战时金融政策。

战时金融措施,须赖强有力之机构以运用之,始克应付非常。故于抗战发生后,政府即立饬中中交农四行组织联合办事处于上海,由四行各派代表共同研讨,并督促各行共同担负战时金融使命,以坚实中央金融枢纽。同时就各地成立四行联合办事分处,建立地方金融主干,以收指臂相顾之效。去年八月复颁布战时健全金融机构办法纲要,改组四行联合办事总处,使成为一执行国民政府战时金融政策之组织,负指挥监督四行业务之责。且规定该总处理事会主席,在非常时期由财政部授权,对四行为便宜之措施,或代行其职权。其后邮政储金汇业局、省市地方银行及商业银行之业务,亦归该总处指挥监督。于是中央金融机构益加充实健全,金融周转亦更且灵活敏捷,而敌伪之金融侵略,亦可以迅速应付矣。

此外,又实行分区处理金融办法,详密规定:(一)沦陷区之金融机关,应予适当之保留,以为与敌伪斗争之据点;(二)附近陷敌区域之金融机关,不得随意撤退,并须抢购物资,移运后方;(三)距敌较远区域之金融机构,应妥善策应前两区域金融,以收指臂相顾之效;(四)后方应迅速完成金融网,以担负协助经济复兴之使命。

(7)采取稳健发行政策,以免通币膨胀。

我国发行向采稳健政策。抗战之前,发行数额原属太少,不但边远地方之人民,咸苦筹码不足,即在腹地各市面,亦尚有通货紧缩之感。迨战争发生以后,抗战建国同时并进,通货之需要,更形迫切,发行数额自须当增加。但发行数额之是否逾限,不在乎数目之多少,而全以是否适合于社会之需要,及已否超过饱和点以上而定。若依此以衡量我国之现在发行额,实不能谓其已超过饱和点,政府为尊重银行制度及法律,并未如战时其他国家之干预发行,故发行权仍在银行,发行准备仍依法由发行准备管理委员检查监督,政府不过依照法令,负行政监督之责而已。由此观之,我国通货膨胀一点,自可毋庸置虑。

(8)增税及推行储蓄,以吸收游资,使法币回笼。

战时军需浩繁,财政支出巨大,因此流通于市面之游资,亦相应增多,自须设法吸收,并使法币回笼,充裕银行头寸,使用于正当有用之途,而免助长投机。吸收游资之道,主要者即为增税与储蓄。

关于战时税政之措施,首当一述者,即为建立直接税系统,以所得税、遗产税、非常时期过分利得税及印花税为其中坚。所得税税收,不但不因战区之日益扩大而减小,且反较前倍增。非常时期过分利得税,原规定于廿八年一月一日起征收,后因故展缓至今年开始实际征课,遗产税亦已于今年七月开始征收。就目前国税税收情形而论,直接税已由战前之第六位,进居第三位。至于间接各税,如烟酒税、卷烟税、转口税等税率,亦已酌为增加。统税范围,亦在筹议推广中。

关于储蓄之提倡与推行,其主要措施为:(一)举办节约建国储金,由全国官商各银行及邮政储金汇业局经收,现各行局皆已举办,推行颇为普遍;(二)发售节约建国储蓄券,由中央信托局中国、交通、农民银行及邮汇局,经财部核准发行,以与节约建国储金并行;(三)举办外币定期储蓄存款,存户可以英美法及其他政府核准之外币存入,到期时仍照原存外币支取本息,亦可以法币按商汇牌价折合外币存入。

此外如有奖储蓄、劝募公债及奖励资金内移，亦皆有助于资金之吸收，而移用于正当之用途。

(9) 统制物价，以安定币值。

物价为币值之反面，物价跌即币值涨，物价涨即币值跌。故安定币值必须安定物价。惟战时通币增多，生产减退，物价上涨，几为一种必然现象。故必须加以有效之统制，始能期其稳定。我国统制物价之办法，最初实施者为评定物价，借政府及社会之力量评定公平价格，使物价不至过分上涨，以安市面。迨廿八年十一月底四联总处订定《平定日用必需品价格方案》并经呈准由经济部设立平价购销处购办大批日用物品，平价销售，以抑制一般商店之抬高物价，是为积极平定物价之始。此外如取缔货物押放，通令各银行禁止以货品作押款，并不得代理客商买卖货物；如便利汇兑，规定凡自海外采购生产机器原料及本国无代替品之必需品，得申请照商汇牌价，核给外汇；凡向口岸采购日用必需品，运销后方，得依照便利内汇办法，请由四行以低率汇来承汇货款，以减轻商品成本；如由四行办理贴放，促进生产，以调剂商品之供求，是则以金融手段，辅助平定物价之重要措施。凡此种种，其目的均在平抑物价，以冀安定币值者也。

五、结　论

综上所述，吾人可知法币已早为我抗战立下一坚固不拔之金融基础。吾人赖法币之运用，战时金融，得以安稳如常；战时财政，得以应付裕如；而对敌经济战亦恃以顺利进行。故吾人谓"抗战需要法币，法币支持抗战"，实非过言也。

（原载《训练月刊》1941 年第 2 卷第 2 期）

如何运用中美平准基金

一、外汇平准基金之作用

设立平准基金,按预定计划买卖外汇,其作用可有二种结果:一为稳定汇价,二为缓和物价上涨之势力,兹请分别言之。

(1) 稳定汇价

汇价系价格之一种,为供求关系所决定。设其水准与经济情形相适合,则全年国际收支总额,可望相抵。惟因季节变动关系,外汇市场之供求,容有短长,若有外汇平准基金相机买进卖出外汇,以为调节,可使汇价稳定。且平准基金运用之结果,必无损益,以买进卖出之数额可以相抵也。

设汇价之水准,不与经济情形相适应,则全年国际收支总额,难望相抵,若汇价失之过高,国际收入将不敷支出,而平准基金运用之结果,将逐渐消耗,其消耗之数等于收支之差额,除非平准基金能源源补充,其数额虽大,亦有消耗尽罄之一日,此时汇价将续落,以至于自然水准,而与经济情形相适应。以往法币汇价,虽有中英外汇平准基金之支持,仍不免下降,其故在斯。

汇价水准是否与经济情形适合,要以国际收支是否相等为衡。国际收支项目中以贸易为大宗,变动亦最敏捷。但汇价与贸易有密切之关系,汇价低,能刺激输出,以造成出超,而使国际收入大于国际支出,汇价高,能刺激输入,以造成入超,而使国际收支不利于我,惟有合理汇价,方能维持国际收支之平衡,而汇价亦得赖以维持于不堕。然汇价为货币对外价值之表征,所以合理汇价或汇价之自然水准,在自由经济制度下,应等于两国货币购买力之比,亦即等于两国物价指数之反比,是为购买力平价,故就汇价之长期趋势言,若非有外力(例如管制)之干涉,应与平价相符合。今我国正从事于长期抗战,巨额战费之筹措,须有合理适度之把注,由是而通货数量渐有增加,汇价物价之变动,当此战时要所难免;若欲防止汇价之连续下落,势须筹有巨额平准基金以为调节运用之需,其理至明,毋俟赘言。

由此观之,运用平准基金,以维持汇价之稳定,可有二种情形:一为维持合理汇价。在此情形下,平准基金之运用,只在消除季节变动,而不变更其长期趋势,且基金将不至有所消耗。一为维持过高(或过低)汇价。在此情形下,平准基金之运用,一面消除其季节变动,同时变更其长期趋势,而基金将逐渐消耗(或增多)。今中美英平准基金借款协定,业经签定,其运用之目的如何? 对于上述两种不同情形,似应预加慎重考虑也。

(2) 缓和物价上涨之势力

卖出外汇,即是收进法币。买进外汇,即是放出法币。今若运用平准基金之目的,仅属消极的调节汇市季节变动,而不变更汇价之长期趋势,则平准基金管理委员会买进之外汇,必约略等于卖出之外汇,对于平准基金既无损益,对于法币之流通量,亦无增减之影响。今若运用平准基金之目的,非仅在调节汇市季节变动,而在积极的抛售外汇吸收法币,以减少市场上法币之流通量,而解除物价上涨之部分势力。如是则不独过高之汇价,可借以保持,即于平定物价,亦确有裨益,惟平准基金将逐渐消耗,若非能继续举借外债,源源补充,则其附随之弊害,亦殊值考虑也。

平准基金会卖出之外汇,若皆用于购买我国必需之货物进口,则卖出外汇愈多,输入货物亦愈多。今物价为供求关系所决定,货物之供给既增,除非有其他影响,物价自将低落,况目前我国各地物价上涨之程度悬殊,就重庆、成都、昆明、桂林、西安、上海六地之趸售物价指数观之,昆明、重庆上涨最速,廿九年十二月时,各增至十一倍以上;上海最慢,计涨四倍半;次为桂林,涨至五倍余。又就衣食必需品之物价观之,米价在桂林为22元,在重庆为180元,相差达158元。盐价在西宁为22元,在贵阳为134.4元,相差达112.4元。纱价在香港为国币1 392.3元,在嘉定为5 200元,相差达3 807.7元,此种地域差异,自系运输工具不敷或运输成本过高所致。倘平准基金管理委员会采取奖励输入运输工具及器材之政策,凡请购外汇用以采办运输工具器材及油料等,特别予以优待(例如给予差别汇率),则运输工具器材及油料等之输入,必将增多,运输能力必将增大,而物价之地域差异,或可减少。如是则物价先涨且速之地区可得平抑之益,而物价后涨之地区,亦可避免因他处物价上涨而涨之势力,亦属有利。

由此观之,外汇平准基金之运用,除稳定汇价外,尚有平抑物价之功,当此物价高涨之秋,此种作用实堪注意。惟运用外汇平准基金以平定物价,所能收效之程度如何? 不可不加研究者也。

二、对于物价之影响

运用外汇平准基金以平定物价，所能收效之程度如何？可分两方面言之：

（1）卖出外汇、吸收法币以紧缩法币之流通量，对于平抑物价之功效如何？

（2）卖出外汇，购进我国所需之外国货物，以增加货物市场之供给，对于平定物价之效能如何？

欲解答前一问题，必先知物价与法币流通额之关系，流通额之统计较难，只能就发行额代之。试以民国廿六年底至廿九年之物价水准与法币发行额之关系比较观之，则知发行额增加之速度缓，而物价上涨速度大。依二七年底之比例，如发行额增加 1%，则物价上涨 1.057%。依廿八年底之比例，如发行额增加 1%，则物价上涨 1.127%。廿九年且更有加甚。假若物价之上涨，全由于法币发行额增多所致，并无其他原因，则此后每增加发行额 1%，将使物价上涨 2% 以上。反之，倘能使发行紧缩 1%，则至少足以使物价下落 2%。

以上仅系假定物价上涨与法币发行额增多有关而言，但目前物价上涨之原因甚多，法币发行额增多，仅为其原因之一。此外如生产不足、运输困难及操纵居奇等，皆属重要原因。欲分析此等原因，并决定各原因对物价之影响程度，本宜用相关方法（Correlation method）以求之，惟资料不全，难将此等因素对物价之影响分开。兹为简便计，姑用减缩方法（Deflation method）以除去法币数量对物价上涨之影响，而求出其他因素对物价之影响程度。则其他因素之变动，确亦居重要之位置。

根据报章所载，美国助华日趋积极，今后借款或可望源源继续。而业经签字之一万万元（其中五千万元为平准基金）借款，不过其开端耳，今设五千万美元平准基金（据报所载此外尚有英国借款一千万镑，约合四千万美元，亦系充平准基金之用）在一年之内，悉数售出，并用以输入我国必需物资，依现在美汇行市每法币一百元合美币五元计算，则售出五千万美元可收回法币十万万元（倘售出平准基金较五千万美元为多，则尚不止此数）。若依上述物价与发行额之关系推论之，当发行额增加 1%，则物价上涨 1.6%，今若运用平准基金之结果，则可消减最近物价上涨势力 80%。换言之，物价上涨问题可以解决过半矣，此种结果殊堪重视也。

兹请解答第二问题。

后方生产不足,物资缺乏,不足以供给前后方大量之需求,实为物价上涨之重要原因。缓和之道,平衡之方,自须从增加物资供给着手。谋物资供给之增加,除积极促进国内生产外,尚须谋国外物资之输入,以减少物资供给不足之程度,而求物价之稳定。

事实上我国军需民用物品,多赖国外输入之接济,凡五金电料类之各种成品,交通上所必需之汽油车辆器材,以及卫生医药上之用品等,几无不仰给于国外。抗战以来,国际运输路线,日渐阻滞,致使此种产品输入不易,其价格之上涨程度,远较国内产品剧烈,如就二十九年十二月重庆趸售物价指数而论,五金电料类与燃料类,几为总指数之二倍。是知一般物价水准之日渐升高(即货币购买力之逐渐低落),其重要原因实为输入物价之飞涨,故为缓和物价上涨之趋势,似非积极购进国外上项物品,以增加国内市场货物之供给不可。

欲自国外购进大量物资,以适应国内之需求,有下列两个前提,一须国营民营实业机关,获得外汇之充分供给,以便采购外国物资。二须国际交通路线具备充分运输能力,以便运入所购之货物。关于前者,只须外汇平准基金供给正当需要之一切外汇,即可解决,毋庸赘言。至于后者,当此南洋风云日紧,国际路线日渐阻滞,以及国内运输困难万状情形之下,毕竟能自外国输入几何物资,殊属疑问。然而事在人为,倘能善用外交力量,同时积极发展国际运输路线,则未始无增进之余地。

就国外交通言之,香港向为我国进出口物资之转运中心,货物运输,又素借英美商轮。在此南洋情势日渐紧张情形之下,我输入物资,容有中途被日人掠夺之可能,此宜运用外交力量,以取得英美友邦之切实合作。必要时,请其护航至香港及其他可以转运入口之地,例如仰光及伊洛瓦底江口。仰光至腊戍有长九百余公里狭轨之缅甸铁路,每月可有一万二千吨之运量,今后自须与缅甸政府合作改进,增加其运量,以便利我国外物资之输入。又由伊洛瓦底江口至八莫,可以通航,全程约千余公里。由八莫通腊戍有三百余公里长之公路。水陆并进,运量已甚可观。若每月总运输量,可达一万八千吨之谱(若再加改进,尚可扩大),如更能就口岸至内地之运输,同时加以改善,则每月运量较之过去增加数倍决非难事。设以如此新增之运量,分配若干于抢运目前最急需之金属电料及医药等,不数月则此类物品在国内市场之供给,差足敷供所求,虽其价格容或不能抑低,但必较以前为稳定。是则外国物资之输入确有平定物价之功。输入愈多,效果愈大,殆可断言也。

我国物价之上涨，原因固多，然运输困难，以致各地物资不能互相调剂，实为其重要原因之一。今各区域间物价上涨之程度不同，而同种物价各地价格相差悬殊，即可见其由于运输困难之故。果若有充分运输工具自湖南运米以接济四川之军粮民食，则川湘两地每市担米价相差何能达三百元之谱，于此可见增强运输力量之重要。目前运输困难之原因，不外车辆与汽油均感不敷所致。如去年七月间滇越路线阻塞以后，汽油输入维艰，因之，重庆汽油价格由五月间之每听七十元，至十二月即涨为一百六十元，尤为显著。油价涨，则运输成本增高，运价不得不随之越级上腾，各地物资既因运输工具缺乏，无法运出，即使能运出，因须担负高额运费之故，遂有价格相差悬殊与畸形暴涨之现象。故在今日后方公路运输，仍占主要地位情况之下，自应积极谋公路运输之改进，其道不外改善现有工程，增加车辆与充实燃料之供给。若平衡基金之运用采积极步骤鼓励公私各方面尽量购入车辆，车辆运至口岸后，即可输入物资，以增加运输量。运输量既大增，则对于物价之贡献，必甚可观。今若将新增之巨大运输量，以一部分配于汽油之输入，再加国内汽车已有半数使用酒精柴油等代用品，则所输入之汽油，除供给各路军民需要外，尚有余裕，可贮之以备非常之需。如是则汽油价格因缺货而暴涨之现象，必可完全消除，而汽车运价自亦将随之减低。又若后方货车，因平准基金会之鼓励政策（如对运输工具之采购特给优遇汇率），由若干万辆增至若干万辆，则运输能力较前增加倍蓰，此与流通物资调节供求必大有裨益。

三、外汇平准基金之运用技术问题

欲发挥平准基金之功能，必须研究运用之技术，务使基金不虚耗，以冀获得最大效果。欲达此目的，则对下列三点应慎加研究。

甲、建立后方外汇市场而放弃维持上海黑市汇价。

乙、新建外汇市场之汇率。

丙、核售外汇之原则。

兹请分述之如次：

(甲) 建立后方外汇市场而放弃维持上海黑市汇价

政府对于上海外汇黑市，向取维持政策，其间虽为适应环境，曾数度放弃之，然皆为时甚暂。此种政策在过去，颇有维护币制之功，而于坚定华北、华中人民对法币之信用，以巩固其向心力，尤足称道。然时过境迁，情势大

变,以前所认为有利者,今已不复存在,而为流弊则仍如往昔,未尝稍减,故今日实有放弃维持上海黑市汇价之必要。其理由如次:

(1) 便利日伪套取外汇

上海外国租界,非我政权能及,无法控制。若我采取维持黑市汇价,欲其有效,必须无限制供给外汇,以满足市场上之一切需要,既予日伪以套取外汇之便利,又与政府当初所采取之审核请购外汇制度相反。今日伪榨取法币之方法甚多,而所得之法币无穷,以有限之平准基金,何能应付无穷之套取,故维持上海黑市汇价,直似以金沙填补无底洞,为不可能之事,是乃智者所不欲为者。

(2) 便利上海进口贸易并使日人得利用我平准基金以购进其所需要之物资

华中、华北出口贸易所得之外汇,早为日方所统制,故由上海进口贸易所需要之外汇,不能取自出口贸易,须仰给于平准基金及其他来源。且在上海进口之货物多为日方所利用,据《密勒氏评论》载称,在沪进口之平滑油及汽油几全数为日本所购去,以为该国驻华机械化部队及空军之使用,而棉花则大部分为日本驻华纱厂所购进。如是则维持上海黑市汇价之结果,适足使日人利用我平准基金,以输入其所需要之物资,利用我之国力以攻击我国,此何异于赞助其推进以战养战之政策?

汇价之稳定,原有促进国际贸易之功,当此长期抗战,国内物资奇缺之时,尤有鼓励进口贸易之作用。上海黑市汇价因平准基金之支持,虽有几次剧变,然每当剧变风潮过后颇为稳定,故自廿六年以来之进口贸易继涨不已,而入超数额亦与年俱进。若以英镑为计算进出口贸易值之单位,四年来上海对外贸易状况有如下表:

上海进出口贸易进值表　　　　　单位:1 000 英镑

	二十六年	二十七年	二十八年	二十九年
进口值	30 286	16 175	35 588	48 789
出口值	24 116	9 546	14 946	22 417
入超额	6 170	6 629	20 642	26 392

注:转录 *Finance and Commerce*。该报贸易值,系按黑市平均汇价折合英镑。

倘进口之货物,皆为本国必需物品,且为国民所消费,则进口贸易额之增大,并无不利。诚如上节所述,进口货物多为日人所利用,则进口愈增,日人受利愈大,即对我之弊害愈大。况入超额随进口货值之增长而益大,因之平准基金之消耗益速，如平准基金无充分供给来源加以补充，终将用尽，而汇价亦难以维持矣！过去上海黑市汇价再三放弃支撑，以致发生暴跌，职是之故。汇价暴跌足以影响人心而摇动币信，其发生之原因，在于平准基金之消耗。其消耗之原因在于进口贸易之无法统制，而进口贸易之不能统制，由于我政权之所不能及。然则运用平准基金以维持上海黑市汇价，实属无益之事，有百害而无一利。

（3）在经济上上海与后方之贸易关系趋于隔绝

异地（不论国内或国外）货币价值之发生联系，其基本原因，为贸易关系之存在，若两地之贸易关系断绝，则货币价值之联系失去基础。今上海之物资因浙、闽、粤海岸之被日封锁及后方运输困难之故，殊难流入后方，而后方之物资久经政府严禁运沪，以防资日，是则上海与后方之贸易关系，濒于隔绝。所以上海法币价值与后方法币价值之联系，可谓业已切断。且就事实言，自去年十二月以后，因上海对后方物资移动困难之故，后方物价之涨落，几已不复受上海黑市汇价之影响，故维持上海黑市汇价不能再视为稳定后方物价之手段。

（4）在金融上上海已失去坚守据点之价值

以往上海为我国在沦陷区之最后金融据点，亦是日我双方金融力量战斗之场所，现在此种情形，已成过去。盖昔日日人对上海金融界所施之压力，仅为搜括法币以套取外汇，手段虽甚毒辣，但尚属一种金融策略。今者变本加厉，日伪已采取政治压力及恐怖手段以打击我方在上海之金融界。因此我方在上海之金融据点，能否保守，殊成问题。当此国际情势逆转，上海租界法院已有一部被伪方强制接收，租界华董亦已有伪方人员加入，将来势必愈演愈烈，在沪四行或有被迫撤退之虞，盖单纯之金融力量决不能与政治力量及恐怖手段相对抗也。政府银行且有不能立足之势，则更无继续维持汇市之必要，日益显明。

（5）在政治上上海已渐失去维系沦陷区民心作用

当国军西移之后，政府与沦陷区人民之关系大有赖于法币价值之维系，因法币价值之稳固，虽经日人造谣中伤与破坏，终不能动摇人民对法币之信心。故维持上海黑市汇价，颇有助于沦陷区民心之维系，然此种维系作用已因年来上海黑市汇价之屡次跌落，后方物价之继续上涨，及日伪在沦陷区域强制使用伪币之故，渐次低减。吾人虽不敢谓维持人心之作用已至完全消失之地步，但可得而言者，若目前放弃维持上海之黑市外汇，其可能引起之不良反响必不若在二十七八年时代之大。且若放弃维持上海黑市汇价，行于后方外汇市场建立之后,则对于法币信用,决无恶影响之可言,倘新建汇市之汇价能保持稳定,法币信用殊有重新振作之望,尤属可欢迎之事。

关于维持黑市汇价之政治影响,尚可从另一立场观察之。黑市汇场稳定,既可促进输入,以增加沦陷区内之物资,又能安定币值,以免物价上涨。当此国家从事于长期抗战,后方人民正在艰苦奋斗,且受物价高涨之压迫,而彼沦陷区内人民仍得在物资充足物价安定中度其如常生活,对照之下,未免相差悬殊。夫避难就易,乃人之天性,此所以沦陷区内人民将有"乐不思蜀"之姿态,而无复怀念我政府矣。然则所谓保持黑市汇价之稳定,以维系沦陷区内人心之内向者,其结果适相反,笔者殊不以为然也。

上述经济上、金融上及政治上之现象为昔日主张维持上海黑市外汇之主要理由,今已时过境迁,均已不复存在,则放弃维持上海黑汇价之政策,可以决矣。

维持上海黑市汇价政策,既须放弃,则必另建外汇市场以代替之,此外汇市场应建设于后方,其理由有三:

(1) 国内应有一受政府控制之外汇市场

当一国对外贸易未完全断绝时,应有一外汇市场,以供应并调整国际收支,如此则政府可借汇价之升降,以协助贸易政策之推行,在战时政府为实行管理外汇之便利计,外汇市场必须置于政府控制之下,故应设于后方,不能设于国外或租界中。

(2) 战时经济金融中心之内移

战事发生以后,沿海一带之厂商大多迁来后方营业,银行业之迁移情形亦正相似。如中中交农四大银行之总行或总管理处均已迁至重庆办公,且其分支行处已在后方构成一新金融网,至其他重要商业银行亦多在后方设立行处营业,是则我国战时经济金融中心渐次集中于后方之重庆。今外汇市场为重要金融活动之一,与经济事业息息相关,无论就理论或事实言,均应随经济金融中心而内移。

(3) 供给后方正当需要之外汇

经济中心既已移至后方,为便利厂商请买外汇,以购取外国机器原料,而从事于生产建设起见,固须有供给外汇之市场,而政府为吸收后方法币,以减少市场上法币之流通量而缓和物价上涨势力计,亦宜在后方建立外汇市场,以利政策之推进。

基于上述之理由,今后平准基金之运用区域,应限于后方,以重庆为中心,并视事实之需要,于西安、昆明、桂林、金华等地设立办事处,或委托中国银行代理,在后方外汇市场建设完成后,应即放弃维持上海黑市汇价。

(乙) 新建外汇市场汇率之决定

汇率之高低,关系平准基金之效能者甚巨,决定汇率之条件有属于客观者,有属于主观者。就我国目前情形而言,客观之标准有三:(1)购买力平价。盖我所以需要外汇,因欲借外汇以购取外国军火及商品等物,外人之所以需要中国货币,固欲借中国货币以购取中国货物,故两国货币之交换比值,应等于外国货币对于外国货物之购买力与中国货币对于中国货物之购买力之比值,是为购买力平价。购买力平价在完全自由经济之情况下,堪称为决定汇率之可靠标准。然在战时,国家对经济金融之活动大多加以管制,故购买力平价已丧失其原有之一部分性能,但仍可用作决定汇价之参考。(2)最近发行金公债之折算率。政府于本年春发行英金公债一千万镑,折算率为法币每元合英金四便士半,美金公债五千万元折算率为每百元合美金七元五角。以与黑市汇价相较,高出40%以上,此系由于金公债之利率较低,且含鼓励人民认购之意。新建外汇市场之汇率,当较金公债之折算率为低,方为合理。故金公债之折算率,不妨视为新汇率之上限。(3)上海黑市汇率。现行上海黑市汇率英汇为三便士二左右,美汇为五元二角左右,有时且有续落至五元相近者,据此以观,则不妨规定五美元为新汇率之下限。

至若国内外经济之现状,平准基金之大小及其补充来源与政府所采取之外汇政策等,皆可视作主观的条件。在理论上,上述六种标准之平衡点,当为最合理之汇率。

此次平准基金系由英美两国贷予者,今后可望源源贷予者,恐唯美国是赖,且就目前世界之局势观之,能供应我大量物资者,恐亦只有英国及美元系统之国家,故新外汇市场之汇率,应放弃钉住镑价而以对美元之汇价为准,实际汇价可以美金公债之折算率七元五角为上限,参照目前之黑市汇价,以五元为下限,在五元至七元半之间,由基金会斟酌主观情形决定之,法币对他种外币之汇价,可以根据美汇行市推算之。

(丙) 后方外汇市场应加管理,而以供给厂商之正当需要为原则

后方外汇市场应加管理,此殆无疑义者,盖自由经济之理论已成时代潮流之过去,其弊端显著,毋待赘言。自上次世界经济恐慌发生以来,举世各国为谋经济复兴,对国内重要经济部门之活动多加管理,其涉及国家间者,如国际汇兑之管理,尤为普遍,而其管理方法亦最周密。至于战时为谋集合

外汇以取得国外之物资,管理外汇更属迫切需要。

外汇市场之管理其主要内容为汇率、地点、手续及用途四项;而用途一项尤为管理外汇之核心。欲使外汇管理有明确之目标,必须对用途加以限制,欲求外汇管理有良好效果,必须用途限制得当。我国实行管理外汇,开始于二十七年三月所公布之购买外汇请核办法,此法仅对购买外汇之地点及申请手续加以限制,而于用途一项,并未提及,故该法除有防止日伪套取外汇之作用外,无甚意义可言。其后二十八年七月又有进口物品申请购买外汇规则之施行,对申请外汇之用途始加以限制,凡进口商进口之物品不在禁止之列而为国内所必需者始得申请购买外汇。此项规定远较以前进步,惜对用途限制过严,审核手续过繁,而商人请购买外汇多未得核准,于是请汇一层,徒具虚名,一般厂商乃不得不向黑市购买外汇,故目前之管理外汇,实无甚效果可言,此皆格于事实,未能抓住管理外汇之核心故也。

今后管理外汇应以维持供给厂商正当需要之外汇为原则,此原则之用意有二:(一)供给厂商之需要。此次中美平准基金成立之意义,似在供给商业性质之需要,以冀稳定法币之对外汇价,且基金数额颇小,事实上不能供应战时外汇之全部需要,故商汇与非商汇之供给,似必分开办理。新基金之运用,当以供给厂商之外汇为限,至于军政外交机关及文化事业所需之外汇,应向财政部申请核购。(二)供给正当之需要。平准基金运用之目的,在向外国购取有关抗战之一切物资,故供给外汇应以"正当需要"为限。所谓正当需要,一方面限于物资之购取,以免资金逃避及投机情事发生,一方面限于与抗战直接有关及民生必需之物资,以免非必需品之源源输入而耗损基金实力。基金之运用既限于供给厂商之正当需要,实际办理时,应按此原则严格执行。为便利申请与审核计,凡属于正当需要范围内之物资,应一一列举公告,至申请手续及审核规则务求简便易行。凡申请外汇之经审查合格者,即由审核机关发给准购外汇通知书,以便凭证向指定之银行购取汇票。总之,今后核售外汇,务使一切正当需要,皆能获得满足,且手续简单迅速,使请购外汇者皆感到便利,盖非如是恐不能达到运用基金之目的也。

四、建立后方外汇市场与管理内汇

限制内汇之主要原因,在减少沪港外汇市场上之法币头寸,而减轻其对汇价之压力。其次在于券料之缺乏,不能付出汇款,今既放弃维持沪港外汇市场,则在券料所容许之范围内,似可放宽限制。后方工业生产不足,若干民生日用必需品,皆须仰赖港沪工厂出品之供应,则放宽内汇限制,实为必要。但内汇开放后,则如沪港外汇市价因政府之放弃维持而暴跌,或将引起资金流入后方,用以套取外汇,是则外汇管理方面所应注意者也。设卖出外汇,以货物上船起运为交割之条件,则套汇之事,不致发生。

放弃上海黑市汇价之维持后,则上海法币汇价有跌落之可能,以致引起法币内流,其结果,将使后方法币之流通量增大,更加促成物价之上涨。然法币为偿付货价及清理债务之手段,决非立时可以完全脱离流通界而转入内地,即使此事确属可能,因其为数有限,至多只能引起物价一定量之上涨,固不足虑也。

五、结 论

外汇平准基金之运用,原意在安定币值。币值有所谓对内价值与对外价值之别,汇价为其对外价值之表征,而物价即其对内价值之倒数。欲安定币值,以巩固币信,必须稳定汇价与物价。今我国物价上涨,较汇价为烈。若以廿六年为基期,就上海言,在廿九年底时物价涨至473.6,汇价则涨至505.5;就重庆言,汇价虽无行市,然大致与上海汇价加内汇率20%相近似,可假定之为606.5,而物价已涨至1 129.5。其他如成都、昆明、西安等地物价之涨势,均与重庆相若,且涨风仍烈。是则物价问题远较汇价问题为严重。欲解决物价问题,固须从实施管制入手,然亦可以运用外汇基金以缓和其上涨之势力。盖物价上涨之原因,既为通货数量增加及战时生产能力缩减暨运输困难等有关,则卖出外汇收回法币,正所以解除物价上涨之部分的原因。同时,平准基金委员会售出之外汇,多用于购进交通工具与器材,可增强运输力量,有利物资之流通;倘若用以输入日用必需品,则能充实市场之供给,正所以减少货物之缺乏程度。是故平准基金之运用,实可以稳定汇价与缓和物价为目的,能并行而不悖。

设中美平准基金之运用,果以稳定汇价与安定物价为目标,则凡正当需要之外汇,无不如数供应,且手续简单迅速,同时实行集中外汇,严禁黑市,汇价自可稳定,至其安定物价之功效如何,前节业经述及,即最少能缓和本年物价涨势80%,当此物价问题严重之秋,此种效果殊值重视。

建立后方外汇市场,并放弃维持上海黑市汇率后,非但外汇市场易于管理,使日伪无法套取外汇,且可在金融上取得主动或自主地位,并得放宽内汇之限制,以便利物资之流通,其利益实不容蔑视者也。

以物资为中心之我国经济政策

一 绪 言

抗战四年余,经济方面所有之问题固多,要以物价继续飞涨为目前最迫切之问题。自廿九年春季以来,全国各地物价,一律猛涨,至卅年年底时,高者(如重庆)涨至二十余倍,低者亦几达廿倍。而一般薪俸阶级之公务员,其薪津所得,虽略有增加,然总不过三倍,工厂工资,在重庆已增至十三倍,不可谓不多,然与其生活费之增加速率相较,犹不及其半,是故一般政府官吏与产业工人,虽尚未至炊骨易子,要亦可谓急矣。再就财政言,政府支出预算,亦将达战前之十倍,不可谓不大,然若论其购买力,则尚不及战前廿分之一,故预算虽增,而财政之困难尤深。综此以观,物价之继长增高,实属目前最严重之问题,若不力谋有效之解决,其情势必日趋恶劣,可能影响整个社会秩序与军民之作战力量。物价高涨之原因,主要约有两端,一为军需浩繁,预算庞大所引起法币发行量之增多;二为物资不足。而物资不足之根本症结,在于(甲)后方生产力薄弱,物资产量稀少;(乙)后方运输困难,以致国内产品流通不畅,与国外物资之来源阻塞;(丙)囤积居奇投机操纵之事盛行,更增加物资流通之阻力,而使市场上物资之供给益稀。欲谋有效之解决,或减轻物价继续高涨之趋势,惟有力谋后方物资供给之增加,与法币流通量之收缩,故今后财政金融经济政策,实有待于针对现实,重加检讨与厘订之必要。

二 通货与物价

甲 法币发行量与财政预算

抗日战事发生以来,因战费浩大,国家岁入常不敷岁出。其差额不免以增发法币为抵补。因之,法币发行量,不免随财政预算之加大而增加,财政预算,又因物价之上涨而增大,如此循环不已,如不速谋根本解决,法币发行之增加与物价之上涨,宁有已时!

乙　物价与法币量

物价上涨,为战时必然现象,本无足异;所可注意者,乃在其上涨之速率如何耳。我国物价,自七七事变发生,以迄廿九年三月,各地各种物价,虽皆上涨,然速率甚缓,为势不猛,对于整个经济,并无若何威胁。惟其后涨势渐猛,潜在威胁力与日俱增。至廿九年六月以后,其上涨之速率,已超过法币发行量增加之速率。依照吾人之估计,假设物价之上涨,纯由于法币发行额增多所致,并无其他原因(事实上物资不足同为重要原因),则法币发行额对物价之影响,虽亦逐年加深,但并不甚猛:照廿六年底之比率,法币发行额每增加1%,则物价大致上涨0.93%;照廿七年底之比率,法币发行额每增加1%,则物价上涨亦大致为1%;照廿八年底之比率,法币发行额每增加1%,则物价上涨约为0.99%;照廿九年底之比率,法币发行额每增加1%,则物价上涨约为1.81%;照卅年底之比率,法币发行额每增加1%,则物价上涨约增加2.38%。就法币发行额与物价指数之比率观之,廿六年及廿八年底之数值,皆略小于1,此殆系廿六年8月16日实施安定金融办法限制提存及廿八年稻谷丰收之影响乎。若然,则通货与物资对物价之关系,固极密切也。

丙　吸收法币应取之措施

法币之继续增发,其主因在于财政收支之不能相抵,今卅一年度岁出预算闻达相当之巨额,且此额系最俭省之数,无可再减,而岁入或尚不及其三分之一,如是,则本年度财政收支差额对于增发法币之压迫,仍难避免。欲谋收缩法币流通额,以安定物价,而维持国家财政与民众生计,惟有使已发之一部分法币回笼,同时以收回之法币或存款抵补财政收支差额。如是则本年财政金融措施,似宜采取下列办法,以冀收缩法币流通量。

子　建立证券市场

信用卓著之公司股票债票、政府公债及其他特许票据,宜并行交易,以便吸收游资,而公司厂商之欲举借贷款贴现者,应由经手银行分别情形,劝其优先增发证券或发售存货,以获致所需之资本,其不足之数,始酌贷信用补助之。

丑　发行金公债

此项公债,定为年息五厘,自第六年起,均分十年偿清本息,准人民以法币按中央银行挂牌汇率折合外币购买,其发行及兑付本息事宜,由中中交农及邮储汇局五行局代理之。为增强信用计,到期公债本息以此次美英政府之巨额贷款为担保。但届时持票人自愿按照当时国币汇率折算,兑取国币者听。

寅　发行美元英镑汇兑凭票

此项美元英镑汇兑凭票,分十元、百元、千元、十镑、百镑五种,以中央银行为发票行,美国纽约联邦准备银行及英国伦敦英伦银行为承兑行,准人民以法币按中央银行挂牌汇率折算购买,此后得自由按市价转让,并可在证券交易所拍卖。但持票人如欲兑现或在美英国境内支付时,须向平准基金委员会洽换正式汇票;美联邦准备银行与英伦银行仅对正式汇票有兑付之责。为加强信用计,此项汇票之发行,可由平准基金委员会出面声明,保证随时兑付。

卯　发行金票

将中中交农四行所有之金银,集中于中央银行,铸成金条银条,金条每条重一公斤,成色为九成,银条之重量与成色,照中央造币厂之原规定。中央银行依照金条银条之枚数,分别发行同数金票银票,准人民以法币依市价购买,并得自由转让或在证券交易所拍卖。此项金票银票之兑现,只限在中央银行总行为之。至中中交农四行及经济部采金局收兑金银工作,应即停止,并恢复金融自由买卖。

辰　举办长短期外币存款

准人民以法币按中央银行挂牌汇率折合外币存储,并以政府最近所得美元贷款之一部分,作为准备,并运入美钞,以备支付到期存款本息。

巳　发行节约建国金储蓄券

准人民以法币按照中央银行挂牌汇价折合购买,并以政府最近所得美币贷款之一部分作为准备,并运入黄金,以便兑付到期本息。

午　加强管理银行限制其资金活动

切实审核调查及限制各行庄放款之用途,使贴放款项,以辅助生产为范围;一面准许商业银行及钱庄在中央银行开户往来,用转贴现方式,予以融通资金之便利,而减少其对比期存款之需要,使银行钱庄渐成为票据承兑所之地位,同时限制其每日贴放余额,非得事先核准,不得超过卅年底之贴放余额。

未　压低市场利率

依民法之规定,严格取缔比期存放款利率,此事中央银行已在办理中,应继续加紧进行。

申　推行保险事业

仿照节约建国储蓄运动,大规模推行人寿保险、农作物保险、畜牧保险、社会保险、陆地兵险、水陆运输保险,以吸收民间游资。

酉　提高税率并扩充范围

中国现行之租税,除田赋改征实物外,其余各税税率均甚低,为谋增加收入并均衡负担计,应酌量增加税率,而直接税尤宜扩充范围,使田赋与其余诸税之税率相均衡,使农民与工商之负担公平。

戌　试办纸币税

货币之流通,按次抽缴百分一至百分五之税,其税率由财政部命令定之。

亥　控制陷区法币内流

今后敌伪对陷区法币,势将加紧压迫。今后陷区法币,或有大量内流之可能,政府应预筹控制之措施。其办法可在陷区边境要道,设立检查队,进口行人须经检查,凡携巨额法币者,强迫存入中、中、交、农四行之任何一行,分期支付,以封锁大宗法币。

三　物资与物价

甲　物资不足之程度

物价原为物资总量与货币总量之对比,故物价变动之因素,计有两种:其一属于货币方面,其二属于物资方面。近年来我国货币之流通量,因有省钞敌票伪币之推行,其总量实无法统计。若根据后方及华中法币发行额增加之情形,加以计算,就物价指数除以发行指数,以消去物价高涨属于货币方面之因素,则其所残余之变动,可视为纯由于物资方面之因素而来。如照此计算,则廿六年以来,纸币发行量即使不变,物价亦将因物资不足或供需失调之故而上涨,至卅年时,将升高一倍余;而事实上因法币发行量增加甚速,物价指数不仅升高一倍,而涨高达廿余倍。惟卅年夏季,因受粮食供需失调之影响,六月份物价指数(232)反较十二月份(215)为高,而发行不仅未减,且有增加。若将卅年六月及十二月情形平均计之,则法币发行量指数为1.101,物价指数与法币发行量指数之比为224,若将此两数分别以其和除之,则可窥知物价上涨原因之属于通货方面者,占80%,其属于物资方面者,占20%。

物资不足与通货增加之相对重要性,除上列估计外,尚可用他法求之。

就理论言,凡物资之供给充裕,对于一切需要恒能满足,而物价如仍上涨,自不能认为由于物资不足之原因,当系由于通货增加之故,是以此等物价所编成之指数,应能代表通货膨胀之程度。依此原则,由四行联合办事总处趸售物价指数所用之物品中,选出合于此条件之四项物价,引用原有权数,编成指数如第一表甲之第三行,又由西南经济研究所趸售物价指数所用之物品中,选出合于此条件之十五种物价,用简单几何平均法,编成指数如第一表乙之第三行。此两指数之编制方法各异,而其结果则极相似:在卅年十二月时,各约为廿六年之廿倍。是则目前重庆物价,设无物资不足之原因,亦将较廿六年时高出廿倍。今若将此通货膨胀指数,用物价总指数除之,所得百分数,可视为物价变动因素中之属于通货方面者,其百分余数可视为物价变动因素之属于物资方面者。如是,则今日物价高涨因素中之属于物资方面者,约占 1/3。

如上所述,今日后方物价问题,固与财金融有密切之关系,然物资不足之因素,亦殊未可忽视。考我国战时物价猛涨之风,实始于廿九年三月下旬纱价之飞腾,而纱价飞腾之原因,则由于货缺。在廿九年二月中旬时,渝市存纱不多,同时以运输阻滞,来货不易,奸黠商人,遂乘机囤积操纵,纱市渐感供不应求。至 3 月 19 日以后,纱货奇缺,纱价乃扶摇直上,廿支双马牌棉纱,在一周之内,上涨约达一千元,自二月至三月一个月间,约上涨一倍,此为物价问题严重化之嚆矢。又廿九年秋,稻谷歉收,而湘赣之米,以运输困难,未能接济川省之需要,大粮户见此情势,乃储谷不肯出售。同时亦有奸商乘机购囤以牟利,遂造成粮荒之局面,自八月至十二月,上涨三倍,至翌年七月,共涨七倍半,于此可见物资不足因素对于物价之作用,实骤而急,最能动摇人心。设若吾人细察物价问题严重化之起源与过程,则廿九年春季纱价与秋季粮价之剧变,要为其中最显著之大事,如是则物资不足之情势,其严重性不特不亚于通货膨胀,容或过之。故民生日用必需品之增产,必须积极推进。况目前新加坡、仰光情势严重,滇缅路或即阻塞,外国物资将无从输入,即使尚能输入,其数量必极微小。故今后经济政策,必向自给自足之途径迈进,凡农工矿各业,其产品为国防民用所不可或缺者,皆须积极扶助,对于此等事业所需资金之贷放与投资,非但不宜紧缩,实有斟酌扩大之必要。但非谓产业之扶植与信用之投放,可不择事业之门类与缓急,自须与当前环境相配合,务求集中人力、物力于必需品之生产,同时经济的使用资金于最急要之产业,以达到促进生产与安定金融之鹄的。

第一表甲　重庆市五种重要物品之躉售物价指数

1937年等于100

	总指数与类指数之比	总指数	类指数	加权综合数	盐（1/10市担）（自流井花盐）	猪肉（1/5市担）（五花肉）	绸（1/5匹）（木机大绸）	肥皂（1/5箱）（吉星牌）
1937	100.0	100.00	100.00	11.24	0.93	4.63	3.00	2.68
六月	100.9	100.52	101.42	11.40	0.92	4.80	3.00	2.68
十二月	99.2	104.78	103.91	11.61	1.00	4.80	3.20	2.68
1938								
六月	91.3	127.59	116.55	13.10	1.01	4.80	4.33	2.96
十二月	92.8	145.88	135.41	15.22	1.05	5.20	4.67	4.50
1939								
六月	98.7	190.12	187.63	21.09	1.23	6.40	6.47	6.99
十二月	91.6	284.52	260.59	29.29	1.36	10.00	10.40	7.53
1940								
六月	87.9	555.34	485.26	54.88	1.88	16.00	22.00	15.00
十二月	65.2	1 225.73	799.20	89.83	6.51	34.66	28.00	20.66
1941								
六月	56.9	2 142.07	1 218.95	137.01	11.01	56.00	46.00	24.00
十二月	75.7	2 748.63	2 080.87	233.89	20.14	109.75	53.50	50.50

第一表乙　重庆市十五种供求相应物品零售物价指数

基期：廿六年上半年=100　　公式：简单几何平均

	1937年		1938年			1939年			1940年			1941年	
	六月	十二月		六月	十二月		六月	十二月		六月	十二月		六月	十二月
总指数与类指数之比%	99.9	82.8		66.9	60.8		64.2	63.3		60.8	63.1		65.5	66.1
总指数15项	102.2	106.7		133.1	170.0		223.6	340.1		592.7	1 223.7		1 652.2	3 043.1
类指数15项	102.1	88.3		89.0	103.3		143.6	215.4		360.5	771.7		1 082.4	2 011.2
玉蜀黍（市石）	99.7	67.3		55.4	58.0		67.7	126.5		263.9	989.4		1 797.8	2 330.1
高　粱（市石）	100.1	69.5		63.9	95.4		93.5	142.5		245.2	908.3		1 438.2	2 159.1
黄　豆（市石）	100.1	75.9		77.4	93.5		121.0	167.8		285.2	855.8		1 616.4	2 523.1
猪　肉（市担）	107.5	107.5		107.5	116.5		143.4	224.0		346.3	854.2		1 254.5	2 402.1
牛　肉（市担）	83.5	85.6		97.0	85.6		136.6	169.2		480.3	805.1		1 590.2	2 324.2
酱　油（市担）	100.0	100.0		100.0	100.0		100.0	169.3		166.7	725.0		1 185.4	2 286.4
白　糖（市担）	100.0	106.2		94.2	97.4		145.4	327.7		455.7	882.3		817.8	1 727.8
大曲酒（市担）	92.0	82.1		87.4	102.2		126.7	200.3		294.1	881.6		1 117.1	2 118.7
花　盐（市担）	100.0	108.7		109.4	114.1		133.7	169.6		204.3	709.1		1 203.3	2 261.1
榨　菜（市担）	158.2	144.2		84.8	101.8		148.5	211.8		314.1	469.2		682.2	1 818.2
纺　绸（匹）	100.1	98.5		136.5	136.5		191.9	293.5		656.8	862.1		985.2	2 114.0
夏　布（匹）	97.3	80.5		78.1	97.3		167.2	182.4		563.2	942.2		790.3	1 519.8
白口铁（公吨）	100.0	109.4		135.3	211.8		458.8	1 000.0		1 000.0	1 070.6		1 247.1	2 341.2
生黄牛皮（市担）	106.9	43.2		48.6	60.4		103.7	145.6		276.9	474.7		570.0	1 218.8
肥　皂（箱）	100.0	100.0		114.0	160.0		260.0	280.0		500.0	500.0		800.0	1 593.4

乙 物资不足状况之一斑

以上所言物资不足,约占物价上涨原因 1/3,系指一般情形而言。若分别考之,则各种物资之供需状况互异:有供过于求者,如桐油、猪鬃、药材等是;有供求相济者,如第一表乙所列物品是;有供不敷求者,如花纱、布、大小五金、西药、颜料等是。至供不敷求之物品中,其不足之程度,自不相同,兹就日用必需之花纱布,试估计其供求概况,以便窥知物资不足情况之一斑:

子 棉布棉纱及棉花需要量之估计

据聂光垹、朱仙舫氏估计,每人每年平均消费布量为粗布六码(14 磅重之布为准)、中等布三码(以 11 磅布为准)、细布一码(以 5.5 磅布为准),共为十码。通常布每匹约有四十平方码,即宽一码,长四十码,故每人平均消费粗布 0.15 匹,中等布 0.07 匹及细布 0.025 匹。

又按战前每年动力机织及手工机织布之产量,合计 95 000 000 匹,再加布贸易入超 500 000 匹,共为 96 500 000 匹,此为总供给量,亦即需要量。设全国人口总数为四万万,则每人每年需要布量约为 1/4 匹,即十码。此与聂、朱两氏之估计相符。故本文所用之每人每年消费布量,即以十码为准。

今 24 支以下之纱,每件约可制(手织或机织)粗布 30 匹;32—42 支纱每件约可制机织 11 磅中等布 40 匹;60—80 支纱每件约可制机制 5.5 磅细布 80 匹。按此标准,可由布之需要量求得纱之需要量。又中国纱每件重为 420 磅即 381.024 市斤。而花纺纱之耗折甚微,则每件纱之纺成,需 3.8 市担,故花之需要量可由纱之需要量推求之。

欲求后方对于纱布之需要量,可从估计人口着手,兹试估计如次:

第二表甲 大后方人口数估计表(单位千人)

省别	自由区域对全省人口百分率	自由区域内人数
苏	—	0
浙	0.6	12 000
皖	0.4	9 300
赣	0.7	11 000
鄂	0.4	11 000
湘	0.9	25 000
川	1.0	52 706
康	1.0	968
冀	0.1	2 860
鲁	—	0
晋	0.2	2 320

续表

省别	自由区域对全省人口百分率	自由区域内人数
豫	0.4	13 600
陕	1.0	9 780
甘	1.0	6 716
青	1.0	1 196
闽	0.8	9 000
粤	0.5	16 000
桂	1.0	13 385
滇	1.0	12 042
黔	1.0	9 919
东四省	—	0
察	—	0
绥	0.3	620
宁	1.0	978
新	1.0	4 360
西京市	1.0	206
总计		224 956

若依上表人口数 224 956 000 人，共需布 56 239 000 匹：内粗布 33 743 400 匹，中等布 16 871 700 匹，细布 5 623 900 匹。折合纱数，得纱 1 616 872 件：内粗纱 1 124 780 件，中等纱 421 793 件，细纱 70 299 件。折合花数，得花 6 160 282 市担：内粗绒棉花（绒长在八分之七吋以下）4 285 412 市担，中等绒棉花（绒长在八分之七吋至一又八分之一吋之间）1 607 031 市担，细绒棉花（绒长在一又四分之一吋以上）267 839 市担。

今若仅以川、康、滇、黔、桂、湘、豫、陕、甘、宁、青、新十二省为准，则其人口及所需之纱布量约如下表（见第二表乙）：

第二表乙　后方十二省人口及其所需之纱布量

	人口（千人）	粗布（千匹）	粗纱（件）	中等布（千匹）	中等纱（件）	细布（千匹）	细纱（件）
川	52 706	7 905	263.5	3 953	98.8	1 318	16.5
滇	12 042	1 806	60.2	903	22.6	301	3.8
黔	9 919	1 488	49.6	744	18.6	248	3.1
桂	13 385	2 008	66.9	1 004	25.1	335	4.2
康	968	145	4.8	73	1.9	24	0.3
陕	9 780	1 467	48.9	734	18.4	245	3.1
甘	6 716	1 007	33.6	504	12.6	168	2.1
宁	978	147	4.9	73	1.9	24	0.2
湘	28 294	4 244	141.5	2 122	53.1	707	8.8

续表

	人口 （千人）	粗布 （千匹）	粗纱 （件）	中等布 （千匹）	中等纱 （件）	细布 （千匹）	细纱 （件）
豫	34 290	5 144	171.5	2 572	64.3	857	10.7
新	4 360	654	21.8	327	8.2	109	1.4
青	1 196	179	6.0	89	2.2	30	0.4
共计	174 634	26 195	873.2	13 098	327.5	4 366	54.6

故后方十二省每年需布 43 659 000 匹，内包括粗布（14 磅）26 195 000 匹，中等布（11 磅）13 098 000 匹，细布（5.5 磅）4 366 000 匹。折成纱 1 255 300 件，内包括粗纱 873 200 件，中等纱 327 500 件，细纱 54 600 件。若以此为准，则纱每件平均可织布 34.7 匹。又若纱折成花，共需 4 782 793 市担，内包括粗绒花 3 326 992 市担，中等绒花 1 247 775 市担，及细绒花 208 026 市担。

据经济部秘书厅之估计，后方人口共有 200 000 000 人，按每人每年消费布十方码计，后方人民共需布 50 000 000 匹，再加军用布假定为 5 000 000 匹，两项合计约共需布 55 000 000 匹，折合纱约为 1 600 000 件，折合花约为 6 100 000 市担。此与上列估计约略相等。惟据农本局之估计，整个后方全年需要布 250 万匹，折合纱为 70 万件，折合花为 300 万市担。此与上列估计数相差甚大，以其估计方法不详，无从评议。原来布之需要，弹性颇大，设使战时尽量节缩消费，其结果，需要量可减为平时之半或甚至以下，则吾人之估计数，似可视为整个后方全年需要量之最大限度，农本局之估计数，可视为需要量之最低限度。

丑　花纱布供给量之估计

（一）布之供给

据估计，整个后方现有动力织布机约 4 000 台，每年最高生产能力可达 299 万匹，但以空袭被炸残缺或疏散装用缺少动力等原因，在前数年，约仅实产 1 146 800 匹，再加手工织布实产约 900 万匹，两共约 10 146 800 匹。惟据某机关之估计，内迁工厂补充设备及增设小型织布机后，去年动力机每月约可产布 285 449 匹，全年约可产布 3 425 388 匹。如是再加手工织布 900 万匹，则后方动力与手工织布合计每年约可产 12 425 388 匹。此数与上列估计，约略相似。故上列估计数字，似尚无大差，姑即用为标准。

（二）纱之供给量

廿九年后方动力纱锭开工 108 000 枚，产纱 68 632 件，此外有七七及三一等纺纱机 36 000 架,及手工纺锭 525 000 锭,产纱 440 000 件,两者合计约共为 508 000 件。又据某机关报告截至去年底止,动力纱锭可增加为 131 700 枚,月产 9 142 件,年产 110 704 件,若再加手工纺纱 440 000 件,共可产 550 700 件。但据另一估计,动力纺纱机约可年产 70 000 件,手工纺纱约可年产 300 000 件,两共约可得 370 000 件,此数与上列估计略有出入。兹假定前一估计数为最高产量,后一估计数为最低产量,似亦属合理。

（三）棉花之供给量

据农本局之估计,后方棉花生产量为陕豫区 120 万担,襄樊区 30 万担,洞庭湖区 40 万担,浙东区 40 万担,川中区 50 万担,共计 280 万担,此与中央农业试验所之估计数亦颇相近。

寅　花纱布供需概况之估计

花纱布之需要与供给量,既经估计如上,试将各项估计数字,列表比较如次,

第三表　花纱布供需概况

（甲）布之供求概况比较：

	最高（千匹）	最低（千匹）
布之需要量	56 239	25 000
布之供给量	12 425	10 500
供不敷求之差量	43 814	14 500

（乙）纱之供求概况比较：

	最高（千件）	最低（千件）
纱之需要量	1 616	700
纱之供给量	550	370
供不敷求之差量	1 066	330

（丙）花之供需概况比较：

	最高（千担）	最低（千担）
花之需要量	6 160	3 000
花之供给量	2 800	2 800
供不敷求之差量	3 360	200

【附注】若以最低需要量与最高供给量相较,则不足之数,布为 3 575 千匹,纱为 150 千件,花为 20 万担。

第四表　若干种供求不相应物品涨价情形

廿六年上半年＝100

	二十六年十二月	二十七年十二月	二十八年十二月	二十九年十二月	三十年十二月
洋钉	144.8	675.9	1 628.1	2 048.7	15 655.7
花线	186.6	497.5	1 119.4	1 421.4	12 470.9
铅皮	169.2	660.7	1 459.0	4 528.1	10 867.4
石灰	97.9	230.3	664.3	1 923.1	8 981.7
新闻纸	150.9	452.9	1 013.1	2 761.0	8 286.1
新铅丝	132.7	485.6	1 232.2	2 766.2	7 856.4
洋钢	118.2	384.8	1 232.6	4 188.5	7 739.3
小大英香烟	141.8	367.8	803.9	2 541.9	7 537.7
僧帽洋烛	147.9	415.1	803.9	2 123.6	7 076.3
毛呢	96.6	294.1	681.1	2 848.3	6 576.2
煤油	88.0	258.9	849.6	3 149.5	6 429.1
快靛	123.9	196.5	984.8	1 079.8	5 041.3

【附注】西药中若干普通物品如奎宁丸、慰欧仿之类，已进入有行无市之状态，最近或将演成无行无市之严重局面，至于其他比较不甚普通之西药，更无论矣。

由此观之，纱布棉花之供给量，似皆不及最低需要量。而其价格在廿九年内均约上涨二倍余，在卅年内，各约上涨一倍半左右（见第四表）。原来花纱布尚不属于最不足物资之列。至于若干五金、电料、西药及化学原料，其不足程度尤深，涨价亦特甚（见第四表）。此等物资，既为国防民生所必需，而最感不足，若不积极扩张生产建设，以增加产量，则物价一时恐不易安定。

丙　紧缩政策与合理发展

论者或谓年来物价继续高涨，系通货膨胀之结果，认为政府应即厉行紧缩政策。此种主张，自亦有其见地。正如上文所述，物价上涨之因素，三分物资，七分通货，准此以论，似未可厚非。然细考之，年来通货增加，乃由于财政收支之不能平衡，而财政收支之不能平衡，乃由于巨额之军费支出，此为战时必然现象，无可减免。至国家预算中之经济建设费，在廿六年七月至廿九年底之三年半中，共计为 3.8 亿元，在卅年度中，国家预算之经济建设费为 1.4 亿元，为数既甚微小，对于通货膨胀之影响，实不足道。设使政府果行紧缩政策，将此经济建设费取消，其于缩减通货，果能发生若何功效？固属疑问。再查国家预算中所列之经济建设项目，皆系重要轻重工业及水利事业,均属急需,不容缓办,亦不可废止。至于经四联总处核准贴放之四行贷款,一本该处既定金融方针,纯属促进生产与协助平价性质(以辅助食盐生产贷款占大多数),亦未可削减。且其贷放总额,亦约与四行及两局(即中中交农四行及中信、储汇两局)之储蓄存款相若,并非以发行法币为贷款之手段,实与通货膨胀无甚关系。况今日国内物资不足,国际通路阻塞,正宜扩张生产力,积极增加必需物品之生产,以减除物资不足促成物价暴涨之威胁,故就目前经济环境言,吾人主张一方面应积极扩张必需品之生产,以增加物资之供给;一方面应积极推进节约消费,以减少物资之需要,而谋物资供需之相应。

四　今后应采取之经济政策

物资不足,既具有促起物价暴涨之威力,而其来势,又骤且速,足以扰乱市场,动摇人心;若物资之增产,能与通货之增多,保持均衡,则物资当无猛涨猛落之可能,故提高生产力以增加物资之生产量,其作用实较收缩通货为要。准此而言,如何使物资能供需相济,实为今后厘定经济政策之中心问题。今后我国经济施政,似应遵循下列原则:

(一)矫正重视通货而忽视物资之思想,并彻底改革过去重视外汇准备之观念,确立今后积极增加后方物资供给之观念。

(二)加强后方军需民用所需物品之生产机构,并充分动员及运用人力物力,建立最低经济自给之基础。

(三)经济的使用人力物力。建设事业之举办,以在短期内,能供应军民所需物资者为度,限制一切缓不济急之建设,同时必需之工业及其他生产建设,应不计成本,积极进行。民营部分,即有亏折,亦应由政府酌量补助。

(四)出口货之生产,应以便于运输,不妨碍自给经济之生产力,并为友邦所必需者为限。因目前国际交通困难,运费昂贵,以输出货物为获得外汇之手段,殊不经济,不若举借外债以取得对外支付力为有利。盖如此则大部分生产出口货之人力物力,可以移用于自给经济之生产。

(五)加强运输机构,以利国外物资之输入与国内各地物资之流通调剂。

(六)厉行节约消费,以减少物资之需要,而免除浪费。

根据上列原则,今后之经济政策,应取下列途径:

甲　加紧增加国内生产

　　子　确定生产计划调整生产机构

　　各种必需品生产事业所需数量,应由主管机关确实统计,通盘筹划,其所需之器材原料,应统筹配给；一切生产事业之设立,均须经事前之审核及事后之监督；对各种生产机构,尤应使其能互相配合联系,例如有多少原料,只准设多少工厂,如工厂扩充或增加,即应设法增产原料,以免脱节,而致影响工业之生产效率。

　　丑　增加工业区之动力厂,扩大动力之供给

　　生产事业所必需之电动力,应加速建设装配,必要时可将仅供市民电灯用之电机,拆运至缺乏电动力之工业区,用以供给该区工业所需之动力。

　　寅　充分动员人力参加生产工作

　　利用学校学生、教职员、商人、公务员及其家属之闲暇,厉行劳动服务,并征集闲散男女,服后备兵役,加以训练后,屯集若干地区,参加有计划之粗放生产工作。

乙　加强运输机构

　　子　加速开办国际航空运输线

　　国内一时不能生产或生产不足之必要物资,皆须加速向国外抢购运入。今太平、印度两洋局势,在最近期间,似将渐趋严重,国际交通日益困难,自应从速开办密切那至昆明及撒地亚至西昌之航空运输线,以便抢运国外物资。

　　丑　加强国内运输机构

　　目前国内交通困难,各省区之物资,不能交流而相调剂,应即加强运输机构,增大运输能量,必要时,应不计成本,扩充航空运输,以利物资之流通,而不致停滞,尤须利用公路旁边添建小型轻便铁道,将江河中之木船配备小型动力推桨机,以扩大运量,并节省人工。

丙　努力抢购国外及陷区物资

　　子　奖励抢购运邻近区域物资

　　指定必需物品若干种,如汽油、火油、棉纱、棉布、五金、电料、药品等,鼓励资本家及商人向国外及陷区大量购运。凡能证明系外来者,由政府照市价收买,并给以相当之奖励。如能妥定办法,努力宣传,使一般知此为名利双收之事,当可望有相当效果。

丑　组织抢购物资商人

由社会部会同贸易委员会等指导抢购物资之商人,组织团体,由政府予以金融上及运输上之便利,以利物资之大量抢购。

寅　严禁物资运往陷区

加紧查禁军民必需品运往陷区,并在陷区边境,利用原有检查机构及军队,严密查缉走私,违者一律以汉奸论罪。

丁　积极调整出口货生产或其用途

子　限制生产

原有出口物品,除猪鬃、毛皮、药材等,因友邦需要甚殷,且轻便仍可出口外,所有今后不能出口,亦不易作其他用途,且不能久藏之出口货,应限制其生产,将生产此类物品之人力、物力,计划地移用于其他生产事业。

丑　改变用途

若干物品,虽一时不能出口,但可改作他用者,应尽量改变其用途。例如桐油可作特制汽车之燃料且能提炼氧气,应大量制造桐油汽车,以资利用,并充分动员科学人才,加以提炼。若干物品虽不能出口,但可代其他物品之用者,应尽量推行代用。例如生丝麻纱,可代替棉纱织品,应尽量设法减轻丝麻之生产成本,以利推广代用。

寅　培养整理

若干物品,现在一时虽不能出口,但其资源,非短时所能培养,且在战后须赖以为出口之大宗者,则可乘此时机,加以培养整理。如茶树、桑树等,可伐去其老树,培植新株。暂在新株空隙间,种植各种杂粮,以增副产,一面更由政府视各地实际情形,酌予补助。

戊　加强管理物资

子　统制奢侈品之销售

市上现有之奢侈品,应由政府普遍检查,照成本征购后,以高价统销;或加以登记后,由政府标定高价,仍归原商店出售,并规定其大部利润,缴纳政府,以吸收有钱者之一部分购买力。

丑　统制重要必需品

选定若干数量较大之日用必需物品,实行统购统销,按生产数量,作平均合理之分配,并力求生产与消费相配合。

寅　慎重统制之人选

推行统制经济之各部门主管长官,对于统制经济,必须为具有信仰与热忱之人,非如此,则统制方案,每不能切实执行。

己　厉行节约消费

子　节制消费量

管理公共消费场所,节制物品之消费量。

丑　限制购买量

利用消费合作机构,限制个人家庭及团体购买物品之数量,选择少数重要物品,先在大都市试办。

寅　提倡代用品

按各种物品之产销实况,有计划地倡导人民以成本低廉物品代替高贵物品(例如以豆浆代替牛乳),或以华贵物品代替粗制低廉物品(例如听任富有者服用丝织品,以补纱布之不足),并普遍宣传代用方法。至代用品之发明创制,如西南化学工业厂所创之云丝与云丝棉胎(即以麻代棉),尤须予以奖励。

卯　工业标准化

经济部颁布《奖励工业技术条例》,原有鼓励发明美观及新式样之规定,应加修正补充,以免工业品大小式样之庞杂,今后应鼓励农工业品之标准化,俾可互相配件代用,而求生产与使用之经济。

以上所拟经济政策,大部系刘攻芸、徐景薇、许性初、寿勉成、杨荫溥、朱通九、朱祖晦、金天锡、侯哲荂、邹宗伊、沈光沛、侯厚培、冯克昌及作者等在一月初旬聚谈之共同意见,特此附志。

(原载《财政评论》1941年第6卷第1期)

国际货币基金与中国

现在的世界,是列国竞存争雄的世界,我们不能希望他马上变成一个大同的理想世界,至多希望能达到列国协和共存:在政治关系上,彼此主权独立,自由平等,无所谓统治国与殖民地;在经济关系上,彼此分工合作,自由贸易,无所谓经济壁垒与生活水平的悬殊;在社会关系上,彼此民族平等,自由移民,无所谓优秀民族与劣等民族的人为歧视。就目前局势言,要做到自由移民并废除殖民地,时机尚未成熟,决难做到的,我们的最大希望,只可鼓吹国际经济合作主义,以求《大西洋宪章》第四、第五点之实现,亦即努力于列国经济关系的自由平等。

据我们的推想,战后世界的经济关系上,大约有四个不平衡的因素存在着:

第一,世界货币的准备金(黄金)的分配,将要比较战前更加畸形,在一九三〇年时美国有备用黄金约四十六万万美元,占全世界的黄金百分之三八。自一九三四年至一九四一年之八年中,由世界各国流入美国之黄金,达一百六十七万万美元。依此趋势以推测战后情形,则黄金将有五分之四以上的数量集中于美国。设各国要实行金本位货币,都有准备不足之虑。

第二,国际资金之流动性,将来更难与国内资产相调和配合。这不但是由于外汇的缺乏,亦且由于国内资产流动性的增加。流动资产对总资产之比率,在战争期内已经增加很大,这是由于一方面通货流通量、中央银行存款、商业储蓄银行存款增加很多,他方面物资因消耗于战争而减少故也。

第三,制成品和原料品物价之相对的长期转移,似将于战后继续进行着。这种转移,已使输出原料和农产品国家的贸易条件逐渐恶化,此后将使恶化程度更加深刻。

第四,世界各国对于美元外汇之缺乏趋势,将继续存在,其原因在于世界各国对美国货物的需要量,常较美国对其他各国货物的需要量为小。

要使这种不平衡的经济关系,回复并维持于平衡状态,自非实行国际经济合作不能成功。又在此四个因素中,有三个是和金融有关系的,所以国际金融合作,是最切要,亦似乎是比较容易做到的。

国际金融合作之后,能否解决上列问题,自然要看合作的方式和合作的程度。然至少应该能满足下列三个需要或目标:

甲、防止或避免各国币制的崩溃,及因币制崩溃而起的经济混乱;保证多难的世界列国,可把一切烦难问题解决,而毋庸求诸竞争性的货币贬值、关税壁垒、两方清算或汇兑统制等办法。

乙、使多方清算的贸易回复,国际分工合作程度加深,人力与资源获得更有利的运用,以维护经济的平衡发展,保持最高水准的就业和所得。

丙、借给列国短期支付工具和长期建设资金,使各国获得充分时间,以校正其不平衡的经济情形,并从事于经济复员和建设。同时维持各国货币汇率的稳定。

金融合作的方式,简括说来,可有四种方式:

(一)列国都采行金本位制。在上次欧战以前,世界各国大都采行金本位币制,纸币的发行,要有黄金为兑现的准备,故货币的发行量,与黄金的保有量,其间有密切关系。在自由汇兑与自由输出输入黄金之机构下,上列三个需要,大体上还能满足,自十九世纪后半叶至二十世纪的初叶,可以说是金本位币制的全盛时代。在这时期里,列国间未尝发生竞争性的货币贬值、关税壁垒、汇兑统制等事;国际贸易可以说是自由的;人力和资源的利用,以及受业和所得的水准,亦大约几近乎饱和点了。在上次欧战后,因受战时影响,经济组织发生重大变化,金本位币制不复能发挥原先的功能了。

(二)交错往来的金融市场。在不同币制本位各国之间,例如银本位时代的中国与其他金本位国,在自由汇兑、自由处分金银之机构下,若金银比价平定时,亦大体可以说能解决了上列三个需要。然若金银比价发生剧烈变动,譬如在一九三三至一九三四年间,因银价急涨,中国的物价与汇价发生剧变,整个经济蒙受其害。所以只凭交错往来的金融市场,国际金融问题是不能得到满足的解决的。

(三)两方清算或汇兑统制,在此次世界大战之前,国际汇兑早已不自由。轴心国统制汇兑最严,而德国更实行两方清算制,以为统制汇兑制度下便利贸易的一种手段。这种制度无法清算三角或多角式的贸易债权和债务,所以世界贸易不能发达,国际分工以及人力资源的利用,都不能达到最高度,国际经济总在不平衡状态下进行着。所以两方清算制是不能满足前列三种需要的。

(四)设立国际机关担负国际金融责任。自然的机构或方式,如金本位币制及交错往来的金融市场,未暴露其弱点以前,可以发挥功能来满足我们的需要。然一经破损失败之后,有理性的人类似乎不致再依旧把他恢复起来。两方清算制在理论上方法上,虽都不值得我们赞扬,然而他是一种代替那自然方式而兴起的一种人为机构,他的缺点和经验,都是将来进步的一块基石。国际临时咨询协商式的合作,如历次国际经济会议和一九三六年的英美法三国协定,都没有法定的官式组织来担负合作的任务。所以一方面缺乏永久性,他方面不能使合作更顺利更有效率。因此设立国际机构以担负国际金融责任,是现时势所必需的。英美财部之建议书及联合国专家宣言都是这个看法。

英国政府所提出的通货计划,是以国际清算联合制度,作为解决战后国际经济合作问题之一初步贡献。其他国际经济问题之解决计划,如贸易政策,主要生产品价格之稳定,发展经济之中期长期投资等,将继续提出。此计划的主旨,在制定一般可以接受之国际付款方法,并保证每一国货币汇价的变动,是有计划的措施结果,而非片面的行动;在使任何国家因支付外国债务而发生困难时,可免除过分负荷,并得有充分时间以为适宜措施而逐渐恢复平衡;在促进国际贸易之稳定发展,借以改进参加国之生活水准。

该计划规定班柯为国际通货,并以一定分量之黄金规定其价值。但此非一成不变,将来可视情形而予以增减。依该计划之规定,各国可以黄金兑换班柯,但不得以班柯换取黄金。如是则黄金可不至畸形的集中于某一国家。是故班柯可以说是一种管理币制,黄金只不过用作管理的一种手段。

国际联合清算制,只为各国中央银行间提供一种结账方法。各会员国的国际收入和国际支出,得依照联合清算当局所认可的汇率,向联合会划账清算。清算联合会账上的贷借两方,必然相等,所以不必由参与国分担任何资本。又国际联合清算制采用银行原理,创造信用,予各会员国以透支之便利,则国际收支逆差国可避免其因对外支付条件之失利而引起国内通货及信用紧缩之不良影响。故联合清算制实含有膨胀性。联合清算会依据各会员国对外贸易数量,决定该国对联合清算会欠债或透支的最高额。此数额初以战前三年贸易总值的平均数为标准,以后依贸易之进展情形,逐年修订之。如是则英国所可得之透支额为最大,若以一九三七年为例,英帝国占总额百分之三十三(英王国占百分之十五),美国百分之十二,中国百分之一。

美国之计划,包括国际平准基金及联合国发展建设银行二种,此二案之精神,互相贯通,其方法相辅相成。平准基金之用意,在供应短期资金,稳定各国货币汇价,以便利国际贸易,而增进世界经济繁荣。联合国银行之用意,在供应长期资金,及协助私营金融机关对外投资,以发展各国经济。故美国计划之主旨,大体和英国相似。

国际平准基金之货币单位,称为优尼塔,其价值等于一百三十七厘又七分之一重的黄金(相当于美币十元)。优尼塔之黄金价值,非经会员投票权百分之八十五以上之通过,不得更改。各国可以黄金兑换优尼塔,亦可以优尼塔兑换黄金(在美国修订案内,此点已修改:平准基金会得买卖黄金,并无对优尼塔兑现为黄金之义务)。是故优尼塔可以说具有金本位币之本质。这与班柯略有不同,班柯只是一种清算国际收支的单位,他的黄金价值可以随经济情形而变更,并不能兑换为黄金。

平准基金制之要旨,为确保各会员国在平时能获得合理需要的外汇。各会员国需要支出之外汇,可以本国货币按照规定汇率向平准基金会购得之,反之,各会员国持有之外汇,可以同样汇率卖与基金会。这是平准基金的运用原理应用于国际方面的一个办法,和清算制的转账办法很不相同。

平准基金会之基金,总额为五十万万美元,由会员国分担之。会员国可以本国货币向基金会购买之外汇数额,与其所摊认的基金数额,有密切的关系。在通常情形下,基金会可以接受会员国的货币数额,在一年内不得超过他所认摊基金额的百分之二十五,各年的累积数(连同基金的国币部分在内)不得超过二倍。每会员国所可认摊的基金数额,依照协定的公式(这公式的组成,含有黄金、外汇、贸易总额,以及国民所得等重要因素)。据英国报纸所载,国民所得额之百分之二十,黄金外汇额之百分之五,贸易额之百分之十,再参酌该国经济潜力而拟定认摊额度计算出来,称为限额。如是则美国以拥有大量黄金及雄厚国富,其所摊的限额,约可达百分之三十五,英国约在百分之十五左右,中国约在百分之三点五,较英制所规定者为大。由此看来,若依英国计划,英国可在联合清算局里操持大权,如依美国计划,则美国可在平准基金管理局里握有大权。这是两个计划的另一重要不同处。

英美两计划的基本原理和方法,以及管理权的分配,既有重大的差别,讨论起来,两国的意见,自然不容易调和。美国舆论方面如《纽约时报》,曾发表论文反对英美计划,并主张于战后从速恢复金本位。英国方面大家都反对金本位,称他为一九二五年的硬板短褂。正式的世界货币会议,自然不能以根本不同的两个计划作为讨论的基础。此所以自从去年四月英美提出方案,过了一年,未即召开正式会议,要先有联合国专家预备会议,研究出一个合理可行的妥协方案。联合国专家宣言,便是具备这种意味的一个新计划要领。

联合国专家宣言的精神，比较的近乎美国计划，合作的方式是采取平准基金制度，基金的总额定为一百万万美元，参加国摊认基金的额度，亦即该国可以本国货币向国际平准基金会购买外汇的标准，由参加国协商决定之。依初步的估计，大约美国的额度为二十五万万美元，占第一位，英国（不包括自治领及印度殖民地）为十二万五千万美元占第二位，苏联为十万万元，占第三位，中国为六万万美元（原为三万五千万美元，因中国经济潜力甚大并得美国之赞助，乃改增至此数）占第四位。金本位币制的色彩，比较美国原提计划，已大为减轻。第一，各国所认摊的基金，其中应缴黄金之数，至多占百分之二十五。第二，会员国货币汇价，须以黄金表示之，但于商得基金会同意后，可在百分之十之限度内伸缩之，此后若有必要，更可经基金会当局的通过，再增减汇价至百分之十。第三，会员国向基金会购买外汇时，如其所有黄金及可兑换为黄金的外汇数额超过于其额度，或在一年内有所增加，基金会得要求用黄金支付其所购外汇的一部分。此外联合专家宣言更容纳英国计划（II 之 3 节）及中国代表之建议和美国舆论的督导（如 G.H. Williams 氏的《战后经济建设》，载《外事月刊》一九四四年一月号），明白规定一个过渡时期，使会员国获得充分时间，以调整其国际经济关系。对于资本的移动，如非属于生产性质，会员国得加以管制，此亦是吸收英国计划的优点而加以规定的。

从中国的立场来说，经长期抗战之破坏，在经济方面，需要外资来帮助建设；在币制方面，需要外国金融的协助，来稳定币值，所以很希望有一个国际金融机构，并愿意参加工作，共同担负起世界经济合作的使命。惟有国际经济互助合作，才能很顺利地解决各国的经济问题，提高他们的信用，稳定汇价，便利贸易，使资源得到最善的利用，国民就业及所得达于最高的水准。中国政府接受美政府的邀请而参加货币会议，是一个贤明的举措，美英政府借给中国以大额的外汇，增加中国的经济力量，并得在基金会中占着第四位的重要地位，便是一种友谊的合作精神的表现。

依照联合国专家宣言要领来看，中国所认摊的基金额度为六万万美元，应缴黄金之数，或为此额度的百分之二十五，即一万五千万美元，或为我政府所保有的黄金和外汇数额的百分之十。中国可选择此两数中之小者，以为缴纳黄金的标准。依我们的估计，中国政府所有外汇和黄金额，不过六万万美元。若以此为准，则中国只须交纳六千万美元的黄金。又因中国的版图，有很大部分被敌人占领蹂躏，得减交黄金百分之二十五。所以中国只须实交四千五百万美元的黄金，其余五万五千五百万美元的基金，可以国币抵付之。如是中国对基金的担负，并不很重。

中国的国际贸易，向来是入超的，每年入超额，大约在一万万美元左右。此外船费、电报费及外资利息的支出，亦年达数千万美元。幸有大宗华侨汇款可以抵付一大部分，国际收支逆差，尚不至于过大。依照联合国专家宣言第三章第二节C的规定，在一年之内，中国可用国币向平准基金会购买外汇的数额，不得超过一万五千万美元（即六万万元之百分之二十五）；历年累积的净购额不得超过六万四千五百万美元（平准基金会所可保有会员国的国币数额，最高不得超过其认摊基金额度的二倍，今中国的认摊基金额度为六万万美元，其中有四千五百万美元为黄金，其余五万五千五百万美元为国币，此后若用国币购买六万五千五百万美元的外汇，则平准基金会将共有十二万万美元价值的中国国币，适为中国认摊基金额的二倍）。假若中国国际收支逆差额，每年平均达一万五千万美元，则于四年又四个月后，中国不可以国币再向平准基金会购买外汇。这是一个硬性的规定，亦是平准基金会使会员国注意于调整国内外经济情形的一种手段。根据以往的经验来看，这对于中国并无不便之处。一国的经常国际收支，不应该让他有很大的逆差，更不可任令其继续存在而不更正的。

国际收支逆差若是累年的继续下去，这断非由于季节变动，而是由于国内外经济的基本不平衡，凡会员国发见这种情形，就该变更汇率或用其他方法（如紧缩财政通货或变更国内物价工资，以与国外经济相适应，然而依照以往的经验，这种方法不如变更汇率的便利），来纠正他。或谓国际收支的长期不平衡的情势，可以国际投资银行的长期借款，用为抵补。这是错误的见解，与联合国专家宣言及联合国发展及建设银行的规定不符。所谓国际收支，原包括长期资本贷借在内，长期资本借入额以及其他一切国际收支之总数，不足以抵付应付之数时，始有逆差，故累年逆差是由于国内外经济的基本不平衡而来，必须更正此基本的经济不平衡，才能使国际收支回复平衡。若谓投资银行的长期贷款，用来帮助弥补长期的国际收支逆差，那么投资银行的主要使命，在于贷款于逆差国抵补其累年国际逆差，而不在于协助经济建设和开发了。

总之，联合国专家宣言，是融铸英美计划的精华而成的，根据这宣言而制定的实施方案，无疑能防止战后各国币制的崩溃，可以使多方清算的贸易回复，足使各国货币汇价稳定，尤其重要的，若干经济力薄弱的国家，可以得到短期支付工具和长期建设资金，平安地渡过困难时期，以逐渐的步骤纠正其不平衡的经济情形。所以这个国际金融合作方案，非独可以解决世界金融问题,且同时为世界经济合作和世界和平开辟了一条平坦大路。战后中国须要立即致力于经济建设,所需于外国资本和技术的帮助,至多且大。这个国际金融合作,自然可以增加各国对中国的认识,因此可以促进外国资本和技术的输入,加速中国的经济建设,中国经济完成之后,可以增加维持世界和平和繁荣的力量。

(原载《新经济》1944年第11卷第4期)

附 录

厉德寅经济思想研究

全面抗战时期厉德寅的外汇政策研究

徐 昂

1937年8月13日,淞沪抗战爆发,金融中心上海处于日军炮火的攻击和摧残之中。全面抗日战争在中国经济最发达的地区展开,中国经济金融顿时陷入危机,中国法币的国际汇率受到日本多维度的攻击,危机四伏。战时汇率问题关系法币制度与财政金融的维持,对中国的抗战事业意义重大,成为这一时期中国政府最为关切的财经问题之一。

1934年8月,从美国威斯康星大学学成归国的厉德寅入职南京中央大学,教授经济统计学、货币银行学、国际贸易汇兑等课程。自全面抗战爆发至1940年7月,他跟随中国政府内迁,先后为庐山、芷江、重庆等地中央政治学校继续教授经济学、统计学。他在1939年11月被任命为重庆国民政府四联总处统计科科长,主管金融调查统计、研究工作,并在1941年6月改任中美英平准基金会研究室主任,直至1943年5月平准基金会基本运作结束,这期间主管基金的外汇和金融市场统计工作。1943年6月以后至抗战胜利结束,他就任交通银行设计处副处长,主管行务的统计与设计工作;同时作为重庆国民政府经济部参事,拟签物价统计报告,并研究物价政策。在抗战局势最危急的几年里,厉德寅以自身所长投身外汇政策及相关经济研究,为国民政府抗战经济政策的制定发挥了一名经济学家的重要作用。

一、深入研究汇率维持问题

1. 任职"四联总处"

上海从19世纪后半期起,银行国际汇兑业务发达,具备统一行市的外汇市场即已存在。1935年国民政府实行币制改革,为稳定法币对外汇价,明确规定应由中央银行、中国银行、交通银行无限制买卖外汇。此后,中国的法币汇率始终平稳,但到1937年7月卢沟桥事变后,一些中外进出口商人和持有法币的投机者纷纷购买外汇,企图逃避风险,投机牟利。1937年下半年的提取存款的高潮过去后,中日战事扩大,海岸交通阻断,中国经济遭到重大打击。华北伪联合准备银行成立后,大量发行钞券,套取法币调换外汇。1938年3月14日,中国不得不采取外汇审核办法,统制汇兑,进入以限制存款提现作为阻碍逃资手段的半放任政策时期。在到8月中旬的期间,中国政府则坚持统制外汇的官方市场而放任外汇黑市,实际上,任何个人无法以官价购得外汇。中国的外汇申请审核制度实际未能有效执行:政策本身无法切断资金外逃(尤其是金融界)的路径;中央银行总行或其香港通讯处,无法获得其他银行的外汇用途清单;外商银行于3月28日停止维持法定汇价,开始自由挂牌买卖外汇,暗中支持市场实际汇价。于是在法定汇价以外,产生了实际公开运行的外汇"黑市"。

当时,国民政府在金融领域采取了一系列的措施,最重要的两项是成立"四联总处"和防范通货膨胀的恶化。1939年10月,在重庆正式成立中央银行、中国银行、交通银行、中国农民银行四银行联合办事总处,简称"四联总处"。蒋介石亲自担任四联总处理事会主席,对日常重要事务直接饬办,并任命财政部政务次长徐堪兼任四联总处的秘书长。

1939年11月,厉德寅即被任命为重庆国民政府四联总处统计科科长。他的研究工作随即围绕战时金融展开,负责完成了大量的金融调查统计和经济指数研究。四联总处成立初期的工作中心就包括了调节发行,以安定金融;核定汇款,以融通资金等。四联总处下设两个委员会:战时金融委员会(下设发行、贴放、汇兑、收兑金银和特种储蓄五处)和战时经济委员会(下设特种投资、物资和平市三处)。从组织架构看,控制物价与稳定金融事关抗战大局,而法币信用背后的外汇问题是核心环节。① 这是因为法币地位的确立从一开始即施行无限兑换外汇,与英镑、美元的汇价挂钩。

2. 研判外汇市场形势

1938年3月政府实行外汇统制以后,官方价格和黑市价格(即市场实际交易价格)最初并无差别,外汇统制还挫败了敌伪套取外汇的企图。为了抵御日元集团对原有英国在华特权和商业利益的取代,上海的英商银行开始暗中支持法币的汇率。具体的做法是:根据前一阶段汇率自由变动的趋势拟定一个略高于八便士的合理标准汇率。当黑市汇价高过于标准汇价,便无限制地买进外汇;当市场汇率低于标准汇价,便无限制地卖出外汇。

---

① 洪葭管:《中国金融通史》,中国金融出版社2008年版,第387页。

外商银行此举暂时平息了外汇投机,资金外逃有所减轻,同时有助于坚定华北华中地区对法币的信心。

不过,厉德寅此时就已意识到,这一结果可能误导财政部认为维持黑市价格的可行性,从而转向承认并维持黑市的外汇政策。①他指出通常管理或统制外汇的主要目的,原在不丧失黄金和外汇准备的条件下,维持比较自由市场汇价更高一点的汇率。然而,战时中国的外汇市场不可能依靠市场自身维持平衡,政府采取外汇统制的主要目的,就是要时刻防止日伪吸收法币套取外汇,发动货币战。②

1938 年五月以后,黑市汇价开始下跌,与法定汇价的差异逐渐显著。6月 14 日(6 月中汇价最底的一日),黑市汇价跌到 $8\frac{1}{8}$ 便士,相当于官价的 57%,市场开始不安。国民政府内部也有不同政策意见,主要分为两派。一部分人主张在上海维持法币汇价,认为汇价与法币信用相关,关系到物资进口与稳定战时经济;继续在上海租界内供应正当进口商人所需的外汇,也有助于英、美等国对中国抗战的同情与支持。中国银行董事长宋子文就坚信只有拥有外汇资源和外汇头寸,一方面以法币售予华侨,换取侨汇,一方面在外汇市场上抛出外汇收进法币,法币的价格就能维持。③另一部分人不主张在上海租界内出售外汇、维持法币汇价,反对把来之不易的外汇投放上海市场,认为此举等同任由日伪套汇,不如将外汇市场移至重庆。④

在争论之中,国民政府一方面在平民无法请准购汇的情况下,坚持原定法价(即合英币 1 先令 $1\frac{1}{4}$ 便士),另一方面,与英商汇丰和麦加利银行达成 1 000 万镑的借款,成立平准外汇基金,来支持黑市 $8\frac{1}{4}$ 便士的汇价。

事实正如厉德寅担心的那样,1939 年 3 月 9 日中英合组外汇平准基金委员会成立后,开始向黑市投入外汇,依照 8.35 便士的平准汇率,无限制地购买外汇,试图以此稳定汇价。这样,政府在名义上固定原有的法定汇价,而在事实上公开承认市场汇率,并以全力维持市场汇率。

---

① 厉德寅:《我国当前外汇问题的出路》,《新政治》1939 年第 3 卷第 1 期。
② 厉德寅:《再论维持外汇与黑市汇价》,《时事月报》1939 年第 21 卷第 1 期。
③ 洪葭管主编:《中央银行史料》,中国金融出版社 2005 年版,第 591 页。
④ 社会各界也出现了各种意见,有的主张根据经济实情,重新确定汇价,并设法维持;有的主张坚持有名无实地维持原定官方汇价;有的主张先支撑黑市价格,以免摇对法币的信心;还有的主张由政府把官价和黑市价格的差额发还或津贴出口商人。

虽然市场汇率十分稳定,但平准基金的损失巨大而迅速,仅两个月便耗1 000万镑平准基金的大半。于是,外汇平准基金不得已于5月中再增加1 500万英镑,按照市场汇价,折合法币72 700万元。但敌伪套取外汇、贸易入超和逃亡资本组合成无底的漏洞。①6月7日平准基金停止依8.25便士的汇率供给外汇,汇价由此大落。9日,平准基金会下调汇率为6.5便士,但只坚持了40天便告失败。7月18日外汇平准基金委员会停止出售外汇法币信用再次动摇。对此,厉德寅指出"财政当局只顾港沪少数商贾的利益,或别有苦衷,而忽略了民族利益"。中英平准基金耗损2 000余万镑的外汇,却于事无补,反而引起民众悲观情绪,同时在政策上从不断加强统制的政策趋势,向自由汇市倒退。②

1939年7月1日以后,国民政府开始实行主动贬值政策,以期恢复法币信用,试图挽救不断下跌的黑市汇率。根据财政部新颁布的《进口物品申请购买外汇规则》,其中规定"凡经核准购买之外汇,由指定之中国或交通银行按照法价售给,但申请人须缴纳按法价与中交两行挂牌价格差额之平衡费"。相关的《出口货物结汇领取汇价差额办法》也做了收取差价手续费的规定,即名义上保持法价,而实际上贬低了汇价。这种做法其实在当时的德国、匈牙利已行之有效。厉德寅并不赞同这样的政策,认为中国情形特殊,必须切割官方汇市与黑市的联系。

事实再次证实了厉德寅的论断,国民政府试图同时举借外债,加强平准基金,继续维持黑市汇率,但借款的落空最终搁置了维持黑市的汇率政策,市场汇率也从6.5便士一路下跌到3.5便士,法币的市场汇价已不及官方汇价的四分之一。政府为加强外汇管理而制定的外汇结算、促进出口和限制进口的政策均未能阻止汇率的下跌。为此,厉德寅在1939年发表《我国当前外汇问题的出路》,再次呼吁财政当局:"把法币的问题重加考虑,认清了问题的核心,再做对症下药的措施,才能达到巩固法币信用的目的。"③

3. 呼吁放弃维持黑市,重订外汇管理

关于核心的外汇汇率问题,厉德寅认为战时外汇问题的核心在于维持官方汇价,其重要意义在于维持人民对法币的信用,避免抗战危局下财政金

---

① 5月19日,日本开始做低日元和伪币对法币的比价,收买法币,以便套取我外汇平衡基金的外汇准备。这一时期,国民政府在一定程度上误以为日元和伪币行将崩溃,未能及时筹划对策,以致6月初,敌伪抛出大批法币套取外汇,外汇市场一时供不应求,谣言四起,酿成挤兑风潮。

②③ 厉德寅:《我国当前外汇问题的出路》,《新政治》1939年第3卷第1期。

融的崩溃。厉德寅对维持汇价的方法作了充分的研究。当时维持汇价的可选方式有两种,一是维持原有法定汇价,二是重新制定新的法定汇价。而这两种方式的共同目的,都是使人民能够获得"正当需要"的外汇;同时维持货币购买力,停止汇价的不断下跌。①

厉德寅对全面抗战爆发以来的法币发行数额进行了跟踪研究。经过统计分析,他发现通货膨胀对国内物价上涨的影响相对第一次世界大战时期西欧的影响较小,但物价有不断上涨趋势。在此情况下,法币外汇价格维持固定不变,未随购买力平价之变动而变,进口商将从物价上涨中获得巨大利益。进口受到刺激,则国内对外汇的需求将随之增加,超出政府准许额度的部分即形成黑市需求。因此,黑市存在的原因在于外汇价格"钉住"、国内物价上涨以及自由的私营进口贸易。

另一方面,厉德寅论证了战争环境下的国民政府并没有维持黑市汇率的充分实力。当时的日本先后采用滥发"联银券"及"华兴券"、伪币及军用票强购民间货物等方式大量榨取、吸收、没收沦陷区的法币,同时控制了海关收入(尤其是江海关)。1938年6月至1939年5月间,日本就总共吸收法币2亿元,并以之不断套购国民政府外汇,"循环不已,无有终止"。厉德寅依据其所做的统计,认为"除非有继续不断的巨额外汇收入",否则有限的外汇平准基金会在短期内用尽。而国民政府两项主要外汇收入(出口贸易与华侨汇款),均已减缩;在1938年10月广州沦陷以后,中国只有依靠西南少数边关(如蒙自、思茅、腾越、龙州)出口;原本用侨汇捐助政府抗战及购买公债的侨民家属也大量移居国外。在没有足够外部援助的情况下,国民政府想要维持黑市汇价,"直似以金沙填补无底洞,为不可能之事"。

厉德寅不仅从可行性上否定了政府维持黑市汇价的做法,还论证了政府不应该采取这种政策。

第一,政府对黑市汇价的维持,必须放弃对黑市采取审核制度,因为只依靠行政手段统制黑市,只能催生汇价更低的、新的黑市。而无限制供给外汇(包括非正当的外汇需要),都会使得日本源源不断地套取到外汇资源,进而破坏法币制度。

第二,外汇平准基金向黑市投入外汇以后,日本改从上海大量进口物资,大规模地利用这些外汇资源。例如,当时占进口货总值约四分之一的进口棉花多数是由驻沪日本纱厂购进。日军在华机械化部队和空军使用的平

---

① 厉德寅:《维持外汇法价与黑市汇价》,《时事月报》1938年第19卷第7期。

滑油及燃料也从上海购入,利用平准基金进行结汇。此外,上海市面大量非必需品和奢侈品均需通过黑市购汇(1939年第一季度奢侈品占进口总值3%左右),从而占用了平准基金的外汇资源。

第三,厉德寅利用海关数据,统计得出1939年中国贸易入超不断增大,较1938年同期增加近3 000万元法币维持黑市汇价,并创开战以来的新纪录。这些进口货物"为日利用者已多",仅天津、胶州二埠入超就达9 000万元,进口值升至13 000万元以上;而且1939年1月至4月,有约9 600万元的货物来自日本,多数须以外汇支付。这无异于用外汇平准基金的外汇资助日本的侵略战争。①

厉德寅进一步推论,要做到人民能获得"正当需要"的外汇,且维持供给,需要实现两点:第一,通过举借外债("此事政府正在进行中,闻有可能性,然未敢定也")或从黑市秘密收买外汇,并筹备充足之外汇基金。他认为在缺乏外汇基金的情况下,难以实现旧法定汇价的维持,而应该在外汇补充到一定数量,"重订外汇法价并切实维持此新法价"。虽然新的法定汇价将引起人民误会,但能够有利于外汇基金的筹措、符合变化中的战时经济环境并阻抑外汇流入向黑市。②

关于平衡对外收支,他提出了五种方法:(1)激励国内生产事业,增加生产量,以供消费,以供输出;(2)开辟交通路线,尤须整理内河运输及修筑湘黔与川滇缅铁道,以利输出;(3)征收逃资,以充实外汇基金;(4)开辟川湘金矿以补充外汇基金;(5)限制法币发行额,以维持法币之购买力。③

国际贸易是国际收支平衡的最重要方面,"欲谋对外收支之平衡,必须统制贸易"。至于统制贸易的方法,厉德寅列举贸易货款清算协定制、以贸易货制、偿债协定制、国营贸易制、比例限额制、购买外汇请核制、进口许可证制七种,并认为国民政府正在施行类似"购买外汇请核制"只是次优选择,这种制度对于各类进口,"无一般之限制"。他认为国营贸易最适合战时中国,"一面可增加输出,一面可尽量限制输入"。④

二、提出"隔离黑市政策"

1. 总结中英平准基金教训

1935年11月实行法币政策起,至战时中国政府实行统制外汇以前,法

---

① 厉德寅:《隔离外汇黑市之建议》,《财政评论》1939年第2卷第4期。
②③④ 厉德寅:《维持外汇法价与黑市汇价》,《时事月报》1938年第19卷第7期。

币对外汇价始终维持在一定水准,加之人民得以依法价买卖外汇,不受限制,法币信用和金融行市总体稳定。1938年3月14日,政府开始统制外汇之后,人民之需要外汇,必先依法请求政府核准,方得向中央银行购买,凡政府认为不必要商品进口和贸易以外不必要的需要,均不能获准购买外汇,于是产生了私行购买外汇的需求,成为外汇黑市的起源。

厉德寅在1938年12月1日中国经济学社年会上就表示:"假使外汇黑市无法解决,法定汇率以及法币信用是不能维持的。"换言之,要巩固法币的信用,必须推行隔离黑市政策,使中国后方各省市和黑市所在区域隔离,以消去黑市汇率变动对于法币信用的影响,且统制后方各省市对外汇兑和贸易,同时查禁后方黑市。①遗憾的是,国民政府当局并没有很快采纳这意见。

自从中英平准基金试图维持黑市,原先一先令二便士半或美元二角九分七五的法定汇率,在事实上已等同虚设。这也为日本破坏法币提供了直接目标:只要向黑市汇率进攻,法币信用自然受到威胁。正如厉德寅所指出的,中英平准基金根本无法维持外汇的无限制买卖,日本则有计划、有步骤、有目的地利用平准基金套取外汇,进而打破黑市汇价,以摇动法币的信用。至此,日本的主要目的已不是套取外汇获利,对黑市价格的打击将愈发凶猛。在间接资敌外汇、助敌进口以外,贸易入超的趋势也将进一步压迫中国财政与金融的抗战能力。因此,厉德寅始终坚持:以无限制买卖方法维持黑市汇率,不仅难以实现,并且害多利少。②

1939年7月18日以后,随着汇率的崩溃,中英平准基金办法已告失败:在法定汇价丧失作用的情况下,政府支持黑市汇价,并不是妥善的政策。外汇平准基金委员会对于黑市供给外汇,事实上是等于承认了黑市;黑市实际成为公开交易市场,反过来牵制了法币价值的变动。③

面对中国金融市场受汇率影响面临崩溃的局面,厉德寅调查了黑市外汇供给的三种来源(偷运出口的货款、逃资和华侨汇款),进而指出外汇黑市的危害。其一,外汇因有黑市而不能集中于政府或国家银行。除第一款受政府统制的出口所得外汇由中交两行承购外,大多数战时外汇成为黑市外汇的供给。(外汇的收入,大约有下列数款:输出货款,华侨汇款,外国使领人员及驻华军队之费用,外人在华旅费,对外投资之本息利润等。)1938

---

①② 厉德寅:《我国当前外汇问题的出路》,《新政治》1939年第3卷第1期。
③ 厉德寅:《再论维持外汇与黑市汇价》,《时事月报》1939年第21卷第1期。

年1月至7月期间,共仅约4 600万元法币进入政府银行,从而削弱了政府动用外汇购买军火及民生必需品(如药品、汽油、汽车、钢铁、机器等)等资源的能力,进而造成冲击外汇固定价格。实际汇价一旦跌落,即直接威胁到法币信用,并造成恶性循环,汇价愈跌,物资愈缺,物价愈涨。外汇价格的稳定成为国内市场价格变动的支配因素。其二,国内外汇需求将因黑市的存在而不断增加。根据国民政府的核准外汇分配计划,65%的外汇将用于军需,15%用于建设事业,4%用于文化事业,15%用于辅助工商,其他占1%。厉德寅了解到在后四类中,除约40种商品以外,"一律不准购买外汇"(即不必要的输入商品)。厉德寅当时无法获得每月的外汇核准数据,但估算出国民政府"早已不犹豫地动用外汇基金,以弥补收支之差额"。厉德寅观察到,"三炮台大前门香烟口红胭脂等奢侈品仍充斥市场",黑市外汇的增加,只能促使进口商抬高物价,政府的外汇缺口则愈发严重,同时官方汇价与黑市汇价对购买力平价都将不断跌落。其三,黑市抑制了中国对外出口。一方面,国内市场物价的腾贵将造成生产成本的提升,出口货物将丧失竞争力;另一方面,国民政府控制区域内的出口只能按照固定汇价结算,而沦陷区同样的出口货物将获得1.835倍的法币收益,从而削弱了国统区的经济活力。①

厉德寅指出战时中国的外汇黑市与当时苏联、德国等国家不同,表现在:其一,中国黑市汇价的变动,大致与购买力平价相符,而外国则不然。其二,中国黑市是人民唯一可获得外汇的汇市,"无异于公开自由汇市,政府不加查禁,亦无法禁止";而外国黑市为政府严密查禁,只能秘密买卖外汇。因此,中国黑市汇价与法币信用直接有关,"法币购买力之维持,间接为黑市汇价之维持"。②因此黑市作为实际的公开汇市,很难真正消除,更可行的目标是避免国民政府统治区内的法币信用受到黑市的负面影响。退而言之,只要使黑市汇价不在下跌,实际官方汇价也能得到支撑。③

消除黑市汇价变动对于法币信用的威胁,理论上有三种方式:"(甲)邀请友邦协同根本禁绝黑市;(乙)维持黑市汇价于一定之水准,使无甚变动;(丙)隔离黑市,使黑市汇价之变动,不能影响法币之信用。"

实际上,上海的外汇黑市在当时没有禁绝的可能性。以上海为大本营,香港、天津以及游击地区的商埠、城市都有外汇黑市。各处黑市汇价,直接或间接取决于上海市价,交易数额也较小。厉德寅指出若要彻底消灭黑市,

---

①②③ 厉德寅:《维持外汇法价与黑市汇价》,《时事月报》1938年第19卷第7期。

则必先消除上海的黑市,这就需要英、美、法等租界主权国诚心合作,愿意协同禁绝黑市。此点等同于要求英、美、法三国政府需要充分勇气和决心,不顾日本的威胁,在中日金融战场上站在中国的一边。①现实是,英国在上海、香港拥有极大的各类权益和经济利益,外资银行中最具实力的英商银行又是外汇黑市的参与投机者。因此,在外汇黑市无从强制消灭的情况下,切断黑市对法币的影响成为唯一的选择。

2. 设计"隔离黑市政策"

至1939年7月以后,国民政府每周核准的外汇数额大都在5万镑以下,不足请购数额的5%。民间外汇需要,"几全数仰给于黑市"。这意味着一旦上海黑市汇价"跌风摇动",法币信用将受黑市拖累。因此,厉德寅认为中国政府不仅不该维持黑市汇价,还要在黑市汇价进一步发生剧烈波动以前,切断黑市与未沦陷地区的联系,即"隔离黑市政策"。②

由于贸易与汇兑流通的存在,各地的物价之间也因相关地域的货币价格的涨落而变化。厉德寅以1931年以后的德国为例,认为控制一地物价水准和货币价格不受外部影响的方法,就是厉行贸易与汇兑的统制,阻隔区域间的市场联通机制。"隔离黑市之用意,即欲使我后方各省区之物价水准,勿受黑市所在区域物价水准涨落之影响",从而使后方各省区内货币对外汇价不受黑市影响。

他认为:"凡我后方各省区输往港沪及游击区域之一切货物,如同输往外国,一律须结售外汇(或由国营),否则不得出口。又凡自我后方各省区汇款至港沪及游击区域,视若汇款至外国,必属正当需要而有充实证明,并经管理当局核准,方得汇出。否则不得汇出。自港沪及游击区域汇款至后方各省区者,亦同此办法。"隔离黑市必须实现三步骤:

第一步,政府应对"正当需要"之范围、请购手续,厘定明确的执行章则,使外汇请核政策避免因标准不一,而失去民心。

第二步,在隔离港沪及游击区域之后,后方各省区内法币对外汇兑,只允许根据政府法定汇价,严格查禁黑市。同时,将后方法币与上海及游击区域中的法币隔离开来,"如同两种不同之货币",上海黑市汇价之变动,如同他国币汇价之变动,不能影响于我后方各省区内法币之信用。此种情形,可比"德国登记马克在伦敦市场之汇价,其涨落不能影响于自由马克之

---

①② 厉德寅:《隔离外汇黑市之建议》,《财政评论》1939年第2卷第4期。

信用"。

第三步,对于日伪将吸收的法币,偷运至抗战后方套取外汇,可以通过严格的核准制度禁绝。至于申请外汇用以购运货物出口,则"非先结售外汇,不得出口"。厉德寅还积极建议实行国营贸易,断绝敌对势力在抗日后方换取物资的可能。①

黑市的存在是客观事实,但黑市汇价是国民政府战时的外汇实力所无法承受的。在此情况下"维持汇价"的目标其实是维持一个政府和市场都可以接受的汇价,其本质仍是围绕法币信用的维持。厉德寅提出了一系列具体措施以供采用,核心是切断黑市,使之不对未沦陷地区的外汇市场产生影响:

(一)依据经济现状,重新厘定法币汇价,并照新定法价切实管理维持之。

(二)管理外汇以非陷敌区域为限,陷敌区域之外汇市场任其自由发展。

(三)对于陷敌区域之汇款和贸易,严加限制或课重税或禁止。

(四)中交总行之未迁渝者,由政府命令其立即迁入,使金融重心归宿于政府所在地,不得停留于港沪。

(五)设法增加并集中政府权力所及地域(陷敌区域除外)之外汇供给,同时惩罚逃资及在外国之资产。

(六)审核外汇需要之性质,分别限制或禁止外汇之购买。

(七)关于生产消费方面,对于有外国市场之货物(如桐油、红茶等)奖励生产并节约甚或禁止在国内消费,以增出口货物以换得外汇。

(八)关于财政者,增开新税并提高旧税之税率,以增加税收,而减少入不敷出之赤字财政差额,来缓和钞票发行额之增速。

(九)关于金融方面,依照廿六年九月颁布的办法,限制银行存户之提款,以减低流通量。

(十)由国库津贴华侨汇款千分之五,以资鼓励,使华侨汇款,得集中于政府之手。②

其中第一、六条是为了确立新的外汇官价,开展外汇管理;第五、七、十

---

① 厉德寅:《隔离外汇黑市之建议》,《财政评论》1939年第2卷第4期。
② 厉德寅:《再论维持外汇与黑市汇价》,《时事月报》1939年第21卷第1期。

条是通过回收逃逸外汇、增加出口、集中侨汇等方式,增强政府外汇储备和维持汇价的能力;第二、三、四条是从空间上切断黑市与中国政府控制区域内外汇市场的物理联系;第八、九条是抑制通胀速度,维持购买力平价本身,缓和汇市压力。

伴随隔离政策,黑市汇价对交战区法币的影响也会减弱,因为黑市将无力独自支持对此类法币的无限制套汇。此时,日方即便回收大量法币,也没有实际的益处。厉德寅还指出,为避免日本对此类法币采用强制手段,只有在军事上加强游击队的实力,才能从根本上保证游击区内法币的流通。①

虽然政府无法隔离游击区内的黑市,但游击区内的法币仍需要维持,政府"不可不注意"。厉德寅进一步考虑到,政府隔离黑市并放弃以政府维持黑市汇率,必会引起黑市汇率的短期波动,并呈现一种下跌趋势。这种趋势会威胁到中日交战区域(或游击区)内法币的信用和价格,也会动摇沦陷区内中国人民和英美各国贸易集团对法币的信心。这种情况依旧助长了"日圆集团"或"日满支经济协同体"的封锁势力。

他认为直接受益于黑市外汇的主要是"少数买办阶级、资本家及外汇投机者",这些人本对法币信心动摇,或逃资国外,或利用汇率变化以为投机买卖而图利,扰乱金融市场。而英、美等国要继续确保在华贸易利益,则可选择在不消耗外汇基金之条件下,援照1938年8月至1939年3月期间暗中支持上海黑市汇率的旧例,选定符合交战区经济现状的汇率。因此,政府只需顾及沦陷区与游击区内的法币购买力,而只要保证法币信用优于伪币及军用票,法币就很难被大量兑换为后者,最差的情况也只是被收藏,暂时退出市场。

不过,在中日货币战中,非沦陷区以外的法币受到了日本货币战的巨大威胁。游击区内的法币生存问题,不能只依靠国民政府的金融政策,还需政治、外交、军事的支持。厉德寅指出,英国接受日本之要求,将天津租界及北平东交民巷内存银全数交给日伪政府,就是在支持日伪"联银券"的发行,直接削弱了法币的信用。因此,各国是否承认所谓"联银券""华兴券"是沦陷区日元集团能否稳固的最大问题。因此,外交在中日货币战中仍有重要地位,尤其事关游击区内法币对伪钞的防卫战。②

---

① 厉德寅:《我国当前外汇问题的出路》,《新政治》1939年第3卷第1期。
② 厉德寅:《隔离外汇黑市之建议》,《财政评论》1939年第2卷第4期。

三、积极献策中美英平准基金会

1. 研究新的平准基金运作机制

1941年4月1日,由中国国民政府代表宋子文、中央银行代表李幹在美国华盛顿与英、美两国财政部签订合约,在中国设立新的中美英平准基金委员会,以稳定法币在外汇市场上的价格。其中,美方提供5 000万美元,中方拨给2 000万美元,英方提供500万英镑。另外1939年成立的中英平准基金1 000万镑亦由该会接收和运用(故英方先后共认1 000万镑),合计总额为1.1亿美元。①

中美英平准基金借款协定达成以后,新的平准基金实际由三国共同商议管理。美、英两国都认为作为借款方,应当对基金管理有所话语权,而重庆方面蒋介石与财政部长孔祥熙则认为事关中国外汇与金融稳定,中国应当占据主导权。最后,新的平准委员会设委员5人:中国3人,英、美各1人,主席由中方担任。委员会的秘书均是经济学家,先为林维英,1941年7月改由冀朝鼎担任。②厉德寅实际是代表中国政府财政部,长期担任平准基金会研究室主任,主管基金管理委员会的外汇和金融市场统计工作,直至1943年5月该平准基金会基本运作结束。

厉德寅在中美英平准基金的研究工作,直接服务于基金会的政策制定,使得相关政策制定能够围绕中国的抗战事业,而不仅仅是外汇市场的稳定和外商银行的利益。而平准基金的运作对战时国民政府平衡国际收支、提供货币供应、疏通物资生产和贸易与实行金融体系管理均有重要意义。

外汇平准基金的作用在于压制投机和调节季节变动,通过抛出或收买外汇,平衡市场供需,避免汇价受投机买卖的影响。厉德寅认为中国的平准基金会有别于俄、德、意各国的管理外汇机构,既不能将汇价抬高至自由市场的汇价上方,亦不能根据外汇需要的性质,限制或禁止购买。事实上,除非通货膨胀不止,法币的购买力平价"不至于有跌无已",黑市汇价的长期趋势也是如此。即便政府不予支撑,黑市汇价也会维持在某个最低点。③

厉德寅指出一系列的"隔离黑市"措施的成功,最终有赖于良好的外汇

---

① 吴景平:《美国和抗战时期中国的平准基金》,《近代史研究》1997年第5期。
② 吴景平:《蒋介石与战时平准基金》,《民国档案》2013年第1期。
③ 厉德寅:《再论维持外汇与黑市汇价》,《时事月报》1939年第21卷第1期。

管理。尤其是法定汇价一旦严重偏离实际经济状况,外汇管理将十分艰难。他认为如果在1939年3月11日中英外汇平准基金委员会成立以前,就降低官方汇价,自然引起社会不安,但要比迟至6月7日重新调整黑市汇价或7月18日黑市汇价猛跌所造成的恐慌情形要好。外汇平准基金委员会的成立,实际使黑市汇价变成半官方的汇价,等于承认其实际汇价的地位,削弱了原有政府汇价的市场效力。他还认为,中国沿海的对外贸易已经被日本控制,"几无我方收购(洋货)之余地";在日本的外汇与贸易管理政策下,中国政府也无法从沦陷区获得日方外汇。①

外汇平准基金,可以按预定计划买卖外汇,其作用一为稳定汇价,二为缓和物价上涨趋势。汇价水平的高低与国际收支平衡有紧密关系。国际收支项目中以贸易为大宗,变动也最敏捷。当汇价水平与经济情形相匹配,则国际收支平衡,平准基金买进卖出的数额可以相抵;当汇价水平过高,则国际收入将不敷支出,而平准基金逐渐消耗,消耗之数等于收支的差额,直至基金耗尽,汇价则将跌落至自然水平。在中、美、英三国平准基金成立以前,中英外汇平准基金对汇价的支持,即属这种情况。

厉德寅认为平准基金的目的及相应的运作机制应当慎重考虑。一种选择是,维持合理汇价,只用于消除季节变动,而不变更其长期趋势,不过分消耗基金。另一种选择是仿效中英平准基金的运行,在消除汇价季节变动的同时,以消耗基金为代价,改变汇价长期趋势。后一种选择也会带来其他益处:维持汇价就需要抛售大量外汇,收进法币,减少了市场上的法币流通量,同时售出的外汇能够缓和物价上涨的趋势。

依据事实数据,厉德寅进一步研究了平准基金外汇政策对国内物价的实际影响。在紧缩法币流通量方面,他发现发行额增加愈多,物价上涨增速越快;相反,高位发行量1%的紧缩也能使物价下落2%。他计算仅美国借予的5 000万美元平准基金若在一年之内,悉数售出用以进口必需物资,可同时收回法币10亿元,消减最近物价上涨势力80%。

在增加市场供给方面,中国大后方生产力不足,各类军需民用物资缺乏,平准基金能够提供支持进口的大量外汇。而大规模进口物资,又需要满足两个条件,一是国营或民营的实业组织能从平准基金获得充分外汇,以便采购外国物资;二是国际交通路线具备充分运输能力。当时,香港作为抗战初期中国进口物资的转运中心,已经受到日军侵略的威胁,有被夺取的可

---

① 厉德寅:《隔离外汇黑市之建议》,《财政评论》1939年第2卷第4期。

能。厉德寅提出应当与英美等航运国交好,获得两国在必要情况下的护航;同时考虑发展东南亚一带的转运港口,比如仰光及伊洛瓦地江口。他指出从仰光至缅甸北部的腊成有300多公里长的公路,中国的对外贸易可以借此水陆并进,每月物资总运输量可达1.8万吨左右。

除了扩充海外物资进入中国的渠道外,厉德寅还建议改善中国内地到口岸的运输条件。理论上,较高的汇价会促进物资进口,能同时缓解国内物资供应的紧张,进而平抑物价。但厉德寅研究了重庆、成都、昆明、桂林、西安、上海六地的批发物价指数,发现物价上涨程度悬殊。鉴于大量进口的物资无法真正输送到抗战大后方,他据此建议平准基金管理委员会采取奖励输入运输工具及器材的政策,"凡请购外汇用以采办运输工具器材及油料等,特别予以优待",以此鼓励运输工具和油料的进口,增加运输能力,平抑内地快速上涨的物价。

2. 建言改良外汇管理体系

为最大限度地发挥平准基金的功能,避免再度发生虚耗基金,厉德寅进一步研究了大后方外汇管理的系统化改进方案。

第一步,建立后方外汇市场而放弃维持上海黑市汇价。这是厉德寅始终坚持的一个观点。到了中美英平准基金设立之时,中国的主要口岸均被日本封锁,上海与抗战大后方的贸易联系也已趋于隔绝。大后方的法币价值与上海法币价值之间,也没有了实质上的关联,更不受上海黑市汇价的影响。加之日伪采取政治压力及恐怖手段以打击国民政府在上海的金融力量,上海作为中、日双方金融力量博弈的据点,意义已经不大。而在政治上,上海已渐失去维系沦陷区民心作用,只要大后方法币价格维持,沦陷区对法币的信心不会有进一步的恶劣影响。

第二步,在后方新建立外汇市场之汇率,代替黑市汇率。通过此举实现重庆国民政府对法币外汇市场的重新控制,以便实行相关战时统制经济的政策,并调整国际收支。同时,外汇市场的内迁也能辅助战时经济金融中心的内移。当时中、中、交、农四大银行的总行或总管理处均已迁至重庆办公,并在大后方形成新的金融网,其他重要商业银行亦多在后方设立营业处,外汇市场自然应当随之迁至重庆。厉德寅认为,经济中心的内迁也是为了战时生产建设的需要。从对法币流通和物价变动的控制角度看,应当迅速放弃维持上海黑市,外汇市场"限于后方,以重庆为中心,并视事实之需要,于西安、昆明、桂林、金华等地设立办事处,或委托中国银行代理"。

建立新的外汇市场,关键在于确立新的官方汇率,这关系平准基金的使用效用。厉德寅认为,虽然在战争状态下,多数国家对经济金融有所管制,但购买力平价仍然是制定新汇率标准的重要参考。美国同意对华平准基金借款,表现了美国对中国抗战的支持日趋积极,厉德寅期望"今后借款或可望源源继续"。他认为当时世界各国只有美国有能力向中国供应大量物资,因此新汇率"应放弃钉住镑价而以对美元之汇价为准"。结合其他因素,他建议参考美元公债折算率的上限和黑市汇价的下限,由平准基金会在5元至7.5元之间决定,并以之为对其他外币的换算标准。

第三步,加强后方外汇市场管理,以供给厂商的正当需要为原则。厉德寅认为,查禁黑市固然重要,例如"凡用黑市汇票购运之商品,如经查出,一律充公",断绝黑市的外汇需求。但同样重要的,是政府或中央银行应当明白列举"正当需要外汇"请购办法并维持供给,树立人民的信心。他指出国民政府未能执行好自己制定的法令,人民依法申请,未必能获得"正当需要"的外汇,有时被迫向黑市购得外汇,而外国人则反而可依规定章则请准购得外汇。另外,商品量与通货量是影响货币购买力的二元素。"前者虽因战事而减少,但甚有限,故其危险性少。后者每因军政费之需要,汇价暴跌,不可制止。"厉德寅指出国民政府在1938年7月以后未曾正常公布法币发行额,大量增发货币具有潜在危险性,"应有相当限制"。①

大后方新的外汇市场管理,主要内容有汇率、地点、手续及用途四项,尤以用途为核心。厉德寅认为1939年7月前的中国外汇管理,只对申购外汇的地点和手续进行了限制。在施行《进口物品申请购买外汇规则》之后,"对用途限制过严,审核手续过繁,而商人请购买外汇多未得核准",一般厂商只能转向黑市购买外汇,外汇管理效果不佳。

厉德寅指出中美平准基金的成立初衷,似乎在于供给商业性质的需要,并稳定法币汇价。中美平准基金的实际数额还不能完全供应战时外汇的全部需要,故可以分为商汇与非商汇两部分,以此确保厂商能够以正当理由申请到外汇。同时,物资的购取不仅项目限于与抗战直接有关的物资或民生必需,且要使手续简便易行。

中国内地运输困难,各地物资难以互相调剂,是物价上涨的重要原因。尤其是民用物资的运输,普遍缺乏车辆和汽油,运费成本很高。而改良主要

---

① 厉德寅:《维持外汇法价与黑市汇价》,《时事月报》1938年第19卷第7期。

的公路运输成为改善物流的主要手段,包括改善已有道路工程和增加车辆与充实燃料供给。他建议平衡基金,鼓励公私各方面尽量购入车辆和燃料,车辆运至口岸后,可随即用于输入物资,以增加运输量。

第四步,在管理后方外汇市场同时,适当放宽内汇市场。国民政府曾经为了减少沪港外汇市场上的法币头寸,减轻汇价压力,对内汇市场进行限制,避免内地法币外流。厉德寅认为,随着抗战大后方的建设需要,内汇能够促进物资生产和流通。政府放弃沪港外汇市价以后,为防止抛售外汇,投机内汇,出口方面也需要以货物上船起运为交割外汇的条件。他认为放弃黑市,可能引起上海法币的内流,但只要法币用于偿付货价及清理债务,不脱离实体流通,对大后方物价上涨的刺激是有限的。①

厉德寅还指出,外汇请核对于向上海及游击区域的汇款也应明白规定正当需要汇款的范围及手续。对于正当需要的汇款,应当免除现行40%的高额汇水。高额汇水只是增加了银行的"过分得利",但无异于盲目剥削了正当的汇款,使许多后方军民无法接济留居沦陷区的家眷。②

1941年8月13日,中美英平准基金委员会开始在香港正式办公,中国汇市开始稳定下来。与厉德寅的建议相似,8月18日起,凡购买外汇的申请均集中在新基金办理,按高于黑市汇率的新汇价供应外汇。1941年12月8日,太平洋战争爆发,日军占领香港和上海租界,两地平准基金委员会办事处遂告结束,外汇平准业务随之转移至重庆办理。从1942年7月10日起,重庆的外汇挂牌定为1美元合法币20元,如同固定汇率,直到1946年3月4日外汇市场再度开放。

在全面抗日战争时期,厉德寅积极投身于外汇政策的研究,发挥了经济学家的重要作用,对抗战各个阶段的重要外汇政策提供了深刻而翔实的分析。鉴于战时政府部门的运作方式和原始档案的公布情况,厉德寅作为"四联总处"和平准基金会调查统计工作的负责人,执行了许多无法留名的实际工作。以消除外汇黑市影响为核心的研究,只是他在战火中的思想成果之一。在国民政府内部的政策争论中,他并没有因所在财政部的部门立场,而放弃客观严谨的科学分析,甚至坚定地指出国民政府的政策弊端和危害。在平准基金会的工作中,他从抗战大局的需要出发,坚持了中国政

---

① 厉德寅:《如何运用中美平准基金》,《财政评论》1941年第6卷第1期。
② 厉德寅:《我国当前外汇问题的出路》,《新政治》1939年第3卷第1期。

府外汇政策的自主性和独立性,而非"乞怜于外国以求取其援助"。他的"隔离黑市"和重订外汇管理的方案,经得起历史的验证,对于财政当局均有重要的资政价值。这都是源于他始终以国家的利益、民族大义和人民经济生活的安定作为研究工作的出发点。

厉德寅农村金融思想及历史价值

苗书迪　贺水金

　　1937年7月日本开始全面侵华,中国大片土地相继沦陷,国民政府统治区域的农产品生产大大减少,农业生产能力愈益萎缩。随着政府机关、军队、工商企业、文化教育部门和大量难民的内迁,口粮需求急剧增加,粮食问题日益凸显。经济作物的减少还直接影响到外贸出口与内迁工厂的原料供应,出口农产品的数量削减影响到国民政府财政经济的稳定,工厂原料的无法满足也抑制了产业部门的生产能力。大后方各省长期处于军阀割据和混战的动乱之中,农业生产力遭到严重破坏,农民借贷率居高不下,债务负担沉重,若论扩大农业生产,实属不易。由此,支持战时农业生产极具必要性及重要性,修建农田水利工程、推广良种与肥料、改进生产工具、开垦荒地等被提上日程,但种种举措"均有赖大量资金之协助也"①,故国民政府的战时农贷政策被赋予了多重含义。

　　为应对抗战期间金融管理之需要,1937年8月国民政府设立了四联总处(即中国银行、中央银行、交通银行、中国农民银行四银行联合办事总处的简称)。四联总处成立之初,主要使命为联合与协调四行业务,以配合国民政府贯彻战时经济金融各项方针。1939年四联总处进行改组,不仅参与各项经济金融大计之决策与筹划,且承担督导国家相关行政机构和银行贯彻执行相关政策的责任,成为国民政府的中枢金融机构。同时在制度层面开始重视农村金融的发展,在四联总处战时金融委员会下设立农业金融处,对全国所有农贷事宜负统划督促及联络之实,并成立农贷审核委员会和农业金融设计委员会,负责农业金融政策的设计与监管执行。

　　厉德寅于1939年11月被调任四联总处统计科科长,主管金融调查、统计、研究工作,在此期间他出于对现实的关怀与制度的思考,利用扎实的统计学功底,撰写数篇论文分析了战时农村金融的发展现状,并提出了切实可

---

① 姚公振:《中国农业金融史》,中国文化服务社1947年版,第300页。

行的农村金融发展路径,其论点精要鲜明,引起时人关注。《农贷消息半月刊》1941年第5卷第1期在转载厉德寅之文《树立兼营式农业合作金融制度刍议》时加了这样的编者前言:"厉先生以客观之态度,论述中国目前所需要之农业合作金融制度,再以精锐之眼光,肯定之主张,提供树立兼营式农业合作金融制度意见,印成单行本,分送各机关参考。编者接读该文后,深佩立论正确而有独到之处,特转载本刊,以飨读者。"厉德寅对战时农村金融发展的数据统计详实,问题分析精辟入里,改革方案兼具适用性与实用性,其思想在国民政府农村金融政策的调整中也得到了具体体现。难能可贵的是,厉德寅切实关注到了中国农村金融发展的特色,并开始思考农业金融制度的中国化探索,虽时过境迁,其思想仍能为当下实践提供有益启发。

一、厉德寅对战时农村金融的统计与分析

抗战初期国民政府为保障后方农业生产,仅1937年下半年及1938年,不同部门关于农业金融政策颁布了至少8则条规,内容涉及农产品押放贷款、农业合作贷款、农业贷款范围及成数等,均旨在引导督促各行局增办农贷业务,扩大放款范围,提高放款成数,以刺激农业生产发展,增强抗战之必备坚实力量。因此,农贷数额确有显著增长,一般盛赞抗战以来农贷之成绩者,也多指这方面。在此基础之上,厉德寅基于数量统计,还洞若观火地剖析了农贷事业"优于量而拙于质"的问题所在,实属更进一步。

对于抗战时期农贷机构的放款统计,国民政府、时人及学者多分析国家行局的数额变化,特别是对中国农民银行、中国银行的农贷数据分析最为完备,忽略了各省地方银行及农民银行、各省合作金库、各省办理合作事务机关的农村放款表现。厉德寅在其文《三年来之农业金融及今后改进之途径》中统计分析了1937—1940年国家行局、各省银行、各省农民银行、各省合作金库、各省政府部门与合作机关等各类农贷机关的放款数据,①更完整地勾画出了抗战初期农贷机关组织的结构表征,为后续农村金融机构的组织体系调整奠定了基础,也为后世研究战时农业金融提供了丰富的史料。新中国成立后对战时农贷研究的经典成果,即黄立人的《论抗战时期国统

---

① 厉德寅:《三年来之农业金融及今后改进之途径》,《经济汇报》1940年第2卷第1—2期。本文数据均来自于此,不再一一注明。

区的农贷》,①被当代学者引用多达73次,其对抗战初期农贷机关及农贷数额的统计分析即来自厉德寅之文;康金莉对1937年、1938年办理农贷机关及农贷数额统计②也来源于厉德寅之数据;龚关在分析战时农贷规模的扩大时也多引用了厉德寅之分析。③

按照机关性质及放款区域,厉德寅主要将各类农贷机关分为农本局及三行、各类地方银行及农民银行、各省合作金库、各省合作事业机关及其他。1937年因战时爆发,情形紊乱,统计样本有7家农贷机关,"其他"为3 920 328.76元,占总额的14.5%,归入了表1中的*3,造成此项在1937年的偏大。1938年及1939年统计样本更加丰富,各类农贷机关多达28家,计算严密,重要贷款机关均已列入,除商业银行未具报外,可谓遗漏甚少,故其文所列表格数据至少可表示全国农贷之大概情形。

表1 1937—1939年各类农贷机关合作放款统计表

农贷机关类别	1937		1938		1939	
	放款结余数	结余数所占百分数	放款结余数	结余数所占百分数	放款结余数	结余数所占百分数
中国农民银行	14 605 059.47	53.98	29 451 345.90	47.50	47 787 913.20	42.52
农本局	671 836.24	2.48	4 322 226.17	6.97	12 927 803.50	11.48
中国银行	3 149 420.00	11.64	11 794 538.00	19.02	14 976 200.00	13.30
交通银行	—	—	1 522 141.00	2.46	1 166 403.09	1.04
*1各省地方银行及农民银行	2 112 191.00	7.86	5 685 895.33	9.17	15 639 219.95	13.89
*2各省合作金库	1 344 177.00	4.97	7 997 241.29	12.90	15 850 556.15	14.08
*3各省办理合作事务机关及其他	5 173 264.76	19.10	1 224 957.38	1.98	4 263 802.20	3.79
合计	27 055 958.47	100.00	61 998 345.07	100.00	112 611 898.15	100.00

注:1937年结余额数据*1包括广东省银行、福建省银行;*2指江西合作金库;*3包括实业部合作事业处及其他机关。1938年*1包括四个省银行、一个农民银行、三个地方银行;*2指四川及江西二个省合作金库;*3包括贵州省政府等七个机关。1939年统计样本中*1包括六个省银行、二个农民银行、三个地方银行;*2指四川、江西、浙江三个省合作金库;*3包括经济部合管局等十个机关。此表根据厉德寅原文之第一表、第二表、第四表综合可得。

---

① 黄立人:《论抗战时期国统区的农贷》,《近代史研究》1997年第6期。
② 康金莉:《民国时期中国农业合作金融研究(1923—1949)》,科学出版社2014年版,第201页。
③ 龚关:《国民政府与中国农村金融制度的演变》,南开大学出版社2016年版,第196—200页。

在农贷机关的数量结构上,能够看出抗战初期农贷数额的增减情况。合作放款结余总额由抗战爆发后的停顿之势到农村贷款的扩大,1938年放款结余数约为上年的1.3倍,1939年放款结余数又为1938年的131.64%,因此厉德寅评价道"就增加数及增加率而言,均不得谓为不速"。

难能可贵的是,厉德寅还重点分析了各农贷机关相对地位的变化,这为后续农贷组织体系的调整打下了基础。1938年农本局、中国农民银行、中国银行、交通银行的结余额共占总额的75.97%,超过各项农贷机关全体贷款额的四分之三,1939年略有下降,也占68.25%,可见国家行局占据农贷市场之主导地位。厉德寅还全面剖析了国家行局内部力量的强弱变化,其中,中国农民银行比重虽略有下降,但仍占据绝对优势地位;农本局发展迅猛,所占比重由1937年的2.48%提高至1939年的11.48%;中国银行相对地位下降;交通银行在三行中所占比重最小。各省合作金库的农贷地位在各省地方银行及农民银行之上,厉德寅对此分析道:"省合作金库为现有农业金融机构之中层组织,一方面向各金融机关透支款项,一方面供给各县合作金库资金,既可省去各金融机关直接对各县合作金库贷放手续之麻烦,而各县合作金库间资金之运用,省金库也可善为调剂,故其地位在全国农贷事业发展中,日见重要。"其对合作金库在农业金融事业的定位分析与国民政府之后续改革大致相同,之后县合作金库的快速铺设及中央合作金库的筹建也似在情理之中。各省地方银行及农民银行之农贷数额相对低下,厉德寅认为"多由于各行资力薄弱,大多未加注意或注意而未尽厥力,实为主因"。合作机关及其他办理农贷之机关,其本身原非金融组织,放款数额之微小纯属必然。

厉德寅详细统计了各农贷机关的放款对象,综合来看,放款于合作社为最多,占总数47.23%,足证战时农贷发放大多借合作社为推进之机构。次为合作金库,占27.21%,合作金库历史极短,为农业金融中之新兴机构,三年来能有如此成绩,可见各方对合作金库推行之努力。合作金库贷款之对象为信用合作社及各种合作联合社,故亦可包括在合作社贷款中,合作社与合作金库两者共占总数的74.44%,因此厉德寅认为合作社在我国农贷事业中之地位重大,为农业金融之基层组织。

同时,厉德寅还关注到了各农贷机关对合作放款与农业贷款的不同态度,这是在以往研究中被忽略的地方。基于各农贷机关合作放款与农业贷款在总放款额中的比重,厉德寅发现了"在合作放款中各类机关放款集中之程度不若全国农贷集中之程度"的特征,认为中国农民银行兼顾合作放款与其他放款,而农本局与交通银行对其他放款颇为重视。中国银行与之相反,省合作金库因受法令之限制,几乎全以合作放款为对象,故在合作放款中占较重要之位置,各省地方银行与农民银行较之省合作金库对其他放款更为重视。此类分析为农业金融的发展路径选择奠定了基础。重视合作金融的发展则自然会重点扶持合作金库的扩张,农本局与各省地方银行则将被选择性忽视,这也与后续农贷制度的演变不谋而合。

表2 1939年各项农贷机关放款对象比较表

放款对象		农本局,中国农民银行,中国银行,交通银行	*1各省地方银行及农民银行	*2各省省合作金库	*3各省合作事业机关及其他	合 计
合作社	数额	52 978 745.54	8 043 700.79	6 509 219.52	3 945 669.93	71 477 335.78
	占比	46.90	45.85	40.26	84.77	47.23
合作金库	数额	30 377 235.13	812 895.60	9 293 338.73	688 728.28	41 172 197.74
	占比	26.89	4.63	57.48	14.80	27.21
农 会	数额	2 560 477.15	5 630 103.53	—	20 332.66	8 210 913.74
	占比	2.27	32.09		0.44	5.43
农 场	数额	328 270.79	77 851.49	—	—	406 122.46
	占比	0.29	0.44			0.27
其他农民借款团体	数额	1 560 201.0	828 081.86			2 388 282.9
	占比	1.38	4.72			1.58
农业指导改进机关	数额	59 223.33	981 715.99	—		1 040 939.32
	占比	0.05	5.60			0.69
其 他	数额	25 096 706.2	1 167 983.41	364 000.00		26 628 689.6
	占比	22.22	6.66	2.25	—	17.60
合 计	数额	112 960 859.5	17 542 332.85	16 166 558.25	4 654 730.87	151 324 481.5
	占比	74.65	11.59	10.68	3.08	100.00

注:*1. 包括六个省银行、二个农民银行、三个地方银行。
*2. 包括四川、江西、浙江三个省合作金库。
*3. 包括经济部合管局等十个机关。

在农贷地域结构上,厉德寅完备地统计了28家农贷机关之每一家在各省的贷款数额,不仅分析了各主要机关的放款地域结构与省份集中度,还分析了总放款额的省份分布,对放款地域结构的论证实为充分,表3仅为简略摘之以分析其主要结论。1939年农贷区域遍及二十省,但分布极不平衡,正如厉德寅所评价的"全国农贷事业繁荣中颇有偏枯之感"。放款最多之省份首推四川,占全国28.08%,以一省之范围,放款数占全国四分之一以上,可见该省在农贷地位上之重要。江西次之,第三为江苏,放款最少者为绥远,几可忽略不计。四川、陕西、云南、贵州、西康、甘肃等后方六省,占全国总额的46.61%,但六省彼此间亦相差悬殊,"此种现象除土地、人口之因素外,尚受交通及政治之影响"。

表3 1939年放款分省统计表

省份	放款数额	百分数	省份	放款数额	百分数
四川	42 495 869.34	28.08	江西	11 889 312.62	7.86
陕西	10 334 462.38	6.83	河北	1 811 936.00	1.20
云南	1 888 868.12	1.25	山东	3 721 045.88	2.46
贵州	9 880 887.76	6.53	广东	2 149 601.82	1.42
西康	505 275.68	0.33	绥远	6 650.00	0
甘肃	5 422 265.78	3.58	河南	4 559 444.95	3.01
湖南	7 262 288.32	4.80	福建	3 390 596.10	2.24
湖北	8 158 093.21	5.39	山西	28 267.53	0.02
广西	10 064 622.45	6.65	浙江	4 828 338.69	3.19
江苏	11 827 741.49	7.82	其他	2 007 727.74	1.33
安徽	9 091 185.60	6.01	合计	151 324 481.46	100.00

注:统计样本为28家全国或地方各类农贷机关,统计区间自1939年6月至1940年2月。

基于以上组织结构、贷款对象、贷款区域等的分析,厉德寅指出了战时农村金融发展的问题,"关于办理农贷机构者,缺乏完整之体系,既有全国性者、省单位者、县单位者,还有农民组织者,各种机关林立杂处,不相统率,步调各异。关于农贷机关业务者,无一贯之政策,放款种类太狭,几乎全系短期之信用贷款,其间较长之水利贷款,农本局虽曾举办,其数甚微,至于长期之农地贷款,则未与闻焉。贷款之区域,萃趋于交通便利物产富饶之地,荒乡僻野,则相率裹足不前。贷款之手续,颇为繁琐未能顾及农民之教育程度。放款之数额当不能应农民之需要,或对申请数额,任意削减,致失去原来之效用,他如放款之利率、申请之审核、还款之方式,各机关自立准则,从无一致之规定。历来贷款最主要对象之信用合作社,其组织极不健全,流弊甚大,农贷实惠多未及于贫农,故当二十八年底时,农业金融情形之纷乱,已至极点,行局间业务之冲突,时有所闻。"①寥寥数语将国民政府战时农村金融发展的问题概括全面精准,后人对此问题的评析几乎全出自于此。

二、厉德寅农村金融发展思想

在对战时农村金融全面系统分析的基础上,厉德寅提出了如今仍闪着智慧闪光的农业金融发展思想,梳理如下。

第一,厉德寅提出农业金融制度的改革在参照各国宝贵经验基础上应依据本国国情推进。自20世纪二三十年代始,学人纷纷介绍德国、日本、法国、美国等国家农村金融发展经验,中国也开始从国外移植其新式农村金融制度。但由于历史传统、社会经济、政府政策等多重异质因素,国民政府时期农村金融制度的构建并不理想。厉德寅认为农村金融在欧洲、美洲、亚洲的许多国家推行已久,能够总结出共同趋势,各国积累的丰富多样的经验教训值得中国吸取,尤其是如美国等后起国家的政府在农村金融建设上的重要作用更值得中国政府借鉴。同时,厉德寅还清醒地认识到"各国有其特殊之政治经济文化背景,致演成各种类型之农业金融制度",强调应依据国情推进农业金融的发展,"吾人固不应呆板模仿任一国之农业金融制度,但应参照其经验,以供吾国建立农业金融制度借鉴"。②

早在清末时政府就已开始仿效德国、法国土地信用银行及日本劝业银行筹建殖业银行、劝业银行等。南京国民政府上台后,以更积极的姿态推进农村金融制度的建设,在制度设计、机构的设置与调整、资金的投入上都有所行动,但所建立的制度并不是逐步完善,而是偏离系统完整性,其原因之一即忽视了中国问题的特殊性。特别是合作金融的推行尤为典型。合作经济体制发源于19世纪中期的西欧并发育良好,是农村金融发展的可靠基础,但20世纪20年代引入中国后,农村合作社加速组建,30年代后合作金库也得到发展,却因国内外经济社会发展条件的不同,合作组织异化为丧失合作精神的商业性、政治性组织,数次政策调整均未涉及根本问题,农村合作金融的基础摇摇欲坠。再如,仿效美国联邦农业金融局而于1936年创设了农本局,但农本局的商业性质与1935年10家商业银行组成的中华农业

---

①② 厉德寅:《我国农业金融制度之展望》,《经济汇报》1941年第3卷第9期。

合作贷款银团雷同,实际业务运营又与中国农民银行多有重叠与纠纷,不得不重新调整。忽略国情的政策调整导致试错成本巨大,也使得国民政府逐步丧失经济基础与政治基础。

关于农业发展与农村金融的关系,厉德寅认为政府若发展农业,必借助农业金融。农业金融为推进农业政策之重要工具,"运用农业金融力量以推行农业政策者,如政府欲建立家庭农场以培植自耕农,或鼓励某种作物之栽培或限制某种作物之种植,或稳定农产品在市场之价格,凡此种种均可假借农业金融之机能,加以控制与推进达到预期目的"。但因农业生产与资金使用的特殊性,"农业金融不能与储信业务相提并论,不可由普通银行兼营,而应独立自成系统"①,国家须为农业金融成立一种专门金融制度,政府对农业金融施以特殊待遇或辅助。

因此,厉德寅重视农村金融制度的健全,强调制度建设是推进农村金融的当务之急。鉴于战时初期农业金融体系的紊乱复杂,他提出"吾人欲调整农业金融,必须建立一个健全之农业金融制度,使已往之经营不致垂废,未来之设施有准则可循"。而国民政府仅在现存弊端丛生的农村金融制度体系的基础上缝缝补补,厉德寅也承认"抗战期间,一切设施应以配合抗战需要为前提,凡非当务之急者,亦不宜多事更张",但又进一步指出"但制度关系国家百年大计,其内容体系应早日确定"。而南京国民政府并没有提供有效的制度供给,过度干预与无效干预并存,在近代中国农民缺乏自我组织合作社内在动力和机制的条件下,农村金融的发展沿着既存的路径演化,变革曲折且绩效低微。因此,应清楚的认识到,"非建立一完善之制度不可,国家一切活动部门如此,农业金融亦然"②。

第二,厉德寅关于合作金融与农村金融的认识更加清晰。今人对国民政府时期农村金融与合作金融的分析多混作一谈,较少分析其关系与区别。针对近世合作金融制度派所主张之"以农业金融为手段,而以推进合作事业为目的",厉德寅对此的分析是辩证的,但在抗战之非常时期,他更注重的是农业金融,认为"合作与农业金融之关系,在于合作为手段,而以推进农业金融为目的"③。

合作金融在农村金融中占有重要地位,从农贷机关对合作社与合作库的贷款占一半以上即可见一斑,健全发展的合作组织与完善运行的合作

---

① 厉德寅:《我国农业金融制度之展望》,《经济汇报》1941年第3卷第9期。
②③ 厉德寅:《树立兼营式农业合作金融制度刍议》,《浙光》1941年第8卷第5—6期。

金融机制能够降低农村金融发展的成本。但学者们也普遍认为，真正意义上的合作金融制度在抗战前"资金归农"的热潮中因过早商业化而没有建立起来。厉德寅抓住了合作金融演化中问题的关键，即基层合作组织——农村合作社之素质提升问题，认为"年来放款对象之合作社，因量之发展过于迅速，徒具形式，无论在组织上与活动上，皆尚停留于幼稚阶段"，提出"望政府实行普及教育，以提高农民教育之水准，同时扩大宣传，以灌输农民之合作知识，而合作指导员之扶助农民组社，尤须重视合作社之素质，务使基础健全，以利发展"①。

厉德寅在合作社健全的基础上，强调合作金融循序渐进之自下而上的发展程序："初期因农民知识浅薄，资金缺乏，先由金融机关、政府机关及其他不以营利为目的之法团认购提倡股，选举金库之理监事，然不论合作社认股如何微小，至少必占监理事各一席，嗣后社股渐增社员所选之理监事也按比例增加，各机关因所认之提倡股较少而派充之理监事也随之减少，最后达到自营自有自享之境界。"②此观点在彼时合作金库主要依靠外部输血铺设的背景下难能可贵，若以如此路径发展，则合作金库之信用系建筑在各个合作社的结合上，可以取得较大信用，且合作金库作为各金融机关放款合作社之中间机构，可调整各银行办理农贷之分歧情形，使归一致。可惜的是，国民政府的政治性需求并没有重视合作社的健全发展与由下至上合作金融制度的完善，如1940年新县制下合作组织的快速推进，导致诸多弊端愈加严重。

针对抗战初期纷杂的合作金库体系，有学者提出另外设立中央合作金库，厉德寅并不赞同，认为"若坚欲另外设立中央合作金库，无异使现有农行之全部业务移交与中央合作金库，放弃原有之机构、人力及事业不用，而另起炉灶，重新办理，非独在事实上困难万端，无法进行，亦且多事更张，损耗国力"③，而此后的实践也恰恰验证了他的预想。1946年11月中央合作金库成立，意欲重新建立合作金库系统，但中央合作金库与中国农民银行分工不明、纠缠不清，中国农民银行原有辅设的众多省县合作金库仍被视为其准分支机构，中央合作金库只能另起炉灶，农村金融制度的纷乱复杂问题并没有解决，反而更加严重。

---

①② 厉德寅：《三年来之农业金融及今后改进之途径》，《经济汇报》1940年第2卷第1—2期。

③ 厉德寅：《我国农业金融制度之展望》，《经济汇报》1941年第3卷第9期。

第三,厉德寅主张树立兼营式农业金融体系。正如前文分析,战时我国农业金融机关林立杂处,全国性、省际范围、县域农业金融机关相互之间无协同关系,不相统率,特别是国家行局农贷行为各自为政、相互竞争与纠纷问题日益严重。针对农贷机关缺乏完整体系的问题,学界与政界关于农贷机关分营制与兼营制的讨论喧嚣尘上。主张分营制者认为农业金融之长中短三期放款,应由三个独立之农业金融机关分别经营。主张兼营制者,提议由政府设立一个国家农业金融机关,经营一切农贷业务,内分长期金融处、中期金融处及短期金融处等三部,分掌长中短期三种农业信用业务,故其基本精神在于农业金融之长中短三期放款,由一个农业金融机关统筹办理,分部经营,各部之基金会计独立。厉德寅从理论及实践上分析了两者的优劣得失,指出了我国未来农业金融制度应采取的体系。

厉德寅认为农贷分期分办方式将带来农民申请贷款及机关放款成本的上升、稽核监督的不便、长中短期限界定的分歧等,因此认为"分营制困难殊多,效率不强,兼营制则无此等弊端也"。且,厉德寅总结了兼营制的三大优点:一方面,可以免设农业金融行政机关,全国仅一家农业金融机关,可使行政监督与业务执行融成一片,收指臂之效;其次,易于获得资金,一行据有三行之雄厚资本,较易博得社会信用,有利于销售债券,融得资金;最后,有补偿作用,兼办三种农业信用,可分散风险,损益也可互相调剂。鉴于分营制诸多困难与兼营制之现实优点,因此厉德寅主张建立兼营制之农业金融制度。①

关于农业金融组织体系方面的协调设置,厉德寅提出国家农业银行——分行或办事处——县合作金库——各种合作社及联合社之组织体系,具体表现为"以农行为上中级主干,而以信用合作社合作金库为基层组织,形成一种政府扶助式之农业合作金融制度"。②此种体系设计可实现农业金融机关在同一系统之内,保证步调一致,杜绝重复纠纷之弊。同时,还可实现由上而下与由下而上的结合。上层组织之国家农业银行,以此作为全国农村金融政策制定与监督执行机构,统筹全国农贷业务,继而通过分支行实现由上而下的政策贯彻。下层组织为合作金库与合作社,合作社优先认购合作金库资本,若合作社认股不足,由国家农业银行补齐资本额,之后合作社认股增加时,由农行让予之,合作金库的管理权与股份持有数相关,随着合作社认股增加,逐步实现合作社掌握合作金库的管理权,政府由此退

---

①② 厉德寅:《我国农业金融制度之展望》,《经济汇报》1941年第3卷第9期。

居管制监督地位,由农民运用合作组织经营,借此实现有机结合的农村金融体系。厉德寅此种农业金融组织体系的设计兼容了自上而下与自下而上设置的优点,国家意志与基层内生动力相融,是为理想的且循序渐进的演化发展。

三、厉德寅农村金融思想对国民政府政策调整的影响

厉德寅对农村金融的分析是基于当时中国发展的实际情况,其农业金融发展思想不仅具有前瞻性,还具有指导性。实践证明,战时国民政府诸多农业金融政策的调整均带有厉德寅思想之折射。特别是,他拟定的过渡期间推行步骤实际上已带有国民政府战时农业金融政策调整之草案性质,对政策的厘定与变革产生了广泛且深刻的影响。

针对战初农业金融组织体系紊乱的问题,一方面,调整业务几无差别的农本局与中国农民银行,厉德寅主张"现有之中国农民银行,修改章程,增发资金,改组为唯一之国家农业金融机关,供给各种农贷资金。至于农本局之业务,原有农产及农资两部分,今后应将农资部分逐渐收缩,让渡于改组后之国家农业金融机关继续办理,而专营农产部分,并加强其业务,或且增营如美国生产信用公司之业务。如此既便利新制度之推行,又可使农本局集中力量,尽其调整农业产品之使命"[①]。以此思想为先导,1941 年 1 月行政院命令农本局原有农村金融业务移转中国农民银行办理,1943 年农本局由财政部接管,改组成花纱布管制局,至此农本局退出历史舞台。另一方面,调整中国农民银行和其他国家行局的农贷关系,1940 年《农贷办法纲要》提及"各行局经办农贷,分联合办理及分区办理两种,由四联总处规定之"[②],仍没有从根本上解决各行局之间的业务竞争。厉德寅认为"现任参加办理农贷之中国、交通二专业银行,在新制度中,应将其所办之农贷业务逐渐收缩而让渡于改组后之国家农业金融机关办理,并以全力完成办理国际汇兑,发展实业之使命"[③]。以此为先声,1942 年 5 月 28 日四联总处临时理事会通过了《中中交农业务划分考核办法》,为"渐谋专业发展",四联总处分别划分了中央银行、中国银行、交通银行与中国农民银行的主要业

[①③] 厉德寅:《三年来之农业金融及今后改进之途径》,《经济汇报》1940 年第 2 卷第 1—2 期。

[②] 《中央日报》(昆明),1940 年 3 月 4 日。

务,规定"农贷方针及重要农业贷款与投资,应由四联总处理事会核定,交由农民银行承做。中、交两行及中信局现有之农贷业务,应限期收缩,移归农民银行接收办理"①。从此中国农民银行担负起战时农贷供给的使命,一定程度上避免了战时有限资源的无效内耗情况。

至于参加农业贷款的其他金融机构,厉德寅提倡政府部门应对于兼营储蓄业务之商业银行"严加监督,务使办理储蓄业务之银行,将其应对农村合作社之质押放款,及以农产品为质之放款,购买国家农业金融机关所发行之债券,其数不得少于存款总数五分之一。此举不但使农贷资金获得可靠而丰富之泉源,且可减少一般不良银行滥用平民血汗之资金,经营投机事业"②。此建议同样也体现在了之后四联总处的政策调整中。1942年四行专业化之后,四联总处规定"所有兼办储蓄业务之省地方银行及商业银行,应将依照储蓄银行法第七条七、八两款规定运用之普通储蓄存款百分之二十,于三、六、九、十二各月月底解交当地中农行代为投放"③。1943年3月颁布了《中国农民银行收受办理储蓄各行庄应收农贷资金办法》,至少以行政手段保障了农业金融资金的供给,农贷规模才得以不断扩张。

针对农贷发放的地域不平衡问题,厉德寅主张今后对各省农贷资金之分配,不能悉依各省当局之要求,而应该"参照各省可耕地之亩数,重要作物之产量,及以往年农贷额,订正贷放款数额的标准,然后再斟酌国家政策及当时环境等主观因素,加以增减。如此虽未恰如所需,亦必相差不远,庶免偏枯之弊"④。国民政府也逐步意识到农贷不平衡之问题,进行了若干调整。农贷地域分配指向由1940年"本年度农贷暂就后方各省有优先办理,并以四川西康为首要区域"转变为1941年"贷款区域应力求普遍",1942年《农贷办法纲要》要求"各省农贷概由四联总处与各省政府订立农贷协议书(或换函),为各行局办理各省农贷之依据"⑤。抗日战争胜利后,中国农民银行的贷款实施配额管理,年初决定农贷区域配额与贷款种类配额,但由于时局动荡与银行盈利性安全性的考量,农贷区域偏枯问题不可能得到解决。

---

① 重庆市档案馆:《抗日战争时期国民政府经济法规(上)》,档案出版社1992年版,第647页。
②④ 厉德寅:《三年来之农业金融及今后改进之途径》,《经济汇报》1940年第2卷第1—2期。
③ 重庆市档案馆、重庆市人民银行金融研究所:《四联总处史料》(下),档案出版社1993年版,第466页。
⑤ 《中中交农四行局农贷办法纲要》,《中农月刊》1942年第3卷第2期。

农业贷款的对象也不应该局限于农村合作社,考虑实际发展情况,厉德寅认为"合作社一时决难普遍设立,且其素质,因成立过速,并不较他种农民组织为健全",因此放款不能仅以合作社为唯一之农贷对象,"已有之农民团体,如农会,借款协会,及其他社会团体如农场,农业改进机关,农业生产促进机关等,应同视为放款之对象"①。厉德寅关于贷款对象调整的建议也体现在了1940年至1941年的《农贷办法纲要》中,1940年规定贷款对象为农民团体或个人及农业改进机关所经营之事业为范围,1941年农贷对象除了农民团体及农业改进机关外,还增加了凡依法登记之农场、林场、牧场、渔场及农村合作供销代营等机构,此或系战时不及组社之权宜办法,亦可谓农贷办法之进步。

农业生产周期较长的特殊性要求资金使用期也较长,生产要素如化肥、耕牛等投入无法立即收回,短期放贷反而加重农民资金负担,无法改进农业生产。针对农村金融机关多短期借贷的问题,厉德寅认为国家农业银行应统筹兼营长中短三期农贷(信用贷款、水利贷款、土地金融)。国民政府在此方面亦有所行动,1941年4月中国农民银行正式成立土地金融处,经营长期的土地金融贷款。1942年12月四联总处增设土地金融小组委员会,土地金融放款的绝对数量从1942年的253.3万元增加到1945年的31 675.8万元,三年时间增加了125倍。最长可分十年摊还的农田水利贷款也逐步开展,1942—1945年农业水利贷款额占农贷总额的比重均在25%以上。②长中短期农业金融事业均有一定程度的发展。

还有一个不容忽视的问题,即农贷资金的不足。农业金融机关业务范围较广,需款农民较多,但近代新式农业金融机关历史较短,其资本远不及其他银行充实,国家财政短绌导致政府资助不足。又农贷资金须为低利长期之资金,致其筹措范围及方法颇多限制。针对农贷资金的来源问题,厉德寅除了提出向储蓄银行解收20%储蓄存款的对策外,还提出发行土地债券的策略,这也在国民政府农业金融政策中得到了贯彻执行。1942年3月制定公布了《土地债券法》,同年7月发行总额为一亿元,并设法推销,这项举措一直延续至战后。可惜的是,战时发债不易,加之严重的通货膨胀,销售困难重重。厉德寅还提出"国家农业银行,得以其农业票据向国家银行贴

---

① 厉德寅:《我国农业金融制度之展望》,《经济汇报》1941年第3卷第9期。
② 《四联总处抗战以来业务统计表》(1945年),上海市档案馆藏,四联总处档案,档号:Q322-1-128。

现或再贴现"①,这也正是战后中国农民银行资金的重要来源。

四、余 论

厉德寅农村金融思想不仅对国民政府战时政策的调整影响颇大,还具有深刻的现实意义。把厉德寅关于农村金融发展的论述与当下农村金融的深化改革实践联系起来,能够清楚地看到历史的相通性及动态的问题解决的过程。

厉德寅基于对 1937—1939 年农业金融发展的分析基础上,提到"我国农业金融,刻已进入调整时期,则如何调整,确为当前重要问题"②,这也是探索特定历史背景下的"深化改革",虽与新时代下我国金融支农的实践不同,但探索农村金融健全发展的目标是相同的。厉德寅关于国际化和中国化的关系、农业发展与农村金融的关系、合作金融与农村金融的关系等论述,在历史的长河中仍能显现出真理的光彩。针对目前农村资金外流及金融机构撤退、农村金融体系不健全等各种发展困境,也能在厉德寅的分析中找出些许答案。厉德寅提出的若干建议值得当下实践所借鉴,如确定制度之体系、健全合作社之素质、农业金融机关之业务调整等分析,与《乡村振兴战略规划(2018—2022 年)》中"深入推进银行业金融机构专业化体制机制建设"、2021 年中央一号文件"推进农民合作社质量提升,加大对运行规范的农民合作社扶持力度"、2022 年中央一号文件"支持各类金融机构探索农业农村基础设施中长期信贷模式"的政策精神不谋而合。

厉德寅农村金融思想是基于特定历史环境下实事求是的分析,顺应了时代进步的要求和潮流,其极具可行性的发展策略被四联总处采纳推进,取得了良好成效,其思想内核也可为当下农村金融政策制定者提供参考,为农村金融机构的经营管理者提供历史借鉴,这是厉德寅农村金融思想的强劲生命力和历史意义之所在。

---

① 厉德寅:《我国农业金融制度之展望》,《经济汇报》1941 年第 3 卷第 9 期。
② 厉德寅:《三年来之农业金融及今后改进之途径》,《经济汇报》1940 年第 2 卷第 1—2 期。

后　记

2019年8月29日，中国人民大学原常务副校长袁卫教授、唐丽娜老师和上海财经大学的胡宋萍老师来我家访问。他们承担了教育部的重大科研项目"中国统计学科史研究"，希望我能提供有关家父厉德寅的资料。了解了袁教授一行的来意后，心里既高兴又担忧。高兴的是先父是中国最早从事数理统计学和计量经济学研究的博士之一，对于中国计量经济学和数理统计学的开创、建立、教学、推广应用和发展都作出过重要贡献，又由于他曾在抗日战争的最艰难时期在国民政府的中枢金融机构，即所谓"经济作战之大本营"的四联总处任职，后来又到管理和应用外汇的中国平准基金会任职，继而又任职经济部参事等，有机会参与了抗日战争时期许多重大经济政策的讨论，为民国时期发展经济支持长期抗战和经济的历史转型提出了许多充满真知灼见的政策建议和实施方法。时隔八十余年，有学者发掘了

袁卫（右二）、唐丽娜（右一）、胡宋萍（左一）和厉无咎徐琳夫妇

这些历史,并要继续深挖和整理这段历史,心里着实高兴。而令我发愁的是,寒舍在"文化大革命"初期遭受了掘地三尺的抄家,无论书画、照片、笔记、手稿,或是首饰、衣物,通通扫荡一空,已无丁点家严的资料可以提供。尽管如此,我仍应允联系亲友共同参与,以寻找历史遗存。

我妹妹厉无忌接到我的通知后,马上就和威斯康星大学麦迪逊分校联系,学校提供了相关纪录资料。此外,妹妹还联系了研究中国科学社美国分社历史的专家、加州州立理工大学普莫娜分校的王作跃教授,王教授提供了先父为帮助重建中国科学社美国分社与竺可桢、杨孝述、梅贻琦等的来往信件复印件。

2002年厉无忌回国探亲,与哥哥无咎、无畏相聚

所遇最困难的事就是寻找先父的档案,复旦大学称已无厉德寅的档案资料,上海财经大学除了提供一份家严的右派平反资料外也称没有其他档案。正感到茫茫然无处寻觅之际,老朋友王林和他的儿子中欧国际工商学院图书馆馆长杜谦伸出援手,他们求助于上海市虹口区人大常委会副主任陈良,陈良联络了虹口区熟悉档案工作的干部帮助寻找,终于由区公安局提供了一份家严在复旦大学填写的高校教师登记表。

同时,我在一些专业网站和图书馆的民国报刊数据库里找到了许多先父的论文。由于年代久远,不少文档照片都漫漶支离,加上那时出版物的文字都是竖排的,要将其转化成 word 文件亦需耗费大量时间。幸得上海财经大学的胡宋萍老师介绍她学生帮忙录入,特此致谢。还要感谢中国人民大学夏晓华教授,先父的博士论文"The Development of the Correlation Theory and Its Application to Economic Statistics"和在《国立中央大学科学研究录》中发表的论文"A Theory of Correlation"由他精心校对。那博士论文长达 422 页,包含许多复杂的公式,校对是很费力的事。

在搜集整理先父的文章时,令我印象极深刻的有两点:一是对于日本侵略中国满怀义愤,为了救国不惜牺牲一切。这不仅展示在他的许多文章里,也体现在他的实际行动上。当他接到紧急调任安徽省主席挽救危局的蒋作宾来电求助后,立即辞别怀孕在身的娇妻,投笔从戎,毅然奔赴抗日最前线。另一个是他卓越的逻辑推理和运用数理统计理论整理分析数据的能力。民国时期,封建王朝刚被推翻,又经军阀混战和日本入侵,现代社会组织极不完善,各种经济数据十分匮乏。对于抗战时期的物价、汇率、农业贷款等问题,在统计数据不足的情况下,他凭借自己精湛的数理统计功底,进行相关分析,提供了极富说服力的政策研判。

2021 年 4 月 24 日,我借参加清华大学 110 周年校庆机会,拜访了袁卫教授。在这次交谈中,我们详细讨论了编撰《厉德寅经济学文集》的草案。2021 年 8 月,袁教授在他发表的《治学报国:民国时期的统计留学生》文章中也专备一节介绍了先父。正是袁卫教授及其团队自始至终的推动,才促成了这本文集的诞生。

袁卫教授在会议上介绍民国时期的统计留学生

2021 年 8 月 26 日,我与上海社会科学院的王振副院长、王慧敏研究员和卢明明编审等交流了编撰厉德寅文集的情况,并建议上海社会科学院的经济史研究部门能从中选择几个课题进行深入研究,得到了他们的重视和力挺。于是,在王振副院长的关怀下,《全面抗战时期厉德寅的外汇政策研究》和《厉德寅农村金融思想及历史价值》两篇论文问世,并作为附录收录于本书,可以说这两篇论文对本文集起到了画龙点睛的作用。

我要感谢上海社会科学院《上海经济》杂志的前主编卢明明先生,他读了先父的有关史料后,感慨万千,特地为本书写了一首七律诗《题咏厉德寅巨擘》:"画水歌山灵气冲,槐堂村里育鸾龙。厉庐嫡子超侪众,庠序先鞭向主峰。治学标新开化境,献谋抗战建戎功。谁知运变沦戈壁,坚劲胡杨花怨红。"诗写先父从"画水歌山"的东阳农村走向世界,为中国引进和开拓了数理统计学,又投身于中国抗日战争的经济战线出谋划策;谁知命运多舛,1958年在反右运动中被发配到青海德令哈的荒滩改造。或许他会像戈壁滩上坚韧的胡杨那样悔恨自己的花太耀眼而遭劫难!这首诗概括了家父可歌可泣的一生。

我还要感谢柯力先生,他是荣获"CCII 国际双年奖 20 年 20 人"接力棒纪念大奖的设计师,他为本文集设计了具有高度艺术性的封面,灵活运用图像元素营造出强烈的感官冲击,凸显了本书的精髓。

在多方共同努力下,本书终于在先父诞生 120 周年纪念日前夕编撰完成,感谢所有为此作出贡献的朋友们!

厉无咎
2022 年 8 月 24 日